Java Gently

INTERNATIONAL COMPUTER SCIENCE SERIES
Consulting Editor **A D McGettrick** University of Strathclyde

Java Gently

3RD EDITION

Judith Bishop

Computer Science Department
University of Pretoria

An imprint of **Pearson Education**

Harlow, England · London · New York · Reading, Massachusetts · San Francisco
Toronto · Don Mills, Ontario · Sydney · Tokyo · Singapore · Hong Kong · Seoul
Taipei · Cape Town · Madrid · Mexico City · Amsterdam · Munich · Paris · Milan

Pearson Education Limited
Edinburgh Gate
Harlow
Essex CM20 2JE
England

and Associated Companies around the world

Visit us on the World Wide Web at:
www.pearsoneduc.com

First published 1997
Second edition 1998
Third edition 2001

ISBN 0 201 71050 1

British Library Cataloguing-in-Publication Data
A catalogue record for this book can be obtained from the British Library

Library of Congress Cataloging-in-Publication Data
A catalog record for this book can be obtained from the Library of Congress

10 9 8 7 6 5 4 3 2 1
05 04 03 02 01 00

Typeset by 30
Printed in Great Britain by Henry Ling Ltd., at the Dorset Press, Dorchester, Dorset

To dear Nigel
whose passion for science
guides and challenges me in all I do;
with love and admiration

CONTENTS

LIST OF EXAMPLES AND CASE STUDIES

PREFACE TO THE THIRD EDITION

Java Gently is a first programming text. It aims to teach students, as well as those fascinated by the possibilities of their computers and the Internet, how to program, and how to do it in the best possible style in the Java programming language. In the process, *Java Gently* covers all the fundamental structures of the Java 2 language and most of its core libraries and utilities. In terms of programming, it covers object-orientation, software design, structured programming, graphical user interfacing, event-driven programming, multithreading, networking and an introduction to data structures.

A philosophy of teaching Java

Teaching Java as a first language is now the accepted thing to do in universities, colleges and even high schools. Educators have realized that Java has several unique features that not only make it suitable as a language that will equip students for future courses and careers, but also make it a language that students want to learn. Java is fun, Java is interesting and Java is not all that hard if taught in a careful way. Why is this so?

1. Java is small, encompassing a limited number of features that can be used sensibly together.

2. Java is object-oriented, which enables programs to reflect the real world and reduces repetition and errors.

3. Java provides for full graphical user interface (GUI) and multimedia (sound, image and animation) facilities, and promotes GUI programs as applets associated with web browsers.

4. Java provides built-in multithreading features and facilitates programming on the network in a variety of ways.

Given this list there seem to be two possible approaches to presenting Java as a first teaching language. The first is immediately attractive: start at point 3; go straight into GUI, multimedia, applets and the whole network environment, thereby catching the students' interest and showing them how modern and different Java really is. The second approach is to start at the beginning, laying a sound foundation of basic concepts, and then moving on to the newer aspects.

Java Gently does *some of both*, as they both have advantages. Starting with applets and GUI is exciting, but requires so much underlying knowledge of objects that even if students learn the outer shell of programs parrot-fashion, they may never fully understand what they are doing. On the other hand, proceeding at a steady pace through all the background first is a sound policy, but can be both boring and overwhelming.

Java Gently's approach

The approach I have devised is three pronged and hinges on Java's three main selling points: it is network-enabled, small and fosters reuse. So we start off with programs that show how the web is used, but then move straight into covering the basic concepts. In so doing, we introduce the idea of packages (libraries or application program interfaces, APIs) early on and employ three especially written for the book. These get students started on meaningful input–output in an object-oriented way, without hiding basic concepts. Then applets, multimedia, graphics and so on can be introduced properly, to students who have already encountered classes, objects, instantiation and inheritance, and know how to handle them.

Approach is not everything, however, and *Java Gently* uses three other tried and tested teaching techniques:

- diagrams everywhere;

- explanation by example;

- multiple-choice quizzes and problems after every chapter.

There are also three kinds of diagrams used throughout the book:

- **Model** diagrams, which show the structure of the program at the class and object level, while still revealing the basic components such as methods and variables and the interaction between them;

- **Form** diagrams, which show the syntax and semantics of each new Java construct in a way that mirrors its usage in practice;

- **Algorithm** diagrams, which show the flow of small programs, and also serve to illustrate new concepts such as exceptions and multithreading.

In the third edition, definite improvements have been made to the diagrams in the book. Firstly, the class diagram notation has been made easier to draw and has been brought into line with unified modelling language (UML – although UML itself is not appropriate for programming at this level). Then the form diagrams have been expanded to include a semantics section and all the forms are collected at the end of the book to form a useful reference to the language constructs and selected APIs. Many of the algorithms have also been reworked for clarity.

Examples

There are over 80 complete fully worked examples, together with test data and output and 30% of these are new in the third edition. Each example has been carefully chosen so that it both illustrates the feature that has just been introduced, and also solves a real problem in the best possible Java style. Most of the examples have a 'real-world' flavour, which reinforces the need for a programmer to understand the user's problem, and to write programs in a user-friendly way. For example, new examples that occur several times in the book are:

- Curio Store,
- Pizza Delivery,
- Flag Designer,
- Currency Converter.

As soon as a new feature is introduced, it becomes part of the repertoire of the programmer, and will re-emerge in subsequent examples when needed. As the book progresses, the examples get longer and more challenging.

Teaching programming *vs* teaching Java

For a first-year course, it is no longer sufficient just to teach a language. The expectation of today's computer users is that the whole computing milieu will assist in the solution of day-to-day problems. In addition to explaining syntax and the construction of a well-formed program, a programming textbook for this century has to include techniques for problem solving.

Java Gently is indeed such a modern textbook. Each worked problem – and there are over 80 of them – is introduced with a typically inexact statement. This is then refined in the process of devising a solution. Where applicable, the appropriate technique is selected from those previously discussed, and then we proceed to algorithm development. As an additional aid, algorithms are illustrated with structured diagrams, and important techniques are discussed, highlighted and identified for reuse later on. The important programming paradigms of:

- structured programming,
- object-oriented programming,
- class design,
- abstraction,
- software reuse, and
- generality

all receive attention, and examples are carefully chosen to show how these techniques can encourage correctness and efficiency. For example, there are discussions on guidelines for class design, on the relationship between arrays and classes, on the interplay between loops and exceptions, and on the different ways of implementing data structures, to mention just a few.

Order of topics

The topics are grouped into chapters to enable an easy introduction to programming right at the beginning. The order of statements as covered is: output, assignment, for, invocation, input, if, exception, while, do, switch. This grouping does not follow that of a Java reference manual, nor of a book intended for someone who already knows programming. It is a pedagogically tried and tested order, which gets the student through the fundamentals of Java, gently, but without undue delay and fuss.

Most of the chapters contain an even mix of class, control and data issues, plus some Java specialities. My experience has shown that this integrated approach to the order of topics has tremendous benefits for motivation and understanding, and that students are able to get ahead and accomplish more in a shorter time, without compromising their assimilation of the principles of Java and programming. The key points of the order of all the material are:

- rapid entry to genuine programming problems;

- the power of object-oriented programming presented with realistic examples that use more than one class and more than two objects right from the start;

- exceptions introduced early on and explained as a natural way to control flow between classes;

- 'no fuss' discussion of features that are simple in Java (such as class structure) but in-depth treatment of potentially difficult topics (such as casting and cloning);

- hash tables grouped with arrays to show their efficacy in providing for non-integer indices;

- three custom-made input–output packages, which are used from Chapter 4, and explained in full in Chapters 7 and 14;

- almost full coverage of the awt (Abstract Windowing Toolkit) facilities, but geared towards examples, together with an intoduction to Java's Swing set;

- applets presented through a viewer and a browser, and the differences between applets and applications explained once the student can genuinely appreciate the issues;

- multithreading used for animation and the development of interesting applications;

- socket programming to illustrate simple client–server or peer-to-peer systems such as chat servers and RMI to show the power of Java in a distributed environment;

- database access via an ODBC–JDBC (open database connectivity – Java database connectivity) bridge to a common database system, with simple to understand set-up steps;

- coverage of some of the JFC (Java Foundation Collection) for algorithms and data structures ranging from sorting and searching through stacks, queues, lists and bit sets.

Teaching aids and the web site

Java Gently contains:

- over 80 fully worked examples and case studies;

- summaries after each chapter;

- multiple choice quizzes at the end of each chapter, with solutions;

- over 100 exercises;

- an active web site;

- special `Display`, `Stream` and `Graph` classes for augmenting Java's input–output;

- notations for algorithms and models resulting in over 70 diagrams;

- a unique way of presenting Java syntax and semantics to the novice programmer.

All examples have been tested and run and are available on a web site that will be actively maintained and updated. The web site at

www.booksites.net/bishop

also contains:

- web pages that introduce the book;

- all the examples for downloading, either individually, in chapters or in one go;

- frequently asked questions;

- error list;

- discussion board;

- future plans for the book;

- e-mail contact with the author and the *Java Gently* team.

This web address mirrors the one at www.cs.up.ac.za/javagently.

Who the book is for

The book is intended for students learning to program for the first time in Java, and who have access to the Java Development Kit from Sun, running on PCs, Macs or Unix. There is no reliance in the book on any of the myriad of development environments that are available. Students would normally be in their first year at a university or college, and could be in the science, engineering, commerce or liberal arts faculties: the examples are sufficiently wide-ranging to cater for all. The book does not require mathematical experience, and would certainly be accessible for school pupils taking computer science in senior years. Because there is an emphasis on facts and examples, rather than long discussions, the book would also be suitable for experienced programmers or hobbyists who wish to pick up Java quickly.

The book is based on many courses given in Java since 1996, and on courses in other languages presented to science and engineering students at first-year university level since 1980. Included are many of the class-tested examples and exercises from these courses. All examples have been tested on JDK 1.3 on Intel PCs with Windows NT and Linux, and the majority of them also on an iMac and PowerBook G3 with Java 1.1.6 on Mac OS9 and CodeWarrior 4. The browser used for the applets was primarily Netscape Communicator with HotJava and Internet Explorer occasionally.

Because technology, and especially Java, is advancing at a rapid rate, it may be that a new version of Java is available simultaneously with this book. Consult our web site for the latest information and for program updates.

Acknowledgements

This third edition of *Java Gently* has been greatly influenced and improved by the many people from all round the world who took the trouble to write in and share their experiences and ideas. In particular, I would like to acknowledge the input of Jens Kaasbøll of the University of Oslo and Uwe Kastens of the University of Paderborn who made extensive critiques of the object-oriented parts of the book.

Once again I am grateful to the technical staff and research students in the department who continued to help solve numerous problems of a rapidly moving Java on multiple platforms, in particular Basil Worrall who has devoted many hours to ensuring that the programs are correct and compatible with the text and the web site, and in spotting errors. Basil is also responsible for the model diagrams, for the database example, and for updating several of the later programs. I could not have wished for a more able and faithful assistant, but any errors that remain are my own.

Johnny Lo has also kept the *Java Gently* web site up to date and running, answering questions and queries on a daily basis with Basil. The contributions of earlier members of the *Java Gently* team must be acknowledged once more: Louis Botha, Tony Abbott, Alwyn Moolman, John Botha, Graeme Pyle and Daniel Acton. I thank my department for the equipment provided, and for the non-stop dial-in service which enabled me to work late into the night. Doing so would also not have been possible without Beethoven, Brahms and the Beatles, and the cheerful e-mails from all my friends on the Pacific West Coast.

The software we used came from Sun, Microsoft and Apple and I pay tribute to these giants in the computer industry for the ease of use and stability that we so often take for granted. The book was prepared on an iMac with Microsoft Word 98 and most of the programs developed there using CodeWarrior 4, and on a Windows NT workstation using JDK 1.3 and TextPad 4, all a pleasure to work with.

Pearson Education has once again provided outstanding professional service in the editorial and production departments in getting this book to print on time: my gratitude especially to Martin Sugden, who put up with more than he had bargained for, and to Kate Brewin, Martin Klopstock, Bridget Allen and their teams.

Finally, as always, I thank Nigel for his support and assistance with the difficult problems that always occur late at night, and to my dear sons William and Michael for their understanding and patience with my months of preoccupation with the book. They are still learning Pascal, but I hope that when they enrol at university soon, they will reap the benefits of their forbearance, and enjoy Java as I do.

Judith M. Bishop
Pretoria, South Africa
November 2000

THE DEVELOPMENT OF *JAVA GENTLY*

The following have contributed to the development of *Java Gently* since the first edition.

Kevin Boone	University of Middlesex
Alan Dearle	University of Stirling
Hans Geers	Technical University of Delft
Priscilla Griscom	University of New Haven, Connecticut
Mark Harman	University of North London
Matthew Huntbach	Queen Mary and Westfield College, University of London
Brendan Hodgson	University of Durham
Steven Jenkins	Iowa State University
Mike Joy	University of Warwick
Uwe Kastens	University of Paderborn
Jens Kaasbøll	University of Oslo
Frank Martin	London Guildhall University
Nicholas Measor	University of Leicester
Andrew McGettrick	University of Strathclyde
Narayan Murthy	Pace University, New York
Andy Ormsby	University of Sussex
Sagar Pidaparthi	De Montfort University
Jon Rowson	Queen Mary and Westfield College, University of London
Chris Sadler	University of North London
Ivor Spence	Queen's University of Belfast
Janet Stack	University of Glasgow
Steve Webster	Bournemouth University

CHAPTER 1

Introduction

1.1   Welcome to Java

Java is unlike any other language that has gone before. It is designed to work easily within the World Wide Web of computers through commonly available, user-friendly software called **browsers**. All computers these days have a browser – be it Netscape, Explorer or Mosaic – and all browsers are now **Java-enabled**. This means that you can scan through documents stored all around the world, and at the click of a link, activate a Java program that will come across the network and run on your own computer. You do not even have to know that it is a Java program that is running.

The key advantage of being Java-enabled is that instead of just passive text and images appearing on your screen, calculations and interaction can take place as well. You can send back information to the **host** site, get more Java programs, and more documents, and generally perform in a very effective way. Figure 1.1 sums up the circle of activity that takes place with a Java-enabled browser. Java programs that run on the web are actually called **applets** (short for 'little applications'), and we shall use this term from now on.

Another important property of Java is that it is **platform-independent**. This means that it is independent of the kind of computer you are using. You may have a Macintosh, or a

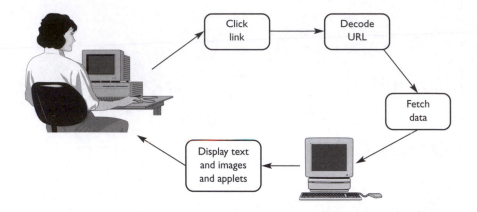

Figure 1.1 *Browsing the World Wide Web with Java applets (URL = Universal Resource Locator).*

Pentium, a Silicon Graphics or a Sun Workstation. Java applets do not mind. They are stored on a **host site** in such a way they can run on any computer that has a Java-enabled browser.

So what does Java-enabled mean? It means that inside the browser there is a program known as a **Java Virtual Machine** (JVM) which can run Java for that particular computer. The Java that comes over the net is in a standard form known as **bytecode**. Your JVM can understand the applet in bytecode and make it work properly on your particular computer. That is why if you get an applet when running under Windows, it will have a Windows 'look and feel' to its buttons and layout. If you pull the same applet down onto a Macintosh, it will look like a typical Mac program. Figure 1.2 sums up this process.

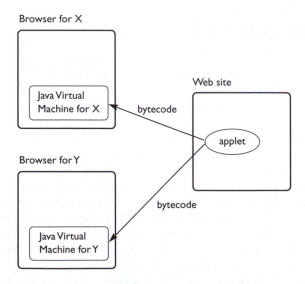

Figure 1.2 *A Java applet going to two different computer types X and Y.*

Enough of theory. What are applets actually good for, and what would one really look like? Let us now consider an example especially set up on *Java Gently*'s web site. This site can be found at the URL[1] http://www.booksites.net/bishop.

The Nature Conservation project

As part of its international outreach programme, the country of Savanna (situated on the grasslands of Africa) is funding a project to make information about nature available on the web. Rather than finding just an electronic book, visitors to the web site will be able to make enquiries about animals, birds or trees that they have spotted, and even to contribute interactively to the information on the site. Consider the web pages from the first version of the site, shown in Figures 1.3 to 1.5. It all looks pretty interesting, and even impressive, but where is the Java?

The fact that it is not obvious is a tribute to Java's usefulness and power. The first web page (Figure 1.3) announces the project and gives the links to the three proposed sections. The birds section is not yet ready, so the link is not enabled. If we click on the

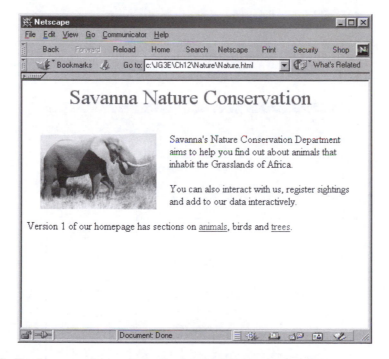

Figure 1.3 *The first page of the web site, showing two links to animals and trees.*

---

[1] The term URL, also referred to in Figure 1.1, stands for Universal Resource Locator. It is a unique reference to a document on the web, usually consisting of a protocol such as http and the name of the site or computer where the item is stored, followed by some subdirectory information.

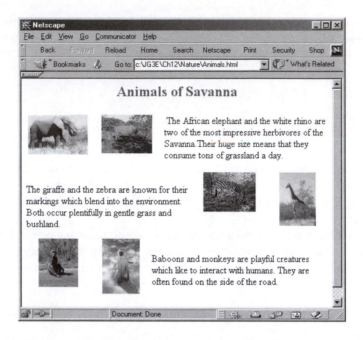

Figure 1.4 *The second web page, showing images and text.*

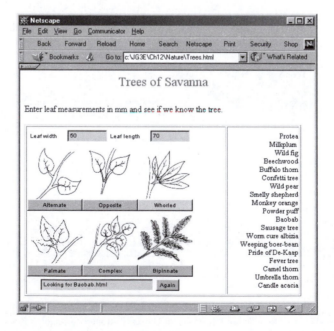

Figure 1.5 *The Trees web page with an applet at the bottom.*

animals link, we get Figure 1.4. The animal section is just pictures at the moment, but the section on trees (Figure 1.5) has a table showing how to codify a tree according to its leaf appearance. You are then invited to enter in three values related to your tree. This is the applet at work, waiting on your machine should you want it. Once it has three values, it calculates a tree code and then asks the browser to bring down from the web site information about that specific tree. For the information as entered, the web page could contain a picture of a baobab tree, plus information about its seeds, flowers and habitat. An example of such a page is given in Figure 1.6. There is more about this applet in Section 12.4.

Should the applet not recognize the combination of leaf appearance and size that you entered, it could give you the opportunity of entering these as a problem for the resident botanists, who will come back to you via e-mail in a few days with whatever information they can glean.

Of course, Java is not just a means for moving information around on the web: it is a real programming language, of the stature of C++, Pascal, Ada and Modula-3. Learning to use Java is what this book is all about, but it also serves as a general introduction to the principles of programming. By the end of the book, you will be able to program Java applications and applets to perform such diverse tasks as inventory control, averaging and sorting marks, computer games and competitions and of course web surfing.

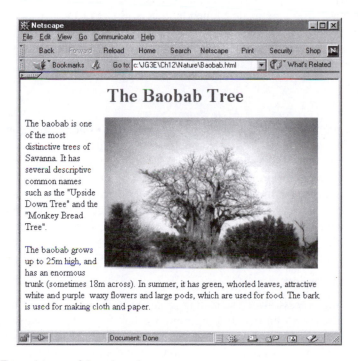

Figure 1.6 *The web page of the selected tree.*

1.2   Software development

Computers consist of hardware and software. When one buys a computer, or uses it in the laboratory, the tendency is to focus on the hardware: how much memory does it have, what is the speed of the processor and so on. These are factors in using a computer, but they are not the most important. It is of course annoying if, for example, one runs out of disk space, but at least a plan can be made to store some of the information somewhere else, or even delete it, to make room.

We would claim that the software that the computer comes with is what really determines its quality. In this section, we shall briefly run through the software components that are necessary for programming in Java, and show how they interact. The description is intended to be a general one, not specific to any particular make or supplier of software. Then we shall outline the stages of software development. The next section shows how these are tackled in this book.

The programming process

The programming process is the activity whereby programs are written in order to be stored and made ready for execution or running. The programs can be run on the same computer on which they were written, or they can be fetched over the web in the manner we have already described. Programming these days needs the support of many software packages, themselves programs developed by others. Some of the software comes with the computer you buy, some you can purchase later, and some you can get as freeware, shareware or applets over the web. In order to develop your own programs, you will need at least an operating system, an editor and a compiler.

Operating systems

The core software loaded onto a computer is its **operating system**. Some operating systems are specific to certain types of computers – for example MacOS is intended for Macintosh – and others are designed to run on a variety of different designs. Windows, Unix and its derivative, Linux, are examples here. The operating system provides the necessary interfaces to the hardware: reading from disk, writing to the screen, swapping between tasks and so on. It also looks after files and provides commands for the user to move files, change their names, etc. Through the operating system, we activate the next level of software.

Editors and compilers

The programming process involves creating a sequence of instructions to the computer, which is written in the particular programming language. The creative process is expressed through an **editor**, of which there are many on the market. Once ready, the program is submitted to a **compiler**. The function of the compiler is two-fold. In the first instance, it makes a thorough check on the validity of what has been written. If there are any errors (called **compilation** or **syntax** errors) then these must be corrected and the program resubmitted for compilation. Activating the Java compiler can be done at a simple level by typing in the following to the operating system, where `Trees.java` is the file we created through the editor:

```
javac Trees.java
```

Once the program is free of compilation errors, the compiler enters a second phase and translates the program into a form that can run on a computer. For compilers for most other languages this form will be the native machine instructions of the particular computer's processor. For Java, though, it is the Java Virtual Machine that is the target of compilation, no matter what the computer is that will ultimately run the translated program.

Although the compiler checks the grammar of the program and can look for quite a range of potential errors, it cannot detect errors in the logic. For example, in the applet shown in action in Figure 1.5, it would be quite possible for a careless programmer to read the width value as the length and the length as the width by mistake. These are known as **logic** errors (also known as **execution** errors).

Logic errors can be avoided by

- carefully structuring the program in the first place,

- following good programming guidelines, and

- reusing existing pieces of program instead of rewriting everything from scratch each time.

However, sometimes the only way to detect a logic error is to run the program and see what happens. This is the second last stage of the software development process. The program is **executed** or **run** by activating it through the operating system. In Java we would activate an ordinary program by a command such as

```
java Trees
```

Some logic errors can be detected by carefully testing the program with well-chosen test data. After finding and correcting an error, the test should be re-run because it is very easy to introduce some other error while fixing the first. All of these topics are covered in this book. The programming process is summed up in Figure 1.7.

Development environments

Because the edit–compile cycle repeats itself over and over again in the programming process, software exists which combines editing and compiling and enables one to switch between them at the touch of a button. Examples of such Java systems are TextPad, Kawa, VisualJ++, VisualAge and JBuilder. An integrated development environment (IDE) also includes facilities for managing large projects, perhaps involving several programmers. Another feature is an enhanced editor for creating user interfaces by designing them on the screen.

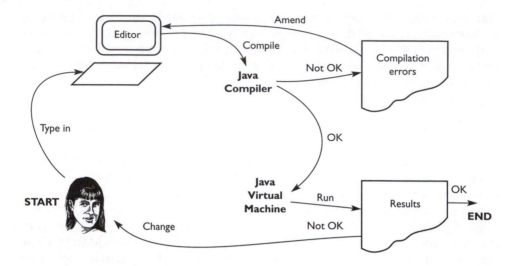

Figure 1.7 *The programming process in Java.*

An advantage of some Java IDEs is that, like Java itself, they are platform-independent, so that you can continue working in the same environment even if you change computers. A disadvantage of IDEs is that they are not always intuitive and sometimes take a while to learn to operate effectively.

Maintenance

It is suprising, but true, that Figure 1.7 represents in industry terms only about 30% of the programming process. The hard programming starts after the product has been delivered and it begins its useful life. Then it has to be **maintained**, an activity similar to the maintenance on an airplane: essential and sometimes costly. Maintenance for software includes fixing errors, making user-required changes and adding enhancements. A primary aim of a programmer even when learning to program should be to make maintenance as easy as possible. Throughout the book we shall mention ways of achieving this goal.

1.3   The approach of this book

Java Gently teaches programming by example. There is a tried and tested progression of examples which leads you from first principles to the more complex constructs in the language. Each example is carefully chosen so as to use only those features that have been covered, and each example uses the features correctly. Achieving this balance means that the order of topics covered has to be precise. While it is possible to dip into the later chapters of the book, the first five should be covered sequentially. They form the core and are closely interlinked.

Each example follows a sequence of steps which is usually:

- problem

- solution

- algorithm

- class design

- example

- program

- testing.

The problem is a short statement in the user's terms of what needs to be done. The solution starts to give an idea as to what approach should be followed to solve the problem, including what software can be reused from elsewhere. The algorithm forms the nub of the problem-solving process. Each program is a complete, running Java program and can be found on our web site given on page 3. The example and testing help to make the programs realistic.

Algorithms

An **algorithm** is a precise, unambiguous statement of steps to follow to solve a problem. Algorithms can be expressed in a variety of ways and we shall use a mixture of English and lines and arrows to express the concepts of decision making and repetition. The resulting diagrams are formal enough to show the structure of the program yet informal enough to be written with the minimum of fuss. For example, in the Trees applet, there are three values to be entered. The algorithm for getting all three in, in any order, before proceeding, would be represented as in Figure 1.8.

In general the flow of the algorithm is downwards. Sideways arrows indicate action to be taken if the condition is true. Often, the algorithm will need to be repeated, and the line from the bottom and up the left joins around the top again to show that this should happen.

Class design

Java is an object-oriented language, which means that a program in Java is composed of interrelated objects. *Java Gently* describes programs in terms of their objects and the relationships between them using a simple set of blocks and lines. The notation used is based on the UML (Unified Modelling Language), with additions to make it more suitable for the level of programming that we are tackling, and to make visible all of Java's interesting features. For example, we distinguish clearly between classes and objects, and make provision for depicting arrays and hash tables clearly. An example of a model diagram related to the Nature project is given in Figure 1.9.

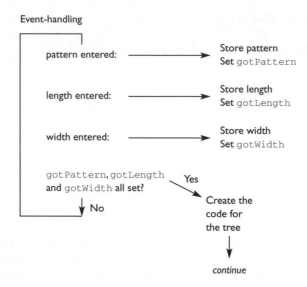

Event-handling

pattern entered: ───────────▶ Store pattern
                               Set `gotPattern`

length entered: ───────────▶ Store length
                               Set `gotLength`

width entered: ───────────▶ Store width
                               Set `gotWidth`

`gotPattern`, `gotLength`   Yes
and `gotWidth` all set? ╲
                          ╲
                   No ▼   ▶ Create the
                             code for
                             the tree

                              ▼
                          continue

Figure 1.8 *A sample algorithm.*

PizzaDelivery1 is a class (shown with dashed lines), and there is an object (shown with solid lines) created from the class. The object has three variables, suitably initialized to values, and seven methods. The calling structure of the methods is indicated in the diagram. There is much more about this notation in Chapters 2 and 3.

Program

Programs are written in programming languages. There are many such languages, but relatively few are available on all kinds of computers. Those that have achieved more or less

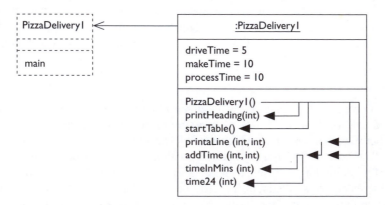

Figure 1.9 *A sample model diagram.*

universal use include Pascal, Ada, FORTRAN, COBOL, BASIC, C++, Lisp, Prolog, Modula and now, of course, Java. Java was developed in 1993 under the name of Oak, and achieved popularity in 1996 when Sun Microsystems launched their Java compilers free on the web.

Java programs look like stylized English, and examples can be found on any page of this book. The form of a program is important: any mistakes will cause the compiler to reject your efforts. It is therefore necessary to learn the syntax of the language precisely. To assist you in this endeavour, *Java Gently* has a unique approach. When a new construct is introduced, its **syntax** and its **semantics** are shown precisely in a **form** that not only explains how a feature is constructed, but also gives an indication of how it should be laid out in a regular way. An example of a simple form is:

If-statement

```
if (condition) {
    statements1;
}
else {
    statements2;
}
```

Evaluate *condition*. If it is true, execute *statements1*; if it is false, execute *statements2*.

The else-part is optional: if it is not included, a false condition causes execution to move to the statement after the if.

The meaning of the bold face and italics will become clear as we start introducing Java statements.

Summaries

At the end of each chapter there are summaries that give a quick description of the main points of the chapter, and also list all the Java keywords, libraries and features covered, as well as the forms and model diagrams. The forms are also listed at the back of the book in the appendices.

1.4   Getting started with Java

If you do not have Java development facilities where you are studying or working, then you will want to set them up for yourself. The Java Development Kit (JDK) is Sun's free gift to the Java programming community. You can download, install and use it as free-ware. The JDK gives you a full reference compiler and interpreter for the very latest version of Java. There is also a directory on documentation for all the Java libraries (known as APIs or application programming interfaces) and a directory called the Java tutorial. Both of these are worth downloading if you have time and space. The JDK, the API documentation and the tutorial each occupy about 10 MBytes on disk, so you are looking at about 30 Mbytes all together.

The following instructions regarding acquiring and installing the JDK are correct at time of writing.

Downloading the JDK

To download the JDK, first don't. In other words, find out whether it is available locally on your server or on a CD from your organization. Only if you cannot get the system you want nearby, go to Sun's site www.javasoft.com and choose the 'Products and APIs' from the list of options. Look from there for the JDK. You will be asked about your machine and operating system, and then you can download. You should also print out the web page associated with the download, which tells you how to install and test the system.

Once you have got the JDK, you will need to install it. Follow the instructions carefully, especially the instructions on setting the path and classpath. .

Testing the system

To test whether you have installed the system correctly, use a simple text editor of your choice to type in the first Java program shown in Example 2.1 and save it in a file called `Welcome.java`. Keep your editor open while opening up a command line window as well (Unix or MS-Dos). Here type in

```
javac Welcome.java
```

The JDK compiler will take the file and compile it. If you made no typing errors, the command prompt will be returned. If there are error messages, go back to the edit window, fix the Java program accordingly, then recompile.

Once you have a clean compilation, the compiler will have created a file called `Welcome.class`. To run the program, type in

```
java Welcome
```

(Note: do not add the word 'class' here.) The program should produce output on the next line in the command window.

The `javagently` package

Once you get started with Java, you will encounter the need to interact with your program, and an easy way to do this is provided by a special classes in the `javagently` package written for this book. Details about the package and how to install it are given in

Sections 4.2 and 4.3 and there is a full listing of the classes in the chapters that follow. You do not have to type the package in if you can fetch it from the web (as described in Section 4.3).

The documentation and tutorial

The additional information supplied with the JDK is invaluable. The documentation gives a hypertext view of all Java's libraries, with detailed descriptions and examples of each method. This is the Java programmer's 'help', and is accessed through your browser. The tutorial consists of a collection of articles written by different people at different times and at different levels. It is not comprehensive, in that it is not intended to cover all of Java or to replace textbooks, but it does give insight into how and why certain parts of Java were developed, and the sample programs form a good addition to those in a book.

Java integrated development environments

Although the JDK is free and many people use it solely, there are more elaborate systems on the market, as described in Section 1.2. Some of the IDEs make use of their own compilers, though more are now switching to the approach of making use of Sun's compiler, which is deemed to be more up to date.

IDEs in common use include Sun's Java Workshop, Microsoft's Visual J++, Symantec's Café, Borland's JBuilder, IBM's VisualAge for Java, Tek-Tool's Kawa and Metrowerks CodeWarrior (available from your local computer store or computer representative). All the above are available for PC platforms using Windows 95 or NT or later. In addition, Java Workshop runs under Solaris on Suns and CodeWarrior is available for the Macintosh.

There is also a simpler class of IDE that concentrates on editing and compiling, without going into project management. The nicest of these is TextPad, available from sales@textpad.com.

Web sites for Java

Java is a web language and there are several excellent sites that discuss Java issues, and have Java articles and Java resources for downloading. Four in particular are worth watching:

- www.javasoft.com – Sun's Java site, regularly updated with topical articles and news about Java products and use;

- www.gamelan.com – incredible collection of Java resources, information and applets;

- www.javaworld.com – a monthly online magazine devoted to Java;

- www.booksites.net/bishop – the web site for this book and its companion texts.

1.5   The *Java Gently* web site

The first edition of *Java Gently* came out together with a web site whose initial purpose was to be a repository for the programs in the book. Since May 1997, the site has grown into an active web site, with readers from all over the world contributing to the discussions, making suggestions, and informing us of their ideas about Java and the book. The number of hits is over 100 000 and growing daily.

On the web site, you can find the following:

- About the book

- Summary of the chapters

- List of institutions using *Java Gently* for teaching

- All the examples for individual viewing or downloading in bulk

- Answers to frequently asked questions

- A discussion board, watched over by the author and the JG team

- Messages about Java of immediate interest

- Other material available from the author on Java

- List of known errors in the book

- Plans and dates for future versions and editions of *Java Gently*

- Link to the publisher's site.

In addition to providing a great deal of information, the web site can be used in two innovative ways. Firstly, for lecturers with access to online facilities in the classroom, the programs can be displayed and viewed directly from the site. I have used this method in teaching, and have found it more effective than first copying the programs onto transparencies. The ability to move rapidly between programs, to save, compile and run very quickly, makes for a dynamic teaching environment.

The second innovation of active web sites such as *Java Gently*'s is that you can interact with a team that can answer questions and discuss Java issues. This team starts at the author's institution, the University of Pretoria, but ultimately includes all the *Java Gently* readers who access the web site and are prepared to share their expertise. In other words, you are not alone out there.

The web site is updated regularly and comments and suggestions are always welcome. All queries are answered and contributions acknowledged.

SUMMARY

It is often said that programming is fun. It certainly can be, and *Java Gently* tries to make it so. Support is available from many sources around the world, and also from the *Java Gently* web site. However, no matter how much you enjoy learning to program – and I sincerely hope you do – I hope that you will also remember the following, adapted from the immortal words of Rudyard Kipling:

> *If you can keep your head when all about you*
> *Are losing theirs and blaming it on you,*
> *If you can trust yourself when all men doubt you,*
> *But make allowance for their doubting too;*
> *If you can wait and not be tired by waiting,*
> *If you can fill the unforgiving minute*
> *With sixty seconds' worth of Java run,*
> *Yours is the Web and everything that's in it,*
> *And – which is more – you'll be a programmer, thank SUN!'*

QUIZ: TO GET YOU STARTED

1.1   What does a compiler do?

1.2   What is the difference between a compilation error and a logic error?

1.3   What is the clock speed of the computer you are using?

1.4   How much memory does your computer have?

1.5   What is the capacity of the disks you are using?

1.6   Would this textbook (including all the spaces) fit on your disk, assuming one printed character per byte of memory?

1.7   List all the computer applications that you come into contact with in the course of an ordinary week.

1.8   Have you ever been on the wrong end of a computer error? If so, could you tell whether the mistake was in the program or was caused by the data that were read in?

1.9   Find out the name, version and creation date of the computer, operating system and compiler that you will be using.

1.10   Get into *Java Gently*'s web site and try out the Nature system. The address is http://www.booksites.net/bishop.

CHAPTER 2

Simple programs

In this chapter we give a broad overview of the different parts of a Java program and how they fit together. Using three carefully chosen examples, we are able to explain the concepts of object-oriented programming so that, by the end, we shall be able to create and run simple programs that have tangible results. The programs are written in the best Java style, and form the pattern for solutions to follow.

2.1 Three starter programs

To start this chapter we shall look at three small programs that illustrate various aspects of Java programming. The first is a simple text-based program, the second uses drawing and colours, and the third defines and sets up some objects. We use them as a starting point for introducing programming in Java, and for enabling you to start using the computer straight away. To this end, there are several simple amendments you can make to the programs, which will give you a reason to get to grips with your editor and programming environment.

| EXAMPLE 2.1 | Welcome |

The aim of our first program is to display the message Welcome to Java Gently!. The program is:

```
class Welcome {

  /* Welcome program  by J M Bishop Dec 1996
   * ----------------Java 2 April 2000
   * Illustrates a simple program displaying a message.
   */

    Welcome () {
      System.out.println("Welcome to Java Gently!");
    }

    public static void main (String [ ] args) {
      new Welcome ();
    }
}
```

and it does indeed, if run, display the required message on the screen as follows:[1]

Welcome to Java Gently!

At this stage we shall note only a few points about the program. Firstly, the text between /* and */ is called a **comment** and is there to help explain to the reader what the program does. It is not **executed** (or **run**) by the computer. Secondly, the text in quotes after println is known as a **string** and is what is actually displayed. The rest of the program is part of the outline that always accompanies a Java program. We shall learn more about this structure soon.

Exercise: Run the Welcome program. (See Section 1.4 for details.) Change it so that it includes your name in the message, e.g. Welcome to Java, Peter! Change it again so that it prints out more than one line of greeting, or underlines the greeting using hyphens. Experiment and use the opportunity to become familiar with your programming environment.

| EXAMPLE 2.2 | Drawing a flag |

One of the advantages of Java is its built-in facilities for graphics, colour, animation, sound and so on. Here is a very simple program to display a flag in a window:

---

[1] From now on, Java programs, and parts of them, are shown in Courier font with output in bold.

```java
import java.awt.*;
import java.awt.event.*;

class FlagMaker1 extends Frame {

  /* Flag drawing program    J M Bishop April 2000
   * --------------------
   * Illustrates colour and simple graphic output
   */

FlagMaker1 () {
    add ("Center", new Flag());
    // Enable the program to end when the window is closed
    addWindowListener(new WindowAdapter () {
      public void windowClosing(WindowEvent e) {
        System.exit(0);
      }
    });

    // Set the frame's title and size and activate the drawing
    // described by the paint method.
    setTitle ("A Flag");
    setSize (300, 200);
    setVisible (true);
  }

  public static void main (String [ ] args) {
    new FlagMaker1 ();
  }
}

class Flag extends Canvas {
  public void paint (Graphics g) {
    // Draw the flag using coloured rectangles
    g.setColor (Color.black);
    g.fillRect (40,40,200,40);
    g.setColor (Color.red);
    g.fillRect (40,80,200,40);
    g.setColor (Color.yellow);
    g.fillRect (40,120,200,40);

    // Label the drawing
    g.setColor (Color.black);
    g.drawString("Germany",100,180);
  }
}
```

The output produced by the program is shown (not in colour, unfortunately) in Figure 2.1.

Figure 2.1 *Graphical output from the* `FlagMaker` *program.*

FlagMaker1 is a slightly longer program than `Welcome` and has two classes – the `Flagmaker1` class and the `Flag` class which comes along with it. `FlagMaker1` performs various housekeeping duties with respect to setting up a new window for the flag, but the real substance of the program – drawing the flag – occurs in `Flag`'s `paint` method. Each of the lines such as

```
g.fillRect (40,80,200,40);
```

draws one of the coloured bars. The numbers in brackets are measurements in pixels (screens can have 600 or more pixels across). In order, the numbers in the list after `fillRect` represent:

- *x*-coordinate of the top left of the rectangle;
- *y*-coordinate of the top left of the rectangle;
- width of the rectangle;
- height of the rectangle.

For a flag with horizontal stripes, the only value that changes is the *y* one, moving down from the top of the screen. There is more about graphics in Chapter 10.

The rest of the program can be described as 'baggage': necessary Java instructions that give us access to the graphics facilities, but that are not particular to our problem. In brief, these are:

- importing the graphics packages we need (`awt` and `awt.event`);

- enabling the window to be closed;

- adding the flag to the centre of a window (or `Frame`, as Java calls it);

- creating a graphics window of a particular size and title.

The program in Example 2.2 also illustrates the use of Java's second type of comment: the one-liner, introduced by //. Either kind of comment is acceptable. The advantage of // is that it is automatically ended by the end of a line. On the other hand, many programmers regard the /* */ pair as more elegant. The convention for using the paired comment symbols is to have the closing */ underneath the /*, as shown in these programs.

Being able to program in a graphics environment is an essential skill for today's programmers, but there is a lot of detail to learn, much of which is repetitive and can be looked up when needed. We therefore leave graphics to the second half of the book and will concentrate on ordinary object-oriented programs while we learn the fundamentals of programming, and of how to do this well in Java.

Exercise: Run the `FlagMaker1` program and check that the flag comes out in the right colours for Germany (black, red, yellow[2]). Now alter the program to show another similar flag such as the Netherlands (red, white, blue) or Ethiopia (green, yellow, orange) instead. Alter the size of the window and flag to display a much larger image.

EXAMPLE 2.3	Curio Store

Our third example emphasizes what an object-oriented program looks like in Java. Objects hold information about real-world items (such as curios) and each class of objects identifies the actions (or methods) that can be made on the items. Let us suppose that we wish to computerize the stock of a curio store. In this very simple program we do little more than create three objects from the `Curio` class and print out their values, but we could imagine methods such as sell and enquire and check stock being added to later versions of the program. Because we know that there will be more versions, we call this program `CurioStore1`.

---

[2] The yellow should be gold, but unfortunately the proper shades of colours for the flags cannot be selected from the simple options we have available now.

```java
class CurioStore1 {

  /* Curio Store No. 1 by J M Bishop April 2000
   * ------------------
   * Illustrates the basic form of an object-oriented program
   */

  // Declare three object variables
  Curio mugs, tshirts, carvings;

  // The constructor for the program is
  // where the initial work gets done
  CurioStore1 () {
    // Create three objects with different initial values
    mugs = new Curio("Traditional mugs", 6, "beaded in Ndebele style");
    tshirts = new Curio("T-shirts", 30, "sizes M to XL");
    carvings = new Curio("Masks", 80, "carved in wood");

    // Print out a header
    System.out.println("The Polelo Curio Store sells\n");

    // Print the values contained in each of the objects
    mugs.write();
    tshirts.write();
    carvings.write();
  }

  // All programs must have a main method
  public static void main (String [ ] args) {
    // Start the program running from its constructor
    new CurioStore1 ();
  }
}

class Curio {

  // Declare variables related to a curio
  String name;
  int price;
  String description;

  // The constructor copies the initial values
  // into the object's variables
  Curio (String n, int p, String d) {
    name = n;
    price = p;
    description = d;
  }
```

```
    // a method to output the values of the object's variables
    void write () {
      System.out.println(name + " " + description + " for G" + price);
    }
  }
```

The output from the program will be:

```
The Polelo Curio Store sells

Traditional mugs beaded in Ndebele style for G6
T-shirts sizes M to XL for G30
Masks carved in wood for G80
```

`CurioStore1` has almost the same structure as the `FlagMaker1` program. It has two classes – `CurioStore1` and `Curio`. The `main` method in both cases just serves as an entry point into the program's constructor where the real work gets done. In this program, three objects are declared, created and then their values are written out.

For each curio, three values are specified – the name, the price and a short description. In the `Curio` class, these values are copied into the object, so that they are available when we have to write them out. Notice that writing the values uses a different order of the values from that used when the object is created, i.e. name, description, price, as opposed to name, price, description.

As we shall see soon, a class such as `Curio` describes fully the information regarding a real-world entity. Within a program such as `CurioStore1` (which is also set up as a class), objects of the class `Curio` are created.

Exercise: Following the pattern established in the program, add a fourth curio to the shop, say woven baskets. Think of a price and a description for the new curio and go through the steps to get the object created and printed. Recompile and rerun the program, and check that it works.

2.2   The structure of a program

Basic concepts

We start our study of Java by noting precisely how to write down the instructions that introduce a Java program. In so doing, it is necessary to introduce several concepts informally, which will be formally introduced again as we proceed. Some of these are already fairly familiar from the examples in the previous section.

- **Program** is a general term used to describe a set of one or more Java classes that can be compiled and run.

- **Class** describes the variables and methods appropriate to some real-world entity.

- **Object** is created from a class by means of the new statement. The process of creating an object is called **instantiation** or **object creation**.

- **Variable** contains a value that a method can work on. Some variables contain simple values such as `price`, other variables refer to entire objects, such as `mugs`.

- **Identifier** is the name of an entity in Java, such as a class. `CurioStore1` is such an identifier, so is `carvings`.

- **Keyword** is a word that has a special meaning in Java and cannot be used as an identifier, such as `class` or `new`.

- **Statement:** the work of a program is done through its statements. A statement causes some action, such as to instantiate an object or to call a method to print out a message.

- **Method** groups together statements to provide a structured functionality for a Java object. A method is defined with an identifier and its own body of variables and statements. It is activated by calling it via its identifier. Examples are `main`, `write` and `paint`.

- **Constructor:** every class has a special method called a constructor that is activated when an object of that class is instantiated. The constructor has the same identifier as the class.

- **Parameters:** a method can have variations based on values supplied to it in parentheses. For example, the calls to create each of the curios in the `CurioStore1` program have different lists of parameters.

Figure 2.2 illustrates the structure. It is not necessary at this stage to understand everything about these concepts right now: they will be re-introduced formally as we go along. However, Java is a very integrated language, and sometimes the explanation of one concept refers to another. That is why we listed the concepts briefly first above, and will proceed to take them further as the chapter progresses.

Model diagrams

Missing from Figure 2.2 is the object: where is it? The object that constitutes the program that is run is instantiated in the `main` method through the

```
new Welcome ();
```

statement. The object view of a Java program is illustrated by means of a model diagram, of which there are many in this book. Figure 2.3 shows a model diagram for the `Welcome` program. The notation used draws on the popular UML notation, but is extended to illustrate more concepts at the basic level at which we are working while we learn to program in Java.

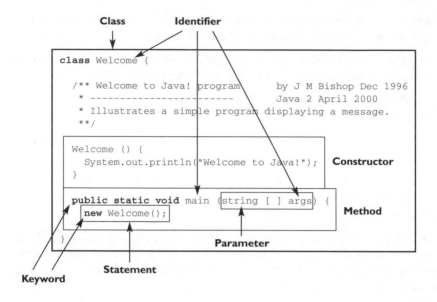

Figure 2.2 *The structure of a program.*

In model diagrams, both class and objects are boxes with three sections – identifier, variables and methods. A class is descriptive, so it is shown with dotted lines, whereas an object represents a real entity in storage and is shown with solid lines. Consider first the class box: it is called `Welcome`, it has no variables and it has one method – `main`. On the right is the object of the class `Welcome`. Since this object does not have a identifier itself, we give the class identifer preceded by `:`. The object does not have any variables itself, only a constructor which has the same name as the class.

These diagrams can also show the work of the classes by using boxes with turned-over corners, as shown in Figure 2.4. The contents of these boxes can be Java, abbreviated Java or plain English.

Syntax forms for Java

Java is a language and as such has a syntax. In this book, Java's syntax is explained by means of form boxes and examples. The following pattern gives the format we must use for a simple program.

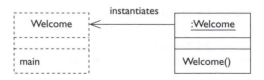

Figure 2.3 *Model diagram for the* `Welcome` *program.*

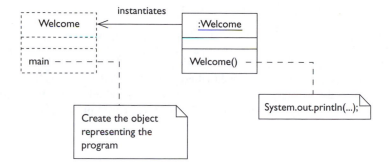

Figure 2.4 *The Welcome model diagram with method explanations.*

```
Simple program

class Classid {
  Classid () {
    data and control
  }

  public static void main (String [] argname) {
    new Classid ();
  }
}
```

The top line of the form gives the name of the Java concept being defined. The contents of the box give the syntax of the concept, in the usual layout that would be used for it. There are three kinds of words in a form, with the following meanings:

- *Italics* are used for identifiers, or other more higher-level program parts, that we fill in with something that matches, e.g. *Classid* could be `CurioStore1`.

- **Bold** is used for Java keywords that must be there, e.g. **class** or **new**. (Note that in the text of the book, though, we leave the keywords in plain program font.)

- Plain – identifiers and symbols that have to be in these positions but are neither keywords, e.g. `main` and `[ ]`, nor placeholders for other identifiers (as in the first point).

Consider again the `Welcome` program in Example 2.1:

```
class Welcome {

  Welcome () {
    System.out.println("Welcome to Java!");
  }
```

```
public static void main (String [ ] args) {
   new Welcome ();
 }
}
```

We see that the three optional parts have been filled in with the *Classid* as `Welcome`, the data and control as the single `println`, and *argname* is called `args`. These parts are underlined for clarity. Everything else is fixed or consequential on the choice of the class name.

Java semantics

Whereas syntax tells us how a program should be structured and what elements are needed in what order, there is still the meaning of any particular arrangement of those elements to consider. The meaning will tell us what effect that part of the program will have. We therefore consider the **semantics** of a construct, as well as its syntax.

There is no accepted way of expressing Java semantics, other than by describing what happens in fairly precise English. In order to make the description easier to refer to, we shall, where relevant, couple a semantic part to a syntax form as follows:

Simple program

```
class Classid {
   Classid () {
      data and control
   }

   public static void main (String [] argname) {
      new Classid ();
   }
}
```

The Java system calls the `main` method which instantiates the program via a `new` on the constructor for *Classid*. Execution of the program proceeds from the constructor and ends when the last statement in sequence has been reached.

The semantic description in a form is precise and therefore necessarily brief. The text after the form usually gives much more explanation, as well as essential examples.

Identifiers and keywords

Names in computer languages are called **identifiers**. An identifier in Java consists of letters, underscores and digits, but must start with a letter. Spaces are not allowed, and capital and small letters are considered to be different so that `CurioStore1` is not the same as `Curiostore1`. If an identifier consists of more than one word, to make it easier to read, the convention is to use capitals to start the inner words.

In the `Welcome` program, the following are all identifiers:

```
Welcome        System         out            println
main           String         args
```

A further convention is that all identifiers, except those for class identifiers, start with a small letter, so we can see immediately that in the above list, `Welcome`, `System` and `String` are all classes.

Keywords are those identifiers reserved for Java's use and may not be used by the programmer for anything else. Thus we cannot call the name of a program 'class', for example, as that word is reserved. In the `Welcome` program, the keywords are:

```
class          public         static         void           new
```

The full list of Java's keywords is given in Table 2.1, divided up alphabetically into three main categories. There is no need to memorize this list: new keywords are introduced as they are needed, and summarized at the end of each chapter.

Table 2.1 *Java keywords*

Data	Control	Objects
boolean	break	abstract
byte	case	class
char	catch	extends
double	default	implements
false	do	import
final	else	instanceof
float	finally	interface
int	for	native
long	if	new
short	return	null
static	switch	package
transient	synchronized	private
true	throw	protected
void	throws	public
	try	super
	while	this
		volatile

Java symbols

In addition to identifiers and keywords, the outline of a Java program includes various **symbols**, of which the most frequently appearing are the following:

- ■ { } curly brackets, which are used to identify a group of statements as a class or a method and so on.

- ■ ( ) parentheses, which are used to group a list of items, even if the list has only one item or none, as can be seen in the parameters in the `Welcome` program.

- ■ ; a semicolon, which is used at the end of each statement.

- ■ , a comma to separate items of a list, whether it is in parentheses or not.

- ■ [ ] square brackets for identifying special kinds of identifiers (explained below).

The curly brackets of a program must match for each class and method. In the form, the outer set refers to the class and the inner sets refer to the constructor and to the `main` method. By ending statements with a semicolon, there can be several statements to a line, but most of the time Java programmers stick to one statement per line. There is more about the layout of a program at the end of Section 2.4.

The creation and running of a program

Following on from the discussion in this section, we can interpret what is meant by each of the lines of the `Welcome` program. The introduction of the class name is clear. Thereafter, we have a constructor and a single method called `main`. `main` has three keywords in front of it – `public static void` – that must be there but that we shall study properly later. Suffice to say that when the Java Virtual Machine is activated by running the Java command, as described in Chapter 1, it must be given the name of a class. It then looks for a `public static void` method called `main` in the class of that name, and starts running the program from there. The parameter in the syntax form is there so that information can be transmitted to the program when it starts up. There is more about this Java feature in Chapter 4.

  The `main` method creates an object of the class of the program and calls its constructor. In this case, the `Welcome` constructor is called and the statement to call `println` is executed. The constructor ends with its } and goes back to where it was called from, i.e. `main`. `main` then ends and the program terminates successfully. Figure 2.3 showed a model diagram for the `Welcome` program.

2.3   Basics of object orientation

Classes

As we have already experienced, a Java **program** consists of a set of one or more interdependent classes. **Classes** are a means for describing the properties and capabilities of

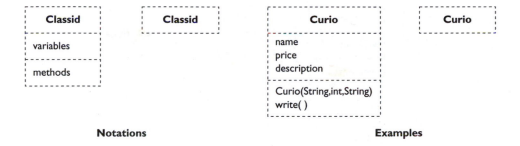

Notations   Examples

Figure 2.5 *Notations for a class.*

the objects in real life with which the program deals. For example, our `CurioStore1` program has a class for curios and `FlagMaker1` has a class for flags. Once we have a class, we can create many objects of that same class. Classes can also be related to each other in a hierarchy, as we shall see in Chapter 9.

A class is represented by one of the diagrammatic symbols in Figure 2.5, depending on the level of detail we want to show. 'id' is short for identifier, so `Classid` means class identifier. Notice that `Classid` will always start with a capital letter.

The `Curio` constructor (which is also a method) declares the types of its parameters which are needed when a curio is instantiated.

Objects

An **object** is a concrete realization of a class definition. It is usually associated with a noun, such as a tree or a book, a curio, a student or a flag. As such, it has various properties and capabilities. The process of generating new objects for a program is referred to as creating an **instance** of a class. When a class is instantiated, the properties it describes become the object's **variables** and its capabilities become the object's **methods**. In the case of a `Curio` object, we have three variables – `name`, `price` and `description` – and we have two methods – the constructor and `write`. Together the variables and methods of a class are called its **members**. The notation with an example is shown in Figure 2.6.

Variables

A **variable** constitutes storage in the computer which can hold values that change. Simple variables hold numbers, for example. An **object variable** holds a reference to the storage where an object is to be placed. Variables do not in themselves have symbols, but are shown as identifiers in the variables section of the relevant class or object. If the value is a simple one, we use an equals sign followed by the value. If it is an object, we can show an arrow with a solid head going out to the object. (We do not have to: it depends on how much detail we want in the diagram.)

For example, a `Curio` object such as `mugs` is part of the `CurioStore1` object and the two of them together look as shown in Figure 2.7.

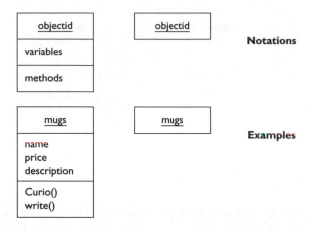

Figure 2.6 *Notations for an object.*

There are six variables depicted in Figure 2.7: can you see what they are?

The reason why we underline object identifiers is to emphasize that they do not exist in the object itself. No object in Java has its own identifier: the identifier is associated with a variable. Sometimes even the object variable's identifier is not known, as in the case of the object variable created in main methods, in which case we use the notation `:Classid`.

Depicting instantiation

It will frequently be necessary to show an object and the class it is instantiated from. For this dependency we use a dotted arrow, as in Figure 2.8. Here we have chosen to use the compact form of the objects and classes, to emphasize the dependency.

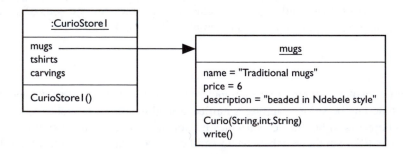

Figure 2.7 *Example of an object variable and an object.*

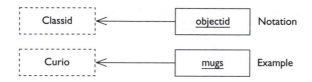

Figure 2.8 *Relationship between an object and its class.*

Declaring object variables and creating objects

To declare an object variable, we use the following form:

Declaration of an object variable
`Classid objectid;` `Classid objectid1, objectid2, ... objectid n;`
An object variable with the identifier *objectid* is declared and given a value `null`. There may not be duplicate object variable identifiers in a class.

At this stage, the object itself does not exist and any attempt to access any of the variables or methods described by its class will fail. For example, taking a snapshot of the `CurioStore1` program just as the constructor starts, we would have Figure 2.9, which shows three object variables, all set to a special value null. Then to create the object itself, we use the form:

Instantiation of an object
`objectid = `**`new`**` Classid (parameterlist);`
A new object is created for the object variable referred to by *objectid* according to the specifications of the class *Classid*.   The constructor of *Classid* is called with the *parameterlist* given (if any). The constructor can use the list of parameter values as it wishes (see the end of the section for further details).

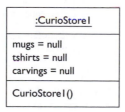

Figure 2.9 *Declared object variables.*

As an example, consider the `CurioStore1` program again. In it we declare three object variables, effectively announcing that these identifiers will be used for objects of this class:

```
Curio mugs, tshirts, carvings;
```

and then we have the statements:

```
mugs = new Curio("Traditional mugs", 6, "beaded in Ndebele style");
tshirts = new Curio("T-shirts", 30, "sizes M to XL");
carvings = new Curio("Masks", 80, "carved in wood");
```

where each object is instantiated using '= new' as the signal to create an instance of the class by assigning storage for the data required by a `Curio` object. For each object the `Curio` constructor is called, which causes the initial values as specified in the parameter list to be put into the object. Figure 2.10 shows a snapshot of the situation after the `mugs` and `tshirts` have been instantiated as objects and just before the `carvings` object is handled. In this diagram, we do not show any classes, since we are concentrating on the instantiation process.

Let us distinguish carefully here between an object variable, and the actual object. When the program begins, the `main` method is executed and it creates an object for the `Curiostore1` class. This object has three object variables in it. Each of them potentially refers to a curio object. Until the actual creation happens (via the execution of the '= new'), the variables contain a null reference. Thus `carvings` is shown as `null`,

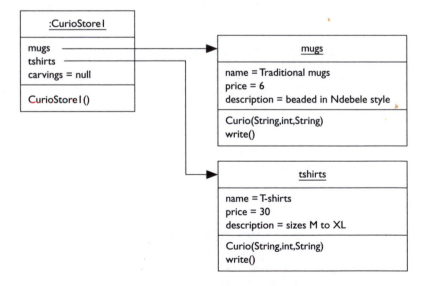

Figure 2.10 *Diagram of* Curio *objects being created – shows a snapshot of the situation after the* mugs *and* tshirts *have been instantiated as objects and just before the* carvings *object is handled.*

whereas the other two object variables are shown pointing off to their created objects, complete with initial values.

Accessing members of an object

To access the members of an object, we use the dot operator as described in the form:

Accessing members of an object
`objectid.variableid`
`objectid.methodid ()`
`objectid.methodid(parameters)`

Examples of this dot operator in the programs in Section 2.1 are:

```
g.drawString ("Germany",100,180);

mugs.write();
```

The objects involved are `g` and `mugs`, and the methods are `drawString` and `write` respectively. We can also access the variables of an object, as in:

```
mugs.price
tshirts.description
```

Manipulating object variables

We said when defining variables that their values can change. The most common way of changing a variable's value is by **assignment**, using an equals operator, as we have already seen in the `Curio` constructor, i.e.

```
Curio (String n, int p, String d) {
  name = n;
  price = p;
  description = d;
}
```

Here the values of n, p and d are assigned and stored in the variables `name`, `price` and `description` respectively. Now what does it mean to change the value of an object variable? An object variable may refer to an object if it has been through an instantiation process. It is quite in order to change it to refer to another object. If we are going to do so, then we would set up an object variable with a fairly generic name, for example:

```
Curio checked;
```

Then we could have the following sequence of statements which goes through the three kinds of curios one by one and writes their values:

```
checked = tshirts;
checked.write();
checked = carvings;
checked.write();
checked = mugs;
checked.write();
```

Of course, this sequence is somewhat artificial, but it does illustrate the use of object variables. Figure 2.11 goes through the steps of the process, explaining it further. The objects in the diagram are shown as plain rectangles, without their usual contents. At this point, when we call `checked.write()` it is the `write` method in the `tshirts` object that is called, and it will be the values of the `tshirts` object that are written. After the next assignment, `checked` refers to the `carvings` object.

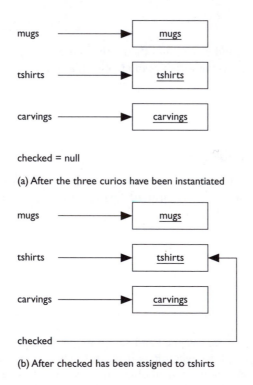

(a) After the three curios have been instantiated

(b) After checked has been assigned to tshirts

Figure 2.11 *Manipulating object variables.*

Constructors and their parameters

A constructor has three distinct roles:

1. When the class has a main method, it performs work of a program (as in Examples 2.1 and 2.3).

2. If the program involves graphics, the constructor is responsible for creating the frame, its size and so on (as in Example 2.2).

3. When the class is a descriptive one for the creation of several objects, the constructor is used to copy the initial values into the object's variables (as in the Curio class of Example 2.3).

The third role requires that we understand something about parameters at this stage. Consider the beginning of the Curio class and its constructor:

```
class Curio {

  // Declare variables related to a curio
  String name;
  int price;
  String description;

Curio (String n, int p, String d) {
  name = n;
  price = p;
  description = d;
}
...  and so on
```

Three variables are declared, and the constructor lists three corresponding parameters – two strings and an integer, known in Java as an int. There will be more about integers in the next chapter, but for now all we have to know is that they are numbers and that they can be copied into variables that are also integers using assignment via the equals sign. So when we create a curio using, for example,

```
mugs = new Curio("Traditional mugs", 6, "beaded in Ndebele style");
```

"Traditional mugs" is matched up with the parameter n and copied into the variable name; 6 is matched up with p and copied into price and "beaded in Ndebele style" is matched with d and copied into description. Java will not allow the parameters to be mixed up: they must match in their types, i.e. strings for strings and integers for integers.

2.4   Beginning with output

Having covered the fundamental structure of a Java program with our examples, we can now consider how to write a simple program that displays something on the screen. In programming parlance what goes to the screen is called **output**, but programmers often use the terms write, print, output and display interchangeably. Unlike many other languages, there is no special statement for output in Java. All output is handled by methods in classes supplied by the language. Thus in order to print, we have to know *which* methods to call.

The methods we are looking for are called `println` and `print`. They are found in a built-in Java class called `PrintStream`. Within the special, universally available class called `System`, there is already a `PrintStream` object defined, called `out`, which is automatically connected by Java to the screen of your computer. Therefore from these three components:

- the class `System`,

- the object `out`, and

- the methods `print` and `println`,

we can construct the correct method call statements for displaying output. Because these method calls will be used so often, we refer to them as output statements as a shorthand. The simple form of Java statements to display a piece of text is:

Output statements

`System.out.println (string);`
`System.out.println (string1 + string2 + ... + stringn);`
`System.out.println ();`
`System.out.print (string);`
`System.out.print (string1 + string2 + ... + stringn);`

`Println` outputs the string or list of strings and ends the line of output. `Print` does not end the line. `Println` on its own gives the effect of ending or skipping a line.

As this form indicates, Java only prints strings, although we shall see later how the effective conversion of numbers to strings means we can print those too. When several strings are to be printed on one line, they are joined by a + (more on this below).

Strings for printing

A **string literal** is any sequence of characters enclosed in quotes, for example

```
"sizes M to XL"
"Licence No. CFD678GT"
"€5.95 per kg"
```

Although string literal is the correct term, much of the time we just use the word **string**. If a quote itself is needed in the string then a backslash \ precedes it. The backslash does not form part of the string, but enables the next character to do so. An example is:

```
"He said \"No\""
```

which is the string *He said "No"*. Calling the `println` method displays the string given as a parameter and ends the line of printing. (The '`-ln`' in `println` is short for 'line'.) Thus, the statements

```
System.out.println("€5.95 per kg");
System.out.println("He said \"No\"");
```

will cause the following to be displayed:

```
€5.95 per kg
He said "No"
```

(The symbol € is the currency symbol for the euro, the European common currency.)

The `print` method works in a similar way except that it does not end the line, so that a subsequent `print` or `println` will continue on the same line from the last point reached. The string is optional for the `println` method. If `println` is called on its own, then it will finish the current line. This facility can also be used to obtain a blank line, as in:

```
System.out.println ("€5.95 per kg");
System.out.println ();
System.out.println ("He said \"No\"");
```

which would give as output:

```
e5.95 per kg

He said "No"
```

Note that any Java method call that does not provide parameters (the items in brackets) must still have the brackets. To obtain several blank lines, we can use several `println` calls in a row, as in:

```
System.out.println();
System.out.println();
System.out.println();
```

Alternatively, we can make use of another special character, \n, standing for 'new line', as in:

```
System.out.println ("\n\n\n");
```

EXAMPLE 2.4   Displaying a warning

Problem   Display a warning message on the screen that the computer might have a virus.[3]

Program   This program is very simple, and similar to that in Example 2.1. It has a class, a constructor and a main method, followed by several output statements which when executed will display the box shown below.

```
class DisplayWarning {

    /* Displaying a warning program        by J M Bishop Aug 1996
     * --------------------------          Java 1.1 October 1997
     *                                      updated and Java 2 April 2000
     * Illustrates the form of a program and the use of println.
     */

    DisplayWarning () {
      System.out.println("----------------------------");
      System.out.println("|                          |");
      System.out.println("|        W A R N I N G     |");
      System.out.println("|   Possible virus detected |");
      System.out.println("|    Reboot and run virus   |");
      System.out.println("|       remover software    |");
      System.out.println("|                          |");
      System.out.println("----------------------------");
    }

    public static void main (String [] args) {
      new DisplayWarning ();
    }
}
```

Testing   The output produced by this program would be:

```
----------------------------
|                          |
|        W A R N I N G     |
|   Possible virus detected |
|    Reboot and run virus   |
|       remover software    |
|                          |
----------------------------
```

[3] A virus is a program that can infect your computer and cause damage to fields on the disk and so on. This program does not itself detect a virus: it just prints out the warning message.

Concatenation

One final point about strings and printing: What happens should a string be too long to fit on a single line of a screen when we are writing a program? We cannot go on to the next line. We have to end the string and start a new one, joining the two together with a plus operator. This is known formally as **concatenation**. An example of concatenation would be:

```
System.out.println ("Your tree is not known to us. Would "+
        "you like to submit details of it by WWW or " +
        "courier?");
```

There are many more examples of long strings in the programs that follow, as well as in the next example.

EXAMPLE 2.5	Curio shop table

Problem We want to write out the details of the stock in the curio shop, but using a table with the details that we have recorded neatly lined up.

Solution Instead of making use of the `write` method, we are going to access each field separately, for each object, using the dot notation. A statement such as

```
mugs.write();
```

is replaced by

```
System.out.println(mugs.item+"\t"+mugs.description+"\t"+mugs.price);
```

where \t will tab to the start of a next set number of characters. The statement will print out

```
T-shirts                sizes M to XL                30
```

When put together with similar statements for the other two curios, the output will be:

```
The Polelo Curio Store
=======================

Items                   Descriptions                Price per item
-----------------------------------------------------------------
Traditional mugs        beaded in Ndebele style     6
T-shirts                sizes M to XL               30
Masks                   carved in wood              80
```

Notes:

1. The long string for the underline was split over two lines, but had to be divided into two and concatenated.

2. The size of a tab on output could vary: on our machine it was a mere four characters so we had to adjust the number of tabs used with each object in order to get the values neatly lined up.

Layout

How the program is written down, in terms of lines and spaces, does not have an effect on how the output appears. Only what is inside the quotes is actually displayed when the program executes. When the output statements display strings, there is no gap in the output if the string in the program had to be split into different pieces joined by +. In the same way, blank lines or comments in the program do not have any effect on the output. Therefore, the following statements will cause the same output to be displayed as before:

```
System.out.println("€5.95 " + "per kg");


                System.out.println();
  System.out.println("He " +
"said \"No\"");
```

The point is that the instructions given to the computer do not *have* to be in any special layout. We usually write them neatly one underneath each other, and we also use **indenting** to make groups of statements stand out, but there is no formal rule that says this should be so. Other points about the layout of the program are:

- more than one statement can be written on a line;

- statements can be split over several lines (but strings cannot);

- statements are ended by semicolons.

2.5   Simple calculations

Like calculators, computers are very good at doing calculations. In this section we look at how to do simple integer-based calculations in Java, and how to assign the results to a variable. In the next chapter we shall study other kinds of calculation as well.

Types

We have already discussed earlier in the chapter how objects store their data in variables. In Java every variable has a **type** and only those of the same type can be used together.

Put in simple terms, this means that we cannot mix strings and numbers, nor could we mix trees and curios. We can separate variables into those that represent object types (such as `mugs` being an object variable of type `Curio`) and those that represent **primitive** types. Java has eight such built-in primitive types, which we shall examine in Chapter 3. Here we look at only one, that for integers, called `int` in Java.

Declaring variables

Variables may be declared anywhere in a Java class or method or any other group of statements delimited by { and }. Such a group of statements is known as a **block**, and we shall see them in use later. Usually declarations are grouped at the beginning or end of the block. The form of a primitive variable declaration is one of the following:

Primitive variable declaration

```
type id;
type id₁, id₂, ... idₙ;
type id = value;
```

Creates a variable according to the type and assigns the identifier to it.

The third form optionally gives an initial value to the variable. If there is no value, a default is set (such as 0 for numbers).

Identifiers may not be duplicated in any block of statements between { and }.

The declaration introduces one or more variables of the given type. The last form can be used to initialize a variable at the same time as declaring it. Examples of declarations of integer variables are:

```
int temperature;           // in degrees Celsius
int oldWeight, newWeight;  // in kilograms
int price;                 // in graz
int maxMark = 100;
```

As mentioned in the form, identifiers must be distinct within a block.

It is worthwhile keeping declarations neat and tidy, with the identifiers and types lined up. It is also a useful habit to indicate what the variables are to be used for, if this is not immediately obvious from their identifiers, as well as to give some supporting information regarding the units that are intended, as shown in the first three examples.

When variables are declared we have the option of specifying an initial value or of receiving a **default initialization**. For the numeric types, the default is zero. It is quite safe to rely on the default, but many programmers prefer to make their initializations explicit.

Expressions

Expression is the term given to formulae in programming languages. Expressions consist of **operands** which are numbers or variables, and **operators**, which in the case of the `int` type start out with the usual brackets, multiplication, division, addition and subtraction. The way in which expressions are written in programming languages is somewhat different from the normal way of writing them. The main differences are that:

- multiplication is indicated by an asterisk `*`;

- division is indicated by a slash `/`;

- denominators follow numerators on the same line.

The implication of the last point – writing on one line – is that we use more brackets in Java expressions than we would in ordinary mathematics. Division that would usually be written as a fraction has to be split into two bracketed parts separated by a slash. For example, consider some simple formulae and their Java equivalents:

Formula	Expression in Java
$\dfrac{euros}{rate}$	`euros/rate`
$\dfrac{30test + 20project + 50exam}{100}$	`(30*test+20*project+50*exam)/100`

An important consideration is that in Java the division operator `/` works at two levels: integer and real. If both the values are integer, it performs integer division, otherwise it performs real division. Integer division is not usually what one wants, for example 1/2 will produce 0. However, it does have its uses, as shown in Example 2.6 later on in this section. We consider real division in Section 3.1.

As well as the usual four operators (or five, if we regard / as having two meanings), use is often made in programming of finding the remainder after integer division. The operator used to represent this **modulus** is `%`. Examples of its use are:

```
23 % 2    which gives   1
 6 % 6    which gives   0
81 % 11   which gives   4
```

Java, like other modern languages, also provides special operators for adding or subtracting one. These are `++` and `--`. These are most useful in the context of assignment, which we discuss next.

Assignment

Having declared a variable, we can now use an **assignment** to give it the value of an expression. The assignment statement has the form:

Assignment statement

```
variable = expression;
variable ++;
variable --;
variable op= expression;
```

The value of the expression calculation is put in the variable. This statement
  applies to all variables, primitive and object.

++ and -- add one and subtract one from the variable's value (only for numeric
  variables).

op= applies the operator between the existing value of the variable and the expression and assigns the result back into the variable (only for numeric variables).

The effect of an **assignment statement** is to evaluate the expression and to assign the
resulting value to the variable indicated by the identifier. The equals sign which indicates
the assignment is read 'becomes'. Thus if we write:

```
temperature = 24;
```

we would read it as 'temperature becomes 24'. The value of the expression is 24, and this
is assigned to the variable `temperature`. In the next sequence:

```
oldWeight = 65;
newWeight = oldWeight - 5;
```

`oldWeight` is assigned the value 65, and is then used to calculate the value for the variable `newWeight` which is 60.

Assignment requires that the types of the expression and the variable are the same.
Thus we cannot assign something of type `int` to a `Curio` object. Assignment is also the
means for assigning and creating objects, as we have already seen with statements such as

```
mugs = new Curios("Traditional mugs", 6, "beaded in Ndebele style");
```

Here the instantiation is essentially an expression, which produces a value that is the reference to the new object, and this is assigned to the `mugs` object variable.

In programming, a common operation is to add 1 to a counter. For example, we might
have the assignment:

```
int total;
total = total + 1;
```

Since this is such a common kind of assignment, it seems wasteful to have to type the
variable's name twice in every case. Thus there are special assignments defined to abbre-
viate common increments and decrements as shown in the form.

i++ or i+=1 mean the same thing: 'add 1 to i', whereas 'i+=2' means 'add 2 to i', and so on. Thus the example above becomes:

```
total++;
```

If we were always adding 5, then we would use

```
total += 5;
```

One way to remember that the increment operator is += and not =+ is that the latter, in an assignment, could be misinterpreted as assigning a positive value, not adding it. That is,

```
total =+ 5;
```

would treat +5 as a constant and assign it to `total`.

The shorthand forms can be used with the other operators as well, most typically minus and multiply. Thus if we were always doubling a value, we could say:

```
int power;
power *= 2;
```

Precedence

In Java, the normal **precedence** rules for operators apply, with brackets coming before division and multiplication, which are performed before addition and subtraction. The precedence groups for arithmetic operators are as follows, with operators within a group being evaluated from left to right:

Operator precedence (arithmetic)	
group 0:	( )
group 1:	++ -- + (unary) - (unary)
group 2:	* / %
group 3:	+ - + (concatenation)

Group 0 operators have highest priority.
The operators within a group are evaluated from left to right.

The precedence in Java (which matches that of another popular language, C) is such that one seldom needs to use parentheses to make an expression clear.

Printing expressions

The explanatory examples so far have used calls to the `print` and `println` methods to print **strings**. It is also possible to print **numbers** and, indeed, to print the results of calculations. For example, to print 4 times 5 less 2 we would have

```
System.out.println (4 * 5 - 2);
```

which would print out

```
18
```

Similarly, we can print out the values of expressions involving variables, for example,

```
int hoursPerDay = 24;
System.out.println (7 * hoursPerDay);
```

which would print

```
168
```

The number is printed with exactly as many digits as needed. If more careful formatting is required, we need to employ additional Java utilities, which are discussed in Chapters 4 and 7.

The `toString` method

What if we want to print more than one value out, or a mixture of numbers and strings? We saw in the previous section that several strings can be printed out in one print call if they are joined by a concatenate (plus) operator. The same applies here. However, now we have to understand what is going on behind the scenes.

The concatenate operator joins strings. When it finds something else to its left or right – for example, a number – it looks for a `toString` method defined by the class, which can convert that value to a string. All the built-in types have `toString` methods and classes such as `Curio` can easily define them. The + operator can then perform the concatenation and the printing proceeds. For example, we can say:

```
System.out.println (7 + " days is "
                    + (7 * hoursPerDay) + " hours");
```

which would print

```
7 days is 168 hours
```

The number and the expression were converted to strings and joined up with the other two strings to make the full message. Notice that it is important to include spaces in a string that is adjacent to a number, since such spaces are not otherwise inserted.

| EXAMPLE 2.6 | Fleet timetables |

Problem   Savanna Deliveries Inc. has acquired new vehicles that are able to travel faster than the old vehicles (while still staying within the speed limit). They would like to know how this will affect journeys.

Solution   Times are represented in a 24 hour clock, such as 0930 or 1755. We need to find out how an arrival time will change, based on an average reduction in the total journey time of 15%. Therefore, we need to be able to subtract times to find the journey time and multiply the result by 0.85, representing a 15% reduction. The question is how to do arithmetic on times.

Algorithm   Times consist of two parts – hours and minutes. In order to do subtraction and multiplication on times, we have to convert them to minutes first, perform the calculation, then convert back. Assuming we can do this, the overall algorithm is:

> **New fleet**
> Set up the departure and arrival times.
> Calculate journey time in minutes.
> Reduce journey time by 15%.
> Add the new journey time to the departure time to get the new arrival time.
> Print out new journey time and new arrival time.

The first conversion involves splitting an integer into two parts. To do this, we need to divide by 100, giving the hours, and get the minutes by taking the remainder. The algorithm with an example is:

> **Convert to minutes**
> | | |
> |---|---|
> | Time is | 0715 |
> | Find hours from time /100 | 7 |
> | Find minutes from time modulo 100 | 15 |
> | Set minutes to hours * 60 + minutes | 435 |

Converting back is similar. The algorithm is:

> **Convert to hours and minutes**
> | | |
> |---|---|
> | Minutes are | 435 |
> | Set hours to minutes /60 | 7 |
> | Set minutes from minutes modulo 60 | 15 |
> | Set time to hours * 100 + minutes | 715 |

Program   The program to handle one journey is quite simple. The departure and arrival times of a particular vehicle are initialized with the variables. In Chapter 4 we shall see how to read them into the program instead. Remember that division of integer values yields an integer result, so that the algorithms above have a direct translation into Java.

```
class FleetCalculator {

    /* The Fleet Calculator Program          by J M Bishop Aug 1996
     * ---------------------------           Java 1.1 Oct 1997
     *                                       update and Java 2, Apr 2000
     * Works out the new arrival time for vehicles that
     * do a journey in 15% less time.
     *
     * Illustrates expressions and assignment.
     * Includes use of the modulo operator %
     */

    FleetCalculator () {

        int reduction = 85;
        int depart24 = 900;
        int arrive24 = 1020;

        int newArrive24,           // 24 hour clock time
            departMins,            // minutes in a day
            arriveMins,
            oldJourneyMins,
            newJourneyMins,
            newArriveMins;

    // convert the initial times to minutes
        departMins = depart24 / 100 * 60 + depart24 % 100;
        arriveMins = arrive24 / 100 * 60 + arrive24 % 100;

    // calculate the old and new times
        oldJourneyMins = arriveMins - departMins;
        newJourneyMins = oldJourneyMins * reduction / 100;

    // create the new arrival time in minutes and
    // then in a 24 hour clock time
        newArriveMins = departMins + newJourneyMins;
        newArrive24 = newArriveMins / 60 * 100 + newArriveMins % 60;

    // Report on the findings
        System.out.println("Departure time is "+depart24);
        System.out.println("Old arrival time is "+arrive24);
        System.out.println("Old journey time is "
                            +oldJourneyMins+" minutes");
        System.out.println("New journey time is "
                            +newJourneyMins+" minutes");
        System.out.println("New arrival time is "+newArrive24);
    }

    public static void main (String[] args) {
        new FleetCalculator ();
    }
}
```

Notice that we use six different variables to keep all the values relevant at any one time. They are also given names that indicate their meaning well.

Testing To test the program, we choose some suitable departure and arrival times and set them in the program. Running the program gives:

```
Departure time is 900
Old arrival time is 1020
Old journey time is 80 minutes
New journey time is 68 minutes
New arrival time is 1008
```

More about testing

This is our first program that involves calculations that can differ from run to run of the program, if we change the initial values. We must therefore test that the calculations we do will work correctly for all possible values. Clearly, running the program for every single possible time would be very time-consuming with the Java skills we have right now, but we can choose a representative selection of data values and test the program with them.

Errors in programs usually occur on boundary values, such as zero, or the last possible value. Also, what will the above program do if it is given a completely unexpected value, such as a negative percentage or an arrival time before the departure time? What we usually try to do is to devise a sequence of test values where we vary one and keep the others static, then move on to vary the next value. Here is a selection of data sets to try:

percent	depart24	arrive24	
0	900	1020	
100	900	1020	
115	900	1020	tests what happens if the new cars are slower
50	900	1020	
1	900	1020	tests small percentages
85	0	1020	
85	1019	1020	tests very small journey times
85	1100	1020	tests incorrect departure time
85	2400	1020	tests what happens with the last possible 24 time
85	900	2359	

The above list is not exhaustive, but gives you an idea of what to try. Of course, it will be very tedious changing the program each time to test new values. Soon we shall see how to keep a program and just type in values which can be read into the variables.

SUMMARY

This chapter introduced programming at two levels. At the high level, we looked at classes and objects, how they are defined and instantiated, and some of the finer details such as constructors. The discussion was preceded by the presentation of three programs that illustrated the basic concepts needed for object-oriented programming, such as classes, objects, constructors, methods, parameters and statements. One program, `FlagMaker1`, had the elements of simple graphics. Object-orientation continued into accessing members of objects and assigning object variables.

On a lower level, we discussed the syntax for identifiers, keywords, assignment and printing, and began with elementary calculations based on expressions and assignment. Concatenation was seen as being a very useful facility for joining several values in a single output call. The common types `int` and `String` were introduced so as to enable a good range of programs to be tackled right from the start. Notations for syntax forms and sematics were defined and used throughout the chapter. Model diagrams based on UML made an appearance, and will be further explained as we progress.

Concepts related to the following keywords were discussed

```
class     new
int       null
```

The following keywords were used, but their meaning will be more fully explained later:

```
import    void
public    extends
static
```

The following classes, objects and methods from Java's packages were introduced and used extensively:

```
System.out.println    String
System.out.print      toString
```

The following were introduced specifically for the drawing program (`FlagMaker1`):

```
java.awt              System.exit
java.awt.event        setTitle
Frame                 setSize
add                   setVisible
addWindowListener     g.setColor
WindowAdapter         g.fillRect
windowClosing         g.drawString
WindowEvent           Color. ... a colour name
```

Their meaning is fully discussed Chapters 10 and 11.

Syntactic and semantic forms were given for the following concepts:

Simple program
Declaration of an object variable
Instantiation of an object
Accessing members of an object
Output statements
Primitive variable declaration
Assignment statement
Operator precedence (arithmetic)

Model diagram notation was developed for:

class
object
object variable
instantiation

QUIZ

2.1 When the `Welcome` program is run, the first statement to be executed is

(a) the constructor
(b) `System.out.println("Welcome to Java!");`
(c) `new Welcome();`
(d) the `main` method

2.2 To change the colour of drawing to green, we use

(a) `setcolour(green)`
(b) `setcolor(green)`
(c) `g.setColor(Color.green)`
(d) `setColor(Color.green)`

2.3 A comment that begins with `//` must end with

(a) `//`
(b) the end of a line
(c) `*/`
(d) `}`

2.4 The following can be used as identifiers in a Java program:

(a) `out`, `println` and `args`
(b) only `out` and `println`
(c) only `println` and `args`
(d) none of them

2.5 To insert a new line between the printing of two values using `println`, we need

(a) `+ "n" +`
(b) `newline()`
(c) `"\n"`
(d) `+ "\n" +`

2.6 To add 10 to `points`, we would use:

(a) `points + 10`
(b) `points += 10`
(c) `points =+ 10`
(d) `points ++ 10`

2.7 The purpose of a constructor is to:

(a) create space for objects
(b) create space and initialize objects
(d) initialize objects
(d) run the program

2.8 Access to `Curio.name` will cause a compilation error because

(a) name is not defined in Curio
(b) name must be accessed via a Curio object
(c) name should have parentheses after it
(d) Curio should be spelt with a small c

2.9 If `newArriveMins` has the value 310, what will the formula for computing the 24 hour clock time in Example 2.6 give:

(a) 510
(b) 610
(c) 505
(d) 516

2.10 For the `Curio` class, the instantiation
`Baskets = new Curios ("Masks", 30, 80);`
will cause a compilation error because:

(a) the first parameter must be `"Baskets"`
(b) `Baskets` has a capital letter
(c) `Baskets` is not a class
(d) the parameters do not match that of the `Curio` class

PROBLEMS

2.1 **Flag diagram.** Draw a model diagram for the `FlagMaker1` program (Example 2.2).

2.2 **Olympic rings.** We want to draw the Olympic logo of five interlocking rings on the screen, in colour. Use a `Ring` class that has the colour and position of a ring as constructor parameters and then write another class that creates five `Ring` objects to complete the logo. Use `FlagMaker1` as a model. (The rings are blue, yellow, black, green and red, with yellow and green being lower.)

2.3   **Curio stocks.** Extend the Curio Store program (Example 2.3) so that it records how many of each curio are in stock, and alter the program wherever it will be affected so that the information for each curio can be output as in:

```
25 Traditional mugs beaded in Ndebele style for G6
```

(Note: We look at curio selling in Example 3.5.)

2.4   **Vertical flags.** In `FlagMaker1`, change the `paint` method so that it shows flags with vertical bars and try out, for example, Italy, France or Mali (green, yellow, red).

2.5   **Weighted averages.** A computer science course has three parts to it: a test, an assignment and an examination, which are weighted at 20%, 30% and 50% respectively. Write a program that will set marks for the three components (out of 100) and print the final mark using the weightings.

2.6   **Fuel consumption.** A motor car uses 8 litres of fuel per 100 km on normal roads and 15% more fuel on rough roads. Write a program to print out the distance the car can travel on a full tank of 40 litres of fuel on both normal and rough roads.

2.7   **Factory shifts.** At a factory, the 24-hour day is divided into three shifts as follows:

Shift 1   from 0000 to 0759
Shift 2   from 0800 to 1559
Shift 3   from 1600 to 2359

Write a program that, given the time on the clock, calculates the remaining length in hours and minutes of the appropriate shift, and also prints out what shift we are in. (Hint: use % and / as in Example 2.6.)

2.8   **Kindergarten.** Children in a kindergarten have names, surnames, the group they are in (rabbits, puppies, goldfish or doves) and the year they will leave the school (a number up to three years from now). Create a `Child` class to hold this information about a child and test it with a program that instantiates six different children and calls a `write` method to print out their details. The year is an integer and the rest of the variables are strings. The `write` method should also calculate the number of years each child has remaining in the school and print it out on the same line as the other information.

2.9   **Kindergarten diagram.** Draw a compete model diagram for your kindergarten program, taking a snapshot after two children have been created.

2.10 **Book.** We are going to develop a program that keeps information about a textbook. Start by defining a `Chapter` class that has variables for a chapter name and number of pages. Using *Java Gently* as test data, instantiate objects of the first four chapters. Then work through the chapter objects again, calculating the total number of pages so far, and the average number of pages per chapter. Before being typeset, each page contains approximately 80% of the information that it finally does. Work through the four objects again, calculating the first page number of the manuscrpt version of each chapter. For example, if chapter one is 20 pages long now, then in manuscript it would have been 20/0.8 = 25 pages long, and chapter 2 would have started on page 26, not page 21.

2.11 **Book diagram.** Draw a complete model diagram for your Book program, taking a snapshot after two chapters have been created.

2.12   **Shuttle bus.** A shuttle bus operates between two terminals of an airport, departing every hour and halfhour. Write a program that, when given a time as an initialized variable, will calculate how long it is until the next bus departs.

CHAPTER 3

Types and methods

3.1 Talking about types

Having examined integer numbers in Section 2.4, we now continue our discussion of types. Java has six numeric types – `int`, `long`, `double`, `byte`, `short` and `float` – which we shall consider first, and two special types, `boolean` and `char`, which we shall look at later. When considering the numeric types, we raise the issue of how to convert from one to the other, so that assignments can be made between variables of different types.

To complete our discussion of the six numeric types, we show their properties in Table 3.1. `byte` is typically used in programs that are dealing with data at the level of the machine. `short` can be a way of saving space, but is not often used in Java. `int` is the usual type for declaring integers, but `long` also frequently appears as it is the default for the result of an integer expression. `float` would be the natural choice for real numbers, except that `double` is the default type for the result of real expressions. So `int`, `long` and `double` are the types of choice in most programs.

Table 3.1 *Details of the numeric types*

Type value	Representation	Initial value	Storage	Maximum
byte	Signed integer	0	8 bits	127
short	Signed integer	0	16 bits	32 767
int	Signed integer	0	32 bits	2 147 483 647
long	Signed integer	0	64 bits	over 10^{18}
float	Floating point	0.0	32 bits	over 10^{38}
double	Floating point	0.0	64 bits	over 10^{308}

The first four numeric types have access to all the operations mentioned already, and can be output as explained in Section 2.4. float and double are real types and have different properties, operations and output formats. A real number is written as one would expect with a decimal point (not comma) as in:

3.1415962
−80.5
0.000007

but we can also write a number in scientific format, or E-format if it becomes very long. This format has one digit before the point and any number as required up to 16 after it, followed by E and an exponent to the base 10. Thus the above three numbers in E-format would be:

3.141592E0
−8.05E1
7E−6

In terms of operations, the real numbers have + * / but no modulus. They also, as mentioned in Section 2.5, treat the division operator differently from integers. In order to force real division, we must ensure that one of the variables is real, or that a constant in the expression is real, which can be done by explicitly adding a decimal point. For example, consider the following expressions:

```
int roughLength = 180;              // in centimetres
double preciseLength = 185.3427;    // in centimetres
double materialNeeded;              // in metres

materialNeeded = roughLength/100;   // will produce 1 metre
materialNeeded = roughlength/100.0; // will produce 1.8 metres

materialNeeded = preciselength/100; // will produce 1.85327 metres
```

Assignment within each type is a permissible statement. Assignment requires that the types of the expression and the variable are the same. Thus we cannot assign something of type `int` to a `Curio`, or even a `double` variable to an `int` variable. However, bearing in mind that even in mathematics the real numbers encompass the integers, we *can* assign integers to reals. So the following is permissible:

```
double rate;
rate = 10;
```

Printing integers and reals

As we have said earlier, when a number is to be printed, Java calls its `toString` method which returns the string version, and this is passed to the `print` method. `toString` has no information about how many digits it should produce, so it gives all of them. `long` integers may yield as many as 10 digits and `double` real numbers up to 17. If the real number's value lies outside the significance of 17 digits, Java resorts to printing the number in E-format. So, how would Java print the following numeric expressions?

Number	Printed as
10	10
650	650
2001	2001
14.75	14.75
1.6213	1.6213
1/1.6213	0.6167889964843027
123456789	123456789
0.000000001	1.0E-9
1.0/2	0.5
1/2	0

Only the last one is surprising, but remember that Java regards / as an integer operator if both the values are integers. In integer terms, the result of 1 divided by 2 is 0.

Clearly, the problem with the above scheme is the long real numbers. In order to achieve finer control, we shall either have to use a custom-built input–output (IO) package or we shall have to delve into Java's large range of formatting classes in the `java.text` package. We leave these issues to Chapters 4 and 7.

The `Math` class

Java provides for the standard arithmetic and trigonometric functions one would expect even on a good calculator through a special class, `Math`. `Math` belongs to the package `java.lang` which is the only one that is automatically imported into every program. Therefore we can use `Math` functions at any time. The following form summarizes some of the main ones.

Math class methods (abbreviated)

```
final double PI
double pow (double, double)
double sqrt (double)
double atan (double)
double cos (double)        // in radians
double sin (double)        // in radians
double tan (double)        // in radians
double toDegrees (double)
double toRadians (double)
double random ();
int round (float)
long round (double)
value abs (value)          // where value can be int, long, float, double
value max (value, value)   // where value can be int, long, float, double
value min (value, value)   // where value can be int, long, float, double
```

PI is a constant value set to the value of π to about 10 digits.

pow raises the first parameter to the power of the second. If the second is fraction, then pow acts as a root function (see examples below).

The four trigonometric methods all operate in radians of a circle, represented by 2π. Thus 360π is 2*PI and 90π is PI/2.

Values or expressions in degrees or radians can be converted from one to the other.

The random method returns a real value between 0 and 1, which can be manipulated to get other ranges (see below for examples).

The round methods will round the value of the parameter to the next greater integer (see below for examples).

abs gives the absolute (or positive) value of the parameter.

max and min give the maximum or minimum respectively of the two parameters.

abs, max and min have four versions for the four types listed. The result is of the same type as the parameter given.

What we see here is that most methods take double values and produce double again, but some of the methods have different variations based on type. The Math class is interesting from several points of view:

- It is the first built-in Java class that we are studying in detail.
- All its methods are what are known as class methods, a concept that we must now define.
- All its methods are typed, rather than void, also concepts that we must now define.

First let us look at some examples to get the flavour of how the class is used, then come back to the definitions. Here are some typical uses of the Math class.

```
double squareRoot, cubeRoot, sinOf90, x;
int player1, player2, winner, diceRoll;

squareRoot = Math.sqrt(x);
cubeRoot = Math.pow(x,3);
sinOf90 = Math.sin(Math.toRadians(90));
winner = Math.max(player1, player2);
diceRoll = Math.round(Math.random()*6);
```

EXAMPLE 3.1   Math class investigation

Just to show how the Math class is used, we give a simple program to generate two random numbers and print out the larger, using max.

```
class RandomInvestigation {

  RandomInvestigation () {
    double random1, random2;
    random1 = Math.random();
    random2 = Math.random();
    System.out.println("The numbers are: " + random1 + " and " + random2);
    System.out.println("Max is " + Math.max (random1, random2));
  }
  public static void main (String [] args) {
    new RandomInvestigation ();
  }
}
```

```
The numbers are: 0.8084638874747664 and 0.8945058642673429
Max is 0.8945058642673429
```

Going back to the 'all on one line' way of writing expressions, we see that to raise to a power, we have to call a method, as in

x^2 `Math.pow(x,2)`

When writing out formulae, the trigonometric functions are called like this:

$\sin x$ `Math.sin(x)`

Another useful method in the Math class is that for rounding a real number to an integer in the usual way. Examples are

```
Math.round (6.6)      7
Math.round (6.3)      6
```

However, Java does not behave quite as expected here. It assumes that any expression involving real numbers produces a double result. Therefore the `round` method for doubles is called and that only produces a long result, not an integer. If we really want the result as an integer, then we shall need to do an explicit conversion, as discussed below. First we must clear up the definitions of class method and function.

Class methods

When we have created objects from classes, we have seen that the methods specified in the class were then made available from the object and were accessed via *objectid.* *methodid()*. The exception was the `main` method: when an object was instantiated from a class with a `main` method in it, that method did not show up in the model diagram as being part of the object: it remained in the class. See Figure 2.3 to confirm this statement. The reason for the difference is that `main` was declared as `static`, and therefore there was only one `main` method, and it belonged to the class itself. When the Java Virtual Machine looked for the `main` method to run, it would look for *Classid*.main().

The `Math` class has done the same thing. All its methods are declared as static, so that we do not create an object in order to use them: we use them directly via the class name.

Typed methods

There will be more about typed methods or functions in the latter part of this chapter. Here we just note that methods that are specified as having types (as are all the `Math` class methods) can be used in expressions. The method performs the required calculation on the given parameters and returns a value of the specified type. That value acts as a variable in any expression and is therefore deemed to be a function.

Conversions between types

It is possible to convert between numeric types, but why would we wish to do this? A common example is that of calculations which result in real values, but that then should be displayed as integers for ease of understanding. So far, two specific conversions have been discussed:

1. Rounding a `double` number up to a `long` using `Math.round`.

2. Assigning an `int` to a `double` number.

Another kind of conversion applies across the board to the numeric types in order of size. Consulting Table 3.1, this means that we can assign `byte` values to any other type, `short` to anything but `byte`, and so on. But what about the other direction? Suppose we want to 'down-size' a `double` to a `float`. In this case we have to use a **type cast**. The type cast takes the form:

Type cast

(type) *expression*

The *expression* is converted into a value of the *type* given, if its value is compatible with *type*. If the expression is not compatible, an error results.

For example,

```
float kilograms;
double estimate = 45;
kilograms = (float) (estimate * 1.2);
```

The proviso is that the value of the expression must be compatible with the values that can be stored by the type. Referring to Table 3.1, we could not cast a `short` value of 1000 into a `byte`, since it would not fit. Java will report a compilation error (if the value is deducible at compile time) or otherwise a runtime error.

In the case of real to integer type casts, any fractional part is discarded, and the cast will proceed provided the whole number part of the expression is compatible. For example,

```
(int) 6.3          gives 6
(int) 6.8          gives 6
```

However, casting a value of 1000.678 into a `byte` will still not work.

3.2   Repetition with for-loops

Computers, like all machines, are very good at doing the same thing over and over again. In a program, such repetition can be formulated as a **loop**. There are two kinds of loop possible in Java, as in most languages – **for-loops** and **conditional loops**. In this section we look at for-loops; the conditional ones are introduced in Chapter 5. In Java, both loop forms rely on conditions, though for-loops use them primarily for counting.

Simple conditions

Conditions govern the decisions made in programs as to alternative paths to follow. A condition yields a value **true** or **false**. Another name for a condition is a **boolean expression**.[1] Boolean expressions are covered in full in Chapter 4. Meanwhile, we can use the

---

[1] Named after George Boole, the nineteenth-century mathematician.

six comparison operators to compare the results of numeric expressions and control the working of a for-loop. The conditional operators are:

```
==      equal to
!=      not equal to
>       greater than
<       less than
>=      greater than or equal to
<=      less than or equal to
```

So, for example, the following are all valid conditions:

```
i < n
temperature > 0
mark >= 50
```

The form of a for-loop

The basic and most common Java for-loop is specified in the following form:

Simple for-statement

```
for (int var = start; check ; update) {
   body
}
```

---

var is initialized to the value of the expression in *start*, the *check* involves a condition based on *var*. If the check true, the *body* is executed. Each time round the loop, *var* is changed by means of the *update* and the *condition* checked again until it becomes false. Note that the check is done only when the loop comes round to the for-statement: it is not monitored continuously. *body* consists of zero or more statements.

For example, the commonest loop is arguably

```
for (int i = 0; i < n; i++) {
   doSomething(i);
}
```

The loop variable `i` is given a starting value of 0 and the condition is checked. The loop then starts executing its body and the `doSomething` method is called. On its return, the loop goes to perform the increment on its variable, then checks whether its condition is still true. If so, the body is repeated, the loop variable is incremented and the condition is checked again. When eventually the condition becomes false (when `i` exceeds `n`), the loop has completed all its repetitions, and control proceeds to the next statement.

Now consider the following example to print out five rows of stars

```
for (int i = 0; i < 5; i++) {
   System.out.println("**********");
}
```

Are we sure that five and not six rows are printed? Once the initialization has been completed (and it happens only once) the sequence in which the other three parts of the loop are executed is:

1. check

2. body

3. update

Taking it slowly, i starts at 0. It is checked against 5, a line of stars is printed and i is incremented to 1. When i gets to 3, the stars are printed, i is incremented to 4, checked against 5, more stars are printed, and i is incremented to 5. Now it is checked that it is *less than* 5 and fails. The loop then ends and control continues after the end of the block. We can therefore verify that five rows are printed, as in:

```
**********
**********
**********
**********
**********
```

It is good practice to have a standard way of writing simple for-loops. If we want to run a loop *n* times, we can choose between:

```
for (int i=1; i<=n; i++) ...
```

and

```
for (int i=0; i<n; i++) ...
```

The first version is perhaps easier to understand. However, many related sequences in Java, especially arrays (as discussed in Chapter 6), use zero as a starting point. It has therefore become conventional to start loops at zero, and the second form is usually preferred.

EXAMPLE 3.2   Multiple labels

Problem   Ms Mary Brown of 33 Charles Street, Brooklyn, would like to print out several return addresses which she is going to photocopy onto sticky labels.

Solution   We checked with Ms Brown and confirmed that, for the time being, she is happy to have the labels one underneath each other. (Later on we shall see how to fill a page with labels.) The solution is to take the body of the `DisplayWarning` program in Example 2.4 and put it in a loop.

Program   The program follows on quite easily. Note that we follow each label by two blank lines to separate them. For now, we build into the program the number of labels, but later we shall see how to let this factor vary with each run. Unlike the previous examples, here the body of the loop consists of several statements.

```
class LotsaLabels {

  /* Displaying a warning program    by J M Bishop  Aug 1996
   * --------------------------      Java 1.1 October 1997
   *                                 updated and Java 2, April 2000
   * Prints many labels
   * Illustrates a simple for-loop
   */

  DisplayWarning () {
    for (int i = 0; i < 8; i++) {
      System.out.println("---------------------------");
      System.out.println("|                         |");
      System.out.println("|   Ms Mary Brown         |");
      System.out.println("|   33 Charles Street     |");
      System.out.println("|   Brooklyn              |");
      System.out.println("|                         |");
      System.out.println("---------------------------");
    }
  }

  public static void main(String[] args) {
    new DisplayWarning ();
  }
}
```

Testing   Running the program is very simple, and there are no additional paths to test, as there are no calculations involved. The output will display many labels.

Using the loop variable

The loop variable serves to record the current iteration of a loop and its values can be used in various ways, some of which are:

- in an output statement;

- in simple arithmetic;

- as part of the bounds of another loop.

Together, these three facilities make looping much more interesting. Take the first use. We can number the star lines printed earlier as follows:

```
for (int i=0; i<5; i++) {
  System.out.print(i*10);
  System.out.println(" **********");
}
```

which would print

```
0 **********
10 **********
20 **********
30 **********
40 **********
```

although the first line is a bit off. Now consider how to print out the first 10 even numbers. There are actually two ways. We can have a loop from 0 up to and not including 10 and write out double the loop variable, as in:

```
for (int number = 0; number < 10; number++) {
  System.out.print((number * 2)+" ");
}
System.out.println();
```

which will produce:

```
0 2 4 6 8 10 12 14 16 18
```

The other way is to do the doubling in the update part, which would be:

```
for (int number = 0; number < 20; number+=2) {
  System.out.print(number+" ");
}
System.out.println();
```

To print the first 10 odd numbers requires a bit of thought. If `number * 2` is an even number, then `number * 2 + 1` or `number * 2 - 1` is an odd number. Choosing one of these expressions, we have:

```
for (int number = 0; number < 10; number++) {
  System.out.print((number * 2 + 1)+" ");
}
System.out.println();
```

which will produce:

```
1  3  5  7  9  11  13  15  17  19
```

EXAMPLE 3.3   Conversion table

Problem   The Savanna Oceanography Laboratory measures temperatures of lakes in Celsius, but some of the technicians want the values in Fahrenheit. The managers have agreed to put up conversion tables around the laboratory. You have to write the program to generate the conversion table.

Solution   Use a loop to go through the range of temperatures required, writing out the one temperature and then its conversion.

Algorithm   The algorithm for a conversion table needs a heading, and then a sequence-printing loop, as described in the discussion above. What will the required range of C values be? Well, if these are water temperatures, they could range from 5 to 20.

Program   The program follows on easily. Notice that we call `Math.round` to get the answers out as integers. To get reasonable layout, we use the escape character `\t` for tab. Notice that we take care to keep the operands for the division as real numbers to ensure accuracy.

```
class TemperatureTable {

  /* The Temperature Conversion Program    by J M Bishop Aug 1996
   * --------------------------------    Java 1.1
   *                                     updated April 2000
   * Displays a simple table converting Celsius
   * to Fahrenheit for a given range.
   *
   * Illustrates using the loop variable
   * in expressions in the loop
   */

  TemperatureTable () {
    System.out.println("Temperature Conversion Table");
    System.out.println("============================");
```

```
      System.out.println();
      System.out.println("C\tF");
      for (int c = 5; c <= 20; c++) {
        System.out.println(c+"\t"+ Math.round(c*9.0/5 + 32));
      }
    }

    public static void main (String [] args) {
      new TemperatureTable ();
    }
}
```

Testing   The program output follows. At the command line, we could redirect the output to a file, print the file and pin the table up on the wall, as in

```
java TemperatureTable > temptable.out

Temperature Conversion Table
==============================

C           F
5           41
6           42
7           44
8           46
9           48
10          50
11          51
12          53
13          55
14          57
15          59
16          60
17          62
18          64
19          66
20          68
```

Other looping options

1. **Backwards.** We note that loops can also count backwards using -- . Thus, to print the sequence

```
10  9  8  7  6  5  4  3  2  1  0  -1  -2  -3  -4  -5  -6
```

we could say

```
for (int n = 10; n >=-6; n--) {
  System.out.print(n + "  ");
}
System.out.println();
```

2. **Empty.** It may also happen with a loop that the starting condition may already exceed the finishing one. In this case, the loop body is not executed at all. In the statement

```
for (int n = 0; n < finish; n++) {
  System.out.print(n + "  ");
}
System.out.println();
```

if finish is negative, the loop will be in this situation, and only a blank line will be printed.

3. **Nested.** Loops within loops is a third option. Here, the body of a loop may itself contain a loop, as illustrated in the next example. The rule here is that the loop variables of the loops must be different to avoid confusion.

4. **Endless.** Sometimes we have other ways of stopping a loop than by counting up or down. As we shall see in the next chapter, working with a graphical user interface enables the user to stop a program by pressing a button on the screen. To make a for-loop perform without ever stopping, we leave out the check part as in:

```
for (int i = 0; ; i++)
```

i will still increase with each iteration, and can be used as usual in the loop. If i is not needed, then we could say

```
for (; ;)
```

but this is not very good practice and a conditional loop, covered in Chapter 5, would be a better choice. However, until then we shall use an endless for-loop when needed.

5. **Unfinished.** Later on in Chapter 4 we will find that there are circumstances when we want to stop a loop in the process of an iteration. There is a special statement called break which will immediately pass control to the end of the loop. break is used in conjunction with the if-statement, also covered later in Chapter 4.

3.3 Making methods

The concept of a method was informally introduced in Section 2.2 and we have already used methods such as `println` and `write`, and referred frequently to the `main` method and to constructors. We now look at why methods are important in programming, and show how to declare our additional methods.

An object consists of variables and methods that operate on them. Formally, the object **encapsulates** the data and its actions. In order to provide a clean and safe interface to objects, we choose the methods so that it is seldom, if ever, necessary to refer to the variables directly. This is not to say that we cannot do so, but that the encapsulation principle saves time and produces programs that are less error-prone.

Declaring a method

A **method** is a group of variables and statements that is given a name and may be called upon by this name to perform a particular action. There are several grades of methods, and we start with the simplest, known as a void method. The form of such a method declaration is:

Simple void method declaration

void *methodid* () {
    variables and statements
}

Declares *methodid* to stand for the block of variables and
    statements given.
The method may make use of the variables that are
    declared by itself or its object.

`void` indicates that the method can be called to perform an action in a self-standing way; for example `println` is such a void method. An example of a simple void method would be:

```
void report () {
  System.out.println("The Polelo Curio Store sells\n");
  mugs.write();
  tshirts.write();
  carvings.write();
}
```

which could be added to the `CurioStore1` program. Creating a method like this is a **declaration**. The identifier `report` is declared to introduce the performing of the given statements.

A method may make use of the variables that are declared by itself or its object. Thus `report` can 'see' the three object variables `mugs`, `tshirts` and `carvings` and make use of them freely. In the same way, the `write` method of a `Curio` object, which is:

```
void write () {
   System.out.println(item + " " + description+" for G" + price);
 }
```

accesses its own three variables.

Calling a method

If a method is declared as `void`, it is called by mentioning its identifier. The form is:

Simple void method call
methodid ();
The method is entered and its statements executed until completion.

For example, to print a report, all we need to say from within the `CurioStore1` constructor (or anywhere else in `CurioStore1`) is:

```
report();
```

the effect of which will be to print as before:

```
The Polelo Curio Store sells

Traditional mugs beaded in Ndebele style for G6
T-shirts sizes M to XL for G30
Masks carved in wood for G80
```

Void methods for structuring

One of the prime uses of void methods is to provide for a longish method to be broken up in to separate logical pieces. Take, for example, the `FleetCalculator` program (Example 2.6) which is nearly a page long. As we can see from the comments, the program devides nicely up into sections, and one way of emphasizing this is to use methods. Thus we would have a constructor of the form:

```
FleetCalculator () {
  convertInitialTimes();
  calculateJourneyTimes();
  convertNewTimes();
  reportFindings();
}
```

Each of the carefully named methods then contains exactly the statements that `FleetCalculator` used to have. The variables that were previously declared inside the constructor are moved to the object level so that all the methods can access them. For example, the first method would be:

```
void convertInitialTimes () {
  departMins = depart24 / 100 * 60 + depart24 % 100;
  arriveMins = arrive24 / 100 * 60 + arrive24 % 100;
}
```

3.4 Passing parameters and returning results

Methods can be made more powerful by allowing their effect to differ each time the method is called. When we declare the method we list the parameters that we want, together with their types, and then when the method is called, values for these parameters must be supplied in the correct order. For example, using one of our well-known constructors as an example, consider the declaration

```
Curios (String n, int p, String d)
```

and the call

```
mugs = new Curios ("Traditional mugs", 6, "beaded in Ndebele style");
```

We are required to supply as parameters a string, an integer and a string, in that order: any other arrangement will be rejected. The identifiers given to the formal parameters are local only to that method and have no reference outside it. That is why constructors are responsible for copying their parameters into variables defined by the class for its objects. For example, we have:

```
class Curios {
  String item;
  int    price;
  String description;
```

```
Curios (String n, int p, String d) {
  item = n;
  price = p;
  description = d;
}
```

. . . and so on

Although we refer to the items in both the method declaration and its call as parameters, strictly speaking the declaration introduces **formal** parameters, and the call provides **actual** parameters. The formal parameters are treated as variables and the actual parameters are potentially expressions which are evaluated before being passed into the method.

The form for a list of formal parameters is:

Formal parameter declarations
`(type field, type field ...)`

whereas the form for actual parameters is:

Actual parameters
`(expression, expression, ...)`

The number, types and order of the formal and actual parameters must match exactly, as shown in the example that follows. In addition, formal parameters form part of the variables of a method, and in consequence all these identifiers should be distinct. For example, if there is a formal parameter called p, then we cannot have a variable declared in the method with the identifier p. It is quite convenient, especially in constructors, to use single-letter identifiers for formal parameters, to avoid conflicts with variables that have genuine explanatory names.

The form for a method with parameters is:

Void method declaration

`void` *methodid* `(`*formalparameters*`) {`
  variables and statements
`}`

Declares *methodid* to stand for the block of variables and statements given. The formal parameters must have identifiers distinct from those of the variables. The method may make use of the variables that are declared by itself or its object.

The form of a method call is:

Void method call
methodid (*actualparameters*);
The actual parameters are matched one by one with the formals and the values of the actuals copied in to the formals. The method is entered and its statements executed until completion.

EXAMPLE 3.4   A rainfall histogram

Problem   The Meteorological Department of Savanna would like a graph of the rainfall for each month of a year.

Solution   How do we draw a graph? For rainfall, a histogram is usually a good idea. We can show the months down the vertical axis, and draw the histogram going outwards across the screen, with centimetres on the x-axis. Here is what we would hope to achieve.

```
Savanna Rainfall
================
for 2000
5     | ************************25
6     | *****************16
7     | ********************************32
8     | ********8
9     | ******5
10    | ********************20
11    | *******************19
12    | ***********************23
13    | ********8
14    | ***********************************35
15    | ****************************28

      ======================================================
      +         +         +         +         +         +
      0        10        20        30        40        50
                              cm
```

In order to write a program to do this, we draw on all the techniques we have explored so far, and set up the following plan:

1. Decide how to print a single histogram bar for a given value *h*, including scaling *h* to fit on one line if necessary. This function is given to the `bar` method. It has an additional parameter for the *y*-axis label (the year).

2. Generate a random number up to 40 to represent rainfall.

3. Set up a call to the `bar` method with the formula as a parameter.

4. Put the call to `bar` in a loop over the number of months (12).

5. Design the `println` statements for the heading and final axis using loops.

Program Put all together, the program is quite long, but the comments help to explain it. Notice that we have placed the main method first, and followed it by the `bar` and `axis` methods which it calls. Unlike some other languages, Java does not mind in which order methods are declared.

```
class RainfallHistogram {

    /*
     * Rainfall Histogram Program          by J M Bishop April 2000
     * --------------------------          adapted from GrowthPlan in
     *                                     JG2E Oct 1997
     * Displays a histogram of rainfall for each month
     * where the rainfall is generated randomly.
     *
     * Illustrates parameter passing of variables
     * and for-loops.
     */

    RainfallHistogram () {

    // The headings
        System.out.println("Savanna Rainfall");
        System.out.println("================");
        System.out.println("for 2000");

    // Display a bar for each year and then the final axis
        for (int year = 5; year <= 15; year++) {
            bar(year, Math.random()*40);
        }
        axis ();
    }

    void bar(int label, double h) {
    // Draws a single histogram bar labelled
    // with the years and consisting of the given
    // number of stars
```

```
        System.out.print(label+"\t|");
        int stop = (int) Math.round(h);
        for (int star = 0; star < stop; star++)
            System.out.print('*');
        System.out.println(" " + (long) h);
    }

    void axis () {
    // Draws a horizontal axis with ticks+1 divisions
    // labelled in steps of 10. Each division is 10
    // characters wide.

        int ticks = 5;

    // Print the line
        System.out.print('\t');
        for (int line = 0; line < ticks*10; line++)
            System.out.print("=");
        System.out.println("=");

    //Print the ticks
        System.out.print('\t');
        for (int n = 0; n < ticks; n++)
            System.out.print("+           ");
        System.out.println('+');
    // Label the ticks, including the last one
        System.out.print('\t');
        for (int n = 0; n <= ticks; n++)
            System.out.print(n*10 + "         ");
        System.out.println();

    // Label the whole axis
        System.out.println("\t\t\t\tcm");
    }

    public static void main (String [] args) {
      new RainfallHistogram ();
    }
}
```

Testing The output has already been shown. This example is extended in the problems at the end of the chapter to obtain different graphs for different data.

Model diagrams for methods

Methods appear in model diagrams and are listed in the methods section of the objects instantiated from classes. Typically, model diagrams do not show the details of methods, but if these are pertinent, we can do so using the turned-down corner box already shown in Figure 2.4. If, within a class, we would also like to indicate which methods call which others, we can do so with arrows. Figure 3.1 shows the program from the previous example as a model diagram.

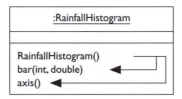

Figure 3.1 *Model diagram for the* `RainfallHistogram` *program, showing methods.*

The methods are shown with the types of their parameters, which is useful information. As we have already seen, we can provide explanations for methods via turned-down corner boxes. These symbols can also stand for methods on their own, as shown in Figure 3.6 later on. Figure 3.2 shows the rainfall program with explanations for the methods. The text is taken directly from the comments in the program – or vice versa.

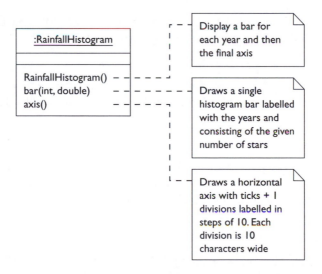

Figure 3.2 *A model diagram for the* `RainfallHistogram` *program, with method explanations.*

Objects as parameters

As an example of parameter passing, consider having an `inStock` variable for `Curio` objects. Then when we sell some curios, we would update the `inStock` variable. There are three ways to do this:

1. The `update` method accepts the number of items sold.

   ```
   void update (int sold) {
      inStock -= sold;
   }
   ```

   So if we sold three mugs, we would call

   ```
   mugs.update (3);
   ```

2. The `update` method accepts the new number of items:

   ```
   void update (int newStock) {
      inStock = newStock;
   }
   ```

   Once again, if we sold three mugs, we would call

   ```
   mugs.update (mugs.inStock-3);
   ```

   The calculation is done on the calling side. The advantage of this method is that we can use it to completely reset the stock (say, after a fire) with just:

   ```
   mugs.update (50);
   ```

3. We can access the `inStock` variable directly, without using a method at all, as in:

   ```
   mugs.inStock -= 3;
   ```

   This would be considered to be the least attractive solution, since it allows `inStock` to be manipulated in any sort of way. On the other hand, it provides for all the variations mentioned in 1 and 2, and so is a possibility.

Results of a method

When we call a method of an object we affect that object's variables and in a sense that is considered a result of the call. The new values of the object's variables are now available to the caller and can be inspected. However, sometimes we would like to explicitly transmit results back to the caller, for ease of processing, or because we would like to protect the copies in the object in some way. Protection is covered later, but it is provided for in Java.

If we have only one result to transmit back, then a typed method is ideal, as described below. If we would like to transmit more values back, then we have to create a class that includes details of all the values we want. We pass an object of this class to the method. It fills in the new values, and these are then available through the actual parameter on return. Rather than embark on an artificial example, we shall defer further explanation of this process to the Case Study at the end of the chapter.

3.5   Typed methods

Typed methods are very common in Java programming, because they provide a simple way of getting a result back from a method, and they are easy to use in expressions. Another name for a typed method is a **function**, and we note that there is a whole branch of computer science devoted to functional programming. As an example of a typed method, consider the conversion from times in the 24 hour clock to minutes, as needed in Example 2.6. Since this operation is performed at least twice in the program, we could create a method for it as follows:

```
int timeInMins (int time24) {
  return time24 / 100 * 60 + time24 % 100;
}
```

The call to a typed method constitutes an expression and can be used wherever an expression of that type is permitted. Typically, typed methods would be called in assignments, as parts of expressions, or in output statements. Calling the conversion method defined above could be done by:

```
departMins = timeInMins(depart24);
arriveMins = timeInMins(arrive24);
```

Here, the method is called twice, with a different variable as the actual parameter in each case. Within the method, the values are known by the common name of `time24`.

Defining methods, whether they represent part of small programs, or subdivisions of a class's operation, enables us to cut down on repetition. It provides a means of creating a structure for a program, since the name of a method can be carefully chosen to reflect the action it performs. Readability is also enhanced.

Although we are concentrating on variables here, we note that objects can also be formal parameters, in which case the matching actual parameter must also be an object. To complete the formalities, we give the forms for typed methods:

Typed method declaration

```
type methodid (formalparameters) {
  variables and statements
  return value;
}
```

Declares *methodid* to stand for the block of variables and statements given.

The formal parameters (if any) must have identifiers distinct from those of the variables.

The method may make use of the variables that are declared by itself or its object.

The return statement may appear anywhere in the method block. It specifies a value of correct type which becomes the value of the method at the point of call.

The form of a method call is:

Typed method call

```
methodid (actualparameters);
```

The actual parameters are matched one by one with the formals and the values of the actuals copied in to the formals.

The method is entered and its statements executed until completion, whereupon the value returned by the method is the result of the call.

| EXAMPLE 3.5 | Selling from the curio store |

Problem   The owner of the curio store, Sam Nelson, would like to use the program to record stock and sales.

Solution   The way to tackle the solution is to examine what features the class for curios needs to provide. Then we adapt `Curio` and check it by adding new calls to its methods from the new program `CurioStore2`.

Design   Without doubt, there must be a variable recording the stock. We could set the contents of the stock via the constructor, as we do with all the other variables, but in fact stock is slightly different. It can be updated continually. Therefore we need a method that adds to the stock level, and the constructor sets it to zero initially. Next we have to be able to sell items, and at this stage we simply submit the number sold, and the stock level is altered accordingly. In addition, we have a `sell` method that returns a string value that says what has been sold, as a sort of receipt. The reason we do this is that otherwise the caller of the method has to access the object again to print details of the sale.

Figure 3.3 shows the model diagram for the new design. In this diagram, we have included information about the types of the variables and parameters in the two classes. The diagram shows `CurioStore2` object, and one of the `Curio` objects. We have left out the classes, because they are well known and do not contain any new information. The complete diagram would be similar to Figure 2.10, but with the additional methods added.

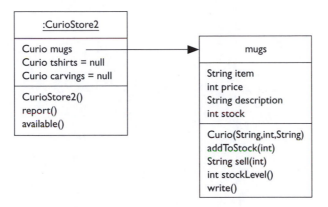

Figure 3.3 *Model diagram for* `CurioStore2` *– snapshot taken just after* `mugs` *is instantiated.*

Program The revised program is now:

```
class CurioStore2 {

    /* Polelo Curio Store No. 2          by J M Bishop April 2000
     * -----------------------
     * The shop with stock levels and a sell option
     * Illustrates methods in an object-oriented program
     */

    public static void main (String [ ] args) {
        // creates the class's (i.e. program's) object
        new CurioStore2 ();
    }

    // declare three objects
    Curio mugs, tshirts, carvings;

    // The constructor for the program
    // where the initializing and main work gets done
    CurioStore2 () {
```

```java
        // instantiate the objects with different initial values
      mugs = new Curio("Traditional mugs", 6, "beaded in Ndebele style");
      tshirts = new Curio("T-shirts", 30, "sizes M to XL");
      carvings = new Curio("Masks", 80, "carved in wood");

      // print out a report
      report ();

      // Now stock the shop for each curio
      mugs.addToStock(10);
      tshirts.addToStock(50);
      carvings.addToStock(5);

      // Report on stock levels
      available();

      // Sell something. The sell method returns a string with
      // a "receipt" we can print.
      System.out.println(tshirts.sell(8));

      // Report on stock levels again
      available ();
   }

   void report () {
      System.out.println("The Polelo Curio Store sells\n");
      // use the objects' access to toString to print their contents
      mugs.write();
      tshirts.write();
      carvings.write();
   }

   void available () {
      System.out.println("Available are "+mugs.stockLevel()+" "+
         tshirts.stockLevel()+" "+carvings.stockLevel()+
         " curios respectively\n");
   }
}

class Curio {
   // An inner class giving details of and actions on a curio.
   // Will be expanded as the project progresses.

   // Declare the fields, including a new one for stock
   String item;
```

```
    int price;
    String description;
    int stock = 0;

    // The constructor copies the initialization into the fields
    Curio (String n, int p, String d) {
      item = n;
      price = p;
      description = d;
    }

    // Three new actions available on curios
    void addToStock (int n) {
      stock += n;
    }

    String sell (int n) {
      stock -= n;
      return "Sold " + n + " " + item;
    }

    int stockLevel () {
      return stock;
    }

    void write () {
      System.out.println(item + " " + description + " for G" + price);
    }
  }
```

Testing   The output from the program is given as:

```
The Polelo Curio Store sells

Traditional mugs beaded in Ndebele style for G6
T-shirts sizes M to XL for G30
Masks carved in wood for G80
Available are 10 50 5 curios respectively

Sold 8 T-shirts
Available are 10 42 5 curios respectively
```

There are obviously some improvements that we can make to the output, and these are taken up in the problems at the end of the chapter. There is also much scope for testing the program, but this time we shall leave this aspect until we can read in data.

| EXAMPLE 3.6 | Large conversion table |

Problem   The Oceanography Laboratory was so pleased with the table we produced (Example 3.3) that it has asked us to do one for a larger range of temperatures, but to arrange it so that the whole table fits on the screen or on a page.

Solution   We know how to do the conversion, so what we need to think about is how to arrange the layout of the table. A standard computer screen has lines 80 characters wide. Each pair of temperatures will occupy no more than 16 characters. We can therefore fit five columns on the screen. For temperatures from 0 to 99, this gives 20 lines, which will fit nicely on a screen or a page. We can then use nested loops to get the desired effect.

Algorithm   We can tackle the solution from the top. We know how to print one line because we did it in Example 3.3. It is:

```
System.out.println(c+"\t"+ Math.round(c*9.0/5 + 32));
```

We can therefore set up a loop to print 20 such lines. The printing of the lines can go in a void method.

Program   Let us define the following values:

```
int colsPerLine = 5;
int maxLineNo = 20;
```

The lines will be numbered by the loop from 0 to 19 (that is, up to but not including 20) with a loop variable `line`. Printing one line can be put in a method, `outaLine`, with its own loop and loop variable, say `col`. Then the expression for the Celsius value on a given line and column will be:

```
thisline * colsPerLine + col
```

In order to clarify the program, we make some improvements at the point where the above expression would appear. Firstly, we create a typed method to perform the conversion from Celsius to Fahrenheit. Then, because the Celsius value appears twice – once when it is printed out and once when it is used for the conversion – we assign it to a local variable, `c`.

Finally, tabs are set so that the columns line up, for both the headings and the values. However, notice that the numbers will be left-justified by Java, rather than lined up on the right, as would be more natural. The full program has plenty of comments to explain what is happening.

```java
class LargeTemperatureTable {

  /* Large Temperature Table Program    by JM Bishop Sept 1996
   * ------------------------------      Java 1.1
   *                                     updated April 2000
   * Produces a conversion table from Celsius to Fahrenheit
   * for values from 0 to 99.
   *
   * Illustrates for-loops, methods for structuring,
   * typed methods and parameters.
   */

  int colsPerLine = 5;
  int maxLineNo = 20;
  String gap = "\t\t";

  LargeTemperatureTable () {

    // First print the headings
    System.out.println("\t\tTemperature Conversion Table");
    System.out.println("\t\t=============================");
    System.out.println();

    for (int col = 0; col < colsPerLine; col++)
      System.out.print("C   F" + gap);
    System.out.println();

    // Second, print the table:
    // For each of the lines required, the outaLine
    // method is called with the line number as a parameter
    for (int r = 0; r < maxLineNo; r++)
      outaLine(r);
  }

  void outaLine(int thisline) {
    /* Using the information given by the parameter as
     * to which line this is, the method calculates the
     * Celsius values for that line and displays them with
     * their Fahrenheit equivalents
     */

    for (int col = 0; col < colsPerLine; col++) {
      int c = thisline * colsPerLine + col;
      System.out.print(c + "   ");
      System.out.print(fahrenheit(c) + gap);
    }
    System.out.println();
  }
```

```
// a simple conversion function
long fahrenheit(int celsius) {
  return Math.round(celsius*9.0/5 + 32);
}

public static void main(String[] args) {
  new LargeTemperatureTable () ;
}
}
```

Testing   Running the program confirms that it does produce the required effect, and the right answers.

```
         Temperature Conversion Table
         ==============================
```

C	F		C	F		C	F		C	F		C	F
0	32		1	34		2	36		3	37		4	39
5	41		6	43		7	45		8	46		9	48
10	50		11	52		12	54		13	55		14	57
15	59		16	61		17	63		18	64		19	66
20	68		21	70		22	72		23	73		24	75
25	77		26	79		27	81		28	82		29	84
30	86		31	88		32	90		33	91		34	93
35	95		36	97		37	99		38	100		39	102
40	104		41	106		42	108		43	109		44	111
45	113		46	115		47	117		48	118		49	120
50	122		51	124		52	126		53	127		54	129
55	131		56	133		57	135		58	136		59	138
60	140		61	142		62	144		63	145		64	147
65	149		66	151		67	153		68	154		69	156
70	158		71	160		72	162		73	163		74	165
75	167		76	169		77	171		78	172		79	174
80	176		81	178		82	180		83	181		84	183
85	185		86	187		87	189		88	190		89	192
90	194		91	196		92	198		93	199		94	201
95	203		96	205		97	207		98	208		99	210

Example 3.6 illustrated methods and parameters well. However, the call to `outaLine` used just a single variable, `r`, each time. Methods and parameters become more interesting when the actual expression passed to the formal parameter is computed from several values, as shown in the case study.

3.6   The type `boolean`

Before we go on to a substantial case study, we introduce the seventh primitive data type in Java, `boolean`.

Conditions

As we saw in Section 3.2, conditions govern the decisions made in programs as to alternative paths to follow. A condition yields a value `true` or `false`. Another name for a condition is a **boolean expression**. Boolean expressions use the six comparison operators to compare the results of numeric expressions. The conditional operators are:

`==`	equal to
`!=`	not equal to
`>`	greater than
`<`	less than
`>=`	greater than or equal to
`<=`	less than or equal to

The result of such an expression can be stored in a **boolean variable**. For example, given the declarations:

```
boolean isaMinor, isaPensioner;
int age;
```

we can store various facts about the age of someone as:

```
isaMinor = age < 18;
isaPensioner = age >=65;
```

and display these later using:

```
System.out.println ("Driver's licence denied:" + isaMinor);
```

If your age is 15, then `isaMinor` would be true so the statement would print:

Driver's licence denied: true

As another example,

```
System.out.println ("It is " + isaPensioner +
            " that you can ride the bus for free.");
```

will for a 15-year-old display:

It is false that you can ride the bus for free.

Boolean expressions

There are also the boolean operators, which can be combined with boolean variables and conditions:

&	and
		or
^	xor, the exclusive or
!	not

For the expression (x & y) to be true, both x and y must be true; for the expression (x | y) to be true, either x or y or both can be true. There is also a precedence between the operators, so that in the absence of parentheses, & will always be evaluated before |. The results of the operators are summarized in Figure 3.4.

and &	false	true		xor ^	false	true
false	false	false		false	false	true
true	false	true		true	true	false

or |	false	true		not !	
false	false	true		false	true
true	true	true		true	false

Figure 3.4 *Boolean operator tables.*

Referring back to the earlier example with the minor and pensioner conditions, suppose we make the declarations:[2]

```
boolean isEmployed, isaYoungWorker, isaVoter, isaTaxpayer;
```

Then further facts can be deduced as follows:

```
isaYoungWorker = isaMinor & isEmployed;
isaVoter = ! isaMinor;
isaTaxpayer = isaVoter | isEmployed;
```

Boolean operators can be combined to express more complex conditions. For example, if both minors and pensioners can go free on the buses provided they are not working, then we have:

---

[2] It is useful habit to preface boolean variables with 'is' or 'isa' so that expressions that use them read more naturally.

```
boolean freeBus = (isaPensioner | isaMinor) & !isEmployed;
```

The brackets are needed so that the | is evaluated first.

Boolean operators are very useful in conjunction with the comparison operators in establishing detailed conditions. As an example, consider an expression for deciding whether school should be cancelled because it is too cold or too hot:

```
goHome = temperature > 40 | temperature < 0;
```

In Java, the precedence between the comparison operators and the boolean ones is such that the comparisons will always be executed first (that is, they have higher precedence). In other languages, the reverse is true, and many programmers are used to putting brackets around conditions. You might often see an expression such as the go home test written as:

```
goHome = (temperature > 40) | (temperature < 0);
```

On the other hand the concatenation operator does take precedence over & and |. To print out a&b and a|b, we cannot use:

```
println(a&b + a|b);
```

because + will try to operate on the central b + a, and will report an error. Instead, we introduce brackets:

```
println((a&b) + (a|b));
```

Java also has 'short circuit' versions of *and* and *or* which are the && and || operators respectively. In the case of

```
c && d
```

d will be evaluated only if c is true. Similarly, for ||, once c has been established as true, d is ignored. A nice example of such operators is establishing whether one date (comprising three integers) is earlier than another. The statement – quite long – would be:

```
boolean earlier = y1 < y2 ||
                  (y1 == y2 && m1 < m2) ||
                  (y1 == y2 && m1 == m2 && d1 < d2);
```

By using short circuit operators, evaluating the expression stops as soon as the answer is known for certain. This example might save a bit of time, but there are also cases where it is essential that one condition be protected by another. Suppose we wish to know whether a curio stock level (in a curio object called checked) is below 5. However, we are not certain whether checked does or does not refer to an object that has already been created. If this case we can use:

```
boolean lowStock = checked != null && checked.stock < 5;
```

The form summarizes the precedence of the boolean operators and comparisons.

Operator precedence (boolean)
group 0:   ()
group 1:   !
group 2:   &
group 3: |
group 4:   &&
group 5: ||

Comparison of objects

The comparison and boolean operators only work for primitive types. If we want to compare objects, then we have to define corresponding methods ourselves. For example, suppose we would like to be able to compare prices of curios. We could add the following typed method to the `Curio` class:

```
boolean cheaper (Curio c) {
   return price < c.price;
}
```

The method is called with the first operand as the object, then the dot operator, and then the second operand as the parameter. For example, we could have:

```
mugs.cheaper (tshirts)
```

which, given the definitions set up earlier in Chapter 2 where mugs cost G6 and t-shirts G30, would return false. Methods for the other operators, particularly equals, can also be defined in a similar way. If we wanted to do so for the original curio class, we would need to compare two strings and an integer. But a string is also an object, so we must first know how to compare strings.

Comparison of strings is also done through methods. In this respect, we list here the comparison methods for strings, from the `String` class. There is more about `String` in Chapter 7.

String comparison methods
int compareTo (*String*)
int compareToIgnoreCase (*String*)
boolean equals (*String*)
boolean equalsIgnoreCase (*String*)

The `compareTo` methods produce an integer as follows:

less than	negative
equals	zero
greater than	positive

which means that a string comparison looks like this:

```
name1.compareTo(name2) < 0
```

which means essentially name1 < name2.

Now we can apply these methods to defining equality of curios. The method we would add to `Curio` would be:

```
boolean equals (Curio c) {
  return name.equals(c.name) && price == c.price
        && description.equals(c.description);
}
```

equals could be called as in:

```
System.out.println("Matching curios found is " + checked.equals(mugs));
```

3.7 Case Study 1: Pizza Delivery 2U

In this case study we look at how to design a class from scratch for both a specific purpose, and so that it can be used more widely later. This dual requirement is a common one and, if met, enables us to get the maximum benefit from our programming effort. We start with a concrete specification of the problem, with a reasonable solution, and then move towards a more durable product. In the process, we shall learn more about the use of objects in both for-loops and parameters.

Problem

Pizza Delivery 2U is interested in giving more accurate delivery times to its customers when they order pizzas. From the time of the call to the pizza arriving, there are two factors to be taken into account: the length of the queue at the pizza oven (i.e. the number of orders already in the system), and the area in which the customer lives. Customers in areas close by will have faster deliveries than those in areas further away. Pizza 2U makes deliveries in four identifiable areas, and would like to have a quick look-up table next to the phone for times from 9am to 11pm and queue lengths from 0 to 5, in these four areas.

Solution

This sounds like a tall order, but in fact, we can bring considerable experience already to our assistance:

- recognizing repetition and controlling it through methods and loops;

- knowing how to print a table, as in Example 3.3 (Temperature conversion);

- knowing how to convert times and add them, as in Example 2.6 (Fleet timetables).

With these in hand we can break the solution down to printing one table for area x, four times (x varying from 1 to 4). Then the table itself will show queue lengths across the top and the times in the given range down the side. If we take times in 15 minute intervals, we shall get a table something like the following:

```
Pizza 2U Delivery estimates for Area 1
=======================================

Time now              Queue length
            0     1     2     3     4     5
900        915   920   925   930   935   940
915        930   935   940   945   950   955
930        945   950   955   1000  1005  1010
945        1000  1005  1010  1015  1020  1025
...
```

Initial design

Attacking the problem from the top, we can postulate the main part of the program as drawing a table consisting of headings and then a number of lines, and this being repeated for each of the four areas. Each line is handled by a `printaLine` method that we do not specify yet, and the only real thinking we need to do is for the loop that controls `printaLine`. Since we want rows labelled for times from 9.00 to 23.00, in intervals of 15 minutes, this is not so difficult. The constructor for the first version of the program is:

```
PizzaDelivery1 () {
    for (int area = 1; area<= 4; area++) {
        printHeading(area);
        startTable();
        for (int time = 900; time < 2300; time = addTime(time,15))
            printaLine(time, area);
    }
}
```

The methods that we now have to fill in are underlined. The first two concern headings, and are simple enough. Let us next look at `printaLine`. It has a much simpler structure than the similar method, `outaLine`, in the temperature table program, because there is only one value per column and each row starts with a provided time. The loop will run over the queue lengths (0 to 5, as specified in the problem formulation) and all we have to do is work out what value gets printed in the column. The answer is that it is the time of the order plus all the unavoidable times for

- waiting in a queue – 5 minutes times the length of the queue;
- cooking the pizza – 5 minutes;
- handling the order – 10 minutes;
- delivering it – 5 minutes per area crossed.

After some thought, we can come up with the following formula for one value in the table:

```
addTime (orderTime, queue*makeTime + processTime + a*driveTime)
```

In other words, we postulate an `addTime` method. The method will be typed in order to return the new time.

Now we can work on `addTime`. It takes a time, represented as an integer but for a 24 hour clock, and adds minutes to it. So the method header must be:

```
int addTime (int t, int m) {
```

We deliberately use `t` as the formal parameter identifier, to keep the method very general. Now we can capitalize on the work already done in Example 2.6 in converting times. There were two statements that converted times from the 24 hour clock to minutes and back again. These were:

```
arriveMins = arrive24 / 100 * 60 + arrive24 % 100;
newArrive24 = newArriveMins / 60 * 100 + newArriveMins % 60;
```

If we formulate these expressions as methods, they become:

```
int timeInMins (int t) {
  return t / 100 * 60 + t % 100;
}

int time24 (int t) {
  return t / 60 * 100 + t % 60;
}
```

Now the `addTime` method can take the easy path: it calls one of the others to convert the given time to minutes, then adds the minutes specified, then converts the whole thing back again. This is done in:

```
int addTime (int t, int m) {
   return time24(timeInMins(t) + m);
}
```

Of course, with such a simple method, we could have just replaced its contents wherever we needed to, so that

```
addTime (time,15)
```

would have become

```
time24(timeInMins(time) + 15)
```

However, the use of the identifier `addTime` adds to the readibility of the program, and we do use the method more than once, so it is worthwhile.

Model diagram

The model diagram for the program is shown in Figure 3.5. The arrows in the method section indicate who calls whom. Unlike the curio store programs, there are no additional objects in this program, the focus being on methods. But the model diagram does tell us quite a bit apart from providing a neat summary of the methods and their parameters, as it shows the calling structure as well. Once the calling structure becomes more complicated than this, we can create a separate diagram, as shown in Figure 3.6.

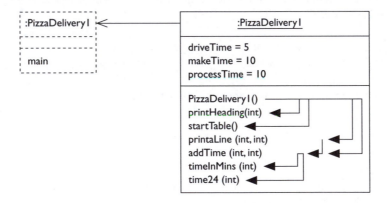

Figure 3.5 *Model diagram for* `PizzaDelivery1`.

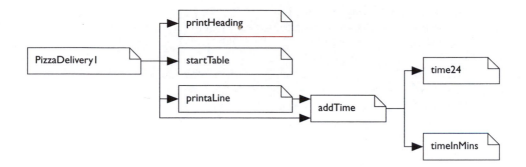

Figure 3.6 *Call model diagram of* `PizzaDelivery1` *methods.*

Program 1

Finally, we can put the whole program together in Java itself:

```
class PizzaDelivery1 {

  /* The Pizza Delivery Program version 1    J M Bishop  May 2000
   * =======================================
   *
   * Works out the time for delivering pizzas based on
   * queue length and area of delivery.
   * Illustrates reuse of methods, method calling and loops
   * Test version with 1 area and times from 900 to 1300
   */

  int driveTime = 5;    // per area;
  int makeTime = 5;     // in a queue
  int processTime = 10; // per order

  PizzaDelivery1 () {
    for (int area = 1; area<= 1; area++) {
      printHeading(area);
      startTable();
      for (int time = 900; time < 1300; time=addTime(time,15))
        printaLine(time, area);
    }
  }

  void printaLine (int t, int a) {
    System.out.print(t+"\t");
    for (int queue = 0; queue <= 5; queue++)
```

```
        System.out.print(addTime(t,
            queue*makeTime+processTime+a*driveTime) + "\t");
      System.out.println();
    }

  int timeInMins (int t) {
    return t / 100 * 60 + t % 100;
  }

int time24 (int t) {
    return t / 60 * 100 + t % 60;
  }

  int addTime (int t, int m) {
    return time24(timeInMins(t)+m);
  }

  void printHeading (int area) {
    System.out.println("Pizza 2U Delivery estimates for "+
      Area "+area);
    System.out.println("==================================="+
      "=====\n");
  }

  void startTable () {
    System.out.println("Time now        Queue length");
    System.out.print("            ");
    for (int queue = 0; queue <=5; queue++)
      System.out.print("   "+queue+"   ");
    System.out.println();
  }

  public static void main (String [] args) {
    new PizzaDelivery1 ();
  }
}
```

Testing

The program has been set up to only print a table for one area, and to stop the times at 1300, just to keep the table manageable. The output looks like this:

```
Pizza 2U Delivery estimates for Area 1
==========================================
```

Time now	Queue length					
	0	1	2	3	4	5
900	915	920	925	930	935	940
915	930	935	940	945	950	955
930	945	950	955	1000	1005	1010
945	1000	1005	1010	1015	1020	1025
1000	1015	1020	1025	1030	1035	1040
1015	1030	1035	1040	1045	1050	1055
1030	1045	1050	1055	1100	1105	1110
1045	1100	1105	1110	1115	1120	1125
1100	1115	1120	1125	1130	1135	1140
1115	1130	1135	1140	1145	1150	1155
1130	1145	1150	1155	1200	1205	1210
1145	1200	1205	1210	1215	1220	1225
1200	1215	1220	1225	1230	1235	1240
1215	1230	1235	1240	1245	1250	1255
1230	1245	1250	1255	1300	1305	1310
1245	1300	1305	1310	1315	1320	1325

How do we check the results? We do it in two ways. Firstly, we take the statements in the program and reason about them. This we have more or less done during the development. The other way of checking a program like this is to do some hand calculations. Take a random spot in the table, e.g. at 1100 with a queue of 2. The delivery time can be calculated as:

$$1100 + (2*5 + 10 + 1*5) = 1100 + 25 = 1125$$

which tallies with the results. More checking should be done at the borders of the table, e.g. at the end of a row, and also when the time goes over the hour, as in the row starting with 1145.

The problem revisited

Given the above investigation, we would like to assess whether a class for times would be a good idea. Although using integers to represent times did work, it was incorrect, because ultimately 915 did not mean nine hundred and fifteen minutes, but nine hours and 15 minutes. It would be better to represent a time as two integers – the hours and the minutes. This implies that we should have a class for times.

So the task is to construct such a class, and in order to test it out, we shall use it in our existing Pizza Delivery program. This way we can compare outputs to ensure they remain the same, and we can assess how much more complex using a class makes the programming. The fact is that the program will look slightly more complex, but it will have been built in a more structured way and will be more maintainable and flexible.

Java's `Date` and `Calendar` classes

Before embarking on the development of a class for times, we should look to see whether Java itself provides one. We do not wish to duplicate what has already been set up. If we go to Java's online documentation and search for 'time', we find that it occurs first in a `Date` class. `Date` has only a few methods, which are shown in the form below. It represents the time as the number of milliseconds since 1 January 1970. It will not be convenient to create times if we have first to calculate milliseconds.

Java's `Date` class

```
Date ()
Date (long Date)
long getTime ()
void setTime(long time)
boolean after (Date when)
boolean before (Date when)
int compareTo (Date anotherDate)
// plus the usual methods for toString etc.
```

Then Java also has a `Calendar` class which has extensive methods for handling dates and times, and for doing arithmetic on them, but not for handling times alone: a time must always be prefaced by a year, month and day. As such, `Calendar` is more elaborate than we need. We can therefore go ahead with the design of a `Time` class, confident that we are not duplicating effort.

Class design for `Time`

In designing a class, we look at

- the variables that make up its object;

- its constructors;

- the methods required by programs that might use it.

Looking at the variables, we find that there is no need for anything beyond the hour and minute for the purposes we have in mind. Of course, the class could be extended to cope with seconds, and this is taken up in the Problems.

The constructors are interesting. We need to supply the hour and minute information to the class. The class can, if necessary, deduce the hour and minute from a variety of formats. These could be:

- two integers – the hour and minute, e.g. (11, 30);

- one integer, where the first hundreds and thousands are used for the hours, as we did before, e.g. 1130;

- a real number, where the fractional part represents the minutes, e.g. 11.30.

Constructors can be provided for all of these. Finally, we recognize that one time can also be created from another time, which gives us a fourth constructor. These are, then:

```
class Time {
  int hour;
  int min;

  Time (int h, int m) {
    hour = h;
    min = m;
  }

  Time (int mins) {
    hour = mins / 60;
    min = mins % 60;
  }

  Time (double t) {
    hour = (int) t;
    min = (int) t*100 - hour*100;
  }

  Time (Time t) {
    hour = t.hour;
    min = t.min;
  }
  ...  and so on
```

Figure 3.7 shows the model diagram for `Time` together with some objects created using the different constructors.

The first method to be developed is going to be `addTime`. The question is: how does `addTime` look in a class, and how would it be called? The answer is: quite differently from before, in all respects. We have already seen that when a class is instantiated to create an object, method calls for that object use the dot operator. In the case of the time to which we are adding minutes, the time itself is the object in question. Therefore the call

```
time = addTime(time,15)
```

will become

```
time.addTime(15)
```

The object will be altered by adding the parameter of 15 minutes to its data. From this, we can deduce that `addTime` is going to be a void method. The addition of the minutes itself turns out to be simpler than before, because we already have the time split into its constituent parts:

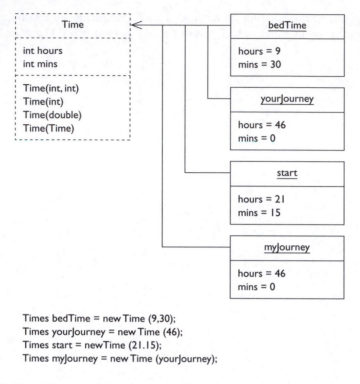

Times bedTime = new Time (9,30);
Times yourJourney = new Time (46);
Times start = newTime (21.15);
Times myJourney = new Time (yourJourney);

Figure 3.7 *Model diagram of the construction of some* `Time` *objects.*

```
void addTime (int m) {
  min += m;
  hour+= min / 60;
  min %= 60;
}
```

The method makes good use of the special assignment operators, which update the left-hand side variable. Thus the first statement could read: 'add m to min' or 'min becomes min plus m'.

What other methods are required? Well, we shall want to display a time, and could set up a `write` method, but in general it is not good practice to have output statements in general classes such as `Time`. Instead, we shall define a `toString` method, which can be automatically called by `println`, as described in Section 3.1. There may be other methods, but we shall add them after considering how to test `Time` in a program.

Testing the class

It is useful to be able to test a new class with a program that already works. So we take our first Pizza Delivery program and rework it. Looking at the original program, we can see that the changes are going to occur where times are mentioned, which are underlined in the following extract:

```
PizzaDelivery1 () {
  .. omit some lines
  for (int time = 900; time < 1300; time=addTime (time, 15))
      printaLine(time, area);
  }
}

void printaLine (int t, int a) {
  System.out.print(t+"\t");
  for (int queue = 0; queue <= 5; queue++)
    System.out.print(addTime(t,
      queue*makeTime + processTime + a*driveTime) + "\t");
  System.out.println();
}
```

For-loops with objects

The first change is that we rename the program, so as to keep both versions. The crucial next question is how do we loop over times, when they are objects? It turns out that the for-loop is far more powerful than just an integer counter, and its general form is:

For-loop

```
for (start; check; update) {
  body
}
```

---

start and *update* are assignments, and *check* is some condition based on the variables mentioned in *start* and *update*.

The loop begins by executing the *start* statement, then the *check*. If the *check* is true, do the *body* followed by *update* and *check*. When *check* returns false, exit the loop.

In other words, the start statement does not have to assign a number to an integer: it can be any appropriate initialization. So let us define two time objects to start with, as:

```
Time open  = new Time (9.00);
Time close = new Time (13,0);
```

We have deliberately used two different constructor calls here, just to emphasize their use. The first sends over a real number, and the second uses two parameters. Now, the start of the loop is simply

```
Time ofDay = open
```

where `ofDay` is going to be the loop variable. Working with the translation that we have already made from integers to objects, the update section of the loop is:

```
ofDay.addTime(15)
```

How do we specify the condition? The obvious formulation is

```
ofDay < close    // won't work
```

but as we discussed in the previous section, we cannot use conditional operators such as < on objects. The condition has to be defined and implemented as a method, so that the call would be

```
ofDay.lessThan(close)
```

where `lessThan` returns a boolean value based on a condition that it evaluates. We can now write out the full loop with its body, as:

```
for (Time ofDay = open; ofDay.lessThan(close); ofDay.addTime(15)) {
  printaLine(ofDay, area);
}
```

As with any other for-loop, `ofDay` starts at `open`, then starts the cycle of

- check against `close`;
- execute the body;
- update with 15 mins by calling `addTime`.

A model diagram showing the objects of the for-loop is given in Figure 3.8. As `ofDay.addTime` is called each time round the loop, 15 minutes gets added to the `ofDay` object. However, as can be seen from the diagram, `ofDay` is the same object as `open`. Thus `open` will change as well. If `open` changes like this, we will need to recreate it for each area table. Instead, what we need to do is to create a copy of `open` for `ofDay`, which can be done easily through our fourth constructor, and the loop becomes:

```
for (Time ofDay = new Time(open); ofDay.lessThan(close);
        ofDay.addTime(15)) {
  printaLine(ofDay, area);
}
```

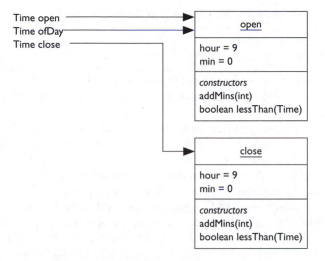

Figure 3.8 *Model diagram of an object loop for times.*

This is an excellent example of how the diagrams have shown up a problem, which we can then remedy in the Java implementation.

Objects as parameters

Moving on to `printaLine`, it would seem that the translation of the call to `addTime` would be simple, and the equivalent for-loop would be:

```
for (int queue = 0; queue <= 5; queue++) {
    t.addTime(queue*makeTime + processTime + a*driveTime);
    System.out.print(t + "\t");
}
```

If we put a print statement in this loop and show the values of the four times we are dealing with, we will get a trace of the values of the variables concerned as the two nested loops – one in the constructor and one in `printaLine`.

open	close	ofDay	t	queue
09:00	**13:00**	**09:00**	**09:00**	0
09:00	13:00	09:15	**09:15**	0
09:00	13:00	09:35	**09:35**	1
09:00	13:00	10:00	**10:00**	2
09:00	13:00	10:30	**10:30**	3
09:00	13:00	11:05	**11:05**	4
09:00	13:00	11:45	**11:45**	5
09:00	**13:00**	**12:00**	**12:00**	0
09:00	13:00	12:15	**12:15**	1

If we use this loop and run the program, the table part of the output will be:

```
9:0        9:15       9:35       10:0       10:30      11:5       11:45
12:0       12:15      12:35      13:0       13:30      14:5       14:45
```

which is wrong. The second line should begin with the time at 9:15, not 12:00. The 12:00 has obviously crept in by ofDay, an actual parameter to printaLine, being contaminated by t, its formal parameter.

Here we see the effect of passing objects as parameters, and how it is different from passing primitive typed values. In PizzaDelivery1, when the integer time value was passed into printaLine, the method received a copy of the value, and could work on it, without disturbing the original. t did change on each line, getting the six different values required for the table. But back in the constructor, it still had its original value for the order time, which was then incremented and became the start of the next line.

However, when an object is passed, its value is not copied, only a reference to where the original is. So any changes to the formal parameter affect the actual parameter directly. To obtain the effect we need, though, is quite simple: we must remember to make a local copy of the parameter inside the method ourselves. This is where our fourth constructor – often called a **copy constructor** – comes in again. The correct method is:

```
void printaLine (Time t, int a) {
  Time ofDelivery;
  System.out.print(t+"\t");
  for (int queue = 0; queue <= 5; queue++) {
    ofDelivery = new Time(t);
    ofDelivery.addTime(queue*makeTime + processTime + a*driveTime);
    System.out.print(ofDelivery + "\t");
  }
  System.out.println();
}
```

Each time we want to enter a new value in the table, we create a new time object with a copy of t in it, alter it, print it out, and then Java disposes of it for us when ofDelivery is reset again to t. The trace now becomes

open	close	ofDay	t	ofDelivery	queue
09:00	**13:00**	**09:00**	**09:00**	null	0
09:00	13:00	09:00	09:00	**09:15**	0
09:00	13:00	09:00	09:00	**09:20**	1
09:00	13:00	09:00	09:00	**09:25**	2
09:00	13:00	09:00	09:00	**09:30**	3
09:00	13:00	09:00	09:00	**09:35**	4
09:00	13:00	09:00	09:00	**09:40**	5
09:00	**13:00**	**09:15**	**09:15**	null	
09:00	13:00	09:15	09:15	**09:30**	0
09:00	13:00	12:15	09:15	**09:35**	1

which can be checked as correct.

Program 2

Finally we list the entire class and test program, all put together:

```
class PizzaDelivery2 {

  /* The Pizza Delivery Program version 2    J M Bishop  May 2000
   * =====================================
   *
   * Works out the time for delivering pizzas based on
   * queue length and area of delivery.
   *
   * Illustrates the design of a Time class and the use of such
   * objects in methods and for-loops.
   */

  int driveTime = 5;    // per area;
  int makeTime = 5;     // in a queue
  int processTime = 10; // per order

  PizzaDelivery2 () {
    // Set the loop for one area only
    for (int area = 1; area<= 1; area++) {
     printHeading(area);
     startTable();
     Time open = new Time (9.00);
     Time close = new Time (13,0);
     for (Time ofDay = open; ofDay.lessThan(close);
            ofDay.addTime(15)) {
       printaLine(ofDay, area);
     }
    }
  }

  void printaLine (Time t, int a) {
    Time ofDelivery;
    System.out.print(t+"\t");
    for (int queue = 0; queue <= 5; queue++) {
      ofDelivery = new Time(t);
      ofDelivery.addTime(queue*makeTime+processTime+a*driveTime);
      System.out.print(ofDelivery + "\t");
    }
    System.out.println();
  }
```

```
class Time {
  int hour;
  int min;

  Time (int h, int m) {
    hour = h;
    min = m;
  }

  Time (int mins) {
    hour = mins / 60;
    min = mins % 60;
  }
  Time (double t) {
    hour = (int) t;
    min = (int) t*100 - hour*100;
  }

  Time (Time t) {
    hour = t.hour;
    min = t.min;
  }

  void addTime (int m) {
    min +=m;
    hour+= min / 60;
    min %= 60;
  }

  boolean lessThan (Time t) {
    return hour < t.hour | (hour==t.hour & min < t.min);
  }

  public String toString () {
    return hour + ":" + min + " ";
  }
}

void printHeading (int area) {
  System.out.println("Pizza 2U Delivery estimates for "+
    "Area "+area);
  System.out.println("===================================="+
    "=====\n");
}
```

```
void startTable() {
  System.out.println("Time now        Queue length");
  System.out.print("          ");
  for (int queue = 0; queue <=5; queue++)
    System.out.print("  "+queue+"  ");
  System.out.println();
}


public static void main (String [] args) {
  new PizzaDelivery2 ();
}
}
```

The output is:

```
Pizza 2U Delivery estimates for Area 1
=========================================

Time now  Queue length
          0        1        2        3        4        5
9:0       9:15     9:20     9:25     9:30     9:35     9:40
9:15      9:30     9:35     9:40     9:45     9:50     9:55
9:30      9:45     9:50     9:55     10:0     10:5     10:10
9:45      10:0     10:5     10:10    10:15    10:20    10:25
10:0      10:15    10:20    10:25    10:30    10:35    10:40
10:15     10:30    10:35    10:40    10:45    10:50    10:55
10:30     10:45    10:50    10:55    11:0     11:5     11:10
10:45     11:0     11:5     11:10    11:15    11:20    11:25
11:0      11:15    11:20    11:25    11:30    11:35    11:40
11:15     11:30    11:35    11:40    11:45    11:50    11:55
11:30     11:45    11:50    11:55    12:0     12:5     12:10
11:45     12:0     12:5     12:10    12:15    12:20    12:25
12:0      12:15    12:20    12:25    12:30    12:35    12:40
12:15     12:30    12:35    12:40    12:45    12:50    12:55
12:30     12:45    12:50    12:55    13:0     13:5     13:10
```

SUMMARY

This is a crucial chapter in that it discussed assignment and looping, as well as primitive types and expressions and the full range of method options. We concentrated on three of the six numeric types, namely int, long and double, as well as boolean. Preparing expressions from these using operators gives a wide range of possible formulae, augmented by the functions available in Java's Math class and the comparisons in Java's String class. How Java prints integers and reals was also discussed, with a promise to improve on the formatting options in Chapters 4 and 7.

For-loops are very powerful in Java and we looked at the full range of for-loop usage for integer types, viz. forwards, backwards, empty, nested, endless and unfinished. Then methods were discussed and care was taken to present the issue of declarations vs call and formal parameters vs actual parameters clearly. Once again there are several real examples, and the chapter ended with an extensive case study on a pizza delivery system. The case study revealed how objects can be used in loops and the practical issues associated with handling objects in expressions and as parameters.

Concepts related to the following keywords were discussed in this chapter:

```
boolean           int
break             long
byte              return
double            short
false             static
float             true
for               void
```

The following keywords were mentioned but will be further defined later:

```
char
final
while
```

The following entities from the Java libraries were also discussed:

```
Math              round
PI                abs
pow               max
sqrt              min
atan              String
cos               Calendar
sin               compareTo
tan               compareToIgnoreCase
toDegrees         equals
toRadians         equalsIgnoreCase
random            Date
```

And finally, we presented the following forms related primarily to methods:

Math class methods (abbreviated)
Type cast
Simple for-statement
Simple void method declarations
Simple void method call
Formal parameter declarations
Actual parameters

Void method declaration
Void method call
Typed method declaration
Typed method call
Operator precedence (boolean)
String comparison method
Java's `Date` class
For-loop

QUIZ

3.1 If we pay one-third of our income in tax after subtracting a rebate, how would this formula for tax be expressed as a Java expression?

(a) `1/3*income - rebate`
(b) `1/3 * (income - rebate)`
(c) `(income - rebate) / 3`
(d) `income/3 - rebate`

3.2 How many stars will this loop display?

```
for (int star = 9; star < 0; star++) {
   System.out.print('*');
}
```

(a) 9
(b) 0
(c) 10
(d) 8

3.3 Which for-statement can be used to loop over the decades of the 20th century (i.e. 1900, 1910,..., 1990).

(a) `for (int year = 1990; year <= 1990; year ++)`
(b) `for (int year = 1990; year < 2000; year ++)`
(c) `for (int year = 1990; year <= 1990; year +=10)`
(d) `for (int year = 1990; year <= 1990; year +10)`

3.4 If `x` is a `double` and has the value `-3.00000000008`, what will be printed by `System.out.print(x)`?

(a) `-3.00000000008`
(b) `-3.0`
(c) `-3.0E-11`
(d) `-3.8E-10`

3.5 The keyword(s) that every typed method must have is:

(a) `void`
(b) `return`

(c) `break`
(d) `public static void`

3.6   If we declare `String name = "John"`, the expression `name == "John"` will yield false. Why?

(a) should be an = not an ==
(b) `name` and `"John"` are different objects
(c) `"John"` will be automatically packed to eight characters and so have four spaces after it.
(d) there should be parentheses around the expression

3.7   If we want to check that two curio objects `a` and `b` have the same name and price, but we do not mind about the description, we could use:

(a) `a.name == b.name & a.price == b.price`
(b) `(a.name == b.name) && (a.price == b.price)`
(c) `a.name.equals(b.name) && a.price == b.price`
(d) `a==b & (a.description != b.description || a.description == b.description)`

3.8   Given the assignment in the `PizzaDelivery1` program `time = addTime(time,15)` what would it become in the `PizzaDelivery2` program when there is a `Time` class containing an `addTime` method?

(a) `time = Time.addTime (time, 15);`
(b) `time.addTime(time,15);`
(c) `time = addtime (15);`
(d) `time.addTime(15);`

3.9   To get a random number between 1 and 6, we would use:

(a) `number = Random(6)+1;`
(b) `number = Math,random(6);`
(c) `number = (int) (Math.random()*6 + 1);`
(d) `number = Math.random()*6;`

3.10 If we have two integers to return from a method, we can use:

(a) an object as a parameter
(b) an object as a return value
(c) two parameters
(d) answer (a) or (b)

PROBLEMS

Note: Problems 3.2 to 3.4 are of the size of the Pizza Delivery case study and make use of skills gained in the whole chapter. Most of the other problems relate to loops and methods and are intended to be smaller and more focused on a single task.

3.1   **Large table diagram.** Draw a model diagram and a call diagram (as in Figure 3.3) for the `LargeTemperatureTable` program in Example 3.6.

3.2   **Marathon runners.** There are five main contenders for the Savanna Marathon Race. They come from England, Germany, Italy, Spain and Norway. The organizers of the race receive the following information about each runner: name, country, age, best marathon time so far (in hours and minutes).

- Create a class that will represent a marathon runner. You could use the `Time` class for the best time. Usually marathon times are around 2 hours.

- Write a short program to test that you can create five runners of the class successfully.

- Now write a `Race` program that will create the runners, then generate randomly a final time for the race for each, and print out the list of runners, indicating all their details, plus this time and their new best time. (Use the `Math.min` method here.)

Note that we cannot easily at this stage work out the winner of the race, but will come back to this problem in Chapter 4.

3.3 **Weight watchers.** Two friends have been trying to lose weight over several weeks. The first started off weighing 100 kg and 98 cm waist, and the second started off weighing 85 kg and a 95 cm waist. Each week they record their new weight and waist measurement and work out who lost more in each category.

- Design and program a class for recording their progress in terms of current weight and waist measurements.

- Test the class out by creating objects for two people.

- Now write a program to run for six weeks, where each week new weight and waist measurements are generated which are roughly similar to those currently held (for example, current weight ± up to 1.5 kg and current waist ± up to 2 cm). Print out the new measurements and store them back in the objects, and also print out who lost more in each case.

- Keep a running total of losses and at the end print out the total loss.

3.4 **World times.** An e-commerce company in London, UK, deals with people all over the world. Sometimes it has to follow up orders by telephone, in which case it needs to know what the time is in a specific time zone. London operates on Universal Time (UT). Print out a table of times for the hours 0:00 to 23:00 for another city such as Vancouver (−8 hours from UT), New York (−5 hours), Cape Town (+2) or Sydney (+10). Use the `Time` class, augmenting `addTime` first to rotate around the clock, as discussed earlier.

3.5 **Conversions.** A conversion table can be viewed as a general algorithm. Establish this fact by adapting the program in Example 3.3 to print out the conversion from miles to kilometres (1 mile = 1.6 km) and again to print dollars to graz ($1 = G0.45).

3.6 **Other tables.** Take the large conversion table program and alter it to produce other tables, such as:

> Celsius to Fahrenheit
> miles to kilometres
> litres to gallons
> dollars to your currency

Use typed methods for the conversions.

3.7 **Voting.** A board of directors consists of three members, each of whom has a two-way switch marked yes/no. When votes are taken, a lamp comes on if the yes votes are in the majority. The circuit that implements the turning on of the lamp is represented by the boolean function

$$L = a \ \& \ (b \ | \ c) \ | \ b \ \& \ c$$

Write a program that writes a table of the alternate yes/no values for a, b and c, and the value of L. Implement L using a boolean method.

3.8   **Accurate times.** For the marathon runners, it is anticipated that seconds and tenths of a second will be recorded for their times. Augment the `Times` class to have this extra field (you could use a double variable). Test the class out with a small test program.

3.9   **Ten green bottles.** A campfire song that can go on a bit is:

> There were ten green bottles hanging on the wall,
> Ten green bottles hanging on the wall
> And if one green bottle should accidentally fall
> There'll be nine green bottles hanging on the wall.
> Nine green bottles hanging on the wall
> And if one green bottle should accidentally fall
> There'll be eight green bottles hanging on the wall.
>
> etc.
>
> One green bottle hanging on the wall
> And if one green bottle should accidentally fall
> There'll be no green bottles hanging on the wall.

Using nested backward loops, as discussed in Section 3.2, design an algorithm to print out such a song, and program it to start with 5 green bottles.

3.10   **Labels.** Adapt the program in Example 3.2 to print three labels with your name and address across the page, and do this eight times to fill the page. If you line the output up carefully, you can photocopy it on to standard-sized sticky labels.

3.11   **Clearer tables.** The conversion table of Example 3.6 is not quite right because the values increase across the page, rather than down, which is more normal. Work out how to change the program so as to print the values increasing in columns.

3.12   **Timetable.** It is always useful to have a blank timetable to fill in for one's lectures. Write a program that will print out such a timetable, with Monday to Friday across the top, and the hours 8 to 15 down the left. The timetable should have suitable borders.

3.13   **Histogram.** A histogram is generally a useful graph to draw. See if you can create a class based on that in Example 3.4 which includes bar and axis methods and can be called to print histograms for a variety of data. Test it by

(a)   generating random numbers to represent temperatures for a given month (between say 10 and 30 degrees Celsius)
(b)   mapping the value of sin x against values of degrees from 0 to 90.

3.14   **Birthdays.** The probability of two people in a group of n having the same birthday is

$$p(n) = 1 - \frac{365}{365} \times \frac{364}{365} \times \frac{363}{365} \times \ldots \times \frac{364 - n + 1}{365}$$

Write a program to evaluate and print this probability for groups of 2 to 60 people. Draw a table of n and $p(n)$ for values of n from 10 to 50. If you completed Problem 3.13, plot the values for $10, 20, \ldots, 50$ on a histogram.

3.15 **A number triangle.** Write a program that uses for-statements and `print/println` statements to produce the following triangle on the display. Read in the number of lines required (five are shown here).

```
1
2 2
3 3 3
4 4 4 4
5 5 5 5 5
```

Adapt the program to print the triangle so that the numbers are centred, as below. Adapt it again to print the triangle upside down. This is called Pascal's triangle.

```
    1
   2 2
  3 3 3
 4 4 4 4
5 5 5 5 5
```

3.16 **The Fibonacci series** consists of a series of numbers in which each number is the sum of the two preceding ones, i.e.

```
1   1   2   3   5   8   13   21   34   55 ...
```

Write a program to display the first 50 terms of the series. Using a nested for-loop, adapt the program so that it displays only every third number. What do you notice about the numbers?

3.17 **Times tables.** In the olden days, exercise books used to have multiplication tables printed neatly on the back. These would be arranged three across and four down, with each row being of the form:

```
4 times table      5 times table      6 times table
1 x 4 = 4          1 x 5 = 5          1 x 6 = 6
2 x 4 = 8          2 x 5 = 10         2 x 6 = 12
3 x 4 = 12         3 x 5 = 15         3 x 6 = 18
4 x 4 = 16         4 x 5 = 20         4 x 6 = 24
5 x 4 = 20         5 x 5 = 25         5 x 6 = 30
6 x 4 = 24         6 x 5 = 30         6 x 6 = 36
7 x 4 = 28         7 x 5 = 35         7 x 6 = 42
8 x 4 = 32         8 x 5 = 40         8 x 6 = 48
9 x 4 = 36         9 x 5 = 45         9 x 6 = 54
10 x 4 = 40        10 x 5 = 50        10 x 6 = 60
11 x 4 = 44        11 x 5 = 55        11 x 6 = 66
12 x 4 = 48        12 x 5 = 60        12 x 6 = 72
```

Write a program that makes good use of methods and parameters to print out a complete set of all the first 12 multiplication tables.

3.18 **Leavers.** Add to the `Child` class in the Kindergarten program (Problem 2.8) a boolean method that returns whether or not a child is leaving this year. Decide where the year value should be declared and accessed: as a constant in the main program, passed as a parameter, as static within the class, or some other option.

3.19 **Manuscript.** Change the program in Problem 2.10 (Book) so that the class records the number of manuscript pages and add a method to calculate the final number of pages, based on an 80% reduction. Check the class with a test program, generating 15 chapters with a random number of manuscript pages between 20 and 50.

3.20 **Chessboard.** A chessboard consist of eight rows of eight squares, where the squares are alternate black and white. Write a program to draw a chessboard, where most of the program consists of a `paint` method with two nested loops and two calls to `fillRect`.

CHAPTER 4

Input and output

In this chapter we focus on input and output and introduce two custom-made Java classes that give a simple yet powerful means of interacting with a program. By being able to read in values to a program, we change its state. Two other ways of changing the state are by means of explicit selection (the if-statement) and reacting to exceptions. Using the IO classes both on the screen and with files requires that we know how to create and use packages, which is also covered.

4.1 Inputting interactively

A program will most often need to acquire values for its variables from the outside world. Such values form the data for the program and could consist of tables stored on disk, replies to questions or just lists of values to be typed in. The term **stream** is applied to the sequence of data items that will come from one source. Thus the keyboard is modelled by a stream, as is a file on disk. In this section we look at keyboard input, and follow it by looking at file input and output in Section 4.5.

Input streams

The Java equivalent of `System.out` is `System.in`. Although `System.in` is also a predeclared object, its class is `InputStream`, which is an **abstract** class in Java terms. Abstract classes are covered fully in Chapter 9, but what we need to know here is that we cannot always create objects of abstract classes. The `System.in` object must be supplied as a constructor parameter to another class called `InputStreamReader`, thereby creating a usable object. In addition, keyboard input works best when buffered, so we then pass this object to another class, `BufferedReader`, and all is set up.

We acknowledge that this is a complex way of handling matters, but the following form shows that the actual programming involved is not excessive.

Declaring the keyboard for input

```
import java.io.*;

BufferedReader stream = new BufferedReader
        (new InputStreamReader(System.in));
```

Imports the `java.io` package.
Creates an `InputStreamReader` object based on the `System.in` object and uses this to create a `BufferedReader` object, which is given the identifier *stream*.

Before the class in which the declaration is to appear, we must import the `java.io` package in which the three classes mentioned above are defined. Then the declaration declares a new stream, connected to `System.in`, with all the facilities of the `BufferedReader` class. A typical such declaration is:

```
BufferedReader in = new BufferedReader
        (new InputStreamReader(System.in));
```

which will declare `in` as the stream that is connected to the keyboard. In Section 4.5 we shall see how to connect streams to files as well.

One side effect of reading is that something could go wrong; for example the data might end unexpectedly or have the wrong format. Such events are called **exceptions** and we shall see later in the chapter how to deal with them. However, Java requires that we indicate in every method those exceptions that can occur. Therefore if we are going to read, we need to add the phrase

```
throws IOException
```

after the method declaration for each method that does reading, and any method that calls it and does not handle the exception. This process is shown in Example 4.1.

Reading strings

Similar to the `println` method, the `BufferedReader` class provides a `readLine` method which will read in a full line of text to the given string. The form is:

Reading a string

```
string = stream.readLine();
```

Gets a whole line of data as a string from the given *stream* and assigns it to *string*.

Notice two differences between this form and that for printing:

■ The suffix is `-Line` not `-ln`;

■ The method is typed, not void, so is called in an assignment, not on its own.

EXAMPLE 4.1   Greetings

Problem   Suppose we would like to greet someone in French.

Solution   Write a program with the greeting built in and ask the user to type their name.

Program   The program is quite straightforward. Apart from following the form for connecting to the keyboard, we also remember to throw `IOException` from both the constructor and `main`.

```
import java.io.*;

class Greetings {

    /*  A simple greetings program   by J M Bishop  Oct 1996
     *  -------------------------     Java 1.1  Dec 1997
     *                                updated May 2000
     */
```

```
Greetings () throws IOException {

   BufferedReader in = new BufferedReader
            (new InputStreamReader(System.in));

   System.out.print("What is your name? ");
   String name = in.readLine();
   System.out.println("Bonjour " + name);
   }


   public static void main (String args []) throws IOException {
      new Greetings();
   }
}
```

Testing   Here is a sample run, using plain type for the input and bold for output as before.

What is your name?
Pierre Marchand
Bonjour Pierre Marchand

Remember that `readLine` reads a whole line from the keyboard, until Return is pressed.

Java's approach to reading numbers

Java can easily read values of the other types of data if they are already in binary form and stored in a file. However, if we want to interact with a program from the keyboard, Java's idea is that we should read a string and do the conversion explicitly in the program. The conversion routines are supplied with object classes associated with the primitive types, as well as through special classes available in the `java.text` package (discussed in Chapter 7). The same classes can be used for output formatting.

   Although powerful, these classes are not simple to use, which is a shame because reading a number is, after all, an operation that we may need to perform frequently. Here is what a read of a real number would look like:

```
double d = Double.valueOf(in.readLine()).doubleValue();
```

Of course, such complexity can be easily hidden in a method and similar methods can be made for integer numbers and the other types. Then, we could collect the methods together and create a class that will provide the functionality required. This is exactly what *Java Gently* does.

   In fairness, it must be said that the `java.text` classes are well put together and make for very versatile programming in the international context, as they cover such input as percentages and currencies, as well as numbers.

4.2   User-friendly input–output

From the above, we realize that input of numbers in Java is even more difficult to manage than output. The full details of Java's input facilities, as discussed in Chapter 7, *are* powerful, but Java itself does not present a simple alternative. Using raw Java input can distract one from the primary purpose of learning to program and more importantly from that of solving realistic problems. For this reason, we have devised two classes for use with this book:

- `Display`, which is a generalized graphical user interface, showing input and output at the same time;

- `Stream`, which is a simple means of input and outputting text-based data with a Java console, command window or text file.

`Display` was written especially for a recent sister book, *Java Gently for Engineers and Scientists*, and presents an easy-to-use graphical user interface (GUI) control. `Stream` is based on a class called `Text` which was written in 1997 for the first edition of *Java Gently* and has been successfully integrated into programs by many thousands of users. In this edition, the nature of the `Text` class is completely reworked to be object-oriented, while still retaining the simple interface that made it so popular. The new class is called `Stream`, but the old class `Text` is still available for compatibility.

The `Stream` class is discussed later in this section, and again later in this chapter when files are covered. In between we look at the `Display` class and show how it enables programs to interact meaningfully with users.

Java Gently's GUI `Display` Class

Let us first look at a display produced by a simple program to repeatedly add two numbers, as shown in Figure 4.1. The display is divided into two sections, the left-hand side for input and the right-hand side for output. Both sections are visible at the same time. They are also **scrollable** so that they can have more boxes or lines that the screen can show at once. Thus one can go back and look at earlier results from the program.

At the bottom of the display are two control **buttons**: a large Ready bar, which provides interaction between the user and the program being written; and a small Close button on the right-hand side, which will shut down the window and the program using it.

It would of course be possible to program such a display from scratch in Java for a particular program, and we shall certainly learn how to do so in Chapter 10. However, doing so involves quite a lot of tedious GUI programming, which can make simple programs into monsters. The look and feel of the `Display` class is just what we would want in such a program, but what we have done is applied the principle of reusability and programmed it once, for multiple use.

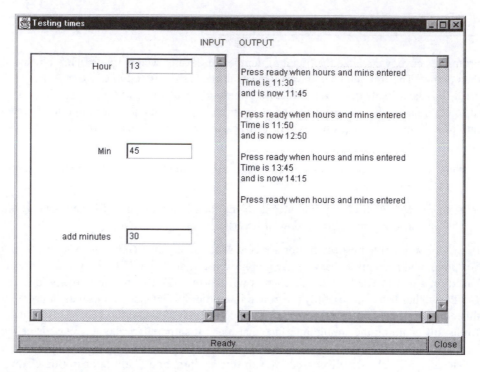

Figure 4.1 *The display produced by a simple program.*

The output section

From the point of view of the output section of Figure 4.1, we see that the program would go through three steps:

- Display an introductory message about the data required.

- Tell the user what to do when the data are ready.

- Get the values from the input section, do the computation and display the results.

This program is set up to repeat these steps until the Close button is pressed. Thus the output section presents the active flow of the program in the usual way.

The input section

The input section presents the data values that the program may wish the user to change. The steps involved in using this section are:

1. The program initially tells the display what data values need to be altered. For each of these, a label alongside a standard sized box is drawn. Initial values can be supplied for the boxes, which is a very useful facility for testing programs, as the user does not have to think of new data for every field.

2. The user makes changes to the values in the boxes as required. Not all need to be changed, and values can be repeatedly overwritten until correct.

3. The user presses the Ready bar. The Display fetches all the values from the boxes, updates its internal table of values and passes control back to the program.

4. The program gets whatever values it needs (presumably all of them) and continues with its calculations and output.

For further runs of the program with different data, steps 2 to 4 are repeated.

The `Display` class's methods

Having looked at the `display` class informally, we now list the methods it provides and describe the function of each method in a comment.

The `Display` class	
new Display (*String*)	// sets up a new Display object with a title
void println (*String*)	// prints a string in the output section
void prompt (*String, value*)	// makes a box in the input section with the given string label and an initial value which is int, double or string
void ready (*String*)	// prints a message then waits for ready bar to be pressed
int getInt (*String*)	// gets the int value that was set that label
double getDouble (*String*)	// reads the double value that was set with that string label
String getString (*String*)	// gets the int value that was set with that label

An entire program can be written using just the first five methods. The next two – `getDouble` and `getString` – are merely variations on `getInt`.

Starting up the `Display` class

The first step in using the `Display` class is to create a `Display` object. A declaration is:

```
Display display = new Display ("Add two numbers");
```

In this instantiation, the object name is `display`, with a small d, whereas the class is `Display`, with a capital D. This is the only time that we refer to the class name, so there will be no confusion later on. Of course, we could call our display object anything we like, for example:

```
Display myWindow = new Display ("Add two numbers");
```

or even

```
Display d = new Display ("Add two numbers");
```

In any one program, there could be more than one display, but this is rather unlikely. Therefore, it is better to stick to a standard name, and to use it in all your programs. We use `display` in this book. A similar convention is that of using `i` for loop variables: it is accepted usage, even though `i` is itself not a very expressive identifier.

The parameter supplied to the `Display` class when the object is created is the name of the window, and it is displayed in the top line, as we can see in Figure 4.1, and in the tab if we minimize the window while doing something else.

Next we have to write out the initial instructions in the output screen. `Display` reuses the well-known method name `println`, and all we learnt about output in Sections 2.4 and 3.1 applies. The `println` for the display in Figure 4.1 is:

```
display.println("Test data set number " + i);
```

The only difference between this statement and a text-based one is that we sent the string to our display instead of to `System.out` (which has a very specific and somewhat old-fashioned connection to the console screen or DOS-window).

Inputting via the display

We now consider how input is done on a GUI display. Each data item is identified by the label shown next to it. To get a data item onto the input section, we use `prompt`, for example:

```
display.prompt("Hour",11);
```

Eleven will be the initial value, but there is no reason why we could not have said

```
display.prompt("Hour", 0);
```

or even

```
display.prompt("Hour", a);
```

where the inital value is stored in `a`. The program asks that the user indicates when the data are ready, by calling `ready` as in:

```
display.ready("Press ready to add");
```

The message is displayed and the Ready bar (which may have been momentarily grey) becomes active.

To get the data out, we first press the Ready bar. Don't forget that part! Without the action of pressing the bar, there is no way for the program to know when the user has finished making alterations. We then call one of the three `get` methods, depending on the type of data we want, e.g.

```
h = display.getInt("Hour");
```

The string supplied here identifies which of the boxes in the input section is relevant. The `display` object returns the current value and assigns it to the variable as shown. Values can be picked off in any order, so that the following is perfectly valid (although a bit eccentric):

```
m = display.getInt("Mins");
h = display.getInt("Hour");
```

EXAMPLE 4.2   Testing the `Time` class

In Case Study 1 we tested the `Time` class using a previous program which printed a table – the Pizza Delivery system. It would have been simpler to just read in values and test that way, but we had not yet covered input. Now we can hook up a simple test program to `Time` and test it thoroughly. The output was shown in Figure 4.1 and the program is:

```
import javagently.*;

class TimeDisplay {

    TimeDisplay () {
      Time time, newTime;
      Display d = new Display ("Testing times");
      d.prompt("Hour",11);
      d.prompt("Min",30);
      d.prompt("add minutes",15);
      for (; ;) {
        d.ready("\nPress ready when hours and mins entered");
        int hour = d.getInt("Hour");
        int min = d.getInt("Min");
        time = new Time (hour, min);
        d.println("Time is " + time);
        time.addMins(d.getInt("add minutes"));
        d.println("and is now " + time);
      }
    }
```

```
// Put the Time class here

  public static void main (String [] args) {
    new TimeDisplay ();
  }
}
```

We see that the program sets up the display and the input boxes in the initialization phase. Thereafter it enters an endless loop. This is not a problem because the program will end when the Close button is pressed by the user, not when the program thinks it has performed enough iterations! The `ready-get-println` sequence follows and then the computations are done. This program forms a model for many of the interactive input–output programs that follow.

Notice that we import a new package called `javagently`: this is where the `Display` class is kept. We look at how to set up the `javagently` package on a computer in the next section. You may need to refer to that section if you wish to run the above program (or your laboratory may already be set up with `javagently` installed).

Testing   What values should we use for testing? The principal method that we are testing is `addTimes`. So we want to have various times, and various amounts of minutes to add to them. The place where things could possibly go wrong is in the borders between different hours and days. The following is a reasonable selection:

hour	min	addmins	expected answer
23	30	15	23:45
23	30	29	23:59
23	30	30	00:00
23	30	60	00:60

Immediately we discover that our `Time` class is deficient in that it does not roll over to the next day. The answer for adding 30 mins to 23:30 is given as 24:00. Now as an exercise, extend the `Time` class so that it does handle midnight correctly.

Java Gently's `Stream` class

The class defined for input–output for *Java Gently* is called `Stream`. It provides eleven methods: four for opening up input and output, four for getting input and three for formatting output. These are shown in the following form:

The Stream class

```
Constants
---------
READ = 0,
WRITE = 1;


Constructors
------------
Stream (InputStream filename)
Stream (String filename, int how)


Input
-----
int     readInt ()
double  readDouble ()
String  readString ()
char    readChar ()


Output
------
void println  - for objects, String, int, double, char
void print    - for objects, String, int, double, char
void close()


Output - class methods
----------------------
String format (int number, int align)
String format (double number, int align, int frac)
```

The first constructor is used when the InputStream is known, as when connecting to the keyboard.

The second constructor is used to connect files, and the *how* parameter indicates
   whether the file is for reading or writing.

The four input methods operate on the Stream object and fetch the next item on
   the stream, interpreting it as the type given. If it is not the correct type, the
   method will return for another item. All items must be delimited by a space or
   other punctuation mark.

println and print operate exactly as they do for System.out.

close must be called on any file opened for writing, so that the contents are
   preserved for later.

The format methods are class methods and therefore are called as
   Stream.format. Full details are given below of how they operate.

If we want to set up the keyboard, then we use the first constructor, which is especially designed for this purpose, as in:

```
Stream in = new Stream (System.in);
```

We can then use the set of four read methods. `readInt` and `readDouble` return numbers as required. `readString` is not exactly the same as the built-in method `readLine` because all of the `Stream` class's methods have the property that multiple values can be typed on a single line. This feature is illustrated in the next example and exploited in the Olympic medals system (Example 4.10). `readChar` reads a single character. All of the four reading methods rely on the item being read being 'delimited' by something such as a space, tab, comma or end of line. Unfortunately, this means that we cannot read successive characters, only those separated by such delimiters.

Usually, for simple interactive input, we have `System.out` connected to the screen (automatically) and by means of the statement above, `in` connected to the keyboard. A typical use of writing and reading would be:

```
System.out.print("Enter your age: ");
int age = in.readInt();
```

The two `format` methods provide a means for controlling numeric output by converting a number to a string. These methods are not in any way connected to a stream, so they can be used with data going to files or to the standard output, `System.out`. What does it mean that they are class methods? We discussed this concept in Section 3.1 with the `Math` class. To recap, compare:

```
double y = Math.sin(x);
```

```
mugs.write();
```

`sin` is an example of a class method, whereas `write` is an ordinary object (or instance) method and is called via the object itself. Class methods exist once only in a class and are referred to by the class identifier. So `format` will be called via the class name `Stream`.

With the formats, the `align` parameter specifies the minimum number of characters that should be used to print the number. Thus if the number is 123 and the align parameter is 6, there will be three spaces in front of 123 when output. In this way, numbers can be neatly lined up in columns. The `format` methods have the property that if the number will not fit in the gap given, the gap will be expanded to the right, and the digits before the decimal point will be printed in full anyway. For real numbers, the `frac` parameter is definite: there will always be that number of digits in the fractional part, and any further digits are truncated. For example, suppose we say:

```
System.out.println(Stream.format(x, 10, 4));
```

then for various values of x we get:

```
-1234.5678          -1234.5678
1234.56789           1234.5679
45.67                  45.6700
4                       4.0000
```

```
4.56789                4.5679
0                      0.0000
123456789              123456789.0000
777777.88888           777777.8889
```

Finally, there are methods for opening and creating files, and for duplicating the `print` and `println` facilities on them (more about which later).

`Stream` is part of the `javagently` package. How to compile, store and access this package is covered in in the next section. The `Stream` class is not at all long, and is discussed in full in Chapter 7. Now we look at an example that uses `Stream` to good advantage.

Constants

The careful reader will have noticed that in the `Stream` class form, there are two constants defined, and they are written with capital letters. In Java, we can declare variables with initial values which are also their final values, i.e. the value may not change, ever. The syntax form is:

Constant declaration

`static final` *type CONSTANTID = value;*

The `CONSTANTID` is declared and given the specified value. The value may not be changed.

It is conventional to write constants with capital letters. An example of another constant that we have seen is `Math.PI`. Examples of constants that we might set up are:

```
static final double KMTOMILES = 1.6;
static final int MILLENNIUM = 2000;
```

EXAMPLE 4.3   Large temperature table formatted

As an example of using the `Stream` class for formatting output, consider how we could improve the table printed out for temperature conversions in Example 3.6. We relied there on tabs to space out the columns, but this did not work when the numbers were different lengths: the first few rows of the table were aligned more to the left.

By simply changing the `print` statements in the `outALine` method to be:

```
System.out.print(Stream.format(c,6));
System.out.print(Stream.format((int) fahrenheit(c),5));
```

we get the following more correct effect. Notice that there is a slight complication in the writing out of the Fahrenheit value. The method we defined uses `Math.round`, which returns a `long` result, so in the original program we left the `fahrenheit` method as returning a `long` type. However, `format` needs an integer. Therefore we must first cast the result before it can be accepted.

```
Temperature Conversion Table
==============================
```

C	F	C	F	C	F	C	F	C	F
0	32	1	34	2	36	3	37	4	39
5	41	6	43	7	45	8	46	9	48
10	50	11	52	12	54	13	55	14	57
15	59	16	61	17	63	18	64	19	66
20	68	21	70	22	72	23	73	24	75
25	77	26	79	27	81	28	82	29	84
30	86	31	88	32	90	33	91	34	93
35	95	36	97	37	99	38	100	39	102
40	104	41	106	42	108	43	109	44	111
45	113	46	115	47	117	48	118	49	120
50	122	51	124	52	126	53	127	54	129
55	131	56	133	57	135	58	136	59	138
60	140	61	142	62	144	63	145	64	147
65	149	66	151	67	153	68	154	69	156
70	158	71	160	72	162	73	163	74	165
75	167	76	169	77	171	78	172	79	174
80	176	81	178	82	180	83	181	84	183
85	185	86	187	87	189	88	190	89	192
90	194	91	196	92	198	93	199	94	201
95	203	96	205	97	207	98	208	99	210

EXAMPLE 4.4   Alternative greetings programs

The `Stream` class has a forgiving nature: it will detect bad numbers and permit you to type them in again. It allows – and ignores – blank lines and spaces between data items. It does not allow them inside strings, so, if we write a `Stream` version of the greetings program, only one of Pierre's names would appear:

```
import java.io.*;
import javagently.*;

class Greetings2 {
```

```
  Greetings2 () {
    Stream in = new Stream (System.in);

    System.out.print("What is your name?");
    String name = in.readString();
    System.out.println("Bonjour " + name);
  }

  public static void main (String [] args) throws IOException {
    new Greetings2 ();
  }
}
```

What is your name? Pierre Marchand
Bonjour Pierre

`Greetings2` detects only a single word: that is, Pierre, not Pierre Marchand. `Stream` does actually allow multiple items on a line; we just have to be aware that we want them. So a third version of the greetings program for a two-word name would be:

```
import java.io.*;
import javagently.*;

class Greetings3 {

  Greetings3 () {
    Stream in = new Stream (System.in);

    System.out.print("What is your name?");
    String name = in.readString();
    String surname = in.readString();
    System.out.println("Bonjour " + name +" "+ surname);
  }

  public static void main (String [] args) throws IOException {
    new Greetings3 ();
  }
}
```

What is your name? Pierre Marchand
Bonjour Pierre Marchand

Although forgiving, `Stream` is very firm, and if it wants two names it will get them or die in the attempt. Thus the second call to `readString` will wait until another string is entered.

Inputting sequences

One of the most common conditions that we shall have to check for, one way or another, is the end of input. There are five ways to handle input of varying lengths:

1. **Know or state in advance** how many items there must be and keep a running count.

2. **Precede the data by a count** of how many items there actually are, and keep a running count.

3. Make use of an **end-of-file exception** to mark the end of the items.

4. Put a **special terminating value** at the end of the items, such as zero or 999.

5. Use a GUI interface to signal end of data by **pressing a button** or something like that.

The first two methods are applicable to counting-loops, since they rely on the number of items being known before reading starts. In some cases, this might not be a restriction, for example if we take one reading every hour, then we know that 24 readings will be entered. We use method 2 in Example 4.6.

In method 3, the number of items is not relevant; rather, the reading stops when a certain condition is achieved. The condition is signalled by an exception, and we see how to use these in Section 4.6. Method 4 is applicable to conditional loops, and is discussed in Chapter 5. Finally, method 5 relies on the presence of a class such as the display, as we have just seen in this section.

4.3   Creating and accessing packages

The `Display` and `Stream` classes are stored in a package called `javagently` and in order to access the class, a suitable import statement must be added to the program, i.e.

```
import javagently.*;
```

The `javagently` package currently contains three classes:

```
Stream
Display
Graph
```

We explain briefly how to use `Graph` later in the book. If we want only the `Stream` class then

```
import javagently.Stream;
```

would be equally effective.

Since `javagently` is our own package, it does not come precompiled with the Java Development Kit or with the Java IDE you may be using. We therefore first have to create it before the import statement will work, and we can run the programs in Section 4.2. Follow these easy steps:

1. At a level above that where you are working, create a directory called `javagently`.

2. Download the files you want (e.g. `Display` and `Stream`) from the web site into this directory or type them in from Section 7.3 (`Stream`) or Section 13.4 (`Display`).

3. In this directory, compile `Stream.java` and `Display.java` (and `Graph.java` if you have that too).

4. There will now be corresponding class files in the `javagently` directory, including some for supporting classes that these classes use.

5. Using the method particular for your machine, add the directory immediately above `javagently` to your classpath (not to the path). Thus one adds something like `C:\mywork\` to the classpath, not `C:\mywork\javagently\`.

6. Put

   ```
   import javagently.*;
   ```

   at the start of your program.

Figure 4.2 summarizes the result of these steps for a typical situation on a PC.

An import statement in a Java class causes a look-up process via the classpath. Thus we include the `C:\COS110\` directory in the classpath, because that is where `javagently` resides. Any and all of the Java classes in `chap4`, or anywhere else under the `COS110` directory, can now make use of `javagently` through importing. If you have not already done so, fetch `Display` and `Graph` into the `javagently` directory as well and repeat steps 2, 3 and 4 above.

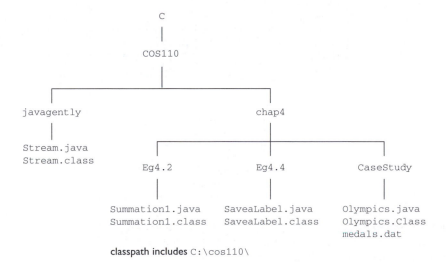

Figure 4.2 *Example of a directory structure for using the* `javagently` *package.*

Model diagrams for packages

Packages also have a notation when we draw model diagrams. It is shown in Figure 4.3 with examples. The arrow symbol for importing a package is the same as for instantiating, and the difference is clear because one cannot instantiate a package. Thus the `Greetings3` program could be drawn as in Figure 4.4. This shows that the `Greetings3` object (created from the `Greetings3` class, which is not shown here) imports two packages. One is a Java package that we do not expand here, and the other is the user-defined package with three classes.

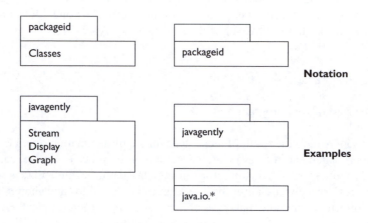

Figure 4.3 *Class notation for packages.*

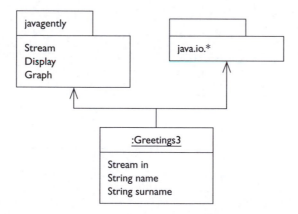

Figure 4.4 *Model diagram for the* `Greetings3` *program showing packages.*

4.4   Selection with if-else

Having used comparisons and booleans already in Chapter 3, we can proceed to the if-statement. Two methods of changing the values of variables have been covered so far: assignment and reading in. We now consider how to check the values in variables, and choose alternative actions based on the result of the check. Java has two **selection** statements known as the if-statement and the switch-statement. We look at the **if-statement** here, and the **switch-statement** in the next chapter.

Form of the if-statement

The general form of the if-statement is:

If-statement
| ```
if (condition) {
   statements1;
}
else {
   statements2;
}
``` |
| Evaluate *condition*. If it is true, execute *statements1*; if it is false, execute *statements2*.
The else-part is optional: if it is not included, a false condition causes execution to move to the statement after the if. |

The condition is a boolean expression as covered in Section 3.6. Examples are:

```
speed > speedlimit
(age >= 16) & (age < 75)
isaMinor
year == 1066
day != 29
initial != 'J'
time.lessThan(close)
answer.equals("Yes")
```

In the if-statement we refer to the block of statements following the condition as the **then-part** and to the statements following the `else` as the **else-part**. The whole if-statement is executed as follows. First, the condition is evaluated. If this result is true, the then-part is executed, and the else-part is skipped. If the result is false, the then-part is skipped and the else-part is executed. A simple example would be:
```

```
if (number >= 0) {
  System.out.println("Positive")
}
else {
  System.out.println("Negative");
}
```

In the form of the if-statement, the `else` is given in italics. This means that it is optional and the statement can be used in an 'if-then' version. For example,

```
if (day == 25) {
  System.out.println("Christmas, Hooray");
}
```

We start illustrating the if-statement by showing a classic algorithm, that of finding the highest number.

EXAMPLE 4.5   The highest number

Problem   Find the largest in a sequence of numbers.

Solution   A program can read in the numbers one at a time, remembering the highest so far, and updating this if necessary. We note that negative numbers should be catered for as well.

Algorithm   This is a very interesting algorithm as it illustrates the process of induction. We start by assuming that we have found the highest of n numbers. Then the $n+1$th number is read. To find the highest of the $n+1$ numbers, all that needs to be done is to compare the new number with the highest so far and, if it is higher, to replace the highest. This process can then be repeated for as long as required.

The question is, how does the process start? Well, the highest number of a sequence that is one long must be just that number. So we start by reading in one number, make it the highest and proceed from there.

Program   We shall take input from the keyboard, and use the `Stream` class for reading.

```
import java.io.*;
import javagently.*;

class HighestValue {

  /* The Highest Value Program    by  J M Bishop  Aug 1996
   *  -------------------------    Java 1.1 October 1997
```

```
 *                                    Java 2 and new Stream class
 *                                    May 2000
 *
 * Finds the highest in a list of numbers.
 * Illustrates the if-statement
 */

HighestValue () {

  Stream in = new Stream (System.in);

  System.out.println("*****  Finding the highest number *****");

 // Find out how many numbers will be coming
  System.out.print("How many numbers (1 or more)?");
  int n = in.readInt();

 // Start off the sequence
  System.out.println("Type them in");
  System.out.print("1>");
  int highest = in.readInt();

 // Read and check the rest of the numbers
  int number;
  for (int i = 2; i <= n; i++) {
    System.out.print(i+">");
    number = in.readInt();
    if (number > highest) {
      highest = number;
    }
  }

  System.out.println("That's enough, thanks");
  System.out.println("The highest number was " + highest);
 }

 public static void main(String[] args) throws IOException {
   new HighestValue ();
 }
}
```

Testing   It is a good idea to test such an algorithm with the first number being the highest, then with the last, and then with one in the middle. Another test would be to have all the numbers except one equal. This is left up to the reader, but here is one run:

```
*****  Finding the highest number *****
How many numbers (1 or more)?   5
Type them in
1>   56
2>   -99
3>   23
4>   70
5>   -4
That's enough, thanks
The highest number was 70
```

EXAMPLE 4.6   Averaging readings

Problem   A scientific expedition is taking various readings throughout the day and wishes to produce the average of the readings. However, any readings that fall outside a given whole number range should be discarded.

Solution   The problem falls into two parts:

- handling the input of the readings and reporting of the results; and
- checking and averaging the readings.

Design   In the program, the bit concerning the if-statement looks like this:

```
if (reading >= min & reading <= max) {
  total += reading;
  n++;
  d.print("K");
}
else {
  d.print("X");
}
```

In other words, if we have a valid reading within range, we add it in, increment *n*, and also print out a symbol that indicates that the reading was OK. Otherwise we give the reading an X and do not include it in the calculations.

The program also illustrates how to stop by entering a string in a display box. We do not want to stop by pressing the Close button, because then we shall lose the final output with the crucial average. This is achieved by having a boolean variable called done and a string that we read after each value, i.e.

```
status = d.getString("Finished?");
done = status.equals("Yes");
```

done is checked in the for-loop at the top.

Program   The complete program is:

```
import javagently.*;

class ReadingsAverages {

  /* Averaging readings (Display version)   J M Bishop May 2000
   * --------------------------------------
   *
   * Works out the average of readings within a certain range
   * Illustrates the if-statement
   */

  Display d = new Display ("Averaging readings");

  ReadingsAverages () {

    double total = 0;
    double reading;
    int min, max;
    int n;
    boolean done = false;
    String status;

    d.prompt("Minimum",0);
    d.prompt("Maximum",100);
    d.ready("Press ready when min and max adjusted");
    min = d.getInt("Minimum");
    max = d.getInt("Maximum");
    d.println("Min is "+min+" and max is "+max);
    d.prompt("Next reading",0);
    d.prompt("Finished?","No");
    d.println("Press ready after entering each reading");
    d.println("Enter Yes when finished");
    for (n = 0; !done;) {
      d.ready();
      reading = d.getDouble("Next reading");
      d.print ("   " + reading);
      if (reading >= min & reading <= max) {
```

```
            total += reading;
            n++;
            d.print("K");
          }
          else {
            d.print("X");
          }
          status = d.getString("Finished?");
          done = status.equals("Yes");
      }
      d.println("\n Average "+" for "+n+" readings is "+
          Stream.format(total/n,8,3));
    }

    public static void main (String [] args) {
      new ReadingsAverages ();
    }
  }
```

Model diagram   In order to emphasize that the Stream and Display classes are both used via objects, we include a model diagram for this program (Figure 4.5). The diagram spells out the differences between the classes and objects clearly. ReadingsAverages is a class and has one static method, main. main creates an object of the class, and the object has one object variable and a constructor. The constructor has several variables of its own, all primitive or string. The object variable, d, when created, is a Display object and has all the methods from that class as shown.

Figure 4.5 also shows the notation for a package, which is a box with a tab above it. Two packages are imported into the class ReadingsAverages, namely java.io and javagently.

This diagram is complete. Although not mentioned in the program, we know that javagently uses java.io, so we import it too. ReadingsAverages, as a class, imports the javagently package. ReadingsAverages as an object using its Classid, instantiates its class. This object has one variable and one method, but we show the variables of that method as well. The variable d is created as a Display object and has the eight methods it specifies. Finally, we show this association with an arrow back to the Display class in the javagently package.

Testing   Typical output at the end of a run would be as in Figure 4.6. When choosing test data, we should ensure that we always exercise all parts of the if-statements. Here we have just one if-statement, so we make sure that some of the data will result in a K and some in an X. We should also include values that are the minimum and the maximum.

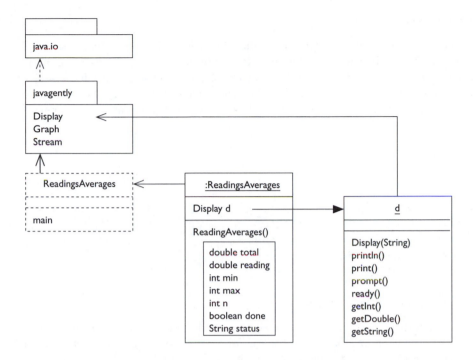

Figure 4.5. *Model diagram for the* `ReadingsAverages` *program.*

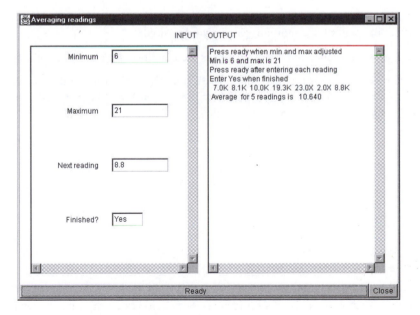

Figure 4.6 *Display from the* `AveragingReadings` *program.*

Successive else-ifs

Sometimes there are more than two possibilities that need to be considered. One way in which this is done is by **successive else-ifs**. The condition of the first if-statement eliminates one case, leaving the rest to the else-part. The else-part in its turn introduces another if-statement which selects out another condition and leaves the rest to its else-part, and so on. Else-ifs are illustrated nicely in an example that assigns a grade for various ranges of marks, thus:

```
int marks;
char grade;

if       (marks >= 80) grade="A";
else if  (marks >= 70) grade="B";
else if  (marks >= 60) grade="C";
else if  (marks >= 50) grade="D";
else                   grade="E";
```

Notice a few points about this statement:

- The conditions are carefully ordered, so that each eliminates a certain range of marks. Thus, the line that writes out a D for anything over 50 will be reached only when it has already been established that the mark is under 60.

- The last class, E, is given for all the rest of the marks, and does not need a condition.

- The layout of successive if-statements is important for readability, and should try to reflect the pattern of conditions as much as possible.

- the statements appear on the same line as the condition for clarity of reading.

A secondary consideration is that the most frequently occurring conditions should be checked first. If it is more likely that people will fail, then it will be marginally more efficient to arrange the order of the conditions thus:

```
int marks;
char grade;

if       (marks < 50) grade="E";
else if  (marks < 60) grade="D";
else if  (marks < 70) grade="C";
else if  (marks < 80) grade="B";
else                  grade="A";
```

As another example, suppose we have over 300 students in a class and need to divide them up into three different rooms for lectures. We decide to do this alphabetically, based on names. Looking at the list, we see that the surnames Jonson and Paulus start the second and third hundreds, respectively. We can set up a method as follows to return the name of the classroom that a student will be in:

```
String room (String name) {
  if (name.compareTo("Jonson") < 0) {
    return "OPV 2-23";
  }
  else if (name.compareTo("Paulus") < 0) {
    return "GW4-10";
  }
  else {
    return "EBE 4-21";
  }
}
```

which would be called as in:

```
System.out.println("Your lecture room is "+room(you));
```

As an exercise, augment the room method to count the number of names for a given room.

4.5   File input and output

Although it is a relief to be able to enter input to programs at last, interactive testing can rapidly become tedious. It is often better to keep the data in a file and read from there. Certainly for large amounts of data this is essential. The `Stream` class has already been set up to connect files for both input and output. To read from a file called `mydata`, all we need is:

```
Stream in = new Stream ("mydata");

double x = in.readDouble();
```

In a program, one can have several streams of either sort open for input simultaneously.

Outputting to a file

It is very useful to be able to send output to a file. Not only does it make it easy to retain the results and print them out, but very often programs produce too much output to appear sensibly on the screen. Furthermore, we may produce data that are never seen by humans, but which serve as input to some other program. Using `Stream` again, we have:

```
Stream fout = new Stream ("results.out", Stream.WRITE);
```

To write out numbers to a file where a neat format is not necessary, we just use
`println`. But if there is more than one number on a line, then we must ourselves separate the numbers by spaces, otherwise they will not be able to be read in again. For
example, if x is 4.5 and y is 0.001, then

```
fout.print((x) + (y));
```

then what will appear on the file is

```
4.50.001
```

So the better course of action, even for a file, is to use formatted output via the `Stream`
class, as in:

```
fout.print(Stream.format(x,10,4)+ Stream.format(y,10,4));
```

An important consideration for output files is that they must be closed before the program
ends, otherwise all the writing done to them is lost. The method in `Stream` is:

```
fout.close();
```

EXAMPLE 4.7   Part codes

Problem   The Savanna Technical Laboratory has a file of some 200 parts used in its
products. The technicians wish to assign serial numbers to the parts, starting with the
code for the laboratory, which is 5000.

Solution   Regard the parts as lines of text and copy them to a destination stream, adding
on the part numbers. To add flexibility, the starting number can be read from the keyboard
in response to a query.

Example   Given a disk file called `parts.dat` containing parts such as

```
Widgets, curly
Widgets, plain
Gadgets, purple
Thingies, bolted
Ghizmos, striped
```

the required table will be written to a file `parts.out` with numbers starting at 5000,
as in:

```
5000  Widgets, curly
5001  Widgets, plain
5002  Gadgets, purple
5003  Thingies, bolted
5004  Ghizmos, striped
```

Program The program makes use of four streams – fin, fout, in and out. Only out is predefined by Java, so the other three are declared in the program. Yet they are each going to be declared in a different way. System.in can be opened as a Stream object, because we want to read numbers from there. The output file is also a Stream object, but of the WRITE sort. And the input file uses Stream with Stream.READ.

Because we have not yet learnt how to stop reading from a file, we have set the number of parts at five for now.

```java
import java.io.*;
import javagently.*;

class PartCodes {

  /* The Part Codes program   by J M Bishop 1990
   * ----------------------   Java 1.1 July 1999
   *                          updated May 2000
   *                          for Stream class
   *
   * Assigns numbers to parts read from a file.
   * Illustrates file input and output.
   */

  public static void main(String args []) throws IOException {
    new PartCodes ();
  }

  PartCodes () throws IOException {

    Stream in   = new Stream (System.in);
    Stream fin  = new Stream ("parts.dat",Stream.READ);
    Stream fout = new Stream ("parts.out",Stream.WRITE);

    int number = 0;
    String part;
    System.out.println("****** Parts from parts.dat file ******");
    System.out.print("Part starting number? ");
    number = in.readInt();
    System.out.print("Writing to file parts.out");
```

```
        for (int i = number; i < number+5; i++) {
          part = fin.readLine();
          fout.println(i+"   "+part);
          System.out.print('.');
        }
        System.out.println();
        fout.close();
      }
    }
```

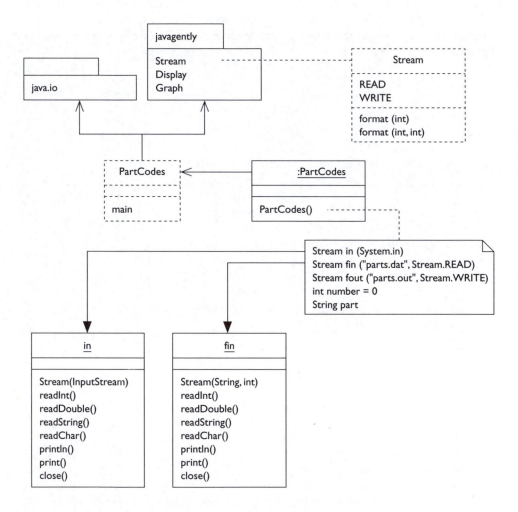

Figure 4.7 *Model diagram for the* `PartCodes` *program.*

Testing   When run, the following will appear on the screen:

```
****** Parts from parts.dat file ******
Part starting number?  5000
Writing to file parts.out . . . . .
```

We have used a time-honoured technique here of showing what is happening while a file is being read. Each time round the loop, we print a dot on the screen to signify another line read. For very long files, this enables the user to see that the program is still running.

Model diagram   Finally, we show a model diagram again (Figure 4.7), to see how Stream appears in this notation. An interesting feature of this diagram is that it shows clearly the difference between the methods associated with a `Stream` object and those belonging to the class. Both `in` and `fin` are `Stream` objects, but `fout` has not yet been initialized (to save space). The constructor shown on `fin` will copy its parameters into variables in the `fin` object. These variables are private to `Stream` objects and therefore are not shown here. There is more about private variables in Chapter 8.

4.6   Handling exceptions

If-statements provide a means of control over the state of the current method. We can check the values of data to which we have access and react accordingly. But what happens if a condition is set in another method and we, the caller of the method, should react to it? The if-statement is not powerful enough to handle this. We need another construct. That construct is the try-catch statement, which relies on exceptions. An example of such a statement, just to show where we are going, would be:

```
try {
  for (;;)
    number = Stream.readInt(fin);
    total+=number;
}
catch (EOFException e) {
  System.out.println("All the data read");
}
```

Java's role in Web programming puts it in the position of the old adage that 'if things can go wrong they will': a user could disconnect, a file could have been deleted, incorrect input could be entered, a host server might be unavailable. In order to operate within such a volatile environment, Java has a special concept known as an **exception**.

An exception is an object that signals that some unusual condition has occurred. Java has many predefined exception objects, and we can also create our own. The point about exceptions is that they are intended to be **detected** and **handled**, so that the program can continue in a sensible way if at all possible. Should an exception occur outside our immediate environment, we shall be informed as to what has happened. We then have the opportunity to handle the situation that has arisen. If we do not react, the method we are in is terminated and the exception is sent to the method that called us. This process may repeat until eventually an unhandled exception will pass to the Java Virtual Machine which will terminate the program.

Figure 4.8 illustrates the process of one method calling another and having a handler ready for a possible exception. Depending on how the rest of method A is structured, it may be able to continue operating after it handles the exception, or it may exit.

Now let us consider a concrete example related to the readings program. It is cumbersome to type the values in interactively, if there are a lot of them, and if they are put on a file, it is unlikely that a user of a program will wish to count precisely the number of values to be entered beforehand. It would therefore be useful to be able to detect in some other way that the data are at an end. The third method mentioned in the list above is to use Java's exceptions.

In the fundamental reading methods supplied with Java, a check is made each time as to whether the input has been exhausted (either by the file ending or by the user indicating end-of-input in the usual way on the keyboard). If the check turns up true, then the read method causes an EOFException (for end-of-file exception). The readings program can then react to it.

Catching an exception

To react to a predefined exception such as EOFException, we have to do two steps, called **try** and **catch**:

- **Try:** create a block around statements where the result of any method calls or other operations might cause an exception, and preface the block with the keyword try.

- **Catch:** follow the try-block with one or more handlers prefaced by the keyword catch.

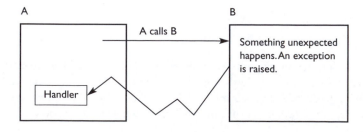

Figure 4.8 *The process of exception handling.*

A **handler** is itself a block and contains statements related to reporting the exception or error, and getting the program back on track. The form for these statements is:

Try-catch statement

```
try {
    statements in which an exception
    could be raised, including method calls in
    which exceptions could be raised
}
catch (Exceptiontype e1) {
    statements to react and recover
}
catch (Exceptiontype e2) {
    statements to react and recover
}
... and more catches
```

If an exception is raised in the try-block which matches one of the *Exceptiontypes* in the parameter list of one of the catch-blocks, then control is transferred to that catch-block, and then execution continues at the end of the construct. If no appropriate catch-block is present, the exception is thrown immediately to the next enclosing method.

So the matter of reading till the end of a file would be handled by:

```
try {
  for ...
    number = Stream.readInt(fin);
    Do something with number
}
catch (EOFException e) {
  display.println("All the data read");
}
```

The parameter e is of the type of the exception. There is a method defined for e, i.e. getMessage. This can be useful as we shall see later if we catch some more general exception, such as IOException, and then want to print out the specifics.

Note that on the keyboard, the user types in data and, when finished, presses the character which the system uses for ending the stream. This may be cntrl-D, cntrl-Z or esc, for example. The presence of this special character is detected by the Stream class and is relayed to the caller by throwing the EOFException.

Throwing exceptions

We have already seen that input–output operations cause exceptions to be thrown, and that this has an effect on the corresponding method headers. Formally, the two steps for throwing exceptions (those that we do not catch) are:

- **Throw:** if the exception is not dealt with at all, it will automatically be passed up to the calling method; if we catch it and deal with it partially, we can still pass it up with a throw statement.

- **Declare:** mention in the method declaration which exceptions it could throw back to its caller.

EXAMPLE 4.8   Part codes with exceptions

Now let us adapt the `PartCodes` program so that the number of products is unlimited, and the program can detect when the file ends. In the program below, the lines that change from Example 4.7 are underlined.

```
import java.io.*;
import javagently.*;

class PartCodes {

  /* The Part Codes program    by J M Bishop 1990
   * ---------------------      Java 1.1 July 1999
   *                            updated May 2000
   *
   * Assigns numbers to parts read from a file.
   * Illustrates handling an EOF Exception.
   */

  PartCodes () throws IOException {

    Stream in  = new Stream (System.in);
    Stream fin = new Stream ("parts.dat");
    Stream fout= new Stream ("parts.out");

    int number = 0;
    String part;
    System.out.println(
        "****** Parts from parts.dat file ******");
    System.out.println("Part starting number? ");
    number = in.readInt(i);
```

```
        System.out.print("Writing to file parts.out");

        try {
          for (int i = number; ; i++) {
            part = fin.readLine();
            fout.println(i+"  "+part);
            System.out.print(".");
          }
        }
        catch (EOFException e) {
          System.out.println("\nData complete");
        }
        fout.close();
      }

    public static void main(String args []) throws IOException {
      new PartCodes ();
    }
  }
```

In other words, the ending of the loop is no longer in the for-statement as a condition, but is taken over by and signalled in the reading of the file.

One might wonder why the main method and constructor still need to have the `throws IOException` clause, when we are catching an exception. The reason is that there is another exception lurking around – `FileNotFoundException`. We now look at the way in which it can be handled.

Recovering from an exception

The previous example showed how we could handle an exception in order to conclude a program gracefully. There may also be cases where we do not wish to end the method, but to go back and retry the operation that caused the exception. An example of such a situation is the opening of a file. If we have the file name incorrect, we may wish to give the user the chance to enter another name. The algorithm is shown in pseudocode in Figure 4.9.

If we go back to the `PartCodes` program where we open the file, we can protect that statement and put a loop around it as follows.

```
    /* Declare the keyboard stream, and initialize
     * the file stream to go there too.
     * Java requires that objects used later on definitely
     * have a value, and within a "try" one cannot be sure
     * that a value has been assigned.
```

```
   * The same applies to giving filename an initial value.
   */

// Pre-assign the file to the keyboard, in case
Stream fin = new Stream (System.in);

// give five tries for the correct file name
for (int tries = 1; tries <= 5; tries++) {
  try {
    display.prompt("File name");
    display.ready("Press ready");
    filename = display.getString("File name");
    fin = new Stream (filename);
    display.println(filename +" opened successfully");
    break;
  }
  catch (FileNotFoundException e) {
    display.println(filename + " not found");
    if (tries<5) {
      display.println("Enter another name.");
    }
    else {
      display.println("Too many tries: ");
      display.println("Connected to keyboard by default");
    }
  }
}
```

These statements would be called at the start of the constructor. In the next example, we shall see how to make a useful method out of them and add them to an existing class and package. We notice several points about them meanwhile.

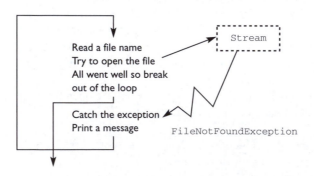

Figure 4.9 *An algorithm for opening a file securely.*

It is a rule that any value that is set inside a try-block must be regarded as potentially unset because the exception could occur before it is assigned. The compiler checks this rule. The implication is that these variables should be given default values first. In the case of the file name, that is easy enough. In the case of the file itself, we have to be careful. We cannot assign the file to any name at all because it might not exist. Therefore we use the only sure file object, which is `System.in`, the keyboard.

Using a for-loop around the try limits the number of guesses at a file name. If the user cannot enter a valid file name within five tries, the program gives up and tries to limp along from the keyboard. Within the catch-block, we detect whether this is the last try or not and display an appropriate message.

If the file is opened successfully, then we want to get out of the loop before the five tries are up: hence the break-statement at the end of the try.

EXAMPLE 4.9   Secure file opener

Since opening a file is probably going to be a facility that will be needed in various programs, we shall see how to set it up as a standard utility in its own package, just like `Stream` in `javagently`. If we are writing our own package, the same steps as above apply, with the additional requirement that the class and its methods must be declared as public.

The design of the `open` method requires some thought. We could have just created another constructor for `Stream`, with an extra parameter specifying how many tries must be allowed. The problem with this approach is that we have to disturb the `javagently` package, and we would prefer to regard it as fixed and unchangeable, since the whole of this book relies on it. Rather, we postulate a second package, called `myutilities` which we shall use for new ideas such as this one. Into the package go classes, not methods, so we need a name for the class. Let's call it `Filer`.[1]

Inside `Filer` is the `open` method, and we declare it as follows:

```
public static Stream open (String filename) throws IOException {...}
```

`open` is public, because it is going to be used outside of a single program. It is `static`, because we are not going to create a `Filer` object, but start from scratch and create a `Stream` object as the result of the method. The parameter is the tentative file name supplied by the program: inside `open`, we shall connect to the keyboard so that if necessary alternative names can be typed in. Finally, the exception may be thrown if we end up not getting a successful open within five tries.

Here is the new `open` method enclosed in a class called `Filer` and destined for a package called `myutilities`:

---

[1] There is an earlier class in the second edition of *Java Gently* called `FileMan`, which relied on the `Text` class, and so by creating a new name, we can maintain upward compatibility.

```
package myutilities;

import java.io.*;
import javagently.*;

public class Filer {

    /* The Filer class            by J M Bishop  June 2000
     * ---------------------       Java 1.2
     *                             based on the FileMan class
     *                             from June 1997
     *
     * Provides for a file to be opened, with five tries at a
     * correct file name.
     * Illustrates the use of exceptions in for-try loops..
     */

    public static Stream open (String filename) throws IOException {

        Stream in = new Stream (System.in);
          if (filename.equals(" ")){
          System.out.print("File name?");
          filename = in.readString();
        }

        for (int count = 0; count < 5; count ++) {
          try {
            return new Stream(filename, Stream.READ);
          } catch (FileNotFoundException e) {
             System.out.println(filename+" does not exist.");
             if (count < 4) {
               System.out.println("Try again");
             }
             filename = in.readString();
          }
        }
      throw new FileNotFoundException ();
    }
}
```

The code has some interesting features, most important of which is that at the end of the loop, if no valid file name is entered, the `FileNotFoundException` is thrown again explicitly. The idea is that the exception should be picked up by the calling program and dealt with. The throw replaces the printing of the message 'Connected to keyboard by default' since in order to be general, we should leave further action up to the caller. Using `Filer` is shown in Example 4.10.

Number exceptions

Another important exception is the `NumberFormatException` which is raised when an attempt is made to convert a string into a number, and the type is incorrect. For example, an integer cannot have a decimal point and numbers cannot have strange characters in them. Consider the input section of Example 4.6. There are two integer numbers to read, and one double. If the user enters a real number where the two integers are expected, the corresponding `get` method will fail. We can protect the initial reading section as follows:

```
for (;;) {
  try {
    display.ready("Press ready when min and max adjusted");
    min = d.getInt("Minimum");
    max = d.getMax("Maximum");
    // successful so
    break; // from the loop
  }
  catch (NumberFormatException e) {
    display.println("Error in input: "+e.getMessage());
    display("Minimum and maximum should be integers");
  }
  // go and try again
}
```

In this case we chose to force the user to enter valid data by using an endless loop.

Another exception related to numbers is `ArithmeticException` which will be raised if there is an invalid calculation, such as division by zero.

EXAMPLE 4.10   Olympic medals

Problem   The number of gold, silver and bronze medals won at the Olympic Games by each country has been stored in a file. We would like to display these results, as well as the total number of medals for each country.

Solution   We start by imagining a loop very similar to that in the readings program, using the `EOFException` (Example 4.8). The data are stored in a file, so we do not prompt for input, and we get four values at a time – country, gold, silver and bronze. Country will be a string, and the other three will be integers. Sample test data would be:

```
Australia  9  9  22
China  16  22  12
Cuba  9  8  8
France  15  7  15
```

In fact, this part of the program is fairly straightforward. The part we want to be careful about is to check whether the file name is valid. Here we shall use `Filer`.

Program   We shall first give the program, then describe its constituent parts.

```
import java.io.*;
import javagently.*;
import myutilities.*;

class Olympics {
   /* Olympic medals program    revised J M Bishop Dec 1996
    * ---------------------    Java 1.1 October 1997
    *                          updated for Stream and Filer
    *                          May 2000
    *
    * Reads in and totals medals gained by countries in an
    * Olympic Games.
    * Uses Filer to open the file.
    * Illustrates ending with an exception (the try-for sequence).
    */

   Olympics () throws IOException {
     System.out.println("**** Olympic medals ****");
     System.out.println();

     Stream in = new Stream(System.in);
     // default the file to the keyboard
     Stream fin = new Stream(System.in);

     try {
       System.out.print("What file for the medals statistics?");
       String filename = in.readString();
       fin = Filer.open(filename);
     }
     catch (FileNotFoundException e) {
       System.out.println("Five tries up");
       System.out.println("Connecting to keyboard by default");
     }
```

```
      String country;.
      int gold, silver, bronze, total, all = 0;
      System.out.println("\nCountry\t\tGold\tSilver\tBronze\tTotal");

      try {
        for (;;) {
            country = fin.readString();
            gold = fin.readInt();
            silver = fin.readInt();
            bronze = fin.readInt();
            total = gold + silver + bronze;
            System.out.print(country);
            if (country.length() < 8) {
              System.out.print("\t");
            }
            System.out.println("\t"+gold+"\t"+silver+"\t"+bronze+
              "\t"+total);
            all += total;
        }
      } catch (EOFException e) {
        System.out.println(all+" medals won.");
      }
    }

    public static void main (String[] args) throws IOException {
      new Olympics ();
    }
  }
```

Algorithm   The first try-catch does not in itself have a loop, but there is one in `Filer`, which it calls. `Filer`'s loop is a for-try one, to enable five tries at opening the file. If `Filer` fails, then the `catch` in Olympics is executed and a message is printed out. `fin` was preset to `System.in`, so in this case, we can carry on with input from the keyboard – it works pretty well. The input and calculations are phrased inside a try-for loop, so that as soon as the end of data is detected, the loop ends and we print the final message.

Testing   As expected, the output from the program is:

```
**** Olympic medals ****

What file for the medals statistics? medlas
medlas does not exist.
Try again
What file for the medals statistics? medals
```

Country	Gold	Silver	Bronze	Total
Australia	9	9	22	40
China	16	22	12	50
Cuba	9	8	8	25
France	15	7	15	37
Germany	20	18	27	65
Hungary	7	4	10	21
Italy	13	9	12	34
Poland	7	5	5	17
Russia	26	21	16	63
South.Korea	7	15	5	27
Spain	5	6	6	17
Ukraine	9	2	12	23
United.States	43	32	25	100

519 medals won.

SUMMARY

There are two ways of changing the state of a variable: by assignment and by reading in values. In order to read in Java, we have first to connect to a stream. Thereafter we can read strings. Through the `Stream` class we can also read numbers and characters. In addition, files can be declared as streams for both input and output. Programs can receive and send data to multiple streams.

There are also two ways of changing the course of the program based on conditions that occur. The if-statement is suitable for checking the local state within a method. It can have an else-part, as well as successive else-ifs. When the condition occurs in another method, it is signalled back by means of an exception. Exceptions can be caught and handled. There are standard ways of recovering from an exception and trying again.

Useful classes can be made into packages, which can be reused by means of the `import` statement. The `javagently` package is a special package defined especially for this book. `myutilities` is a package that we can add our own classes to.

The following keywords are defined in this chapter:

catch	package
else	throws
if	try
import	public

The following entities from Java's libraries were discussed:

java.io	System.in
BufferedReader	readLine

and from our own libraries

```
javagently        myutilities
 Display             Filer
 Stream
```

and exceptions

```
 IOException              NumberFormatException
 FileNotFoundException    ArithmeticException
 EOFException
```

and forms

Declaring the keyboard for input
Reading a string
The Display class
The Stream class
Constant declaration
If-statement
Try-catch statement

QUIZ

4.1 The statement for connecting to the keyboard is

(a) `Stream in = System.in;`
(b) `Stream in = new Stream(System.in);`
(c) `Stream in = Stream (System.in);`
(d) `Stream System.in = new Stream(System.in);`

4.2 We have a display set-up, and a box called "File name" in the input section. Why does `display.getString(filename)` give the message `ERROR: No such input label:?`

(a) filename should be in quotes
(b) the method is `readString`, not `getString`
(c) we must press the Ready bar first
(d) `getString` needs the exact box name, i.e. "File Name"

4.3 For PC users: if the `Stream` class has been compiled in a directory called `C:\Book\JG\javagently` what should be put in the classpath to get access to `Stream`?

(a) `Stream.class`
(b) `C:\Book\JG\javagently\`
(c) `C:\Book\JG\`
(d) `C:\`

4.4 From a sequence of numbers coming in, we want to write out only those between 30 and 40. What would be the correct if-statement to control this process?

(a) `if (number >=30 & <= 40)`
(b) `if (number >=30 | number < 40)`
(c) `if (30 <= number >= 40)`
(d) `if (number >= 30 & number <= 40)`

4.5 The program using the `Stream` class is expecting three integers to be read from a file into the variables a, b and c, what will happen if b is a string in error, given the data 45 2r3   67   84?

(a) `a=45 b=67 c=84`
(b) `a=45 b=23 c=67`
(c) `a=45 b=undefined c=67`
(d) `a=45` program crashes

4.6 The program using the `Display` class has three integer boxes with values 45 67 84. The ready bar is pressed and then the first value is changed by the user to 55. Three `getInteger` calls then follow. What will be the values of the three integers?

(a) `55 67 84`
(b) `45 67 84`
(c) `error 67 84`
(d) `45 55 67`

4.7 We wish to read all the numbers off a file and there are 210 of them. If we specify a try-for loop as

```
try {
   for (int i = 0 ; i <=10; i++) { ...
      int n = in.getInteger();
   }
}
catch (EOFException e) {
   }
```

how many numbers get read?

(a) 200
(b) 210
(c) 10
(d) none

4.8 The correct statement for gaining access to Java's input–output classes is

(a) `import java.io;`
(b) `import java.io.*;`
(c) `package java.io;`
(d) `import javagently.*;`

4.9 If x is `456.23458` then what will `display.println(Stream.format(x,4,2))` give (if _ is a space)?

(a) `_456.23`
(b) `456.23`

(c) `456.2`
(d) `456.`

4.10   In Figure 4.7, the `Stream` class has two methods called `format`. These are not shown in `Stream` objects such as `in` and `fin` because:

(a)   they are static
(b)   they have the same name
(c)   it saves space in the diagram
(d)   they need other classes in `javagently`

PROBLEMS

Note: Problems 4.1 to 4.7 pose extensions to earlier problems now that reading and selection are part of our skills base.

4.1   **Conversions again.** Adapt the programs in Prolems 3.5 and 3.11 so as to read in the limits required for the tables.

4.2   **Better filer.** Extend the `Filer` class to have another method, also called open, but which has a parameter specifying how many tries should be allowed.

4.3   **Stopping the song.** Consider Problem 3.9 again. Alter the program so that it will stop after each verse of the song, and wait for some command to continue or not. Alternatively, make it react to a cntrl-Z or cntrl-D by stopping at the end of the next verse.

4.4   **Fuel consumption again.** Adapt the program written for Problem 2.6 so as to read in from a display all the values that may vary.

4.5   **Weighted averages again.** Adapt the program in Problem 2.5 to read in the marks from a file and print each student's average as well as the overall average. Use exceptions to detect the end of the file.

4.6   **Marathon winners.** Picking up from Problem 3.2, set up a display so that the information for a runner can be entered interactively. Extend the program so that it can calculate the winner of the race. (Hint: use Example 4.5 The Highest Number to help you here.)

4.7   **Weight watchers again.** Alter Problem 3.2 so that the data are read in from a display rather than generated as random numbers.

4.8   **Average ages.** A youth club has 24 children grouped in four 'rings'. The children are aged 7 to 11. Write an interactive program to read in the ages for each ring and to work out the average age per ring for a group of 24 children, as well as the average overall age.

4.9   **Splitting files.** Suppose we have a file of numerical readings, some of which are negative and some of which are positive. We wish to create two new files, one with all the positive numbers, and one with the negative numbers, and then go back and print both out from the program, with the positive numbers file first. Use a suitable random number generator to create the files in the first place, allowing for a total of 100 numbers.

4.10   **CD length.** CDs have up to 22 tracks. Using the display to input the time for each track in hours and minutes, calculate the total length of a CD. Use a box with a value of 1 in it, which is changed to zero with the last track, to singal the end of the data.

4.11   **CD length with exceptions.** Redo Problem 4.10 using the ordinary Java console input output (and the `Stream` class) and detect the last track with cntrl-D or cntrl-Z and an exception.

4.12   **Room bookings.** We want to have a system that will allocate the most appropriate room for a class of a given size. We are going to do this problem using only files and the display, although later on (Chapter 6) we will see other ways of handling it.

- Set up a file with names of rooms and the number of people they can hold (between about 50 and 500).

- Start a program with a display that asks for a number of people and the booker's name.

- Read through the file, finding the first room, if any, that is no more than 10% larger than the size required.

- Report on the booking, if successful.

- If not, and if the program detected that a larger room was available, run through the ifle again, getting any room available that will take the number required, even if too large.

4.13   **Room reservations.** We augment Problem 4.12 as follows:

- Now we can actually make a booking, by writing out to a second file the data as read, but with a marker next to the booked room and the name of the booker. This file then becomes the one read in next time, and that room cannot be booked again.

- However, the program can report that the room would be ideal, and is currently booked by the person listed.

4.14   **Experiments.** A laboratory takes readings and the results required are the first reading divided by the second. The readings are stored on a file. Write a program that processes the file but catches an exception when a division by zero is encountered. In this case, the program should ask for both replacement values for the particular reading number, and continue processing until the end of the file.

4.15   **Examinations.** An examination paper has four questions in Section A and four in Section B. Each question is valued at 20 marks. Students must answer five questions in total, with at least two from Section A and two from Section B. If more questions than required are answered, then the first ones are counted and the latter ones disregarded. Unanswered questions are indicated by a zero mark.

Write a program to read in from a file eight marks for each of several students and print out their final marks according to the rules. The output should be made to a file and should echo the input as shown here. If rules are broken, print appropriate messages. Sample data and results are:

Sample Input								Sample Output	
Section A				Section B				Result	Comment
10	15	0	0	20	8	17	0	70	
10	9	7	20	0	0	0	10	36	Too many from A.
5	6	10	0	19	5	3	14	45	More than 5. Too many from B.

4.11   **Rainfall figures.** The rainfall figures in mm are available for each day of the past four weeks. We want to know the total rainfall for each week, the most recent wettest day and the driest week. Write a program that will read in several sets of 28 rainfall figures from a file and write out to another file the three bits of information required together with an echo of the data. Sample data and results would be:

```
Sample data               Sample results
3 0 0 7 8 21 0            39 mm
0 1 1 0 0 0 4             6 mm
9 6 7 0 0 0 0             22 mm
0 0 0 0 0 0 1             1 mm
The wettest day was day 6.
The driest week was week 4.
```

4.17   **Golf scores.** The Savanna Golf Course has nine holes. At each hole, a player is expected to be able to sink the ball in the hole in one to five shots. This gives a course average or par of 30. A player's score for the course is the sum of the numbers of shots for each hole. Depending on past performance, a player is granted a handicap which is subtracted from his or her score to give his or her actual result for a game. Players are also interested in knowing whether they have scored under par or not. When players play together, the winner is the one with the lowest score. If the scoring of a golf game were computerized, sample input and output might be:

Player	Handicap	Shots per hole	Total	Result	Under Par?
1	6	1 3 6 2 1 4 3 2 4	26	20	yes
2	3	2 2 2 2 4 4 4 2 2	24	21	yes
3	2	4 5 4 3 4 1 3 5 4	33	31	no

The winner is player 1 with a handicapped result of 20

Write a program that

■ reads in from a file the shots per hole for several players, catching an exception when the data are finished;

■ calculates each total score, handicapped score and par decision;

■ determines the winning player and the winning score;

■ writes the results together with an echo of the data to another file.

4.18   **Parking meters.** The Savanna Traffic Department wants to decide whether to mount a campaign against illegal parking. A number of traffic inspectors are sent to different zones in the city where parking time is restricted. The different zones have different time restrictions. Each of the traffic officers has to monitor any 10 cars in their zone and record the actual time the vehicle was parked in the time-restricted zone. If 50% or more of the cars were parked for a longer period than allowed, the traffic department will decide to launch a massive campaign. Write a program that

■ reads in from a file the number of zones; the time limit and actual parking-time for ten vehicles for each of the zones;

■ determines the number of cars exceeding the time limit in each of the zones;

- decides whether a campaign should be mounted or not;
- identifies the zone where the situation is the worst and indicates this on the display;
- writes the results and an echo of the input to another file.

Sample combined output might be:

```
Number of zones: 3
Area Limit  Parking times                        Over limit
1     60     20 40 70 35 45 78  34 56 73  5   3
2     45     62 47 68 40 53 62 120  8 15 72   7
3     30     66 32 41 89  7 25  29 33 54 17   6
A campaign must be mounted.
Concentrate on area 2
```

CHAPTER 5

Controlling the flow

5.1 Properties of a good program

The structure of a program indicates how its parts are connected together, and how sound those connections are. One can think of the structure of a bridge: each strut and rivet plays its role, and the whole performs a defined function efficiently. Bridges can even look pleasing. So it is with programs. When we create them we aim to achieve a structure that in the first instance achieves the required purpose, but that is also readable, reusable and efficient. These are the properties of a good program. In this section, we consider such properties.

Correctness

It seems obvious that a program when complete should be correct but we all know that the two properties can diverge widely. Much software these days is released to the world with errors remaining (called bugs). In defence of such software, one must say that programming is one of the most complex engineering tasks that we know, and it is also one of the newest (genetic engineering is perhaps more recent). It is only since the mid-1980s that codified books on software engineering started to appear, and standards of software reliability began to be set by international bodies. So how do we program to achieve correct software? There are two golden rules:

1. Follow good programming practice while writing a program.

2. Test the program thoroughly once it is done.

This book aims to instil good practice by example, and by motivating guidelines that can be followed in any programming activity. Interestingly enough, these are frequently not Java-specific.

Testing is very important, as no matter how hard we try, we cannot always imagine all possibilities that might occur when the program starts running. With simple programs, we can read through the logic and reason about what will happen. With more complex programs (extending over more than two pages, say) and, in particular, programs where the user can alter the course by supplying data, the task is very much harder. Here the careful design of test data pays off.

Readability

In order to reason about a program, we have to be able to read it, and perhaps even discuss it with others. Some of the factors that aid readability are:

- the use of meaningful identifiers, e.g. `timeInMins` instead of `t`;

- careful layout, especially indenting and blank lines;

- comments to explain the function of statements that follow;

- careful choice of types and classes to reflect exactly what is required of the data.

We can also take readability further by starting to develop a **style** of writing that enables us to find what we are looking for quickly, and to communicate effectively within a group of programmers. For example, we may organize our methods so that the declarations always appear before the statements, at the front. Another suggestion is to arrange the methods of a large class alphabetically by name (as shown in Java's API). Software organizations will often set up such guidelines – and expect them to be followed by employees.

Reusability

While some might say that the inaccuracy of software is a major crisis in the industry, of equal concern is the inability of firms to produce software on time. One of the ways in which we aim to alleviate this position is to reuse software that has been tried and tested before. Java's packages are a classic example of reusability: instead of each of us writing a class to store and manipulate random numbers, one is provided.

Reusability works both ways: when writing a new program, we look around for existing classes that can be used or even adapted, and at the same time, we try to write our own classes so that they have a general appeal, without compromising their efficiency or readability in their primary program. Java has specific class constructs which aim to assist with reusability, and these are covered in later chapters.

Efficiency

There is nothing more frustrating than a program that is too slow or too big. Of course, a complex task might require time, memory and disk space, but simple tasks should not. There are many small ways in which we can start out by programming thriftily, while once again not compromising our other goals. Just a few ideas for keeping a program compact are:

- declare variables as needed – do not overdo it;

- maximize the use of methods, thus avoiding copies of common statements;

- do common calculations once and store the result;

- choose the appropriate type for the calculations required, e.g. not always `double`.

Method design

We now look at different ways in which we can group statements to aid readability, reusability and efficiency, and specifically at the questions: when does it make sense to make a method out of a group of statements, and how do we best group methods in classes? The answer to the first question lies in weighing up the following factors:

1. Will the statements be used more than once in the program?

2. Do the statements refer to data that vary with each application?

3. Is the group of statements involved in solving an identifiable subproblem?

4. Is the current method getting too long (more than 20 lines)?

5. Is it likely that the statements might be used again in another program?

If the answer is 'yes' to 1 or 2, then we more or less are obliged to use methods, or the program will exhibit very bad style. If 3, 4 or 5 apply, then it still makes sense to employ methods. Consider the the histogram example (3.4). It could have been written as one set of statements in the constructor, but then we would not have had a bar method to reuse in other programs (as in Problem 3.13) and putting the axis method (which has a very self-contained function) would have made the constructor very long.

Another place, obviously, where methods are necessary is in classes: they form the means by which we communicate with the data stored in an object, as can be seen in both the `Curio` and `Times` classes.

Top-down programming

Although we have so far shown complete programs, they do not, of course, just fall from the sky, correct in every detail. Writing a program starts from a small part and develops. One of the best programming techniques is called **top-down** programming, where we divide the solution up into subsolutions and start by representing each of these as a method call. In this we way get the overall design of the program correct, with the main variables in place. Thereafter, we can take each method and develop it further, maybe even into subsolutions of its own. This process is illustrated in Example 5.2.

Protection and accessibility

All object-orientation languages provide some means whereby variables and methods can be protected from outside interference, for whatever reason. The reasons are explored next, but here we note that Java's accessibility control is provided by modifiers to the declaration of a method or variable, as in the form:

Accessibility control

private *declaration*
public *declaration*
declaration

Members declared as private are only accessible within the object itself.
Members declared as public are accessible by objects of any other class that
  imports the class from which this object is declared.
In the absence of an explicit accessibility modifier, members are accessible by
  objects of any other class in the same package as the class from which this
  object is declared.

Therefore private would be used for variables and methods used in the processes and calculations of a class, which the outside user has no need to see. So far, our classes have not been complex enough to exhibit such a requirement, but we shall see examples in the rock–scissors–paper game case study at the end of the chapter.

Some would argue that default anything, and in this case default accessibility, is bad practice, and that it would be better to make every declaration explicitly private or public. We have avoided doing so in *Java Gently* because the use of private has been not required, and the use of public would be more than we needed. Unless a class is going into a package, such as `Filer` did (Example 4.9) there is no need to extend its accessibility to public.

In model diagrams, we can also assume that default accessibility is in place. To emphasize either public or private, we add a + or – before the variable or method. This usage is shown well in the diagram for the `Stream` class in Section 7. 3.

Guidelines for class design

Methods are a means of grouping statements. At the next level, classes are a means of grouping methods. Specifically, we group together methods that serve a common purpose. For example, the `Math` class in Java provides trigonometrical methods, and the `Stream` class provides input–output methods.

In a class, we can do more than just group methods. We can also include data stored in variables. The design of the class in terms of the methods and data it provides is the cornerstone of object-oriented programming, and central to the way Java is intended to be used. We therefore consider some guiding principles for design here and follow this with an example and a case study, both of which make good use of classes and objects.

1. **Coherence.** A class should be concerned with a single physical entity or a set of similar operations. For example, the `Curio` class defines and manipulates product data; the `Times` class provides operations on hours and minutes.

2. **Separation of concerns.** Even for a single entity, one can have several related classes rather than one class. For example, `Curio` does not provide any output statements apart from `toString`, but we could imagine setting up quite a useful class which could provide nicely formatted output for the variables, much as we were starting to develop in the examples of `CurioStore1` and 2.

3. **Information hiding.** A class should reveal to the user only what has to be revealed and no more. In this way data can be protected from misuse, and the class can operate on a more secure basis. There is also a case to be made for methods to be hidden if they are not relevant to users, but are needed only by the class itself. In order to hide variables, we can declare them as `private`. By default, all data are accessible to classes in the same directory. There is more about accessibility in Chapter 9.

4. **Data access via methods.** Following on from 3, a guideline that is followed in all of Java's standard classes is that data are hidden from the user, but made accessible via carefully named methods, usually called `get` and `set` methods. In this way the data are protected from inappropriate changes. For example, Java's `Date` class (see Case Study 1 in Chapter 3) does not reveal the time fields themselves, but provides `getTime` and `setTime` methods.

5. **Object initialization.** When an object is created, it is efficient to copy in values for all its initial values, so that these can be used later. This is in preference to supplying the values repeatedly as parameters. For example, with the `Curio` class, we set up the initial values for each curio object, and unless we changed them, they are always available. Of course, some values must change, such as stock, but the aim is to keep method calls as simple as possible. This guideline was tested to the full in Case Study 1.

Other guidelines will be mentioned as the need arises.

5.2   Conditional loops with while- and do-statements

This book introduced loops early in order to emphasize the power of programming in handling repetitive tasks in a simple way. The two kinds of loops examined so far have been:

- counting loops based on the for-statement;

- indeterminate loops based on the for-statement, but with breaks and exceptions providing for exits from the loop when certain conditions or signals are encountered.

As was explained in the discussion on exceptions, the place where the exception is thrown is often one call level lower than the place where it is caught. The implication is then that the condition for the loop to end is hidden, except in so far as it is conveyed in a meaningful exception name, such as `EOFException`.

We now consider a third and important group of loops: those based on conditions that are visible and detectable where the loop itself is defined.

The form of conditional loops

Conditional loops are phrased in terms of while- or do-statements. A general form of a loop using the while-statement is:

While-statement

```while (condition) {```
   ```statements```
```}```

The *condition* is evaluated. If true, the *statements* are executed, then the *condition* is evaluated again. This process is repeated until the *condition* becomes false, in which case execution proceeds at the end of the loop.

An example of a simple while-loop is

```
int number = 0;
while (number <= 10) {
  System.out.println(number+" ");
  int number = (int) Math.random()*20;
}
```

The loop will definitely start because `number` is set to zero, and entry to the loop is based on `number` being less than 10. `number` is printed out and then a new number is generated randomly between 0 and 20. The condition for stopping the loop is that the number is in the upper part of that range, i.e. number is greater than 10. The loop continues `while (number <=10)`, as it says.

From this example, we see that the statements should at some stage change the condition, or else the loop will perform endlessly. It is also important to initialize any variables before entering the `while`, so that the condition can be correctly evaluated.

Both while- and for-loops can contain `break` statements which will serve to terminate the loop no matter what the conditions. So for example, in the above extract, suppose we want to stop if the number is exactly 5, but only after printing the value, we could write the loop as follows:

```
int number = 0;
while (number <= 10) {
  System.out.println(number+" ");
  if (number == 5) break;
  int number = (int) Math.random()*20;
}
```

This does not have quite the same effect as adding an extra condition, as in,

```
int number = 0;
while (number <= 10 && number != 5) {
  System.out.println(number+" ");
  int number = (int) Math.random()*20;
}
```

since here the occurrence of 5 will be detected before it can be printed out.

EXAMPLE 5.1   Highest common factor

Problem We wish to find the highest common factor (HCF) of two numbers.[1]

Solution One possible solution would be to find all the factors of each number and then compare both lists for the highest one. Fortunately, there is a quicker way!

Algorithm Suppose a and b are the numbers, a is larger than b and their HCF is f. Then $a - b$ and b will also have an HCF of f. If we use this fact, repeatedly replacing the larger of the two numbers by their difference, until the two numbers are the same, then this figure will be the HCF, even if it is 1.

Examples These examples show the algorithm at work.

---

[1] Some people may know the HCF as the GCD – greatest common divisor.

a	b	$|a-b|$
65	39	26
26	39	13
26	13	13
13	13	HCF

a	b	$|a-b|$
99	66	33
33	66	33
33	33	HCF

Program Looking at the program, we see that there are two while-loops. Because we would like to do several runs, and use the `Display` class, we can set up the outer loop as `while(true)`, which is a more elegant construct than `for  (;  ;)` which we used in the past. We know that stopping the program is accomplished by pressing the Close button on the display.

The second while-loop is then nested inside the first. It has two actions to perform: printing out the current values, and then changing *a* or *b*. The condition is easily expressed as `(a!=b)` − *a* not equal to *b*.

```
import javagently.*;

class HCFRepeat {

  /* The HCF Program      by J M Bishop Aug 1996
   * ===============      Display version July 1999
   *                      updated May 2000
   * Calculates the highest common factor of two integers.
   * Illustrates a while loop.
   */

  HCFRepeat () {
    Display display = new Display("HCF");
    display.println("***** Finding the HCF *****");
    display.prompt("Integer a", 567);
    display.prompt("Integer b", 123);
    int a, b;

    while (true) {
      display.ready("Press ready when data has been entered");
      a = display.getInt("Integer a");
      b = display.getInt("Integer b");
      display.println("a\tb");
      while (a != b) {
```

```
        display.println(Stream.format(a,6)+"\t"+Stream.format(b,6));
        if (a > b) {
          a -=b;
        } else {
          b -=a;
        }
      }
      display.println("The HCF is " + a);
      display.ready("Press ready for another data set");
    }
  }

  public static void main (String args []) {
    new HCFRepeat();
  }
}
```

Testing After two runs, we have the display as in Figure 5.1.

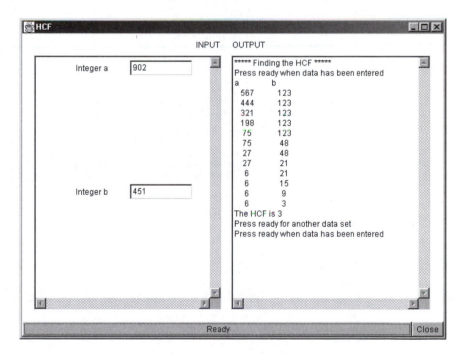

Figure 5.1 *Display output for finding the HCF.*

EXAMPLE 5.2   Curio store open all day

Problem   It is time to work on the curio store again. The functions that we can add, having learnt about while-loops and if-statements, are:

- selling throughout the day, i.e. handling different sales;
- checking whether there is enough stock for a given sale.

Solution   The first step is to look at whether the `Curio` class can stay the same or whether it needs adaptation. In fact, it is fine except that it prints out a receipt, and as we have seen, it would be better if a class modelling a real-world entity has input–output done by the caller. For input, we shall need to know what curio is being sold, how many, and when the store has closed. We shall use the `Display` class here, and aim for results such as in Figure 5.2.

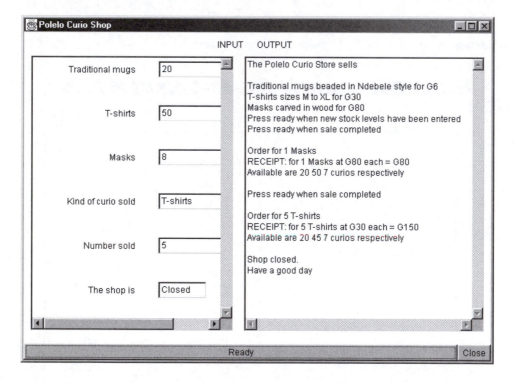

Figure 5.2 *Display output for the Curio Store.*

Algorithm   The program divides neatly into two. First we create the display and the objects. Then we run the store. Using top-down design, we can express this part at a high level as follows:

```
report();
stockTheStore();
openTheStore();

while (open) {
  sellCurios();
  open = display.getString("The store is").equals("Open");
  available();
}
display.println("Store closed.\nHave a good day");
```

`report` and `available` were part of `CurioStore2`, so the three methods that then have to be further developed are underlined. We already had the basics of stocking the store: what was missing was reading the data in. This is simple to do off the display. Opening the store adds the second three boxes on the display, making space for entering sales and indicating when the store is closed. Selling curios is mostly an input–output affair, although we recognize that the `sell` method in `Curio` is inadequate because stock can go negative, i.e.

```
void sell (int n) {
  // stock could go negative
  stock -= n;
}
```

Let us delay handling this point for a moment, and get the program running first. The final aspect of selling is that we enter what has been sold and the program has to go through the list of stocked items to find the reference to that object, as in:

```
Curio curio;

  display.ready("Press ready when sale completed");
  String curioName = display.getString("Kind of curio sold");
  int CurioSold = display.getInt("Number sold");

  if (curioName.equals(mugs.name)) {
    curio = mugs;
  } else
  if (curioName.equals(tshirts.name)) {
    curio = tshirts;
  } else
  if (curioName.equals(carvings.name)) {
    curio = carvings;
  } else {
    display.println(curioName + " is an invalid curio name");
    return;
  }
```

At this point, `curio` holds the reference to any one of the three objects and can be used in what follows, i.e.

```
curio.sell(curiosSold);
display.println("\nRECEIPT: for "+ curiosSold + " "
    + curioName +" at G"+ curio.price+" each = G" +
    curio.price*curiosSold);
```

A model diagram of the `sellCurios` method shows a stage in this process (Figure 5.3). Note that `sellCurios` from the `CurioStore3` object is expanded in the normal way for methods. `sellCurios` has three variables, one of which is a `Curio` variable. If `curioName` is 'T-shirts' then it will match with the name in the `tshirts` object and the `curio` object variable will be set to the same object as `tshirts`, as shown in the diagram. Then when the statement

```
curio.sell(curiosSold);
```

is executed, it refers to the `sellCurios` method of `tshirts`, with the parameter of 4 as read in, and changes will be made to the stock level of `tshirts`, i.e. 50 will become 46.

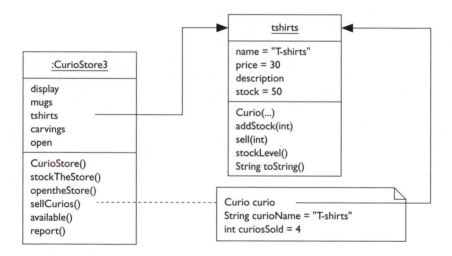

Figure 5.3 *Model diagram of selling curios.*

Program

```
import javagently.*;

class CurioStore3 {
```

```
/* Curio Store Version 3          by J M Bishop April 2000
 * ---------------------
 * This shop has stock levels and a sell option
 * Illustrates working within an object-oriented program
 * Makes use of the Display class for input-output
 */

 public static void main (String [ ] args) {
   new CurioStore3 ();
 }

// Declare objects relevant to all methods
Display display = new Display ("Polelo Curio Store");
Curio mugs, tshirts, carvings;
boolean open;

// The constructor where the initializing and main work gets done
CurioStore3 () {
   mugs = new Curio("Traditional mugs", 6, "beaded in Ndebele style", 20);
   tshirts = new Curio("T-shirts", 30, "sizes M to XL", 50);
   carvings = new Curio("Masks", 80, "carved in wood", 8);

   // print out the initial shop details
   report ();

   // Use methods to perform a sequence of actions
   stockTheStore();
   openTheStore();

   while (open) {
     sellCurios();
     open = display.getString("The store is").equals("Open");
     available();
   }
   display.println("Store closed.\nHave a good day");
 }

 void report () {
   display.println("The Polelo Curio Store sells\n");
   // use the objects' access to toString to print their contents
   display.println(""+mugs);
   display.println(""+tshirts);
   display.println(""+carvings);
 }
```

```
void stockTheStore () {
  display.ready("Press ready when new stock levels have been entered");
  mugs.addStock(display.getInt(mugs.name));
  tshirts.addStock(display.getInt(tshirts.name));
  carvings.addStock(display.getInt(carvings.name));
}

void openTheStore () {
  display.prompt("Kind of curio sold","                    ");
  display.prompt("Number sold",0);
  display.prompt("The shop is","Open");
  open = true;
}

void sellCurios () {
  Curio curio;

  display.ready("Press ready when sale completed");
  String curioName = display.getString("Kind of curio sold");
  int CurioSold = display.getInt("Number sold");

  if (curioName.equals(mugs.name)) {
     curio = mugs;
  } else
  if (curioName.equals(tshirts.name)) {
    curio = tshirts;
  } else
  if (curioName.equals(carvings.name)) {
    curio = carvings;
  } else {
    display.println(curioName + " is an invalid curio name");
    return;
  }
  display.println("\nOrder for "+CurioSold+" "+curioName);
  curio.sell(CurioSold);
  display.println("RECEIPT: for "+ CurioSold + " "
      + curioName +" at G"+ curio.price+" each = G" +
      curio.price*CurioSold);
 }

void available () {
  display.println("Available are "+mugs.stockLevel()+" "+
    tshirts.stockLevel()+" "+carvings.stockLevel()+
    " curios respectively\n");
```

```
      }
  }

  class Curio {

      String name;
      int price;
      String description;
      int stock;

      Curio (String n, int p, String d, int t) {
        name = n;
        price = p;
        description = d;
        display.prompt(name,t);
      }

      void addStock (int n) {
        stock += n;
      }
      void sell (int n) {
        // stock could go negative
        stock -= n;
      }

      int stockLevel () {
        return stock;
      }

      // This method is accessed by println to turn
      // a Curio object into a String.
      public String toString () {
        return name + " "+description+" for G" + price;
      }
  }
```

To handle the low stock level most efficiently, we need to discuss a construct covered in the next section. But first we continue our discussion of conditional loops.

The do-statement

The general form of the do-statement is similar to the while, as shown below. The do-statement starts off by going through its body at least once before checking the conditions. This can sometimes be a desirable property, but in general the while-statement is favoured by programmers.

Do-statement

```
do {
  statements
} while (condition);
```

The *statements* are executed once. Then the *condition* is checked. If it is false, the loop is repeated. When the *condition* is evaluated to true, the loop ends and the next statement is executed.

Developing a conditional loop

Two very important points about conditional loops are that:

- the condition must be initialized;
- the condition must change during the loop.

If the condition is not initialized, then the loop will be working on incorrect or even un-defined information. If it is not altered during the loop, then there will be no chance of its changing and causing the loop to end.

Before going on to a problem, consider a small illustrative example of conditional loops, bearing in mind the importance of formulating them correctly. In order to convey the sense of the looping process, the example makes use of booleans and methods, which have the effect suggested by their names. The example simulates trying to find a pair from a drawerful of mixed coloured socks. We have:

```
PickaSock();
PickAnotherSock();
while (!aPair()) {
  DiscardaSock ();
  PickAnotherSock ();
}
```

The loop is initialized by having two socks in hand: this is essential so that the check for a pair can be correctly performed. The loop is correctly formulated in that the condition will change each time round, as a new sock is selected. There are, however, two crucial flaws in the loop.

Suppose a pair is never found. The condition is not met so the loop continues, but the method to `PickAnotherSock` will eventually fail, and the whole operation will crash. The other problem is similar – suppose there were no socks in the drawer to start with. In this case, neither of the initializing statements can be performed, and the program as it stands will not be able to execute. These two situations can be summed up as:

- guard against not being able to begin;

- guard against never ending.

The remedy is to provide additional conditions as the guards. In this case, we need to know if sufficient socks (that is, at least two) exist to be able to test for a pair, and then we need to know when the drawer becomes empty. Both conditions are based on the number of socks in the drawer, and we assume that this figure can be provided in some way. The corrected version of the loop then becomes:

```
if (NumberofSocksinDrawer >= 2) {
  PickaSock ();
  PickAnotherSock ();
  while (NumberofSocksinDrawer > 0 && !aPair()) {
    DiscardaSock () ;
    PickAnotherSock () ;
  }
}
{At this point, a pair may or may not have been found}
```

There is one final consideration with any conditional loop. If there is more than one part to the condition governing the loop, it may be necessary to know at the end which part caused the loop to stop. In the example, it seems sensible to be able to decide whether the search was successful or not. This is called a **follow-up action**, and is performed by rechecking some of the conditions, as in:

```
if (aPair()) {
  System.out.println("Got a pair of socks.");
} else {
  System.out.println("Bad luck, no pair found.");
}
```

Notice that when conditions are connected (as they often are), one must be careful as to which is tested. In this case, it would not have been correct to test for the drawer being empty as in:

```
if (NumberofSocksinDrawer == 0)
  System.out.println("Bad luck, no pair found.");
else
  System.out.println("Got a pair of socks.");
```

since the pair could have been found on the very last time round the loop. The drawer would also be empty, but that is irrelevant for this purpose.

Exercise: Write the necessary if-statements to report on whether a pair was found or not, whether the drawer was empty initially, or whether it became empty during the search.

5.3   User-defined exceptions

In Section 4.6 we looked at how to react to exceptions which get thrown by the Java system, such as `EOFException` and `FileNotFoundException`. We can also define our own exceptions and use them to signal between classes. Sometimes, exceptions are a more appropriate and cleaner way of controlling a program than an if-statement would be.

To define your own exception, particular to the situation in hand, the form is:

Defining a new exception

```
class name extends Exception {
  public name () { }
  public name (String s) {
    super (s)
  }
}
```

name will be the new exception name. The second constructor will pass any string specified up to the system's
exception system so that it is available for methods such
as `getMessage`.

This definition must be made where both the thrower and catcher can see it. We now have an exception class called name and we can throw exception objects of this class as in:

Throwing an exception

```
throw new name ("message");
```

The *message* is an explanation of the nature of the exception.

Catching an exception proceeds exactly as before, as shown in the form in Section 4.6. The message can be used by the exception handler (the catch-statement) to give informa-
tion to the user by calling the `getMessage` method, or it can be empty (accounting for the two options in the declaration above). Opportunities for using user-defined exceptions arise infrequently in ordinary programming because usually the required signal can be obtained by calling a method which gives the state of the object (or part of it) and then

applying an if-statement. It is only when the state and what it should be compared to are completely hidden in the class that an exception is essential. However, to show how they work, we consider the following example.

| EXAMPLE 5.3 | Checking on stock availability |

Problem   As we saw earlier, we need to watch the stock levels in the Curio Store, and not allow orders that exceed the stock.

Solution   There are actually two ways to solve this problem. We can use an if-statement and call the `stockLevel` method, or we can use an exception.

Programs   The first option is very simple:

```
if (curio.stockLevel >= curiosSold) {
  curio.sell(curiosSold);
    display.println("RECEIPT: for "+ curiosSold + " "
        + curioName +" at G"+ curio.price+" each = G" +
        curio.price*curiosSold);
  }
  else {
    display.println("Not enough stock. "+
        curio.stockLevel() + " available.");
  }
```

The second option, using exceptions, is fairly similar at the calling side, as in:

```
try {
   curio.sell(curiosSold);
   display.println("RECEIPT: for "+ curiosSold + " "
       + curioName +" at G"+ curio.price+" each = G" +
       curio.price*curiosSold);
}
catch (StockException e) {
  display.println(e.getMessage());
}
```

However, to activate the exception we have to define it, say we will throw it, and then throw it. Throwing it means having the if-statement anyway. The definition is:

```
class StockException extends Exception {
    StockException (String s) {
      super(s);
    }
}
```

and the `sell` method in the class becomes:

```
void sell (int n) throws StockException {
  if (stock >= n) {
    stock -= n;
  }
  else {
    throw new StockException
      ("Not enough stock. "+stock+" available.");
  }
}
```

The output in either case is given in Figure 5.4.

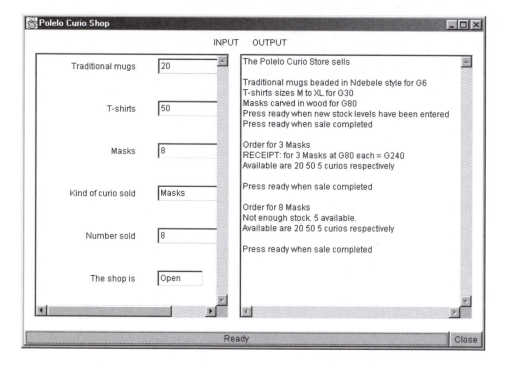

Figure 5.4 *Output from the Curio Store with stock level check.*

There is a good example of user-defined exceptions in Section 15.2.

5.4   The type char

We have already looked informally at strings in Java and they are covered formally in Chapter 7. A string in Java is an object, and a single character in quotes, e.g. "a", is also a string. Java provides a more simple type for single characters, on a keyboard, typically:

A to Z
a to z
! @ # $ % ^ & * ( ) _ + − = { } [ ] : " | ; ' ~ ` ? /

In addition, we can represent some other keyboard characters with the escape prefix:

\b   backspace
\t   tab
\n   new line
\f   new page (i.e. form feed)

Notice that these particular keyboard keys cannot otherwise appear on the screen: they cause special effects when pressed.

Characters in Java are written with a single quote, e.g. 'a' and the following operations are automatically valid for them:

■ assignment;

■ comparison;

■ concatenation to strings.

The result of a comparison for less or greater depends on the order of the characters as set up in Java. What we need to know is that the letters are in order so that 'g' < 'z', for example.

There are several useful class methods defined for characters via char's companion class Character. These are shown in the form:

Character class methods
int   digit (**char** *ch*, **int** *radix*)
char   fordigit (**int** *digit*, int *radix*)
int   getNumericValue(**char** *ch*)
boolean isDigit(**char** *ch*)
boolean isLetter(**char** *ch*)
boolean isLowerCase(**char** *ch*)
boolean isUpperCase(**char** *ch*)
char   toLowerCase(**char** *ch*)
char   toUpperCase(**char** *ch*)
... and 13 others

At first glance, these methods make for some interesting examples in character processing. Unfortunately, the character reading facilities of Java need some more sophisticated ideas, which we are leaving to Chapter 7. Therefore, making full use of these methods will have to wait till then. However, there is one string method that will prove important later on, i.e.

```
char charAt(int index)
```

If we read a character as a string, then `charAt(0)` will convert it to a `char` type.

Finally, Java also provides, through the escape character \u, space for an additional 10 000 characters, which are not available on the usual keyboards. These are called Unicode characters and enable Java to be truly international. There are Unicode sequences for letters in Greek, Cyrillic, Hebrew, Arabic, Tibetan and so on, conforming to international standards where they exist. However, we do not need to be concerned with these while we are dealing in what is called the Latin alphabet.

Casting characters

Characters can be cast to numbers and back. The following conversion is automatic, and therefore all the numeric operators also work on characters:

`char` can be cast to `int` or `long` or `float` or `double`

To convert in the other direction, we use a type cast. So for example, the following is a valid sequence:

```
char digit;
int n;
n = digit;
n++;
digit = (char) n;
```

The efffect of this sequence is to take a character and 'move it on one'. Thus if `digit` started with the value 'j' then it would become 'k'. Because of the neat methods already mentioned for characters, it is unlikely that we will have to cast them to integers, unless we really want to do arithmetic, as in the next example.

EXAMPLE 5.4   Printing out the character set

Problem   We would like to see what additional characters are available on our system.

Solution   We can loop through all the integers from 0 upwards, and show the corresponding character. In fact, experience has shown that the printable characters only start at 32.

Program The program is quite simple as shown below, but has some new features in it. There are two places where arithmetic operations are applied to the character variable: these are underlined. Then we use the Unicode hexadecimal notation for the start and end of the loop. When printed out, these values are in decimal, though, and, as seen from the output, run from 32 to 255.

```java
import java.awt.*;
import javagently.*;

class TestUnicode {

  /* Program to demonstrate Unicode       J M Bishop May 2000
   * ================================
   *
   * Illustrates character casting, unicode
   * and use of hexadecimal
   */

  TestUnicode() {
    for (char code = "\u0020" ; code <="\u00FF" ; code++) {
      System.out.print(Text.format(code,5) + " " + code);
      if (code%10 == 0) {
        System.out.println();
      }
    }
  }

  public static void main (String [] args) {
  new TestUnicode();
  }
}
```

Testing The results are:

32		33	!	34	"	35	#	36	$	37	%	38	&	39	'	40	(			
41	)	42	*	43	+	44	,	45	–	46	.	47	/	48	0	49	1	50	2	
51	3	52	4	53	5	54	6	55	7	56	8	57	9	58	:	59	;	60	<	
61	=	62	>	63	?	64	@	65	A	66	B	67	C	68	D	69	E	70	F	
71	G	72	H	73	I	74	J	75	K	76	L	77	M	78	N	79	O	80	P	
81	Q	82	R	83	S	84	T	85	U	86	V	87	W	88	X	89	Y	90	Z	
91	[	92	\	93	]	94	^	95	_	96	'	97	a	98	b	99	c	100	d	
101	e	102	f	103	g	104	h	105	i	106	j	107	k	108	l	109	m	110	n	
111	o	112	p	113	q	114	r	115	s	116	t	117	u	118	v	119	w	120	x	
121	y	122	z	123	{	124	|	125	}	126	~	127		128	?	129	?	130	?	

131 ?	132 ?	133 ?	134 ?	135 ?	136 ?	137 ?	138 ?	139 ?	140 ?
141 ?	142 ?	143 ?	144 ?	145 ?	146 ?	147 ?	148 ?	149 ?	150 ?
151 ?	152 ?	153 ?	154 ?	155 ?	156 ?	157 ?	158 ?	159 ?	160
161 ¡	162 ¢	163 £	164 ?	165 ¥	166 ¦	167 §	168 ¨	169 ©	170 ª
171 «	172 ¬	173 –	174 ®	175 ‾	176 °	177 ±	178 2	179 3	180 ´
181 µ	182 ¶	183 ·	184 ¸	185 1	186 º	187 »	188 1·4	189 1·2	190 3·4
191 ¿	192 À	193 Á	194 Â	195 Ã	196 Ä	197 Å	198 Æ	199 Ç	200 È
201 É	202 Ê	203 Ë	204 Ì	205 Í	206 Î	207 Ï	208 \<ETH>	209 Ñ	210 Ò
211 Ó	212 Ô	213 Õ	214 Ö	215 *	216 Ø	217 Ù	218 Ú	219 Û	220 Ü
221 Y´	222 \<THORN>	223 ß	224 à	225 á	226 â	227 ã	228 ä	229 å	230 æ
231 ç	232 è	233 é	234 ê	235 ë	236 ì	237 í	238 î	239 ï	240 \<eth>
241 ñ	242 ò	243 ó	244 ô	245 õ	246 ö	247 ÷	248 ø	249 ù	250 ú
251 û	252 ü	253 y´	254 \<thorn>	255 ÿ					

5.5 The switch-statement

The if-statement is a two-way selection statement based on conditions. However, if there
are several simple tests for given values, successive else-if statements can become
unwieldy. Java provides for so-called **keyed** selection with the switch-statement. The form
of the switch-statement is:

Switch-statement

```
switch (switch-expression) {
  case value : statement; break;
  case value : statement; break;
  . . .
  default : statement; break;
}
```

The *switch-expression*, which must be one of the integer types or `char`, is
evaluated and the *value* compared with those listed. If it appears, execution
starts at the corresponding *statement* and continues down statements until
the end of the switch or a break is found. If the switch value is not present,
the default statement is executed. Values may appear only once.

The switch-statement considers the value of the switch-expression and, starting at the
first case value, endeavours to find a match. If a match is found, then the corresponding
statement is executed and the `break` causes control to pass to the end of the whole
switch. The `default` keyword is a catch-all for values that have not been mentioned.
The break-statements and the default part are not strictly compulsory but it is considered

good programming practice to have them. Without a break, control falls through to the next case. This could be useful if the statement part is empty, as shown in the examples that follow.

The switch-expression must produce a value that is an integer or character. It may not be real. The case values are expressions of the same type as the switch-expression, and there may be one or more case values for a given statement. The switch values do not have to be in any order but may occur only once.

As an example, consider the little jingle that gives the number of days in a month:

Thirty days hath September, April, June and November.
All the rest have thirty-one, excepting February alone,
Which has but twenty-eight days clear,
And twenty-nine in each leap year.

If we assume that month has an integer value with January being 1, then a switch-statement can be used to look at the month and set days to the appropriate value as follows (ignoring leap years):

```
switch (month) {
  case 9:
  case 4:
  case 6:
  case 11: days = 30; break;
  case 2: days = 28; break;
  default: days = 31; break;
}
```

As always, the statement mentioned after each case can be a block and include several statements. Such is the situation when establishing the correct number of days for February, taking account of leap years. Instead of doing a calculation of the year (divisible by 4 and so on), we simply require that whether the year is leap or not is passed as a parameter to a method encompassing the switch. Now the breaks become redundant because the return has the same effect.

```
int daysInMonth (int month, boolean leapyear) {
  switch (month) {
    case 9:
    case 4:
    case 6:
    case 11:
      return 30;
    case 2: {
      if (leapyear) {
        return 29;
      }
```

```
      else {
        return 28;
      }
    }
    default: return 31;
  }
}
```

Alternatively, we could have passed the year and done the calculations in `daysInMonth`. Switch-statements are the subject of the next example. The switch-expressions are characters, which is quite often the case.

EXAMPLE 5.5   Exchange rates

Problem   The Curio Store is patronized by many international clients and would like to enable them to pay in any of the major currencies.

Solution   We add an extra box on the input section for a currency sign. Once the amount has been calculated, we read the sign in and use a switch to find the appropriate conversion factor from graz. The receipt is then amplified to include the converted amount, as shown in Figure 5.5.

Algorithm   The solution can be divided into two parts: the entry of the currency symbol, and the the conversion and printing of the foreign currency value. Clearly a switch-statement is ideal for the second part, and it will look something like this:

```
switch (currencySymbol) {
  case '¥': factor = yenExchange; break;
  case '$': factor = dollarExchange; break;
  case 'D': factor = markExchange; break;
  case '£': factor = poundFactor; break;
  case 'G': factor = 1; break;
  default : ...;
}
```

This is the clearest and most efficient way of solving this problem, but it is not the only way. The same effect could be achieved using successive if-else statements as described in Section 4.4. However, it is usually easier to see what is going on in a table as opposed to a calculation, so switch-statements should be used in preference to if-statements where possible.

What should be done in the default case, which would be reached if an invalid symbol is entered? Obviously, a message must be displayed, informing the user that the symbol

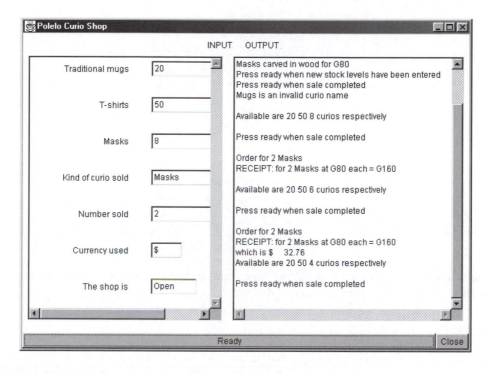

Figure 5.5 *Display from the currency change version of the Curio Store.*

was invalid. But how to try again? One possibility would be to declare and raise an exception. This would be overkill, however, since we have all the information to hand, and we have stipulated repeatedly that exceptions are for cross-class communication.

Instead we declare a simple boolean variable that will be set to true, and should the currency symbol be invalid, it will be set to false. The switch-statement is then encased in a do-statement based on the boolean.

```
void displayReceipt (Curios curio, String curioName, int curiosSold) {
    double factor;
    char currencySymbol;
    boolean symbolRead=true;

    do {
      currencySymbol = display.getString("Currency used").charAt(0);
      switch (currencySymbol) {
        case 'Y': factor = yenExchange; break;
        case '$': factor = dollarExchange; break;
        case 'D': factor = markExchange; break;
        case '£': factor = poundExchange; break;
        case 'G': factor = 1; break;
```

```
        default : factor = 1;
                  symbolRead = false;
                  display.println("Invalid symbol, try again");
    }
  } while (!symbolRead);

  display.println("RECEIPT: for "+ curiosSold + " "
      + curioName +" at G"+ curio.price+" each = G" +
      curio.price*curiosSold);
  if (currencySymbol != 'G') {
    display.print("which is "+ currencySymbol +
      Text.format(curio.price*curiosSold/factor,10,2));
  }
}
```

An extension to this aspect of the Curio Store would be to be able to change the exchange rates each day: this is taken up in a problem later.

When not to use switches

The clarity of the switch makes it a natural choice for many types of selections. However, it cannot be used in situations where the selection is based on conditions. For example, the following is not valid Java:

```
/* NOT VALID JAVA */
switch (number) {
  case < 0: Addtonegatives;
  case = 0: Donothing;
  case > 0: Addtopositives;
}
```

The cases must be actual values. A suitable approach here would employ successive if-else statements.

Another place where switch-statements are inappropriate is for checking strings. A string is a more complex entity than a switch can handle. Later on we shall see how to match strings as keys to values (Section 6.5).

5.6 Case Study 2: Rock–scissors–paper game

There is a popular two-person game in which each player makes a choice of rock, scissors or paper, and who is the winner depends on the following rules:

- rock beats scissors (it can smash them);

- scissors beat paper (they can cut it);

- paper beats rock (it can wrap it).

If both players make the same choice, then it is a draw. We would like to program the computer to play this game against a human. Each will make a choice and the computer will work out who won.

Solution

Programming any two-person game involves several steps:

- Give instructions (or omit them if requested to do so).

- Initialize the state of the game.

- Set up a loop to play the game repeatedly until told to stop.

- Generate the computer's choice.

- Get the user's choice.

- Decide who has won.

- Play again, or if no more required, sign off.

We shall look at each step in turn.

Step 1: instructions

Computer games should always give instructions for new users. These should include not only a description of the rules, but also how to enter replies. Two issues that should always be addressed here are whether replies need to be followed by Return, and whether capital letters are acceptable as well as lower-case letters. Fortunately, in Java we can use a character method to change any input into one or other case, so we can accept both.

Step 2: initialize

We need to ask the question here as to how the computer is to make its choice. Ideally, we want a random choice, and therefore need to use random numbers. The simple random number generator in the `Math` class is fine if we multiply the value by 3 and make it an integer. What values will this yield? If we start with 0 to 0.999 then we will get 0 to 2.999. Taking an integer cast gives us 0 to 2. (You should check this with a small test program.)

Alternatively, we could use the opportunity to learn about a more sophisticated random number generator in the `java.util` package. It works with random objects where the sequence of numbers generated can be initialized from a **seed.** If we let the user type in the seed, then there is little chance of the computer always winning. We can use this class to simulate the throwing of a three-sided dice, by declaring:

```
Random dice = new Random (in.readInt());
```

Then calling the method nextInt() on the dice object will return an integer in the full range of int, positive or negative. To get an integer down to the values 0, 1 or 2, we make it positive and take modulo 3, i.e.

```
mychoice = Math.abs(dice.nextInt()) % 3;
```

Step 3: set up a loop

We are going to use an indeterminate while-loop because the place where we stop the loop (based on a Q being input) is in between getting our choice and getting the computer's choice. We exit the loop with a break. The loop is the main feature of the main class that plays the game, as follows:

```
import java.io.*;
import javagently.*;

class PlayGame {

  /* The Playing Game program      by J M Bishop Aug 1996
   * -----------------------       Java 1.1
   *                               updated June 2000
   * Driver for playing Rocks-Scissors-Paper.
   * Calls methods in the RSP class to get
   * my choice and the computer's choice and
   * display who has won until Q is typed.
   * Illustrates conditional loops and objects
   */

  public static void main (String [] args) throws IOException {
    new PlayGame ();
  }

  PlayGame () throws IOException {

    // This line will change for each game
    RSPGame mygame = new RSPGame ();

    mygame.startGame ();
    while (true) {
      mygame.makemyChoice();
      if (mygame.getyourChoice ()=='Q') break;
      mygame.winner();
    }
    System.out.println("Thanks for playing");
  }
}
```

Step 4: generate the computer's choice

We have already seen that generating choices will be done by random numbers. The computer will be submitting 0, 1 or 2 and the user will be submitting R, S or P. In fact, this will not cause problems.

Step 5: getting the user's choice

Here we have to program defensively. We must check that the character entered is indeed one of the permissible ones. If it is not, we should give a message and try again. A do-loop is in order because the test comes after the input has been done. The basic sequence is:

```
do {
  System.out.print ("Your choice of R S P or Q to stop?");
  yourchoice; = Text.readChar(in);
} while (yourchoice!='R' & yourchoice != 'S'
        & yourchoice != 'P' & yourchoice != 'Q');
```

This simple sequence will force the player to use capital letters. The program has a more sophisticated version. Notice that the initial message serves as an error message as well.

Step 6: decide who has won

This is algorithmically the most intricate part. We have three choices for the computer, and each of these has three outcomes, depending on the player's choice. This could mean a selection statement with nine arms! Fortunately, there is a better way, using a method with parameters.

Let us consider the first case of the computer having a rock. Then, depending on the player's choice, the computer judges the result as:

- scissors – win;

- paper – lose;

- rock – draw.

The same process is repeated for the computer having a scissors, except that the list of player's choices is in a different order. Clearly, a method will be appropriate here, and the result is shown in the program below in method `report`.

Step 7: sign off

We can have a very simple sign off, such as thanking the user, or we can print out statistics on how many games were won either way.

Program

The program follows the strategy outlined above, and makes good use of all the control statements introduced in this chapter (i.e. while, do and switch). The program is arranged in two classes: the structure of the `playGame` class is more or less independent of the game being played, except that it creates the `mygame` object of a particular class, in this case, `RSPGame`. In the `RSPGame` class, there are three private variables and one private method, which are not needed to be seen outside of a game object. Figure 5.6 gives the model diagram for the program.

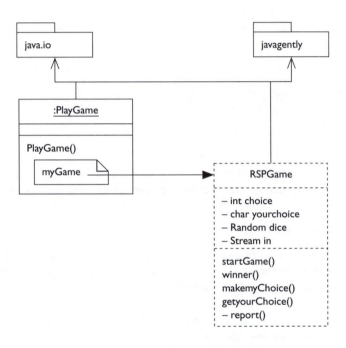

Figure 5.6 *Model diagram for the rock–scissors–paper game.*

```
import java.io.*;
import javagently.*;

class PlayGame {

    /* The Playing Game program        by J M Bishop Aug 1996
     * ------------------------        Java 1.1
     *                                 updated June 2000
     * Driver for playing Rocks-Scissors-Paper.
     * Calls methods in the RSP class to get
     * my choice and the computer's choice and
```

```
 * display who has won until Q is typed.
 * Illustrates conditional loops and objects
 */

public static void main (String [] args) throws IOException {
  new PlayGame ();
}

PlayGame () throws IOException {

  RSPGame mygame = new RSPGame ();
  mygame.startGame ();

  while (true) {
    mygame.makemyChoice();
    if (mygame.getyourChoice ()=='Q') break;
    mygame.winner();
  }
  System.out.println("Thanks for playing");
}
}
import java.io.*;
import javagently.*;

class RSPGame {

  /* The RSP Game class      by J M Bishop Aug 1996
   * ------------------      Java 1.1 Dec 1997
   *                         updated June 2000
   * offers four methods:
   * startGame, getmyChoice, getyourChoice and Winner.
   * getyourChoice returns a character so
   * that we can stop if it was a Q.
   * Illustrates typed methods, switches, loops, Math.random
   * and private members
   */


  private int mychoice;
  private char yourchoice; // R S P
  private Random dice;
  private Stream in = new Stream(System.in);

void startGame () throws IOException {
  System.out.println("Let's play RSP");
```

```
    System.out.println("To show I'm not cheating, start me off by"+
      " giving me a number.");
  dice = new Random(in.readInt());
}

void winner () {
  // In the calls to report, the first parameter is my choice.
  // The second one is the choice that I could beat.
  // The third one is the choice that would beat me.

  switch (mychoice) {
    case 0 : report ('R','S','P'); break;
    case 1 : report ('S','P','R'); break;
    case 2 : report ('P','R','S'); break;
  }
}

void makemyChoice () {
  // nextInt returns an integer in its full range.
  // We have to reduce it to 0, 1, 2
  mychoice = Math.abs(dice.nextInt()) % 3;
}

char getyourChoice () throws IOException {
  do {
    System.out.print("Your choice of R S P or Q to stop ?");
    yourchoice = Character.toUpperCase(
        gameDisplay.getString("Player's choice").charAt(0));
  } while (yourchoice !='R' && yourchoice != 'S'
          && yourchoice != 'P' && yourchoice != 'Q');
  if (yourchoice != 'Q') {
    System.out.print("You drew "+yourchoice+" and ");
  }
  return yourchoice;
}

private void report (char me, char Iwin, char youWin) {
  System.out.println("I drew a " + me);
  if (yourchoice == Iwin) {
    System.out.println("I win");
  } else
  if (yourchoice == youWin) {
    System.out.println("You win");
```

```
        }
        else {
          System.out.println("It's a draw");
        }
      }
   }
}
```

Testing A typical run could go something like this:

```
Let's play RSP
To show I'm not cheating, start me off by giving me a number.
67
Your choice of R S P or Q to stop ? R
You drew R and I drew a S
You win
Your choice of R S P or Q to stop ? S
You drew S and I drew a R
I win
Your choice of R S P or Q to stop ? P
You drew P and I drew a R
You win
Your choice of R S P or Q to stop ? P
You drew P and I drew a P
It's a draw
Your choice of R S P or Q to stop ? S
You drew S and I drew a P
You win
Your choice of R S P or Q to stop ? R
You drew R and I drew a S
You win
Your choice of R S P or Q to stop ? Q
Thanks for playing
```

As you can see, the computer's choices are random, and it does lose sometimes!

Multiplayer game

Multiplayer games are very popular. RSP is a two-player game, but we can, without much effort, show how the computer can play several games at once, just like a grand master in chess. To do this requires threads, which we shall learn about in Chapter 13.

SUMMARY

The while-loop is a basic controlling loop. It checks the condition at the start of the loop. The do-loop checks the condition at the end. In either case, we can check one or more conditions in the middle and exit the loop using a break-statement. Boolean variables are useful when programming while-loops, in order to keep the value of conditions established before the time comes to check whether to continue. The use of while-loops is intimately entwined with reading input data, but it is necessary to handle some of the ending conditions via exceptions.

The switch-statement provides for multiway decision making based on values. Several values can lead to the same statement. The values may only be integers or characters.

In this chapter we defined the following keywords:

```
case                public
char                switch
default             throw
do                  while
private
```

and mentioned this one

```
extends
```

and Java library components

```
Exception           isDigit
super               isLetter
Character           isLowerCase
digit               isUpperCase
forDigit            toLowerCase
getNumericValue     toUpperCase
```

and forms

Accessibility control
While-statement
Do-statement
Defining a new exception
Throwing an exception
`Character` class methods
Switch-statement

QUIZ

5.1   If a method has no accessibility modifier, then it will be visible

(a)   only within objects of its class
(b)   to any object of a class in its package
(c)   to any other object
(d)   not at all

5.2   In the following while-statements, how many characters will be printed if the data are KALAMZOO?

```
int ch = ' ';
while (ch != 'Z') {
   System.out.println(ch);
}
```

(a)   6
(b)   5
(c)   0
(d)   cannot say

5.3   After the following switch-statement, what will value be ?

```
int coin = 5;
switch (coin) {
   case 1: value = 0.01;
   case 2: value = 0.02;
   case 3: value = 0.05;
   case 4: value = 0.20;
   case 5: value = 0.50;
   case 6: value = 1.00;
   case 7: value = 2.00;
   default: value = 0;
}
```

(a)   0.50
(b)   2.00
(c)   5
(d)   0

5.4   What happens when a switch-statement is entered with a value for which there is no case-statement and there is also no default case?

(a)   execution error
(b)   a case-statement is selected at random
(c)   the last case-statement is executed
(d)   nothing happens in the switch, and the program proceeds

5.5   A while-loop ends when

(a)   its condition evaluates to true
(b)   its condition evaluates to false

(c)   its condition evaluates to false or a break is executed
(d)   its condition evaluates to false and a break is executed

5.6   Given a character `ch`, the next character value alphabetically can be obtained by:

(a) `ch ++`
(b) `nextChar(ch)`
(c) `((int) ch) ++`
(d) can't be done

5.7   When we throw a user-defined exception, the exception is a

(a) class
(b) variable
(c) object
(d) formal parameter

5.8   In the case study, how could the following condition be made more efficient?

```
while (yourchoice! = 'R' & yourchoice!= 'S'
   & yourchoice!='P'& yourchoice ! = 'Q');
```

(a) replace the `&` operators by `&&` operators
(b) put brackets around each of the four comparisons
(c) rewrite it as

```
while (yourchoice != {'R', 'S', 'P', 'Q'});
```

(d) can't be done

5.9   A rewrite of the while-loop in the HCF as a do-while loop would be:

(a) `do {if (a>b) a-=b else b-=a;} while (a != b);`
(b) `do {if (a>b) a-=b else b-=a;} while (a == b);`
(c) `if (a!=b) do {if (a>b) a-=b else b-=a;} while (a!=b);`
(d) `if (a!=b) do {if (a>b) a-=b else b-=a;} while (a == b);`

5.10   The idea of keeping input–output out of a class which describes an object and keeping it in the main driving class which instantiates the class is called:

(a) separation of concerns
(b) anti-coherence
(c) information hiding
(d) private accessibility

PROBLEMS

Note: the first eight problems relate to formulating loops correctly. Most of them use while- or do-loops, but for-loops could also be appropriate.

5.1   **Plastic.** A librarian covers books with plastic. She has a roll of plastic which is 2.2 m wide and 100 m long. Books range between 20×14 cm and 21×30 cm and a book needs twice its size plus a border of 4 cm all round of plastic. As books come in, she works across the roll.

When a book does not fit (first horizontally, then vertically), she cuts a straight line across the plastic (because it is easier), and starts a new row. Generate random book sizes and show for 20 books, how the plastic will be used.

5.2 **Spelling.** There are certain spellings that have acceptable variations in English. Write a program to analyse some text and make changes to two word endings as follows:

■ -ize becomes -ise

■ -or becomes -our

5.3 **Comments.** A piece of text is stored on file. It is divided into paragraphs separated by blank lines. Write a program which reads in the text and prints it out again, ignoring all text between curly brackets {}. Print suitable warning messages if

■ a { is found inside brackets;

■ a } is found without a matching {.

■ a paragraph ends without a matching }.

At the end of each paragraph print the percentage of text (excluding spaces) that occurred in brackets. *Hint:* This program is a good one for testing character handling, and it will be easier to write with the additional use of boolean variables.

Sample input	Sample output
This is the same length	**This is the same length**
as the comment { This	**as the comment rest assured.**
assured comment is the	***** No ending bracket**
same length as the rest}	
rest assured. {And so	**Comment is 50% of the text**

5.4 **Sensitive drugs.** A sensitive drug cannot sustain a change in temperature of more than 30°C in a 24-hour period. The temperatures are monitored and recorded every two hours. Write a program the laboratory technician can run once a day to determine whether or not to throw the drug away.

5.5 **Engineering apparatus.** A certain engineering apparatus is controlled by the input of successive numbers. If there is a run of the same number, the apparatus can optimize its performance. Hence we would like to arrange the data so as to indicate that a run is coming. Write a program that reads a sequence of numbers and prints out each run of numbers in the form ($n*m$) where m is the number to be repeated n times. These instructions are printed in brackets on a new line, to indicate that they are going to the apparatus. Note that a run could consist of a single number. The numbers are terminated by a zero, which halts the apparatus. Sample input and output would be:

```
sample input and output
20 20 20 20 20 20 20 20 20 20 50
(10*20)
50 50 50 50 60
(5*60)
30
(1*20)
```

```
30 30 30 90
(4*30)
0
(1*90)
(0)
```

5.6   **Rabbits!** A scientist needs to determine when she will run out of space to house her rabbits. She starts with two rabbits and it is known that a pair of adult rabbits (those more than three months old) produce on average two rabbits every three months. The scientist has space to house 500 rabbits. Write a program that will determine how many months it will be before she runs out of space. Adapt the program to print out a table of rabbit populations (adult, non-adult and total) every three months for five years. Assume no rabbits die.

5.7   **Fibonacci again.** Problem 3.16 involved printing out the Fibonacci sequence. Alter the program so that only every third value is printed out. What do you notice about these values?

5.8   **Contents.** Write a program to produce a contents page for a book using a data supplied in fixed format. The data should be read off a file and the output sent to a printer. Consider the following input:

(First steps (The Computer, 5) (Problem Solving (Definition, 10) (Outline, 15) (Algorithms, 20)) (Programs and Procedures, 25)) (Types and Looping (Types (Integer, 30) (Character, 36) (Boolean, 43)) (Looping (Counting loops, 49) (Conditional Loops, 52)))

The parentheses indicate the chapters, sections and subsections and the numbers following them are the page numbers. Page numbers are only given when there is no further subdivision. The output for the data above would be:

CONTENTS

1. First steps
  1.1 The Computer   5
  1.2 Problem Solving
    1.2.1 Definition   10
    1.2.2 Outline   15
    1.2.3 Algorithms   20
  1.3 Programs and Procedures 25
2. Types and Looping
  2.1 Types
    2.2.1 Integer   30
    2.2.2 Character   36
    2.2.3 Boolean   43
  2.2 Looping
    2.2.1 Counting Loops   49
    2.2.2 Conditional Loops 52

5.9   **Car tax.** There is a special tax on cars in Savanna, which is currently at the following rate:

Net price	Rate
<G25 000	10%
G26 000 to G100 000	G5000
>G100 000	15%

Write a program that prints out the net price, tax and gross price of cars with net prices between G15 000 and G125 000 in steps of G5000.

5.10 **Postage stamps.** Savanna Mail has decided to have machines that print out postage stamps up to a maximum value of G99.99. The stamps have a basic design as follows:

```
-----------
| SAVANNA |
| G14.30  |
| BY AIR  |
-----------
```

The three zones of postage rates per 10 grams are as follows:
(a) 50c
(b) 90c
(c) G1.10

and the postage is doubled for airmail. Write a program that prompts the user for the mass of an article, the zone to which it is going and whether it should go by air or not, and then prints out the correct stamp. Use a class for the stamps, and start the program by creating three objects for the different zones.

5.11 **Setting exchange rates.** Improve the exchange rates program (Example 5.5) so that the rates can be read in before trade begins each day. Use a separate display for this part of the program.

5.12 **Rooms with exceptions.** Consider Problem 4.12. Redo the solution with
(a) while-loops;
(b) user-defined exceptions.

Discuss the relative merits of the different solutions with respect to ease of programming, proper use of the constructs and the length of programs.

CHAPTER 6

Arrays and tables

6.1 Simple arrays

We are beginning to realize that there is a need to be able to store and manipulate multiple values in a program. If there are relatively few values, simple variables can possibly be used, but consider the following example.

Suppose we have several hundred scores between 0 and 19 which have to be analyzed for frequency of occurrence of each score. We could set up 20 counters, one for each score. As the scores are read in, the counter corresponding to the score could be incremented. It would be very unwieldy if we had to invent 20 different names for the counters, and then use a big switch-statement every time one of them needed updating. What we need is the concept of the ***i*th variable** so that we can read a value, say i, and then update $counter_i$. Programming languages provide for this facility with the **array**.

Form of an array

An array is a bounded collection of elements of the same type, each of which can be selected by indexing with an integer from 0 upwards to a limit specified when the array is created. The relevant form is:

Array declaration

```
type arrayid [ ] = new type [limit];
type arrayid [ ] = {values};
```

The first form creates an array variable called *arrayid* which references a sequence of variables known as array elements which are indexed from 0 to *limit*–1. The *type* may be any primitive type or class or another array.

The second form does the same but also initializes each array element to the values given. The limit of the array is the number of elements listed minus one.

Arrays can be declared to contain any type or class, but the index and hence the limit must always be an integer. The limit gives the number of elements in the array, with each element being indexed by a number in the range from 0 to *limit*–1. Examples of array declarations of the first form shown above are:

```
int     frequencies [] = new int [20];
Times   periods []     = new Times [8];
String countryCode [] = new String [175];
```

The `frequencies` array will have 20 integers, numbered 0 to 19. There will be 8 times in the `periods` array, numbered 0 to 7, and 175 strings stored in the `countryCode` array numbered 0 to 174. Notice that array names are frequently, though not always, given as plurals.

The second form creates an array with initial values. The size of the array is then deduced from the number of values given, for example:

```
char vowels [] = {'a','e','i','o','u'};
```

The `vowels` array has five characters, numbered from 0 to 4.

The array model

Java's array model reflects that of its object model, so that we can draw diagrams showing what each of the declarations above means. The notation for an array is shown in Figure 6.1. The array variable is distinguished from other variables by its square brackets. The

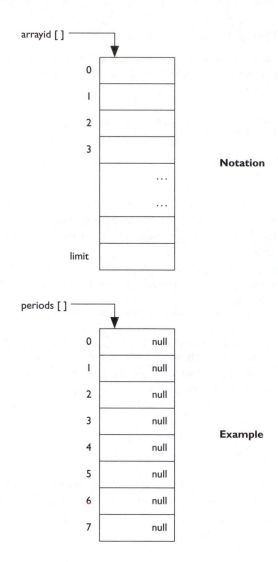

Figure 6.1 *Notation for an array.*

arrow to the array itself will usually go downwards, so that the indices can be listed as well as the array values. We can just have the array identifier, in which case we shadow the box to indicate multiple values.

The array declaration creates space for each element and, if these are primitive types, they are given the appropriate initialization. In this case, integers are initialized to zero. The next declaration of `periods` has elements that are going to be objects. They are not objects yet, but object variables. Each will have to go through its own new process to be created as an object in its own right. Meanwhile, their default values are null, as shown in the diagram.

Accessing array elements

To access an array element, we give the name of the array variable and an index expression enclosed in square brackets. The index is sometimes known as the **subscript**. For example, we could have:

```
periods[3] = new Times (11,0);

for (int i=0; i<20; i++) {
   frequencies[i] = (int) (Math.random*100);
}

countryCode[27] = "South Africa";

System.out.println(vowels[3]);
```

Remember that arrays are always indexed starting at 0, so that the last example here will print the fourth element, which is 'o', not 'i'.

Going back to the array diagrams, consider the one for the `periods` array and what will happen after we assign a new object into `periods[3]`, as above. The diagram will be as shown in Figure 6.2. Thus at this stage we can validly refer to:

```
periods[3].hour
periods[3].addTime(30);
```

but not to any other element of the array, apart from for instantiation or for checking whether the reference is null.

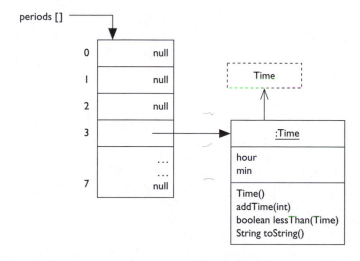

Figure 6.2 *Diagram of the* `periods` *array after one element has been assigned.*

| EXAMPLE 6.1 | Frequency count |

Problem   The frequencies of several hundred scores between 0 and 19 have to be calculated.

Solution   The solution has already been outlined at the beginning of the section. We set up an array and as each score is calculated or read, the appropriate element of the array is incremented. The algorithm is so simple that we go straight on to the program.

Program   The program uses the random number generator to create 100 numbers between 0 and 19 for testing purposes. The important line is

```
scoreFreqs [score]++;
```

which is where the relevant element of the array is incremented.

```
import javagently.*;

class Frequencies {
  /* The Frequencies Program       by J M Bishop Dec 1996
   * ------------------------       Java 1.1
   *                                updated May 2000
   * Counts the frequencies of scores from 0 to 19.
   * Tested by generating random numbers.
   * Illustrates simple array handling
   */

  Frequencies () {

    int maxscore = 20;
    int scoreFreqs [] = new int [maxscore];
    int score;

    for (int i=0; i < 100; i++) {
        score = (int) (Math.random() * maxscore);
        scoreFreqs[score] ++;
    }
    System.out.println("Table of Score Frequencies\n"+
                       "==========================\n\n"+
                       " Score occurred");
    for (int i = 0; i<maxscore; i++) {
      System.out.println(Stream.format(i, 6) +
                         Stream.format(scoreFreqs[i], 6));
    }
```

```
    }

  public static void main (String [] args) {
    new Frequencies ();
  }
}
```

Testing   Sample output would be

```
Table of Score Frequencies
===========================

Score    occurred
  0         2
  1         6
  2         7
  3         2
  4         4
  5         5
  6         2
  7         3
  8         3
  9         9
 10         8
 11         5
 12         7
 13         5
 14         7
 15         5
 16         6
 17         4
 18         6
 19         4
```

It would be interesting to view this table as a histogram: this possibility is taken up in Problem 6.10.

Properties of arrays

Element type

Arrays can be formed of any type or class, from simple types to objects to arrays themselves. The last leads to multidimensional arrays, discussed in detail in Section 6.2.

Size

The size of an array is limited only by the computer's memory, which is usually adequate for most applications. The size is **fixed** at the time that the array is created, and cannot be changed thereafter.

Delayed sizing

The declaration of an array can be done in two stages: one to declare the array name and create the reference, and then later another to set up the storage. This option is very useful when the size of the array is going to be read in as a data item. We can then say:

```
int A [];
```

and later on when a value n has been read in or otherwise calculated, we say

```
A = new A [n];
```

which will establish the full array.

Array operator

The only operator that applies to a whole array is assignment. Assigning one array to another, though, does not create a copy of the whole array. Instead, it copies the references, so that both arrays will refer to the same storage, and changes made to one will affect the other. For example, given the declaration of A above, then if we have the following sequence:

```
int B [];
B = A;
B[3] = 81;
```

both B and A refer to the same elements, as can be seen in Figure 6.3, and both A[3] and B[3] have the value 81.

Copies of the actual values of arrays can be made in the same way as can copies of objects, by a method called **cloning**, and this topic is taken up in Section 8.3. Should we wish to copy an array at this point, we could do it simply by creating a new array and copying each element over using a loop.

Element access

Java is quite firm about allowing access only to array elements that actually exist. Every time an array is accessed, the index supplied is checked against the bounds given in the array declaration. If the index is out of bounds, an `ArrayIndexOutOfBoundsException` is thrown. The exception can be caught and handled, and if it is not, the program halts. For

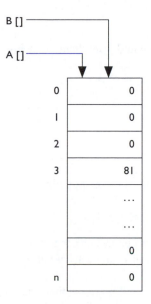

Figure 6.3 *An array referred to by two array variables.*

example, with the above declarations, both `frequencies[100]` and `vowels[5]` would cause errors.

Length

The length of an array can be seen by means of a special property associated with every array, called `length`. Thus

```
frequency.length
```

will yield 20. In other words, `length` returns the limit used in the declaration. Notice that `length` is not a method, but a property, and therefore does not have parentheses after it.

Parameters

Arrays can be passed as parameters to methods. A very convenient feature of Java is that the formal parameter in the method does not have to specify the length of the array it expects. The method can accept arrays of the correct type of any length, and processes them by using the `length` property described above. A prime example is the main method which declares[1]

---

[1] There is an alternative array syntax where the brackets come before the array identifier. This syntax has been used in the main method to date. It means exactly the same as having the brackets after the array identifier.

```
main (String [] args)
```

If there are any arguments, `main` could print them out using a for-loop as follows:

```
for (int i=0; i < args.length; i++)
   System.out.println(args[i]);
```

Array and class interaction

There are at least three different ways in which arrays and classes can interact.

1. An array of a class of objects. For example, Figure 6.2 showed the representation of:

```
Times period [] = new Times [8];
```

Each element of the array can be instantiated as a `Times` object, and then variables and methods applicable to times can be accessed, as in `period[3].hour`.

2. A class containing an array and methods that operate on it. Talking generally, we might have an array `A` inside a class and provide `get` and `set` methods to operate on elements of the array, as in:

```
class IntArray {
   // Example of a private array with get and set methods
   private int A [];

     IntArray (int n) {
       A = new int [n];
     }

     int get (int i) {
       return A[i];
     }

     void set (int i, int x) {
       A[i] = x;
     }

     public String toString () {
       String s = "";
       for (int i=0; i<A.length; i++) {
         s += "   "+ A[i];
       }
     return s;
   }
}
```

A is marked as private because in this class, the only access to the array is via the methods `get` and `set`. A model diagram for `IntArray` is shown in Figure 6.4.

Objects of class `intArray` can be declared, and each one will get its own instance of the A array. For example, we might have:

```
IntArray marks = new IntArray(50); // we expect 50 marks
int m;

for (int i=0; i<50; i++) {
  m = (int) (Math.random()*100);
  marks.put (i, m);
}
System.out.println(marks);
```

The model diagram in this case is shown in Figure 6.5. In this diagram, A is placed at the end of the marks object and is shown in a section with vertical bars: these indicate that A is private.

3. A class containing methods that operate on array parameters (Figure 6.5). The class could be something like:

```
class ArrayUtils {

  static int max (int A []) {
    // finds the maximum element of A, A[i] and returns it
    return A[i];
  }

  static void sort (int A[]) {
    // sorts the elements of A
  }
}
```

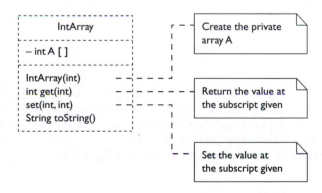

Figure 6.4 *The* `IntArray` *class.*

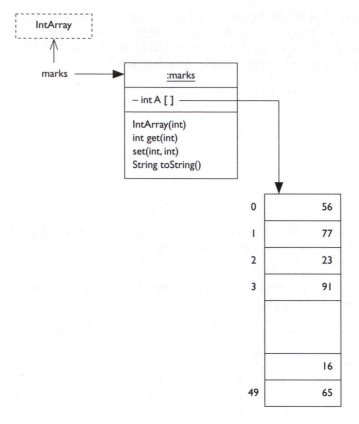

Figure 6.5 *A class containing an array.*

where the contents of max and sort still need to be defined. Notice that these methods are class methods, and that we have a utility type class defined here. To use it, we could say:

```
int frequencies [] = new int [20];
int max = ArrayUtils.max(frequencies);
ArrayUtils.sort(frequencies);
```

Figure 6.6 shows that there exists only one array, frequencies. Each method in ArrayUtils has a formal parameter, which is an array variable. When a call to, say, max is made, the contents of frequencies is copied into A, so that A is now directed to frequencies, and the method operates on that array.

These three techniques are illustrated in the examples that follow.

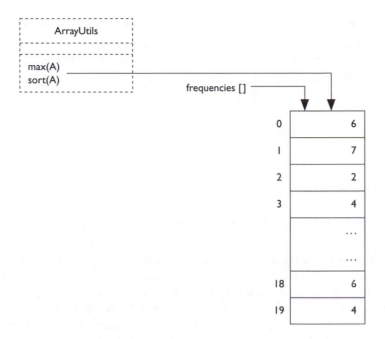

Figure 6.6 *A class with methods that work on array parameters.*

Arrays as an abstraction

In this book, we delayed introducing arrays in order to emphasize the control operations in processing data. Very often, one will find a solution to a problem that makes use of an array, where in fact it is not strictly necessary. Is this wrong? No, it is not wrong; it merely represents a different abstraction of a solution.

Consider the following problem: we need to read in 20 values and find the smallest and the largest. There are two approaches to the solution:

■ Read in the 20 values, keeping track of the smallest and largest 'on the fly', in a similar way to that shown in Example 4.5.

■ Read the 20 values into an array, then scan the array through twice to find the smallest and then the largest values.

Instinctively, the first approach seems more efficient, and on the face of it, it is no more complicated than the second. But the balance changes if we take into account methods we already have in stock. The differences are illustrated in Figure 6.7.

The concept we are highlighting here is called **separation of concerns**. Suppose we already have methods to calculate the minimum and maximum values from a given array (as we already postulated for ArrayUtils above). In the first algorithm, all the operations are mixed up in one process. In the second, we identify three concerns that can be handled separately. These are the reading, finding the minimum and finding the maxi-

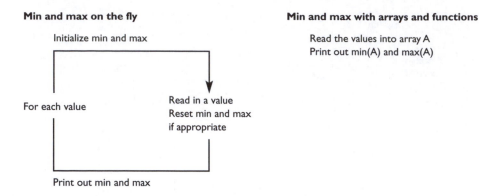

Figure 6.7 *Two algorithms for finding the minimum and maximum in an array.*

mum. The development of each process can proceed independently in time, and they are also identified separately in space as three different methods. In the long run, the second approach can enable us to reap the benefits of readability and be easier to manage.

These ideas are illustrated in Example 6.2, which, strictly speaking, does not need an array, but which uses one to good effect to make an easily understandable program. On the other hand, later examples do need arrays, as did Example 6.1.

EXAMPLE 6.2   Diving competitions

Problem   The judging of diving competitions relies on judges from several countries. In order to avoid bias, such as judges rewarding competitors from their home country with higher scores, the result for a single dive is calculated as the average of all the scores, less the highest and lowest score. We would like to computerize these calculations.

Algorithm   As outlined just above, there are two possible approaches to this problem. The three values required – the sum, and the lowest and highest scores – can all be calculated on the fly while the scores are read in. Alternatively, we can read the values in and then assess them. Assuming we choose the second approach, then there are once again two options. These are to compute the three values simultaneously in a single loop, or to have three different loops, perhaps in three different methods, to calculate them. Since the calculations are really so simple, we shall adopt the first approach this time, and do them all together in one loop.

Class design   Clearly there is scope for a class in this program, but the question is: what should it model? What is the real concept that is worth putting in a class? There are various options:

- One **judge**, with all his or her scores for each dive. If there are three dives then this class would have an array of three integer scores.

■ One **dive**, with all the scores for each of the judges. If there are eight judges, then this class will contain an array of eight integer scores.

As a competition progresses in time over each dive, it makes sense to keep the scores per dive. Elaborations on this theme are considered in the case study at the end of the chapter.

Another consideration when designing classes is that we should endeavour to keep input and output separately. A class that models a physical object should not be tied to input and output streams. The correct way to interface with the outside world is to perform the input–output in a driver part of the program and to use `get` and `set` methods to alter the data. To get the data out in a printable form, `toString` is the standard method to implement.

To start us off, the definition of the `Dive` class without method bodies is:

```
class Dive {

    /* The Dive Class     by J M Bishop Dec 1996
     * ---------------     Java 1.1 October 1997
     *                     adapted from Judge, May 2000
     * Stores and assesses diving scores for one dive.
     * Illustrates arrays
     */


    int minJudge, maxJudge, minScore, maxScore, sum;

    private int scores [];
    private int noOfJudges;

    Dive (int njudges) {...}
    void setScore (int judge, int score) {...}
    void assessScores() {...}
}
```

`Dive` has a constructor that is responsible for setting up the array of the correct size for the number of judges supplied. The array itself is not part of what is publicly available, though. Then whenever a mark is read in, it is entered in the array via `setScore`. When all the values are in, `assessScores` will run through the array and produce values in the five variables indicated. These values are printed out by the calling method using

```
d.println("Scores " + dive.minScore + " from judge "
          + dive.minJudge + " and " + dive.maxScore +
          " from judge " + dive.maxJudge + " excluded.");
```

The relationship between a class for dives and the array of scores falls into the second category of array and class interaction described above. The scores are kept in a class and we have two methods, `setScore` and `assessScores`, to assign them and total them.

Program   Here follows the full class:

```java
import java.io.*;

class Dive {

    /* The Dive Class     by J M Bishop Dec 1996
     *                         Java 1.1 October 1997
     * Stores and assesses diving scores for one dive.
     *
     * Illustrates arrays
     */

    int minJudge, maxJudge, minScore, maxScore, sum;

    private int noOfJudges;
    private int score [];

    Dive (int n) {
      noOfJudges = n;
      score = new int [noOfJudges];
    }

    void setScore (int i, int s) {
      score [i] = s;
    }

    void assessScores() {
        minScore = 10;
        maxScore = 0;
        sum = 0;
        for (int i = 0; i < noOfJudges; i++) {
          sum += score[i];
          if (score[i] <= minScore) {
              minScore = score[i];
              minJudge = i;
          }
          if (score[i] > maxScore) {
              maxScore = score[i];
              maxJudge = i;
          }
        }
    }
```

```
      minJudge++;
      maxJudge++;
   }


}
```

Notice that we could not use the `Math.min` and `Math.max` methods in `assessScores` because we need to record the array element index as well as its value when finding the minimum and maximum, so that we can print out the 'culprits' later.

And here is the program. Notice that we use the `format` method of the `Stream` class to ensure that we get only a reasonable number of fractional digits when the calculations are done. One seems to be standard. In addition, we make use of the `Display` to enable the scores to be entered easily.

```
import java.io.*;
import javagently.*;

class DivingCompetition {

   /* The Diving program     by J M Bishop Dec 1996
    * ------------------      Java 1.1 October 1997
    *                         updated May 2000
    * Uses the Judge class to record the
    * correct scores for dives.
    * Illustrates calling class methods,
    * and typed methods and using arrays
    * in a separate class. */

   Display d = new Display ("Diving Competition");
   int noOfDives = 3;
   int noOfJudges = 8;

   DivingCompetition () throws IOException {

      headings ();

      double result, total = 0;
      // There is one Dives object which records 8 scored
      // and is reused for each dive

     Dive dive = new Dive (noOfJudges);
     int score;
```

```
      for (int i=0; i < noOfDives; i++) {
        d.println("Dive no: "+(i+1));
        d.println("Enter the scores for the judges");
        d.ready("Press ready to continue");
        for (int j = 0; j < noOfJudges; j++) {
          score = d.getInt("Judge "+(j+1));
          dive.setScore(j, score);
        }
        dive.assessScores();
        result = (double) (dive.sum
              - dive.minScore - dive.maxScore)
              / (double) (noOfJudges - 2);
        total += result;
        d.println("Scores " + dive.minScore + " from judge "
            + dive.minJudge + " and " + dive.maxScore +
            " from judge "
            + dive.maxJudge + " excluded.");
        d.println("Result is: " + Text.writeDouble(result,5,1));
      }
      System.out.println("Diving average is : "+
            Text.writeDouble(total/noOfDives,5,3));
    }


    void headings () {
      d.println ("Diving Score Calculator\n" +
                  "=======================\n");

      d.println("For each of " + noOfDives +
        " dives give scores for "+noOfJudges+" judges.");
      for (int i = 1; i<=noOfJudges; i++)
        d.prompt ("Judge "+i,0);
    }


    public static void main (String [] args) throws IOException {
      new DivingCompetition ();
    }

}
```

Testing A test run of the program would produce output as shown in Figure 6.8.

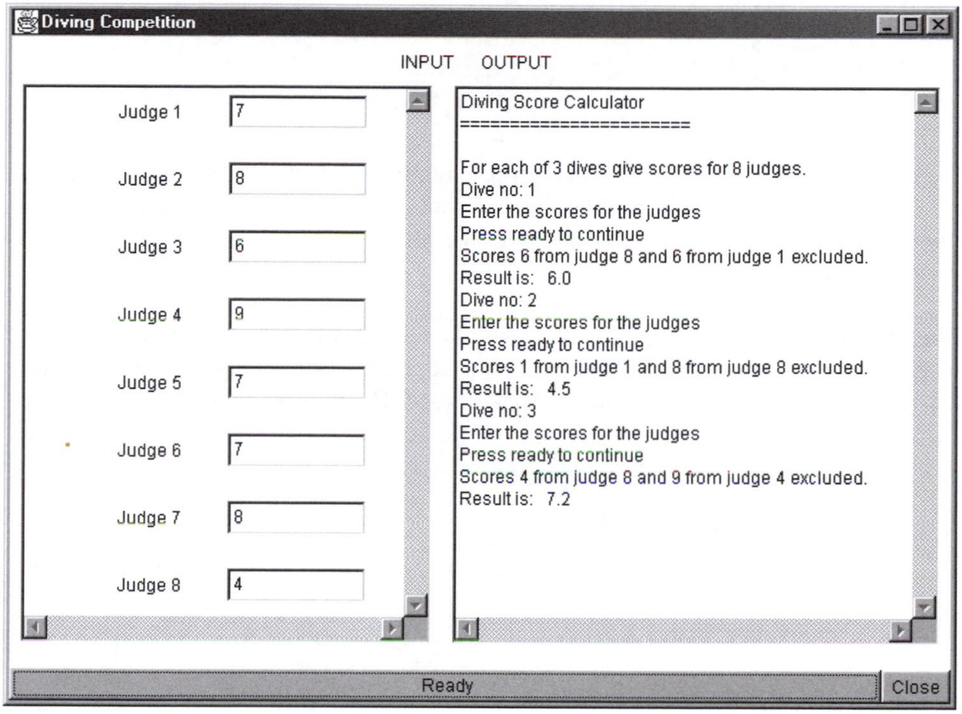

Figure 6.8 *Display from the diving program.*

EXAMPLE 6.3   Statistical analysis

Problem Common statistical operations on array data include calculating the mean and standard deviation. We would like to develop methods for these operations with a view to making them readily available for use from a library, as discussed in Section 4.3.

Approach If we have a set of measurements x_i we can analyze them to find the mean $\bar{x}$ which gives the average measurement, and the standard deviation s, which shows the amount by which measurements are likely to differ from the mean. In other words, the standard deviation indicates the spread of the measurements.

Theory The mean of a set of measurements x_i ($i = 1, \ldots, n$) is defined to be

$$\bar{x} = \frac{1}{n} \sum_{i=1}^{n} x_i$$

and the formula for the standard deviation is:

$$s = \sqrt{\frac{\sum\limits_{i=1}^{n}(x_i - \bar{x})^2}{n-1}}$$

We can allow for expected errors and intrinsic randomness by saying that the result of a set of measurements will be within a certain standard deviation. In many cases we can say that the true result is in the range $\bar{x} \pm 2s$, i.e. the mean plus or minus twice the standard deviation.

Method design   It is straightforward to write a method to calculate the mean, just by using a for-loop. However, the formula for the standard deviation uses the mean, and so has to be calculated after the mean has been decided. The two methods are as follows:

```
public static double mean (double a [], int n) {
   double sum = 0.0;
   for (int i=1; i<=n; i++)
     sum += a[i];
   return sum / n;
}
```

```
public static double stddev (double a [], int n, double ave) {
   double sum = 0;
   for (int i = 1; i<=n; i++)
     sum += (ave - a[i]) * (ave - a[i]);
   return Math.sqrt(sum / (n-1));
}
```

Both methods have an array as a parameter, but notice that we also include n as the number of elements actually in the array. This is because a large array may be used for different numbers of elements. When it is passed to mean or stddev, a.length will give the actual large limit (say 1000) rather than the current usage of the array (say 256). Now let's investigate how to get them into a library.

Expanding the library   Clearly, mean and stddev are two excellent candidates for inclusion in a library of useful routines that we started developing with Filer in Example 4.9. Within Java the structure of such a library is: methods in classes in a package. The Java package that we have already encountered is java.io, and of course the very useful javagently done for this book. The javagently package offers the classes: Stream, Display and Graph.

Rather than add to javagently, we shall use the myutilities package which already has the Filer class in it. The Java way to create the methods in a new class in a new package is:

```
package myutilities;

public class Stats {

  public static double mean (double a [], int n) {
    ... as before
  }

  public static double stddev (double a [], int n, double ave) {
    ... as before
  }
}
```

The above class is placed in a file called `Stats.java` in the usual way, and this class must be in a directory called `myutilities`. It is compiled in that directory, and the classpath is augmented to include the directory *in which* `myutilities` resides. See Figure 4.2 for an example. In other words, we do *not* put `myutilities` in the classpath: we give the directory in which `myutilities` is to be found. Once this has been done, any program that wishes to use the methods simply imports `myutilities.*` and can call the methods as in:

```
ave = Stats.mean (myreadings, number);
```

Notice that both the class and its methods are declared as public, so that they can be seen from other packages, notably the default package associated with ordinary programs.

EXAMPLE 6.4   The lifetime of light bulbs

Problem   Savanna Lights manufactures light bulbs, and bulbs are chosen at random from the production line, to see how long they last. For quality control purposes, there must be regular reports on the mean lifetime and standard deviation in hours.

Algorithm   In setting up the array, we use option 2, discussed above, and declare a large array, from which we use a variable number of elements, depending on how many data items come in. Of course, we also check that no more than the maximum number of elements is entered. The segment of Java to handle such input is:

```
double hourreadings [] = new double[max];
BufferedReader in = Text.open(System.in);
int n = 0;

try {
  for (n=1; n<max; n++)
```

```
      hourreadings[n] = Text.readInt(in);
   System.out.println("Can only take "+(max-1)+" samples");
 }
catch (EOFException e) { }


n--;
System.out.println("That's the data, thanks");
System.out.println("There were "+n+" samples");
```

The intention is that the Stats class methods will process values with $i = 1$ to n. Because the formula for the standard deviation includes division by $n - 1$, we check whether $n = 1$, to prevent a runtime error.

Program

```
import java.io.*;
import javagently.*;
import myutilities.*;

class LightBulbAnalysis {

  /* The light bulb program          J M Bishop 1990, 1998
   * ----------------------           updated May 2000
   *
   * Calculates the average life of light bulbs
   * Uses the mean and stddev methods created
   * in a Stats class in the myutilities package.
   *
   * Illustrates array i/o again
   */

    LightBulbAnalysis () throws IOException {
      int max = 101;
      Display display = new Display("Light Bulb Analysis");

      display.println ("***** Light Bulb Analysis *****\n");
      display.println ("Statistical analysis of the lifetime of "+
                      "light bulbs");
      display.println("with no. of readings < "+max);
      display.println("Enter in the readings pressing ready after each
                      one");
```

```
      display.println("Enter yes for stop with the last reading");
      display.prompt("Hours",0);
      display.prompt("Stop", "no");

      double hourReadings [] = new double[max];
      int n = 0;
      boolean stop = false;

      for (n=1; n<max & !stop; n++) {
        display.ready();
        hourReadings[n] = display.getDouble("Hours");
        display.print(Stream.format(hourReadings[n],6,1)+" ");
        stop = display.getString("Stop").equalsIgnoreCase("yes");
      }
      n--;
      display.println("\nThat's the data, thanks");
      display.println("There were "+n+" samples");

      if (n == 1) {
        System.out.println("Mean = "+
           Text.writeDouble(Stats.mean(hourReadings,n),10,6)+
           " but standard deviation not defined for n=1");
      }
      else {
        double ave = Stats.mean(hourReadings,n);
        display.println("Mean = "+Text.format(ave,6,2)+
                           " hours");
        display.println("Standard deviation = " +
           Stream.format(

           Stats.stddev(hourReadings,n,ave),6,2) + " hours");
      }
    }

  public static void main (String [] args) throws IOException {
    new LightBulbAnalysis ();
  }
}
```

Testing   Any number of values can be read in. In Figure 6.9 we try a random selection of six.

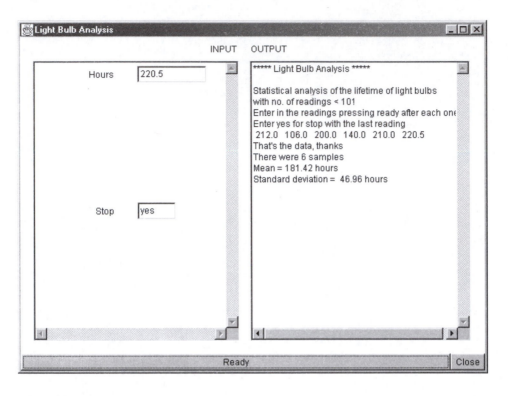

Figure 6.9 *Display of the light bulb analysis program.*

In order to check that the answers are correct, we can work out the formula by hand, or with a calculator. We can also submit controlled test data. For example, 5 values all the same, say 200, should give a mean of 200 and a standard deviation of zero. Try it out. (It does work.)

6.2   Tables

Tables appear commonly in computer applications. The data are arranged in rows and columns. Since Java permits array elements to be of any type, including arrays themselves, arrays of multiple dimensions can be built up, which are known as a **multi-dimensional arrays**. Most of the time, though there will not be more than two dimensions, and the resulting structure is known as a **matrix** or **table**.

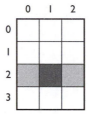

Figure 6.10 *A typical table.*

Consider a typical table 4 by 3, such as that shown in Figure 6.10. In Java, the declaration would be:

```
double table [] [] = new double [4][3];
```

Rows are always mentioned first in the declaration. This enables a single row of the table to be represented. For example,

```
table [2]
```

would give the shaded row in Figure 6.10. Each element of the row can be selected by indexing twice, as in:

```
table [2] [1]
```

which would give the darker element. Figure 6.11 shows the model diagram for such a table.

As an example of how table rows can be manipulated, to swap two rows, i and j, we could say:

```
int row [] = new int [2];
row = table[i];
table[i] = table[j];
table[j] = row;
```

| EXAMPLE 6.5 | Gold exploration |

Problem Savanna Exploration Inc. has obtained data of infrared readings of a portion of desert where gold is believed to be present. The data should show up the boundaries of a gold reef, based on readings that are greater than the average of those around them. Can you help find the gold?

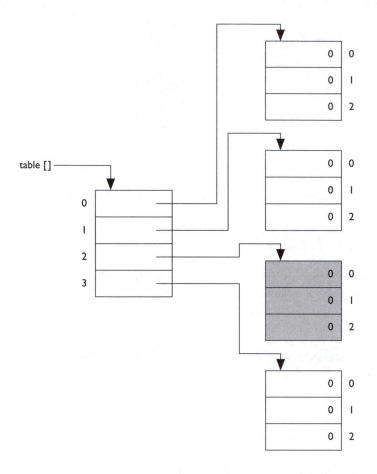

Figure 6.11 *Model diagram for a table.*

Solution The map of the readings can be considered, a point at a time, and a corresponding map printed out showing those with higher than average infrared levels. For example, given the following data on a sample 8 × 8 grid:

```
21  21  22  30  40  21  34  45
21  22  23  30  45  21  37  40
22  23  24  45  46  47  38  39
22  23  24  35  46  47  38  38
23  24  25  36  46  49  37  36
23  24  25  37  39  48  36  35
23  24  25  25  26  25  26  25
23  25  26  27  28  29  30  31
```

we could deduce the corresponding map:

```
******* Savanna Exploration Inc. *****
Will use test data in gold.dat if file open is unsuccessful
  sam.dat does not exist.
Try again
mali.dat
We shall find gold!

Map of possible boundaries of the gold reef
============================================

 0 1 2 3 4 5 6 7
0
1           *   *
2   *     * * *
3         * *
4   *     * * *
5         *   *
6
7
Good luck prospecting!
```

Algorithm   The high-level algorithm is:

Gold exploration
Open the file and create the tables
Read in the data
Assess each point, creating the corresponding map of blanks and asterisks
Print the map

Each of these steps can be refined into double loops scanning the whole table. For example, assessing a point consists of adding up the values to its north, south, east and west and dividing by 4. If the point itself has a higher reading than its neighbours, we mark it as part of the reef on the map. Thus there are two tables: data and map.

```
point = data[i][j];
average = (data[i-1][j]+data[i+1][j]
               +data[i][j-1]+data[i][j+1])/4;
if (point > average) {
  map[i][j] = cover;
}
```

We must also consider how to deal with data points on the edge of the grid. We shall assume that there is sufficient redundancy in the data to allow us to ignore the points on the boundary. Thus we run the assessing loops from 1 to rowmax-1 and 1 to colmax-1 respectively.

Class design   In this solution, there are two data structures, both tables. The elements of the tables are double values and characters respectively. For this reason, there is no need to specify a separate class which models anything and is repeatedly instantiated. However, there is a good call to set up numerous useful methods.

Program   The `Gold` class is:

```java
import java.io.*;
import javagently.*;
import myutilities.*;

class GoldExploration {

  /* The Gold class     by J M Bishop Jan 1997
   *                        Java 1.1 October 1997
   * Transforms raw geological readings into a character map of a
   * possible gold reef.
   * Illustrates two different multidimensional arrays in a class.
   */

  int rowMax = 8;
  int colMax = 8;
  char map [][]     = new char[rowMax][colMax];
  double data [][] = new double[rowMax][colMax];
  char blank = ' ';
  char cover = '*';

  Stream fin;

  GoldExploration () throws IOException{
    introduction();
    getData();
    assess();
    report();
  }

  public void getData() throws IOException {
    for (int i = 0; i < rowMax; i++)
      for (int j = 0; j < colMax; j++)
        data[i][j] = fin.readDouble();
  }

  public void assess() {
    double point, average;
    for (int i = 0; i < rowMax; i++) {
      for (int j = 0; j < colMax; j++) {
        map[i][j] = blank;
```

```
        }
    }
    for (int i = 1; i < rowMax-1; i++) {
        for (int j = 1; j < colMax-1; j++) {
            point = data[i][j];
            average = (data[i-1][j] + data[i+1][j] +
                    data[i][j-1] + data[i][j+1]) / 4;
            if (point > average)
                map[i][j] = cover;
            }
        }
    }

    public void report() {
        System.out.println("Map of possible boundaries of the "+
                    "gold reef");
        System.out.println("================================="+
                    "========");
        System.out.println();
        System.out.print(" ");
        for (int j = 0; j < colMax; j++) {
            System.out.print(j+" ");
        }
        System.out.println();
        for (int i = 0; i < rowMax; i++) {
            System.out.print(i+" ");
            for (int j = 0; j < colMax; j++)
                System.out.print(map[i][j]+" ");
            System.out.println();
        }
        System.out.println("Good luck prospecting!");
    }

    void introduction () throws IOException {
        System.out.println("******* Savanna Exploration Inc. *****");
        System.out.println("Will use test data in gold.dat"+
                    " if file open is unsuccessful");
        fin = Filer.open("");
        System.out.println("We shall find gold!\n");
    }

    public static void main(String[] args) throws IOException {
      new GoldExploration ();
    }

}
```

The `introduction` method makes use of the file opening class we developed in Example 4.9 and which is stored in package `myutilities`. If a file is not found, we open up a default map that we know exists, called `gold.dat`.

Testing   The expected output to the file has already been given. We should test other maps, including one which has all values the same. Here is the output for such input:

```
******* Savanna Exploration Inc. *****
Will use test data in gold.dat if file open is unsuccessful
sam.dat does not exist.
Try again
same.dat
We shall find gold!


Map of possible boundaries of the gold reef
============================================

  0 1 2 3 4 5 6 7
0
1
2
3
4
5
6
7
Good luck prospecting!
```

In other words, if there is no gradient to the data, there is unlikely to be a reef.

6.3   The `Graph` class

Scientific insight relies heavily on visualizing what is going on. It is not as easy to read meaning into tables of numbers as it is to make deduction from a graph, no matter how roughly drawn. Errors can remain undetected in tables more easily than in their graphic equivalents.

Java has very good facilities for drawing at the dot and line level, but constructing a graph from such primitive components, complete with axes, is quite a lengthy process. In order to enable the insight we need at little programming cost, we have devised a very easy to use `Graph` class. As with the other two classes, `Display` and `Stream`, `Graph` will be used as a case study itself later on in the book.

Graph class methods

Here is a list of its ten methods and the four colour constants that Graph defines:

The Graph class

```
//Basic
new Graph ()          - Compulsory instantiation
add(x, y)             - Adds a point to a list
                      - Expects points to come in x-order
showGraph()           - Compulsory call to get the axes and
                        graph drawn and the window made visible


//Advanced
new Graph (graphTitle, xAxisTitle, yAxisTitle)
                      - Version of instantiation with labelling
                        options. Use empty strings if not all
                        titles applicable
nextGraph()           - Starts a new graph on the same axes.
                        One showGraph call applies to all the
                        graphs
setColor(int 0 to 3)  - Choice of black, magenta, blue, red
                        (constants are available instead of
                        numbers)
setSymbol(boolean)    - Deduced from the colour
                        (convenient if colours are being set)
setSymbol(int 0 to 3) - circle, upside down triangle, triangle,
                        square (used if colours are not being set)
setLine(boolean)      - Normally on, can be turned off. Used when
                        lines between points don't make sense
setTitle(String)      - Will appear on a key alongside the symbol
                        and/or in the chosen colour
black, magenta        - constants for colours. Equivalent to 0-3
blue, red
```

To use Graph, we must declare a Graph object as in its simplest form

```
Graph g = new Graph ();
```

or we can supply titles for the graph and axes as explained. Thereafter, all we have to do is add each new (*x*, *y*) point to the graph, and then show the graph. In other words, for a simple graph, we only need three methods.

How `Graph` works

The `Graph` class takes the point supplied to it, and adds it to a list of points. When `showGraph` is called, the minimum and maximum points values for both *x* and *y* are used to determine the scale for the axes. There is no set axes that the points fit onto, and each graph window will therefore have a different set of axes. In the case of the above example, the minimum and maximum values as read off the display are:

x	*y*
10.00	0.0628
50.00	1.5708

The origin and end of each axis are labelled accordingly. No attempt is made to place other labels along an axis, as there is no sure way of predicting what the user would like. The graph provides a rough impression of what is going on: for accurate values, the table printed on the display is used.

Advanced features

Before we get to the extra methods `Graph` provides, we discuss the issue of multiple graphs. Since `Graph` is a class, we can create multiple `Graph` objects, and each will have its own window. A program can therefore add points to different windows. This technique would be appropriate if we wanted the axes to differ.

If, however, we want to compare different graphs on the same axes, then we call `nextGraph`. This method starts up a new set of data points, d, for a new graph, and resets the parameters as follows:

```
d.plotType = black;
d.symbolRequired = false;
d.colorRequired = false;
d.titleRequired = false;
d.lineRequired = true;
```

Using the methods shown above, all of these can then be changed by the program. For example, a full set of changes would be:

```
g.setColor(blue);
g.setSymbol(true);
g.setTitle("Rainfall");
g.setLine(false);
```

There is a relationship between the colour and the symbol: both map onto the integers 0 to 3, and in the absence of instructions to the contrary, the same integer is used for the symbol as that set for the colour. Thus black lines have circles, blue have triangles, and so on. If in the above set of instructions, we want a blue line with circles, we would add:

```
g.setSymbol(0);
```

Although colour is very effective on a screen, it cannot be shown easily in black and white, so graphs that are to be copied into reports should use symbols more often than those that are not. If there is no title, the symbol is still shown in the key at the bottom of the graph. If there is no symbol or title, then the colours are not explained in a key: it is assumed that the user can see them.

EXAMPLE 6.6   Rainfall statistics

Problem   The Savanna Weather Department has kept statistics on monthly rainfall figures for the past 20 years. Now it would like to calculate

- the average rainfall for each month;
- the standard deviation for each month.

Solution   The table of rainfall figures that is provided by a clerk will look something like this:

Year	Jan	Feb	Mar	Apr	May	Jun	Jul	Aug	Sep	Oct	Nov	Dec
1989	20	22	17	14	5	0	0	0	7	12	30	20
1990	22	24	19	12	0	0	3	0	8	15	20	25
1991	17	17	17	15	0	0	0	0	6	17	8	20
1992	10	10	10	5	0	0	0	0	0	12	10	15
1993	10	10	10	5	0	0	0	0	0	12	10	15
1994	20	22	17	14	5	0	0	0	7	12	30	20
1995	22	24	19	12	0	0	3	0	8	15	20	25
1996	17	17	17	15	0	0	0	0	6	17	8	20
1997	25	30	25	15	7	0	0	0	20	15	20	30
1998	25	30	25	15	7	0	0	0	20	15	20	30

The data will be stored in this form in file. As the values are read in, they are stored in a matrix that is indexed by both the years and the months. Since the rainfall for a month seems to be the crucial figure, the matrix should be structured so that a whole column can be moved around at once. To do this, we make months the first subscript, and years the second. In other words, we would like to represent the matrix as in Figure 6.12.

The appropriate Java declarations are:

```
static final int maxyear = 70;
double rainTable [] [] = new double [13][maxyear];
```

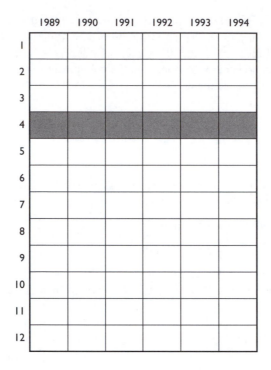

Figure 6.12 *Part of the matrix for storing rainfall data.*

Because it is natural to do so, we run the month subscript from 1 to 12, which means we declare the array as length 13 (allowing for the zeroth element that we will not use). `rainTable[4]` then gives all rainfall for all the available years for April. April's row is the shaded area in Figure 6.12.

Program design This program is a classic read–process–output program, where the input–output is based on files. Therefore we just create one class to handle everything, and call it from the main program. In addition to printing the data out and the results, we would like to draw a graph of the means for the various months and their respective standard deviations. Because the `Graph` class can only have points being added to one line at a time, we store the standard deviations in an array and then loop through them at the end, creating the second graph.

For the actual processing, we shall be able to make use of the mean and standard deviation methods stored in the `myutilities` package's `Stats` class as described in Example 6.3.

Program The program is set up to get data from the specific file `rain.data`. The name could be made a variable and be read in. Furthermore, because the results occupy a lot of space we have not used the display. The results will appear on the console output but we could send them to a file by running the program with a redirection, as in

```
java Weather > weather.out
```

The program follows:

```java
import java.io.*;
import javagently.*;
import myutilities.*;

class Weather {

  /*  The Weather program     by J M Bishop Jan 1997
   *  ====================     Graphics July 1999
   *                          updated June 2000
   *
   *  Calculates mean and standard deviation of rainfall
   *  for each month over the number of years provided.
   *
   *  Illustrates handling of a matrices and passing columns
   *  as parameters.
   *  The data must be in a file in the form:
   *  year followed by the 12 rainfall figures for
   *  the months of that year.
   */

  class RainBase {

    int base = 1950;
    int startyear, endyear = 0; // range from 1950 upwards

    // all arrays declared length 13 so months go from 1 to 12
    double rainTable [] [] = new double [13] [70];
    double averagetable [] = new double [13];
    double stddevTable [] = new double [13];

    Graph g = new Graph("Rainfall", "month", "cm");

    void readIn () throws IOException {
      Stream fin = new Stream("Rain.dat",Stream.READ);
      int actualYear = 0; // e.g. 1989
      int yearIndex = 0; // e.g. 0

      // The actual years are read in and might not be sorted
      // or contiguous. The yearIndex starts at 0 and is
      // used to store the data in an orderly manner.
```

```
      try {
        while (true) {
          actualYear = fin.readInt();
          System.out.print(actualYear+" ");
          if (yearIndex == 0) {
            startyear = actualYear;
          }
          for (int m = 1; m<=12; m++) {
            rainTable[m][yearIndex] = fin.readDouble();
            System.out.print(
                Stream.format(rainTable[m][yearIndex],6,1));
          }
          System.out.println();
          yearIndex++;
        }
      }
      catch (EOFException e) {
        // Pick up the last year of data read in.
        endyear = actualYear;
        System.out.println("Data read for "+startyear+" to "+
            endyear+"\n\n");
      }
    }


    void showResults () {
      System.out.println("Rainfall statistics for " +
          startyear + " to " + endyear);
      System.out.println("=========================" +
          "============\n");
      System.out.println("Month\tMean\tStd Deviation");
      int nyears = endyear-startyear+1;
      double a;
      g.setTitle("Mean");
      g.setSymbol(true);

      for (int m =1; m<=12; m++) {
        averagetable[m] = Stats.mean (rainTable[m], nyears);
        stddevTable[m] = Stats.stddev
            (rainTable[m], nyears, averagetable[m]);
        System.out.println(Stream.format(m,2)+
          Stream.format(averagetable[m],12,2)+
          Stream.format(stddevTable[m],12,4));
        g.add(m,averagetable[m]);
      }
```

```
    g.nextGraph();
    g.setColor(g.blue);
    g.setSymbol(true);
    g.setTitle("Standard Deviation");
    for (int m = 1; m <= 12; m++) {
      g.add (m, stddevTable[m]);
    }
    g.showGraph();
    }
  }

  public static void main (String args [])throws IOException {

    RainBase rain = new RainBase();

    rain.readIn ();
    rain.showResults ();
  }


}
```

Testing   For the data shown above, the output to the file would be as follows, and the graph is shown in Figure 6.13.

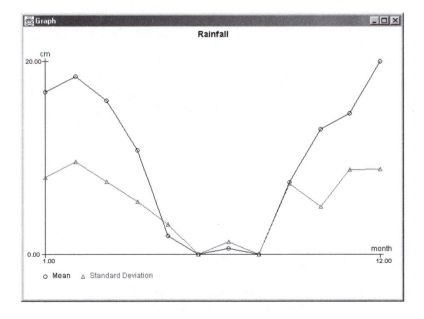

Figure 6.13   *Graphs from the weather program.*

1989	20.0	22.0	17.0	14.0	5.0	0.0	0.0	0.0	7.0	12.0	30.0	20.0
1990	22.0	24.0	19.0	12.0	0.0	0.0	3.0	0.0	8.0	15.0	20.0	25.0
1991	17.0	17.0	17.0	15.0	0.0	0.0	0.0	0.0	6.0	17.0	8.0	20.0
1992	10.0	10.0	10.0	5.0	0.0	0.0	0.0	0.0	0.0	12.0	10.0	15.0
1993	20.0	22.0	17.0	14.0	5.0	0.0	0.0	0.0	7.0	12.0	30.0	20.0
1994	22.0	24.0	19.0	12.0	0.0	0.0	3.0	0.0	8.0	15.0	20.0	25.0
1995	17.0	17.0	17.0	15.0	0.0	0.0	0.0	0.0	6.0	17.0	8.0	20.0
1996	25.0	30.0	25.0	15.0	7.0	0.0	0.0	0.0	20.0	15.0	20.0	30.0
1997	25.0	30.0	25.0	15.0	7.0	0.0	0.0	0.0	20.0	15.0	20.0	30.0
1998	10.0	10.0	10.0	5.0	0.0	0.0	0.0	0.0	0.0	12.0	10.0	45.0

Data read for 1989 to 1998

```
Rainfall statistics for 1989 to 1998
======================================
```

Month	Mean	Std Deviation
1	16.80	7.9833
2	18.40	9.5940
3	15.90	7.5344
4	10.80	5.4528
5	1.90	3.1073
6	0.00	0.0000
7	0.60	1.2649
8	0.00	0.0000
9	7.50	7.3522
10	13.00	4.9441
11	14.60	8.7965
12	23.00	11.5950

Once again, we have chosen realistic data, but that makes it harder to check that the answers are actually correct. Because we have drawn a graph, we can see that the results look correct, and we also know that the mean and standard deviation are working properly, because we tested them previously. That is one of the advantages of working with libraries.

6.4 Sorting and searching

Sorting and searching are very common operations in computing, and many systems provide high-level commands that enable data to be sorted or searched in any specified way. These commands rely on one of a number of algorithms, and every programmer should know at least one sorting algorithm and one searching algorithm by heart. We start by introducing simple ones: selection sort, which performs in time proportional to the square of the number of items being sorted, and linear search which is proportional to the number of items, as its name suggests. Other algorithms (for example, Quicksort and binary search) perform faster, but are perhaps more difficult to understand and remember. They are covered in Chapter 15.

Selection sort

Sorting items means moving them around in a methodical way until they are all in order. A method used by some card players is to sort cards by holding them in the right hand, finding the lowest one and taking it out into the left hand, then finding the next lowest and taking it out, until all the cards have been selected, and the left hand holds the cards in order. The following sequence illustrates how this method works.

Left hand	Right hand
	7 3 9 0 2 5
0	7 3 9 – 2 5
0 2	7 3 9 – – 5
0 2 3	7 – 9 – – 5
0 2 3 5	7 – 9 – – –
0 2 3 5 7	– – 9 – – –
0 2 3 5 7 9	– – – – – –

We could implement this by having two arrays and picking the numbers out of one, adding them to the other. However, there is a way of keeping both lists in the same array, the one growing as the other shrinks. Each time an element is picked out, the gap it leaves is moved to one end, thus creating a contiguous area, which is used to hold the new list. The move is done by a simple swap with the leftmost element of the right hand. So, the example would proceed as follows:

Left hand	Right hand
	7 3 9 0 2 5
0	3 9 7 2 5
0 2	9 7 3 5
0 2 3	7 9 5
0 2 3 5	9 7
0 2 3 5 7	9
0 2 3 5 7 9	

The underlined digits are those that moved at each phase. Each time, a reduced list is considered, until only one element is left. The algorithm can be phrased more precisely as in Figure 6.14.

Because sorting is clearly going to be useful in many contexts, it makes sense to put it in a method from the beginning. The parameters would be the array to be sorted, and the number of items that are active in it. Of course, we shall have to say in the formal parameter what types of item are being sorted. In Section 9.2 we explain how we can relax this requirement.

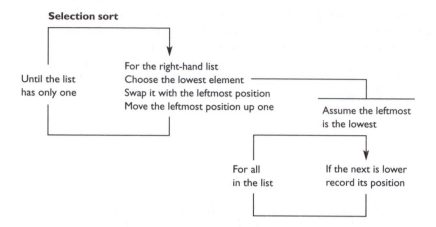

Figure 6.14 *Algorithm for the selection sort.*

```
void selectionSort (double [ ] a, int n) {
  double temp;
  int chosen;

  for (int leftmost = 0; leftmost < n-1; leftmost++) {
    chosen = leftmost;
    for (int j = leftmost+1; j < n; j++)
      if (a[j] < a[chosen]) chosen = j;
    temp = a[chosen];
    a[chosen] = a[leftmost];
    a[leftmost] = temp;
  }
}
```

Sorting is a frequent requirement in computing, and it is useful to have a sorting algorithm handy. The above algorithm can be applied to arrays of any size, and containing any elements, and can be used to sort in descending order just by changing the comparison from < to >. Notice, however, that if we wish to sort from highest to lowest, then the value that moves to the left each time will be the largest, not the smallest. The example sort given here sorts an array of doubles, and uses the < operator for the comparison. If the items being sorted are objects, then < will not work and will need to be replaced by a method, typically called lessThan or compareTo.

Searching

A simple linear search involves proceeding through an array until an item is found or until the end of the array is reached. If we only want to return whether or not the item is there, then a boolean method does the trick, as in:

```
boolean search (double[] a, int n, double x) {
  for (int i = 0; i < n; i++) {
    if (x == a[i])
      return true;
    else
      return false;
  }
}
```

However, if we also want to return where in the array the item was found (so that we can update it, perhaps) then a more complex method is needed. We leave this to Section 15.2, as the above is sufficient as a companion to the sort for now.

EXAMPLE 6.7 Sorting words in a file

Problem The mandate is: 'illustrate sorting and searching'.

Solution In this example, we do not have a particular problem to solve, but need to create the problem to fit a technique we have learnt. A suitable scenario would be to read in every word of a file, construct an array containing only the unique words, sort the array and print it.

Algorithm In diagrammatic terms, Figure 6.15 illustrates the part of the program that creates the array of unique words. After this, we print the array, call the sort, and print again.

Program In using `selectionSort`, we shall be sorting strings. As we have already discussed in Section 3.6, the < operator cannot be used on `String` objects. Instead we use `compareTo` or `compareToIgnoreCase`. The same method will be used in the search. The program follows.

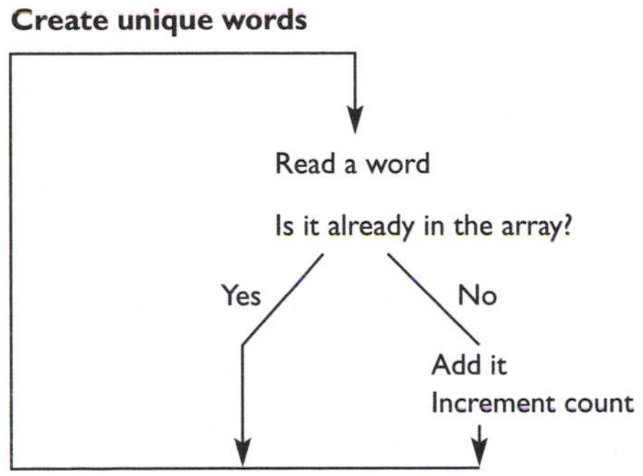

Figure 6.15 *Algorithm for creating an array of unique words.*

```java
import java.io.*;
import javagently.*;
import myutilities.*;



class SortWords {

    /* The Sort Words program    by J M Bishop Feb 1997
     * =====================     Java 1.1 October 1997
     *                           updated June 2000
     * Reads in and then sorts up to 100
     * different words.
     * Illustrates sorting and searching an array.
     */

  void selectionSort(String[] a, int n) {
    String temp;
    int chosen;

    for (int leftmost = 0; leftmost < n-1; leftmost++) {
        chosen = leftmost;
        for (int j = leftmost+1; j < n; j++)
            if (a[j].compareTo(a[chosen])<0)
                chosen = j;
        temp = a[chosen];
        a[chosen] = a[leftmost];
        a[leftmost] = temp;
    }
  }

  boolean search (String[] a, int n, String x) {
    for (int i = 0; i < n; i++)
      if (x.compareTo(a[i])==0) return true;
    return false;
  }

  void report(String[] a, int n) {
    for (int i = 0; i < n; i++) {
      if (i>0 && i % 7 == 0) System.out.println();
      System.out.print(a[i]+"\t");
    }
  }
```

```
SortWords() throws IOException {

  String group [] = new String[100];
  System.out.print("Where are the words? ");
  Stream fin = Filer.open("");

  int count=0;
  try {
    while (count < 100) {
      String word = fin.readString();
      if (! search(group,count,word)) {
        group[count] = word;
        count ++;
      }
    }
  } catch (EOFException e) {
    System.out.println(count + " words read.\n\n");
  }

  System.out.print("Original\n");
  System.out.print("========\n");
  report(group,count);

  selectionSort(group, count);

  System.out.print("\n\nSorted\n");
  System.out.print("======\n");
  report(group,count);
}

public static void main(String[] args) throws IOException {
  new SortWords();
}


}
```

Testing   We have set up the program to use `Filer` to open the file, so we can supply any data we like. Just for interest's sake, the test run below uses the selection sort in a file. In order to maximize the common words, we reorganized the file so that there were spaces between words and symbols. The results are quite interesting.

```
Where are the words? sort.java
30 words read.
Original
========
static    void    selectionSort    (           String    [ ]      a
,         int     n                )           {         temp     ;
chosen    for     leftmost         =           0         <        -
1         ++      j                +           if        .        compareTo
}


Sorted
======
(         )       +                ++          ,         -        .         0
1         ;       <                =           String    [         ]
a         chosen  compareTo        for         if        int       j
leftmost  n       selectionSort    static      temp      void      {
}
```

The output gives some idea of Java's 'collating sequence', in other words how it sorts operators and letters and numbers. Further information on the order of characters can be found in Example 5.4.

6.5   Class-independent tables

In this section we look at a very useful extension of the table concept, that of the dictionary. A dictionary, as the name suggests, has the following properties:

- keys are mapped to values;
- keys and values can be anything;
- there is a fast way of finding a key.

In a real dictionary, words are mapped to explanations, and the speed of searching is obtained because the keys are sorted alphabetically. Knowing this, we can arrive very rapidly at the right place for a word (see Section 15.2 for more on searching).

The problem is that arrays as we have studied them up to now are inadequate to represent the dictionary concept. There are several drawbacks to arrays:

- they are of a fixed size, set inside the program, and cannot grow;
- the index is always an integer;
- the index always starts at zero.

The fixed size restriction can be sidestepped by making the array very large, and working within it. We did this in the previous example (Example 6.7). Although the array was defined as being 100 long, we kept an internal tally of the number of used elements in it, which hovered around 30. For the second restriction, consider the following fairly common, requirement: we would like to store values for each of the letters of the alphabet. An array would be the ideal choice, but we cannot index one with char, nor can we easily convert chars to integers and back. Finally, Example 6.6 has already shown that even if the index is an integer, there are cases where the data does not start from zero. Adjustments are necessary to fit it into a zero-starting array.

Fortunately, Java provides more sophisticated array-handling facilities in the form of standard classes in the `java.util` package. The first class, `Vector`, mirrors the array idea, but removes the fixed size restriction. The second class, `Hashtable` (based on class `Dictionary`), provides a full mapping service in what is also known as an **associative array**.

The `Vector` class

The `Vector` class defines sequences of objects where the sequence can grow in size as required. In fact, it grows automatically, without even being explicitly asked to! Objects are put in and taken out of the vector, using methods. A method is also used to access elements. We shall not look further at vectors in this chapter for two reasons: firstly, the next class is more general and interesting, and, secondly, the terminology used for defining vectors is quite different from Java's other classes, and is quite confusing. `Vector` is part of the `java.util` package.

Hash tables

What we really want is a dynamically sized structure, which also has the property that the indices can be, well, anything. Java's hash tables fit this bill completely. A **hash table** is a collection of pairs of items (key, value). The key is the index to the table and the value is what is associated with the key. We can therefore see that an array is a special case of a hash table, with the key being of type `int`. With hash tables, though, the key can be of any type of object, including `Curio`, `String`, `Times` or whatever. The proviso is that the key cannot be a primitive type, unless it is wrapped in an envelope. We shall deal with envelopes later in this section.

A prime example of a hash table is that kept by the `Display` class, as illustrated in Figure 6.16, based on the display output of Figure 4.1. When we send the input section information about a data field to be shown with a label and an initial value, these are put in a hash table, with the label as the key. Later on, when the program asks for the value, it supplies the label as the key, and gets the value in return.

If we compare Figure 6.16 with the example shown in Figure 6.1, we notice that the essential difference is that with an array table (or matrix) the indices are external to the table, whereas here they are part of it – the key part. Also, values are not inserted contiguously from the beginning: there may be gaps. This does not affect the access of the data. In fact, it makes it faster!

A word about the term 'hash' table. Hash refers to the fact that the items are not stored sequentially in the table, but in a manner that makes them efficient to retrieve. In fact, in a

Key	Value
Min	45
Hour	13

Figure 6.16 *An example of a dictionary or hash table.*

fairly empty table, the efficiency can approach that of an array. As a result, hash tables are not ordered by key, and if we print out what is in one, the items will appear in some seemingly random order. A dictionary, on the other hand, would be expected to also keep items in recognizable order.

Declaring and accessing a hash table

Before looking at the form for a hash table, we note that there is one special class in Java called `Object`. As we shall see in Chapter 9, all objects are compatible with this class. Therefore the `Hashtable` class has keys and values that are `Objects`, and we can then insert our own objects of any class into it. Some of the ways of declaring and manipulating a hash table are summarized in the form:

Hash table declaration and access

```
Hashtable tableid = new Hashtable ( );

void      put (Object key, Object value);
Object    get (Object key);
boolean   containsKey (Object key);
boolean   contains (Object value);
void      remove (Object key);
```

The constructor creates a `Hashtable` object called *tableid* with some
  default number of entries of which both the key and the value are of
  the general class `Object`.
The five methods access the hash table as explained by their names.

For example, suppose we wish to associate names with times. We could do the following:

```
Hashtable timesOfDay = new Hashtable ();
Times time;

timesOfDay.put ("Noon", new Times (12,0));
timesOfDay.put ("Midnight", new Times (0,0));
timesOfDay.put ("Evening news", new Times (22,00));
time = (Times) timesOfDay.get ("Noon");
```

The last statement will successfully get the time 12:00 out of the table. But why does the cast to (Times) appear in the assignment? The reason is that hash tables are potentially available for any kinds of objects. The result type of a get is Object. In order to ensure that we have obtained an object of type Dates, Java requires that we **cast** the Object.

Enumerations

A class that is closely associated with hash tables is Enumeration. In fact, Enumeration is not a class: it is a special kind of class called an **interface**, described in Chapter 9. In this context, the difference is not important. Enumerations provide a means for iterating over a collection of objects. The form for declaring an enumeration, and the methods for it, are:

Enumerations

```
Enumeration e = table.keys();

Object nextElement ();
boolean hasMoreElements ();
```

e is an Enumeration object based on the keys of the given *table*.
e.nextElement() will return the nextElement in the key list as a
    variable of type Object.
e.hasMoreElements() will return true or false based on whether
    the key list has been exhausted yet.

Once we declare an enumeration on a given sequence of objects (such as keys is), nextElement will repeatedly provide the next element, and we can ask it to do so until hasMoreElements becomes false. For example, consider the hash table timesOfDay that we were beinning to set up above. The loop for printing out the keys will be:

```
for (Enumeration e = timesOfDay.keys(); e.hasMoreElements(); i++) {
   String s = (String) e.nextElement();
   display.println(s);
}
```

which could print out (depending on the particular hash in place):

```
Midnight
Noon
Evening news
```

Notice that because of the casting required (as explained just above), the update part of the loop is done as a separate assignment in the body, rather than along with the initialize and check parts, as is usual with for-loops.

Accessing values in a hash table

Now that we can access the keys one by one, we can also get the corresponding values from a hash table. For this we use the `get` method. So, as an example, the above extract can be expanded to

```
for (Enumeration e = timesOfDay.keys(); e.hasMoreElements(); i++) {
    String s = (String) e.nextElement();
    Time t = (Times) timesOfDay.get(s);
    display.println(s +" "+ t);
}
```

Putting this all together, we can tackle Example 6.8.

EXAMPLE 6.8   Currency converter

Problem   We would like to be able to look up the exchange rate for any country into a currency called ZAR, and do a conversion for a given amount.

Approach   There is an Internet site called `www.xe.net` which has daily updates of worldwide exchange rates. From it, one can obtain a table in text form, a fragment of which looks like this:

```
Currency unit               ZAR/Unit            Units/ZAR
====================== ==================== =================
DZD Algerian Dinars         0.777              12.9
USD American Dollar         4.556               0.2195
ARP Argentinian Pesos       4.556               0.2195
AUD Australian Dollars      3.356               0.2980
ATS Austrian Schillings     0.3614              2.767
BSD Bahamian Dollars        4.556               0.2195
BBD Barbados Dollars        2.265               0.4415
DEF Belgian Francs          0.1231              8.121
```

Omitting the headings, what we have here is a table of five values per row – a code, the country name, its currency and two reciprocal exchange rates. According to the problem statement, the index to the table should be the second field, namely the country. Because country is a string, we cannot store the data in an array, but can use a hash table.

We shall read all the values into a hash table, row by row, and then interrogate the table by the key, which is the country name. If that is a valid name, we can go ahead, get the exchange rate and output how much exchanged currency would be provided.

Class design   Together, the fields that appear on one line above form an object, so what we need to do is create a class for it. This class is unlike those we have set up before in that its primary purpose is not to provide any methods, but to be a receptacle for data. In addition, the class can provide a method for reading the fields in from a file. Let us call this class `Rates`.

Once we have the `Rates` class we can set up a hash table of these objects and interrogate it in the manner explained. Making a guess at the kinds of method we shall need, Figure 6.17 gives a model diagram for the system. The table is shown as an object of class `Hashtable`. Because `Hashtable` is a class in `java.util`, we do not have access to its structure, but we do know it contains keys and values. We therefore depict it as such. The keys are strings and the values are of the `Rates` class.

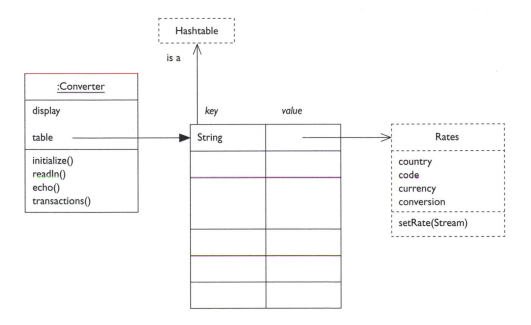

Figure 6.17 *Model diagram for the Converter program.*

Program Firstly, here is the `Rates` class.

```
import java.io.*;
import javagently.*;

class Rates {
  /* The Rates class    by J M Bishop Dec 1998
   * ---------------
   * Stores a country name, currency, code and rate
   */

  String country;
  String code;
  String currency;
  double conversion;

  void setRate (Stream in) throws IOException {
    code = in.readString();
    country = in.readString();
    currency = in.readString();
    // we don't want the first rate,
    // ignore it by reading over it
    conversion = in.readDouble();
    conversion = in.readDouble();
  }

}
```

The `Converter` program follows the lines set out above. Of interest are the lines in the `transactions` method where the objects are retrieved from the hash table, and a type cast is done.

```
c = display.getString("Country");
if (table.containsKey(c)) {
  amount = display.getDouble("Amount");
  r = (Rates) table.get(c);
  ... etc.
```

As usual, the program makes use of the display, and the results are shown in Figure 6.18.

```
import java.io.*;
import javagently.*;
import java.util.*;
import myutilities.*;
```

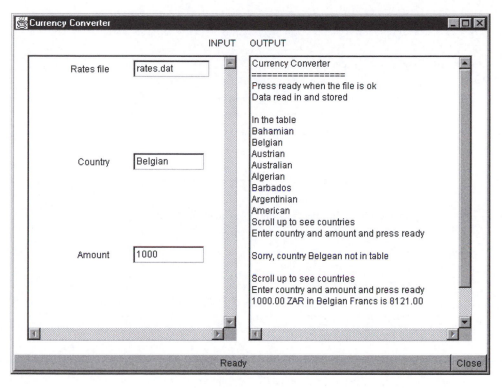

Figure 6.18 *Display from the* Converter *class.*

```
class Converter {

  /* The Converter Program  by J M Bishop Dec 1998
   * ---------------------  updated June 2000
   * Keeps the exchange rates from one currency into
   * many others and enables currency purchases to be
   * estimated.
   *
   * Illustrates the use of hash tables.
   */

Display display = new Display ("Currency Converter");
Hashtable table = new Hashtable();

Converter () throws IOException {
  initialize();
  readIn();
  echo();
  transactions();
}
```

```
// read in each line of data and store in
// the hash table with country as key

void initialize () {
  display.println("Currency Converter\n"+
                  "==================");
  display.prompt("Rates file", "rates.dat");
  display.ready("Press ready when the file is ok");
}

void readIn() throws IOException {
  Rates rate;
  String filename = display.getString("Rates file");
  Stream fin = Filer.open(filename);
  try {
    for (int i = 0; ; i++) {
      rate = new Rates();
      rate.setRate(fin);
      table.put(rate.country, rate);
    }
  }
  catch (EOFException e) {
    display.println("Data read in and stored\n");
  }
}

void echo() {
  display.println("In the table");
  int i = 1;
  for (Enumeration e = table.keys(); e.hasMoreElements(); i++) {
    String country = (String)e.nextElement();
    display.println(country);
  }
}

void transactions () {
  display.prompt("Country", "American");
  display.prompt("Amount", 1000);
  String country;
  double amount;
  String c;
  Rates r;
```

```
        while (true) {
          display.println("Scroll up to see countries");
          display.ready("Enter country and amount and press ready");
          c = display.getString("Country");
          if (table.containsKey(c)) {
            amount = display.getDouble("Amount");
            r = (Rates) table.get(c);
            display.println (Stream.format amount, 6, 2) +" ZAR in "+c+" "
                +r.currency+" is "+
                Stream.format(amount * r.conversion,6,2)+"\n");
          }
          else {
             display.println("Sorry, country "+c+" not in table\n");
          }
        } // while
      } // transactions

    public static void main(String[] args) throws IOException {
      Converter data = new Converter ();
    }


  } // class Converter
```

Testing   The display output from a typical run of the program would be as in Figure 6.18. To test the program thoroughly, we should provide data for well-known currencies. A good idea is to convert ZAR (South African rands) to themselves, and see if the answer is the same. This example is continued in future chapters when we see how to convert from one chosen currency to another.

If the data cannot be found on xe.net, there is a copy of the data file on the *Java Gently* web site under Other Material. Look for a file called curtable.

SUMMARY

Arrays provide for multiple values referred to by the same name. Arrays in Java are of fixed size, but they can have multiple dimensions. There are several ways in which arrays and classes interact, and the correct technique must be chosen for each problem's solution. A useful feature in Java is the ability to declare a method with an array parameter whose length is not specified. Sorting also makes use of arrays, and the selection sort is explained and presented in as general a way as possible.

Finally, we consider how the restrictions of fixed size arrays as well as indexing only with integers can be relaxed. The best answer is to use Java's hash tables which can store values of any class, indexed by any other class, and enable the table to be interrogated and values or keys retrieved. To iterate through the hash tables, we use the enumeration interface supplied along with hash.

QUIZ

6.1   In the `periods` array shown in Figure 6.2, why would the following expression be invalid: `periods[7].mins`

(a)   `mins` is not a method of `periods`
(b)   7 is outside the range of the array
(c)   the 7th object has not been created
(d)   the expression should be `periods[7].mins()`

6.2   Consider the `IntArray` class under 'Array and class interaction'. To create such an `IntArray`, which of the following should we use?

(a)   `IntArray A = new IntArray()`
(b)   `IntArray A = new IntArray(100)`
(c)   `IntArray A[] = new IntArray[100]`
(d)   `IntArray A(100)`

6.3   The statement that ensures that the `Stats` class gets into the `myutilities` package is:

(a)   `imports myutilities;`
(b)   `package myutilities;`
(c)   `package Stats;`
(d)   `import myutilities.Stats;`

6.4   If we create a 10 × 10 table of strings, then the string in the fifth row and first column is referred to by:

(a)   `table [5][1]`
(b)   `table [5,11]`
(c)   `table [4][0]`
(d)   `table [4][1]`

6.5   When using the `Graph` class, the method that we must call to see the graph is

(a)   `showGraph( )`
(b)   `nextGraph( )`
(c)   the constructor
(d)   `setVisible(true)`

6.6   The reason why the `selectionSort` method has a parameter n as well as the array A is because:

(a)   the length of A is not known inside the method
(b)   we may only want to sort some of A's elements
(c)   an n value of zero shows that the array may not yet have been initialized
(d)   n is not necessary, actually

6.7 The keys and values of a hash table can be (where anything means object or primitive value)

(a) anything
(b) objects only
(c) key can be anything, value must be an object
(d) value can be anything, key must be an object

6.8 The statement for getting a string value from a hash table called table is:

(a) `String s = t.get( )`
(b) `String s = (String) t.nextElement( )`
(c) `String s = (String) t.get( )`
(d) not enough information given

6.9 If an array is declared as `int A[ ] = {2, 4, 6, 8};` and we try to access `A[5]`, what do we get?

(a) the value 8
(b) the value 0
(c) an `arrayOutOfBoundsException`
(d) a `NullPointerException`

6.10 To get the number of elements in an array A, we use

(a) `A.length( )`
(b) `length(A)`
(c) `A.length`
(d) `A.length-1`

PROBLEMS

6.1 **Growing arrays.** Arrays are of fixed size, but we can actually replace an array by a larger one if it gets too small. If A is declared as an array, instantiated to a certain limit and then is the subject of an `ArrayOutOfBoundException` when too many elements are added, we can invoke a `grow` method which creates a new array 50% larger, copies the values over and returns the new array reference as its result. Write such a method and test it with a small program.

6.2 **Distance table.** In map books one often finds a distance table which consists of the names of important towns across and down and the distances between them in the matrix. However, we cannot implement such a table directly in Java because the rows and columns are strings not integers. A solution is to have a hash table of town names where the value is a number that indexes into the table. Write a program to

■ construct such a system from up to 20 town names on a file and randomly generated distances between 50 and 1000 km;

■ use the display to query the distance between any two town names.

6.3 **Sorted rings.** Improve the program of Problem 4.8 (average ages) so that the children's names, ages and ring (a letter from A to D) are read into objects, and the objects are stored in an array. Then sort the array by age and print out the children's details. Can you also sort them by name or by ring?

6.4   **Assessing lecturer performance.** Savanna University has instituted a lecturer (or instructor) assessment scheme. Lecturers are evaluated on several criteria such as knowledge, manner, rapport with the class, lecturing aids, and so on. Students are asked to rate the lecturers on a scale of five, where each value is given a specific meaning. For example, part of the questionnaire might read:

Voice	Amount of material
lively and varied	satisfactory
fairly lively	rather too much
satisfactory	lacking
rather dull	far too much
monotonous	insufficient

Five marks are given for the first answer, four for the second, and so on down the scale. The answers are presented in a file where, for each question, the number per answer has already been calculated

```
R N Smith
6 November 2000
COS101 Programming Principles
80 students
Voice 16 35 20 9 0
Material 37 20 11 10 2
...
```

The output will then look something like this:

```
R N Smith
6 November 2000
COS101 Programming Principles
Voice
a       Lively and varied     20% ********************
b       Fairly lively         44%
********************************************
c       Satisfactory          25% ************************
d       Rather dull           11% **********
e       Monotonous            0%
```

We would like to write a program to process lecturer evaluations.

■ Decide on the files that will be needed for the data, and finalize the format of the data.

■ Decide on the classes that will be needed to store the information appropriately while the program is running.

■ Decide on whether arrays, hash tables, both or neither are needed.

■ Write the program and test it thoroughly.

6.5   **Book chapters again.** Expand the class begun in Problems 2.10 and 3.19 so that it includes more information about each chapter, such as a list of up to seven sections, the number of problems, the ten letters that are the answers to the quiz, and anything else you can think of. Design an interactive program that has options for reading in new data about chapters as the book develops, and for printing out the current state of the book. Note that there are already three arrays here: the array of chapters, an array of sections (which is a class of its own with string names and integer page numbers) and an array of quiz answers (which are characters).

6.6   **Public holidays.** Using a hash table, set up a facility to type in store the public holidays for your country, together with their days for this year. Then using the `Display` class, enable the user to read in a holiday name, and be given the date back. As an interesting expansion to this problem, enter every day of the year in another, larger hash table, so that given a date, the name of the holiday can be produced, if there is one.

6.7   **Mains voltage.** The mains voltage supplied by a substation is measured at hourly intervals over a 72-hour period, and a report made. Write a program to read in the 72 readings and determine:

■ the mean voltage measured;

■ the hours at which the recorded voltage varies from the mean by more than 10%;

■ any adjacent hours when the change from one reading to the next is greater than 15% of the mean value.

The program should display a graph of the voltage over the 72 hours, using the `Graph` class.

6.8   **Useful methods.** Write a class with methods that take an array of integers as one of their parameters and do the following:

■ find the maximum of all the elements;

■ determine whether all the quantities in the array are equal;

■ determine the number of times a value greater than a given level occurs.

We would also like to add the following facilities:

■ find the maximum of all the elements, plus all the positions where it occurs;

■ determine the range of values spanned by the array.

Discuss why these two will be more difficult and propose a class-array design that might be able to provide for the methods.

6.9   **Standard passes.** The Senate at Savanna University has decreed that at least 75% of students in each course must pass. This means that the pass mark for each course will differ. Write a program that will read in a file of marks and determine the highest pass such that the Senate's rule applies.

6.10   **Judges' countries.** In Example 6.2, instead of printing out the judges' numbers, we would like to print out the country from which they come. Use an array to set up a list of country names for the judges on duty, and adapt the program to make the output more explanatory. Consider carefully whether to have an array of countries in `judge` alongside the scores, or whether to create another class consisting of a name and a score.

6.11 **Population increase.** Since 1980, the Savanna population statistics have been stored on a computer file, with each line containing the year followed by the total people counted for that year. Write a program that will read this file and find the two consecutive years in which there was the greatest percentage increase in population. The data are not guaranteed to be in strict year order and may need to be sorted first.

6.12 **Bilingual calendars.** Design a program to print out a calendar, one month underneath each other. Then using hash tables, set up versions for the months and days of the week in another language (say, French, Spanish or German), and let the user select which language the calendar should be printed in.

6.13 **Many light bulbs.** Taking the program in Example 6.4, adapt it so that it reads many values from a file, and uses the display. Then adapt it again so that it can accept data from ten different light bulb manufacturers and plot the mean and standard deviations for each. Draw the graphs without lines, as there is no connection between the manufacturers. Use a random number generator with a Gaussian distribution to create the data if you like.

6.14 **Comparative assessment.** Most lecturers would like to know how they are doing in comparison with other lecturers. Thus we keep a file that contains the current average score for each of the questions. As we process a new questionnaire, we read the current average, merge it with the new score and at the end of a program run, write out the new averages back to the file. Implement this extension. If lecturers can choose which questions they use, does this affect whether one should use an array or a hash table to store the averages while the program runs?

6.15 **Birthday graph.** Use the `Graph` class to print a graph of birthday probabilities from Problem 3.14.

6.16 **Sum of squares.** Write a typed method that is given two integers as parameters, and returns as its value the sum of the squares of the numbers between and inclusive of the two parameters. Show how to call the method to print the value of $\sum i^2$ where i runs from 1 to 10. How would the program change if the data were to be read in and stored initially in an array?

6.17 **Online room bookings.** Redo Problems 4.12 and 14.13 so that the room bookings are kept in an array or hash table while the program runs.

CHAPTER 7

Formatting

In this chapter we consider the various ways that Java provides for formatting text, both internally and externally. Initially, Java did not have much in this regard, but Java 2 has extensive facilities for handling data in a manner that is locale-dependent. This means that programs can present themselves in the most appropriate style for the country in which they run. In many ways, such presentation details could be regarded as not essential in a first course, but we give them here to show how different Java is from languages that preceded it. In this chapter, Section 7.1 is essential reading for what follows, and Section 7.2 contains very useful information. Sections 7.3, 7.4 and 7.5 can be covered later if necessary.

7.1 Strings and string handling

Strings were the first data items that we introduced in *Java Gently* and they have been used extensively since. It is now time to take a formal look at what they really are and what facilities are available for them. Strings are special in Java for several reasons:

- `String` is a class so that strings are instantiated as objects from variables.

- There is a special notation for string constants which is a shorthand for creating string objects with known contents, for example `"America"`.

- Strings, unlike other objects, have an operator defined for them, i.e. the + for concatenation.

- Once created, the contents of a `String` object cannot be changed.

- Another class, `StringBuffer`, enables changes to the contents of a string.

- There is a difference between an empty (but initialized) string and a null (i.e. not initialized) string.

So, for example, if we make the declaration:

```
String big = "hippopotamus";
```

an object will be created and initialized (without us using `new`) and will be referred to by the variable called `big`, as in Figure 7.1.

The `big` object is shown with raw data, but no variable and method sections as we are used to. The reason is that `String` is a Java class that we do not see inside. We can, however, access some of its methods, as we shall see below.

Compare this declaration with a similar one for `Time` (as defined in Case Study 1 in Chapter 3):

```
Time noon = new Time (12,0);
```

Here the constant is given in brackets and the `new` operator is used.

Regarding empty and null strings, consider the following two statements:

```
String s1;
String s2 = " ";
```

`s1` will have the special value called null until it is given some other string value. Such a string is not valid for string manipulation methods, and if an attempt is made to access it, a `NullPointerException` will be thrown by the Java system. `s2`, on the other hand, can be used in string manipulation: it just has no characters in it. The difference between the two is brought out in Example 7.1.

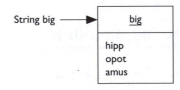

Figure 7.1 *Example of how a string is stored.*

The strings created in quotes or read into objects of the `String` class cannot be altered. There is another Java class, `StringBuffer`, which allows for this sort of thing, but we shall not discuss it in this book.

String operations

The `String` class has several constructors, some of which are shown in the next form:

Creating a string

```
String s = "chars";
String ();
String (String value);
String (char[] value);
String (char[] value, int offset, int count)
String (StringBuffer buffer)
```

The first form, with the assignment to a string literal, is the most common.
The next two create an empty string and provide a copy constructor respectively.
Strings can also be created from character arrays, in whole or in part, as well as
    from a `StringBuffer` variable.

Many methods are available in the `String` class; the form shows a selection of them:

Manipulating strings

```
// class methods
   String   valueOf (int i)
   String   valueOf (double d)
   ... and 9 others

// instance methods
   char      charAt (int index)
   int       compareTo (String s)
   boolean   equals (Object obj)
   int       indexOf (String s)
   int       indexOf (String s, int fromindex)
   int       length ()
   String    substring (int begin, int end)
   Boolean   startsWith (String prefix)
   char []   toCharArray ()
   String    toLowerCase ();
   String    trim ();
   ... and 33 others
```

`length` will give the length of string. Notice that unlike for an array, this is a method call, so the brackets are required. Although a string cannot be indexed directly, it is made up of characters and the character at any index position can be obtained via `charAt`. The whole string can also be transformed into a character array if required. For example,

```
String big = "hippopotamus";
char study [] = big.toCharArray();
```

produces an array of length 12 with each character from the original string. `indexOf` operates as a searching mechanism, enabling one to find a substring in a string. So, for example,

```
String big = "hippopotamus";
int bang = big.indexOf("pop");
int fizz = big.indexOf("up");
```

will produce 3 in `bang` but −1 in `fizz`. Similarly, a substring can be extracted, as in

```
String small = big.substring(3,5);
```

which would give `"pop"` in `small`.

`compareTo` and `equals` enable the values of strings to be compared since we cannot do so with boolean operators (see Section 3.6). The difference between assigning object values and their references was also covered in that section, and applies as well to strings. So now we note how the comparison methods would be used. `equals` returns a boolean as expected; for example:

```
String big = "hippopotamus";
String small = bigOne.substring(3,5);
System.out.println (big.equals(small));
```

will give false. The `compareTo` method provides a straight alphabetical comparison and produces −1, 0 or +1 depending on less than, equal to or greater than. So, for example,

```
String big = "hippopotamus";
String small = big.substring(3,5);
System.out.println (big.compareTo(small));
```

will produce −1. In other words, 'hippopotamus' does come alphabetically before 'pop'.

One of the common operations in programming is to convert strings to numbers and back again. The `valueOf` methods can take any of the primitive types and produce a string from it. We would only want to use `valueOf` if we want to keep the string in the program for a while, rather than print it out immediately.

| EXAMPLE 7.1 | Removing double spaces |

Problem   Standards have been set up that indicate that in typed paragraphs, there should only ever be single spaces. We would like to process existing text and replace any double spaces with single ones.

Solution   We can read a file a line at a time, looking for double spaces using the string method `indexOf` and proceed accordingly.

Algorithm   String manipulation algorithms can be very tricky. This one is best taken in stages. Let us start by reading one line of text and printing out the line together with the position of the first occurrence of a double space. Assuming `fin` is a `BufferedReader`, the Java would be:

```
s = fin.readLine();
System.out.println(s.indexOf("  ",s) + " " + s);
```

If we enclosed this in a program to process a whole file, we could get output such as

```
0    Algorithm String manipulation algorithms can be very tricky.
33   This one is best taken in stages.  Let us start by reading one
-1   line of text and printing out the line together with the
52   position of the first occurrence of a double space.  The Java
10   would be:
```

which indicates that the first line has a double space at the beginning; the second and fourth lines have doubles somewhere in the middle; the third line has no double space, so `indexOf` returns –1; and the last line has a double space at the end, that is, after the colon.

To find more than one occurrence of double space in a string we shall have to loop round, checking from where we left off each time. The basic loop looks like this:

```
startingFrom = 0;
while (true) {
spaceAt = s.indexOf("  ",startingFrom);
if (spaceAt==-1) break;
s = s.substring(0,spaceAt)+" "
   + s.substring(spaceAt+2,s.length());
startingFrom = spaceAt+2;
}
System.out.println(s);
```

In other words, we recreate `s` each time from the part from 0 to the double space, plus a single space, plus the remainder of the string. We know we have finished processing the string when the `indexOf` method returns –1.

Program The full program incorporates these sections, and also checks for the end of file. It does so by looking for a null string. For testing purposes, the program is set up to read from the keyboard, but the `fin` stream could just as easily be directed to a file of the user's choice using `Filer.open`.

```java
import java.io.*;
import javagently.*;

class Spaces {

  /* Removing spaces program    by J M Bishop Dec 1997
   * ----------------------     Java 1.1
   *
   * Replaces double spaces by single.
   * Illustrates use of string handling methods.
   */

  public static void main (String args []) throws IOException {
    System.out.println("Program to convert double spaces");
    System.out.println("to single ones.");
    Stream fin = new Stream(System.in);

    String s = "";
    int spaceAt, startingFrom;
    try {
      while (true) {
        s = fin.readLine();
        if (s==null) throw new EOFException();

        startingFrom = 0;
        while (true) {
        spaceAt = s.indexOf(" ",startingFrom);
          if (spaceAt==-1) break;
          else if (spaceAt==0)
              s = s.substring(1,s.length());
          else s = s.substring(0,spaceAt)+" "
                + s.substring(spaceAt+2,s.length());
          startingFrom = spaceAt+2;
        }
        System.out.println(s);

      }
    }
    catch (EOFException e) {}
  }
}
```

Testing The following shows some simple test data entered interactively, which cover many of the cases we set out to detect.

```
Program to convert double spaces to single ones.
Line one  with one double.
Line one with one double.
Line one  with   two.
Line two with two.
Line three ends with one.
Line three ends with one.
  Line four starts with one.
 Line four starts with one.
Line five has a   triple.
Line five has a  triple.
```

Obviously, there are many improvements that could be made to this program, and they are picked up in the Problems at the end of the chapter.

The `StringBuffer` class

As we have mentioned, strings themselves are immutable. If we want to change the length or contents of a string, we basically have to break it up into bits and rejoin them, making a new string, as explained in Example 7.1. `StringBuffer` is an alternative class which provides methods such as `append`, `insert` and `setcharAt`, all of which enable efficient alterations to existing strings.

Strings and character arrays

Unlike other languages, strings in Java are definitely different from character arrays. However, conversion between the two is possible, as mentioned above. The next example shows where such conversion would be very useful. The general idea is that in order to read in individual characters, we first read a string, convert it to an array, and peel off each character in turn. If we just read characters, we have to separate each by a space, which is quite artificial in most circumstances.

EXAMPLE 7.2 Counterfeit cheques

Problem Counterfeit cheques are in circulation and the banks have discovered that they all have the same distinctive properties. In the 10-digit cheque number, if there are:

■ three or more zeros in succession, and/or

■ four or more non-zeros in succession,

then the cheque could be counterfeit. We would like the computer to assist in warning of a possible counterfeit.

Solution   When the cheques are handled by a bank's computers, the first thing that is read is the number. For the purposes of this example, we could write a program to read in cheque numbers and to analyze them for the above properties. The analysis could detect the occurrence of either of the runs described above and if either is found then the cheque can be marked as suspect.

Algorithm   The algorithm for analyzing a number involves reading it in, digit by digit, and counting the number of zeros and non-zeros. However, these have to occur in runs, so once a run is 'broken', the relevant count will be reset. It will therefore be necessary to remember that a critical count was reached at some stage: this is best done with a boolean variable. Figure 7.2 shows what the algorithm looks like.

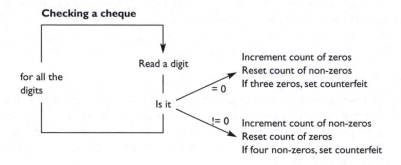

Figure 7.2 *Algorithm for checking a cheque.*

Program   The first version of the program follows the algorithm closely, making use of two methods for clarity. The digits will be read as characters, but one of the features of the `Stream` class is that any items must be delimited by what is known as 'white space' – spaces, ends-of-lines, tabs. Thus the digits of the cheque have to be entered with spaces following each one, so that they can be read using `readChar`.

```
import java.io.*;
import java.io.*;
import javagently.*;

public class ChequeDetector {

    /* Counterfeit cheque detector    by J M Bishop Sept 1997
     * --------------------------      Java 1.1 October 1997
     *                                 updated July 2000
```

```
 * Checks a cheque number for the occurrence
 * of >= 3 zeros
 * or >= 4 non-zeros in a row
 * The digits of the number must be separated by spaces.
 *
 * Illustrates if-then-else and characters
 */

static final int noOfDigits = 10;

boolean counterfeit = false;
int countOfZeros = 0;
int countOfNonzeros = 0;

ChequeDetector () throws IOException {

  Stream in = new Stream (System.in);

  System.out.println("****** Checking for counterfeits ******");
  System.out.println("Enter a cheque number of ten digits "+
      "separated by a space and ending with a return");

  char digit;

  for (int i = 0; i < noOfDigits; i++) {
    digit = in.readChar();
    if (digit == "0")
      recordZero();
    else
      recordNonzero();
  }
  if (counterfeit)
    System.out.print("\tCOUNTERFEIT");
  else
    System.out.print("\tOK");
  System.out.println();
}

void recordZero() {
  countOfZeros ++;
  countOfNonzeros = 0;
  if (countOfZeros == 3)
    counterfeit = true;
}
```

```
void recordNonzero() {
  countOfNonzeros ++;
  countOfZeros = 0;
  if (countOfNonzeros == 4)
    counterfeit = true;
}
public static void main(String[] args) throws IOException {
  new ChequeDetector();
}


}
```

Testing   Cheque numbers should be chosen so as to test the special cases. For example, sample runs of the program with input and output might be:

```
****** Checking for counterfeits ******
Enter a cheque number with digits separated by a space
0 0 0 3 3 0 0 4 4 0
        COUNTERFEIT


****** Checking for counterfeits ******
Enter a cheque number with digits separated by a space
0 0 3 3 3 0 0 3 3 3
        OK


****** Checking for counterfeits ******
Enter a cheque number with digits separated by a space
4 4 4 4 0 0 5 5 0 0
        COUNTERFEIT
```

Improvement   Now we consider how to remove the restriction that the digits of a cheque number have to be separated by spaces. Instead of using `readChar`, we read a string, convert it to a character array, and strip off characters one by one. The main loop then changes from:

```
char digit;

for (int i = 0; i < noOfDigits; i++) {
  digit = in.readChar ();
  if (digit == "0")
    recordZero();
  else
    recordNonZero();
}
```

with data such as 1 0 0 6 7 0 2 2 1 5 to

```
String s = in.readString();
char digits [ ] = s.toCharArray();

for (int i = 0; i < digits.length; i++) {
  if (digits[i] == "0")
    recordZero();
  else
    recordNonZero();
}
```

with the much more conventional data such as 1006702215.

7.2   Tokenizers and envelopes

We mentioned in Chapter 4 that reading numbers was somewhat awkward in Java, and introduced the `Stream` class as a means for providing these simple facilities. In the next section we now look at the inside of that class, to see how it actually performs its task. But first we have to examine two more important Java features: the tokenizer and the envelope.

Tokenizers

We have already mentioned that Java is slightly deficient in the input arena, and that the `Stream` class was created to make up for the problem. Java's approach is to read strings, and to provide a very efficient means of breaking a string up into tokens and then to convert the token to the required type. Tokens are substrings separated by a character such as a comma, a space or a tab. In this way we can pick off substrings from the input and pass them to the string versions of the envelope class routines for conversion in order to get the values we want. For example, in the following sentence, there are 10 tokens which roughly correspond to the words.

> Where e're you walk, cool gales shall fan the glade[17].

The methods provided by the `StringTokenizer` class, which is in `java.util`, are:

`StringTokenizer` declaration and access

```
StringTokenizer (String s);
StringTokenizer (String s, String delimiters);
StringTokenizer (String s, String delimiters,
                 boolean returnasTokens);
String nextToken ();
String nextToken (String delimiter);
boolean hasMoreTokens ();
int countTokens ();
```

Having read in a string, we declare a tokenizer on it, as in:

```
StringTokenizer T = new StringTokenizer (S);
```

We then look through the tokens, checking for the end, as follows:

```
while (T.hasMoreTokens()) {
  System.out.println(T.nextToken());
}
```

Given the sentence above, the following would be printed:

```
Where
e're
you
walk,
cool
gales
shall
fan
the
glade[17]
```

Changing the delimiter set

We can also change the default delimiters from the usual space, tab and end-of-line, to something else. For example, if we were analyzing a program, we would want semicolon, brackets and so on also to be delimiters. Otherwise they will be part of the tokens. Suppose we have the following statement as data

```
spaceAt = s.indexOf(" ",startingFrom);
```

With default delimiters, the tokens would be:

```
spaceAt
=
s.indexOf(" ",startingFrom);
```

which probably is not what we wanted. We would want more detail. We could get a better effect by declaring:

```
StringTokenizer T = new StringTokenizer (S," .(,); =:", false);
```

which increases the delimiter set and excludes delimiters from the tokens. This gives:

```
spaceAt
s
indexOf
" "
startingFrom
```

which is more like it. We now consider how envelopes and tokenizers are used in the `Stream` class.

Envelopes

Before we can look inside the `Stream` class, we first have to know about envelopes. One of the strict rules in Java is that values of primitive types and objects cannot be mixed. For most of the time, this causes little inconvenience, but there are times when a standard package requires an object, and we wish to send it, say, a value of type `int`. In order to do so, we first place the value in what is known as an **envelope** class, thus making it an object. The envelope class provides access to the value and also has various conversion methods available.

The Java `lang` package has envelope classes associated with each of the primitive types, which classes are called `Boolean`, `Character`, `Double`, `Float`, `Integer` and `Long` (notice the capital letters). As their names suggest, they provide class-level versions of their respective primitive data types.

As an example, the important methods of the `Integer` class are given in the following form:

`Integer` and `int` conversions

```
Integer   (int value);          // constructor

Integer   valueOf (String s);

int       intValue ();
int       parseInt (String s);
String    toString (int i);
// and 15 other methods in the Integer class
```

The constructor takes an `int` value and wraps it up as an `Integer` object.
`valueof` will create an integer value from a string and put it in an `Integer` object.
`parseInt` is similar, but the result is put in a primitive `int`.
`intValue` will unwrap the `Integer` object into an `int`.
`toString` converts a primitive integer to a `String`.

The constructor and the instance method provide for moving back and forth between types and classes. Thus if i is an `int`,

```
Integer Iobj = new Integer (i);
```

makes an object out of it. To get the `int` back so as to print it, say, we use:

```
System.out.println(Iobj.intValue());
```

The other selected methods convert from strings and back. The other envelope classes have corresponding methods. We saw the `Character` class in Section 5.4.

7.3   Inside the `Stream` class

What really goes on behind the scenes in the `Stream` class? We now have covered enough of the language to explain this useful addition to our programming repertoire. The class is not long, but it does make use of tokenizers and envelopes. The methods provided by the class were given in Chapter 4, and are repeated here:

```
The Stream class

Constants
---------
READ = 0,
WRITE = 1;


Constructors
------------
Stream (InputStream filename)
Stream (String filename, int how)


Input
---
int      readInt ()
double   readDouble ()
String   readString ()
char     readChar ()


Output
------
void println - for Objects, String, int, double, char
```

```
void print - for Objects, String, int, double, char
void close()

Output - class methods
----------------------
String format (int number, int align)
String format (double number, int align, int frac)
```

The first constructor is used when the InputStream is known, as when connecting to the keyboard.

The second constructor is used to connect files, and the *how* parameter indicates whether the file is for reading or writing.

The four input methods operate on the Stream object and fetch the next item on the stream, interpreting it as the type given. If it is not the correct type, the method will return for another item. All items must be delimited by a space or other punctuation mark.

Println and print operate exactly as they do for System.out.

close must be called on any file opened for writing, so that the contents are preserved for later.

The format methods are class methods and therefore are called as Stream.format. Full details are given below of how they operate.

The Stream class is intended to be instantiated as stream objects, as we have seen many times already. Once created, Stream objects can use the input methods. The two format methods are not, however, dependent on objects and can be called at any stage to format a number as a string with a given number of digits, composed of a set of methods which can be called in any order. There is no initializing to be done, so the methods must be sure to initialize themselves.

Algorithms

The general algorithm for each of the reading methods is illustrated by that for reading an integer. The routine can initialize itself by detecting a null token. If this is the case, it reads a line and generates the tokenizer. It then calls nextToken, to get a token, and tries to convert the token to a number. Both statements can go wrong and throw an exception.

- The call to nextToken can fail if there are no more tokens. The appropriate action is therefore to read another line.

- The conversion can fail if the substring forming the token does not represent a number of the proper kind. Here we just print a message and try again.

If both statements complete successfully, the method exits. This method is therefore an excellent example of exception handling. It is:

```
public int readInt () throws IOException {
  if (T == null) refresh();
  while (true) {
    try {
      return Integer.parseInt(T.nextToken());
    }
    catch (NoSuchElementException e1) {
      refresh ();
    }
    catch (NumberFormatException e2) {
      System.out.println("Error in number, try again.");
    }
  }
}
```

The class contains interesting statements in each of the numeric conversion methods. The integer one uses the parse method from the `Integer` envelope class:

```
return Integer.parseInt(T.nextToken());
```

However, the `Double` class does not have a corresponding parse method, and the conversion is a bit more complex:

```
return Double.valueOf(item.trim()).doubleValue();
```

Let us consider what this statement does. `item` is a string returned from the tokenizer. Working from the inside outwards, we first trim it of spaces, using a method from the `String` class. Then we call the `Double.valueOf` method to convert the string to an object of type `Double`. Finally, we take the object out of its envelope and turn it into a `double` type. This statement is certainly worth putting into a typed method!

The `format` methods make use of `java.text` package, which is the subject of the next section. Meanwhile, we list the complete class below:

The `Stream` class

```
package javagently;

import java.io.*;
import java.util.*;
import java.text.*;


public class Stream {

  /* The Stream class    by J M Bishop and B Worrall May 2000
```

```
 *  ================        on suggestion from Jens Kaasbøll
 *                          based on the Text class Aug 1996
 *                          by J M Bishop and A Moolman
 *
 *  Provides simple input from the keyboard and files.
 *  And formatted output to the screen and files.
 *
 *  Constructors
 *  ------------
 *  public Stream (InputStream in)
 *  public Stream (String filename, int why)
 *
 *  Input
 *  -----
 *  public int     readInt ()
 *  public double readDouble ()
 *  public String readString ()
 *  public char    readChar ()
 *
 *  Output
 *  ------
 *  public void println   - for Objects, String, int, double, char
 *  public void print     - for Objects, String, int, double, char
 *  public void close()
 *
 *  Output - class methods
 *  ----------------------
 *  public String format (int number, int align)
 *  public String format (double number, int align, int frac)
 */


private BufferedReader in;
private PrintWriter out;
private StringTokenizer T;
private String S;

public static final int
READ = 0,
WRITE = 1;

public Stream(InputStream i) {
in = open(i);
}


public Stream(String filename, int how)
```

```
                throws FileNotFoundException, IOException {
     switch(how) {
        case READ: in = open(filename); break;
        case WRITE: out = create(filename); break;
     }
  }


  private BufferedReader open(InputStream in) {
     return new BufferedReader(new InputStreamReader(in));
  }


  private BufferedReader open(String filename)
                    throws FileNotFoundException {
     return new BufferedReader(new FileReader(filename));
  }


  private PrintWriter create(String filename) throws IOException {
     return new PrintWriter(new FileWriter(filename));
  }

  public String readLine () throws IOException {
     refresh();
     return S;
  }

  public int readInt () throws IOException {
     if (T==null) refresh();
     while (true) {
        try {
           return Integer.parseInt(T.nextToken());
        }
        catch (NoSuchElementException e1) {
           refresh ();
        }
        catch (NumberFormatException e2) {
           System.out.println("Error in number, try again.");
        }
     }
  }
  public char readChar () throws IOException {
     if (T==null) refresh();
     while (true) {
        try {
           return T.nextToken().trim().charAt(0);
        }
        catch (NoSuchElementException e1) {
           refresh ();
```

```
        }
    }
}

public double readDouble () throws IOException {
  if (T==null) refresh();
  while (true) {
    try {
      String item = T.nextToken();
      return Double.valueOf(item.trim()).doubleValue();
    }
    catch (NoSuchElementException e1) {
      refresh ();
    }
    catch (NumberFormatException e2) {
      System.out.println("Error in number, try again.");
    }
  }
}

public String readString () throws IOException {
  if (T==null) refresh ();
  while (true) {
    try {
      return T.nextToken();
    }
    catch (NoSuchElementException e1) {
      refresh ();
    }
  }
}

private void refresh () throws IOException {
  S = in.readLine ();
  if (S==null) throw new EOFException();
  T = new StringTokenizer (S);
}

private static DecimalFormat N = new DecimalFormat();
private static final String spaces = "                    ";

public static String format(double number, int align, int frac) {
  N.setGroupingUsed(false);
  N.setMaximumFractionDigits(frac);
  N.setMinimumFractionDigits(frac);
  String num = N.format(number);
  if (num.length() < align)
```

```
        num = spaces.substring(0,align-num.length()) + num;
     return num;
    }

  public static String format(int number, int align) {
    N.setGroupingUsed(false);
    N.setMaximumFractionDigits(0);
    String num = N.format(number);
    if (num.length() < align)
       num = spaces.substring(0,align-num.length()) + num;
    return num;
    }
  }
}
```

Figure 7.3 shows the model diagram for `Stream`. It shows clearly those parts that are class members and those that are instantiated, as well as the public and private accessibility of each member (using + and -). `Stream` provides for each object the five instance methods and two class methods shown as public. The `open`, `create` and `refresh` methods are used by the public methods and are private. Similarly, the constructor parameters are copied into private input–output variables and the other two private variables, `T` and `S`, are used for the tokenizing as we have already described.

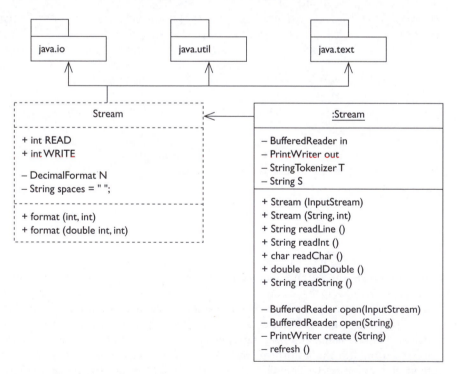

Figure 7.3 *Model diagram for the* `Stream` *class and a typical* `Stream` *object.*

7.4 Formatting numbers

In the `format` methods of our `Stream` class, we made use of features of the `java.text` package. In this section we describe and assess this built-in approach to writing numbers.

The concept of a formatter

Java differs from other languages in that the formatting for numbers is not given in the print statements, but in a separate object. Then in the print statement, the relevant format object is joined up with the item to be printed. Several format objects can exist in a program together at any one time, and they can be used and reused at will.

The formatters that are available in `java.text` are

```
DateFormat
SimpleDateFormat
NumberFormat
DecimalFormat
MessageFormat
```

We discuss the date formatters in the next section and concentrate on number formatters here.

`NumberFormat` and its subclass `DecimalFormat` provide facilities for formatting all kinds of numbers, including percentages and currencies, in various forms. First we create a format; then we can customize it in two ways:

- for particular formatting requirements, such as the number of fractional digits to be printed for a real number;

- for different **locations** around the world, which have different conventions for decimals, currency symbols, thousand groups and so on.

The latter is a very powerful aspect of Java and puts the language in a class of its own for world-wide computing. Let us first look at how locales are set in Java.

The computer's locale

Java is very much an international language, and it provides for internationalization in numerous ways. The idea is that as programs move around the world on the Internet, they can present themselves in local parlance to users. For example, in the United States, dates are written with the month first, whereas in other countries either the year or the day comes first. If you are using an operating system such as MS Windows, you can access the regional settings in the control panel and see where your computer thinks it is. Computers often come set by default for English (United States), so you could experiment and change the setting. Notice that if you change the country, other settings change automatically, such as the currency symbol and the date format.

Java provides a class in the `java.util` package that enables a program to interrogate the computer's settings and print them out. The class is called `Locale`, and some of its facilities are given in the following form:

The `Locale` class

```
Locale (String language, String country, String variant);
Locale (String language, String country);

// Constants
   Locale CANADA;
   Locale CANADA_FRENCH;
   Locale CHINA;
   Locale CHINESE;
   Locale ENGLISH;
   Locale FRANCE;
   Locale FRENCH;
   Locale GERMAN;
   Locale GERMANY;
   Locale ITALIAN;
   Locale ITALY;
   Locale JAPAN;
   Locale JAPANESE;
   Locale KOREA;
   Locale KOREAN;
   Locale PRC;
   Locale SIMPLIFIED_CHINESE;
   Locale TAIWAN;
   Locale TRADITIONAL_CHINESE;
   Locale UK;
   Locale US;

// class methods
 void Locale   getDefault();
 void          setDefault(Locale newLocale);

// instance methods
String  getCountry();
String  getDisplayCountry();
String  getDisplayCountry(Locale inLocale);
String  getDisplayLanguage(Locale inLocale);
String  getDisplayLanguage();
String  getLanguage();
String  getName();
// and 10 others
```

As you can see, the `Locale` class starts off with two constructors. We can create a new locale if we know the language and country we want. Thereafter, there are two class methods, one of which provides the other option: a locale object can be created from the default setting in the machine. The second class method is used in conjunction with regular object declarations to set up one of the locales that follow as constants. The constants include only a limited number of locales, but Java is not restricted to these, as it can and will fetch other information from the machine, as shown in the following example.

The bulk of the class is made up of instance methods and, as is usual, there are several variations on each theme, which are not shown here. Let us explore these practically.

EXAMPLE 7.3   Where am I?

Problem Find out which geographical region and which language the computer running a program uses.

Solution The obvious solution is to pull in the `Locale` class and find out the necessary information. Once we have done that, we will extend the specification slightly and create another locale to see the effect on the various properties that are returned when interrogated.

Program The program looks at the local machine's locale, and then creates a locale for Germany.

```
import java.util.*;

class WhereAmI {

  /* The program for finding Where Am I?   by J M Bishop Dec 1997
   * ----------------------------------
   *                                     updated July 2000
   * Illustrates the use of classes in Java packages
   * and the facility of changing locales.
   */

  public static void main (String [ ] args) {
    new WhereAmI ();
  }

  WhereAmI () {
    Locale here = Locale.getDefault();

    System.out.println("My Locale is " + here);
    System.out.println("Country: " + here.getCountry());
```

```
System.out.println("Language: " + here.getLanguage());
System.out.println("Country:  " + here.getDisplayCountry());
System.out.println("Language: " + here.getDisplayLanguage());
System.out.println();


Locale there = new Locale("GERMAN","GERMANY");
there.setDefault(Locale.GERMANY);
System.out.println("New Locale is " + there);
System.out.println("Country:  " + there.getCountry());
System.out.println("Language: " + there.getLanguage());
System.out.println("Country:  " + there.getDisplayCountry());
System.out.println("Language: " + there.getDisplayLanguage());


    }
}
```

Testing   The output when run on my Windows computer was:

```
My Locale is en_SOUTH AFRICA
Country: SOUTH AFRICA
Language: en
Country: United States
Language: English

New Locale is german_GERMANY
Country: GERMANY
Language: german
Country: Deutschland
Language: Deutsch
```

What this says is that the computer detects that it is in South Africa and the main language is English ('en'). However, for display purposes, it will use the conventions of the United States, as South Africa is not currently one of the options in its list. If we then create a new locale and declare it as Germany, we see that the country and language will in fact be completely localized. Interestingly enough, when I run the same program on my iMac, I get

```
My Locale is en_US
Country: US
Language: en
Country: United States
Language: English
```

```
New Locale is german_GERMANY
Country: GERMANY
Language: german
Country: GERMANY
Language: german
```

which shows that I have not set up the computer correctly and/or MacOS does not have as much support for locales as does Windows.

The `NumberFormat` class

`NumberFormat` is an abstract class, which means that we cannot create objects by instantiating it, but can get object instances from the class itself. The meaning of abstract classes will become clear in Chapter 9. Creating a format is done by class methods, as given in the form:

Creating number formatters
NumberFormat getInstance () NumberFormat getCurrencyInstance () NumberFormat getNumberInstance () NumberFormat getPercentInstance ()
Each of these returns an object on which various methods related to formatting apply.

Each of the four creation methods has a corresponding version that mentions a new locale, other than the default one, that should be used. A locale is a region of the globe where certain local conditions such as language, currencies and time prevail. Typical locales would be `Locale.US` or `Locale.GERMANY`.

To use a format object, the following instance methods apply. Since all the other numeric types can operate within `long` and `double`, only two methods are needed.

Using number formatters
String format (double *number*); String format (long *number*);
When used on number formatters, these methods provide more compact and sensible formatting than that available in `println` statements.

So, for example, to compare the default writing of numbers with the default settings of the formatter, consider:

```
NumberFormat N = NumberFormat.getInstance ();

System.out.println(Math.PI + " " + 10000);
System.out.println(N.format(Math.PI) + " " + N.format(10000));
```

which would print out

```
3.141592653589793 10000
3.142 10,000
```

Thus the number formatter structured the numbers in a much more pleasing way, although the printing out of numbers with commas is not very common, except in financial matters in some countries such as the USA. So we would want to customize the format in most cases. To do so, we make use of the following instance methods:

Customizing a number formatter

void setMaximumIntegerDigits (int *newvalue*);
void setMinimumIntegerDigits (int *newvalue*);
void setMaximumFractionDigits (int *newvalue*);
void setMinimumFractionDigits (int *newvalue*);
void setGroupingUsed (boolean *newvalue*);

The setMaximum methods will cause values to be truncated when written.
The setMinimum methods will cause spaces (integer part) or zeros (fraction part) to be written.
Groupings refers to whether or not a comma, a space or some other locale-dependent symbol should separate thousands.

For each of the set methods, there is a corresponding get method which can, if needed, provide the current settings. Note that it is a good idea to use short identifiers for formatters since, with format, they tend to clutter up print statements.

Formatting real numbers

To see the effect of changing the various settings for real numbers, the best example is to dissect a Stream.format method. It is:

```
public static String format(double number, int align, int frac) {
  N.setGroupingUsed(false);
  N.setMaximumFractionDigits(frac);
  N.setMinimumFractionDigits(frac);
  String num = N.format(number);
  if (num.length() < align)
    num = spaces.substring(0,align-num.length()) + num;
   return num;
  }
```

The three `set` calls establish that there must be no grouping of thousands and that the number of fractional digits is fixed. If we set the minimum but not the maximum then we would get spaces as padding, whereas usually we want zeros in fractions. The number is then formatted and put into a local string, because there is one adjustment to be made. The number formatter has a default setting of 1 for the minimum integer digits, so we will always get a number such as 0.567 rather than .567. If we set the maximum to (`align - frac`) then we will get numbers of fixed width, but there will be leading zeros, not spaces. Therefore we add the extra spaces by means of string manipulation instead.

Setting the maximum integer digits has another danger: Java will truncate anything else. Thus with a maximum digits of 3, 1000 will be printed as 0. In general therefore, the `Stream` class is still a useful tool.

In the `DecimalFormat` class there is a facility to set up a pattern to be used in formatting. However, creating a pattern such as ###0.### requires string handling as well if the number of hashes is a variable. We shall consider patterns again when customizing dates.

Currencies

As part of the number formatting facilities, we can get any currency printed out nicely.[1] To print a number as a currency, we use:

```
NumberFormat C = NumberFormat.getCurrencyInstance();
System.out.println (C.format(10000));
```

which could give in return:

```
$10,000.00
```

Currencies are fun because Java will pick up the correct currency formatting and currency symbol from the computer and use it. Example 7.4 illustrates what happens.

---

[1] Percentages seem to be somewhat problematic at present, so we shall not consider them here.

| EXAMPLE 7.4 | Currency conversion table |

Problem We would like to investigate the effect of locale changes on the printing of currencies.

Solution We set up a small test program that gets five exchange rates and then prints out a table with the amount converted from graz.

Program The program is very simple. A currency format is created for each of the locales that are involved. The rates are read in and then the converted amounts printed.

```java
import java.text.*;
import javagently.*;
import java.util.*;
import java.io.*;

class Currency {

  public static void main (String args []) throws IOException {

    Stream in = new Stream ("rates.dat",Stream.READ);

    System.out.println("Currency conversion table");
    System.out.println("=========================");
    System.out.println();
    System.out.println("The exchange rates are:");
    System.out.println("graz\tdollars\tpounds\tyen\tmarks\tfrancs");
    double d = in.readDouble();
    double p = in.readDouble();
    double y = in.readDouble();
    double m = in.readDouble();
    double f = in.readDouble();
    System.out.println("1\t"+d+"\t"+p+"\t"+ y+"\t"+ m+"\t"+ f);
    System.out.println();

    NumberFormat Nd =
          NumberFormat.getCurrencyInstance(Locale.US);
    NumberFormat Np =
          NumberFormat.getCurrencyInstance(Locale.UK);
    NumberFormat Ny =
          NumberFormat.getCurrencyInstance(Locale.JAPAN);
    NumberFormat Nm =
          NumberFormat.getCurrencyInstance(Locale.GERMANY);
    NumberFormat Nf =
          NumberFormat.getCurrencyInstance(Locale.FRANCE);
```

```
for (int graz = 1000; graz < 10000; graz+=1000)
  System.out.println('G'+Text.writeInt(graz,3) + '\t' +
    Nd.format(graz/d) + '\t' +
    Np.format(graz/p) + '\t' +
    Ny.format(graz/y) + '\t' +
    Nm.format(graz/m) + '\t' +
    Nf.format(graz/f));
  }
}
```

Testing   The output from the program will be:

```
Currency conversion table
=========================
```

```
The exchange rates are:
graz      dollars      pounds       yen           marks         francs
1          4.8845      8.047        0.0378        2.7361        0.8174


G1000     $204.73      £124.27      ¥26,455.03    365,48 DM      1 223,39 F
G2000     $409.46      £248.54      ¥52,910.05    730,97 DM      2 446,78 F
G3000     $614.19      £372.81      ¥79,365.08    1.096,45 DM    3 670,17 F
G4000     $818.92      £497.08      ¥105,820.11   1.461,93 DM    4 893,56 F
G5000     $1,023.65    £621.35      ¥132,275.13   1.827,42 DM    6 116,96 F
G6000     $1,228.38    £745.62      ¥158,730.16   2.192,90 DM    7 340,35 F
G7000     $1,433.10    £869.89      ¥185,185.19   2.558,39 DM    8 563,74 F
G8000     $1,637.83    £994.16      ¥211,640.21   2.923,87 DM    9 787,13 F
G9000     $1,842.56    £1,118.43    ¥238,095.24   3.289,35 DM    11 010,52 F
```

The output is very interesting, considering that we did no work ourselves!

Inputting formatted data

We have concentrated up to now on outputting data. The `java.text` package also provides for inputting formatted data in each of its classes. Formatted data are distinguished from unformatted data in that the items need not be delimited by spaces and so on, but must appear in particular columns in the input line. They may even abut each other as in the following:

```
76 89123 45 10 6100
```

If this is interpreted with a format of maximum and minimum digits as 3, then the resulting numbers are 76, 89, 123, 45, 10, 6 and 100.

The general term for getting input data in Java is **parsing**, which is analogous to formatting for output. However, data these days are very seldom presented without delimiters of some sort, and in general tokenizers, as discussed in Section 7.2, are adequate for most needs. A distinct disadvantage of parsing via the formatters is that the results are presented as objects, so one still has to do the conversion to primitive types.

7.5   Dates, calendars and time

The `Date` class, which is part of the `java.util` package, represents dates and times in a system-independent way. Its complete specification is given in the form:

```
The Date class

Date ();
Date (long date);


boolean after (Date when);
boolean before (Date when);
boolean compareTo (Date d);
boolean equals (Object obj);
long    getTime ();
long    setTime (long time);
String  toString ();
```

`Date` starts off with two constructors. The first one, which has no parameters, will put the computer's current date and time in the new object. Thus if we say

```
Date today = new Date ();
```

we create an object containing today's date and time, as taken from the computer's clock. The second constructor creates a date from the number of milliseconds from some arbitary date. In `Date` itself, there is no easier way to create a specific date, and we need another class, `Calendar`, for this purpose.

After the constructors come the methods, and the interesting ones to us at this stage are `getTime` and `toString`. Given a date object, we can print it straight through `println` as follows:

```
System.out.println(today);
```

`today` will first be converted to a string and then printed. The conversion is carried out by the `toString` method, which should be present in all classes that want their objects to be printed. The format for the conversion means that the date will always be printed in the following form, shown with an example:

```
Day Month Date Hours:Mins:Secs Zone Year
Tue Jul 04 17:11:54 EST 2000
```

If the zone of the computer is not one of Java's recognizable time zones, then an offset from GMT is given, as in

```
Tue Jul 04 17:11:54 GMT+00:00 2000
```

Other formats are possible via `java.text`, as discussed below.

Originally in Java 1.0, the `Date` class was much bigger and included methods for getting and setting parts of the date, among others. These functions have now been taken over by another much more complex class, `Calendar`. Rather than itemize `Calendar`, we just list here the parts we shall need for the next example:

- constants indicating the various fields, e.g. `YEAR` or `MINUTE`;

- constants for the days and months, e.g. `MONDAY` or `DECEMBER`;

- a class method that creates an object, i.e. `getInstance`;

- instance methods for getting and setting parts of the date, i.e. `get` and `set`.

`get` and `set` require field parts to be specified, for example

```
int y = get(Calendar.YEAR);
set (Calendar.YEAR, 2001);
```

In addition, `set` can be given three values, year, month and day, but note that it is best to use the constant names provided for the months, e.g. `Calendar.MAY` not 4.

EXAMPLE 7.5   Shopping days

Problem   We would like to calculate the number of shopping days to Christmas, assuming that we are already in the month of December.

Algorithm   Given the assumption that we are already in December, the algorithm is very simple, as we only have to subtract the dates of the two `Date` objects. Working from November or October would require more calculating skills than we want to use in this illustration.

Program

```
import java.util.*;

public class Shopping {

    /* Shopping Program          by J M Bishop Dec 96
     * ----------------          Java 1.1 by J M Bishop Dec 97
     *                           updated July 2000
     * Calculates the number of shopping days to Christmas,
     * and is only meant to be run in December.
     */

    public static void main(String[] args) {
      new Shopping ();
    }

    Shopping () {
      Calendar today = Calendar.getInstance();
      Calendar christmas = Calendar.getInstance();

      christmas.set(
          today.get(Calendar.YEAR), Calendar.DECEMBER, 25);

      System.out.println("Only run this program in December!");
      System.out.println("Christmas is on "+ christmas.getTime());
      System.out.println("Today is "+ today.getTime());

      System.out.println("There are "
              +(christmas.get(Calendar.DATE)-
                today.get(Calendar.DATE))
              +" shopping days to Christmas.");
    }
}
```

Counting lines within the main method, the two dates are declared on lines 1 and 2 as `Calendar` objects using the `getInstance` class method to set them up. Lines 3 and 4 make the program independent of which year we are in, by getting the year from today to set the year for Christmas.

Lines 5 and 6 print out the two dates and then on line 8 we subtract their day numbers for the final message. Notice here that we have to put the subtraction expression in brackets so that the result of it, which is an integer, is the expression which is converted to a string for printing. The compiler will complain if we do not do this. (Try it and see.)

Testing   The results of a test run of the program would be:

```
Only run this program in December!
Christmas is on Mon Dec 25 10:17:01 GMT+02:00 2000
Today is Tue Dec 05 10:17:01 GMT+03:00 2000
There are 21 shopping days to Christmas.
```

Date formatting

In the same way as we can format numbers and currencies, we can also format dates. From the DateFormat class of java.text we create a formatter with a specific style, being one of DEFAULT, FULL, LONG, MEDIUM or SHORT. Thus instead of the simple

```
System.out.println("Today is "+ today.getTime());
```

in the above program, we can be more specific and say:

```
DateFormat D = DateFormat.getDateInstance(DateFormat.FULL);
System.out.println("Today is "+ D.format(today));
```

which would print out the more user-friendly version of:

```
Tuesday, July 4, 2000
```

The various options are explored in the next example. Similarly, we can select a time formatter and print the time in a variety of ways. The method here is getTimeInstance.

Date parsing

A useful feature of the DateFormat class is the method to parse a date from a string. It enables us to read dates. For example, if we declare an ordinary date formatter as:

```
DateFormat DF = DateFormat.getDateInstance();
```

and have data such as

```
15-Jul-2000
```

we can read it with:

```
Date D = DF.parse(in.readString());
```

parse can raise an exception, so it is necessary to catch it here or mention it in all the methods associated with the call. Catching it is shown the following test program:

```
import java.text.*;
import javagently.*;
import java.util.*;
import java.io.*;

class TestDates {

  public static void main (String args []) throws IOException {
    new TestDates ();
  }

  TestDates() throws IOException {
    System.out.println("Type in a date as dd-mmm-yyyy');
    System.out.println();
    Stream in = new Stream(System.in);
    String s = in.readString();
    System.out.println("String is :"+s);
    DateFormat DF = DateFormat.getDateInstance();
    Date d = new Date();
    try {
      d = DF.parse(s);
      System.out.println("Date is :"+d);
    } catch (ParseException e) {
      System.out.println("Error in date " + s);
    }
  }
}
```

```
Type in a date as dd-mmm-yyyy

15-Jul-2000
String is :15-Jul-2000
Date is :Sat Jul 15 00:00:00 GMT+03:00 2000

Type in a date as dd-mmm-yyyy

15-Mei-2000
String is :15-Mei-2000
Error in date 15-Mei-2000
```

The default date format is the simple one shown above. Of course, other date formats can be insisted upon by changing the style of the formatter, as shown in the next example.

EXAMPLE 7.6   Formatting and parsing dates

Problem   Illustrate the various options for input and output of dates in Java.

Solution   The solution, as always, is to set up a test program. The one that follows is carefully crafted not only to give the necessary illustrative output, but also to exercise some of the other interesting aspects of date formatting in Java. Specifically:

- date formats can be sent as parameters;
- the parse method throws a `ParseException` which indicates a date in the wrong form.

Program   Notice that we have set the program up for the UK locale which will put the day before the month. It is easy to change this statement. The default is US, which would put the month before the day. See Example 7.7 for more on dates and locales.

```
import java.text.*;
import java.util.*;
import javagently.*;
import java.io.*;

class CustomDates {

  /* Testing date formatting    by J M Bishop Dec 1997
   * ----------------------    Java 1.1
   *                           Java 2 July 2000
   *
   * Writes dates in multiple formats and
   * prompts for dates back in the same form.
   */

  Stream in = new Stream (System.in);
  Date d = new Date ();
  Date my = new Date();

  void echoDate(String style, DateFormat Din,DateFormat Dout)
                    throws IOException {
    System.out.println(style+"\t"+Din.format(d));
    String s = in.readLine();
    System.out.println("\t\t\t"+s);
    try {
      my = Din.parse(s);
    }
    catch (ParseException e) {
      System.out.println("Invalid date "+s);
    }
```

```
      System.out.println("\t\t\t"+Dout.format(my));
  }

CustomDates() throws IOException {

  Locale.setDefault(Locale.UK);
  DateFormat DS = DateFormat.getDateInstance(DateFormat.SHORT);
  DateFormat DM = DateFormat.getDateInstance(DateFormat.MEDIUM);
  DateFormat DL = DateFormat.getDateInstance(DateFormat.LONG);
  DateFormat DF = DateFormat.getDateInstance(DateFormat.FULL);
  DateFormat DD = DateFormat.getDateInstance(DateFormat.DEFAULT);

  echoDate("SHORT",DS,DF);
  echoDate("MEDIUM",DM,DF);
  echoDate("LONG",DL,DF);
  echoDate("FULL",DF,DF);
  echoDate("DEFAULT",DD,DF);
}

public static void main (String args []) throws IOException {
  new CustomDates();
}

}
```

Testing

```
SHORT      04/07/00
30/04/00
           30/04/00
           30 April 2000
MEDIUM     04-Jul-00
15-Oct-00
           15-Oct-00
           15 October 2000
LONG 04 July 2000
25 September 2000
           25 September 2000
           25 September 2000
FULL 04 July 2000
7 January 2000
           7 January 2000
           07 January 2000
DEFAULT    04-Jul-00
Jul-04-00
           Jul-04-00
Invalid date Jul-04-00
           07 January 2000
```

We notice two points from this output:

1. Java seems to have a Year 2000 problem! It is not until the date style is given as LONG that a four digit year is allowed on input.

2. In FULL style, the day (e.g. Tuesday) should be requested as well.

Time zones

In its mission to be a truly world-wide and web-oriented language, Java provides for detecting the time zone of the computer running the program. From the time zone, the zone code, the offset from Universal Time[2] and information about daylight saving can be established.

EXAMPLE 7.7   Testing time zones

What follows is a test program to show the information that can be deduced about the computer's time zone.

```
import java.util.*;

class WorldTime {
  /* Time Zone program    by J M Bishop December 1997
   * -----------------    Java 1.1
   *                      updated July 2000
   * Uses the Java libraries to display
   * time anywhere in the world.
   */

  public static void main (String [ ] args) {
    new WorldTime();
  }

  WorldTime() {
     TimeZone here = TimeZone.getDefault();
     Date today = new Date();
     System.out.println(today);
     System.out.println("We are in " + here.getID() + " time zone");
     System.out.println("with " + here.getRawOffset()/3600000 +
                        " offset from UTC");
```

[2] Universal Time is taken from 0° longitude and used to be known as GMT (Greenwich Mean Time).

```
      System.out.println("Daylight Savings Time used here is " +
                         here.useDaylightTime());
      System.out.println("and being now in Daylight Savings Time is "
                         + here.inDaylightTime(today));


  }
}
```

Testing

```
Tue Jul 04 17:11:54 EST 2000
We are in EST time zone
with -5 offset from UTC
Daylight Savings Time used here is true
and being now in Daylight Savings Time is false
```

Once you have run the WorldTime program, it is quite fun to change your time zone and run it again. On a Windows system, you do this by going into Help, selecting time zones and clicking the arrow. You are given a map of the world and can select any vertical time zone slice, as well as a specific region for that zone.

Localized date formatting

In the previous section we discussed locales and showed how the locale of a program can be changed, thus indicating a different display language. By using locales, we can obtain dates printed in different languages and different formats. We can even create our own, if the language is not one known to the Java Locale class (the full list is given in the Locale form above).

EXAMPLE 7.8   Multilingual dates

Problem   We would like to demonstrate Java's ability to print dates in various languages.

Solution   Use the DateFormat and Locale classes.

Algorithm   Printing the dates can be done by a method

```
void printDates (Locale L) {

  System.out.println("We are in " + L.getCountry() +
    " speaking " + L.getLanguage());
```

```
   DateFormat D = DateFormat.getDateInstance();
   System.out.println(D.format(today));

   D = DateFormat.getDateInstance(DateFormat.FULL);
   System.out.println(D.format(today));
   System.out.println();
}
```

This will give the country and language, then print the date in default form (quite short) and full form (but without the time). To call it, we use:

```
   Locale.setDefault(Locale.GERMANY);
   printDates(Locale.getDefault());
```

In other words, we overwrite the default locale of the computer, and pass this to `printDates`. The result should be:

```
We are in DE speaking de
14.12.2000
Donnerstag, 14. Dezember 2000
```

Java is providing quite an impressive facility here.

Program   The program put together with several such changes of locale is:

```
import java.util.*;
import java.io.*;
import javagently.*;
import java.text.*;

class VaryDates {

   /* Vary Dates program    by J M Bishop December 1997
    * ------------------     Java 1.1
    *                        updated July 2000
    * Uses the Java libraries to display
    * dates for different locales.
    */

   Date today = new Date();

   void printDates (Locale L) {

     System.out.println("We are in " + L.getCountry() +
        " speaking " + L.getLanguage());
```

```
      DateFormat D = DateFormat.getDateInstance();
      System.out.println(D.format(today));

      D = DateFormat.getDateInstance(DateFormat.FULL);
      System.out.println(D.format(today));
      System.out.println();
   }

   VaryDates () {

     System.out.println(today);

     Locale genuine = Locale.getDefault();
     printDates(genuine);

     Locale.setDefault(Locale.GERMANY);
     printDates(Locale.getDefault());

     Locale.setDefault(Locale.UK);
     printDates(Locale.getDefault());

     Locale.setDefault(Locale.FRANCE);
     printDates(Locale.getDefault());

     Locale.setDefault(Locale.US);
     printDates(Locale.getDefault());

     Locale.setDefault(Locale.JAPAN);
     printDates(Locale.getDefault());

   }

   public static void main (String [ ] args) throws IOException{
     new VaryDates ();
   }

}
```

Testing   Running the program gives:

```
Tue Jul 04 11:23:19 GMT+03:00 2000
We are in SOUTH AFRICA speaking en
04-Jul-00
Tuesday, July 4, 2000
```

```
We are in DE speaking de
04.07.2000
Dienstag, 4. Juli 2000

We are in GB speaking en
04-Jul-00
04 July 2000

We are in FR speaking fr
4 juil. 00
mardi 4 juillet 2000

We are in US speaking en
04-Jul-00
Tuesday, July 4, 2000

We are in IT speaking it
4-lug-00
martedì 4 luglio 2000

We are in JP speaking ja
2000/07/05
2000?7?5?
```

The displaying is not always perfect, but there certainly are a variety of formats and the words do come out in different languages. It is interesting to note if we switch locales to Japan, it is already tomorrow, and the date has changed to 5 July. Java also cannot print the Japanese characters so does its best with numbers.

Extension As promised, we can also teach the computer about new locales. To do this, we declare a new locale as in

```
Locale Afr = new Locale("Afrikaans","Suid-Afrika");
```

Then we have to pull in another class called `DateFormatSymbols` in which we can set the names of the days and months in the new language. For example, the months go like this:

```
String AfrMonths [] = {"Januarie", "Februarie", "Maart", "April",
        "Mei", "Junie", "Julie", "Augustus", "September",
        "Oktober", "November", "Desember"};

DateFormatSymbols DAfr = new DateFormatSymbols(Afr);
DAfr.setMonths (AfrMonths);
```

Then we set up the format patterns for the country, using a string pattern. The pattern facility is provided in a subclass of `DateFormat` called `SimpleDateFormat`, and typical format declarations would be:

```
SimpleDateFormat Dshort = new SimpleDateFormat("yyyy/MM/dd");

SimpleDateFormat Dfull = new SimpleDateFormat
                   ("EEEE dd MMMM yyyy", DAfr);
```

`Dshort` specifies a pattern; `Dfull` specifies a pattern and a set of `DateFormatSymbols` which will include all the names of months, etc. Putting this all together, we get the following statements which can be put at the end of `VaryDates`.

```
String AfrMonths [] = {"Januarie", "Februarie", "Maart",
    "April", "Mei", "Junie", "Julie", "Augustus", "September",
    "Oktober", "November", "Desember"};

String AfrDays []= {"Saterdag", "Sondag","Maandag", "Dinsdag",
    "Woensdag", "Donderdag", "Vrydag"};

Locale Afr = new Locale("Afrikaans","Suid-Afrika");
Locale.setDefault(genuine);

DateFormatSymbols DAfr = new DateFormatSymbols(Afr);
DAfr.setMonths (AfrMonths);
DAfr.setWeekdays (AfrDays);

System.out.println("We are in " + Afr.getCountry() +
    " speaking " + Afr.getLanguage());

SimpleDateFormat Dshort = new SimpleDateFormat("yyyy/MM/dd");
System.out.println(Dshort.format(today));

SimpleDateFormat Dfull = new SimpleDateFormat
                   ("EEEE dd MMMM yyyy", DAfr);
System.out.println(Dfull.format(today));
```

The output would be:

```
We are in SUID-AFRIKA speaking afrikaans
2000/07/04
Dinsdag 04 Julie 2000
```

There are more facilities available in all these classes, and you can look them up in the Java API help.

SUMMARY

Strings are not arrays in the Java context, but are objects instantiated from a special `String` class. They have their own properties and characteristics. Conversion methods between strings and character arrays and between strings and numbers do exist. However, the conversions sometimes need the help of envelope classes, which turn variables into objects. Strings can be processed by means of tokenizers. Together these facilities combine to provide the power needed by the `Stream` class, which is used for all the simple input in this book.

Output formatting is provided for extensively in Java. Numbers, currencies, percentages and dates can all be customized for specific formats, as well as for locales. Choosing a locale causes the language and format of output to be adapted to the conventions of that country. Time zones can also be specified and interrogated.

In this chapter we introduced no new keywords, but concentrated on the following Java APIs:

```
String                      Numberformat
  valueOf                     getInstance
  charAt                      getCurrencyInstance
  indexOf                     getNumberInstance
  substring                   getPercentInstance
  startsWith                  format
  toCharArray                 setMaximumIntegerDigits
  toLowerCase                 setMiniumumIntegerDigits
  trim                        setMaximumFractionDigits
StringBuffer                  setMinimumFractionDigits
StringTokenizer               setGroupingUsed
  nextToken                 Date
  hasMoreTokens               after
  countTokens                 before
Integer                       getTime
  valueOf                     setTime
  intValue
  parseInt
```

and exceptions

```
NoSuchElementException       ParseException
NumberFormatException
```

and forms

Creating a string
Manipulating strings
`StringTokenizer` declaration and access
`Integer` and `int` conversions
The `Stream` class
Creating number formatters

The `Locale` class
Using number formatters
Customizing a number formatter
The `Date` class

7.1 If `name` is a `String` variable, which expression will correctly return the first position of the letter 'e' if it exists?

   (a) `name.indexOf('e')`
   (b) `name.startsWith('e')`
   (c) `indexOf(name,'e')`
   (d) `name.charAt('e')`

7.2 If we have the data '$567.89' in the string price, how would we get the cents as a string?

   (a) `price.substring(price.indexOf('.'), price.length()-1);`
   (b) `price.startsWith('.',price.endsWith('9'));`
   (c) `price.substring(price.indexOf('.')+1,price.length())`
   (d) `price.substring('.',price.length);`

7.3 If `tragic` is a `Calendar` object, how would we set it to 31 August 1997?

   (a) `tragic.set(1997,Calendar.August,31);`
   (b) `tragic.set(31, 8, 1997);`
   (c) `tragic.set (1997, 8, 31);`
   (d) `tragic.set (1997, Calendar.AUGUST, 31);`

7.4 To read in 10 digit cheque numbers properly, we had to first read a string and convert it to a `char` array. Why?

   (a) there is no `readChar` method in the `Stream` class
   (b) chars have to be followed by spaces when read
   (c) 10 digits is too long to read as an integer
   (d) we can't compare strings and characters

7.5 If a string and a tokenizer are set up with

```
String s = "A678230056 7";
StringTokenizer T = new StringTokenizer(s, "0123456789", false);
```

what will the tokens be if we loop through all of them?

   (a) A67230056 and 7
   (b) 7
   (c) A and 7
   (d) A and space

7.6 If we have a price as an `int` and want to put it in a hash table, it has to be wrapped up as an object. The expression to do this is:

   (a) `(Integer) price`
   (b) `new Integer (price)`

(c) `price.Intvalue()`

(d) `Integer (price)`

7.7 In the `Stream` class, the format methods are declared as static because

(a) they deal with output, not input

(b) they are not related to any `Stream` object

(c) there are two of them with the same name

(d) they do raise `IOExceptions`

7.8 What will be printed after the following sequence?

```
NumberFormat N = NumberFormat.getInstance();
N.setGroupingUsed(false);
N.setMaximumFractionDigits(4);
N.setMinimumIntegerDigits(4);
System.out.println(N.format(Math.PI)+" "+ N.format(10000));
```

(a) `3.1416 10000`

(b) `0003.1416 10000`

(c) `3.1416 10000.0000`

(d) `3 10000`

7.9 A locale can be set by

(a) a Java program

(b) the user via the operating system

(c) both of these

(d) neither of these

7.10 If our `Locale` is set to Germany, and we type in a date such as 07-May-2000 what will happen if we are using parsing on a `DateFormat`?

(a) the computer interprets it the date as intended, i.e. 7-5-2000

(b) a `parseException` is raised

(c) May defaults to zero, i.e. January

(d) we are asked to enter the date again

PROBLEMS

On string handling

7.1 **Validating codes.** Course codes at Savanna University have a precise form: three capital letters followed immediately by three digits. Write a class for such codes, and include methods to create, convert to a string and check a code for validity. Test the class with a small test program.

7.2 **Palindromes.** A palindrome is a word or sentence that reads the same forwards as backwards, disregarding punctuation. Famous palindromes are:

Madam, I'm Adam

Able was I ere I saw Elba.

Write a boolean method that will check whether a given string is a palindrome or not. Call the method from a test program.

7.3   **Converting names.** A very old file of people's names was created using all capital letters. Convert it to the usual capital and lower-case letters. Take account of initials. Set surname prefixes such as Du or Von with a capital. Examples are:

M A STORE	M A Store
J. FOX-ROBINSON	J. Fox-Robinson
P DU PLESSIS	P Du Plessis

On tokenizers

7.4   **Indexing programs.** A useful feature when programming is to know where each identifier occurs. Write a program that will index a program in this way, producing an alphabetically sorted list of identifiers, with all the line numbers of the program on which they occur.

7.5   **Concordance.** A concordance is a list of words similar to an index, where the position of each word – its page number and line number – in a piece of text is indicated. The difference between a concordance and an index is that a concordance considers all words except common ones such as 'and', 'the' and 'is'. Write a Java system to create a concordance from a piece of text at your disposal. Use tokenizers and hash tables. (Hint: the hash table will have the words as keys and the page/line numbers as values. Since the words could occur more than once, the value will have to be an array of numbers, and will have to have an upper limit, say 10 occurrences recorded.)

7.6   **Egalitarian minutes.** The Council of Savanna University has decreed that in future all minutes of meetings will omit titles of those speaking. Instead of Prof. Brown, committees may choose between John Brown, Brown, JB or John, depending on circumstances. However, in any one document, only one convention should be used. Your task is to process a document, looking for titles, i.e. Prof. Dr, Mr, Ms, Miss, Rev., remove them, and replace the name that follows with the selected form.

To solve this problem, the program will need information regarding the names of the people. For example, if the John Brown format is chosen, and the program encounters Prof. Brown, then it must be able to find John from somewhere. There are two options:

■ Interact with the secretary or whoever is running the program and get the information that way. This is simple to set up but could be tedious and error prone when running.

■ From the attendance and apologies lists at the beginning of the document, construct a hash table with the necessary information. Assume that these lists give everyone's details in full, e.g. Prof. John Brown (JB). Make use of the `String` method `startWith` to find the lists.

You will have to decide how the hash table is going to be arranged, i.e. what the key is, but remember that we can search the keys and the values, and customized searching can also be added.

On formatting

7.7   **Multiple word names.** A problem we detected earlier (for example in the Olympic medals program in Example 4.10) is that we cannot have names with spaces in them. The reason is that a space delimits the whole name, so it cannot be *in* the name. We solved the problem by changing the data so that names such as United.States were written with a full stop in the middle. Now that we know more about formatting, what would be the best approach to employ for a method that could read such names? Assume that the names are lined up in columns of a fixed size and that no other data items will be in that column. Write a suitable method to read multiword names, include it as part of a class called `Formatters` in your `myutilities` package and use it to remove the data restriction from the Olympics program.

7.8   **Better price formatting.** Consider Problem 5.9 again (car tax). Use number formatter to help print out the car prices in the correct format for the currency for a country with which you are familiar.

7.9   **Variable formatting.** To give yourself practice with using formatters, write a program that will print out real numbers (randomly generated) in a format specified via the display. This means using a pattern of the form ###0.### where the number of hashes before and after the point could vary.

On dates, calendars and time

7.10   **Birthdays.** The `after` and `before` methods of the `Calendar` class in the `java.util` package will return true or false depending on the relationship between the instance object and the parameter. For example,

```
new calendar (1951, Calendar. DECEMBER, 14). before
              (new Calendar (1951, Calendar. December, 1))
```

will be false. Write a program that sets up your birthday and the day of Easter this year and displays the result of each of the three relations – before, equals and after – between the two dates.

7.12   **Your own dates.** Choose another country not supported by the standard locales and customize Java to reflect the language and conventions of that country, as we did in Example 7.8. Investigate the APIs via Java's help and try to customize the currency formatting as well. The approach is very similar to that for dates.

7.13   **Public holidays again.** Referring to Problem 6.6, use Java's `Date` class for the dates. Find the holidays for one of the countries listed in the `Locale` class's form in Section 7.4 and set up the program to print out the dates in the correct format for that country. Public holidays around the world can currently be found on

http://www.globalsources.com/TNTLIST/TRAVEL/HOLIDAYS.HTM.

CHAPTER 8

Objects at work

Java is an object-oriented language and, in earlier chapters, we introduced and used both objects and classes in many examples. Now that we have covered the basic constructs of Java, it is time to look at the real power of objects, and how they are used in larger programs. In this chapter we discuss objects using a case study of a typical inventory program. In the next chapter we go on to look at further capabilities of objects, such as inheritance, interfaces and abstract classes, and explore some more examples. This chapter starts with a Coffee Shop example, goes on to revise some basic object principles and then continues with the example as a case study.

8.1 Designing an object-oriented program

We now consider the design and development of an example that will make considerable use of classes and have many objects instantiated from them.

| EXAMPLE 8.1 | Nelson's Coffee Shop |

Problem Nelson's Coffee Shop is looking to computerize its inventory. It would like to investigate what information it needs about coffee stocks and what operations it should incorporate to handle them.

Solution At this stage we are not going to write the whole inventory program! We are just looking at the definition of the objects. In so doing, though, we shall bear in mind that while coffee may be the main selling item at the shop, it may in the future also sell pastries, ice creams and so on.

Definition The shop does not sell just one kind of coffee, but many kinds, such as Java, Colombian, VIP and Kenyan. Coffee is going to be a class, and we shall create different coffee objects. In looking at stocks of coffee, we can list the data items that need to be taken into account when recording information about a particular kind. Such a list is the starting point for an object definition. At the same time, we take a guess at the general type of each data item. The first such list is shown in Table 8.1. String, real, integer and date all have existing equivalents in Java.

Table 8.1 *Data items for the coffee class*

Item	Type
Name	string
Price	double (graz)
Amount in stock	integer (kilograms)
Reorder level	integer (kilograms)
Barcode	string
Sell-by date	date

Looking at this list, we notice that it is too simple. Whereas the first five properties refer to coffee in general, the sell-by date is going to differ for each *batch* of coffee as it comes into the shop. What this means is that a batch is another object. Not only must it record the date, but it also keeps a count of the number of kilograms of coffee for that date. The main coffee object will keep a cumulative total. This relationship is illustrated in Figure 8.1.

The next part of the definition concerns the operations. We treat these in two groups: those for a kind of coffee (Table 8.2) and those for particular batches (Table 8.3). Starting with the coffee, there is a list of operations that seem likely. Some of these have implications for batches.

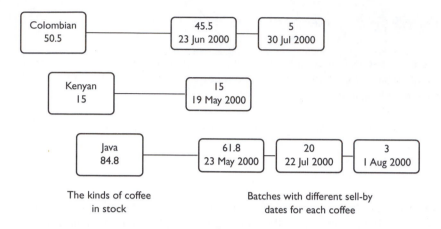

The kinds of coffee in stock

Batches with different sell-by dates for each coffee

Figure 8.1 *Multiple classes and objects for the coffee shop.*

We can see that there is a hierarchy between the two types of objects: coffee objects call batch operations, but not vice versa. The method to remove old stock will consider each batch in turn and nullify a batch if it finds it is too old. Similarly, selling coffee could bring a batch down to zero.

How can an object be removed? It will all depend on how the batch objects are arranged. The only grouping structure we know of so far is an array, and we can immediately see that it is a singularly inappropriate structure if we want to delete items: all those following will have to move up, or we have to handle gaps.

Of course there is a better way, but in order not to extend this part of the example for too long, we shall tackle that in Section 8.3, and return to the coffee shop in Section 8.4. Consequently, we will not implement the methods to sell coffee or remove old stock at this point, and will be content to keep batches in an array.

Table 8.2 *Operations on coffee kinds*

Operations on coffee	Implications for batches
Prepare to enter stock	
Display coffee kind's data	
Check reorder level	
Change price	
Add stock	Add a new batch
Sell coffee	Subtract stock from relevant batches
Remove old stock	Check sell-by date

Table 8.3   *Operations on coffee batches*

Operations on batches	Implications for coffee
Add a new batch	
Display data about a batch	
Check how much is available	
Check sell-by date	
Sell	

Classes   Now we can try to express the design in Java. Starting with the specification of the `Batch` class:

```
class Batch {

   /* The Batch class   by J M Bishop Oct 1996
    * ----------------   Java 1.1 October 1997
    * for products with sell-by dates.
    * Can be tested with the Coffee class.
    */

   private double inStock;
   private Date sellByDate;
   private DateFormat DF = DateFormat.getDateInstance();

   Batch   (double k, Date d) { }
   double  available ( ) { }
   boolean sell (double k) { }
   void    display () { }
}
```

The details of the methods have not yet been filled in. Let us first look at how they are used. To create a new batch, the `Coffee` class will include a statement of the form:

```
freshBatch = new Batch (kilos, roastDay);
```

The new batch will have to be linked to the other batches in some way, but we shall leave that issue for the time being. When coffee is sold, the method responsible must first check the availability in the oldest batch and sell as much as it can there. If the order is not complete, the next batch is offered. Let us assume that in an array of batches, batch `B[i]` contains the oldest coffee. The statement to call it to sell `k1` kilograms will be:

```
B[i].sell(k1);
```

If we needed to reduce stock from another batch, identified by B[j], then

```
B[j].sell(k2);
```

would refer to a different stock and date. The two would not be confused, because they are in different objects.

With respect to accessibility, Batch is always going to be used with Coffee, so there is no need to make it public at this stage. The four methods it provides to the Coffee class can therefore also have default accessibility. However, the fields a batch uses should not be accessed from outside, and therefore are declared as private.

The definition of the Coffee object proceeds in a similar way. Its outline is:

```
class Coffee {

    /*  The Coffee class        by J M Bishop Oct 1996
     *  ----------------         Java 1.1 October 1997
     *                           updated August 2000
     *  keeps an inventory of batches of coffee of a
     *  particular kind
     */

    Coffee () { }

    Coffee (String s) { };

    void     prepareToStock (Stream in) { }
    boolean newBatchIn (Stream in) { }

    void     display () { }
    double  sell (double k) { }
    boolean stocksLow () { }
    void     changePrice (double p) { }
    void     checkSellByDate () { }

    private String name;
    private double price;    // per kg
    private double stock; // kgs
    private double reorder; // kgs;
    private Batch B [ ] = new Batch [10];
    private int batches = 0;
    private DateFormat DF = DateFormat.getDateInstance(DateFormat.DEFAULT,
                    Locale.UK);
}
```

As with a batch, the variables are all declared as private, which means that they cannot be altered from outside, only from methods within the class itself. The constructor has no parameters, and in fact does nothing either: all the setting of values is done inside `prepareToStock`. Why did we do it this way? The reason is that the details of the coffee will be read from a file; they are not available in the program itself. In the next version of the program, we will add a second constructor.

Both the `prepareToStock` method and `newBatchIn` will be reading data, and they open and close their own data streams. The model diagram so far is shown in Figure 8.2. All the variables in both classes are declared private (see Chapter 5), indicated by a minus sign. The array of batches kept in `Coffee` is declared as of the class `Batch`, and this instantiation is shown by the arrow. One of the elements of the array has been instantiated as a `Batch` object.

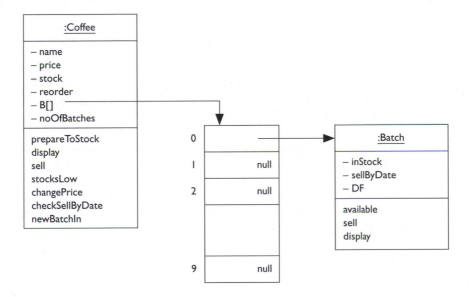

Figure 8.2 *Model diagram for the* `Coffee` *and* `Batch` *classes.*

Data   An important consideration for the operation of the reading in of coffee is how the data should be arranged. We choose to keep it on file at this stage, becuase it is easier to test the program that way. The alternatives, that of prompting the user on the screen, line by line, or of using the display, are really rather tedious.

The data can be arranged on file as follows:

```
name
price reorder-level
stock sell-by-date      (repeated for each batch)
0
```

with an example that matches Figure 8.1 being

```
Colombian
59.95 10
45.5 23-Jun-00
5 30-Jul-00
0
Kenyan
60.75 10
15 19-May-00
0
Java
63.50 30
61.8 23-May-00
20 12-Jul-00
3 1-Aug-00
0
```

The zero after each set of batches is necessary to enable the loop to end. (See Section 5.2 for a discussion on this issue.) The date is going to be read in as a string and converted to a `Date` object. How this is done was discussed in Section 7.5.

Program   And finally we have the program. It consists of three classes, `Batch`, `Coffee` and main program, `CoffeeShop`. The latter contains a little test main program that causes the data to be read in and printed out. Nothing else happens at this stage, but of course we have achieved a lot: we have written a large-ish object-oriented program, and it contains two kinds of user-defined objects. Just as a matter of interest, can you count how many other kinds of objects it contains as well?

```
import java.io.*;
import java.util.*;
import java.text.*;

class Batch {

   /* The Batch class                        by J M Bishop Oct 1996
    * ---------------                         Java 1.1 October 1997
    * for products with sell-by dates.
    *
    * To be used with the Coffee class
    */

  Batch (double k, Date d) {
     inStock = k;
     sellByDate = d;
  }
```

```java
double available ( ) {
  return inStock;
}

boolean sell (double k) {
  inStock -= k;
  System.out.println("Sold "+ Stream.Format(k, 1, 1) +" from batch "+
                     DF.format(sellByDate));
  return inStock <= 0; // sold out
}

void display () {
  System.out.println("\t\t"+DF.format(sellByDate) +
        " : " + Stream.Format(inStock, 4, 1) + "kg");
}

private double inStock;
private Date sellByDate;
private DateFormat DF = DateFormat.getDateInstance(DateFormat.DEFAULT,
                   Locale.UK);

}


//=====================================================
import java.io.*;
import java.util.*;
import javagently.*;
import java.text.*;

class Coffee {

  /*  The Coffee class        by J M Bishop Oct 1996
   *  ----------------        Java 1.1 October 1997
   *                          updated August 2000
   *  keeps an inventory of batches of coffee of a
   *  particular kind
   */

  Coffee () {
  }

  Coffee (String s) {
    name = new String (s);
  };
```

```
void prepareToStock (Stream in)
              throws IOException {
   name = in.readString();
   price = in.readDouble();
   reorder = in.readInt();
   batches = 0;
   stock = 0;
  }


  boolean newBatchIn (Stream in) throws IOException {
    double amount;
    Date sellby;
    String s;

    amount = in.readDouble();
    if (amount == 0) // batch completed
      return false;
    else {
      stock += amount;
      sellby = new Date ();
      s = in.readString();
      try {
        sellby = DF.parse(s);
      } catch (ParseException e) {
        System.out.println("Error in date " + s);
      }
        B[batches] = new Batch (amount,sellby);
        batches ++;
        return true;
      }
    }


    void display () {
      System.out.println(name+" @ G"+
            Stream.format(price,1,2)+" per kg");
      for (int i = 0; i < batches; i++) {
        B[i].display ();
      }
      System.out.println("\t" + Stream.format(stock, 1, 1) +
            "kg in stock. Reorder level is "
            +reorder+"kg\n");
    }
```

```
    private String name;
    private double price;    // per kg
    private double stock; // kgs
    private double reorder; // kgs;
    private Batch B [ ] = new Batch [10];
    private int batches = 0;
      private DateFormat DF = DateFormat.getDateInstance(DateFormat.
                             DEFAULT, Locale.UK);


}



// ========================================================

import java.io.*;
import java.util.*;
import java.text.*;
import javagently.*;
import myutilities.*;

class CoffeeShop {

  /* A test Coffee Shop program     by J M Bishop Oct 1996
   * --------------------------     Java 1.1 October 1997
   *                                updated August 2000
   * checks that data can be read into the
   * Coffee and Batch classes, and printed out again.
   * Uses an array to store several objects of each.
   */

 public static void main (String [] args) throws IOException {

    Stream in = Filer.open("coffee.dat");

    Coffee C [ ] = new Coffee [10];
    int kind;

    // Introductory messages
    System.out.println("Nelson's Coffee Shop");
    System.out.println("Inventory control");
    System.out.println("Stocking from coffee.data");

    // Read in the data for the coffees
    for (kind=0; kind<10; kind++) {
```

```
        try {
          C[kind] = new Coffee ();
          C[kind].prepareToStock (in);
          boolean morebatches = true;
          while (morebatches)
            morebatches = C[kind].newBatchIn (in);
        }
        catch (EOFException e) {
          System.out.println("That's the shop stocked for today\n");
          break;
        }
      }

    // Display all the details
    DateFormat DF = DateFormat.getDateInstance(DateFormat.FULL);
    System.out.println("The contents on " + DF.format(new Date()));
    for (int i = 0; i<kind; i++)
      C[i].display();
    }
  }
```

Testing   For the data above, the output would be:

```
Nelson's Coffee Shop
Inventory control
Stocking from coffee.data
That's the shop stocked for today

The contents on Thursday, August 3, 2000
Colombian @ G59.95 per kg
      23-Jun-00 : 45.5kg
      30-Jul-00 :  5.0kg
   50.5kg in stock. Reorder level is 10.0kg

Kenyan @ G60.75 per kg
      19-May-00 : 15.0kg
   15.0kg in stock. Reorder level is 10.0kg

Java @ G63.50 per kg
      23-May-00 : 61.8kg
      12-Jul-00 : 20.0kg
      01-Aug-00 :  3.0kg
   84.8kg in stock. Reorder level is 30.0kg
```

8.2 Properties of objects

We now look at more of the properties of objects, and how they can be manipulated in a program.

Using references

We have seen references being used for parameter passing from Chapter 3 onwards, and object variables have formed part of the declarations of classes in a natural way. Another use of references is to form a **list** of objects of the same kind. Such a list would be useful in overcoming the problem we had in the previous section of having to set an upper limit on the number of kinds of coffee, because we were using an array. In the next section we shall look at built-in Java classes for creating and manipulating lists, but here we can sketch a simple way of making one from scratch.

To make a list of coffees, we add a `Coffee` variable to the `Coffee` class, which will link to the next `Coffee` variable, i.e.:

```
Coffee link;
```

and the constructor inside `Coffee` will be changed so that an existing `Coffee` object is supplied, onto which this one is linked, as in:

```
Coffee (String s, Coffee c) {
  name = s;
  link = c;
}
```

Declaring a variable of type `Coffee` gives a variable with a value. If we instantiate a coffee, we use

```
Coffee coffees = new Coffee ("Java", null);
```

and get an object with the potential to join up to another `coffee` through the link. The object diagram at this stage is Figure 8.3.

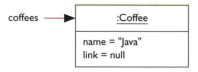

Figure 8.3 *The first item on a list.*

Now if we repeat the instantiation for another object using `coffees` as the link, and assign the result back into `coffees`, i.e.

```
Coffee coffees = new Coffee ("Colombian", coffees);
```

we get Figure 8.4. And so it could continue. The list will continue to grow, with new coffees being added at the front, and the last one always being Java. The actual variable name `coffees` will be associated with a different object after each assignment. The other coffee objects will not have identifiers and will be reachable only through a link.

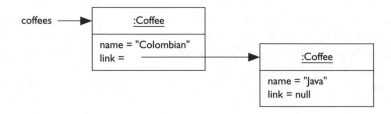

Figure 8.4 *Two items on the list.*

EXAMPLE 8.2   Illustrating a list

Problem   Illustrate how a list of objects can be built up.

Solution   The discussion on how to solve the problem is given above. Here we give a small program that tests this technique, creating a list of five coffee names read from a file and then printing them out.

Program

```
import javagently.*;
import java.io.*;

class LinkTest {

   /* The LinkTest program      J M Bishop Aug 2000
    *
    * Small test program to
    * Illustrate linking of objects through references
    */

   LinkTest () throws IOException {
   Coffee coffees = null;
```

```
String name;
Stream in = new Stream ("names.dat", Stream.READ);

// create a list headed by coffees
System.out.println("Coffees on the list");
for (int i=0; i<=4; i++) {
  name = in.readString();
  System.out.println(name);
  coffees = new Coffee (name, coffees);
}

System.out.println("Coffees on the list");
// Copy the head of the list
Coffee list = coffees;
// Print out the list
for (int i=0; i<=4; i++) {
  System.out.println(list.name);
  list = list.link;
}
}

public static void main (String args []) throws IOException {
  new LinkTest();
}
}

class Coffee {
  /* Small test class with a link */

  Coffee (String s, Coffee c) {
    name = s;
    link = c;
  }

  String name;
  Coffee link;
}

}
```

An interesting point of the program is that after we have read the names in and created the list, we then make a copy of the head into the object variable list and use it to link back through the objects. To illustrate what is happening, the situation with variables after the first name has been printed will be as in Figure 8.5.

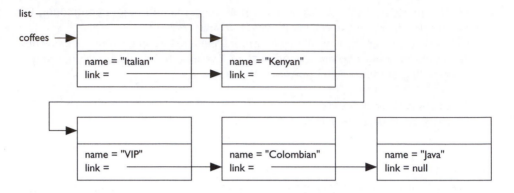

Figure 8.5 *A linked list with two object variable as heads.*

Thus the list called `list` is gradually degenerating as each name is printed, and will eventually be null. The creation of a list in this way means that the data is 'stacked' in the list and comes out backwards if printed, as shown in the test.

Testing

```
Coffees read in
Java
Colombian
VIP
Kenyan
Italian

Coffees on the list
Italian
Kenyan
VIP
Colombian
Java
```

We should also check what happens to the program if the file is empty. To do this properly, we would need to rewrite the reading loop with an exception handler, and the printing loop as a while-loop. The latter point is taken up next.

Using `null`

We already know that object variables start off with the special value `null` on declaration. If we try to access members of a null object, then Java will raise an exception, called a `NullPointerException`.[1] We can test if an object is null before continuing. For example, if s is a `String`, we can say if `(s == null)`.

A use of such a comparison would be in printing out a list when one did not know how long it was. In other words, the second loop in Example 8.2 could be rephrased as a while-loop with a condition as follows:

```
Coffee list = coffees;
// Print out the list
while (list != null) {
   System.out.println(list.name);
   list = list.link;
}
```

Reasoning about this loop we see that it will correctly print the last name, Java, then move on to a null link, and terminate. Just for interest's sake, we could also phrase the loop using an exception as follows:

```
Coffee list = coffees;
// Print out the list
try {
   while (true) {
      System.out.println(list.name);
      list = list.link;
   }
}
catch (NullPointerException e) {// end reached
}
```

The `this` identifier

Every object can access all of its members by name. The full name for a member is `this.member`, where `this` is an identifier signifying the current object. When there is no ambiguity over member names, the use of `this` is unnecessary. We would employ `this` in a case where a method has a local field or parameter with the same name as that defined in the class: then we can refer to the class field by its full name, prefixing it with `this`.

For example, we could rephrase the `Coffee` constructor in Example 8.2 as:

```
Coffee (String name, Coffee c) {
   this.name = name;
   link = c;
}
```

In this book we have chosen to give constructor parameters one-letter identifiers, as their meanings are immediately determined by the variables that they are copied into. As

---

[1] It should of course be a `NullObjectException`, but Java shows its C++ influences here.

shown here, we could also use the same name for a parameter and its corresponding variable, employing `this` to make the assignment unambiguous.

The `Object` superclass

In Java there is a superclass above all other classes, called `Object`, which we have already seen in use in Section 6.5. `Object` is central to the theory of classes in Java. Java achieves generality by using objects of different classes in the same parts of the program, while just calling them all `Objects`. This principle is important in cloning, which is discussed below.

Object equality

There are two implications of objects having references as their values. The first concerns **equality**, as we have already mentioned in Section 7.1. A straight comparison such as

```
B[i] == B[j]
```

will compare the *references* of two batches: that is, do they refer to the same object? It will not compare the values of the objects, which is probably what we intended. To compare the values themselves (all together as a group) we use an `equals` method which we must define for each new class of objects. Because `equals` is user-defined, the user (us) must decide on what basis to establish equality. Suppose we decide that two batches are equal if they have the same sell-by date: it does not matter how many kilograms of coffee is in each of them. Therefore, the equals method is:

```
boolean equals (Batch b) {
  return (sellByDate.equals(b.sellByDate));
}
```

Because dates are also objects, we had to use the `Date`'s class `equals` method to perform the date comparison, so there are actually two comparisons going on, at two levels.

Object assignment

The second implication of the way objects are stored is for **assignment**. Assigning one object variable to another, for example

```
tempBatch = B[i];
```

will copy the *reference*. To copy the values, we need to clone[2] the object using a method that once again must be defined for each new class as shown in the following form:

---

[2] For clone, read copy if you like.

Clone declaration

```
class Classid implements Cloneable {

  Declarations of Classid's variables

  public Object clone ( ) {
    Classid obj = new classname (parameters);
    Copying statements
    return obj;
  }

}
```

The prototype *clone* method creates a new object of this class and then has statements to copy the values of all the current object's variables into the new object's variables. The new object variable is returned as the value of the clone.

An additional point is that cloning is a special operation in Java, and therefore any class that wants to clone must implement the `Cloneable` interface and indicate this on the class declaration, as shown in the form. Interfaces are discussed in the next chapter: what we need to know here is that the `Cloneable` interface has a `clone` method that we implement.

Figure 8.6 illustrates the difference between the assignment of object variables and the cloning of objects.

For assignment, `temp1`'s reference becomes the same as `B[0]`'s. Any changes made to `B[0]` are reflected in `temp1`. With cloning, a copy of the object is made, and `temp2` refers to the copy. Now `temp2` and `B[0]` can change independently.

As mentioned earlier, each class is responsible for defining what is meant by `equals` and `clone`. For our example, a clone for `Batch` could be:

```
public Object clone () {
  Batch x = new Batch (inStock,null);
  x.sellByDate = new Date(sellByDate.getTime());
  return x;
}
```

Cloning a batch involves copying both data items, the stock and the date. `inStock` is a primitive variable so it can be assigned or supplied in the constructor to the new object, as is done here. Copying the date means making a new date object and supplying the existing one to its constructor.

Class conversions

In Section 3.1, we saw that primitive variables of different types can be converted into each other if this is meaningful. The same applies to object variables. In particular, there

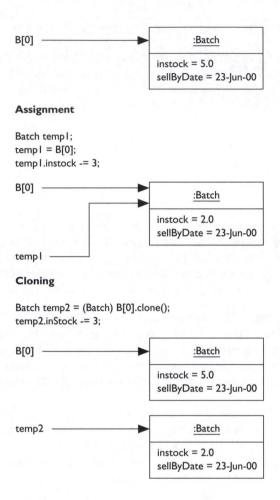

Assignment

```
Batch temp1;
temp1 = B[0];
temp1.instock -= 3;
```

Cloning

```
Batch temp2 = (Batch) B[0].clone();
temp2.inStock -= 3;
```

Figure 8.6 *The difference between assignment and cloning.*

are methods defined for the Java superclass, `Object`, which can be used by other objects. However, before the results are assigned, an explicit type cast must be made. `clone` is one of these methods. Thus to clone a `Batch` and print it out would require:

```
Batch tempBatch = (Batch) B[0].clone();
System.out.println(tempBatch);
```

Calling the `clone` method on `B[0]` will return an `Object`. It must return an `Object` because that is what the `Cloneable` interface requires. But we can convert it to a `Batch` by mentioning the class name. You can insert the clone method into `Batch` and the above statement into `Coffee` and check that it all works.

Modifiers

Classes and members of classes can be given modifiers which indicate how they be used. Not all modifiers apply to classes: some are for members (methods, variables) only. Table 8.4 gives a summary of the meaning of some of Java's main modifiers, together with the section of this book where the topic is fully discussed.

Table 8.4 *The meaning of some of the modifiers applicable to classes and members, together with the sections where they are discussed*

Modifier	Class	In	Member	In
No modifier	Accessible only within its package	5.1	Accessible only within its package	5.1
`public`	Accessible anywhere its package is	4.6	Accessible anywhere its class is	4.6
`private`	n/a		Accessible only within its own class	5.1
`protected`	n/a		Accessible within its package and its subclasses	9.2
`abstract`	May not be instantiated	9.4	A method is not implemented here but in a subclass	9.4
`final`	May not be subclassed		A value may not be changed A method may not be overridden	8.2 9.2
`static`	A top-level class, not an inner one	8.2	Class member accessed through its class name	3.1
`synchronized`	n/a		Other methods may not operate on the same data at the same time	13.3

We have already used `private` and `public` in classes. They are explored again in the next chapter together with the other protection modifiers, default and `protected`, after inheritance has been introduced. `Abstract` is also covered in Chapter 9, and `synchronized` in Chapter 13. We consider the last two here. Although they do not have a modifier, mention is made of inner classes, and these are picked up again in Chapter 11.

Static members

When a class is instantiated, then the object so created has variables of that class accessible to the class's variables through the object name. This is by now a familiar process. However, there is another option whereby members exist once only for all objects of that class. Such members are declared as static and are accessed by their class name in the dot notation. They are also known as **class members**. Static was discussed earlier in Section 3.1.

Take two examples. The `java.lang.Math` class discussed in Section 3.1 has several good methods for doing mathematical calculations, but they are not tied to object creation: the values are submitted through parameters and the answers returned by the method results, as in

```
y = Math.sin(x);
```

For variables, we would use static when we want to collect or associate a value with an entire class. For example, in the `Curio` class, when items are sold, we could also keep track of the total stock and number sold over time. A skeleton of a new `Curio` would be:

```
class Curio {
  // An inner class giving details of and actions on a curio.
  // Has been expanded with a stock parameter
  // and two methods to add and sell stock
  // Now also keeps track of total stock and numbers sold

  String name;
  int price;
  String description;
  int stock;

  static int totalStock = 0;
  static int totalSold = 0;

  // The constructor copies the initialization into the fields
  Curio (String n, int p, String d, int t) {
    name = n;
    price = p;
    description = d;
    display.prompt(name,t);
  }

  // Three new actions available on curios
  void addStock (int n) {
    stock += n;
    totalStock += n;
  }

  void sell (int n) throws StockException {
    if (stock >= n) {
      stock -= n;
      totalstock -= n;
      totalSold += n;
    }
```

```
      else
        throw new StockException
          ("Not enough stock. "+stock+" available.");
    }

  ... other methods as before
  }
```

In the program that uses `Curio`, the `CurioShop`, we can then refer to these totals as follows:

```
  display.println("Total stock now: "+Curio.totalStock+
                  " having sold "+ Curio.totalSold);
```

There is a complication with static. If a method is called from a static one, then it must also be static. The same applies to all variables declared in the class: if they are used from a static method, they must be static. Thus it is important not to use static methods for structuring a program. The problem is that the `main` method has to be static. Therefore anything it calls or uses must also be static. For this reason, we have throughout the book made the main method only call the constructor, and in an anonymous way without using a variable to declare the new object.

Constants

Recall from Chapter 4 that constants in Java are defined with the modifiers `static final`, as in:

```
  static final retirementAge = 60;
```

We have already seen that the declaration modifier `static` makes the item into a class member. Thus constant declarations can occur only at the class level, and not inside methods, even inside `main`. The second modifier, `final`, indicates that the contents of the field cannot be changed during the program: in other words, it is constant.

When variables are declared we have the option of specifying an initial value or of receiving a **default initialization**. For the numeric types, the default is zero. However, it is usually clearer to explicitly give each variable a starting value. How does such an initialization differ from a constant declaration? The fundamental difference is that once constants are set, they cannot be changed again. With variables, the values can change through assignment.

Arrays and objects can also be constants; for example, the following are valid:

```
  static final int daysInMonth [] = {31.28.31.30.31.30.31.31.30.31.30.31};
  static final Time midnight = new Time (12, 0);
```

Inner classes

In Java 1.1, classes achieved 'first class' status in that they can now be declared any-where, and can be used as parameters, and as local members to other classes, methods and blocks. Table 8.5 summarizes the four kinds of inner class that can be used:

Table 8.5 *Types of inner class*

Inner class type	Defined as	Used for	Comments
Nested top-level	Static member of another class	Grouping classes	Name includes enclosing class name
Member	Ordinary member of another class	Helper class, or for sharing members among classes	■ Gives access to enclosing instance of other class ■ Special syntax for this, new and super ■ Cannot have static members
Local	Member of a method of block	Adapter class to be passed as a call-back, e.g. in event handling	Same as for member
Anonymous	Unnamed member of a method or block	One-off objects defined and instantiated where needed	■ Same as for member ■ No name or constructor ■ Is only instantiated once ■ Defined in an expression

A **nested class** is just like any other class, but it is grouped inside another class for ease of development and handling. Often it is not convenient to have every class in a dif-ferent file, and with nested classes, we can keep them together. By declaring the class as static, we indicate that it is to have the same top-level status as the enclosing class. Nested classes can be imported from within their enclosing class. In a way, they are similar in effect to Java's package concept.

Member classes are typically helper classes for the enclosing class. They are not visi-ble outside it, but can make use of all its members, private or not. While an inner class may not have the same name as its enclosing class, it can have the same name as other member classes of other enclosing classes, thus cutting down on the number of names one has to invent in a big system. Member classes are regarded as elegant and worth using. In fact, Example 8.2 was written in this style, with the `Coffee` class being inside the `TestLinks` class. In several other programs up to now, the classes such as `Curio` or `Rates` could have been included in the main classes `CurioStore` or `Converter`.

Because of the ability to use one's own members and those of an enclosing class, member classes can distinguish two versions of `this`. An unqualified `this` refers to the member class, whereas to refer to the enclosing class we preface `this` with its name. Similar extensions are made for `new` and `super`. A notable restriction of member classes is that they may not have static members. Any static members (including constants) that are required by a member class must be grouped in the top-level class.

Anonymous classes perform the same function as local classes with the restriction that they do not have a name and therefore can be instantiated only once, at the point where they are defined. They are very useful with Java's event handlers, which we shall study in Chapter 11. To give the flavour of such a class, here is a typical usage:

```
f.addWindowListener(new WindowAdapter () {
  public void windowClosing(WindowEvent e) {
    System.exit(0);
  }
});
```

`WindowAdapter` is an interface (see Section 9.2) that needs to have a `windowClosing` method defined, so that it can be called at the appropriate moment for the window called `f` here. So we create a new anonymous class as a parameter to the `addWindowListener` method. The whole class is passed as a parameter and at the appropriate moment, `windowClosing`, as here defined, will be called. Anonymous classes are used often in Chapter 10.

Local classes are much the same as anonymous ones, except that we give them names and they can have more than one instantiation. The choice as to which to use is 90% a matter of taste.

8.3 Lists and iterators

One of the problems with arrays is that they are rigid, both in size and arrangement. One cannot remove an element without pushing all the later elements up, and this takes time and effort. Hash tables, discussed in Chapter 6, get away from both of these restrictions, but they store the data in a somewhat unconventional way ('hashed'). The classical alternative to an array is the **linked list**, and we shall spend this section looking at the one defined in Java, and how it integrates with Example 8.1.

In an array, items are stored sequentially, and we know that item $i+1$ follows item i. In a linked list, the items are regarded as self-standing, but connected together by **links**. These links can be made and broken, and thus we can have a structure that, unlike an array, can grow and shrink at will while the program is executing.

Suppose we have some string objects already created in a linked list as in

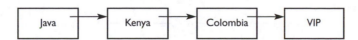

If the object with 'Colombia' in it needs to be removed, then we can just arrange to redirect the links as in the next diagram. Java will then **garbage collect** the space that the unwanted object occupied and it will be no more.

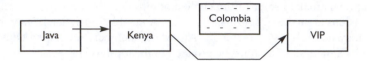

In the same way, we can add new objects to the list at any given position.

Java's List classes

Building on the ideas embodied in Example 8.2 and discussed here, it would be fairly simple to define a class that will handle lists in this manner. However, in the transition from Java 1.1 to Java 1.2, a large number of classes were added to the `java.util` package which handle lists in many different forms. We shall therefore rather learn how to use these with the aim of modifying the Coffee Shop program accordingly.

The general term for all kinds of lists and other structures is a **collection**. There is more about collections in Chapter 15, so here we confine ourselves to lists. There are four classes which Java provides under the general heading of an `AbstractList`. These are: `LinkedList`, `ArrayList`, `Vector` and `Stack`. `Vector`, as we saw briefly in Chapter 6, represents an indexable sequence of objects that does not necessarily have a fixed size. `Stack` stems from `Vector` and has the restriction that additions and removals are permitted only at one end. `ArrayList` is very similar to `Vector`. However, `LinkedList` is closer to our needs, because removing is going to be more efficient if we can change the links, as we saw above.

The specification for `LinkedList` is given in the following form:

`LinkedList` class (abbreviated)

```
void clear()
void add (Object item)
boolean contains(Object item)
boolean remove (Object item)
int size ()
// plus 20 more mainly related to indexed lists
```

`clear` will remove any elements that have been added to a `LinkedList` object.
`add` adds the object to the end of the list.
`contains` will search for an occurrence of the object parameter and return true or false. It relies on equality being defined for the objects.
`remove` will remove the first occurence of the object with a value equal to the parameter `item`.

In most cases, adding to the end of a list is fine, but we shall see just now how to add in the middle of the list as well.

For example, we could create a list of curios as follows:

```
LinkedList curioList ();
curioList.add(new Curio("Traditional mugs", 6,
              "beaded in Ndebele style",20));
curioList.add(new Curio("T-shirts", 30, "sizes M to XL", 50));
curioList.add(new Curio("Masks", 80, "carved in wood", 8));
```

If we define equality of curios based on the name variable as follows:

```
public boolean equals (Curio c) {
  return name.equals(c.name));
}
```

then we can use contains to check for a curio, and remove one from the list.

```
System.out.println("T-shirts"+ are in the shop is "+
                   curioList.contains(new Curio("T-shirts",0,"", 0));
curioList.remove(new Curio("T-shirts",0,"", 0));
```

Our example is slightly inefficient since it would have been better to define an object for T-shirts and then use this in the checks. But the above will work.

List iterators

There is now obviously the question of how do we move around in the list? Suppose we wish to print out the whole list. In the above form, we deliberately omitted the methods that used indices (as an array would), thus begging the question as to how we get each element in turn. The answer is to use an iterator. An **iterator** keeps track of the position in a list, and can be used in a for- or while- or do-statement to loop through the list, looking at each element in turn. Iterators are interfaces, which in this context means that they supply added methods to the class of objects they can iterate through, i.e. LinkedLists. They are very similar to enumerations, which were introduced in Section 6.5.

To create an iterator we use:

Creating an iterator

```
ListIterator listiter = list.listIterator();
```

Given a list, listiter will then make available the methods below.

Then we have the following methods available through the ListIterator class:

Class `ListIterator`

```
boolean hasNext ()
boolean hasPrevious ()

Object next ()
Object previous ()

void add (Object item)
void remove ()
void set (Object item)
```

`hasNext` and `hasPrevious` check if the end of a list has been
  reached, either from the front or the back.
`next` and `previous` move the iterator forwards or backwards.
The `add`, `remove` and `set` methods provide a safe means to change
  the list while moving through it. `add` will insert the object parameter
  immediately before the object that would be returned by the next call
  on `next`. `remove` deletes the object most recently returned by
  `next`, and `set` alters the value of the next object.

Put together, the form for iterating through a list with a for-loop is:

A for-loop with a list iterator

```
for (ListIterator listiter = list.listiterator (); listiter.
    hasNext (); ) {
  item = listiter.next ();
  body
}
```

As an example, consider a list based on simple objects that have only a numeric field. To
create the list based on random numbers until a 3 is found we would do the following:

```
Random r = new Random ();
LinkedList list = new LinkedList ();
int number = 0;
while (number != 3) {
  number = r.nextInt ();
// adding to the end of the list
  list.add(new Integer (number));
}
```

Then to print the list out, we use the iterator in a for-loop:

```
for (ListIterator listiter = list.listIterator(); listiter.hasNext();)
   System.out.println(listiter.next());
```

Doing something more complicated, suppose we wish to add one to each number in the list. We could use `set` quite safely as follows:

```
for (ListIterator listiter = list.listIterator(); listiter.hasNext();){
   number = listiter.next().intValue();
   number++;
   // replaces the object fetched by next
   listiter.set(new Integer(number));
}
```

Linked lists and iterators are the tools we shall need to make the Coffee Shop more extensible.

8.4 Case Study 3: Nelson's Coffee Shop

Opportunity

Nelson's Coffee Shop wants to make the stock of coffee types and batches dynamic: that is, the number does not have to be set at the start, and batches (and coffees) can be removed when sold out. The solution, of course, is to take advantage of the `LinkedList` class just described.

Algorithms

The algorithmic part of the system relates to handling sales. These will be entered from an orders file with the name of the coffee followed by the number of kg. First of all, the main program must find the relevant coffee in its list, then call the sell method in that `Coffee` class. Two things can go wrong:

- the type of coffee is not found;

- there is not enough in stock.

In both cases, the program prints out a suitable message.

Moving now to selling, this algorithm is more complex than one would first imagine. It has to check each batch in turn, using it up and then moving to the next one if there are still kilograms outstanding on the order. The algorithm reduces to that shown in Figure 8.7. The rest of the program follows in a similar vein or is fairly simple.

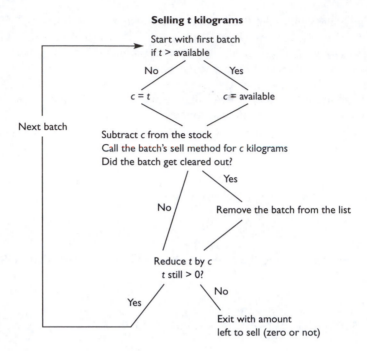

Figure 8.7 *Algorithm to sell coffee.*

Converting the program

It turns out that the Batch class is independent of how it is put together in a structure. In other words, whether we have arrays of batches, or lists of batches, does not matter to the Batch class. The Coffee class, however, will have to change slightly. We shall call the new class Coffee2. In the Coffee class where there is an array, replace it with

```
private LinkedList batchStock = new LinkedList ();
```

This statement has the effect of creating an object that can be altered by the LinkedList methods, and those of list iterators. The counter, noOfBatches, is deleted as it is no longer needed. Adding a new batch becomes a call to add, as in:

```
BatchStock.add(new Batch (nextStock,stockDate));
```

The loop at the end to print all the batches will use a list iterator, that is,

```
for (ListIterator list = batchStock.listIterator(); list.hasNext(); ) {
  Batch batch = (Batch) list.next();
  batch.display();
}
```

The reason why the extra local object, batch, is necessary is as follows. batchStock is a LinkedList, and it has access to all the LinkedList methods. But they are all defined in terms of the superclass Object. There is nothing that ties the LinkedList in Coffee2 to the Batch class. We do put batches in it, but to get batches out, we must convert objects of class Object to Batch. Then the assignment can take place. We now have a local reference to the current object in the list, and can call Batch's display method on it.

Another place where care must be taken over precisely which objects we are dealing with is in the section of the program which finds a coffee. This is:

```
//Find the right coffee by name in the CoffeeStock list
Coffee2 foundBlend = null;
Coffee2 orderBlend = new Coffee2(orderName);
ListIterator list = coffeeStock.listIterator();
boolean found = false;

while (list.hasNext()) {
  foundBlend = (Coffee2) list.next();
  if (foundBlend.equals(orderBlend)) {
    found = true;
    break;
  }
}
```

We cannot of course use == to compare the name of the required coffee with each of the coffees in stock. In the first place, the name is a string, and the coffees are of class Coffee2. That is why we must create a temporary coffee object. Secondly, we must make sure as before that the item that comes off the list is designated as a Coffee2 object, so that the equals method defined for Coffee2 is called. This method is defined to look only at the blend names, not the price and so on.

An interesting question is why did we not use the contains method supplied by LinkedList? The reason is that contains returns only a yes/no answer, and does not give us a reference to the object in the list. We could find its position via some of the LinkedList class's indexing methods, but we are not covering those in this book. They can be found in the Java API documents online.

The list of Coffee2 objects is created in exactly the same way as the batches, using LinkedList's add method.

A diagram showing the main classes in the system is given in Figure 8.8. All the un-arrowed dotted lines indicate that the class has variables of the class lower down in the diagram. Thus CoffeeShop2 has LinkedList, Coffee2 and Stream object variables. The arrowed lines indicate the imports from the two packages involved here. The ListIterator is shown associated with the LinkedList class.

From the diagram we can deduce that Batch does not do any input. There are other classes which are not shown, notably Date, imported from java.util and used by the three main classes. DateFormat, imported from java.text is another one.

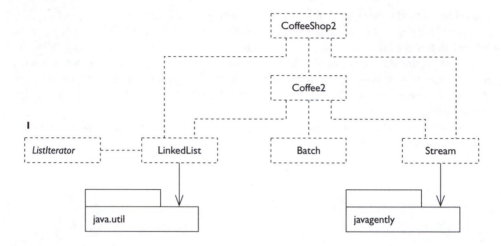

Figure 8.8 *Classes in the dynamic coffee shop. The* I *above* ListIterator *marks it as an interface, as explained in Section 9.3.*

Program

Given the options for inner classes explained in Section 8.2, how should our three classes be arranged? CoffeeShop2 is a top-level, main program type class. Should Coffee2 and Batch be declared as inner classes? In fact, the answer is no. Batch is the likeliest candidate for inclusion, but remember that it is also used by the previous version of the system, so it should then remain separate. (It does not have to, as it could be a nested class and therefore accessible to other classes.) For ease of changes and compilation, we leave Coffee2 on its own as well. The program is therefore in three compiled files:

```
import java.io.*;
import java.util.*;
import javagently.Stream;
import java.text.*;

class Coffee2 {

   /* The Improved Coffee class       by J M Bishop Oct 1996
    * -----------------------         Java 1.1 October 1997
    *                                 substantially updated
    *                                 and Java 2 May 2000
    * Keeps an inventory of batches of coffee of a
    * particular kind or blend using
    * a Linked List from java.util.
    */
```

```
private String name;
 private double price;    // per kg
 private double stock; // kgs
 private double reorder; // kgs;
 private LinkedList batchStock = new LinkedList ();

 public Coffee2() {
     /* empty constructor, because all values
      * are read in via prepareToStock
      */
 }

 public Coffee2(String s) {
     name = new String(s);
 }

DateFormat DF = DateFormat.getDateInstance(DateFormat.Default, Locale.UK);

 void prepareToStock(Stream in) throws IOException {
     name = in.readString();
     price = in.readDouble();
     reorder = in.readInt();
     stock = 0;
     newBatchIn(in);
 }


 boolean newBatchIn(Stream in) throws IOException {
   double nextStock = in.readDouble();
   if (nextStock == 0)
     return false;
   else {
     stock += nextStock;
     Date stockDate = new Date ();
     String dateString = in.readString();
     try {
       stockDate = DF.parse(dateString);
     } catch (ParseException e) {
       System.out.println("Error in date " + dateString);
     }
     batchStock.add(new Batch(nextStock, stockDate));
     return true;
   }
 }
```

```
double sell(double ordered) {
    double kgInBatch;
    Batch currentBatch;

    for (ListIterator list =
            batchStock.listIterator(); list.hasNext(); ) {
        currentBatch = (Batch) list.next();
        if (ordered > currentBatch.available())
            kgInBatch = currentBatch.available();
        else
            kgInBatch = ordered;
        stock -= kgInBatch;
        boolean soldOut = currentBatch.sell(kgInBatch);
        if (soldOut) {
            System.out.println("Batch now empty");
            list.remove();
        }
        ordered -= kgInBatch;
        if (ordered <= 0)
            break;
    }
    System.out.println("Stock report:");
    display();
    return ordered;
}

boolean equals(Coffee2 c) {
    return name.equals(c.name);
}

void display () {
    System.out.println(name+" @ G"+
        Stream.format(price,1,2)+" per kg");
    for (ListIterator list =
        batchStock.listIterator(); list.hasNext(); ) {
      Batch batch = (Batch) list.next();
      batch.display();
    }
     System.out.println(Stream.format(stock, 1, 1)+"kg in stock. Reorder
        level is "+ reorder+"kg\n");
  }
}
```

```
import java.io.*;
import java.text.*;
import java.util.*;
import javagently.Stream;

class CoffeeShop2 {

  /* The Coffee Shop program Version 2  by J M Bishop Oct 1996
   * -------------------------------  Java 1.1 October 1997
   *                                  Java 1.2 May 2000
   *
   * Includes the ability to sell batches of a
   * particular kind of coffee, starting at the oldest.
   *
   * Illustrates the use of the java.util LinkedList
   * and ListIterator classes
   */

  CoffeeShop2 () throws IOException {

    LinkedList coffeeStock = new LinkedList ();

    stockUp(coffeeStock);
    inventoryReport(coffeeStock);
    makeSales(coffeeStock);
  }

  void stockUp(LinkedList coffeeStock) throws IOException {
    Stream in = new Stream("coffee.dat",Stream.READ);
    System.out.println("Stocking the shop");
    while (true) {
      try {
        Coffee2 coffee = new Coffee2();
        coffee.prepareToStock(in);
        coffeeStock.add(coffee);
        boolean morebatches = true;
        while (morebatches)
          morebatches = coffee.newBatchIn(in);
      } catch (EOFException e) {
        System.out.println("That's the shop stocked for today");
        System.out.println();
        break;
      }
    }
  }
}
```

```
void inventoryReport(LinkedList coffeeStock) {
  System.out.println("Nelson's Coffee Shop");
  System.out.println("Inventory control");
  System.out.println("The coffee stock on "+
          DateFormat.getDateInstance().format(new Date(DateFormat.FULL)));
  for (ListIterator list =
        coffeeStock.listIterator(); list.hasNext();) {
    Coffee2 current = (Coffee2) list.next();
    current.display();
  }
}


void makeSales(LinkedList coffeeStock) throws IOException {

  Stream orderFile = new Stream ("orders.dat",Stream.READ);
  System.out.println("Coffee sales");

  while (true) {
    try {
      String orderName = orderFile.readString();
      double orderAmount = orderFile.readDouble();
      System.out.println("Order for " + orderName + " "
          + orderAmount);
      System.out.println("=====");

      //Establish that the blend exists
      Coffee2 foundBlend = null;
      Coffee2 orderBlend = new Coffee2(orderName);

      ListIterator list = coffeeStock.listIterator();
      boolean found = false;

      while (list.hasNext()) {
        foundBlend = (Coffee2) list.next();
        if (foundBlend.equals(orderBlend)) {
          found = true;
          break;
        }
      }

      if (!found)
        // None of that name
        System.out.println("Sorry, we're out of that blend.\n");
      else {
        // Start selling
```

```
            double remainder = foundBlend.sell(orderAmount);
            if (remainder > 0) {
              System.out.println("Could not match "+remainder+"kg\n");
            }
          }

        } catch (EOFException e) {
            System.out.println("\nShop closed");
            break;
        }
    }
  }

  public static void main (String [] args) throws IOException {
    new CoffeeShop2 ();
  }
}
```

Testing

The original data file was:

```
Colombian
59.95 10
45.5 23-Jun-00
5 30-Jul-00
0
Kenyan
60.75 10
15 19-May-00
0
Java
63.50 30
61.8 23-May-00
20 12-Jul-00
3 1-Aug-00
0
```

Let us now add the following orders file:

```
VIP 2
Kenyan 15
Kenyan 2
Java 70
Colombian 46
Colombian 3
```

The intention is that the first order's name will not be found. Then all the Kenyan coffee will go in the second order and the third order will not be able to be processed. The Java order will need to take coffee from two batches, as will the first Colombian. The last order is a straightforward one. The detailed output is as follows:

```
Stocking the shop
That's the shop stocked for today


Nelson's Coffee Shop
Inventory control
The coffee stock on Thursday, August 3, 2000
Colombian @ G59.95 per kg
        23-Jun-00 : 45.5kg
        30-Jul-00 :  5.0kg
50.5kg in stock. Reorder level is 10.0kg


Kenyan @ G60.75 per kg
        19-May-00 : 15.0kg
84.8kg in stock. Reorder level is 30.0kg


Java @ G63.50 per kg
        23-May-00 : 61.8kg
        12-Jul-00 : 20.0kg
        01-Aug-00 :  3.0kg
132.25kg in stock. Reorder level is 30.0kg


Coffee sales
Order for VIP 2.0
=====
Sorry, we're out of that blend.


Order for Kenyan 15.0
=====
Sold 15.0 from batch 19-May-00
Batch Now Empty
Stock report:
Kenyan @ G60.75 per kg
0.0kg in stock. Reorder level is 10.0kg


Order for Kenyan 2.0
=====
Stock report:
Kenyan @ G60.75 per kg
0.0kg in stock. Reorder level is 10.0kg
```

```
        Could not match 2.0kg

        Order for Java 70.0
        =====
        Sold 61.8 from batch 23-May-00
        Batch now empty
        Sold 8.2 from batch 12-Jul-00
        Stock report:
        Java @ G63.50 per kg
             12-Jul-00 : 11.8kg
             01-Aug-00 :  3.0kg
        14.8kg in stock. Reorder level is 30.0kg

        Order for Colombian 46.0
        =====
        Sold 45.5 from batch 23-Jun-00
        Batch now empty
        Sold 0.5 from batch 30-Jul-00
        Stock report:
        Colombian @ G59.95 per kg
             30-Jul-00 : 4.5kg
        4.5kg in stock. Reorder level is 10.0kg

        Order for Colombian 3.0
        =====
        Sold 3.0 from batch 30-Jul-00
        Stock report:
        Colombian @ G59.95 per kg
             30-Jul-00 : 1.5kg
        1.5kg in stock. Reorder level is 10.0kg


        Shop closed
```

We have explained in detail how to use Java's `LinkedList` class. In Chapter 15 we look at the some similar classes Java provides. The mission of this book is to teach you more than just the syntax. It aims to teach you the fundamental principles of programming as well. Knowing how to use APIs from a library is one of those principles. You may not know how to program a list class in a first course, but at least you will have understood how one works, and will be able to apply this knowledge in other circumstances later on in your programming career.

SUMMARY

This has been a crucial chapter in the development of programming skills. It has included specific details about objects, how to use them in a grand plan, and the model of a linked list as the alternative data structure to an array. Full details of the meaning of protection modifiers and inner classes have been spelt out, clarifying the relationship between packages, classes and methods.

The declarations of object variables results in a reference to an object, whereas the values of primitive variables are stored directly. The implications of this model are that equality and copying of objects have to be done via the equals and clone methods. `Clone` relies on the superclass, `Object`, and therefore class conversions become necessary.

Lists are a prime alternative to arrays for storing sequences of data. They have the advantage that they can grow and shrink dynamically as items are added and removed. All programmers should know how to set one up. Java provides the `LinkedList` and `ListIterator` classes for this purpose.

This chapter explained the following keywords:

```
this
final
static
```

and introduced these, for later explanation:

```
protected
abstract
synchronized
```

and Java APIs

```
Object              contains
clone               remove
Linked list         size
add
```

and forms

```
Clone declaration
LinkedList class
Creating an iterator
Class ListIterator
A for-loop with a list iterator
```

and the concepts of

```
modifiers
inner classes
```

QUIZ

8.1   In the first Coffee Shop program (Example 8.1) the compiler would prevent access to
`C[0].name` (i.e. there would be a compilation error) because:

(a)   `C[0]` has not been instantiated
(b)   name is declared as private
(c)   0 is not a valid index for the array
(d)   a value for name has not been read in yet

8.2   If cloning for the `Time` class has been defined and `today` is a `Time`, then which of the
following is valid?

(a)   `Time temp = (Time) clone(today);`
(b)   `Time temp = Time.clone(today);`
(c)   `Time temp = (Time) today.clone();`
(d)   `Time temp = today.clone();`

8.3   The `LinkedList` supplies method `contains`, used as in `L.contains(x)`. It relies on

(a)   there being a hash table of objects
(b)   `equals` being defined for the objects in the list
(c)   the object x being in the list
(d)   the object x not being in the list

8.4   The difference between the `add` method in `LinkedList` and in `ListIterator` is:

(a)   none
(b)   where the object gets added in the list
(c)   the need to provide an object cast or not
(d)   whether the object can be removed afterwards

8.5   When iterating through a list `L` with a list iterator `Lit`, getting the next element is done with:

(a)   `L.getNext( )`
(b)   `L.next( )`
(c)   `Lit.hasNext( )`
(d)   `Lit.next( )`

8.6   In terms of the operations available for it, an array is more like

(a)   an object
(b)   a string
(c)   a primitive value
(d)   something quite distinct from any of these

8.7   If we declare a method `Coffee equals ()`, we must also

(a)   declare it public
(b)   declare it private
(c)   declare a clone for `Coffee`
(d)   do nothing else

8.8   A difference between a nested class N and a member class M is

    (a)   nothing
    (b)   M need not have constructors
    (c)   M can see the members of its enclosing class
    (d)   N cannot have static members

8.9   The `ListIterators` in `Coffee2` and in `CoffeeShop2` both produce, when iterating, variables of type

    (a)   `Batch`
    (b)   `Object`
    (c)   `Coffee2`
    (d)   `Date`

8.10   In Example 8.2, at the end of the program, the list variable has the value

    (a)   `coffees`
    (b)   `Java`
    (c)   `null`
    (d)   undefined

PROBLEMS

8.1   **Interactive orders.** Nelson's is not just a mail-order business: he has a shop where customers can come in and buy. Add to the program in Case Study 3 a facility for using the display to enter an order.

8.2   **Gold customers.** In the orders file, some orders are identified as coming from Gold Card customers. Each day, these should be given priority in processing. Achieve this by altering the `Coffee2` program to read the orders into a list, except that if an order is from a Gold Card customer, it is processed immediately and not added to the list.

8.3   **Batches in order.** The `LinkedList` used by Nelson's Coffee Shop always adds new nodes to the end of the list. The data in the `orders.dat` files were carefully arranged so that for the batches, the oldest batches were listed first and therefore would get sold first. If batches are arriving at different times of day, one could not always ensure that this happened. In the `Batch` class, add a new method that can find the correct position for a new batch, based on its sell-by date. Then write another adding method for the program, say, `insert`, that will add the new batch in the correct date position.

8.4   **Coffees in order.** Using the same philosophy as in Problem 8.3, we would like to keep the coffee types in alphabetical order. Write a method for the `Coffee2` class which will find the correct position for a new coffee, and then use the same `insert` method to insert it.

8.5   **Club database.** Choose an activity with which you are familiar and design a class and object structure to store information about the people, equipment or events associated with the activity. Add methods to access the information.

8.6   **Weight watchers club.** Working from Problem 3.3, augment the class so that each person has a goal weight. Then set up a list of several weight-conscious people with their appropriate values, and let the program run. When someone reaches their goal weight, congratulate them and remove them from the list. People can be added at any time interactively.

8.7 **Savanna Marathon.** The Savanna Marathon attracts thousands of runners each year, but gives gold medals to only the first 20 who finish. Change the class developed in Problem 3.2 slightly so that it has no string data, but has runners identified by numbers. This will enable the data (including the time for the race) to be generated randomly in the program. Create a linked list of some 1000 runners. Then loop through the list, finding the best 20 times. Print these out for the gold medals.

8.8 **Weather statistics again.** In Example 6.6, the matrix for storing data is declared of a given size once the first and last years are read in. Suppose we do not wish to read these in in advance. Draw a diagram of how the data could be stored as an array of linked lists instead. Redo the program using the simple list technique of Example 8.2.

8.9 **Publishing a book.** Working from Problems 6.5, 3.19 and 2.10, set up a system that creates a manuscript for a book, as described, using a linked list this time. Then, keeping the manuscript intact, create a final version of the book's details by cloning each chapter into a new linked list. Let the program be interactive so that last-minute changes can be made and the page numbers and so on will be automatically updated where necessary.

8.10 **Curio Shop.** Now is the time for the Curio Shop to go live. Using the Coffee Shop as a model, set up data that can be read in each day, and have both filed and interactive orders. Process them as required. Flag reorder levels and produce regular reports.

CHAPTER 9

Abstraction and inheritance

Object-oriented programming has several ways in which the use of classes is made more powerful. We have already been using classes extensively for what is known as **composition**, in other words, creating an object in a class based on another class. An example of this would be the array of batches kept in the `Coffee` class. Two other concepts that we shall now study are **abstraction** and **inheritance**.

9.1 Class power

Abstraction

Abstraction enables a class or method to concentrate on the essentials of what it is doing – its behaviour and interface with the world – and to rely on the details being filled in at a later stage. In a way, we can think of it as a more elaborate form of parameter passing, but this time at the class level. Java has two ways of providing abstraction – **abstract classes** and **interfaces**.

For example, so far, all our classes have related to concrete descriptions of natural items, such as curios, marks and coffee. If we wanted to perform an operation on all these classes, such as sorting arrays of curios, arrays of marks or arrays of coffee, then up until now we would need to have three different sort methods, or we would have to convert them all to the superclass `Object`, and work on them at that level. We saw the use of `Object` for this purpose with hash tables, but it is not an ideal solution, since the essential definition of the original class is lost. Abstraction allows us to maintain the security of the class concept, while at the same time cutting down on repetition and aiding reuse – two of our goals right from the start.

Abstract classes and interfaces both concentrate on methods, allowing us to define and use a method by a common name, but the method can be implemented in a variety of ways. The differences between the two techniques will become clear as we proceed.

Inheritance

With **inheritance**, we concentrate on defining a class that we know about, and leave open an option to define additional versions of it later. These versions will inherit the properties and characteristics of the original class, and do not need to repeat them in their specification. In this way we build up hierarchies of classes and can focus changes and additions at the right level. This technique is called **incremental development**, and is an important outcome of inheritance. We shall see an example of it in Case Study 4.

A more high-level consequence of inheritance is known as **specialization**. Because all the classes in the hierarchy belong to the same family, they have the same type in Java's typing mechanism, and one can be used where the other might be required. Consider the diagram in Figure 9.1. As in Chapter 1, we postulate a `Nature` class consisting of animals, trees and birds. Animals could be herbivores or carnivores. Possible herbivores are elephants and rhinos. Now the field holding the name of the animal could be right in the top class, in `Nature` itself, since all animals, trees and birds will need a name. Similarly a method to write the name would also be placed here. If we had an elephant object and wanted to write the name, the method that would be called would be the one in `Nature`. However, peculiar to an elephant would be its tusk length. This field and a method to display it would be kept in `Elephant` itself. Along the way in the hierarchy, there could be a tally of how much grass a herbivore eats a day. Since this applies to all herbivores, we store the information in the `Herbivore` class. All of these design decisions are illustrated in Figure 9.1.

Figure 9.2 shows the effect of two object declarations on the classes at the lowest level of the hierarchy, `Elephant` and `Rhino`. `jumbo` and `mafuta` each have three variables, but the last one is different in each case. The other two were inherited from classes higher up.

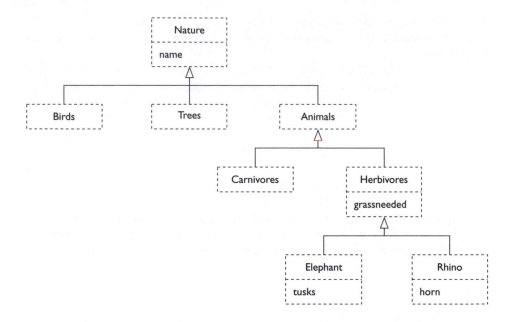

Figure 9.1 *A hierarchy in* `Nature`.

Interfaces

Interfaces are slightly different. An interface is a specification of methods and constants that any class can implement. All classes that implement a given interface are then acceptable wherever the interface name is mentioned. This does not mean that objects of the classes can be assigned to each other, or themselves mixed in any way. The interface is just there to indicate a guarantee of certain behaviour that is important. We have already seen three interfaces: `Enumeration` (Section 6.5), `Cloneable` (Section 8.2) and `ListIterator` (Section 8.3). If we are writing a method which is to work on objects where all that is important is that they are `Cloneable`, then we can declare the objects in the method with `Cloneable` as their type. Detailed examples of interfaces are given in Section 9.3.

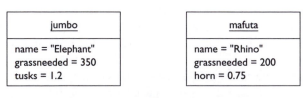

Elephant jumbo = new Elephant ("Elephant", 350, 1.2);

Rhino mafuta = new Rhino ("Rhino", 200, 0.75);

Figure 9.2 *Object declarations in the* `Nature` *hierarchy.*

9.2 Inheritance

Following the informal description of inheritance in Section 9.1, let us look at inheritance in practice in Java. Each new level of class is said to **extend** the class above it. The term conveys the impression that the new class can have more fields and methods than the original. The terms for the different class are **superclass** or **parent** (the original) and **subclass** or **child** class.

Inheritance is also transitive: that means that if *a* is a class and *b* extends it, with *c* extending *b*, then *c* is also related by inheritance to *a*. The same would be true in a family, in this case *a* being the grandparent, *b* the parent and *c* the child. Figure 9.1 shows this kind of hierarchy of inheritance clearly. The process of inheriting is also sometimes referred to as deriving, but in fact Java's term – **extending** – is the most evocative of what is actually happening. There are several issues related to inheritance which we need to define, but which come out nicely in the following example, based on Figures 9.1 and 9.2, so we shall take the definitions afterwards.

EXAMPLE 9.1   The `Nature` hierarchy

Problem   We would like to see how the `Nature` hierarchy can be expressed correctly in Java.

Solution   We declare a class for each of the groups, concentrating on the direct line from `Nature` down to `Elephant` and `Rhino`. Then we write a small test program to create the two objects as in Figure 9.2 and print them out.

Program   The main part of the test program is very short, but we have included the hierarchy classes as inner member classes, as they are so short. The underlined declarations relate directly to getting the hierarchy defined. The rest of the program relates to getting the values into the objects we want to instantiate in the hierarchy, and to printing out such objects.

```
class TestNature {

  TestNature () {
    Elephant jumbo = new Elephant ("Elephant",350, 1.2);
    Rhino mafuta = new Rhino ("Rhino", 200, 0.75);
    System.out.println (jumbo);
    System.out.println (mafuta);
  }

  public static void main (String [] args) {
    new TestNature ();
  }
```

```
class Nature {
  protected String name;

  Nature (String n) {
    name = n;
  }

  public toString () {
    return name;
  }
}


class Animals extends Nature {
  Animals (String n) {
    super (n);
  }
}


class Herbivores extends Animals {
  protected int grassneeded;

  Herbivores (String n, int g) {
    super (n);
    grassneeded = g;
  }
}


class Elephant extends Herbivores {
  private double tusks; // their length
  Elephant (String name, int weight, double length) {
    super (name, weight);
    tusks = length;
  }
  public String toString () {
    return name+"  "+grassneeded + "  "+tusks;
  }
}


class Rhino extends Herbivores {
  private double horn; // its length
  Rhino (String n, int w, double l) {
    super (n, w);
    horn = l;
  }
```

```
  public String toString () {
    return name+"   "+grassneeded + "   "+horn;
  }
  // and more on rhinos
}


}
```

Testing   The output from running the program will be as expected, i.e.

```
Elephant   350   1.2
Rhino   200   0.75
```

Protected accessibility

We have already worked with the different protection modifiers: private, public and default (see Sections 4.6, 5.1 and 8.2). Within an inheritance hierarchy there is a need for another level of accessibility, that of private to the hierarchy. Any member that is declared as `protected` is accessible within its class and any of its subclasses. Therefore `name` and `grassneeded` were declared `protected`, but `horn` and `tusks` were `private` because at present these classes are not subclassed.

Superconstructing

A useful technique in a hierarchy of classes is **superconstructing**. A subclass can call the constructor of a parent to perform initialization on those variables for which the parent is responsible. This divides the work up in a cleaner way.

In Example 9.1, both `Elephant` and `Rhino` are sent values for all three parameters, but they defer to their parent classes as to what should be done with the ones they do not themselves declare. The process bubbles up: `Herbivore` takes care of `w`. It passes `n` up to `Animals`. `Animals` at present does nothing other than pass its parameter up to `Nature`.

Note that the call to the superconstructor must be the first statement in a constructor.

Working within a hierarchy

The purpose of setting up a hierarchy of classes is to enable us to deal at different levels. At the top level, we just need to know about names of natural beings. At each level below that, we have more information and can perform in appropriate ways. The key to this multilevel operation is being able to assign objects freely within a hierarchy. Put formally:

- any object of a subclass can be assigned to an object of its superclass;
- any object of a superclass can be assigned to a subclass with an appropriate **cast**.

When these assignments are done, the object does not change at all: only the compiler's view of it, for typing purposes, is changed. As an example, if we have:

```
Animals a;

a = jumbo;         // okay
mafuta = a;        // not okay: compiler error
mafuta = jumbo;    // not okay: compiler error
mafuta = (Rhino) a; // okay
```

The example shows that we cannot assign variables across levels. `jumbo` and `mafuta` are of quite different classes and it would never make sense to assign them. But, of course, we can work with them together under the `Herbivore`'s banner, or one of the higher ones. The following example shows this:

```
Herbivores greedier;

if (jumbo.grassneeded > mafuta.grassneeded)
  greedier = jumbo;
else
  greedier = mafuta;
```

Notice that a restriction in Java is that a class may only extend one other class: there is no provision for inheriting from multiple classes. However, classes can implement several interfaces, thereby getting much the same effect. (See the next section.)

Shadowing variables

In addition to adding to any inherited data, a subclass can decide to replace data with its own version. It does this by declaring a variable with the same name as one higher up. Mostly we do this to change the type to something more suitable. When the object is created, all the variables still exist, but the higher one is masked out. This is called **shadowing**. For example, if the zoologists working with elephants want to be more precise about what the elephants eat, they could decide to record the grass as a real number. Therefore we would add to `Elephant`:

```
double grassneeded;
```

When dealing with elephants, we shall get this version of the variable. Other classes will get the original integer version from the `Herbivore` class.

It is still possible to get at a shadowed variable by using the **super** prefix. Thus from `Elephant`,

```
super.grassneeded;
```

would refer to the original variable in `Herbivores`.

Overloading methods

Where it makes sense, we can provide different versions of a method, yet keep the same name. The proviso is that the formal parameter lists must be distinct so that there is no confusion as to which method is being called. The prime example here is the two format methods declared in the Display class. These are:

```
String format (int number, int align)
String format (double number, int align, int frac)
```

Overriding methods

A subclass can decide to supply its own version of a method already supplied by a superclass, known as **overriding**. We would use this facility when we start off defining a general or default method in a superclass, and as we get down the hierarchy we can provide more specialized versions.

The classic example here is toString. There is a toString method in Nature, which will print out a name. However, once we have more information about a particular animal, we can define a more detailed toString method, such as that in the Elephant class, which prints out the values of all the variables visible at that level.

Notice that overriding is not the same as overloading. Overloading involves providing several methods with the same name, but with different parameter lists, so that Java sees them as distinct entities. In overriding, the parameter lists are the same, but the methods exist in different, hierarchically related, classes. In the case study below we look at an example of inheritance in a small system. There will be many more examples in the next chapter because inheritance is used extensively in Java's own packages.

Dynamic binding

Overridden methods are more powerful than shadowed variables in the following way. When there are several instances of a method in a hierarchy, the one in the closest subclass is always used. This is true even if an object of the subclass is assigned to an object of the superclass and called from there. Consider the following, using jumbo as an example:

```
Animals a ("An animal");

System.out.println(a);       // calls Animals version of toString
System.out.println(jumbo); // calls Elephant version of toString
a = jumbo;
System.out.println(a);       // still calls Elephant version of toString
```

Overriding uses **dynamic binding** to find the correct method. Each object has a table of its methods and Java searches for the correct versions of any overridden methods at run-time. The default is that methods will need dynamic binding, and this can incur a performance overhead. If we know that a method will not be overridden, we can declare it with the modifier `final`, and save on speed. Dynamic binding is illustrated very well in the case study that follows.

9.3 Abstraction through interfaces

We have suggested that abstraction will cut down on repetition and aid the generality and reuse of the classes we write. Java provides two ways of obtaining abstraction: **interfaces** and **abstract classes**. Let us start with interfaces and then move on to abstract classes in Section 9.4.

An **interface** is a special kind of class which defines the specification of a set of methods, and that is all. The methods together encapsulate a guarantee: any class that implements this interface is guaranteed to provide these methods. We can think of an interface as defining a set of standards, and a class that implements them gets a 'stamp of approval' as having conformed to those standards. Objects of the class can therefore gain access to any methods that need an object with those standards.

The forms for an interface and for a class that implements it are:

Interface declaration
| ```
interface Interfaceid {
  method specifications
}
``` |

Interface implementation
| ```
class Classid implements Interfaceid {
  bodies for the interface methods
  own data and methods
}
``` |

The notation for an interface is the same as for a class, except that we annotate it with an `I` in the top left corner and the name is in italics. Although we said that an interface only has methods, it can also have constants, and these would be listed in the variables section of the class box.

Interfaces allow different implementations of the same idea to exist side by side. The main program can declare variables or arrays where the type of them is the interface class. Then any class that implements the interface is acceptable for instantiating objects. The array can even contain differently classed objects, provided their classes all implement the interface. This technique is illustrated very well in the next example, which involves sorting, and picked up again in the case study. There will also be many occasions to use interfaces in the chapters that follow. Java also has its own built-in ways for offering sorting via its own interfaces, and these are shown with examples in Chapter 15.

EXAMPLE 9.2   Sorting

Problem   The sorting method that we developed in Chapter 6 is obviously extremely useful and we would like to adapt it so that it is independent of what we are sorting.

Solution   We consider what makes a class of objects sortable, and encapsulate this operation (or operations) in an interface called `Sortable`. Then we change the `selectionSort` method so that it works with `Sortable` objects. Thereafter any class that needs sorting must just implement the `Sortable` interface, and it can call the methods of the `Sort` class.

Assuming that we would like to sort countries and students, Figure 9.3 sums up the relationship between the various classes and the interface. What is this x method referred to in the diagram? What makes sorting one class different from another? It is not the assignment of the objects, since this is defined for all types and classes. The answer is that it is the comparison between two items. The comparison triggers the interchange of items, which is how all sorts work. How this comparison is done will differ from class to class. There are two inequalities – less than and greater than. We will use less than in what follows.

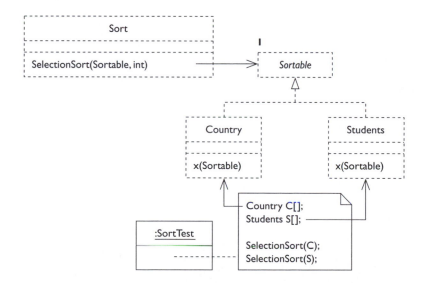

Figure 9.3   *The classes involved in abstract sorting.*

Algorithm   Sorting is obviously a common utility so we shall put it in the `myutili-`
`ties` package. First we set up the `Sortable` interface as follows:

```
package myutilities;

public interface Sortable {
  public boolean lessThan (Sortable a);
}
```

The `Sort` class defined in Section 6.4 must also be changed slightly as follows:

```
package myutilities;

public class Sort {

    /* The Sort class    by J M Bishop  Feb 1997
     *                      revised October 1997
     * Provides one sorting method
     * for arrays of objects of any length.
     * where the objects' class implements the
     * Sortable interface.
     */

  public static void selectionSort(Sortable a [], int n) {
    Sortable temp;
    int chosen;

    for (int leftmost = 0; leftmost < n-1; leftmost++) {
      chosen = leftmost;
      for (int j = leftmost+1; j < n; j++) {
        if (a[j].lessThan(a[chosen])) {
          chosen = j;
        }
      }
      temp = a[chosen];
      a[chosen] = a[leftmost];
      a[leftmost] = temp;
    }
  }
}
```

The array parameter and the temporary variable are both now declared as `Sortable`.
Also the comparison that used to use the boolean relation < now calls the `lessThan`
method on one of the objects, giving the other as a parameter.

Next we include in the class of objects to be sorted an implementation of the lessThan method. For example, a simple Country class would be:

```
import myutilities.*;

class Country implements Sortable {
    /* The Country class    by J M Bishop Dec 1996
     * ------------------    Java 1.1
     * stores a country name and is sortable
     */

    private String name;

    Country(String s) {
        name = s;
    }

    public boolean lessThan(Sortable a) {
        Country b = (Country) a;
        return (name.compareTo(b.name) < 0);
    }

    public String toString() {
        return name;
    }
}
```

In the implementation of lessThan we must first type cast the Sortable object passed as a parameter to a Country. The compareTo method (part of the String class) then operates on the current object's name and the name of the parameter. compareTo returns negative if the result is less, positive if it is more and 0 if it is equal. Note that lessThan, like toString, must be declared as public because it overrides a method in a class in another package.

Program   Now Country, Sortable and Sort can be used in a test program as follows:

```
import java.io.*;
import javagently.*;
import myutilities.*;

class SortTest {

    /* The SortTest program    by J M Bishop Dec 1996
     * --------------------    Java 1.1 October 1997
     *                         revised August 2000
```

```
 * for sorting a table, of countries or integers.
 * Illustrates interfaces and
 * linking up to an independent sorter.
 */

public static void main(String[] args) throws IOException {
  new SortTest ();
}

SortTest () throws IOException {
    Country t [] = new Country[10];
    String s;

    Stream in = new Stream ("Countries.data", Stream.READ);
    for (int i = 0; i < t.length; i++) {
        s = in.readString();
        t[i] = new Country(s);
    }

    System.out.println("Original");
    System.out.println("========");
    for (int i = 0; i < t.length; i++) {
        System.out.println(t[i]);
    }

    Sort.selectionSort(t, t.length);

    System.out.println();
    System.out.println("Sorted");
    System.out.println("======");
    for (int i = 0; i < t.length; i++) {
        System.out.println(t[i]);
    }
  }
}
```

Notice that there is actually no mention of Sortable in the program. In other words, this program could have run with the old sort. The change was effected between the object and sort. What we have gained is the flexibility to sort other classes.

Testing Just to be sure of the sort process, we give the data and output for the program:

```
Japan
Russia
Argentina
```

```
Finland
Ukraine
Spain
Algeria
France
Iceland
Israel
```

Original
========
Japan
Russia
Argentina
Finland
Ukraine
Spain
Algeria
France
Iceland
Israel

Sorted
======
Algeria
Argentina
Finland
France
Iceland
Israel
Japan
Russia
Spain
Ukraine

Extension   What we really want to test is whether we have achieved the objective of independence. A quick way of doing this is to change `SortTest` to sort something else, such as integers. However, remember that `Sortable` is dealing with objects, so we must put the integer in a class. This class can be in an inner one.

```
import java.io.*;
import javagently.*;
import myutilities.*;

class SortTestInt {
```

```
/* The SortTestInt program     by J M Bishop Dec 1996
 *                             Java 1.1 October 1997
 *                             revised August 2000
 * for sorting a table of integers
 * Illustrates linking up to an independent sorter.
 * as well as putting integers in envelopes.
 */

public static void main(String[] args) throws IOException {
  new SortTestInt();
}

SortTestInt () throws IOException {
    OurInteger[] t = new OurInteger[10];
    Stream in = new Stream(System.in);

    for (int i = 0; i < 10; i++)
        t[i] = new OurInteger(in.readInt());

    System.out.println("Original");
    System.out.println("========");
    for (int i = 0; i < t.length; i++) {
        System.out.print(t[i].val+"  ");
    }
    System.out.println();

    Sort.selectionSort(t,t.length);

    System.out.println();
    System.out.println("Sorted");
    System.out.println("======");
    for (int i = 0; i < t.length; i++) {
        System.out.print(t[i] +"  ");
    }
    System.out.println();
}

class OurInteger implements Sortable {

  /* This member class encapsulates an integer
   * as an object and implements Sortable
   * for integers.
   */
```

```
      int val;

      public OurInteger(int i) {
        val = i;
      }

      public boolean lessThan(Sortable a) {
        OurInteger i = (OurInteger)a;
        return val < i.val;
      }

      public String toString () {
        return String.valueOf(val);
      }
    }


  }
```

A run of the program would produce (using data typed in):

```
Original
========
5 8 1 2 0 4 3 7 9 6


Sorted
======
0 1 2 3 4 5 6 7 8 9
```

Before we leave interfaces, we stress that they can only have method specifications in them – no completed methods or variables. However, they can include constants if necessary.

9.4   Abstract methods and classes

The final member of the class power trio is abstract methods and abstract classes. When used together with interfaces and inheritance, they provide a clear and understandable way of putting together large systems.

Abstract methods

Abstract methods provide 'place holders' for methods that can sensibly be mentioned at one level, but that are going to be implemented in a variety of ways lower down. Take for example a sleep method in the `Nature` example. It probably does not make sense to have a general method to describe sleep patterns of all animals. But we do know that all kinds of animals have sleep patterns, and when we are dealing with objects at the `Animals` class level, it would be useful to be able to call the different methods supplied for the different classes at the bottom. What we are looking for is the concept of an abstract method. Thus we declare:

```
abstract void sleep ();
```

in `Animals`. The effect of such an inclusion in `Animals` is to turn it into an abstract class.

Abstract classes

An abstract class is any class with at least one abstract method. An abstract class cannot be used to declare objects any more: the presence of the abstract method means that it is incomplete. It must first be subclassed and the abstract method(s) filled in. In the above example, `Animals` becomes:

```
abstract class Animals extends Nature {
   // All sorts of things here

   abstract void sleep ();

   // and more here
}
```

Now each of the bottom level of classes, such as `Elephant` and `Rhino`, can complete the definition of sleep. If `Herbivore` mentions nothing about sleeping, then by implication it must also be declared as abstract.

How would we use the hierarchy now? Well, all declarations will take place at the bottom, concrete level, for example:

```
Elephant E [] = new Elephants [10];
Rhino R [] = new Rhino [5];
```

But now we cannot declare any `Herbivores` or `Animals` as such (they are abstract). What we have gained is abstraction: we have defined what should be done, and have left it up to other classes to be responsible for doing it.

There are several examples of abstract classes in the Java packages, some of which have already been discussed in earlier chapters (`Date`, `TimeZone`, `NumberFormat` and so on). These classes provide class methods that can be used to create an instance of the class, as we have been doing all along.

9.5 Case Study 4: Veterinary Tags

Problem

The Savanna Veterinary Association several years ago developed a system of tagging pets so that if they were found straying, they could be tracked back to their owners. The tags were small and simple and had the animal's name and owner's phone number on them. If a pet was found by a member of the public, he or she could try to phone the owner in order to return it. However, the S.V.A. found that when owners moved, they did not always update their tags, and so tracking owners was more difficult.

It then started to keep a central register of all tags, so that people could phone in and check whether a pet was recorded missing or not. In addition, it wants to introduce an improved Xtag which has the vet's name on it as well. Obviously, the old system must continue to run, and the new system along with it. The register is being built up over several months, and will consist of old and new tags together.

Solution 1 and class design

The solution is to use inheritance. The old program already exists and runs with the old tags. What we do is define a new tags class, called XTags, which extends the old tag and has the new data item in it. But both can be stored as Tags – the 'family' name – in the register.

The program can be done in one class, with the Tags and XTags classes for the creation of the objects. main calls three methods that do the processing as required. makeTags will be the method that actually creates the Tags objects and puts them in the array, declared as:

```
static Tags register [] = new Tags [100];
```

showTags will display the current register, and checkTags is the facility offered to the public for finding the phone numbers of pets, given the name of their tags.

The original Tags class looks like this:

```
class Tags {

  /* The Tags class          by J M Bishop Januray 1997
   * for keeping data on a pet.
   */

  String name, phone;

    public Tags(String n, String p) {
      name = n;
      phone = p;
    }
```

```
    public String toString() {
      return name+" tel: "+phone;
    }

  }
```

It has a constructor and one method – the standard `toString` method – which enables tags to be concatenated with other strings and used in `println` and other statements where strings are required. The part of `makeTags` which adds a tag to the register is:

```
  Tags tag = new Tags (petsName, ownersPhone);
  register[index] = tag;
```

In `showTags` it is printed out with:

```
  display.println(i+"\t"+ register[i]);
```

Data for the program are in the form of pets names and phone numbers, and are stored on a file. The full original veterinary program is on the web site, but here we press on immediately to the extension to illustrate inheritance.

Solution 2

Now we want to add the `XTags` to the system. The class is given by:

```
  public class XTags extends Tags {

    /* The XTags class      by J M Bishop  January 1997
     * for extended vet tags with vet numbers.
     * Uses inheritance */

    String vet;

    public XTags(String n, String p, String v) {
      super(n, p);
      vet = v;
    }

    public String toString() {
      return name+" tel: "+phone+" Vet's tel: "+vet;
    }

  }
```

Notice several points here. `XTags` has access to the `name` and `phone` variables in `Tags`. It overrides the `toString` method in `Tags`. It declares its own new field, `vet`.

Program

Before we consider the full Veterinary program, let us look at the important section related to inheritance.

```
1.    char kind = Text.readChar(fin);
2.    petsName = Text.readString(fin);
3.    ownersPhone = Text.readString(fin);
4.    Tags tag;
5.    switch (kind) {
6.      case 'p':
7.    case 'P':
8.      tag = new Tags(petsName, ownersPhone);
9.      break;
10.   default:
11.   case 'x':
12.   case 'X':
13.     String vetsPhone = Text.readString(fin);
14.     tag = new XTags(petsName, ownersPhone, vetsPhone);
15.   }
16.   register[index] = tag;
```

The very first line obtains information about whether the pet is to have a tag or Xtag: this is indicated by means of a 'P' (for plain) or 'X' for Xtag. Lines 2–3 are concerned with getting in the common information of pet's name and owner's phone number. Now we use a switch-statement to deal with creating the two types of tags. The Xtag option is also the default because we would like to move the public towards the new version. By using multiple-case labels, we can easily accommodate both capital and lower-case letters.

The statement under case 'P' comes from the old program and creates a new `Tags` object. However, if one of the new tags is requested, then we read in more information and create an `XTag` object, **but in the same tag field**. Whichever tag is created gets assigned into the register, which is still declared of the superclass `Tag`. Because `XTag` inherits from `Tag`, in other words comes from the same family, it is accepted wherever a `Tag` would be welcome. In this way inheritance aids significantly in keeping programs reusable and maintainable.

Now here is the full updated program. The main program instantiates a nested class called `DataHandler`, which is where most of the work gets done.

```
import java.io.*;
import javagently.*;

class VeterinaryTags {

    /* The Vet tagging program   by J M Bishop Jan 1997
     * -----------------------    Java 1.1 Oct 1997
```

```
    *                                  Display class July 1999
    * Keeps a register of pets' tags and enables it to be
    * checked if a stray pet is found.
    * Uses two types of tags.
    * Illustrates inheritance.
    */

public static void main (String args []) throws IOException {
    TagDataHandler vetAssoc = new TagDataHandler ();
    vetAssoc.initialize();
    vetAssoc.makeTags();
    vetAssoc.showTags();
    while (true)
       // ends when close button is pressed on display
       vetAssoc.checkTags();
}

static class TagDataHandler {

  int index;
  Tags[] register = new Tags[100];
  Display display = new Display ("Veterinary tag system");
  BufferedReader fin = Text.open(System.in);

  void initialize () {
    // fin defaults to the keyboard in case there is no file

    display.println("Savanna Pet Tag System");
    display.prompt ("Pet file name", "tags.data");
    while (true) {
      display.ready("Set file name and press ready");
      String filename = display.getString("Pet file name");
      try {
        fin = Text.open(filename);
        break;
      } catch (FileNotFoundException e) {
        display.println("No such file, try again");
      }
    }
  }

  void makeTags( ) throws IOException {
    String petsName, ownersPhone;
    while (true) {
      try {
```

```
      char kind = Text.readChar(fin);
      petsName = Text.readString(fin);
      ownersPhone = Text.readString(fin);
      Tags tag;
      switch (kind) {
        case 'p':
        case 'P':
          tag = new Tags(petsName, ownersPhone);
          break;
        default:
        case 'x':
        case 'X':
          String vetsPhone = Text.readString(fin);
          tag = new XTags(petsName, ownersPhone, vetsPhone);
      }
      register[index] = tag;
      index++;
    }
    catch (EOFException e) {
      break;
    }
  }
  display.println("All "+index+" pets read in.\n");
}

void showTags() {
  display.println("The Pet Register\n");
  display.println("Pet No.  Name and phone no.");
  for (int i = 0; i < index; i++)
    display.println(i+"   "+register[i]);
  display.prompt("Found pet's tag name","Buster");
}

void checkTags() {
  display.ready("\nEnter pet's name as on tag and press ready");
  String info = display.getString("Found pet's tag name");
  boolean found = false;
  for (int i = 0; i < index; i++)
    if (register[i].name.equals(info)) {
      display.println("The pet called "+
        info+" is registered no. "+i);
      display.println("Full info: "+register[i]);
      found = true;
      break;
    }
```

```
        if (!found)
            display.println("The pet called "+
                info+" is not registered.");
    }
  }
}
```

Testing   Figure 9.4 gives a sample run of the program.

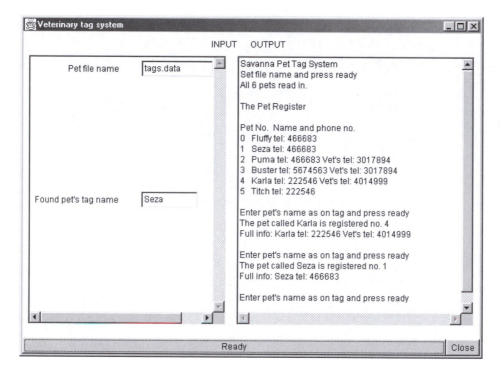

Figure 9.4 *Display from the Vet tagging program.*

Sorting the register

The next step is to make our tags register sortable, which essentially means making objects of the `Tags` class sortable. The first question is: what field do we want to sort on? We could simply sort on pet names, in which case a `lessThan` method would look like this:

```
public boolean lessThan (Sortable secondTag) {
   Tags temp = (Tags) secondTag;
   return (name.compareTo(temp.name) < 0);
}
```

The local object `temp` is needed because we have to cast the parameter (which is of the general interface type) to the specific type `Tags` before we can pick up fields belonging to `Tags`. If we did this, then only `Tags` would implement `Sortable`, and any `XTags` would go back in the inheritance hierarchy to use `lessThan`. There is nothing in an `XTag` that alters the way in which sorting would be performed.

Suppose, however, the association would like to sort on phone numbers. Under the old tags system, this will group together pets for a given owner. But with `XTags`, we would like the vet's phone to be considered instead. Now sorting for `XTags` is different from that for `Tags`. Moreover, how do we define `lessThan` when one of the operands is a `Tag` and the other an `XTag`?

We start by realizing that `selectionSort` will call the method in the class of the first operand. So at a particular place in the sort, if the first operand to be compared is a `Tags` object, we shall arrive at the `lessThan` method for `Tags`. At this stage, the parameter could be either type. Here is what the `lessThan` method will look like:

```
public boolean lessThan (Sortable secondTag) {
   Tags temp = (Tags) secondTag;
   // temp may be a tag or an xTag, so we get
   // the relevant phone field by calling a method
   String secondString = temp.getPhone();
   return (phone.compareTo(secondString) < 0);
}
```

Having got the second operand from the parameter, we are not sure what type it is. So we employ the technique of dynamic binding, and extract via a method the phone number we want. If the second operand is tag, then `getPhone` for `Tags` will be called, which is:

```
String getPhone () {
   return phone;
}
```

If, however, the second operand is an `XTag`, Java will direct `getPhone` to that class, which returns the vet's phone as follows:

```
String getPhone () {
   return vet;
}
```

The `lessThan` method in `XTags` is exactly like the above except that the last line refers to `vet`, as in:

```
return (vet.compareTo(secondString) < 0);
```

As already explained, the second operand will pick up an owner's phone or a vet's phone, depending on the type of the object at runtime. For completion's sake, here is the full `Tags` class:

```
import myutilities.*;

class Tags implements Sortable {

    /* The Tags class           by J M Bishop January 1997
     * --------------           adapted July 1999
     * for keeping data on a pet.
     */

    String name, phone;

    public Tags(String n, String p) {
        name = n;
        phone = p;
    }

    String getPhone () {
      return phone;
    }

    public boolean lessThan (Sortable secondTag) {
      Tags temp = (Tags) secondTag;
      // temp may be a tag or an xTag, so we get
      // the relevant phone field by calling a method
      String secondString = temp.getPhone();
      return (phone.compareTo(secondString) < 0);
    }

    public String toString() {
        return "Owner: "+phone+"  "+name;
    }

}
```

Finally, the main program needs a minor adjustment. It does not implement or mention `Sortable`; all this is handled by the tag classes. All it has to do is call

```
Sort.selectionSort (register,index);
```

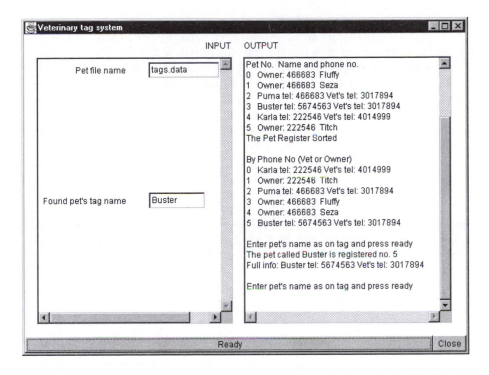

Figure 9.5 *The pets register sorted by phones of vets or owners.*

The ouput from the program after the register is sorted on these phone numbers is given in Figure 9.5. We have altered the way in which each line is printed to emphasize how the sorting is achieved. From the output we can see that Fluffy, Seza and Puma, all owned by the same owner, are sorted separately, because Puma has an Xtag and therefore is sorted on the vet's phone number first.

9.5   Serialization

The careful reader will have noticed that both the last two case studies – the Coffee Shop and the Veterinary Tags – are involved in keeping an inventory of data in memory. The data are initially read in from a text file, and then can be updated (as in selling coffee) or queried (as in checking pet tags). However, there is no provision for preserving the state of the data between one run of the program and the next. Thus both programs are somewhat unrealistic. Clearly, there is a need to save data both while a program is running (in case of a crash) and at the end of a run (so we do not have to start from scratch). In Java, saving data is based on a special facility called serialization.

Serialization is a technique whereby an object can be converted into a simple stream of bytes in such a way that it can be reconstructed correctly later. Once we have such a stream of bytes, we can output it to a file and read it back again. The object that is serialized will usually be a composite of many other objects, such as an array or a hash table or even a linked list. Java can cope with any sort of structure we have learnt so far.

There are two parts to serializing. Firstly, the object to be serialized must declare that it implements the `Serializable` interface. Since this interface is already implemented for the superclass `Object`, the methods it contains do not actually have to be implemented: the declaration simply indicates that the object allows these methods to be called on it. The methods are `writeObject` and `readObject`. They take and return `Objects` and they are declared in the classes `ObjectOutputStream` and `ObjectInputStream` respectively. The following form gives the syntax and semantics of serializing.

Serializing an object out and back in

```
// Write the object out
ObjectOutputStream outstream =
    new ObjectOutputStream (outputStreamObject);
outstream.writeObject(theObject);
outstream.close();


// Read the object back in
ObjectInputStream instream =
   new ObjectInputStream (inputStreamObject);
theObject = (Serializable) instream.readObject();
instream.close();
```

The constructor for *outstream* supplies as a parameter a stream such as a file or an array or a network connection (see Chapter 14). The corresponding constructor for the input stream should supply the same actual stream.

The `writeObject` method will take the given parameter, convert it to a stream of bytes and transfer it to the `outstream`.

The `readObject` method will retrieve the bytes from the corresponding `instream` and reconstruct the structure of the original object, be it an array, list, or whatever.

Both streams should be closed before continuing.

The class of `theObject` must be declared as implementing the `Serializable` interface.

In addition, there are some exceptions that can be raised by the above process. In general these relate to input–output errors (incorrect file names and so on) or class errors (the object did not implement `Serializable`). Thus the method that includes the above forms should catch `IOException` and `ClassNotFoundException`.

In the example that follows and some of the problems we concentrate on serializing data to files. In Chapter 14, we see how we can also serialize across a network.

EXAMPLE 9.3   Illustrating `Serializable`

Problem The statement is 'illustrate `Serializable`'.

Solution   We shall set up a system to serialize any object, then test it out with an array of objects and a list of objects, i.e. the coffees list developed in Example 8.2. With this generality in mind, the design of the method makes considerable use of the `Serializable` interface as a type. The method is:

```
Serializable outAndInAgain (Serializable structure) {
  Serializable copy = null;
   try{
   // Serialize the object
     ObjectOutputStream out =
          new ObjectOutputStream (new FileOutputStream("mydata"));
     out.writeObject(structure);
     out.close();

    // Read the object back in
     ObjectInputStream in =
          new ObjectInputStream (new FileInputStream("mydata"));
     copy = (Serializable) in.readObject();
     in.close();
   } catch (IOException e)
     {System.out.println("IO problem "+e.getMessage());}
     catch (ClassNotFoundException e)
     {System.out.println("Class problem "+e.getMessage());}
   return copy;
 }
```

This is just a test method, because it writes to a file and reads back again immediately – hardly a normal occurrence. Notice that the objects that are passed as a parameter to the constructors for `ObjectOutputStream` and `ObjectInputStream` are files, but based on classes we have not used before. In Section 7.3 when we discussed the `Stream` class, we made use of `FileReader` and `FileWriter`. The difference is that the classes used above handle raw byte streams, whereas the other two, used by `Stream`, work at the character level.

Program The program has two parts. The first part illustrates serializing a small array of student names and marks. The second uses the `Coffee` test class from Example 8.2 and shows how a list can also be serialized in one statement.

```java
import java.io.*;
import javagently.*;

class TestFiles implements Serializable  {

  /* Serializing files                 J M Bishop  April 2000
   * ==================
   *
   * illustrates how easy it is to save and retrieve a data structure
   * to and from a file.
   * The program and the class of objects must declare that they
   * implement Serializable.
   */

  TestFiles ()  throws IOException {
    doItWithAnArray();
    doItWithAList();
  }

  Serializable outAndInAgain (Serializable structure) {
    Serializable copy = null;

    try{
    // Serialize the object
      ObjectOutputStream out =
            new ObjectOutputStream (new FileOutputStream("mydata"));
      out.writeObject(structure);
      out.close();

    // Read the object back in
      ObjectInputStream in =
            new ObjectInputStream (new FileInputStream("mydata"));
      copy = (Serializable) in.readObject();
      in.close();
    } catch (IOException e)
      {System.out.println("IO problem "+e.getMessage());}
      catch (ClassNotFoundException e)
      {System.out.println("Class problem "+e.getMessage());}
      return copy;
  }
```

```
 void doItWithAnArray () {

  Students [] table = new Students [10];
  Students [] copy = new Students [10];
   // Set up test data
  table[0] = new Students("Peter",84);
  table[1] = new Students("John",51);
  table[2] = new Students("Kathy",65);
  int n = 2;

  // Print the original data
  System.out.println("\nThe original table");
   for (int i=0; i<=n; i++)
     System.out.println(table[i]);

  // Make a few changes
  table[1].marks = 58;
  table[2].name = "Cathy";
  table[3] = new Students("Sipho",70);
  n = 3;

  copy = (Students []) outAndInAgain (table);

   //Print the table and the copy
   System.out.println("\nThe copied table");
   for (int i=0; i<=n; i++) {
     System.out.println(copy[i]);
   }
 }

void doItWithAList () throws IOException {
  Coffee coffees = null;
  Coffee copy = null;
  String name;
  Stream in = new Stream ("names.dat", Stream.READ);

  // Read the coffee data from a text file
  for (int i=0; i<=4; i++) {
    name = in.readString();
    coffees = new Coffee (name, coffees);
  }

  // Print out the list
  Coffee list = coffees;
  System.out.println("\nCoffees on the list");
  for (int i=0; i<=4; i++) {
```

```
        System.out.println(list.name);
        list = list.link;
      }

    copy = (Coffee) outAndInAgain (coffees);

    //Print the list as read back
     list = copy;
     System.out.println("\nThe read back list");
     for (int i=0; i<=4; i++) {
       System.out.println(list.name);
       list = list.link;
     }
    }

  public static void main (String args []) throws IOException {
    new TestFiles ();
  }

class Students implements Serializable {

  String name;
  int marks;

  Students (String n, int m) {
    name = n;
    marks = m;
  }

  public String toString () {
    return name + " " + marks;
  }
}

  class Coffee implements Serializable {
    /* Small test class with a link */

    Coffee (String name, Coffee c) {
      this.name = name;
      link = c;
    }

    String name;
    Coffee link;
  }

}
```

Testing The following small test illustrates that the process does work.

```
The original table
Peter 84
John 51
Kathy 65

The copied table
Peter 84
John 58
Cathy 65
Sipho 70

Coffees on the list
Italian
Kenyan
VIP
Colombian
Java

The read back list
Italian
Kenyan
VIP
Colombian
Java
```

SUMMARY

Object-oriented programming is much enhanced in power by the use of abstraction and inheritance. Abstraction enables us to concentrate on the essentials of a method or class: what it must guarantee to the user. The details can then be filled in later, and perhaps by more than one implementation of the abstraction. Java provides interfaces and abstract classes and methods as means of achieving abstraction.

Inheritance serves at least two purposes. We can prolong the life of a system by creating new versions of classes that include new features, but that inherit the old. The two classes are regarded as being of the same family and therefore the child can be used wherever the parent was expected. We can also divide up information into what is essential at any level, creating a hierarchy of classes, all of which can be used together or separately.

Objects need not only exist in memory: they can easily be transferred to a permanent medium after a serialization process.

In this chapter we define the following keywords:

```
extends                abstract
interface              protected
implements
```

and use the following APIs:

```
Sortable               FileInputStream
Serializable           ObjectOutputStream
FileOutputStream       ObjectInputStream
```

The forms that are defined here are:

Interface declaration
Interface implementation
Serializing an object out and back in

QUIZ

9.1   If we wish to add a gestation period to the `Nature` hierarchy, in which class(es) would it logically go?

    (a) `Nature`
    (b) `Animals`
    (c) `Elephant` and `Rhino`
    (d) `Herbivores`

9.2   `TestNature` is prevented from seeing the variable `name` inside class `Nature` because

    (a) `name` is protected
    (b) `Nature` has not been instantiated in `TestNature`
    (c) `Nature` is a superclass of `Elephant` and `Rhino`, not a subclass
    (d) `name` has not been initialized

9.3   In the `Nature` hierarchy, the `toString` method is an example of

    (a) overriding
    (b) overloading
    (c) shadowing
    (d) dynamic binding

9.4   If we wanted to sort the coffee list from Example 8.2,

    (a) we could do it by implementing `Sortable`
    (b) we could do it by implementing `Sortable` and defining a `lessThan` method
    (c) we could not do it because `selectionSort` works on arrays only
    (d) we could not do it because we cannot define a `lessThan` method between two list objects

9.5   If a is an `Animal` object, then it has the following data variables:

(a)   `name`
(b)   `name` and `grassNeeded`
(c)   none
(d)   `name`, `grassNeeded` and either `tusks` or `horn`

9.6   The rule for working within a hierarchy, expressed in terms of P and Q where Q extends P is:

(a)   Q can be assigned to P
(b)   P can be assigned to Q with a type cast
(c)   both A and B
(d)   neither A nor B

9.7   The following is an attempt to implement a `lessThan` method for comparing `Rhinos`' horns:

```
public boolean lessThan (Sortable a) {
  return horn < a.horn;
}
```

It will not compile because:

(a)   `horn` is `private`
(b)   `a` does not necessarily have a horn
(c)   `<` is not defined for double variables
(d)   `lessThan` has already been defined for tusks

9.8   To read a hash table object, `hash`, back that has been written to a file (assuming that a correct connection has been made to an object stream `oos`), we use:

(a)   `hash = (HashTable) oos.readObject();`
(b)   `hash = (Serializable) oos.readObject();`
(c)   `hash = oos.readObject();`
(d)   `hash = new readObject ();`

9.9   If the serializable process raises a `ClassNotFoundException`, then a likely cause is:

(a)   the class was not compiled
(b)   the class was not instantiated
(c)   the class was not declared as implementing `Serializable`
(d)   the class does not exist

9.10   To create an instance of an abstract class we

(a)   define any abstract methods then instantiate the class
(b)   instantiate the class
(c)   instantiate its superclass
(d)   call a class method to create the instance

9.1   **Object illustrator.** Take Example 9.1 and work into it an example of every kind of object property that was mentioned in Sections 8.2 and 9.2. Comment your program fully.

9.2   **A marker system.** Set up a marker system that has a `Students` class consisting of student numbers and marks. There are five marks per student, and each has an associated weight. The weights add up to 100%, and enable a composite final mark to be calculated. The system should be able to be:

■ interrogated to produce a final mark for a student;

■ sorted according to student number;

■ sorted according to mark;

■ requested for a full print out.

9.3   **Extending the marker.** Savanna University is introducing continuous assessment from 2001 and wants to extend the marker system in Problem 9.2 so that new students will have two sorts of marks: *open* marks, which relate to assignments and projects, and *controlled* marks, which relate to tests and examinations. The old kind of marks will remain as well. Decide on how to extend the `Students` class to include this facility and examine carefully what, if anything, of the `Marker` class itself needs to be changed as a result. Get the new system working.

9.4   **Graph drawing.** We would like to investigate abstract methods more carefully. Set up a system that has a basic method for calling the `Graph` class to draw a graph, but where the limits of *x* and the function to be called are supplied by instantiated objects of another class. Thus the limits will come as parameters, and the function will be an abstract method. Instantiate several such objects for functions such as sin, $2x-1$ and so on. Supply suitable limits via the display.

9.5   **Nelson sells ice creams.** Nelson is contemplating selling ice creams at his Coffee Shop during a heatwave. Obviously he has to keep track of stock and watch expiry dates and so on, so that much of the programming associated with keeping ice cream is already part of keeping coffee. Study the Coffee Shop program and its associated classes and investigate how it could be adapted to include ice cream. Should one use interfaces, inheritance or abstract classes, or a mixture? Is a major rewite of the `Coffee` class necessary first?

9.6   **Coffee shop overnight.** Using serialization, adapt the Coffee Shop program so that the state of the stock is preserved between runs of the program. Then include a facility for interactively adding new batches of coffee, so that the system is truly dynamic.

9.7   **Marks all term.** Change the `Marker` program of Problems 9.2 and 9.3 so that the marks are kept in a list, not in an array. This will enable the number of marks to grow as the term progresses. Serialize the marker program so that the data are written away and read back, then added to during a run.

CHAPTER 10

Graphics and user interfaces

10.1 Introduction to the awt and Swing

The real world has been converted to wysiwyg[1] and GUI[2] interfaces, and Java is fully equipped to provide these options. The GUI part is provided inside two packages called `java.awt` – abstract windowing toolkit – and `javax.swing`. From now on we will call them the awt (pronounced 'ought') package and Swing, and know that they are Java's platform-independent approach to user interfacing.

These packages are also completely driven from within the Java language. That means that any graphical layout tools that allow pointing and selecting of the visual appearance of an application, and generate the code for it, are separate from Java itself. These tools do exist, but running them will need a larger computer and more resources than were at first bargained for.

A complete tour of all the facilities available through awt and Swing are beyond the scope of this book. What we aim to do is to reveal the overall structure of the packages and then to introduce several of the most used features through examples.

---

[1] What you see is what you get, prounounced 'wizzywig'.
[2] Graphical user interface, pronounced 'gooey'.

Overall structure of awt

The classes in the awt package can be classified as:

- graphics;

- components, including windows and menus;

- layout managers;

- event handlers;

- image manipulation.

Graphics permits the drawing of shapes, lines and images; the selecting of fonts, colours and so on. **Components** are items such as buttons, text fields, menus and scroll bars. We can put them in **containers** and then choose one of a selection of **layout managers** to arrange them suitably on the screen. The subpackage `java.awt.event` handles external **events**, such as pushing buttons and moving the mouse, through a suite of event **handlers**, **listeners** and **adapters**. Finally, `java.awt.image` is another subpackage, which is used by awt to incorporate **images** in a variety of formats. Figure 10.1 gives an overall picture of the main awt.

There are four main abstract classes – `Component`, `Container`, `MenuComponent` and `Graphics`. Other abstract classes are `FontMetrics`, `Image`, `PrintJob` and `Toolkit`. `LayoutManager` is an interface (along with five other specialized ones not shown), and all the rest are classes, inheriting from the classes drawn above them. Thus `Frame` is a `Window`, which is a `Container`, which is a `Component`.

With all of these different parts to the graphical user interfacing, it is actually hard to know where to start. We shall use a very simple example – the one in Chapter 2 for drawing a flag on the screen – and introduce the various parts of awt as they are needed. In particular, we shall see that there are several ways of achieving very similar effects, and that awt has a rich selection of features from which to choose.

Swing

Swing is a code name for a further set of GUI tools provided in Java. Whereas the awt, as its name implies, provides a common abstraction of GUI tools that can be implemented using the facilities present on any operating system, Swing provides a set of similar tools that are implemented independently of the operating systems. For example, using the awt, a window and a button will have the look and feel of the machine the program runs on. That is because the awt links into the GUI facilities of the operating system. This of course makes awt programs smaller in size at runtime, because much of the code is offloaded to the operating system.

Swing components, on the other hand, are implemented entirely in Java and a Swing window and button will have a Swing look about it, no matter which computer it runs on. Swing programs will be bigger, but they have the advantage that the design of the GUI is

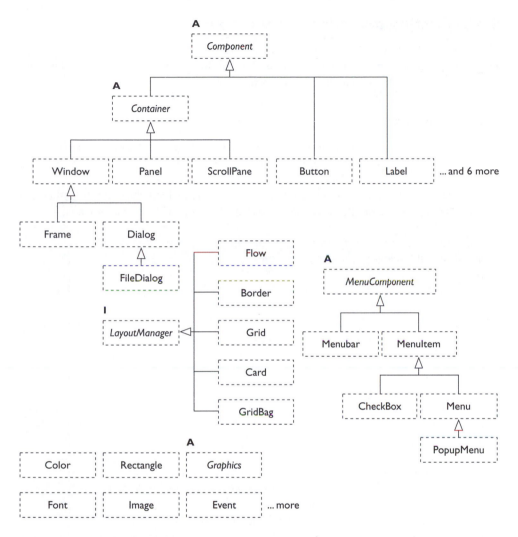

Figure 10.1 *The awt class structure (A indicates an abstract class and I an interface).*

fixed by the designer, and will not suddenly go off the edge of the window, for example, because the buttons of one operating system are slightly larger than another's. However, there is a way of changing the look and feel of a GUI at runtime, to reflect a different operating system.

In this book, we have continued use of the awt, because it is simple and small and the principles of GUI design and event-handling are the same for Swing. There is an example of Swing later, which gives an idea of how it looks. An excellent introduction to Swing is given in the online Java Tutorial on the Sun web site at www.javasoft.com.

10.2 Putting graphics in a window

Graphical interfaces are presented to the user in **windows**. Java has a `Window` class, but in practice we usually use one of its subclasses, `Frame`.

`Frame` – the basic window

We start off with `Frame` as the basic presenter of GUI items. Each application can have several windows and, for each, we declare a class that inherits `Frame` and includes calls to the methods necessary to display information in the window and perform other actions. If we are just dealing with one window, as in Example 2.2 which showed a flag, then the main program's class would also be the one that declares the window. The form is:

Creating a frame

```
import java.awt.*;

class Classid extends Frame {

  Classid {
    setTitle ("title"); // optional
    setSize (width, height);
    setVisible (true);
  }

... somewhere (e.g. in main) we have

  new Classid ();
```

First import the `java.awt` package.
Then the class containing the frame object inherits class `Frame`.
Finally, the class creates an object of itself (as usual) and its constructor
performs three essential functions: setting the title of the window
and its size, and activating the drawing of the frame itself via
`setVisible`.

The three methods are declared in `Frame` and `Component` (which `Frame` inherits). As an example, part of the class declaration and constructor for the flag maker shown in Example 2.2 is:

```
import java.awt.*;

class FlagMaker extends Frame {
```

```
public FlagMaker ( ) {
  add ("Center", new Flags());

  // Set the frame's title and size and activate the drawing
  // described by the paint method in the component we added
  setTitle ("A Flag");
  setSize (300, 200);
  setVisible (true);
}

public static void main (String args []) {
  new FlagMaker ();
}
}
```

Adding graphics to the window

At this point, the awt will look for a `paint` method to add any further graphics to the contents of the window. `paint` is defined

- either in the class that extends `Frame` (as will be seen in Example 10.1);
- or in some other object of a class that extends `Canvas` and that we added to our frame (as in Example 2.2).

The form for a `paint` method, which overrides that defined in `Component`, is:

Redefining the `paint` method

```
public void paint (Graphics g) {
  Calls to methods in Graphics, prefixed
  by g.
}

public void repaint (Graphics g) {
  Calls to methods in Graphics, prefixed
  by g.
}
```

`paint` is called once a component is made visible, and again whenever the window it is in has been hidden and needs to be redrawn.
`repaint` can be called explicitly by the program for the same effect.

The `paint` method is supplied with a `Graphics` object by the runtime system customized for the particular platform (i.e. computer and its operating system) that the program is running on. In this way, Java can take advantage of the good points of any particular platform, and make the awt present a familiar look and feel to the users of different platforms.

The `Graphics` class is quite extensive, but some of its methods are given in the form:

`Graphics` class specification

```
clearRect  (int x, int y, int width, int height)
copyArea   (int x, int y, int height, int width, int dx, int dy)
drawChars  (char [ ] data, int offset, int length, int x, int y)
drawLine   (int x1, int y1, int x2, int y2)
drawOval   (int x, int y, int width, int height)
drawRect   (int x, int y, int width, int height)
drawString (String str, int x, int y)
fillOval   (int x, int y, int width, int height)
fillRect   (int x, int y, int width, int height)
setColor   (Color c);
setFont    (Font f);
// plus 38 others
```

The five draw methods are the most commonly used and enable shapes and text to be displayed. The x and y parameters are pixel values calculated from the top left corner of the screen. Width and height are also in pixels.

`clearRect` clears a portion of the screen and `copyArea` duplicates a portion to another specified place a distance of (dx, dy) away.

`setColor` and `setFont` are examples of similar methods that adjust the appearance of the drawing.

`Color` is a class that contains constants for the 13 usual colours (see below) plus facilities for creating new colours.

The colours provided by `Graphics` are: black, blue, cyan, darkGray, gray, green, lightGray, magenta, orange, pink, red, white and yellow. For example, to draw a red rectangle (as the only output), we would say:

```
public void paint (Graphics g) {
  g.setColor (Color.red);
  g.fillRect (10, 10, 200, 100);
}
```

which starts at a point 10 pixels in from the top left corner of the screen, and draws a red-filled rectangle 200 wide by 100 deep (Figure 10.2).

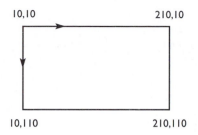

Figure 10.2 *Drawing a rectangle in the* Graphics *package.*

Writing in an awt window with drawString

Working with the Graphics package, the equivalent of println in awt is draw-String. For example, we could say:

```
g.drawString ("Hello Pierre",30,15);
```

which would write the string 'Hello Pierre' 30 pixels in from the left and 15 pixels down from the top of the screen. The size and number of pixels varies from screen to screen, but typically a screen will have 600×400.

The difference between println and drawString is that drawString gives a choice of fonts, font styles and font sizes, and these affect the dimension of each letter. Consequently the positioning of the start of a string can be difficult. We have to use actual numbers to fix the x, y coordinates of the start of a piece of text (as we did above). When trying to get a program to work to one's satisfaction, these numbers can change many times, so it is better to base everything on the relative size of letters. FontMetrics is an awt abstract class that has methods for finding out the size of letters, but sometimes for small programs, using absolute pixel numbers is acceptable. We are now ready for our first example, a very simple one indeed.

EXAMPLE 10.1   Virus warning

Problem   We would like to display a virus warning on the screen.

Solution   Use an awt window and the drawString and rectangle facilities as described above. To make the rectangle striking, we need colour. Colour is provided by the setForeground and setBackground methods in the Component class, using the colour constants defined in the Color[3] class. We will use a cyan background, Color.cyan.

Program   The program follows very simply.

---

[3] Notice that it is color without a 'u', American style.

```java
import java.awt.*;
import java.awt.event.*;
class VirusWarning extends Frame {

    /* The Graphic warning Program    by J M Bishop Oct 1996
     *                                Java 1.1 by T Abbott Oct 1997
     *                                updated 1.2 by J Bishop May 2000
     * produces a warning message on the screen in cyan
     * and black.
     * Illustrates setting up a window, painting in it
     * and enabling the close box.
     */

    VirusWarning () {
      setTitle("Draw Warning");
      setSize(220,150);
      setBackground(Color.cyan);
      setForeground(Color.black);
      addWindowListener(new WindowAdapter () {
        public void windowClosing(WindowEvent e) {
          System.exit(0);
        }
      });
      setVisible(true);
    }

    public void paint(Graphics g) {
      g.setColor(Color.pink);
      g.fillRect(25, 30, 150, 90);
      g.setColor(Color.black);
      g.drawString("W A R N I N G",          70, 60);
      g.drawString("Possible virus detected", 45, 75);
      g.drawString("Reboot and run virus",    50, 90);
      g.drawString("remover software",        60, 105);
    }

    public static void main(String[] args) {
      new VirusWarning ();
    }
}
```

Testing   Figure 10.3 shows the output of the program (reduced to black and white, unfortunately). To stop the program, we click on the Close box on the right.[4] The window closes, and the final statement is a call to `System.exit(0)`. How the program is enabled to close in this way is discussed next.

---

[4] This picture shows Windows output which is similar to Unix; on a Macintosh the Close box will be on the left.

Figure 10.3 *Graphic output for the virus warning program.*

Closing a window

A program that runs in a window needs some way of stopping. One of the accepted methods is for the user to click on the window close box in a top corner. Clicking is an **event** and can be detected by one of the **listeners** in the Event package in the awt. In the main method, we establish a link to such a window listener from the frame being built, by calling the method addWindowListener and instantiating a new version of a window adapter. In the implementation of the adapter that follows we override the WindowAdapter method called windowClosing and perform the appropriate action, which is to call System.exit(0).

The sequence of definitions and actions for closing a window is summarized in the following form:

Closing a window

```
addWindowListener(new WindowAdapter () {
  public void windowClosing(WindowEvent e) {
   System.exit(0);
  }
 });
```

WindowAdapter is a simple abstract class that implements the Window-Listener interface and provides dummy bodies for various methods contained therein. We can decide which to override, and in this case the only interesting method is windowClosing (there are six others). The instantiation of a new WindowAdapter object and the overriding of windowClosing are done as part of the parameter to addWindowListener.

Everything in this form is a keyword (in bold) or an identifier already defined in the awt package (in plain) – except for the event parameter e which is not used, so it can always remain as e anyway. The form becomes a mantra that can be put in the main method of all GUI programs. It uses an anonymous class, as introduced in Section 8.2. The alternative to an anonymous class would have been to supply (new x()) as the parameter and then define x as a local class, with a heading that extends WindowAdapter and a body just the same as that shown here, i.e. an implementation of windowClosing. All in all, the anonymous class is neater.

EXAMPLE 10.2	A weather chart

Problem   Draw a histogram of rainfall figures for Savanna, based on the data of Example 6.6.

Solution   By using Example 6.6, we can get in the data for several years, calculate the mean for each month (as before) and then use this figure to draw a histogram bar in graphics.

Algorithm   The program will follow the pattern described above. The class will inherit Frame. Its main program will contain exactly the same instructions as in our previous example to set up the window properly.

The constructor is rather novel. We shall use it to read in all the data, a task previously performed by a readIn method. The contents, however, do not change. The most important part of the program is how to draw a satisfactory graph. We would like output such as Figure 10.4.

Let us take each of the parts of the chart in turn.

1. **The axes.** Firstly, drawing the lines for the axes establishes a basis for the other parts. 'Zero' on the graph will be at about $x = 50$, $y = 300$, where the values are pixels, and the orientation is as given in Figure 10.2.
2. **The bars.** Next, to draw the bars, we use fillRect and must supply parameters as shown in the graphics form given at the start of this section. In other words, we need a bottom point, a width and a height. The width is some constant, such as 20. The height is the actual value of the month's mean rainfall, which we shall multiply by 10 so that it is decently represented on the screen (that is, a rainfall of 10 mm will use 100 pixels). The y starting point of the rectangle is then y-height where y is our zero point (300, as defined above). Lastly, the x starting point is a bit complicated, because it will vary for each month. The formula is based on the width and on a gap between bars as follows:

```
g.fillRect(month*(width+gap)+gap+x, y-a, width, a);
```

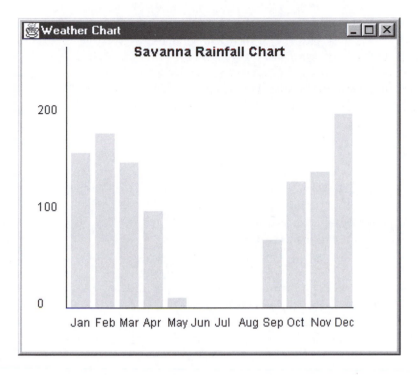

Figure 10.4 *Weather chart drawn with graphics.*

3. **The labels.** Labelling the axes involves two loops which are fairly easy to understand, though admittedly take some time to develop correctly from scratch! The
   x-axis makes use of an array of string names for the months.
4. **The title.** Finally, writing out the title shows how we can change fonts in Java.
   There is a `Font` class which can be instantiated with three parameters: font name,
   style and size. The available font names are: `Serif`, `SansSerif`, `Monospaced`,
   `Dialog` and `DialogInput`. The styles are `PLAIN`, `BOLD` and `ITALIC` and the
   sizes the usual point measurements, for example 12 is normal, 24 is large, and you
   should not go below 8. Changing the font is done for the last `drawString`, so we
   do not need to change it back again.

Program   For what it does, the program is short, compared with Example 10.1 which did
very little. This shows that graphics, like all programming, can be very powerful when repetition is involved. But if every little thing has to be custom-made and mentioned individually,
then the programming can get long and tedious, as we shall see in later examples.

```
import java.io.*;
import javagently.*;
import java.awt.*;
import java.awt.event.*;
```

```
import myutilities.*; // for the Stats class

class WeatherChart extends Frame {

    /* The Weather Charting program    by J M Bishop Dec 1997
     *                                 Java 1.1
     *                                 updated May 2000
     * Draws a histogram of monthly rainfall
     * from data taken over a few years.
     * The data must be in the form:
     * year followed by the 12 rainfall figures for
     * the months of that year.
     * Illustrates simple graphics.
     * Uses the Stats class from myutilities.
     */

    int        base = 1950;
    int        startYear, endYear, nYears = 0;
    double[][] rainTable = new double[12][70];
    String     months [] = {"Jan","Feb","Mar","Apr","May","Jun",
                             "Jul","Aug","Sep","Oct","Nov","Dec"};

    WeatherChart () throws IOException {
      getData ();
      setTitle("Weather Chart");
      setSize(400,350);
      setVisible(true);
      addWindowListener(new WindowAdapter() {
        public void windowClosing(WindowEvent e) {
          System.exit(0);
        }
      });
    }

    public void paint (Graphics g) {
      int x = 50;
      int y = 300;
      int width = 20;
      int gap = 5;
  // the axes
      g.drawLine (x,y,x+12*(width+gap),y);
      g.drawLine (x,y,x,30);
  // labelling the axes
```

```
      for (int m = 0; m < 12; m++)
        g.drawString(months[m],m*(width+gap)+gap+x,y+20);
      for (int i = 0; i <y; i+=100)
        g.drawString(String.valueOf(i),20,y-i);
  // the title
      Font heading = new Font("SansSerif",Font.BOLD,14);
      g.setFont(heading);
      g.drawString("Savanna Rainfall Chart",120,40);
      g.setColor(Color.cyan);
  // the bars
      for (int month = 0; month < 12; month++) {
        int a = (int) Stats.mean
                    (rainTable[month], nYears)*10;
        g.fillRect(month*(width+gap)+gap+x, y-a,width,a);
      }
    }
  }

  void getData () throws IOException {
      Stream fin = new Stream ("rain.dat", Stream.READ);

      int actualYear = 0;       /* e.g. 1997 */
      int yearIndex = 0;        /* e.g. 0 */
      try {
        while (true) {
          actualYear = fin.readInt();
          if (yearIndex == 0)
              startYear = actualYear;
          for (int m = 0; m < 12; m++)
              rainTable[m][yearIndex] = fin.readDouble();
          yearIndex++;
        }
      } catch (EOFException e) {
    /* Pick up the last year of data read in. */
      endYear = actualYear;
      nYears = endYear-startYear+1;
    }
  }

  public static void main(String[] args) throws IOException {
    new WeatherChart ();
  }

}
```

Using a canvas

Once we want to do more than a single paint job (as it were) and have either several windows, or more control over the window we are using, we need to group together graphics in a canvas. A canvas is a component that can be added to a frame and will be painted by the frame's paint method, or supplied as images.

EXAMPLE 10.3	Many flags

Problem We would like to be able to display other flags from the Flag Maker program.

Solution In fact, there are many flags that have the same pattern as Germany's, i.e. three bars across of different colours. For example, the Netherlands is red, white and blue, and Ethiopia is green, yellow and red. We can parameterize the `Flags` class so that the colours are sent at the time a flag is constructed. Then paint is changed to refer to these parameters, rather than to absolute colours.

Program We create a `Flags` class which extends `canvas` and contains the amended constructor and the paint method. Then for each flag we want to make a new frame, i.e. have the flag in its own window. To generalize the operation, we create a `makeFlag` method which instantiates a new frame and then goes through the same motions of setting its title, size, etc. But this time, we explicitly add the canvas into the frame as a component.

One further aspect of a multiframed program is that we can position the frames on the screen starting at a certain *x,y* coordinate using

```
setLocation(x, y);
```

So we number each flag and stagger the windows down the screen, as shown in Figure 10.5. The program follows.

```
import java.awt.*;
import java.awt.event.*;

public class FlagMaker2 extends Frame {

  /** General Flag drawing program       J M Bishop April 2000
   *  ====================
   * Works for several flags as well as different designs.
   * Illustrated inheritance
   **/
```

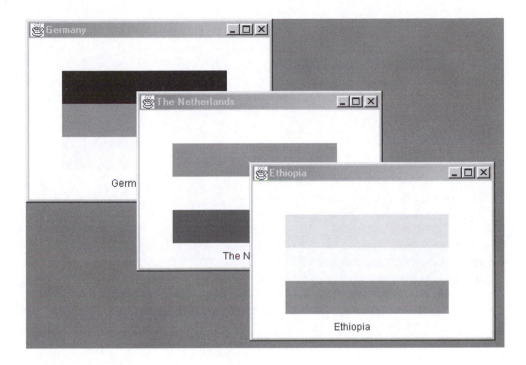

Figure 10.5 *Output from the* FlagMaker2 *program.*

```
public FlagMaker2() {
  FlagCanvas flag;
  flag = new FlagCanvas
          ("Germany",Color.black,Color.red,Color.yellow,0);
  makeFlag(flag);
  flag = new FlagCanvas
          ("The Netherlands",Color.red,Color.white,Color.blue,1);
  makeFlag(flag);
  flag = new FlagCanvas
          ("Ethiopia",Color.green,Color.yellow,Color.red,2);
  makeFlag(flag);
}

public static void main(String [] args) {
   new FlagMaker2();
}
public static void makeFlag (FlagCanvas canvas) {
  Frame f = new Frame();
  f.add(canvas);
  f.setTitle(canvas.country);
```

```
      f.setSize(300,200);
      f.setLocation(75*canvas.flagNo,75*canvas.flagNo);
      f.setVisible(true);
      f.addWindowListener(new WindowAdapter() {
        public void windowClosing(WindowEvent e) {
          e.getWindow().dispose();
        }
      });
    }
  }


//===========================
  class FlagCanvas extends Canvas {

    String country;
    Color bar1, bar2, bar3;
    int flagNo;

     FlagCanvas (String c, Color b1, Color b2, Color b3,int f) {
       country = c;
       bar1 = b1;
       bar2 = b2;
       bar3 = b3;
       flagNo = f;
     }

    public void paint (Graphics g) {
      // Draw the flag from coloured rectangles
      g.setColor (bar1);
      g.fillRect (40,40,200,40);
      g.setColor (bar2);
      g.fillRect (40,80,200,40);
      g.setColor (bar3);
      g.fillRect (40,120,200,40);
      // Label the drawing
      g.setColor (Color.black);
      g.drawString(country,100,180);
    }
  }
```

Awt class and method summary

Before leaving this section, we just tie up a few loose ends related to where the main classes of the awt fit in, and what are the methods they provide that we find are the most useful. Based on the short introduction in Section 10.1 backed up by Figure 10.1, we see

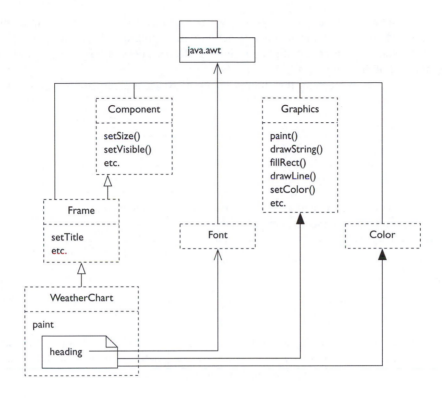

Figure 10.6 *Model diagram for the* WeatherChart *program showing awt connections.*

that we could well have been using Frame, Window, Container and Component, as well as Graphics. In fact, we have mostly been using Component (awt's master class) and Graphics. One method, setTitle, comes from Frame, and Container is used only once we start looking at grouping components, as shown in the next section. To summarize, Figure 10.6 shows a complete model diagram for Example 10.2, with all its connections to the classes in the Java awt package.

10.3 Laying out a GUI

Graphics is only one side of a GUI: the other side is creating a responsive environment through which a user can interact with a program. Java provides a wealth of components for this purpose, as shown in Figure 10.1. These components do not go through the paint method, but are created as objects with certain constructor values, and then added to the frame according to a layout scheme that is currently in place.

The two simplest components are `Label`, which provides for limited text output, and `Button`, which is the basic means for interacting with a program. There are more such components, some of which are studied in later sections. There is a summary of all of them at the end of this section.

The `Label` class provides for the output of simple text via a parameter to its constructor, as in:

Creating a `Label`

```
add(new Label ("some text"));
```

A `Label` object is created with the given text and is added to the current container (usually the current frame).

Thus we could say:

```
add(new Label ("School:"));
```

to get the label `School:` displayed on the screen. `Button` is similar, but has the additional facility of being reactive; that is, we can press the labelled button on the screen and the program can make something happen. This form is:

Creating a `Button`

```
// declare the component
Button buttonid;

// instantiate the object
buttonid = new Button ("some text");
  add(buttonid);
```

buttonid is declared and then instantiated as an object with a given text value.
It is then added to the current container (usually the current frame).

The `add` method is defined in the `Container` class, so what we are doing here is adding the button to the default container of the frame we are working in. We shall see soon how to declare other containers.

The difference between declaring labels and buttons is that labels are passive: you cannot react to them, so it is seldom necessary to make them object variables. Buttons, on the other hand, will certainly be referred to later in the program, so they need to be variables with permanent identifiers. It is also the case that the identifier will be used outside the constructor, which is why we declared it before creating the button.

For example, to set up a `submitButton` and put it in the window, we could say:

```
Button submitButton;

submitButton = new Button ("Submit");
  add(submitButton)
```

Why are there no parameters indicating *x,y* positions on the screen when we add the components to the frame? The reason is that these components (unlike graphics drawings) work with **layout managers.**

Layout managers

Layout managers take over control of the positioning of components that are added to a window, and arrange them sensibly. If the window is resized by the user, the layout manager endeavours to adjust the components in the new area so that they are all still visible and laid out in a similar way relative to each other.

Java has five such managers, but we shall look at only the first three: flow, border and grid. They all implement the interface `LayoutManager`, as shown in Figure 10.1. This interface is part of the awt package, and is made accessible when the awt is imported. The form for incorporating a layout manager is:

Incorporating a layout manager

`setLayout (`**`new`** *`Manager(parameters)`*`);`

One of the five layout managers is instantiated as an object and passed to the `setLayout` method of the current container (e.g. `Frame`) which will then record how components are to be laid out.

The default layout manager for a Java program is `BorderLayout`, but `FlowLayout` is actually more useful for our purposes. It also has the desirable property that it is the default manager for applets. An example layout set up is:

```
setLayout (new FlowLayout(FlowLayout.CENTER,horigap,vertigap));
```

The first parameter indicates that the items added to the frame should be centred: they could also have been left or right justified. The `horigap` and `vertigap` parameters are constants that indicate the minimum distance (in pixels once again) between items in the frame. All three parameters are optional, and `CENTER` is the default for the arrangement expected. Examples of flow layout are given in the sample programs later on.

Reacting to buttons

In addition to closing the window, we now also need to react to buttons being pressed. Like the `windowListener`, there is an `actionListener` defined in `awt.event`. This listener interface has only one method to be implemented: `actionPerformed`. So the strategy for buttons is to link them to the `actionListener`, and to provide a version of `actionPerformed`. The linking is done in the constructor immediately after the button is declared and added to the container. The three statements for a submit button would be:

```
submitButton = new Button ("Submit");
  add(submitButton)
  submitButton.addActionListener (this);
```

The reference to `this` indicates that the current frame will be responsible for defining the `actionPerformed` method. When we set up such a link in the model diagram, it would be useful to distinguish GUI components and listeners from other classes. We choose as the symbol for a component a double-edged box and for a listener a sideways cone. The handler is a normal method symbol. So the above statement would be represented as in Figure 10.7.

`actionPerformed` has one parameter, which is an `ActionEvent`, and it can be successively interrogated to see whether it matches any of the buttons that could be pressed. The following form spells this sequence out:

Reacting to buttons

```
public void actionPerformed (ActionEvent e) {
  if (e.getSource () == buttonname1) {
    statements
  } else
  if (e.getSource () == buttonname2) {
    statements
  }  // etc
}
```

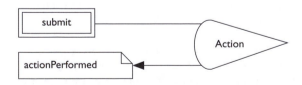

Figure 10.7 *Model for a button, listener and handler.*

If there are several buttons, all with different string labels, then the only way to distinguish between them is to have a sequence of if-else statements, checking for each possibility. A button press is just one kind of event so a diagram such as this will become very useful when the logic of handling events is more complicated. How to handle others will be discussed in Section 11.2.

Extended indentation guidelines

Up until now, indentation in our programs has followed the traditional approach inherited from older languages such as Pascal and C, that is that we indent whenever there is a new method or statement block. Statements within the same block remain at the same level of indentation.

With GUI programming, one finds that there are often very long sequences of statements involved with setting up a number of components on the screen. Each component can have three or more statements associated with it. There is no prescribed order in which the statements have to be executed, but normally we deal with each component in turn and follow a create–link–add pattern. For Java programs, therefore, a new indenting scheme has been introduced that regards the creation of a component as introducing a new level. Then all statements referring to that component can easily be seen. This effect has already been used in the `submitButton` example above, and is evident in the next example and the ones that follow.

EXAMPLE 10.4   Warning with two responses

Problem   Improve the virus warning notice by including two buttons. One should enable the user to acknowledge the message, but wait. In this case, the whole window should turn red. The other button should pretend to force a reboot.

Algorithm   Use the flow layout manager, labels and buttons to achieve the necessary effect. Select background and foreground colours from the `Color` class. For the actions, the Reboot button being pressed causes a simulated reboot in a similar way to closing the window. Pressing the Wait button changes colours as specified. The constructor performs associations between components and listeners. A listener activates `actionPerformed` so that it can react to events.

Program   The program is quite simple, and illustrates the essential sequential nature of GUI programming. The message to be displayed is set up as an array of strings. Each line is displayed through adding it to the frame as a label.The model is shown in Figure 10.8.

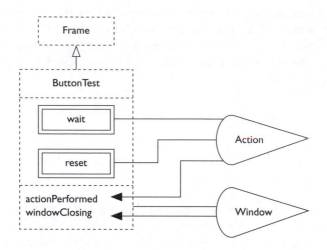

Figure 10.8 *Model diagram for the* `ButtonTest` *program.*

```
import java.awt.*;
import java.awt.event.*;

class ButtonTest extends Frame implements ActionListener {

    /* The Graphic warning Program    by J M Bishop Oct 1996
     *                          Java 1.1 by T Abbott Oct 1997
     *                          updated 1.2 by J Bishop May 2000
     * produces a warning message but when a warning
     * message is pressed, it turns the window red.
     * Illustrates buttons, listeners and the handling of events.
     */

    Button waitButton;
    Button rebootButton;

    String[] message = {
        "W A R N I N G",
        "Possible virus detected.",
        "Reboot and run virus",
        "remover software" };

    ButtonTest ( ) {
    /* The constructor is responsible for setting
     * up the initial buttons and colour background.
```

```
    */
    setBackground(Color.cyan);
    setForeground(Color.black);
    setLayout(new FlowLayout(FlowLayout.CENTER, 15, 10));
    for (int i = 0; i < message.length; i++)
      add(new Label(message[i]));
    waitButton = new Button("Wait");
      waitButton.addActionListener(this);
      add(waitButton);
    rebootButton = new Button("Reboot");
      rebootButton.addActionListener(this);
      add(rebootButton);
    setTitle("Draw Warning");
    setSize(220,150);
    setBackground(Color.cyan);
    setForeground(Color.black);
    addWindowListener(new WindowAdapter () {
      public void windowClosing(WindowEvent e) {
        System.exit(0);
      }
    });
    setVisible(true);
  }

  public void actionPerformed(ActionEvent e) {
    if (e.getSource() == rebootButton) {
      setVisible(false);
      dispose();
      System.exit (0);
    } else
    if (e.getSource() == waitButton) {
      setForeground(Color.white);
      setBackground(Color.red);
    }
  }

  public static void main(String[] args) {
    new ButtonTest ();
  }
}
```

Testing   The first display from this program will be as shown in Figure 10.9.

Figure 10.9 *Output from the* ButtonTest *program.*

Other layout managers

In addition to flow, the other layout managers and their features are as follows:

- **Border.** Allows positioning of items (scroll bars, menus, buttons, etc.) in fixed size borders indicated by a parameter that can nominate the North, South, East or West of the window, with the remainder of the space being the Center.[5]

- **Card.** Overlapping panels of information can be selected by clicking on tabs on the top of each panel.

- **Grid.** The frame is divided into a specified number of rows and columns which can be selected by number.

- **Box.** A layout for multiple components to be laid out either vertically or horizontally. The components will not wrap so, for example, a vertical arrangement of components will stay vertically arranged when the frame is resized. Box belongs to Swing but is fully compatible with the awt.

- **Grid bag.** Fine-grained layout where each component is given exact pixel constraints. Although complex to use, it is the most versatile and portable.

Since LayoutManager is an interface, it is possible to define your own layout manager, with customized (and sometimes very pleasing) results.

---

[5] Note the American spelling once again for Center.

Other component options

Labels and buttons are components, and we indicated that there were other similar classes. To round things off, we name them and indicate their main functions here.

- `TextComponent`, together with its two subclasses `TextArea` and `TextField`, handles multiple lined text, text selecting and editing.

- `Scrollbar` is useful with text and enables the contents of the container to move in the window.

- `ScrollPane` is a container that enables a component with a larger area to be moved underneath it with scroll bars so that a portion is visible at any one time.

- `Canvas` is an additional window area that can be used for drawing in, so as not to interfere with buttons.

- `Checkbox` provides for yes/no or on/off selection. An example would be selecting bold on a tool bar in a text processor.

- `Choice` provides dropdown lists from which choices can be made. One choice can be made.

- `List` is similar to choice except that the items are always on screen, and multiple selections can be made.

- `Menus` can be created on the menu bar of the window, with pull down items. One can be selected at a time. Some options can be made unselectable when necessary.

- `Popup menus` can be created anywhere in a window, and can have side submenus. Items can also be unselected.

- `Print` is a command that can cause all or some of a window to be printed, in hard-copy, to a printer – a most useful feature, as it saves having to go through a screen dump process outside of Java.

Some of these options are used in other examples in this and later chapters.

Panels for grouping

Java provides higher-level groupings of components, which can then be moved around together in a window and are protected from overwriting each other. The first is a panel, which is used to keep groups of like components such as buttons. The panel is then passed to the layout manager as an entity. For example, Submit and Clear buttons could be grouped as follows:

```
Panel p = new Panel ( );
  p.add (new Button ("Submit"));
  p.add (new Button ("Clear"));
add(p);
```

(Notice the use of indentation for the panel once again.) The panel can then be added to the frame in its constructor. In order to get the buttons always at the bottom of the screen, we can use `BorderLayout` and position the panel in the `South` area. `BorderLayout` is already the default manager for frames, while `FlowLayout` is the default for panels. Thus we can leave out calls to set them up, unless we wish to alter the gaps and so on. When adding to the `BorderLayout`, the first parameter selects one of five areas, as shown in Figure 10.10.

The borders are narrow, being deep enough for one component only. Thus a couple of buttons will fit, or a heading, or a scroll bar but no more. An equivalent to the constructor in Example 10.3 is:

```
ButtonTest() {
  // using BorderLayout as the default

  setBackground(Color.cyan);
  setForeground(Color.black);

  Panel m = new Panel ();
    for (int i = 0; i < message.length; i++)
      m.add(new Label(message[i]));
    add ("Center", m);
  Panel p = new Panel p ();
    // use Flow layout as the default
    waitButton = new Button("Wait");
      waitButton.addActionListener(this);
      p.add(waitButton);
    rebootButton = new Button("Reboot");
      rebootButton.addActionListener(this);
      p.add(rebootButton);
  add ("South", p);

  // other statements related to the frame
}
```

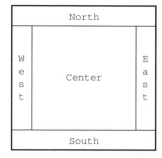

Figure 10.10 *Areas recognized by* `BorderLayout`.

EXAMPLE 10.5	Traffic lights

Problem   The Savanna Traffic Department would like to simulate traffic light times, and watch how pedestrian button requests affect the changing of the lights.

Solution   Design a screen along the lines of Figure 10.11. Then handle the interaction of the lights and buttons as required. Such interaction needs event-based programming, so we shall take it up in Section 11.1 and complete the example there. Meanwhile we shall work on setting up the window ready for action.

Class design   Put the traffic light in a canvas, with the circles, and so on, drawn using methods from `Graphics`. Put the buttons in one panel and the title in another. The model diagram for the program is shown in Figure 10.12. To keep the diagrams simple, we shall leave out the listener for the window closing event from now on. Notice that the diagram shows that the Walk button is not connected to anything yet.

Traffic extends `Frame`, as it must in order to display graphics. The buttons and title objects are both instances of the `Panel` class. `Lights` is a private object that is an instance of a small member class called `LightsCanvas`. `LightsCanvas` inherits from `Canvas` and has a single method, `paint`, which calls methods in `Graphics`.

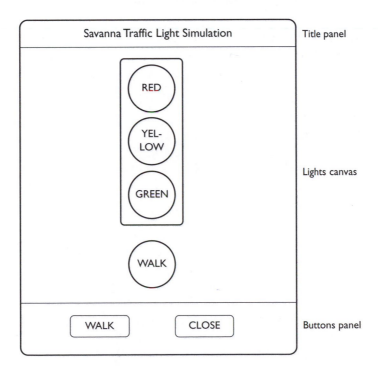

Figure 10.11   *Mock-up of the screen for the traffic light simulation.*

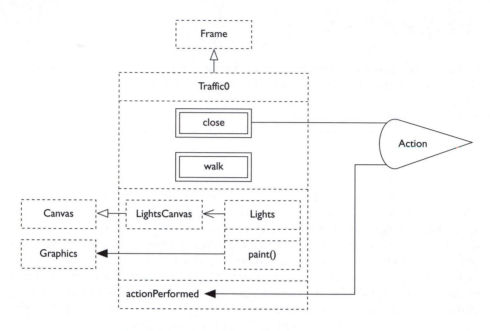

Figure 10.12 *Model diagram for the initial traffic light simulation.*

In this program, we link the Close button up to the appropriate listener, but we do not yet supply any action for Walk: that comes later.

Program

```
import java.awt.*;
import java.awt.event.*;

class Traffic0 extends Frame implements ActionListener {

    /* The first Traffic light program
     *                                 by J M Bishop Oct 1996
     *                       Java 1.1 by T Abbott October 1997
     *                              updated J M Bishop May 2000
     * Displays a representation of traffic lights,
     * in preparation for a simulation.
     *
     * NOTE: The walk button is not activated yet.
     * Illustrates panels and canvases and the
     * BorderLayout manager.
     */
```

```
    LightsCanvas lights;
    Button close;
    Button walk;

    Traffic0() {
      // Add the components
      Panel title = new Panel();
        title.add (new Label("Savanna Traffic Light Simulation"));
      add("North", title);
      lights = new LightsCanvas();
        add("Center", lights);
      Panel buttons = new Panel();
        walk = new Button("WALK");
          buttons.add(walk);
        close = new Button("CLOSE");
          close.addActionListener(this);
          buttons.add(close);
      add("South", buttons);

      // Set up the frame
      setTitle("Traffic Lights version 0");
      setSize(300,200);
      setVisible(true);
      addWindowListener(new WindowAdapter () {
        public void windowClosing(WindowEvent e) {
          System.exit(0);
        }
      });


    }

  public void actionPerformed(ActionEvent e) {
      // Must be the close button
      setVisible(false);
      dispose();
      System.exit(0);
    }

public static void main(String[] args) {
    new Traffic0 ();
}

class LightsCanvas extends Canvas {
  public void paint(Graphics g) {
```

```
        g.drawOval(97, 10, 30, 68);
        g.setColor(Color.red);
        g.fillOval(105, 15, 15, 15);   // red
        g.setColor(Color.yellow);
        g.fillOval(105, 35, 15, 15);   // yellow
        g.setColor(Color.green);
        g.fillOval(105, 55, 15, 15);   // green
        g.fillOval(105, 85, 15, 15);   // walk
        g.setColor(Color.black);
        g.drawString("RED", 15, 28);
        g.drawString("YELLOW", 15, 48);
        g.drawString("GREEN", 15, 68);
        g.drawString("WALK", 15, 98);
    }
  }
}
```

Testing   See Figure 10.13. In colour, the three lights show up well; in black and white the colours are not easily identifiable! To ensure at least an outline for each light, we should add drawOval with the same centre to the corresponding fillOval, using one pixel more in each direction, and drawn in black. For example:

```
g.setColor (Color.red);
g.fillOval (105, 15, 15, 15);
setColor (Color.black);
g.drawOval (105, 15, 16, 16);
```

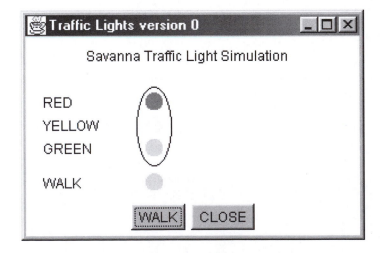

Figure 10.13 *The output of the initial traffic light simulation.*

SUMMARY

Graphics permits the drawing of shapes, lines and images; the selecting of fonts, colours and so on. **Components** are items such as buttons, text fields, menus and scroll bars. We can put them in **containers** and then choose one of a selection of **layout managers** to arrange them suitably on the screen. The subpackage `java.awt.event` handles external **events**, such as pushing buttons and closing a window, through a suite of event **handlers**, **listeners** and **adapters**. Finally, `java.awt.image` is another subpackage, which is used by awt to incorporate **images** in a variety of formats.

Functionally, we distinguish between graphical drawing and graphical user interfaces. Graphics is fun but time-consuming. The graphics methods of Java are available in the `Graphics` class and accessed by calls in redefined `paint` and `repaint` methods. All drawing takes place in a `Frame`, which is a subclass of the abstract class `Component`. In setting up a GUI, there is a wide range of choice of components such as `Button`, `ScrollBar`, `Textfield` and so on. The Swing set is an alternative to the awt and provides a platform-independent look and feel to a GUI.

This chapter has not introduced any new keywords, but has made extensive use of Java's awt API. The classes and methods actually discussed in the chapter were:

```
java.awt                      Frame
java.awt.event                  setTitle
javax.swing                     setSize
ActionListener                  setVisible
  actionPerformed             Graphics
BorderLayout                    drawOval
Button                          drawRect
  addActionListener             drawString
Canvas                          fillOval
Component                       fillRect
  paint                         Color
  repaint                       setColor
  setBackGround               Label
  setForeGround               LayoutManager
  setLocation                 Panel
Container                     System.exit
  add                         Window
  setLayout                     addWindowListener
FlowLayout                    WindowAdapter
FontMetrics                     windowClosing
                              WindowEvent
```

The forms defined in this chapter are:

Creating a frame
Redefining the `paint` method
`Graphics` class specification
Closing a window
Creating a `label`
Creating a `button`
Incorporating a layout manager
Reacting to buttons

QUIZ

10.1   For a GUI program to compile, we must

    (a)   inherit from `Window`
    (b)   inherit from `Frame`
    (c)   `setVisible(true)`
    (d)   call `repaint`

10.2   If we draw a circle using `drawOval(300,20,50,50)` in a frame **600 × 400** then it
    will be positioned

    (a)   towards the bottom of the frame and on the left
    (b)   towards the top of the frame and on the left
    (c)   towards the top of the frame and in the centre
    (d)   right in the centre

10.3   To change the font to sanserif bold we use

    (a)   `setFont (sanserif, bold);`
    (b)   `g.setFont(Font.sanSerif, Font.Bold, size);`
    (c)   `g.setFont(new Font (Font.SanSerif, Font.BOLD, size));`
    (d)   `g.setFont(new Font ("SanSerif", Font.BOLD, size));`

10.4   The default layout manager for a Java GUI application is

    (a)   `Flow`
    (b)   `Border`
    (c)   `Flow centred`
    (d)   no default

10.5   When running a GUI program, pressing a certain button had no effect. The reason is prob-
    ably that:

    (a)   the button was not instantiated
    (b)   the button was not connected to a listener
    (c)   there was no handler for the button's event
    (d)   the button's variable had been assigned to another button

10.6 `ActionListener` is

    (a) a method that is called by the program
    (b) an interface that the program must implement
    (c) a class that the program must inherit
    (d) a method that calls the program when an event happens

10.7 In these two statements in the alternative to Example 10.3 (see Section 10.3) are

```
    p.add (new Button ("Reboot"));
  add("South", p);
```

Which of these answers is true?

    (a) `p` could be before the `add` or as a parameter
    (b) the first `add` refers to a panel and the second to a frame
    (c) if we indented the second `add`, we would have to include `p.` for it.
    (d) `p` is using border layout

10.8 A statement to request border layout would be:

    (a) `setLayout (BorderLayout);`
    (b) `setLayout(new BorderLayout);`
    (c) `setLayout (new BorderLayout());`
    (d) `setLayout(new BorderLayout(), CENTER);`

10.9 In the FlagMaker2 program (Example 10.3) how many frames are in existence at the end of the program?

    (a) one
    (b) three
    (c) four
    (d) none

10.10 The most significant difference between the awt and Swing is that

    (a) Swing methods start with a J
    (b) Swing methods make use of the look and feel of a particular platform
    (c) Swing methods are more efficient
    (d) Swing methods are implemented independently of any particular platform

PROBLEMS

Note: The first three problems relate to the design and programming of GUIs. Handling the events is not essential here: to test the GUI, the handler could just report that a certain event has occurred. Such reporting can be done via `System.out.println` and will be visible on the Java console or MSDos command window.

10.1 **Digital watch.** Design the display and knobs of a digital watch. Make the watch work by changing the time at regular intervals in a loop.

10.2 **Remote control.** Implement a user interface for a remote control for a television set.

10.3   **Cellphone.** Design and program a screen version of a cellphone.

10.4   **Door lock.** Savanna Security makes digital locks for doors that consist of nine keys numbered 0 to 9, and two other keys labelled clear open. When a correct sequence of four numbers is pressed, followed by open, a green light shines. Otherwise a red light shines. Design and program a GUI representing such a lock and test it by having a set of five preset codes in the program, which the user can choose to get the green light.

10.5   **Security system.** The locks prototyped in Problem 10.4 are going to be sold, and need software associated with them. Write a small system to maintain a list of room numbers, people's names and associated codes. Enable new lock details to be entered as new locks are fitted, and codes of existing locks to be changed. Use password protection for changing codes.

10.6   **Advanced locks.** Savanna Security is going to introduce a new advanced lock with three extra keys labelled X, Y and Z. Inherit a new frame from the GUI in Problem 10.4 and include the extra information. Show how the system in Problem 10.5 will run with both kinds of lock with very little alteration.

10.7   **Two traffic lights.** Improve the lights system to display two identical traffic lights on the screen. Investigate having them as two different frames, and as two canvases in the same frame.

10.8   **Better Flag Maker.** The `FlagMaker2` program in Example 10.3 is going to be updated in Chapter 11, but meanwhile we can make some interesting improvements. Instead of having three fixed test objects in the constructor, design and implement a GUI which enables the four parameters (country name and three colours) to be entered interactively.

CHAPTER 11

Event-driven programming

Clearly, responding to events is an important part of GUI programming. Java's `awt.event` package provides the means for listenening for events, recording information about events as they occur, and linking up to user-defined event handlers. In this chapter we consider:

■ how are events classified and corresponding listeners and handlers set up?

■ how can sequences of events be managed?

In preparation, we start off by completing our look at components, paying special attention to text fields, an essential part of user interaction.

11.1 Interaction with text fields

To get text into a GUI program, Java provides a component `TextComponent` with two subclasses, `TextField` and `TextArea`. `TextArea` is for multi-line text and works in conjunction with scroll bars. We shall just consider the single-line text fields. To declare a component as a `TextField`, we use the form:

Creating a text field

```
TextField t;

t = new TextField("initial text",n);
 add(t);
```

The declaration creates an object variable for `t`.
  An object is then instantiated with an initial string of text and a given character width, which influences the length of the box around the text (see below).
add inserts the text field in the current container.

---

n is the number of characters one expects in the field, but will not fully define its width, since the width is also influenced by the font chosen and the layout manager used. However, the field will scroll if the user enters more than n characters, so there is no problem in guessing n incorrectly. Some of the methods available on a `TextField` are:

Text field methods

```
String    getText ();
void      setText ("value");
void      selectText (start, end);
void      selectAll ()
void      setEditable (booleanvalue);
boolean   isEditable ();
```

getText gets any text that has been inserted or typed into the text field and returns it as the value of the typed method.
setText replaces the entire text in the field with the given string.
selectText highlights part of a text field without changing anything; selectAll highlights all the text.
A text field can be available for changing or not, and this state can be set and checked by the next two methods.

`getText` and `setText` are the read and write equivalents for a `TextField`. Each field can also be open for input – that is, editable (the default) – or it can be locked. In the first state, it will be white, and the user must move the mouse there, click and start typing, ending with a return. If it is not editable, the field might be grey and data cannot be entered – this option depends on the computer being used. The need for these two states is illustrated in the next section. Finally, `selectText` allows a given part of the field to be highlighted, usually in blue.

Text fields usually have labels associated with them. To set up text fields to collect a person's name and age together in a `Panel` we would use:

```
Panel p = new Panel ();
  TextField name = new TextField("",40);
    p.add (new Label ("Name"));
    p.add (name);
  TextField age = new TextField("",5);
    p.add (new Label ("Age"));
    p.add (age);
```

which would give:

Name   [_____]

Age   [_____]

Notice that the flow layout manager would have taken care of setting the boxes out neatly in a frame of the right size. If the frame is bigger, the 'Age' label might land on the top row, whereupon some adjustment might be necessary to achieve the desired effect.

Inputting numbers

You may have noticed that there is only one `get` method for `TextField`, and it returns a `String`. Thus we are faced once again with translating the contents of the string to a number, if that is what we want. We discussed this process in Section 7.2, where the following key statement was used for integers:

Translating a string to an integer
`i = Integer.parseInt(s);`
Translates the string `s` into the integer `i`. Will raise a `Parse-Exception` if the string is not in the correct form.

Exactly the same technique can be used in GUI programming. However, a simple statement such as this assumes that nothing will go wrong in the conversion, such as a non-numeric character in the string. The `Stream` class took care of these problems, and one could envisage a similar class being written, called say `GUIText`, which would perform exactly the same function, but with input from a `TextField` instead of a `BufferedReader`. For now we shall live dangerously, and leave the development of `GUIText` as a worthwhile exercise for the reader.

Avoiding input

We mentioned at the end of Section 10.3 that there were several other components in the awt, some of which provide for selections from lists or choices. Essentially, these save the user from typing in a lot of data, and they also create a more secure environment because there is no opportunity for unexpected input. Take a simple example. If we want the user to give us a day of the week, we do not ask for text to be typed into a text field, with all its accompanying checking. Instead we provide a `Choice` list, which gives the seven choices, and the user simply selects one with the mouse. `CheckBox`, `List`, `Menu` and `Popup` have similar uses. An example of the use of a `Choice` is given in the next development of the traffic light program.

| EXAMPLE 11.1 | Traffic lights with buttons |

Problem Looking at the traffic light example, the simulation is intended to consider the effectiveness of different timings for the lights. For example, whether red should be on for longer than green, and so on.

Solution For an easy-to-use simulation, we must have the ability to change the time each light is on. In other words, we must read in new values. Doing so requires

- the selection of one of the four lights;
- the entering of the new duration.

The necessary components can be added to the buttons panel and appear at the bottom of the screen. They are a choice list for the four lights and a duration text field for entering a number of seconds.

Program We have not learnt enough yet to know how to make the lights flash: this will be covered in Chapter 13. However, we can still react to the choosing of the light and setting of the duration by outputting a suitable message alongside the light. An appropriate revised constructor for such a frame is:

```
Traffic1() {
  setTitle("Traffic Lights Version 1");
```

```
    Panel title = new Panel();
      title.add(new Label("Savanna Traffic Light Simulation"));
      add("North", title);

    lights = new LightsCanvas();
    add("Center", lights);

    Panel buttons = new Panel();
      colours = new Choice ();
      colours.addItem("Red");
      colours.addItem("Yellow");
      colours.addItem("Green");
      colours.addItem("Walk");
      buttons.add(colours);

      duration = new TextField("", 3);
        buttons.add(new Label("Duration"));
        duration.setEditable(true);
        buttons.add(duration);

      walkButton = new Button("Walk");
        buttons.add(walkButton);

      closeButton = new Button("Close");
        closeButton.addActionListener(this);
        buttons.add(closeButton);
      add("South", buttons);
  }

  private TextField duration;
  private Choice colours;
  private Button walkButton;
  private Button closeButton;
  }
```

Testing   The output of the constructor is shown in the next example in Figure 11.4.

Although this constructor sets up components for choosing colour and duration, it does not indicate how events relating to such choices will be handled. A link to a handler is set for the Close button, as usual, but we now need to consider how to widen event-handling for more kinds of components, and to look at more complicated event sequences.

11.2 Events, listeners and handlers

The classification of events is tied to the types of components that generate the events, but there is not one event type for each component type. Rather there are 11 **event** types and they are shared by the many **component** types. Each event type has a **listener** associated with it (though `MouseEvent` has two), and each listener requires that a corresponding **handler** must implement one or more of its methods.

For example, we have already seen that a button component is associated with an `ActionEvent` and an `ActionListener` and that the `actionPerformed` method must be implemented. Table 11.1 gives the full list of Java events, listeners and methods with the components they handle. All the listeners are interfaces, so those that are referred to in a program must be listed in the class header.

To understand Table 11.1, let us take an example from the previous program. In it, we defined a choice box, and we obviously will need to react to that. `Choice` is a component that is related to an `ItemEvent`, and needs an `ItemListener`. The method `itemStateChanged` must be implemented. What does such an implementation look like? Well, let us consider a handler we have seen already. When we implemented the `actionPerformed` method in Example 10.4, it looked like this:

```
public void actionPerformed(ActionEvent e) {
  if (e.getSource() == rebootButton) {
     setVisible(false);
     dispose();
     System.exit (0);
  } else if (e.getSource() == waitButton) {
     setForeground(Color.white);
     setBackground(Color.red);
  }
}
```

Thus `ActionEvent` uses the `getSource` method to return the object that caused the event. This object reference can be successively interrogated to establish which event occurred, and then the appropriate action can be taken. `getSource` is a method defined in a class called `EventObject` which is actually so high up in the hierarchy, it is in `java.util`, not `java.awt`! In every one of the event classes, there is a corresponding and more specific method that can be used instead of `getSource`. The problem is one of remembering all the names and return values, as they do not follow a pattern in the same way as the listeners and other methods do, as shown in Table 11.1. For example, for an `ActionEvent`, the alternative method to `getSource` is `getActionCommand` and it returns a string. Thus

Table 11.1 *Classification of events, listeners, methods and components*

Event	Listener	Methods	Components
ActionEvent	ActionListener	actionPerformed	Button List MenuItem TextField
AdjustmentEvent	AdjustmentListener	adjustmentValue- Changed	ScrollBar
ComponentEvent	ComponentListener	componentHidden componentMoved componentResized componentShown	Component
ContainerEvent	ContainerListener	componentAdded componentRemoved	Container
FocusEvent	FocusListener	focusGained focusLost	Component
ItemEvent	ItemListener	itemStateChanged	CheckBox Choice List
KeyEvent	KeyListener	keyPressed keyReleased keyTyped	Component
MouseEvent	MouseListener	mouseClicked mouseEntered mouseExited mousePressed mouseReleased	Component
	MouseMotionListener	mouseDragged mouseMoved	
TextEvent	TextListener	textValueChanged	TextComponent
WindowEvent	WindowListener	windowActivated windowClosed windowClosing	Window

```
if (e.getSource() == rebootButton) {
```

would become

```
if (e.getActionCommand() == "Reboot") {
```

However, for an `ItemEvent` (as generated by a `Choice`) the method is `getItem-Selectable` and it returns a value based on an interface called `ItemSelectable`. To keep things simple, we shall stick to `getSource` as a means of identifying events.

11.3   Case Study 5: The Flag Designer

Problem

We saw in Examples 2.2 and 10.3 that drawing simple flags is quite easy, and can be parameterized for different colours. We would now like to investigate parameterizing the flags to encompass other designs such as flags with vertical bars (e.g. France), and to provide a GUI interface to create a completely new flag design.

Solution

The solution divides into two parts:

- defining the types of flags that can be accommodated;

- providing a GUI interface to select the components for making such flags.

We start with three types of flags, striped, vertical bars and striped with a motif in the centre. Examples of the last two might be as in Figure 11.1. Then there are four colours to select (the fourth being for the motif when applicable), the motif itself and the name of the flag. For motifs, we will offer none, a circle, a star or a star of David. This leads us to a simple GUI as shown in Figure 11.2. Using this interface, we could design an elaborate flag such as the second one in Figure 11.1.

To set up the colours, we use a check box, then select the colour itself from a choice list, which is more efficient than having four choice lists for the colours. The colour choice list will refer to whichever of the items is currently selected in the check boxes.

The program develops in three parts:

- constructing the window;

- reacting to events;

- drawing the flag.

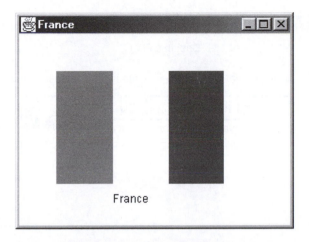

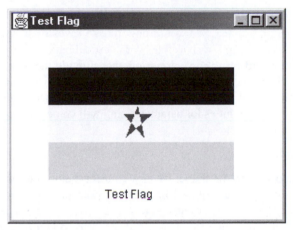

Figure 11.1 *Two types of flag.*

Constructing the GUI

This is a fairly simple GUI with a label and six other components in it. These are identi-fied by the GUI variables we need, namely:

```
CheckboxGroup         flagParts;
Checkbox []           colourCheck = new Checkbox[4];
Choice                colourChoice;
Choice                flagChoice;
Choice                motifChoice;
TextField             nameField;
Button                drawButton;
```

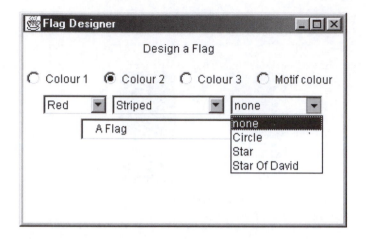

Figure 11.2 *GUI for the Flag Designer program.*

The `CheckboxGroup` and `Checkbox` array together provide the four check buttons at the top of the GUI. Then there are the three choice lists, the text field and the button. Adding all these items to the GUI is tedious, and makes for a fairly long constructor, but there is no other way. Opportunities for parameterizing will come later.

Reacting to events

As we add the components to the frame, we also connect them up to listeners. Referring to Table 11.1, we see that the required listener for both choices and check boxes is `ItemListener` and the other two events go to `ActionListener`. That means that we will need to implement two handlers – `ItemStateChanged` and `ActionPerfomed` – and distinguish within them which component caused the event.

The method to handle the choices and check boxes is fairly complex. There are four blocks following if-statements, and each one handles a different component. In each block, we get the choice that was made using, for example,

```
flagPicked = ((Choice) picked).getSelectedIndex();
```

`getSelectedIndex` is a method applicable to a `Choice` object. `picked` is returned from `getSource` and is of the superclass `Object`, which is why the type cast to `Choice` is needed. In the case of the colour choice, we record the result for the specific stripe or motif, with the default being stripe two. In other words, if we select a colour before we select what the colour is for, that's fine. Finally, the check boxes themselves are scanned to see which has been selected, and the corresponding integer is stored.

```java
public void itemStateChanged(ItemEvent e) {
  Object picked = e.getSource();

  // Distinguish between the four components
  // Colour choice
  if (picked == colourChoice) {
    int selectedColour = ((Choice) picked).getSelectedIndex();
    colour[checkBoxPicked] = listedColours[selectedColour];
  }

  // Flag choice
  else if (picked == flagChoice)
    flagPicked = ((Choice) picked).getSelectedIndex();

  // Motif choice
  else if (picked == motifChoice)
    motifPicked = ((Choice) picked).getSelectedIndex();
  else

  // Check boxes (by default)
  for (int i=0; i<4; i++) {
    if (picked == colourCheck[i]) {
      checkBoxPicked = i;
    }
  }
}
```

`actionPerformed` is somewhat different, as it needs to react to the Draw It button. Doing so involves creating new flag objects, just as was done in the previous versions of the program. What flag objects? Assuming that `actionPerformed` is otherwise struc- turally simple, we can go on to the topic of drawing flags immediately.

Drawing flags

We have a class for drawing a three-striped flag, and a `makeFlag` method for handling all the frame details is:

```java
public void makeFlag (FlagCanvas canvas) {
  Frame f = new Frame();
  f.add(canvas);
```

```
      f.setTitle(canvas.country);
      f.setSize(300,200);
      f.setLocation(200,200);
      f.setVisible(true);
      f.addWindowListener(new WindowAdapter() {
      public void windowClosing(WindowEvent e) {
      e.getWindow().dispose();
        }
      });
  }
```

Drawing a flag with the stripes vertical is perfectly easy. But in order to keep the makeFlag method simple, we would like both of this and third option (with a motif) to be acceptable to it. We can do this through inheritance. If we have

```
class FlagCanvas extends Canvas
class FlagCanvasVerti extends FlagCanvas
class FlagCanvasMotif extends FlagCanvas
```

then any objects of any of the three classes will be acceptable to makeFlag as a parameter.

The only interesting part of the actual drawing process is the stars required in the motifs. Drawing the stars uses preset arrays of points which can be passed to methods called fillPolygon or drawPolygon defined in the Graphics class.

Program

Finally, we give the full program.

```
import java.awt.*;
import java.awt.event.*;

public class FlagMakerGUI extends Frame
                     implements ActionListener, ItemListener {

  /** General Flag designer program     J M Bishop May 2000
   * ======================
   *
   *  Presents a simple GUI for selecting one of
   * three styles of flag, plus three motifs and
   * seven colours for each bar or stripe.
   *
   * Illustrates inherited classes and GUI components
```

```
 * particularly Choices, Checkboxes and Buttons.
 *
 **/


static final int none = 0, circle = 1, star = 2, starOfDavid = 3;
static final int stripes = 0, bars = 1, motif = 2;
static final Color listedColours [] = {Color.red, Color.blue,
                    Color.white, Color.black, Color.green,
                    Color.orange, Color.yellow};


// GUI variables
// *************


CheckboxGroup flagParts;
Checkbox []    colourCheck = new Checkbox[4];
Choice         colourChoice;
Choice         flagChoice;
Choice         motifChoice;
TextField      nameField;
Button         drawButton;


public FlagMakerGUI() {

// Laying out the GUI
// ******************

  setLayout(new BorderLayout());
  Panel intro = new Panel();
    intro.add(new Label("Design a Flag"));
    add("North",intro);
  Panel middle = new Panel();
    middle.setLayout(new FlowLayout());
    flagParts = new CheckboxGroup();
      for (int i=0; i<3; i++)
        colourCheck[i] = new Checkbox("Colour "+(i+1),i==1,flagParts);
      colourCheck[3] = new Checkbox("Motif colour",false,flagParts);
      for (int i=0; i<4; i++) {
        colourCheck[i].addItemListener(this);
        middle.add(colourCheck[i]);
      }
    colourChoice = new Choice ();
      colourChoice.addItem("Red");
      colourChoice.addItem("Blue");
```

```
            colourChoice.addItem("White");
            colourChoice.addItem("Black");
            colourChoice.addItem("Green");
            colourChoice.addItem("Orange");
            colourChoice.addItem("Yellow");
            colourChoice.addItemListener(this);
            middle.add(colourChoice);
         flagChoice = new Choice ();
            flagChoice.addItem("Striped");
            flagChoice.addItem("Bars");
            flagChoice.addItem("Striped with motif");
            flagChoice.addItemListener(this);
            middle.add(flagChoice);
         motifChoice = new Choice();
            motifChoice.addItem("none");
            motifChoice.addItem("Circle");
            motifChoice.addItem("Star");
            motifChoice.addItem("Star Of David");
            motifChoice.addItemListener(this);
            middle.add(motifChoice);
         nameField = new TextField("   A Flag ",20);
            nameField.addActionListener(this);
            middle.add(nameField);
         drawButton = new Button("Draw it");
            drawButton.addActionListener(this);
            middle.add(drawButton);
      add("Center",middle);
    setTitle("Flag Designer");
    setVisible(true);
    addWindowListener(new WindowAdapter() {
      public void windowClosing(WindowEvent e) {
        System.exit(0);
      }
    });
  }

// Variables for the event handlers
int      flagPicked = 0;
int      checkBoxPicked = 0; // colour 1
int      motifPicked = circle;
Color [ ] colour = {Color.red, Color.white, Color.blue, Color.black};
String   name = "A Flag";
```

```java
public void actionPerformed (ActionEvent e) {
  if (e.getSource() == drawButton) {
    switch (flagPicked) {
      case stripes : makeFlag (
           new FlagCanvas (name, colour[0], colour[1], colour[2]));
           break;
      case bars : makeFlag (
           new FlagCanvasVerti (name, colour[0], colour[1], colour[2]));
           break;
      case motif : makeFlag (
            new FlagCanvasMotif (name, colour[0], colour[1], colour[2],
            motifPicked, colour[3]));
    }}
  else if (e.getSource() == nameField)
    name = nameField.getText();
}

public void itemStateChanged(ItemEvent e) {
  Object picked = e.getSource();

  // Distinguish between the four components
  // Colour choice
  if (picked == colourChoice) {
    int selectedColour = ((Choice) picked).getSelectedIndex();
    colour[checkBoxPicked] = listedColours[selectedColour];
  }
  // Flag choice
  else if (picked == flagChoice)
    flagPicked = ((Choice) picked).getSelectedIndex();
  // Motif choice
  else if (picked == motifChoice)
    motifPicked = ((Choice) picked).getSelectedIndex();
  else
  // Check boxes (by default)
  for (int i=0; i<4; i++) {
    if (picked == colourCheck[i]) {
      checkBoxPicked = i;
    }
  }

}

public static void main(String [] args) {
  new FlagMakerGUI();
}
```

```java
   public static void makeFlag (FlagCanvas canvas) {
     Frame f = new Frame();
     f.add(canvas);
     f.setTitle(canvas.country);
     f.setSize(300,200);
     f.setLocation(200,200);
     f.setVisible(true);
     f.addWindowListener(new WindowAdapter() {
       public void windowClosing(WindowEvent e) {
         e.getWindow().dispose();
       }
     });
   }
 }


//============================
  class FlagCanvas extends Canvas {

    String country;
    Color bar1, bar2, bar3;

     FlagCanvas (String c, Color b1, Color b2, Color b3) {
       country = c;
       bar1 = b1;
       bar2 = b2;
       bar3 = b3;
      }

     public void paint (Graphics g) {
       // Draw the flag from coloured rectangles
       g.setColor (bar1);
       g.fillRect (40,40,200,40);
       g.setColor (bar2);
       g.fillRect (40,80,200,40);
       g.setColor (bar3);
       g.fillRect (40,120,200,40);
       // Label the drawing
       g.setColor (Color.black);
       g.drawString(country,100,180);
     }
   }

  class FlagCanvasVerti extends FlagCanvas {

    FlagCanvasVerti (String c, Color b1, Color b2, Color b3) {
      super (c,b1,b2,b3);
    }
```

```java
  public void paint (Graphics g) {
    // Draw the flag from coloured rectangles
    g.setColor (bar1);
    g.fillRect (40,40,60,120);
    g.setColor (bar2);
    g.fillRect (100,40,60,120);
    g.setColor (bar3);
    g.fillRect (160,40,60,120);
    // Label the drawing
    g.setColor (Color.black);
    g.drawString(country,100,180);
  }
}


class FlagCanvasMotif extends FlagCanvas {

  int motif;
  Color motifColor;

 FlagCanvasMotif (String c, Color b1, Color b2, Color b3, int m,
                  Color mc) {
  super (c,b1,b2,b3);
  motif = m;
  motifColor = mc;
}

public void paint (Graphics g) {

  int [] xpoints = {120,150,122,135,142,120};
  int [] ypoints = {90,90,115,80,115,90};
  // Draw the flag from coloured rectangles
  g.setColor (bar1);
  g.fillRect (40,40,200,40);
  g.setColor (bar2);
  g.fillRect (40,80,200,40);
  g.setColor (bar3);
  g.fillRect (40,120,200,40);
  // Label the drawing
  g.setColor (Color.black);
  g.drawString(country,100,180);
  if (motif != 0) {
    g.setColor (motifColor);
    switch (motif) {
    case 1: g.fillOval(125,90,20,20); break;
    case 2: g.fillPolygon(xpoints,ypoints,6); break;
    case 3: g.drawPolygon(xpoints,ypoints,6); break;
```

```
            default: break;
          }
       }
    }
}
```

Testing

Testing a GUI program is quite tedious because the user should go through every combination of possibilities. Certainly the interaction of each component with another should be tested. This cannot be shown here, and the reader is encouraged to do it. Sample output has already been shown in Figure 11.2.

11.4 Managing sequences of events

In terms of the awt's interaction with the user, events are single happenings, but together they can form a chain of events. In other words, a certain event need not always elicit the same response. There may be two or three responses, depending on the events that have gone before.

How do we record what has gone before? In most cases, we use suitably named boolean variables which indicate whether or not a previous event happened. For example, in the panel in Example 10.4 which enabled the selection of a light, and then the entering of a new duration, we could force these two to happen in this order. We may also like to disable both of these components until a Change button has been pressed.

The point is that whatever logic we choose, we must be clear about it and it must contain no dead ends. It is not customary to provide a guide to the user about what to do, since just clicking the buttons will soon make the sequence clear.

EXAMPLE 11.2	Traffic light calibration

Problem We continue with Example 10.4, getting the user interface ready for changing the length of time that a light will shine.

Solution The display has been set up in the revised constructor we developed in the previous example. We need to connect the various components up to listeners and establish appropriate event handlers for their activation. The three components are the colours choice box, the duration text field and the Walk button. At present we cannot do anything about the Walk button, so we leave it unactivated.

To simulate changing the duration of the lights in response to a value typed in, we just write the value next to the light. This means that every time a duration is entered, the central graphic must be redrawn with the new values. The `actionPerformed` event therefore is responsible for calling `repaint`.

Algorithm   A suitable algorithm for the event-handling of the new program is given in Figure 11.3.

Light is initially set to 0 meaning red

| choice | → | Get in the item selected
Set light according to the selection |

| duration | → | Get in the value
Alter the message [light] string to value
Repaint the light canvas |

| close | → | Exit the program |

Figure 11.3   *Event handlers for version 1 of the Traffic Light Calibration program.*

The enhanced model diagram for the new program is given in Figure 11.4.

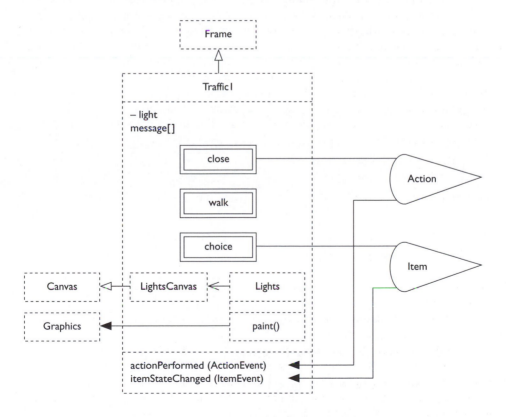

Figure 11.4   *Model diagram for the Traffic Light Calibration program.*

Program

```java
import java.awt.*;
import java.awt.event.*;
public class Traffic1 extends Frame
                    implements ActionListener, ItemListener {

    /* The second Traffic Light program
     *                          by J M Bishop Oct 1996
     *            Java 1.1 version by T Abbott Oct 1997
     *        enhanced and revised by J M Bishop Oct 1997
     *                    updated J M Bishop August 2000
     *
     * Adds options to set the duration for a light to
     * be on, but choice is merely recorded, not
     * acted upon at this stage.
     */

  private LightsCanvas lights;
  private TextField duration;
  private Choice colours;
  private Button walkButton;
  private Button closeButton;

  public Traffic1() {
    setTitle("Traffic Lights Version 1");

    add("North",new Label("Savanna Traffic Light Simulation"));
    lights = new LightsCanvas();
    add("Center", lights);

    Panel buttons = new Panel();
      colours = new Choice ();
        colours.addItem("Red");
        colours.addItem("Yellow");
        colours.addItem("Green");
        colours.addItem("Walk");
        buttons.add(colours);
        colours.addItemListener(this);

      buttons.add(new Label("Duration"));

        duration = new TextField("", 3);
        duration.setEditable(true);
```

```
      duration.addActionListener(this);
      buttons.add(duration);

    walkButton = new Button("Walk");
      // no action yet
      buttons.add(walkButton);

    closeButton = new Button("Close");
      closeButton.addActionListener(this);
      buttons.add(closeButton);
  add("South", buttons);

  // set up the frame
  setSize(350, 210);
  setVisible(true);
  addWindowListener(new WindowAdapter () {
    public void windowClosing(WindowEvent e) {
      System.exit(0);
    }
  });
}

public void actionPerformed(ActionEvent e) {
  if (e.getSource() == closeButton) {
  setVisible(false);
  dispose();
   System.exit (0);
 } else if (e.getSource() == duration) {
   message[light] = duration.getText();
   lights.repaint();
 }
}

public void itemStateChanged(ItemEvent e) {
  if (e.getItemSelectable()==colours) {
   String s = (String) e.getItem();
   if (s=="Red") {light = 0;} else
   if (s=="Yellow") {light = 1;} else
   if (s=="Green") {light = 2;} else
   if (s=="Walk") {light = 3;}
  }
}
```

```
public static void main(String[] args) {
  new Traffic1();
}

private int light = 0;
String [ ] message = {"default","default","default","default"};

class LightsCanvas extends Canvas {
  public void paint(Graphics g) {
  g.drawOval(87, 10, 30, 68);
  g.setColor(Color.red);
  g.fillOval(95, 15, 15, 15);
  g.setColor(Color.yellow);
  g.fillOval(95, 35, 15, 15);
  g.setColor(Color.green);
  g.fillOval(95, 55, 15, 15);
    // walk light is also green
  g.fillOval(95, 85, 15, 15);
  g.setColor(Color.black);
  g.drawString("RED", 15 ,28);
  g.drawString("YELLOW", 15, 48);
  g.drawString("GREEN", 15, 68);
  g.drawString("WALK", 15, 98);
  g.drawString(message[0], 135 ,28);
  g.drawString(message[1], 135, 48);
  g.drawString(message[2], 135, 68);
  g.setColor(Color.black);
  g.drawString(message[3], 135, 98);
  }
  }

}
```

Testing The expected output is shown in Figure 11.5, with two of the durations changed and the others still on default.

The formulation of the traffic light simulation has been deliberately vague on the question of how the lights actually count down and change. In order to make this kind of animation work, we shall need Java's multithreading facilities. Threads are covered in Chapter 13, when the example is picked up again.

Let us consider another example, that of currency converter (Example 6.8). In it, we used the display as the input–output mechanism, but it was rather limited. We can now employ a customized GUI to make the program more professional.

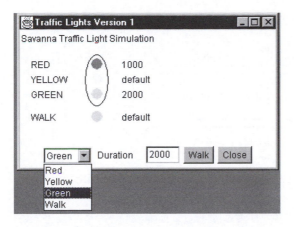

Figure 11.5 *Output from the Traffic Light Calibration program.*

EXAMPLE 11.3   Currency converter with a GUI

Problem   We think that the program for currency conversion developed in Example 6.8 has probably outgrown the `Display` class. We would like to create a better GUI design, and also expand the program so that it can convert from any one currency to another.

Screen design   With all GUI programs, we start by looking a screen design. To speed things up, Figure 11.7 shows the result of our vision: this is the design we would like to achieve. It retains the output text area in the centre of the screen, and then puts two choice boxes on either side. Above and below the text area is the amount text field and a Convert button that activates a conversion and the output.

Given this goal, we need to break the interface down into panels, and decide on the layout for each panel as in Figure 11.6. The overall layout is border layout, so we can put the three main panels in west, centre and east. South and north of the main panel are unused, but could contain a heading or instructions.

The west and east panels are also based on border layout, and have the label in the north and the choice box in the centre. The centre panel is similar, but the north is itself a panel with a label and the text field for amount.

Program design   In moving from the display class, the structure of the program takes a different form. With the display, we are still bound to input, then ready, then output. Once we are in complete control of our own GUI, we have to be prepared to react to events at any time. Moreover, having two countries selected does not mean that a transaction will take place. We need to be able to manage events so that something has been selected from each of the lists before a transaction is allowed.

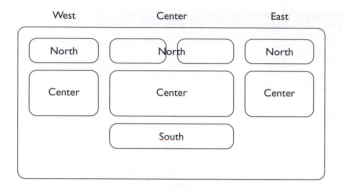

Figure 11.6 *Screen layout for the converter GUI.*

The basic logic is that there are two boolean variables, one for each of the choice lists. They are both initially false. When a country from the choice list is selected, the boolean is set true, as in:

```
public void itemStateChanged(ItemEvent e) {
  String s = (String) e.getItem();
  if (e.getItemSelectable() == fromChoice) {
    fromSelected = true;
    fromCountry = s;
  }
  else {
    toSelected = true;
    toCountry = s;
  }
}
```

The booleans are checked when a conversion is attempted (the Convert button is pressed) and are reset back to false after a successful conversion.

The main program basically initializes the GUI, reads in the rates file, and that's it. There is no endless loop calling the transactions method. Instead, the transactions method is called by `actionPerformed` when the Convert button is pressed.

```
import java.awt.*;
import java.awt.event.*;
import java.util.*;
import java.io.*;
import javagently.*;
```

```
class ConverterGUI extends Frame {

  /* The Converter Program     by J M Bishop Dec 1998
   * --------------------      Display version July 1999
   *                           GUI version July 1999
   *                           updated August 2000
   * Keeps the exchange rates from one currency into
   * many others and enables currency exchanges to be
   * estimated.
   *
   * Illustrates the use of a customized GUI
   * and managed sequences of events
   */

  ConverterGUI () throws IOException {
     DataHandler data = new DataHandler ();
     data.initialize();
     data.readIn();
  }

class DataHandler extends Frame
            implements ActionListener, ItemListener {
  Hashtable table = new Hashtable();

  // read in each line of data and store in
  // the hash table with country as key

  Choice fromChoice, toChoice;
  boolean fromSelected, toSelected;
  TextField amountField;
  TextArea resultField;
  String toCountry, fromCountry;
  Button goButton;

  void initialize () {
    Panel p = new Panel (new BorderLayout());

      // left hand side panel
      Panel q = new Panel();
        q.add ("North",new Label ("From"));
        fromChoice = new Choice();
          fromChoice.addItemListener (this);
         q.add("Center",fromChoice);
        p.add ("West", q);
      // right hand side panel
```

```
        q = new Panel();
         q.add ("North",new Label ("To"));
         toChoice = new Choice();
          toChoice.addItemListener (this);
          q.add("Center",toChoice);
         p.add ("East",q);
       // Centre panel
       q = new Panel(new BorderLayout());
         Panel r = new Panel();
          r.add(new Label("Amount"));
          amountField = new TextField("1000 ");
           amountField.addActionListener(this);
           r.add(amountField);
           q.add("North",r);
          resultField = new TextArea(8,20);
           q.add ("Center",resultField);
           resultField.append("First select the countries\n");
          goButton = new Button ("Convert");
           goButton.addActionListener(this);
           q.add("South",goButton);
        p.add("Center",q);
    add(p);
    setTitle("Currency Converter");
    setSize(610,300);
    addWindowListener(new WindowAdapter() {
      public void windowClosing(WindowEvent e) {
         System.exit(0);
      }
   });
 }

 public void actionPerformed (ActionEvent e) {
   int amount = 1000;
   if (e.getSource() == amountField)
     amount = (int) Integer.parseInt(amountField.getText());
   else
   if (e.getSource() == goButton) {
     if (fromSelected && toSelected)
       transaction(amount);
     else
       resultField.append("First select the countries\n");
   }
 }

 public void itemStateChanged(ItemEvent e) {
   String s = (String) e.getItem();
```

```
    if (e.getItemSelectable() == fromChoice) {
      fromSelected = true;
      fromCountry = s;
    }
    else {
      toSelected = true;
      toCountry = s;
    }
  }

  void transaction (int amount) {
    Rates fromRate = (Rates) table.get(fromCountry);
    Rates toRate = (Rates) table.get(toCountry);
    resultField.append(amount+" "+fromRate.country+" "+
        fromRate.currency+
        "\n in "+toRate.country+" "+toRate.currency+"\n was "+
        Stream.format(amount/fromRate.conversion*
                   toRate.conversion,10,3)+"\n\n");
    fromSelected = false;
    toSelected = false;
  }

  void readIn() throws IOException {
   Stream fin = new Stream("Rates.dat", Stream.READ);
   Rates rate;
   try {
     for (int i = 0; ; i++) {
       rate = new Rates();
       rate.setRate(fin);
       table.put(rate.country, rate);
       toChoice.addItem(rate.country);
       fromChoice.addItem(rate.country);
     }
   }
   catch (EOFException e) {}
   fromSelected = false;
   toSelected = false;
   setVisible(true);
   }
  }

  public static void main(String[] args) throws IOException {
    new ConverterGUI();
  }

}
```

Testing   The GUI for the converter after a few runs is shown in Figure 11.7. Notice that we made the program identify an incorrect attempt at conversion.

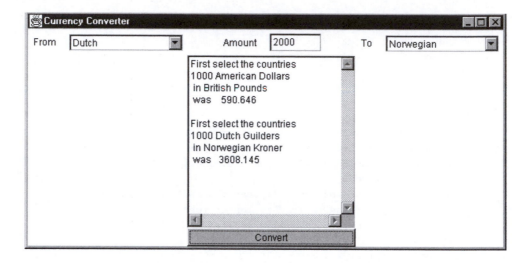

Figure 11.7   *Graphical user interface for the Converter program.*

Case Study 6 also puts into practice the ideas regarding event-handling that we have developed in this section.

11.5   Case Study 6: Supermarket Till

The solution to the following problem exploits different components of a GUI interface as well as event-handling and sequences of events.

Problem

Savanna Grocers wishes to computerize the weighing of fruit and vegetables at its tills. It envisages a display with buttons for the different produce and a space to enter the mass. At present the scales are not directly linked to the till, and there is not a special unit to print a price sticker, but the price of each item should be entered on the usual till slip.

Solution

The sequence of events required is shown in Figure 11.8. Thus if the strawberries weigh 3 kg, we enter 3 in the mass field. The cost per unit is given in graz, let us say G12 per

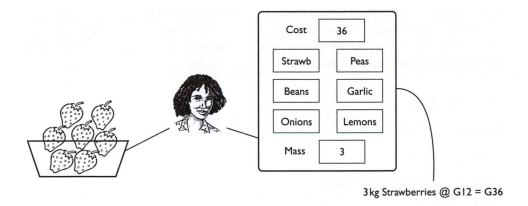

Figure 11.8 *A model for the grocery till.*

kilogram. The mass times unit cost, which is G36, will appear in the cost field, and a line is printed for the complete transaction.

The solution devolves nicely into two parts: the design of the screen and the organization of the event-handling.

The design of the screen

Apart from the mass and cost text fields with their accompanying labels, there must be a button for each type of produce. These can be laid out in rows and columns like calculator buttons. In this case, the best layout manager is not flow, but grid. With `GridLayout` we specify the expected number of rows and columns, and Java will line the components up in these boxes as they are added. The result is more symmetric and fixed than with `FlowLayout`.

All in all, we have three panels on the screen, which fit into a `BorderLayout` as follows:

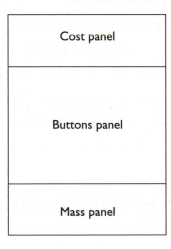

The buttons panel contains a button for each item of produce, plus three others for controlling the till, WEIGH, PRINT and CLOSE. CLOSE is not really needed since the system stops when we close the window, but it could be used to cause the printing of a running total or something like that.

Event-handling

We start by listing the possible events:

WEIGH pressed

produce button pressed (e.g. peas)

mass entered

PRINT pressed

CLOSE pressed

window close

Not all of these are always valid. We want to force an ordering of events for weighing produce so that everything is entered before PRINT is pressed, that is:

these three in any order	press WEIGH
	press a produce button
	click on mass field, enter mass, press RETURN
then	press PRINT

Now we tabulate the events and indicate their effect:

WEIGH	opens up mass field
a produce button	sets unit cost and sets chosen
text in weigh field	sets mass and sets weighed
PRINT	prints the cost and resets everything

However, these effects cannot be achieved if the sequence of events is not correct. So we need to build that in too, with the help of a couple of boolean variables (Figure 11.9).

Data entry

There remains the question as to how to get the basic data into the program: that is, the produce names and their unit costs. Since the items could vary from day to day, and their

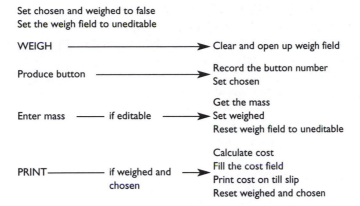

Set chosen and weighed to false
Set the weigh field to uneditable

WEIGH ─────────────────────► Clear and open up weigh field

Produce button ─────────────► Record the button number
Set chosen

Enter mass ──── if editable ──► Get the mass
Set weighed
Reset weigh field to uneditable

PRINT──────── if weighed and ──► Calculate cost
chosen Fill the cost field
Print cost on till slip
Reset weighed and chosen

Figure 11.9 *Handling events in the grocery till.*

prices certainly will, it would make sense to have this information stored in a file. For ease of getting the program up, though, we shall embed a few items in the program for now, and leave the extension to a file as an exercise.

Program

The program is as follows. Notice that in the constructor, we declare one panel, `p`, but instantiate it three times for each of the three different panels we need.

```
import java.awt.*;
import java.awt.event.*;

public class Till extends Frame implements ActionListener {

  /* The Grocery Till program  by J M Bishop Oct 1996
   * ------------------------          Java 1.1 T Abbott and J M Bishop Oct 1997
   *                                   updated August 2000
   *
   *
   * Simulates the operation of a grocery till for
   * up to 12 products, together with the costs per
   * kilogram.
   *
   * Illustrates Panels, different layout managers,
   * (including grid), user event handlers and the
   * handling of events that should occur in a
   * specified order.
   */
```

```java
private TextField weighField, totalField;
private Button[] itemButtons;
private Button weighButton, printButton, closeButton;

public Till() {
  setLayout(new BorderLayout());

  Panel p = new Panel();
    p.setLayout(new FlowLayout());
    totalField = new TextField(6);
    totalField.setEditable(false);
    p.add(new Label("COST"));
    p.add(totalField);
  add("North", p);

  p = new Panel();
    p.setLayout(new GridLayout(5, 3));
    itemButtons = new Button[items.length];
    for (int i = 0; i < items.length; i++) {
      itemButtons[i] = new Button(items[i]);
      itemButtons[i].addActionListener(this);
      p.add(itemButtons[i]);
    }
    weighButton = new Button("WEIGH");
      weighButton.addActionListener(this);
      p.add(weighButton);
    printButton = new Button("PRINT");
      printButton.addActionListener(this);
      p.add(printButton);
    closeButton = new Button("CLOSE");
      closeButton.addActionListener(this);
      p.add(closeButton);
  add("Center", p);

  p = new Panel();
    p.setLayout(new FlowLayout());
    weighField = new TextField(4);
      weighField.setEditable(false);
      weighField.addActionListener(this);
      p.add(weighField);
    p.add(new Label("MASS"));
```

```
      p.add(new Label("Type return after the amount"));
   add("South", p);

   // set up the frame
   addWindowListener(new WindowAdapter() {
     public void windowClosing(WindowEvent e) {
       System.exit(0);
     }
   });
   setTitle("Savanna Grocers");
   setVisible(true);
   pack();
}

public void actionPerformed(ActionEvent e) {
   Object source = e.getSource();
   if (source == closeButton) {
     System.exit(0);
   } else
   if (source == printButton) {
     printItems();
   } else
   if (source == weighButton) {
     resetWeighField();
   } else
   if (source == weighField) {
     readWeighField();
   } else
     selectItem(e.getActionCommand());
   }

  /* Here follows the main control of the program.
   * The event and action handlers above call these
   * methods, which ensure that there is only a reaction
   * if certain conditions (e.g. other previous events)
   * have already been met.
   */

   public void resetWeighField() {
     weighField.setText("");
     weighField.setEditable(true);
   }
```

```
public void readWeighField() {
    if (weighField.isEditable()) {
      weighField.setEditable(false);
      weighField.selectAll();
      kg = (double)Integer.valueOf(
      weighField.getText().trim()).intValue();
        weighed = true;
    }
  }

  public void printItems() {
    if (weighed && chosen) {
      total = kg*unitCosts[select];
      totalField.setText("G "+total);
      System.out.println(kg+"kg "+items[select]+" @ G"+
              unitCosts[select]+" = G"+total);
      kg = 0;
      weighed = false;
      chosen = false;
      total = 0;
      weighField.select(0,0);
      }
    }

  public void selectItem(String item) {
    select = 0;
    while (!item.equals(items[select]))
      select++;
    chosen = true;
  }

  public static void main(String[] args) {
    new Till();
  }

  private String[] items = { "Apples", "Pears", "Oranges",
                    "Potatoes", "Lemons", "Squash",
                    "Onions", "Garlic", "Avocados",
                    "", "", "" };
  private double[] unitCosts = { 6.00, 5.00, 7.00,
                        3.00, 10.00, 4.00,
                        4.00, 12.00, 15.00,
                        0, 0, 0 };
```

```
        private double total;
        private double kg;
        private boolean chosen = false;
        private boolean weighed = false;
        private int select = 1;
    }
```

Examining the `actionPerformed` method, we see that there are five if-statements.
These correspond to the five events, excluding closing a window which is handled separately in the `constructor` as usual. Three of the events are unconditional: CLOSE,
WEIGH and pressing a produce button. They always cause the action as given. The
other two rely on previous events, so that the `weighField` can get input only if it is
editable, and the PRINT button causes a reaction only if `weighed` and `chosen` have
already been set.

Notice the use of a new method right at the end of the constructor, `pack`.Unlike
`setSize`, which needs to be given concrete pixel width and height for the frame, `pack`
waits till the components are positioned, and then adjusts the frame size accordingly.

Testing

The screen looks like Figure 11.10 after onions have been selected. Many more tests are
needed, which can be done online. On the Java console would be printed the following:

```
    12.0kg Onions @ G4.0 = G48.0
```

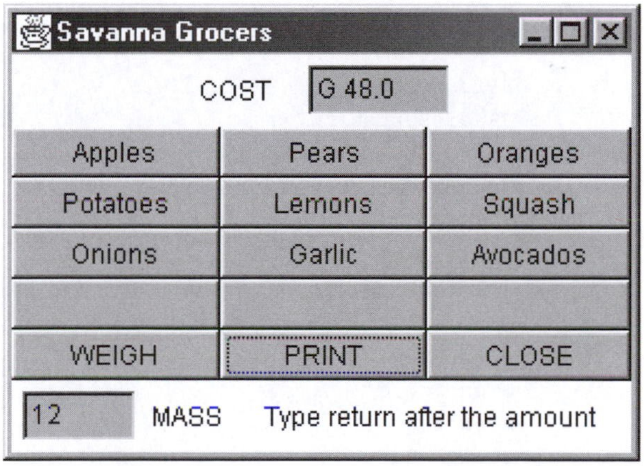

Figure 11.10   *The Till program screen.*

11.6   Case Study 7: The Converter with Swing

Now that we have seen most of what the awt has to offer, we can look at Swing. As discussed in Section 10.1, Swing provides an alternative to the awt which is platform independent. There are whole books devoted to Swing programming, but at the level of an introductory course, the concepts do not add much to the principles we need to know. The aspects that are important in Swing are:

- a slightly different and also larger set of available components from that in the awt, most of them identified with a J prefix;

- the ability to change the look and feel of an entire GUI through one statement;

- extensive facilities for the handling of text on the screen, especially hypertext markup language (HTML) text;

- separating the presentation of a data structure from its representation.

The last point means that in Swing there are facilities to have a GUI that presents data successively, such as an address book, but where the precise way in which the structure is represented is not known by the GUI. The data could be in an array, a list, a hash table or even a database. Adapted from the model–view–controller concept of earlier object-oriented languages, this fascinating advance in programming is beyond the scope of this book, and we shall concentrate on the first two points. To illustrate how Swing is used, we shall rewrite the currency converter program (Example 11.3) using Swing.

Swing components

A selection of the main Swing components is:

```
JButton              JProgressBar
JCheckBox            JRadioButton
JColorChooser        JScrollBar
JComboBox            JScrollPane
JComponent           JSlider
JDesktopPane         JSplitPane
JDialog              JTabbedPane
JEditorPane          JTable
JFileChooser         JTextArea
JFrame               JTextField
JLabel               JTextPane
JLayeredPane         JToggleButton
JList                JToolBar
JMenu                JToolTip
JOptionPane          JTree
JPanel               JViewport
JPopupMenu           JWindow
```

Many of these, like `JButton` and `JLabel`, have matching classes in the awt. Others, such as `JSlider` and `JColorChooser`, are new. In the conversion of the `Converter GUI` program, we shall make use of one new component, `JComboBox`.

`JComboBox` essentially replaces the `Choice` component of the awt, and represents a more general approach towards showing objects in lists in a GUI. In a combo box, the entire object is stored as an item, but only the values picked up by the class's `toString` method are displayed in the list. Thus in the converter program, we want to display the countries in the two choice lists. Instead of adding the country names as items, and then keeping a separate (though corresponding) data structure of the full details of the rate conversions for each country, we store the whole `Rates` objects in the combo box. We define the `toString` method so that the name of the country is displayed, and then when required, the rest of the information can be retrieved.

Updating the `Rates` class

Given the requirement for a `toString` method, we obviously need to update the `Rates` class. There are actually two choices: just create another class of the same name with a `toString` method in it, or make a new class that inherits from `Rates` and that has a `toString` method added. In theory, the latter is the more correct solution. However, we would need to employ a new name for the extended class. Following on from the veterinary tags example (Case Study 4), we could have `XRates`, or even `SRates` or `JRates`. Then every occurrence of `Rates` would have to be replaced with the new name in the program.

Just for the definition of a standard method such as `toString`, such upheaval does not seem necessary. If the new version of `Rates` were used in one of the older converter programs, it would cause no problem at all. For this reason, we decide to stick to `Rates`, and the new version is:

```
import java.io.*;
import javagently.*;

class Rates {
  /* The Rates class    by J M Bishop Dec 1998
   * ---------------    updated by B Worrall Aug 2000
   * Stores a country name, currency, code and rate
   */

  String country;
  String code;
  String currency;
  double conversion;

  void setRate (Stream in) throws IOException {
    code = in.readString();
```

```
    country = in.readString();
    currency = in.readString();
    // we don't want the first rate,
    // ignore it by reading over it
    conversion = in.readDouble();
    conversion = in.readDouble();
  }


  public String toString () {
    return country;
  }


}
```

The `toString` method returns only the country name, which is the value that is going to be used in the combo box list.

The data structure

In the earlier versions of the converter, the country (as key) and the rates objects (as values) were stored in a hash table. Because the whole object is now stored in the combo box, and selection is made directly by clicking on the relevant country, the need for a separate data structure falls away. The combo box *is* the data structure.

Apart from this, the reading in and transaction processing sections of the program remain almost identical. The declaration of the two choice lists is:

```
JComboBox fromChoice, toChoice;
```

The loop to put the objects in the lists is:

```
  for (int i = 0; ; i++) {
    rate = new Rates();
    rate.setRate(fin);
    toChoice.addItem(rate);
    fromChoice.addItem(rate);
  }
```

and the statements to get the rate out are:

```
void transaction () {
  // The to and from rates are loaded directly from the
  // JComboBox and used to create the output
  Rates fromRate = (Rates) fromChoice.getSelectedItem();
  Rates toRate = (Rates) toChoice.getSelectedItem();
  resultField.append(amount+" "+fromRate.country+" "+
```

```
      fromRate.currency+
      "\n in "+toRate.country+" "+
      toRate.currency+"\n was "+
      Stream.format(amount/fromRate.conversion*
      toRate.conversion,10,3)+"\n\n");
   }
```

Look and feel

Since Java programs are portable and can run on any computer, Swing has a means whereby the way in which a GUI looks and feels can either depend on the running computer, or be completely independent of it. In the first case, the GUI will be familiar to users of that computer, but will look different on another computer. In the second case, the GUI will be the same, no matter what, but may look strange to some. The two options are obtained by calling:

```
UIManager.setLookAndFeel
        (UIManager.getSystemLookAndFeelClassName());


UIManager.setLookAndFeel
        (UIManager.getCrossPlatformLookAndFeelClassName());
```

In addition to these options, specific look and feels can be chosen, identified by the classes that embody them, viz:

```
"javax.swing.plaf.metal.MetalLookAndFeel"
"javax.swing.plaf.mac.MacLookAndFeel"
"com.sun.java.swing.plaf.windows.WindowsLookAndFeel"
"com.sun.java.swing.plaf.motif.MotifLookAndFeel"
```

Because of copyright reasons, the Macintosh look and feel will run only on a Macintosh, so one's program should be written so as to include a default. Examples of these GUIs are shown when we test the program below.

Icons

Images are discussed in Section 12.3. In Swing they are more integrated than in the awt. Given a file name, the image object is created, the file is fetched and the image (if it is one) is displayed. JLabel has an option for an image alongside the label, so we have used this in the program below to create a header for the converter's GUI. The statements are:

```
JLabel label = new JLabel ("Savannah Travel",
                new ImageIcon("Elephant.gif"),CENTER);
   p.add("North", label);
```

The program

We can give the whole program. It is not long. In fact, because of the combo box, it is shorter than the previous version. It includes a command line parameter option for selecting a look and feel with the following values:

1. Cross Platform (defaults to Java's own – same as 3)

2. System (selects the one of the system, i.e. 4, 5 or 6)

3. Metal (Java's own)

4. Windows (from Microsoft)

5. Motif (from Sun and Unix)

6. Macintosh (from Apple)

The logic of the program is not quite the same as Example 11.6 in that the managing of the events is omitted. It is more difficult to detect changes with combo boxes.

```
import java.awt.*;
import javax.swing.*;
import java.awt.event.*;
import java.util.*;
import java.io.*;
import javagently.*;

class ConverterSwing extends JFrame {

  /* The Converter Program      by J M Bishop Dec 1998
   * ---------------------      Display version July 1999
   *                            GUI version July 1999
   *                            Swing version B Worrall
   *                            and J Bishop Aug 2000
   * Keeps the exchange rates from one currency into
   * many others and enables currency exchanges to be
   * estimated.
   *
   * Illustrates the use of a customized Swing GUI.
   */

  public static void main(String[] args) throws IOException {
    int look = 0;
    if (args.length > 0)
      look = Integer.parseInt(args[0]);
    new ConverterSwing(look);
  }
```

```
ConverterSwing (int look) throws IOException{
  try {
    switch (look) {
      case 1: UIManager.setLookAndFeel
        (UIManager.getCrossPlatformLookAndFeelClassName()); break;
      case 2: UIManager.setLookAndFeel
        (UIManager.getSystemLookAndFeelClassName()); break;
      case 3: UIManager.setLookAndFeel
        ("javax.swing.plaf.metal.MetalLookAndFeel"); break;
      case 4: UIManager.setLookAndFeel
        ("com.sun.java.swing.plaf.windows.WindowsLookAndFeel");
        break;
      case 5: UIManager.setLookAndFeel
        ("com.sun.java.swing.plaf.motif.MotifLookAndFeel"); break;
      case 6: UIManager.setLookAndFeel
        ("javax.swing.plaf.mac.MacLookAndFeel"); break;
    }
  }
  catch (Exception c) {
    System.out.println("Could not use the specified look and feel"
      + "- defaulting to cross-platform");
  }

    DataHandler data = new DataHandler ();
    data.initialize();
    data.readIn();
  // now control transfers to the user and events are handled
  // via actionPerformed and the transaction() method
}

class DataHandler extends JFrame
                implements ActionListener, SwingConstants {

  JComboBox fromChoice, toChoice;
  JTextField amountField;
  JTextArea resultField;
  JButton goButton;

  void initialize () {
    JPanel p = new JPanel (new BorderLayout());
    // Heading
    JLabel label = new JLabel ("Savannah Exchange",
      new ImageIcon("Elephant.gif"),CENTER);
```

```
        p.add("North", label);
        // left hand side panel
        JPanel q = new JPanel();
          q.add ("North",new JLabel ("From"));
          fromChoice = new JComboBox();
            q.add("Center",fromChoice);
          p.add ("West", q);
        // right hand side panel
        q = new JPanel();
          q.add ("North",new JLabel ("To"));
          toChoice = new JComboBox();
            q.add("Center",toChoice);
          p.add ("East",q);
        // Centre panel
        q = new JPanel(new BorderLayout());
          JPanel r = new JPanel();
            r.add(new JLabel("Amount"));
            amountField = new JTextField("1000 ");
              amountField.addActionListener(this);
              r.add(amountField);
              q.add("North",r);
            resultField = new JTextArea(8,20);
              q.add ("Center",resultField);
            goButton = new JButton ("Convert");
              goButton.addActionListener(this);
              q.add("South",goButton);
          p.add("Center",q);
    getContentPane().add(p);
    setTitle("Currency Converter");
    setSize(610,300);

    setDefaultCloseOperation(JFrame.DISPOSE_ON_CLOSE);
}


public void actionPerformed (ActionEvent e) {
  int amount;
  if (e.getSource() == amountField)
    amount = (int)
      Integer.parseInt(amountField.getText().trim());
  else
  if (e.getSource() == goButton)
    transaction(amount);
}
```

```
      void transaction (int amount) {
        // The to and from rates are loaded directly from the
        // JComboBox and used to create the output
        Rates fromRate = (Rates) fromChoice.getSelectedItem();
        Rates toRate = (Rates) toChoice.getSelectedItem();
        resultField.append(amount+" "+fromRate.country+" "+
                            fromRate.currency+
                            "\n in "+toRate.country+" "+
                            toRate.currency+"\n was "+
        Stream.format(amount/fromRate.conversion*
                    toRate.conversion,10,3)+"\n\n");
      }


      void readIn() throws IOException {
        Stream fin = new Stream ("Rates.data", Stream.READ);
        Rates rate;
        try {
          for (int i = 0; ; i++) {
            rate = new Rates();
            rate.setRate(fin);
            // Here we store the rate elements in the JComboBoxes.
            // Note that the whole rate is stored, but only the
            // elements specified in Rates' toString() method will
            // show up in the list.
            toChoice.addItem(rate);
            fromChoice.addItem(rate);
          }
        }
        catch (EOFException e) {}
        setVisible(true);
      }
    }
  }
```

Testing

The logic of the program does not need testing, but the effect of the look and feel needs to be seen. We show three screen shots (Figures 11.11 to 11.13) which illustrate Java's Metal cross platform look (options 1 or 3), the system's look, which coincided with the Windows platform the test was run on (options 2 or 4) and the Motif look (option 5).

As we said earlier, Swing is a collection of packages, which offers much in the way of GUI programming, but which is indeed a subject of a course in its own right.

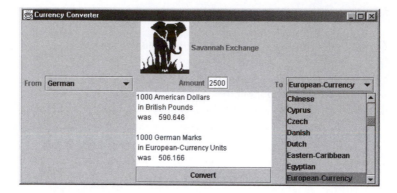

Figure 11.11 *Swing converter with Metal look and feel.*

Figure 11.12 *Swing converter with Windows look and feel.*

Figure 11.13 *Swing converter with Motif look and feel.*

SUMMARY

User input is handled through text fields, as well as menus, check boxes, choice lists and so on. Choices restrict the user's options, but can make interaction more accurate and fast.

Once a screen has been laid out and displayed, interaction with the user begins. Moving the mouse, clicking a button or entering text constitutes an event. Events are linked to listeners and the listeners call back handlers that perform the correct actions. Event-driven programming requires careful algorithm development, especially for events that have to be accepted into a certain order.

In this chapter there were no new keywords. We discussed the following new parts of the awt API. There are other classes and methods mentioned in Table 11.1.

```
TextField                       Choice
   getText                         getSelectedIndex
   setText                         getItemSelectable
   selectText                   getSource
   selectAll                    getActionCommand
   setEditable                  TextArea
   isEditable                      append
parseInt                        javax.swing.*
ActionEvent                      JButton
ItemEvent                        JTextField
ItemListener                     JComboBox
itemStateChanged                 JTextArea
CheckBox                         JLabel
CheckBoxGroup                    UIManager
```

Three new forms were developed:

Creating a text field
Text field methods
Translating a string to an integer

QUIZ

11.1 Reading a `String` value `s` from a `Textfield` `t` is done with

(a) `s = t.readString();`
(b) `s = readString(t);`
(c) `s = t.getText();`
(d) `t.getText(s);`

11.2 If the Traffic program, if there is to be a new light with a green arrow on it, what statement(s) would be needed to add it to the GUI display, without activating it?

(a) `buttons.add(walkButton);`
(b) `walkButton = new Button("Walk");`
    `buttons.add(walkButton);`

(c) `walkButton = new Button("Walk");`
(d) `buttons.add (new Button("Walk"));`

11.3 The best way to control the sequence in which events on certain components occur is to

(a) set all but the required component invisible
(b) set all but the required component disabled
(c) define boolean variables which are set and checked at appropriate points
(d) put each of the components in a separate panel

11.4 What event is caused by typing into a `TextField`?

(a) `TextEvent`
(b) `ActionEvent`
(c) `FieldEvent`
(d) `MouseClickedEvent`

11.5 What is the method used in `ActionPerformed` to decide what kind of event has occurred?

(a) `getEvent()`
(b) `getSource()`
(c) `getText()`
(d) `getAction()`

11.6 An event, in Java terms, is

(a) an object
(b) a class
(c) a variable
(d) a component

11.7 When a new `Frame` is constructed, it appears on the screen

(a) immediately
(b) when `setVisible(true)` is executed
(c) at the end of the constuctor
(d) whenever the paint method is executed

11.8 A statement such as

`closeButton.addActionListener(this)`

can best be interpreted as meaning:

(a) store a reference to the current object with `closeButton` so that an `ActionEvent` on `closeButton` will activate the `actionPerformed` method in the current object
(b) store a reference to the current object with `amountField` so that the `ActionListener` will be called when `closeButton` is pushed
(c) store a reference to `closeButton` with the `actionListener` so that `closeButton`'s event handler can be called when it is pushed
(d) store a reference to `closeButton` with the the current object so that the `ActionListener` can call this object's event handler when `closeButton` is pushed

11.9 We did not need a hash table in the converter program because the data were stored instead in

(a) an array
(b) the Swing components

(c) the file

(d) a linked list

11.10   In the Till program, to turn a selected product button green when it is pushed, we would use:

(a) `itemButtons[select].setBackground(green);`

(b) `itemButtons[i].setBackground(green);`

(c) `(Color.green) itemButtons[select];`

(d) `itemButtons[select].setBackground(Color.green);`

PROBLEMS

11.1   **Shape selector.** A teacher wishes to let toddlers draw shapes (circle, square, triangle) in three colours (red, blue, yellow). The children cannot read. Provide a suitable GUI interface for selecting a shape and colour and for drawing the object at a position given by a mouse click.

11.2   **Improving the grocery range.** Alter the Till program so as to have the items and costs stored on a file and read in at the start of the main program before the window is activated. Will the `GridLayout` size be affected or will it automatically accommodate more buttons? Implement the new program.

11.3   **Till slip.** Create a proper till slip for a weighed item in a separate window, using a pleasing design similar to that of your local supermarket.

11.4   **GUI text.** Implement a companion class to `Stream` (Sections 4.2 and 7.3) for input from `TextFields`.

11.5   **GUI Coffee Shop.** Create a design for a full screen version of Nelson's inventory control program. Rewrite the classes so as to access the screen effectively. Find out what events may occur, and set up a suitable event handlers.

11.6   **Scandanavian flags.** The four Scandanavian countries (Norway, Sweden, Denmark and Finland) have flags that follow a pattern: an off centre cross with a double border. Extend the flag designer program of Case Study 5 to include these as an option.

11.7   **Flag diagram.** Case Study 5 makes good use of inheritance. Draw a complete model diagram for it, showing a snapshot for the program just after the details for a flag have been selected.

11.8   **Swing Till.** Convert the Till program in Case Study 6 to use Swing. Investigate whether the use of Swing's box layout would be a good idea. Details of box layout can be found on the Java API documentation system.

11.9   **Swing GUI's.** Convert into Swing other GUIs you have written from the problems in Chapter 10, or use the flag designer system in Case Study 5.

11.10   **Understanding canvases.** In the traffic light programs (Examples 10.5 and 11.2) we explain how an extra class can be used to have graphics objects which are then displayed on canvases in the main GUI. Follow this technique in adapting the flag designer program in Case Study 5 to display the flag in the same window as the GUI, rather than in a separate one.

CHAPTER 12

Applets in action

12.1 From applications to applets

A great deal of the excitement surrounding Java has had to do with its integration into the World Wide Web. As we shall see, once the mechanics of accessing Java through the web have been sorted out, and we have looked at the facilities available in the standard Java packages, it will be very easy for you to branch off on your own and create applets bounded only by your imagination.

So what is an applet? An applet is a Java program that operates within a browser, and hence can appear in a web page. The applet runs on the user's computer, even though it may have been fetched from far away.

The combination of factors that make this particular (and unique to Java) operation possible is the **interpretation**, rather than full compilation of programs, and the **enabling** of the Java Virtual Machine in all web browsers. Interpretation means that Java applications (which we have studied so far) can move around the web and be executed on a variety of machines. Java browser enabling extends this facility to create the concept of applets. As the name suggests, applets are normally small programs, each devoted to a single task on a single browser page. At this point, the reader might like to refer to the diagrams and screen shots in Figures 1.1 to 1.6, when applets were first introduced in the book.

The advantages of having applets in a web page are that:

- The work is done on the machine where the results are needed, rather than sent there, so there is **less traffic** on the network.

- The user's machine can be **dedicated** to the applet and can run it much faster than could a share of a server machine where the web page resides.

- The **full facilities** of the Java programming language are available,[1] unlike some specially designed web languages which have restricted calculation and structuring powers. In particular, the standard awt is used for user interface communication.

To get an idea of how an applet differs from an application, let us go back to the first awt example in Chapter 9 and convert it to an applet.

Converting an application to an applet

The steps to achieve the conversion are as follows:

1. Check that all **input/output** relevant to the user goes through the awt interface. For example, replace

   ```
   System.out.println("This is a warning");
   ```

   with

   ```
   g.drawString("This is a warning", 0,0);
   ```

2. Remove any means for **stopping** the program (e.g. Close buttons). Applets end when their viewer or surrounding browser pages end. They are not allowed to call `System.exit()`.

3. `Applet`'s **default layout** is flow, so if the frame was relying on border layout by default, add a call to make it specific, thereby overriding flow layout: for example, add

   ```
   setLayout (new BorderLayout ());
   ```

4. Import the `applet` package and in the main **window**, extend `Applet`[2] instead of `Frame`. For example, replace

   ```
   class GraphicWarning extends Frame {
   ```

   with

   ```
   class AppletWarning extends Applet {
   ```

---

[1] Barring some security restrictions discussed below.

[2] `applet` with a small a is the name of the package that is imported; `Applet` with a captial A is the name of the class that is extended.

5. Replace the class's **constructor** by a redefinition of the `init` method, which will be called by `Applet` to make any one-off initializations. For example,

```
GraphicWarning ()
```

becomes

```
void init ()
```

6. Remove the **main** method from the program, as the applet package will take over its functions such as creating a window and setting its size and visibility.

7. Create an **HTML** file that refers to the applet's class file or include HTML instructions (called **tags**) in an existing web page (see form below).

8. **Run** the HTML file through an applet viewer or through a web browser such as HotJava, Netscape, Mosaic or Explorer.

There are some consequences of no longer importing `Frame` (point 4 above). A call to `setTitle` must be removed (applets use the file name as a default title) and any other `Frame`-specific method calls must be replaced by `Applet` ones: for example, `dispose` becomes `destroy`.

Simple HTML

HTML stands for hypertext mark-up language. We need to know only the bare basics of it to run applets. In fact, the form for activating an applet consists of one tag as follows:

HTML tags for an applet

```
<APPLET code="name" width=n height=m>
</APPLET>
```

An HTML page created via the editor of a browser may generate additional tags indicating the start and end of the HTML and the Body, but the above is sufficient.

Point 8 above indicates that there are two ways of running an applet. Let us first consider how to do this through the applet viewer supplied with Java. In the next sections we shall consider how to integrate applets with a browser.

EXAMPLE 12.1   Virus warning applet

Opportunity The warning program has become popular, and others would like to use it.

Response   If the program is changed into an applet, it can be downloaded onto any other machine and run there. (Of course, this is a very simple program that would not draw much on the resources on either side, but we are using it for illustrative purposes.)

Design   Following the steps above, we can convert the application of Example 10.1 into an applet. The HTML file that must be created contains the following:

```
<APPLET code="WarningApplet.class" width=200 height=200>
</APPLET>
```

Program   The program was pretty simple to start with, so it does not require much conversion. Points 2, 3 and 5 above do not apply in this case. Notice that as an applet, it is shorter than the original because the main program has gone: its function has been taken over by the Java runtime system in the browser or viewer.

```
import java.awt.*;
import java.applet.*;

public class WarningApplet extends Applet {

  /* A Warning box in an applet   by J M Bishop Oct 1996
   * =========================   Java 1.1
   * Must be run via its corresponding html file
   * in a browser or the appletviewer
   */

  static private final int line = 15;
  static private final int letter = 5;

  public void paint(Graphics g) {
    g.drawRect(2*letter, 2*line, 33*letter, 6*line);
    g.drawString("W A R N I N G", 9*letter, 4*line);
    g.drawString("Possible virus detected", 4*letter, 5*line);
    g.drawString("Reboot and run virus", 5*letter, 6*line);
    g.drawString("remover software", 7*letter, 7*line);
  }
}
```

Testing   The output from the applet (Figure 12.1) looks exactly the same as that from an application, except that the title bar of the window is set up by the applet viewer as the file's name and there is a clear indication that the window is created by an applet. Figure 12.1 shows the window and a listing of the HTML file.

Figure 12.1 *Applet output for the Warning program.*

How applets work

If an applet does not have a main program, how does it get started, and how does it stop? An applet is started up by the Java runtime system from within a browser (such as Netscape or Explorer) or a special program called an appletviewer. The Java Virtual Machine (JVM) looks to call one of the four methods shown in the form below – if the applet has provided them – at the appropriate time.

Figure 12.2 shows the relationship between an applet and the `Applet` class running in a web browser. The `init` method is called in place of a constructor the first time the browser encounters the tag for the applet. `init` is responsible for providing the initial setting up of the applet, its user interface, its buttons and menus, and any extra threads of control. (Threads are discussed in the next chapter.) The `start` method, on the other hand, is called whenever the web page that the applet is in reappears. `start` could, for example, resume any animation that had been halted.

Applet methods
`init()`
`destroy()`
`start()`
`stop()`

All or some of these four methods should be implemented by any subclass of `Applet`. They are called by the JVM when needed.

`init` initializes any GUI related to the applet as well as starting up any threads (see Chapter 13) and `destroy` kills them and terminates the applet.

`start` will initiate activity such as animation each time the applet is restarted from a web page and `stop` will suspend any such activity.

At this point, the system calls any other methods that the program (in either its application or applet form) has overridden, such as `paint`. In Example 12.1, only the `paint` method is present, as the applet had no reason to define any of the others. The applet then returns to a passive state and waits for something to happen. There are two possibilities: the applet can become invisible, by means of the user scrolling it off the page in the browser, or there can be a normal GUI event such as a mouse down or a button press. If an applet becomes invisible, its `stop` method is called, which has the responsibility of suspending any animation and so on. When it becomes visible again, `start` is called.

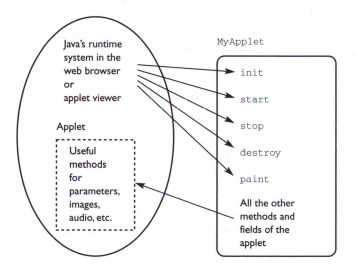

Figure 12.2   *The relationship between an applet and the* `Applet` *class.*

Any of the other events are handled in the normal way via the awt methods redefined in the original program (such as `actionPerformed`).

Finally, a `destroy` method can be provided so that the applet can release any resources it may have before the viewer ends or the browser moves to a different page. If we return to the web page with our applet on it, the applet will start from scratch again, going through its `init` sequence.

The above four methods are defined by the `Applet` class, but are overridden by the user, who provides the functionality. There is also a group of methods defined in the `Applet` class which we can use directly. These include methods to load images, audio and HTML parameters, and to establish where the applet is and where it came from. These methods are introduced in later sections and chapters.

12.2 Applets in browsers

Before Java, web browsers were mainly static, presenting information to the viewer exactly as it was stored at the original site. There were facilities for returning data to the host via form collecting and mailing, but Java's idea of having calculations at the host site is novel. With applets being able to be included in web pages, what comes down the link can now present a dynamic interface to the user (refer back to Figure 1.1).

Work can be done and results can be returned to the host machine. Without Java, the same sequence of events as in Figure 1.1 occurs when web browsing, except that the display includes only text and images.

Where are the applets?

If an applet is stored on a host machine, then it is accessible to any other machine on the Internet via its World Wide Web protocol and name or URL.[3] The `WarningApplet`'s URL would be something like:

```
http://www.cs.up.ac.za/javagently/Examples/Ch12/WarningApplet.html
```

where the HTML file is stored on a web-accessible directory. The class file it refers to must be in the same directory, if it has the simple name as given in the tag:

```
<APPLET code="WarningApplet.class" width=200 height=200>
```

If the applet is in another directory, then the tag must specify its full URL.

We consider now an example of an applet that actually interacts with the user, and compare its operation locally through the applet viewer and remotely via a browser.

---

[3] URL stands for Universal Resource Locator.

EXAMPLE 12.2	Supermarket till applet

Opportunity   The directors of Savanna Grocers see the opportunity of keeping the master version of the supermarket till program in one place, and letting the various tills download it as required. There could well be advantages for updating, for franchising and for changing computers.

Response   Convert the program into an applet as per the instructions. Create an HTML file and access it via a browser loaded on each till.

Program   The changes are absolutely minimal. The constructor changes its name to `init` and the `main` method is removed. Since applets cannot close themselves, we also remove the Close button and the corresponding handler for it in `actionPerformed`.

```java
import java.awt.*;
import java.awt.event.*;
import java.applet.*;

public class TillApplet extends Applet implements ActionListener {


  /* The Grocery Till applet    by J M Bishop Oct 1996
   *       Java 1.1 version     by T Abbott and J M Bishop Oct 1997
   *
   * Simulates the operation of a grocery till for
   * up to 12 products, together with the costs per
   * kilogram.
   * Runs as an applet via its corresponding html file.
   */

  private TextField weighField, totalField;
  private Button[] itemButtons;
  private Button weighButton, printButton, closeButton;

  public void init () {
    setLayout(new BorderLayout());


    Panel p = new Panel();
      p.setLayout(new FlowLayout());
      totalField = new TextField(6);
      totalField.setEditable(false);
      p.add(new Label("COST"));
```

```
      p.add(totalField);
    add("North", p);

  p = new Panel();
    p.setLayout(new GridLayout(5, 3));
    itemButtons = new Button[items.length];
    for (int i = 0; i < items.length; i++) {
      itemButtons[i] = new Button(items[i]);
      itemButtons[i].addActionListener(this);
      p.add(itemButtons[i]);
    }
    weighButton = new Button("WEIGH");
      weighButton.addActionListener(this);
      p.add(weighButton);
    printButton = new Button("PRINT");
      printButton.addActionListener(this);
      p.add(printButton);
    add("Center", p);

  p = new Panel();
    p.setLayout(new FlowLayout());
    weighField = new TextField(4);
      weighField.setEditable(false);
      weighField.addActionListener(this);
      p.add(weighField);
    p.add(new Label("MASS"));
    p.add(new Label("Type return after the amount"));
    add("South", p);

  }


  public void actionPerformed(ActionEvent e) {
    Object source = e.getSource();
    if (source == printButton) {
    printItems();
  } else
  if (source == weighButton) {
    resetWeighField();
  } else
  if (source == weighField) {
    readWeighField();
  } else
    selectItem(e.getActionCommand());


  }
```

```
 /* Here follows the main control of the program.
  * The event and action handlers above call these
  * methods, which ensure that there is only a reaction
  * if certain conditions (e.g. other previous events)
  * have already been met.
  */

  public void resetWeighField() {
    weighField.setText("");
    weighField.setEditable(true);
  }

  public void readWeighField() {
    if (weighField.isEditable()) {
      weighField.setEditable(false);
      weighField.selectAll();
      kg = (double)Integer.valueOf(
            weighField.getText().trim()).intValue();
      weighed = true;
    }
  }

}

public void printItems() {
  if (weighed && chosen) {
    total = kg*unitCosts[select];
    totalField.setText("G "+total);
    System.out.println(kg+"kg "+items[select]+" @ G"+
            unitCosts[select]+" = G"+total);
    kg = 0;
    weighed = false;
    chosen = false;
    total = 0;
    weighField.select(0,0);
  }
}
  public void selectItem(String item) {
    select = 0;
    while (!item.equals(items[select]))
      select++;
    chosen = true;
  }
```

```
    private String[] items = { "Apples", "Pears", "Oranges",
                               "Potatoes", "Lemons", "Squash",
                               "Onions", "Garlic", "Avocados",
                               "", "", "" };
    private double[] unitCosts = { 6.00, 5.00, 7.00,
                                   3.00, 10.00, 4.00,
                                   4.00, 12.00, 15.00,
                                   0, 0, 0 };

    private double total;
    private double kg;
    private boolean chosen = false;
    private boolean weighed = false;
    private int select = 1;
}
```

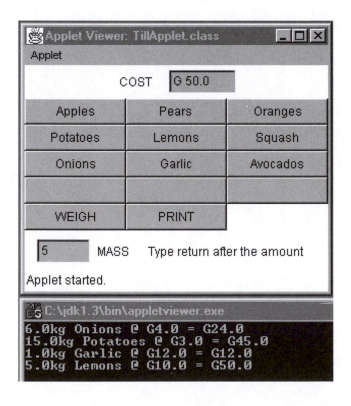

Figure 12.3 *Applet output from the Till program via a viewer.*

Testing If we run the applet via the applet viewer, then the till applet's output is the same as that of the original application, except for the absence of the Close button. Figure 12.3 gives a picture of the screen, together with output that is still being printed for the till slip, that comes out on the command line window. The applet responds to the application in the same way but is closed by closing the applet viewer itself: there is no Close button.

Now if we store the HTML file in a location that is accessible on the web, we can start up a browser (Netscape in this case) and request the location specified. The result is shown in Figure 12.4. There are two differences between what the user sees of the applet in the viewer and browser environments:

- The applet viewer still gives access to the screen for printing. Under the browser, open up the Java console window to see the output (usually available on the File menu).

- The applet viewer can be stopped by closing the viewer's window, whereas under a browser, the applet ends only when the page it is running in is closed.

In all other respects applets behave the same under either environment.

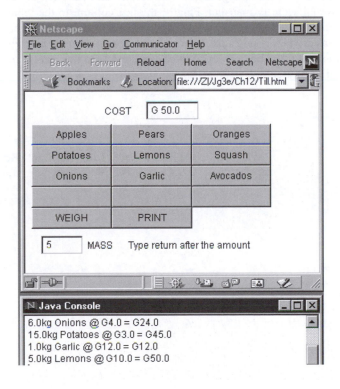

Figure 12.4 *The Till applet running under Netscape.*

Applet security

A potential concern when using applets on the web is that a program you download could be corrupt and cause damage to your system. In every possible way, Java guards against this happening. In the first place, there is a validity check on the bytecode that arrives at your computer. If it had been tampered with en route, your Java Virtual Machine will not run it. Secondly, the JVM itself will not perform any operation that could potentially harm your machine. For example, an applet from far away cannot find out your password, nor can it delete your files. The full set of rules is summarized in Table 12.1.

Let us consider the implications of this table. A Java application is a full program and as such can do anything that is required on your computer. An applet is quite different, and is subject to scrutiny and the rules above. Applets running in the applet viewer can do everything that an application can, except for deleting files. However, once they run within a browser, their activities are curtailed somewhat.

Within a browser, an applet does not end: it ends when the page it is in is replaced by another page. Thus it does not call exit, nor is there any Close box. Applets in web pages are **seamless**, as shown in the case study. The fact that applets cannot read or write the local file system can be a disadvantage. In fact, this restriction can be lifted by the applet user defining a special security manager. Finally, the last column in the table shows that additional restrictions apply to remotely loaded applets, and these are all to the good.

These restrictions are in a good cause, but they can make a programmer's life difficult. The work-arounds that must be employed when an applet cannot read a local file are described next and illustrated in Example 12.3.

Table 12.1 *Applet security*

Operation	Java application	Applet in an applet viewer	Local applet in a browser	Remote applet in a browser
Access local files	✓	✓		
Delete a local file	✓			
Run another program	✓	✓		
Find out your name	✓	✓	✓	
Connect back to the host	✓	✓	✓	✓
Connect to another host	✓	✓	✓	
Load the Java library	✓	✓	✓	
Call exit	✓	✓		
Create a pop-up window	✓	✓	✓	✓

The `PARAM` facility

We are already aware that getting data into an applet cannot always be done by just reading a file. If the applet is running in a browser, then there is a facility to set up data in the web page, and for the applet to fetch it from there. The mechanism is fairly cumbersome, so is best used for one-off set-up type data.

Interaction between applets and web pages is achieved through the `PARAM` facility. `PARAM` operates by having named parameters listed in the HTML document that the applet can read using an `Applet` class method called `getParameter`. Parameters are listed between the `<APPLET>` and `</APPLET>` tag brackets and each parameter must be of the form:

HTML parameter
`<PARAM NAME = "formal" VALUE = "actual">`

`NAME` indicates that the string that follows is the name of the parameter that is being sought. Within the same set of angle brackets, forming a pair, there is the `VALUE` to be assigned to that parameter. The value is also a string, but obviously it can be parsed as a number or whatever other type is required. A possible application of `PARAM` in the till example would be to move the prices of the products from the applet to the web page, specifying them as:

```
<PARAM NAME="garlic" VALUE="12">
```

To access the parameters we use the string method `getParameter` as follows:

```
unitCosts[i] = Integer.parseInt(getParameter(items[i]));
```

Here, `items[i]` is a string, such as `"garlic"`, and `getParameter` will find the parameter with that name and return the corresponding value, which would be the string `"12"`. The `PARAM` facility is used in Example 12.3 and the case study, and is required in some of the problems that follow.

Signed applets

All the above restrictions apply to untrusted code. Some of them could get in the way within a single company, where applets are written at head office and fetched to branches. There may well be the need to read local files at the branches, for example. The JDK provides for applets to be created with digital signatures, via a special utility called the keytool. The company must maintain a small database of trusted applets, which can be entered in the base, with their public and private keys. Then the applet is saved as an archive or JAR[4] and the JAR file is passed through the keytool. The HTML file that is

---

[4] JAR stands for Java archive.

going to run the applet then includes an additional tag to fetch the signed archive file, before the code file it contains is executed.

The above applies to the JDK: other IDEs and browsers may have other ways of declaring and handling trusted applets.

JAR files

A further consideration for applets is their access to user-defined packages, such as `javagently` and `jgeslib`. In the normal course of events, the applet class loader will not be able to find the classes we need if they are in other directories. On the other hand, we cannot just copy all the class files we need into our working directory because then we shall disturb the package and import structure of our program and it will not compile anymore.

Fortunately, Java has a solution. We can create a Java ARchive (JAR) of a package, and then refer to this in the HTML file that sets up the applet. To create a JAR, go to the directory above a package, and activate the JAR tool as in the form:

JAR tool command

```
jar cf packagename.jar packagename\*.class
```

This will create an archive, compressed, of all the class files in the package. For example,

```
jar cf javagently.jar javagently\*.class
```

Then in the HTML file for the applet, add the additional tag

```
archive = javagently.jar
```

Apart from enabling the package structure to be retained on the distant computer, the compression factor of JAR means that the applet code is smaller and can get loaded much faster.

EXAMPLE 12.3   The newspaper competition

Problem   The *Savanna News* runs a weekly competition based on readers' names. A value is assigned to each letter of the alphabet and there is a winning score. If you are one of the readers whose name adds up to the winning score, then you can enter for a prize. To even things out, every name is expanded or contracted to 20 letters, without spaces or punctuation. The competition is repeated every week with different letter values and a different winning score each week. All those who enter have a chance of winning the weekly 1000 graz prize.

Example

```
Alphabet          a b c d e f g h i j k l m n o p q r s t u v w x y z
Values            5 1 3 6 7 9 2 3 7 5 4 1 3 8 9 7 5 4 3 2 1 3 2 4 5 4
Winning score     100
```

Names	Letters used	Score
Judy Bishop	JudyBishopJudyBishop	94
John Smith	JohnSmithJohnSmithJo	100
Roelf van den Heever	RoelfvandenHeeverRoe	118
Timothy Fox-Fox-Robinson	TimothyFoxFoxRobinso	116

So John Smith can enter the competition this week. The others can try again when the letter values change next week.

Now the editor would like the competition to be available on the web so that people can try out their names and get an immediate response.

Solution   Write a Java applet, of course! This competition is ideal for an applet because it contains information that is maintained centrally (the letter values) and that must be protected, but we want everyone to be able to do the calculation. Moreover, doing it by hand is actually quite tedious, so the calculation facility offered by applets is valuable.

Screen design   It is useful to start off with a screen design for the applet, indicating what fields we need to reserve for input and output while iterating with the user. In addition, we can decide what information can be kept in the web page, and what has to go in the applet. Plain text is cheaper to display via HTML than via an applet. Figure 12.5 gives an indication of what the screen could look like.

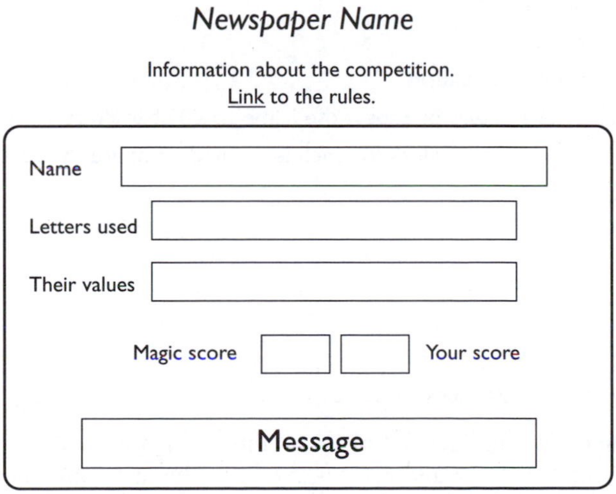

Figure 12.5   *Screen design for the newspaper competition.*

Algorithm   The competition applet splits into two parts. The first one handles the setting up of the screen and the data; the second one handles the input of names and the calculation of the result through a GUI interface. Figure 12.5 gives an idea of the layout. Setting up the data requires more thought.

We want to associate values with characters. In other words, we want a table relating characters to integers. Unfortunately, as we discovered in Section 6.4, Java does not allow arrays to have any index type except integer. Instead, we have to use a hash table, where the characters and corresponding integers are both stored using `put`, and extracted using `get`.

The question then is: how do we get the values into the applet? What we want is for the values to be easily alterable by newspaper staff who may not be programmers. If we create them as fixed constants, then each week we shall have to recompile the program when the values change, which is not convenient. Two other options are:

1.   Have the values stored in the web page as parameters and get them from there.

2.   Connect to a file on the main newspaper computer and read the values remotely.

Either of these suggestions is feasible. How to connect to a remote resource is covered in Chapter 14, so we shall use the parameter facility here. The parameter names will be Score and a, b, c, d and so on for each letter of the alphabet.

The interface has two input fields – the name and an Again button – and five display fields – the letters used, their values, the magic score, your score and a message. Setting up the strings to be displayed is best described in Java itself in the applet below.

For the input, the `actionPerformed` method must handle events on the field and the button. Clicking the Again button will set the fields to their original state, which is easy. Handling the name is more complex. The algorithm required is:

Checking a name for a win

Get the text

Trim it of trailing blanks

Convert it to lower case

Remove all spaces and punctuation

Cut the name to 20 characters or repeat the name to 20 characters

Consult the hash table for the values for each letter and compute the Total

Total is winning score?

Yes   No

Good luck message   Bad luck message

To work on the name, we use several of the methods supplied with the `String` class, such as `trim`, `toLowerCase` and `toCharArray`. The last converts a string into an equivalent array of characters, which is more convenient for our purposes. The extracted name is also an array of characters, as is its equivalent array of letter values. These are both displayed in the output.

Web page   The web page has the headings and the parameters. Here it is, as produced through a browser editor.

```
<HTML>
<HEAD>
  <META HTTP-EQUIV="Content-Type" CONTENT="text/html; charset=iso-8859-1">
  <META NAME="GENERATOR" CONTENT="Mozilla/4.01 [en] (WinNT; I)
   [Netscape]">
  <TITLE>Competition</TITLE>
</HEAD>
<BODY>

<CENTER>
<H1>
<B><FONT COLOR="#3366FF"><FONT SIZE=+2>
<I>Savanna News </I>Competition</FONT></FONT></B>
</H1>
</CENTER>

<CENTER>
<P>
<B>Win G1000 if your name matches the magic score.</B>
</CENTER>
</P>
<CENTER>
<B><A HREF="Rules.html">Rules</A> of the competition.</B>
</CENTER>

<CENTER>
<APPLET CODE="Competition.class" WIDTH=400 HEIGHT=200>
<PARAM NAME="Score" VALUE="100">
<PARAM NAME="a" VALUE="5"><PARAM NAME="b" VALUE="1">
<PARAM NAME="c" VALUE="3"><PARAM NAME="d" VALUE="6">
<PARAM NAME="e" VALUE="7"><PARAM NAME="f" VALUE="9">
<PARAM NAME="g" VALUE="2"><PARAM NAME="h" VALUE="3">
<PARAM NAME="i" VALUE="7"><PARAM NAME="j" VALUE="5">
<PARAM NAME="k" VALUE="4"><PARAM NAME="l" VALUE="1">
<PARAM NAME="m" VALUE="3"><PARAM NAME="n" VALUE="8">
<PARAM NAME="o" VALUE="9"><PARAM NAME="p" VALUE="7">
<PARAM NAME="q" VALUE="5"><PARAM NAME="r" VALUE="4">
<PARAM NAME="s" VALUE="3"><PARAM NAME="t" VALUE="2">
<PARAM NAME="u" VALUE="1"><PARAM NAME="v" VALUE="3">
<PARAM NAME="w" VALUE="2"><PARAM NAME="x" VALUE="4">
<PARAM NAME="y" VALUE="5"><PARAM NAME="z" VALUE="4">
</APPLET>
</CENTER>
</BODY>
</HTML>
```

Applet   Some of the interesting code in the applet includes the extraction of the name from the text field and its conversion into a character array, done by:

```
c = nameField.getText().trim().toLowerCase().toCharArray();
```

getText returns a string. trim and toLowerCase are both string methods that return strings. Finally, toCharArray takes a string and converts it into a character array.

The next section of code takes each element of this array and looks up its letter value in the hash table. The hash table stores strings, so the result of

```
String s = (String) values.get(String.valueOf(d[i]));
```

is a string. To build up another character array of the letter values (which are all under 10 and therefore single digits) we can just extract the first character of the string using charAt. However, to create the score, we do finally have to convert the string to an int. These two lines perform this task:

```
e[i] = s.charAt(0);
total += Integer.parseInt(s);
```

A further point of interest is that we use a variety of fonts in the applet. The ordinary font is:

```
Font g = new Font("SanSerif",Font.PLAIN,12);
```

but for the letters and their values we use a fixed spaced font, set up by:

```
Font h = new Font("Monospaced",Font.PLAIN,12);
```

and then the message uses a larger font:

```
Font f = new Font("Serif",Font.BOLD,20);
```

The Java applet follows. It is not all that long, but is effective.

```
import java.util.*;
import java.awt.*;
import java.applet.*;
import java.awt.event.*;
public class Competition extends Applet implements ActionListener {
    /* The Competition applet      by J M Bishop Oct 1996
     * =======================      Java 1.1 Jan 1998
     * Runs a competition screening mechanism.
     * Illustrates interaction between an applet
     * and a web page.
     */
```

```
private static int winningScore;
private TextField targetField, nameField,
        lettersField, valuesField, scoreField, resultField;
private Button againButton;
private Hashtable values = new Hashtable ();
private String openingMessage = "See if your name is a winner!";
private static final int lettersCounted = 20;
String letters [] = {"a","b","c","d","e","f","g","h","i","j",
      "k","l","m","n","o","p","q","r","s","t","u","v","w",
      "x","y","z"};

public void init () {

  // First, generate the letter values and
  // Create the hash table by using values in the
  // PARAM tags of the web page.
  // Both the key and value are strings.

  winningScore = Integer.parseInt(getParameter("Score"));
  for (int i = 0; i<26; i++)
    values.put(letters[i], getParameter(letters[i]));

  // draw the user interface
  setLayout (new BorderLayout ());

  Panel p = new Panel ();
    Font g = new Font("SanSerif",Font.PLAIN,12);
      p.setFont(g);
    nameField = new TextField ("",40);
      p.add (new Label ("Your name is?"));
      p.add (nameField);
      nameField.addActionListener(this);
    Panel r = new Panel();
      Font h = new Font("Monospaced",Font.PLAIN,12);
      r.setLayout(new GridLayout(2,2));
      lettersField = new TextField("",20);
        lettersField.setEditable(false);
        r.add(new Label("Letters used:"));
        r.add (lettersField);
        lettersField.setFont(h);
        valuesField = new TextField("",20);
      valuesField.setEditable(false);
        r.add(new Label("Their values are:"));
```

```
            r.add (valuesField);
            valuesField.setFont(h);
        p.add(r);
        targetField = new TextField
                       (Integer.toString(winningScore),4);
          targetField.setEditable(false);
          p.add (new Label ("Magic score"));
          p.add (targetField);
        scoreField = new TextField ("",4);
          p.add (scoreField);
          p.add (new Label ("Your score"));
          scoreField.setEditable(false);
      add ("Center", p);

      Panel q = new Panel ();
        resultField = new TextField (openingMessage);
          resultField.setEditable(false);
          Font f = new Font("Serif",Font.BOLD,20);
          resultField.setFont(f);
          q.add (resultField);
        againButton = new Button("Again");
          q.add (againButton);
          againButton.addActionListener(this);
      add ("South", q);
    }

    public void actionPerformed (ActionEvent evt) {
      Object source = evt.getSource();

      // Again resets everything. It is always available
      if (source == againButton) {
        nameField.setText("");
        scoreField.setText("");
        resultField.setText(openingMessage);
      }

      // A name was entered
      else
        handleName();
    }
```

```
void handleName() {
  char c [];
  char d [] = new char[lettersCounted];
  char e [] = new char[lettersCounted];

  // Convert name to lower case and strip blanks
  c = nameField.getText().trim().toLowerCase().toCharArray();
  int n=0;
  for (int i=0; i<c.length & n<lettersCounted; i++) {
    if (Character.isLetter(c[i])) {
      d[n] = c[i];
      n++;
    }
    if (i==c.length-1) i=-1;
  }

  // The stripped down array is now in d[0] to d[n]
  // and we put the corresponding values in e[].
  int total = 0;
  for (int i=0; i<n; i++) {
    String s = (String) values.get(String.valueOf(d[i]));
    e[i] = s.charAt(0);
    total += Integer.parseInt(s);
  }

  // Calculate and compare the score. Display a message.
  scoreField.setText(Integer.toString(total));
  lettersField.setText(String.valueOf(d));
  valuesField.setText(String.valueOf(e));
  if (total == winningScore)
    resultField.setText("Good luck in the lucky draw");
  else
    resultField.setText("Bad luck! Try again next week");
  }

}
```

Testing   The applet can be tested with the names above, or with a variety of other names. The run shown in Figure 12.6 has hit on a name with the lucky score.

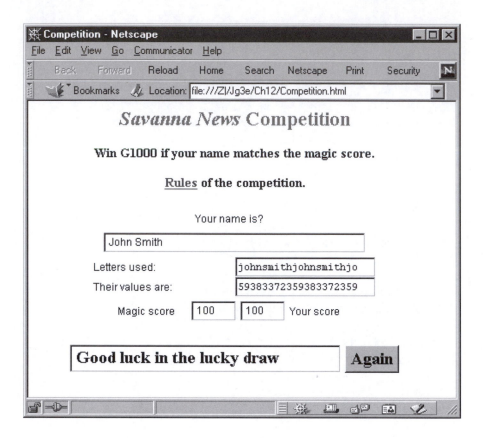

Figure 12.6 *The Competition applet running in Netscape.*

12.3 Sound and images

One of the joys of Java is being able pull sound and images easily and effectively into a program.

Sound

The `Applet` package has an interface called `AudioClip` which has three methods: `play`, `stop` and `loop`. The Applet method `getAudioClip` will return an object that implements this interface, and then we can play that object. The form is:

`AudioClip` declaration and play

```
AudioClip name;
name = getAudioClip (getCodeBase (), filename);
name.play();
```

The `getCodeBase` method in `Applet` finds out where the applet is running, so that the sound can be played there. The file, at the moment, must be an .au file, not a .wav file.

Suppose we have a file called 'ouch.au' and want to play it. The following statements will set this up:

```
AudioClip ouch;
ouch = getAudioClip (getCodeBase (), "ouch.au");
ouch.play();
```

There is also a shorthand version of the above which uses anonymous clips as follows:

```
play(getCodeBase (), "ouch.au");
```

The first form is preferable if you are going to use the clip more than once in a program. Sound is used in Example 12.4.

Images

Images are pixel data that are stored in a file, brought over the network, or created in real time by a graphics engine or video camera. Java has extensive facilities for handling all these, and in particular for addressing the problems of working in a distributed, networked environment. You will have already experienced the varying speeds at which images are downloaded within a browser. One of the more useful options in a browser is to set autoloading of images, meaning that the text will continue to come in while the image is being displayed. Thus we are not held up just for a picture we may have already seen and do not particularly want.

Java can perform the same kind of control through objects called `Observers`. We can also animate images, control flickering and filtering and run through videos at varying speeds. All of this is a topic on its own. In this chapter, we shall look at a simple fetch of a single image, and the usual way of moving it around on the screen.

Like audio clips, Java has a class for images, and the form for getting one is exactly the same as above, with `AudioClip` replaced by `Image`. Thus an example of fetching an image would be:

```
Image me;
me = getImage (getCodeBase (), "bishop.gif");
```

To display the image, we access the `drawImage` method within the `Graphics` class of the awt. The form for displaying an image is:

Display an image

```
g.drawImage (Image imageid, int x, int y,
             ImageObserver observer);
```

The *x* and *y* coordinates specify the top left corner of the spot where the image should be drawn on the screen. In most cases our applet is the observer and therefore we use `this` as the fourth parameter. For example:

```
g.drawImage (me, 0, 0, this);
```

Media tracking

While observers let us carry on with what we are doing while images are being loaded, we may wish to do the opposite: ensure that an image is loaded before continuing. It is important to do so when an applet is loading images in its `init` method. If an image is set to load, and the applet asks how big it is, it may get a spurious answer. So we set a media tracker on it. The form is:

Media tracker

```
MediaTracker tracker = new MediaTracker(applet);
tracker.addImage(Image imageid, 0);
try {tracker.waitForID(0);}
catch (InterruptedException e) {}
```

The tracker will watch the image and when a signal such as the zero (selected by us) is returned, we catch it and deduce that the image has been loaded. The case study uses this method successfully.

Moving images

The technique for moving an image around on the screen is a well-known one. Java just makes it easier. In many other systems, when you take an image and draw it somewhere else, you also have to take care to wipe out the old one. In Java, the use of the `paint` method means that the screen is written correctly as we want it each time. What we have to do is make sure that we specify the coordinates for moving objects in a relative way: that is, using variables rather than constants for their coordinates. Example 12.4 shows how this is done.

Reacting to mouse events

In Section 11.2 we described the different events, listeners and handlers that Java provides. Thereafter, we used mainly the `ActionEvent`, with its associated `ActionListener` and `ActionPerformed` handler method. `ActionListener` is special, because it has only one handler method. If you refer to Table 11.1, you will see that most other events have several methods.

The point is that the listeners are abstract interfaces, and when one uses an interface, you have to provide real versions of *all* its abstract methods, even if you do not use them. Thus to detect a mouse press, we would have to define a `mousePressed` method (which is fine) and also dummy versions of all the other four mouse-related methods in the `MouseListener` class. To save on such wasted coding, the `java.awt.event` package includes for each of the abstract listener interfaces an implementation of it called an **adapter**. The abstract adapter class supplies dummy versions of all the methods in the listener. Then instead of implementing the listener, we inherit the adapter, and override only those methods that we really need. Figure 12.7 shows how this sequence applies to the two mouse listeners available for mouse events. All the methods have a `MouseEvent` as a parameter.

So if an applet wants to listen to the mouse, it includes the following in its `init` method:

```
this.addMouseListener(new MouseHandler());
```

and an inner class called `MouseHandler` where the code for the `mousePressed` event is given. The next example illustrates the use of both the mouse listener and the mouse motion listener.

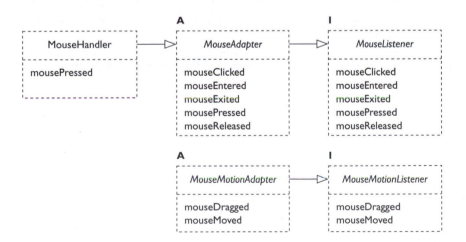

Figure 12.7 *Model diagram of mouse listeners and adapters.*

| EXAMPLE 12.4 | Catching the duke |

Problem   We would like to have a little game where an image moves around the screen, and we move the mouse to try to catch it. The game should have sound as well.

Solution   First we need to get hold of a gif file and two au files – one for a hit and one for a miss. In my experience, the gif files should not be larger than 10 Kbyte and the au files should be at least 6 Kbyte to be playable. These are guidelines: your computer could possibly handle different sizes. Then we shall draw the image and let the user track it with the mouse. Hits will be rewarded by one sound, and misses by another. In order to reinforce the sounds, we shall also print out corresponding messages.

Algorithm   The applet method for moving the image works like this. Once the image has been fetched and drawn, we can obtain its width and height. When the user clicks the mouse, a `mouseDown` event occurs and we can then check if the current mouse coordinates are within those of the image. After reacting with a win or lose sound and message, we repaint the screen, having moved the image. Moving the image is done by adding a random amount to the coordinates that we pass to `drawImage`. The message is displayed in a special browser area called the status bar with the `showStatus` method. As a result, the message does not appear if the program is run with a viewer.

Now consider carefully the dynamics of the system. When do things actually move? Well nothing happens in the applet, unless we activate an event. So the image will remain stationary until we start to move the mouse. Every time the applet detects a `mouseMover` event (as opposed to a `mouseDown` event) it can repaint the screen. Repainting includes changing the *x,y* coordinates, so the image will seem to move randomly as we move the mouse, and we will have to 'chase' it. In order to make the game realistic, we move the image only if a current position coordinate is a multiple of 3. Thus the *x* can change without the *y* coordinate's changing.

Program   The program follows the algorithm and forms described above.

```
import java.awt.*;
import java.applet.*;
import java.awt.event.*;

public class CatchM extends Applet {

    /* Catching the Duke program by J M Bishop Dec 1996
     * ==========================     Java 1.1 Jan 1998
     *
     * Try to catch the duke and hit it by pressing the left
     * mouse button.
     * Illustrates sound, images and movement
     * and mouse handling events. */
```

```
int mx, my, limitx, limity ;
int wins;
int boardSize;
Image duke;

public void init() {
  wins = 0;
  boardSize = getSize().width - 1;
  duke = getImage(getCodeBase(),"duke.gif");
  this.addMouseListener (new mousePressHandler());
  this.addMouseMotionListener (new mouseMotionHandler());
}

class mousePressHandler extends MouseAdapter {

  public void mousePressed (MouseEvent e) {
    int x = e.getX();
    int y = e.getY();
    requestFocus();
    if (mx < x && x < mx+limitx &&
        my < y && y < my+limity) {
      wins++;
      getAppletContext().showStatus("Caught it! Total " + wins);
      play(getCodeBase(), "sounds/ouch.au");
        }
    else {
      getAppletContext().showStatus("Missed again.");
      play(getCodeBase(), "sounds/haha.au");
    }
    repaint();
  }
}

public class mouseMotionHandler extends MouseMotionAdapter {
  public void mouseMoved(MouseEvent e) {
    if (e.getX() % 3 == 0 && e.getY() % 3 == 0)
      repaint();
  }
}

public void paint(Graphics g) {
  // wait till the image is in before getting the
  // size. Can't put these statements in init
  limitx = duke.getWidth(this);
  limity = duke.getHeight(this);
```

```
        int change = boardSize-limitx;

    // draw a boundary
    g.drawRect(0, 0, boardSize, boardSize);

     // calculate a new place for the duke
     // and draw it.
     mx = (int)(Math.random()*1000) % change;
     my = (int)(Math.random()*1000) % change;
     g.drawImage(duke, mx, my, this);
   }
 }
```

Testing   For obvious reasons, it is very difficult to show a test of the program in the book. Figure 12.8 shows a snapshot of the duke and a message, running in the Netscape browser, but this is one case where the you are going to have to get on to the web to see and hear it! The program can be found on the *Java Gently* site.

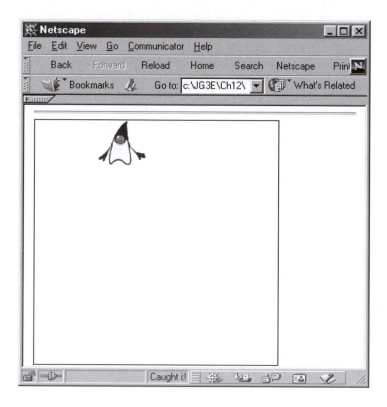

Figure 12.8   *Catching the duke in Netscape.*

12.4 Case Study 8: The Nature Conservation Project

The project to create a web site to show the animals, birds and trees of Savanna was postulated and described in Chapter 1. Now we have sufficient knowledge to examine how such a system is put together, and what the relationships are among the HTML scripts, the Java applets and the images that will illustrate the site.

Web pages

Referring to Figure 1.3, which is the first page of the site, we see that it is a simple display consisting of a heading, some text, an image and two links – to animals and trees. A third link – to birds – is promised but not yet implemented. To create such a page, one can use the interactive editor in a browser such as Netscape, or one can write the HTML directly. Either way, there will be an HTML document which in its simplest form looks like this:

```
<HTML>
<BODY>

<CENTER><P><FONT COLOR="#0000FF"><FONT SIZE=+3>
Savanna Nature Conservation
</FONT></FONT></P></CENTER>

<P></P>

<CENTER><P><IMG SRC="Elephant.jpg" HSPACE=20 HEIGHT=117 WIDTH=178
ALIGN=LEFT></P></CENTER>

<P><FONT COLOR="#000000">Savanna's Nature Conservation Department aims
to help you find out about animals that inhabit the Grasslands of Africa.
</P>

<P>You can also interact with us, register sightings
and add to our data interactively.</P>

<P>Version 1 of our homepage has sections on
<A HREF="Animals.html">animals</A>,
birds and
<A HREF="Trees.html">trees</A>.
</FONT></P>

</BODY>
</HTML>
```

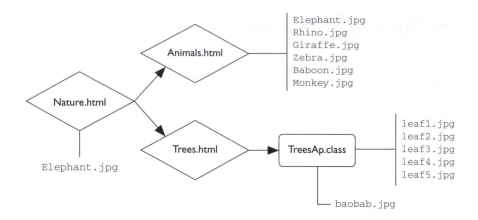

Figure 12.9 *Schematic of the Nature Conservation system.*

The document starts off with some header information. Thereafter the heading is printed in a larger than normal font. The image of the elephant is expected to be in the same directory as the HTML file itself, and it is in JPG format. Various dimensions are specified, and it is indicated that the image will go to the left of any text that follows. The next three paragraphs have the text with the last one including two links to other pages with file names `Animals.html` and `Trees.html`.

`Animals.html` follows a similar pattern, except that it has six images to display. At this stage, a schematic diagram of the system can be built up, as in Figure 12.9. The arrows indicate HTML links and the plain lines indicate images and applets that are included.

Including an applet

The `Trees.html` document presents the web page shown in Figure 1.5. An abbreviated version of the HTML code for it is:

```
<HTML>

<BODY>
<CENTER><P><FONT COLOR="#008000"><FONT SIZE=+2>
Trees of Savanna</FONT></FONT></P></CENTER>

<P>With a twig in hand, find out what your tree is by selecting the
leaf type and giving the leaf measurements in millimetres. Some of the
trees we can identify so far are:</P>

<TABLE BORDER=1 WIDTH="100%">

<TR>
```

```
<TD><APPLET CODE="TreesAp.class" WIDTH=350 HEIGHT=300>
<PARAM NAME="entries" VALUE="19">
<PARAM NAME="tree-1" VALUE="Protea">
<PARAM NAME="codes-1" VALUE="165 175 176">
<PARAM NAME="tree-2" VALUE="Milkplum">
<PARAM NAME="codes-2" VALUE="156 166">

... and more parameters

NAME="tree-19" VALUE="Candle acacia">
<PARAM NAME="codes-19" VALUE="666">

</APPLET>

</TD>

<TD ALIGN=RIGHT><FONT COLOR="#0080FF"><FONT SIZE=-1>
Protea<BR>
Milkplum <BR>
Wild fig<BR>
... and more trees

Fever tree<BR>
Camel thorn<BR>
Umbrella thorn<BR>
Candle acacia
</FONT></FONT>
</TD>
</TR>
</TABLE>
<FONT COLOR="#0080FF"></FONT>
</BODY>
</HTML>
```

Once again, we start with a heading and a short piece of text. Then we want to have an applet next to a list of tree names. An easy way to accomplish this is to set up a table and put the applet in one of the cells and the text in the other. A side effect of using a table is that a nice border is drawn for free.

The applet tag specifies that the applet comes from `TreesAp.class`, and occupies a certain height and width. Thereafter there is a long list of names of trees and values. These are discussed below. The list of 19 trees is given as part of the HTML as well, and it is this list that is displayed in blue on the right of the table.

Getting data into an applet

Consider once again the Trees applet, the output of which was shown in Figure 1.5. The purpose of the applet is to receive three pieces of data – a leaf width, a leaf length and a matching leaf pattern – and to display an image of the tree that might have been found as a result. Figure 1.5 shows the entering of particulars related to the baobab tree, and Figure 1.6 shows the result. This is the one way in which we pass data to an applet – by entering values in fields and clicking buttons.

However, this applet also needs to keep a complete list of trees and their associated particulars. How should this be done? There are three ways:

- Initialize an array with the data, as was done for the till example.
- Use the browser's PARAM facility.
- Read the data off a file using a remote connection.

The PARAM facility seems appropriate here. If we want to have parameters that form an array (such as our 19 trees) then there must be 19 different names for the parameters. If we call them by similar names, such as tree-1, tree-2 and so on, then we can use deft programming to pick off the parameters without listing each by name in the applet. The statement to get a tree parameter's value would be:

```
String tree = getParameter("tree-"+(i+1));
```

Tree codes

The applet constructs a three-digit code from the data entered by the user. Each tree could have several (up to four, say) of these codes, since there is a range of leaf sizes that might apply. So for each tree we need its name, as described above, and we also need a set of codes that can be used to identify it. For example, the second tree (tree-2) called the milk-plum, has alternate leaves of between 40 and 80 cm long and a width between 20 and 30 cm. This reduces to two codes (in a coding system adapted from Moll, Moll and Page[5]), namely 156 and 166. Therefore matching the tree-2 parameter shown above, we need to have a codes-2 parameter like this:

```
<PARAM NAME="codes-2" VALUE="156 166">
```

Of course, nature is notoriously difficult to code, and in reality there are possibly other trees that would fit a 156 or 166 code as well. But in the main, the Molls' system works and so we can proceed to choose a list of curious-sounding trees, enter them in the HTML with their codes, and activate the applet.

[5] Eugene and Glen Moll and Nicci Page, *Common Trees*, Struik, 1989.

Inside the applet

In order to conclude this example, we should look at the details of the applet:

- how the layout is achieved;

- how the tree names and codes are stored and accessed in a hash table; and

- the event-handling necessary to collect the user input and return an image.

These are all explained in the comments associated with the Java that follows.

Another aspect of this applet is that we react to user input by turning the fields green. When all the data have been entered and a tree has been sought, the user clicks the Again button and the fields revert to white. A similar technique could have been employed in the till and competition applets.

```java
import java.applet.*;
import java.awt.*;
import java.awt.event.*;
import java.net.*;
import java.util.*;


public class TreesAp extends Applet implements ActionListener {

   /* The Trees applet      by J M Bishop January 1997
    * =================      Java 1.1 Jan 1998

       Asks for information about the leaves of a tree.
       Codes the information and links to a URL where

       further information about the tree is stored.
       Gets the tree names and codes from an HTML page.
       Illustrates interaction with a browser,
       button arrays, image tracking,
       nested panel layouts and string tokenizers.
   */

   // A TextField, boolean and integer for each leaf part.
   private TextField widthField, lengthField, messageField;
   private Button againButton;
   private boolean gotChoice = false;
   private boolean gotWidth = false;
   private boolean gotLength = false;
   private int c, w, l;

   private Hashtable table = new Hashtable ();
```

```
private String patterns [] = {
  "Alternate", "Opposite",
 "Whorled", "Palmate",
 "Complex", "Bipinnate"};

private Button patternButton [] = new Button[6];


public void init () {
//====================
  // First read in the parameters from the HTML page
    setUpTable();

  // Create the applet screen with two text fields above
  // and one below. In the centre is the grid of nine
  // leaf patterns, each a border panel in its own right
  // with a button in the south and a canvas occupying
  // the rest. The canvas is painted by the leafPattern
  // class. The font is set to 10pt.

  Font f = new Font ("SanSerif",Font.PLAIN,10);
  this.setFont (f);
  setLayout(new BorderLayout(0,0));
  Panel p = new Panel ();
    p.add (new Label ("Leaf width"));
    widthField = new TextField (8);
      p.add (widthField);
     widthField.addActionListener(this);
    p.add (new Label ("Leaf length"));
    lengthField = new TextField (8);
      p.add (lengthField);
     lengthField.addActionListener(this);
  add ("North",p);

  // Create a panel for the nine leaf patterns
  Panel q = new Panel ();
    q.setLayout(new GridLayout(2,3));
    for (int b = 0; b<patterns.length; b++) {
      Panel s = new Panel ();
        s.setLayout(new BorderLayout(0,0));
        s.add ("Center",new leafPattern (this,b));
      patternButton[b] = new Button(patterns[b]);
        patternButton[b].addActionListener(this);
        s.add ("South",patternButton[b]);
      q.add (s);
    }
  add ("Center",q);
```

```
// Follow up with a message and again button
  // at the bottom of the applet.
  Panel r = new Panel();
    messageField = new TextField (30);
      r.add (messageField);
    againButton = new Button ("Again");
      r.add(againButton);
      againButton.addActionListener(this);
  add("South",r);
}

private void setUpTable() {
//==========================
    String s, item;
    StringTokenizer t;
    int code;
    s = getParameter("entries");
    int n = Integer.parseInt(s);
    for (int i = 0; i<n; i++) {
    // extract a tree name from the html
      String tree = getParameter("tree-"+(i+1));
    // read all its codes
      s = getParameter("codes-"+(i+1));
      t = new StringTokenizer (s);
    // store each code-tree pair in the table.
      while (true) {
        try {
          item = t.nextToken();
          code = Integer.parseInt(item.trim());
          table.put(new Integer(code),tree);
        }
        catch (NoSuchElementException e) {
          break;
        }
      }
    }
}

public void actionPerformed (ActionEvent e) {
//=========================================
  Object source = e.getSource();
  String name = e.getActionCommand();
    if (source == widthField) {
```

```
      w = readValue(widthField);
      gotWidth = true;
    } else if (source == lengthField) {
      l = readValue(lengthField);
      gotLength = true;
    } else if (source == againButton) {
      resetFields();
    } else if (name instanceof String) {
      c = 0;
      while (!name.equals(patterns[c])) c++;
      gotChoice = true;
      patternButton[c].setBackground(Color.green);
    }
    if (gotChoice & gotLength & gotWidth)
      findTree ();
  }

private void findTree () {
//=========================
// Calculate the three-part code
  int part2=convertLength();
  int part3=convertWidth();
  int code = 100*(c+1)+10*part2+part3;
// Fetch the tree name from the table if it exists
  String tree = (String) table.get(new Integer (code));
  if (tree == null)
    setMessage("No information on code "+code+" yet.");
  else
    fetchTree (tree);
  }

private void fetchTree (String treeName) {
//=====================================
// Try to get a web page of information on
// the tree.
  try {
   AppletContext context = getAppletContext ();
    String s = treeName+".html";
    setMessage("Looking for "+s);
    URL u = new URL (getCodeBase(),s);
    context.showDocument(u,"_self");
  }
  catch (MalformedURLException e) {
    setMessage("No information for that tree yet");
  }
```

```
   }
   // Code conversion methods
   //=========================

   private int convertLength () {
   // returns a code based on the leaf length supplied
     if (l<=25) return 4; else
     if (l<=50) return 5; else
     if (l<=100) return 6; else
     if (l<=200) return 7; else
                 return 8;
   }
   private int convertWidth () {
   // returns a code based on the leaf width supplied
     if (w<=10) return 4; else
     if (w<=20) return 5; else
     if (w<=40) return 6; else
     if (w<=80) return 7; else
                 return 8;
   }

// Utility methods
   // ===============
   private int readValue (TextField t) {
       int x = Integer.parseInt(t.getText());
       t.setEditable(false);
       t.setBackground(Color.green);
       return x;
   }

   private void clearField(TextField t) {
     t.setEditable(true);
     t.setBackground(Color.white);
     t.setText("");
   }

   private void resetFields () {
     gotChoice = false;
     patternButton[c].setBackground(Color.lightGray);
     gotWidth = false;
     clearField(widthField);
     gotLength = false;
     clearField(lengthField);
     clearField(messageField);
     messageField.setEditable(false);
   }
```

```
   private void setMessage(String s) {
     messageField.setText(s);
     messageField.setBackground(Color.green);
   }

   class leafPattern extends Canvas {
   //===============================
     Image im;

     leafPattern(Applet a, int b) {
       weAre = a;
   // Construct the URL name
       pattern = "leaf"+Integer.toString(b)+".jpg";
   // Get the image
       im = weAre.getImage(weAre.getCodeBase(),pattern);
   // Ensure that the image has been received before
   // the constructor returns.
       MediaTracker tracker = new MediaTracker(weAre);
       tracker.addImage(im, 0);
       try { tracker.waitForID(0);}
       catch (InterruptedException e) {}
     }

     public void paint (Graphics g) {
       g.drawImage(im,0,0,this);
     }

     private Applet weAre;
     private String pattern;
   }
 }
```

Testing   The applet's output is shown again in Figure 12.10. Look at the HTML if you want to be sure of hitting trees. The figure shows the results of the correct values for the baobab tree.

Legal considerations   While writing applets that pull in images seems a great idea, there is a serious consideration: other people's pictures are usually copyrighted. The implication is that we cannot use them freely in our own web pages, even in experimental ones. We must use our own pictures, ones that we own. For this reason, the photographs in Chapter 1 were taken by myself, and the diagrams drawn especially for this book.

   The infrastructure provided by Java's multimedia facilities is so powerful and easy to use that one tends to forget that the content required to fill an applet or web page also has to be created. Look out for shareware images and, when in doubt, ask permission from the author, artist, originator or publisher.

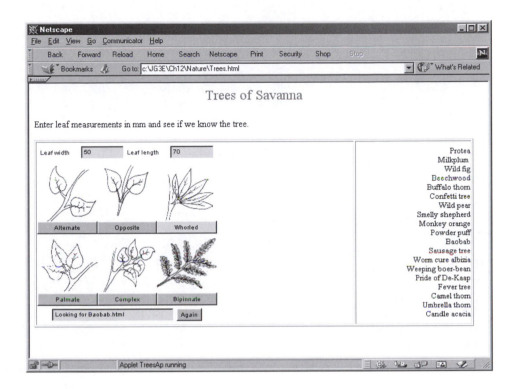

Figure 12.10 *The Trees applet running under Netscape.*

SUMMARY

Applets are similar to applications, but because they run within the context of the `Applet` class and a browser or viewer, they do not need a main method, and all input–output must be through the awt. An applet must have an accompanying HTML file which calls it. This HTML file can be supplied to an applet viewer or to a browser, or can be called from within a web page. Applets run in browsers stop only when the page they are in is discarded. Applets can get data from a web page through the `PARAM` facility. Java provides a considerable amount of security surrounding applets so that they cannot cause damage after coming over the network.

Applets, as well as applications, can make use of sound and images. Both can be simply set up in Java using objects to connect to au and GIF or JPEG files respectively. The images can be made to move on the screen by repainting the screen with new coordinates. Watching and waiting for images to be loaded requires additional programming.

There are no new keywords in this chapter, but the following new API classes and methods are introduced:

```
java.applet.*                    MediaTracker
Applet                               addImage
    init                             waitforID
    destroy                      Observer
    start                        InterruptedException
    stop                         MouseEvent
    getCodeBase                  MouseListener
    getAppletContext                 mousePressed
getParameter                         mouseMove
Image                                mouseDown
    getImage                     MouseAdapter
    drawImage
```

There were seven new forms:

HTML tags for an Applet
Applet methods
HTML parameter
JAR tool command
AudioClip declaration and play
Display an image
Media tracker

QUIZ

12.1 Which of the following best describes what an applet is?

  (a) a program stored on the local hard-drive, run from the command prompt
  (b) a program stored on a remote system that is transferred to the local system and run within a web browser
  (c) a program stored remotely that is executed remotely, with the results transferred to the local system and displayed in the web browser
  (d) a program stored remotely that is executed remotely, with the results transferred to the local system and displayed in the Java console window or command prompt window

12.2 What does interpretation mean, in the sense of a Java program?

  (a) the compiler decides what your code is supposed to mean, then creates an executable file, using a translating dictionary, that will run the program
  (b) the compiler generates byte-code as an intermediate step, which is then stored on the hard-drive as an executable file
  (c) the compiler generates byte-code from your source-code and stores this byte-code in a binary form in a class file. When you run the program, a module called the Java Virtual Machine reads the byte-code and converts it into machine-code, which is then executed in the normal fashion. This ensures that the program can be run anywhere
  (d) the compiler will read any strings you have within your code and translate them into all the languages of the world, so that your program can be run anywhere

12.3   What are the advantages of having applets in web pages?

(a)   less network traffic, faster code execution due to local execution, and having access to the full facilities of Java
(b)   more hits to your web page
(c)   answer (a), as well as enhanced security
(d)   giving a remote programmer access to the user's machine

12.4   An applet stops executing when

(a) a new web page is loaded into the browser
(b) the user clicks on the applet's Close button
(c) a call is made to `System.exit()`
(d) when the user scrolls beyond the applet

12.5   The default layout for an applet is

(a)   `GridLayout`
(b)   `BoxLayout`
(c)   `BorderLayout`
(d)   `FlowLayout`

12.6   HTML stands for …

(a)   Hyperspace Marketing for Mobile Links
(b)   Hypertext Mark-up Language
(c)   How To Make Links
(d)   Hyperlinks, Tables, Movies and Lists

12.7   What is most novel about Java's approach to applets?

(a)   all the books needed to describe it
(b)   doing all the work on the host site
(c)   making more money from web surfers
(d)   genetic engineering to make things smaller

12.8   If an applet includes lines to print to a console (`System.out.println()`), where can the output be found?

(a)   the printer
(b)   the command prompt window
(c)   it does not get displayed anywhere
(d)   in the browser's Java console window

12.9   Which of the following best describes what privileges an applet has that is stored on a remote machine and loaded in a browser?

(a)   connecting back to the host and creating a pop-up window
(b)   accessing local files, running another program, calling exit and creating a pop-up window
(c)   finding out the local machine's name and passwords, formatting the hard-drive and loading a Java library
(d)   no privileges

12.10   What are observers, in a Java applet's context?

(a)   objects in Java that keep track of how much of an image is loaded, allowing the applet to continue execution

(b) objects in Java that keep track of how much of an image is loaded, pausing the applet's execution until the image is fully loaded and displayable
(c) Java methods which can be called to handle remote events
(d) Java methods on the applet's remote machine which are automatically called when a corresponding local listener is called

12.1 **Your trees.** The Nature Project is in its infancy and still needs to be considerably extended to fulfil its mandate of allowing visitors to the site the ability to add new specimens that they identify. If you watch the *Java Gently* web site, you may see new versions of the system as they become available. One improvement you could make on your own is to change the list of trees to reflect your own environment. You should be able to do this by altering only the HTML.

12.2 **Till user's guide.** How to use the till applet is not really intuitive. Set up an HTML page that has some instructions on the left and includes the till applet on the right.

12.3 **Savanna News banner.** If you have a scanner, scan in the masthead from your local newspaper and embed it in an HTML page which surrounds the competition applet. Otherwise create a big heading with a new and interesting font. Include the rules in small print below the competition.

12.4 **Lots of dukes.** Add more dukes to the catching applet. Have each move at a different rate.

12.5 **Letter value update.** Create a separate applet with a password that can be selected by a menu or button from the Competition HTML page and will enable one of the newspaper employees to change the letter values interactively.

12.6 **Nelson's applet.** Referring to Problem 11.5, put the GUI version of Nelson's Coffee Shop in an applet and HTML document.

12.7 **Interactive exchange rates.** Following on from Case Study 7, create an applet to interface to the Bureau de Change.

12.8 **Changing prices.** The prices for fruit and vegetables change often. In the place where the Close button used to be on the Till program, add a button called Reset which will bring up a new window, listing the products and their current prices, and allow the user to type in new prices for any product that changes. The price change should be effective immediately after the window has been closed. Put password protection on the use of this window.

12.9 **Pets lost and found.** Based on the pet tag system devised for the Savanna Veterinary Association (Case Study 4 in Chapter 9), the *Savanna News* wants to set up an online version of its popular Lost and Found column. The idea is that owners who have lost pets will enter details and also a photograph. Those who have found pets can type in tag details as usual and get back the other data. Design and implement such a system using applets and web pages. Images of pets are available for use on *Java Gently*'s web page under Other Material.

12.10 **Cellphone applet.** Convert the cellphone GUI that you developed in Problem 10.3 into an applet. Add event handlers so that typing the keys produces a message on the Java console window. In Chapter 14 we shall see how to make one cellphone communicate with another one.

CHAPTER 13

Multithreading

13.1 Introduction to multithreading

In operating system terms, a program that is running is known as a **process**. An operating system can be running several processes for different users at any one time. Not all of these need be active: they could be awaiting their share of processor time, or they could be waiting for some information, such as user input.

Now within a single process, the same division into separately runnable subprocesses can be made. In Java these are known as **threads** and a program with threads is called **multithreaded**. Each thread looks like it is running on its own. It can communicate with other threads in the same process, though care must be taken when this is done through changing the value of shared variables.

In the same way that the operating system shares time between processes, so it must share time among threads. The fairest way to share is to give each thread a time slice, at the end of which it is suspended and the next thread that is ready to run is given a chance. A less attractive method is for a thread to run until it needs information from elsewhere (another thread, or the user, say), and only then to relinquish control of the processor. The problem with this approach is that a single thread can hog the processor. Most systems are now using the first approach.

Why threads?

Why do we actually need threads? Two particular situations illustrate their value:

1. **User interfacing.** If an applet or graphics application is busy drawing or displaying text, the user may wish to stop this activity. If a Cancel button is provided, we can press the button, but the program will only detect the button press once it has reached a passive state: that is, it has finished computing or outputting and is waiting for events. However, if the button is being handled by a separate thread, the opportunity to react will come around regularly, even while the other computation is proceeding. Figure 13.1 illustrates the time-line associated with two such threads.

2. **Many instances.** Sometimes one wants identical copies of a picture, of multiple windows or of different versions of a computation to be available simultaneously. For example, the set of traffic lights of Example 10.4 could be duplicated and we could watch two or three sets working at once. Each would be handled by a separate thread. In the simple case, the threads will be straight copies of each other and will run independently. Java also allows the threads to communicate and synchronize their activities, as discussed in Section 13.3.

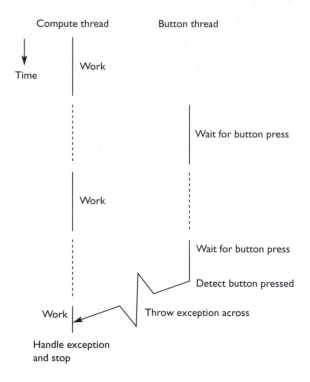

Figure 13.1 *Multithreading for a user interface.*

From the user's point of view, the presence of multiple threads should be transparent. From the programmer's side, though, work has to be done to set up the threads in the first place, to keep them running and to detect when they should finish. During the lifetime of a process, threads can be created and destroyed at will. They are a cost-effective way of handling processor power and memory for non-trivial programs.

13.2 Setting up threads

To 'thread' a program, we first have to identify those methods that can run independently. Usually, these are already in a class and it is the class that becomes a thread, possibly in multiple instantiations.

Thread is a class in the java.lang package, which means that it is always available and no special import is needed. Any class that wishes to be a thread class, must inherit from Thread. In addition, Thread implements the Runnable interface, which has one method, run. Therefore the prospective thread class must implement run as well. Basically, we take the executable part of the class and put it in a run method (allowing run of course to call other methods to assist it as usual).

The main method is by default a thread, and it is from there, or from another active method such as Applet's init, that the other threads are set in motion. As we shall see in later examples, threads can spawn their own threads as well. Let us first consider a simple thread example, then go back to the theory again.

EXAMPLE 13.1   Drawing spots

Problem   Illustrate how threads operate.

Solution   We shall choose a simple example of drawing coloured spots on a applet frame. There will be three threads running together, each drawing spots of different colours.

Program   The program is written as an applet, in which the init method instantiates three threads and starts them up. These threads are of the inner class called Spots, which inherits from Thread. Each of the Spots threads records its colour, then goes into its run loop. The loop calls the draw method to paint one spot and then waits a while (sleeps) and paints another spot.

```
import java.awt.*;
import java.applet.*;
import java.awt.event.*;

public class SpotTest extends Applet {
```

```
/* SpotTest                    J M Bishop Aug 2000
 * ========
 *
 * Draws spots of different colours
 *
 * Illustrates simple threads
 */

  int mx, my;
  int radius = 10;
  int boardSize = 200;
  int change;

  public void init() {
    boardSize = getSize().width - 1;
    change = boardSize-radius;

    // creates and starts three threads
    new Spots(Color.red).start();
    new Spots(Color.blue).start();
    new Spots(Color.green).start();
  }


class Spots extends Thread {

  Color colour;
  // the constructor records the thread's colour
  Spots(Color c) {
    colour = c;
  }

  // a very simple run method
  public void run () {
    while (true) {
      draw();
      try {
        sleep (500); // millisecs
      }
      catch (InterruptedException e) {
      }
    }
  }

public void draw() {
```

```
    Graphics g = getGraphics();
    g.setColor(colour);
    // calculate a new place for a spot
    // and draw it.
    mx = (int)(Math.random()*1000) % change;
    my = (int)(Math.random()*1000) % change;
    g.fillOval(mx, my, radius, radius);
  }
}
}
```

Testing If we run the program, we will notice that the spots do indeed appear seemingly at the same time (Figure 13.2). We say 'seemingly', because although the threads are running together, they are actually sharing a processor. It is just that they can share it faster than we can notice.

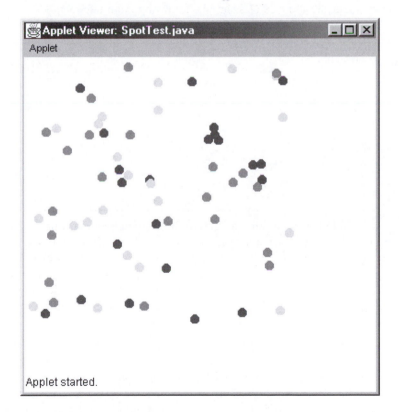

Figure 13.2 *Output from the* SpotTest *applet.*

The `Thread` class

After the above informal introduction to threads, let us consider the `Thread` class more specifically. Creating a thread can be done in two ways:

Thread creation

```
Threadclass threadid = new Threadclass (parameters);
new Threadclass (parameters)
```

In the first form, a thread object is created with the identifier
    `threadid`.
In the second form, the object is created without an identifier.

Among many others, the `Thread` class has the following important methods:

Thread methods

```
instance methods
----------------
start ();
run ();
class methods
-------------
sleep (milliseconds);
yield ();
```

`start` is called from an already active thread (such as main or an applet's `init` method) and calls `run`. This tells the JVM that this thread is ready to run and it will be called when the processor is free.
The thread itself can call `sleep` or `yield` when it has done some work. `sleep` actively suspends the thread for the specified milliseconds, while `yield` will give another thread a chance if one is waiting to run.

A new thread is created in the same way as any other object declaration, as shown in the first form. Alternatively, if there is no need to give the thread a name that its parent knows, we can use the second form, which simply creates a thread of the given class. Threads are dynamically created in Java: we do not need to state in advance how many of a certain kind of thread there will be. Every time a new thread declaration is executed, a new thread object comes into existence.

start, run and sleep are the three important thread methods. After a thread has been created via its constructor, the creating method calls start, which is defined in the Thread class. start will cause run to be called, thus causing the thread to join the operating system's list of threads waiting to run. In a while, it will get its chance for the processor and start executing independently.

run will usually consist of a loop that continues until some condition is met, in which case the loop ends. At this point the run method meets a natural end and the thread dies as a result.

sleep and yield are class methods. Both cause the thread to relinquish the processor. sleep will wait for the specified time, and then the thread will be ready to run again. yield is not needed if the operating system is sharing time among processors, but if it is not, then calling yield is a way for a thread to stand back and give others a chance.

Java also supports priorities for threads. These can be set as a value between 1 (low) and 10 (high) and direct the operating system as to which thread to run next, if there is a choice. Higher priority threads that are waiting to run will always go first.

Converting to threads

Let us consider an example of changing a program to have threads. Take Example 11.2, the traffic light calibration. We would like the lights to rotate through their assigned sequence of red–yellow–green, while the buttons and other choices at the bottom of the screen are still active. In the original program, the constructor sets up the headings and buttons, and then creates a canvas that has a paint method to draw the lights.

First we need to turn LightsCanvas into a thread. In other words, it must

- extend Thread, and

- have a run method which repeatedly executes.

But a class can inherit from only one other class, so we have to adopt the following strategy:

1. Let LightsCanvas extend Thread.

2. Pass an instance of the canvas to a new LightsCanvas constructor.

3. Store the reference to the canvas instance in the thread locally.

4. Call getGraphics to establish the canvas in the window with which the thread is dealing.

The paint method as it exists above is called automatically via the awt. Since we are now going to have independent drawing going on in a single window, we had better have it more under control. In other words, the run method should explicitly cause the drawing to be done.

The simplest run method, as shown in Example 13.2, is given the following form:

The `run` method of a thread

```
public void run () {
  while (!ended) {
    draw (); // or some other statements
    try {
       sleep (500);
    }
    catch (InterruptedException e) {}
  }
}
```

The `run` method is called when the thread starts.

The boolean variable `ended` can be set by some other thread or a main
  program to cause the thread to terminate.

In each iteration of the `run` method, some statements are executed (e.g.
  draw) and then the thread passes control back to the JVM by sleeping. Other threads then have a chance to execute.

The thread may be woken up to run again through the `Interrupted-
  Exception`.

Here we repeatedly draw the picture, waiting at least 500 milliseconds before doing it
again. The `InterruptedException` can be thrown by the system to start the thread up
if its turn has come round in the meantime.

Putting it all together, the new version of the `LightsCanvas`, with a new name, is:

```
class SetOfLights extends Thread {

  SetOfLights (Canvas c) {
    area = c;
  }

  public void run () {
    while (true) {
      draw ();
      try {sleep (500);} catch (InterruptedException e) {}
    }
  }

  void draw ( ) {
    Graphics g = area.getGraphics();
    ... the contents of paint as before
    }
  }
private Canvas area;
```

To create the thread and set it running, we call its constructor and then call `start`:

```
SetOfLights lights = new SetOfLights (area);
lights.start();
```

To stop a thread, we must make it end gracefully. The best way is to have a boolean variable, which is checked in the while-statement of the run method. When a signal comes from the user that the program must end, that boolean will be set to false, and the thread can exit its while-loop and terminate.

In Example 13.2, the complete program for the new Traffic System is shown.

EXAMPLE 13.2   Traffic lights flashing

Problem   The static representation of the lights in Example 11.2 needs to be improved to show the lights actually flashing. Furthermore, we would like to have more than one set of lights operational at any one time, so that we can compare changes.

Solution   Implementing the flashing is a question of awt graphics programming. Displaying several lights can be done with threads. We create a new class for the lights as discussed above, have it extend `Thread`, and repeatedly draw the full set of lights when a New Set button is pressed. The time specified for the sleep will then represent the time that one of the lights is on and the others off. Using a switch statement, we can implement the required green–yellow–red sequence.

Class design   Because we are using threads, the relationship between the classes in awt and those we define is slightly altered. The new model diagram (refer back to Figure 11.4) is shown in Figure 13.3. It excludes some of the buttons and other components that are not necessary for this example.

The differences are those that we have already explained. `SetOfLights` inherits `Thread`, and so cannot also inherit `Canvas` as well. Instead, the canvas, called `area`, is passed as a parameter from `Traffic2`'s `actionPerformed` method to `SetofLights`' constructor. The lights objects are shown as being created inside the `actionPerformed` because this is where they are instantiated, on request from a New Set button. The reference to this canvas is used by the `draw` method to access the methods in the `Graphics` class successfully.

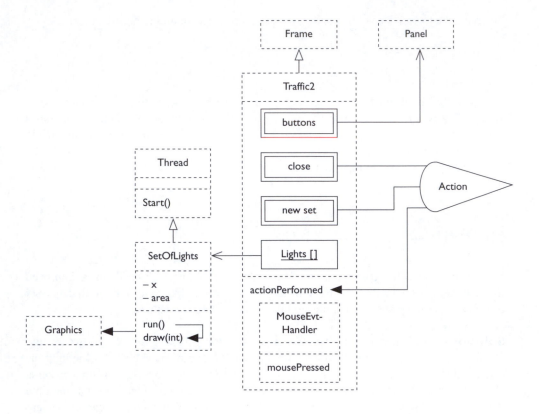

Figure 13.3 *Model diagram for the traffic lights flashing.*

Program The `SetofLights` class is as follows:

```
class SetOfLights extends Thread {

    private int red = 0;
    private Canvas area;
    private int x;
    private boolean alive = true;

    public SetOfLights(Canvas c, int x) {
        area = c;
        this.x = x;
    }
    public void run() {
        while (alive) {
            for (int light = 0; light < 3; light++) {
                draw(light);
```

```
        try { sleep(500);}
        catch (InterruptedException e) { }
      }
    }
  }

  void draw(int light) {
    Graphics g = area.getGraphics();
    g.setColor(Color.black);
    g.drawOval(x-8, 10, 30, 68);
    g.drawOval(x, 85, 15, 15);
    g.drawString("RED", x-90, 28);
    g.drawString("YELLOW", x-90, 48);
    g.drawString("GREEN", x-90, 68);
    g.drawString("WALK", x-90, 98);

    switch (light) {
      case 0:
        g.setColor(Color.red);
        g.fillOval(x, 15, 15, 15);
        g.setColor(Color.lightGray);
        g.fillOval(x, 35, 15, 15);
        g.fillOval(x, 55, 15, 15);
        break;
      case 1:
        g.setColor(Color.green);
        g.fillOval(x, 55, 15, 15);
        g.setColor(Color.lightGray);
        g.fillOval(x, 15, 15, 15);
        g.fillOval(x, 35, 15, 15);
        break;
      case 2:
        g.setColor(Color.yellow);
        g.fillOval(x, 35, 15, 15);
        g.setColor(Color.lightGray);
        g.fillOval(x, 15, 15, 15);
        g.fillOval(x, 55, 15, 15);
        break;
    }

    }
  }
```

The run method has its own inner loop, going through the three light phases.
Depending on which light has to be shown, the switch colours one circle with the

appropriate colour and renders the other two in grey. The program that activates these threads is:

```java
import java.awt.*;
import java.awt.event.*;

public class Traffic2 extends Frame
        implements ActionListener {

  /* The third Traffic Light program
   *                             by J M Bishop Oct 1996
   *             Java 1.1 version by T Abbott Oct 1997
   *         enhanced and revised by J M Bishop Oct 1997
   *                     updated by J M Bishop Aug 2000
   * Enables several sets of lights to
   * operate simultaneously.
   *
   * Illustrates threads and graphics.
   */

    private Canvas area;
    private int lightsPosition = 105;
    private static final int lightsWidth = 150;
    private SetOfLights[] lights = new SetOfLights[3];
    private int nLights = 0, setWanted = 0;
    private Choice colours;
    private Button newSetButton;
    private Button walkButton;
    private Button closeButton;
    private TextField duration;

    public Traffic2() {
      setTitle("Traffic Lights Version 2");
      add("North",
          new Label("Savanna Traffic Light Simulation", Label.CENTER));
      area = new Canvas();
        area.addMouseListener(new MouseEvtHandler());
        add("Center",area);

      Panel buttons = new Panel();
        newSetButton = new Button("New Set");
          newSetButton.addActionListener(this);
          buttons.add(newSetButton);
        colours = new Choice ();
          colours.addItem("Red");
```

```
        colours.addItem("Yellow");
        colours.addItem("Green");
        colours.addItem("Walk");
        buttons.add(colours);

    buttons.add(new Label("Duration"));

    duration = new TextField("", 3);
        duration.setEditable(true);
        duration.addActionListener(this);
        buttons.add(duration);

    walkButton = new Button("Walk");
        // no action yet
        buttons.add(walkButton);

    closeButton = new Button("Close");
        closeButton.addActionListener(this);
        buttons.add(closeButton);
    add("South", buttons);

    // set up the frame
    setSize(350, 210);
    setVisible(true);
    addWindowListener(new WindowAdapter () {
    public void windowClosing(WindowEvent e) {
        System.exit(0);
    }
 });


}

class MouseEvtHandler extends MouseAdapter {
  public void mousePressed(MouseEvent e) {
    int n = e.getX() / lightsWidth;
    if (n < nLights)
    setWanted = n;
    }
}

public void actionPerformed(ActionEvent e) {
  Object event = e.getSource();
  if (event == newSetButton) {
    lights[nLights] = new SetOfLights(area, lightsPosition);
    lights[nLights].start();
```

```
            lightsPosition += lightsWidth;
            nLights++;
            if (nLights == 3)
            newSetButton.setEnabled(false);
        } else if (event == closeButton) {
          for (int i = 0; i<nLights; i++)
            lights[i].alive = false;
          setVisible(false);
          dispose();
          System.exit(0);
        }
      }
    }

    public static void main(String[] args) {
      new Traffic2();
    }
  }
```

The new addition to the button panel is a New Set button. When pressed, it will start up a
new thread for another set of lights. In order to have the lights drawn across the window,
we supply a new *x* starting position, which increases by 150 pixels for each light.

Testing   Figure 13.4 shows the screen with three lights at different phases.

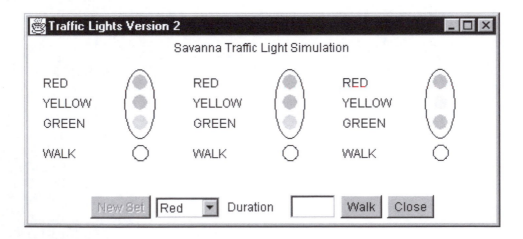

Figure 13.4   *The traffic lights flashing.*

Communication among threads

The threads in the above example are quite independent. However, it is often the case that threads need to pass information between each other – results of subcalculations, or signals to change to another mode of working, for example. Because threads are objects, such communication can use the normal object techniques, such as calling methods or updating non-private variables. On the face of it, there would seem to be no problem in threads communicating in either of these ways. However, conflicts can occur that would cause the program as a whole to give incorrect results. This is the subject of Section 13.4. Meanwhile, we can proceed with the traffic example, and show how simple, non-conflicting communication can be handled.

EXAMPLE 13.3   Traffic lights for walking

Problem   Right at the beginning of the traffic light simulation (Example 10.5) we mentioned the objective of examining the effect of pedestrians pressing the Walk button. The Walk button is present in the control panel of the simulation as it stands. We would now like it to cause the walk light to flash as soon as a red light phase comes around again. Furthermore, we would like to reactivate the choice box and duration field, and pass this information to the flashing lights so that the simulation can become realistic.

Algorithm changes   The first consideration is whether one leaves a single Walk button for all sets of lights on the screen, or whether we alter the screen to have a Walk button under each set. The latter seems more reasonable, but is more difficult to implement because we are using a very simple border layout to keep the lights in the centre panel and the buttons in the south. Therefore we elect to keep the one button, but we select the set of lights we want affected by clicking somewhere in that general area. A mouse listener with a `mousePressed` event is of assistance here.

The second point is what do we actually do once the Walk button is pressed? Well, we must pass the information over to the particular thread running that set of lights. The thread need not react immediately, because the requirement is that it continues through its cycle until it reaches red, and then starts flashing the walk light. We can therefore achieve the communication by having a boolean variable called walk in the lights thread, and setting it to true once the Walk button is pressed.

How do we know which thread to talk to? Well, each thread will need to be recorded in the main program with a name, and the simplest way is to have an array of threads. Depending on the mouse press on the central canvas, we deduce which set of lights is intended, and can make any subsequent press of Walk refer to that thread in the array.

Previously, the lights objects were created inside `actionPerformed`, and the name, `lights`, was reused each time a new one was needed. Now, because we need to keep track of the names of the threads throughout the lifetime of the program, we declare an array of threads as private. Each new thread of the array is activated via a call to `start`.

The final change is to use the choice box and duration field to alter the time that a light stays on. The change is quite simple. Instead of sleeping for 500 ms every time, we let a light sleep for `time[light]` milliseconds. In `actionPerformed`, the values of the `time` array are altered when required.

We do not give a model diagram this time, in order to encourage the reader to understand the program by drawing one.

Program   The final simulation program removes the labels for the lights and replaces them with the current duration.

```
import java.awt.*;
import java.awt.event.*;

public class Traffic3 extends Frame
       implements ActionListener, ItemListener {

  /* The fourth Traffic Light program
   *                                         by J M Bishop Oct 1996
   *                           Java 1.1 version by T Abbott Oct 1997
   *                    enhanced and revised by J M Bishop Oct 1997
   *                                     improved J M Bishop Aug 2000
   * Enables the different lengths of lights
   * entered as durations to be used in
   * practice.
   */

  private Canvas area;
  private int lightsPosition = 105;
  private static final int lightsWidth = 150;
  private SetOfLights[] lights = new SetOfLights[3];
  private int nLights = 0, setWanted = 0;
  private TextField duration;
  private Choice colours;
  private int light;
  private Button newSetButton;
  private Button walkButton;
  private Button closeButton;

  public Traffic3() {
    setTitle("Traffic Lights Version 3");

    add("North",new Label
       ("Savanna Traffic Light Simulation",Label.CENTER));

    area = new Canvas();
    area.addMouseListener(new MouseEvtHandler());
    add("Center",area);
```

```
Panel buttons = new Panel();
  newSetButton = new Button("New Set");
    newSetButton.addActionListener(this);
    buttons.add(newSetButton);
  colours = new Choice ();
    colours.addItem("Red");
    colours.addItem("Green");
    colours.addItem("Yellow");
    colours.addItem("Walk");
    colours.addItemListener(this);
    light = 0;
    buttons.add(colours);

  buttons.add(new Label("Duration"));

  duration = new TextField("", 4);
    duration.addActionListener(this);
    buttons.add(duration);
  walkButton = new Button("Walk");
    walkButton.addActionListener(this);
    buttons.add(walkButton);
  closeButton = new Button("Close");
    closeButton.addActionListener(this);
    buttons.add(closeButton);
  add("South",buttons);

// Set up the frame
    setSize(450, 210);
    setVisible(true);
    addWindowListener(new WindowAdapter () {
    public void windowClosing(WindowEvent e) {
      System.exit(0);
    }
  });

}

public void itemStateChanged(ItemEvent e) {
    String s = (String) e.getItem();
    if (s=="Red") {light = 0;} else
    if (s=="Green") {light = 1;} else
    if (s=="Yellow") {light = 2;} else
    if (s=="Walk") {light = 3;}
}
class MouseEvtHandler extends MouseAdapter {
  public void mousePressed(MouseEvent e) {
```

```
        int n = e.getX() / lightsWidth;
        if (n < nLights)
        setWanted = n;
      }
    }

    public void actionPerformed(ActionEvent e) {
      Object event = e.getSource();
      if (event == newSetButton) {
        lights[nLights] = new SetOfLights(area, lightsPosition);
        lights[nLights].start();
        lightsPosition += lightsWidth;
        nLights++;
        if (nLights == 3)
        newSetButton.setEnabled(false);
      } else if (event == walkButton) {
        lights[setWanted].walk = true;
      } else if (event == duration) {
        lights[setWanted].time[light]=
          Integer.parseInt(duration.getText());
      } else if (event == closeButton) {
        for (int i = 0; i<nLights; i++)
          lights[i].alive = false;
        setVisible(false);
        dispose();
        System.exit(0);
      }
    }

    public static void main(String[] args) {
      new Traffic3();
    }
  }
```

The reaction to the Walk button is to set the `walk` variable in the correct thread to true. The desired thread has been preselected by clicking the mouse somewhere on the screen and dividing by the width of a full set of lights, which we have set at 150 pixels.

The logic associated with the lights proceeds as follows. Each time the red light is about to come on, we need to check if the `walk` variable is set. If so, we go into a separate loop for 10 cycles which keeps the red light on, and alternates the walk light between green and grey. The `run` method is shown in the full class here:

```
import java.awt.*;
class SetOfLights extends Thread {
```

```
private int red = 0;
private Canvas area;
private int x;
private int light;
private boolean alive = true;

// public variables
boolean walk = false;
boolean walkOn = false;
int time [] = {500, 500, 500, 500};

public SetOfLights(Canvas c, int x) {
  area = c;
  this.x = x;
}

public void run() {
  while (alive) {
    for (int light = 0; light < 3; light++) {
      if (light == red & walk) {
        walkOn = false;
        for (int i = 0; i < 11; i++) {
          draw(light);
          try { sleep(time[3]);}
          catch (InterruptedException e) { }
          walkOn = !walkOn;
          }
        walk = false;
      } else {
        draw(light);
        try { sleep(time[light]); }
        catch (InterruptedException e) { }
      }
    }
  }
}

void draw(int light) {
  Graphics g = area.getGraphics();
  g.setColor(Color.black);
  g.drawOval(x-8, 10, 30, 68);
  g.setColor(Color.cyan);
  g.fillRect(x-90,10,70,100);
  g.setColor(Color.black);
  g.drawString(""+time[0], x-70, 28);
```

```
    g.drawString(""+time[2], x-70, 48);
    g.drawString(""+time[1], x-70, 68);
    g.drawString(""+time[3], x-70, 98);

    switch (light) {
      case 0:
        g.setColor(Color.red);
        g.fillOval(x, 15, 15, 15);
        g.setColor(Color.lightGray);
        g.fillOval(x, 35, 15, 15);
        g.fillOval(x, 55, 15, 15);
        break;
      case 1:
        g.setColor(Color.green);
        g.fillOval(x, 55, 15, 15);
        g.setColor(Color.lightGray);
        g.fillOval(x, 15, 15, 15);
        g.fillOval(x, 35, 15, 15);
        break;
      case 2:
        g.setColor(Color.yellow);
        g.fillOval(x, 35, 15, 15);
        g.setColor(Color.lightGray);
        g.fillOval(x, 15, 15, 15);
        g.fillOval(x, 55, 15, 15);
        break;
    }

    if (light == red & walk) {
      if (walkOn)
      g.setColor(Color.green);
    else
      g.setColor(Color.white);
      g.fillOval(x+1, 85, 14, 14);
    } else {
      g.setColor(Color.black);
      g.drawOval(x, 85, 15, 15);
    }
  }
}
```

The walkOn variable is set and unset to control the flashing of the walk light. After ten iterations, walk is reset and the set of lights can proceed to the next normal phase, which would be green. The appropriate change is at the end of the draw method.

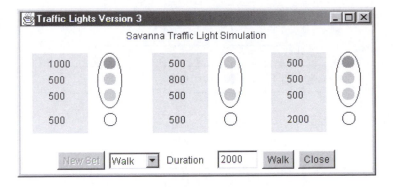

Figure 13.5 *The final traffic light simulation, with variable light duration.*

Testing The program can be run as before, and the Walk button can be pressed for each of the sets of lights at different times, as shown in Figure 13.5. Various durations have been entered, and the simulation is now actually quite useful.

13.3 Synchronization among threads

In the above example, the main program communicated with each thread individually. In other words, we had channels of communication as shown in Figure 13.6. There was no possibility that `Traffic` calling `lights[0]` could interfere with the communication between `Traffic` and `lights[1]`, say. However, suppose for the sake of illustration that the lights threads have each to alter the same variable in `Traffic` (for example, a count of the number of times yellow lights come on). The calling diagram would be as shown in Figure 13.7.

Now there is a chance that the threads could interfere with each other's operation, leading to corrupted values. The corruption could happen like this. Thread 1 starts to increment a variable with value 52 to 53, say. It gets halfway through before it is interrupted by the operating system and Thread 2 is given the processor. Thread 2 reads the current value of the variable, which is still 52, updates it to 53 and continues. Control is eventually passed back to Thread 1 which is still in the middle of the update. It has already read the variable's value as 52 and so writes 53 back. The correct answer would have been 54 (after two updates), but the interference meant that Thread 1 overwrote the update made by Thread 2.

To avoid such a possibility, Java provides means for threads to synchronize their activities. There are two levels of synchronization provided:

- protection of shared resources;

- signalling changes in conditions between threads.

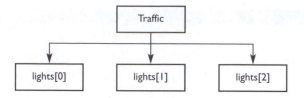

Figure 13.6 *Threads that cannot interfere with each other.*

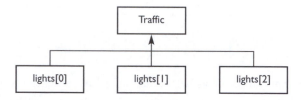

Figure 13.7 *Threads that could possibly interfere which each other.*

Protecting shared resources

In order to protect resources such as variables that could be accessed by several threads at once, we funnel updates through a method, and mark the method with a special modifier shown in the form:

Synchronized method
synchronized *modifiers methodid (parameters)*
There may not be more than one object executing this method at a time.

Java then guarantees that once a thread has gained access to a synchronized method, it will finish the method before any other thread gains access to that or any other synchronized method in that object. Such threads are placed in a queue, awaiting their turn. The thread therefore has exclusive access to the object from within the synchronized method. An object with one or more synchronized methods acts as a **monitor** on its data.[1]

In order not to delay the other threads unduly, synchronized methods should be kept to a minimum and only contain statements that are genuinely sensitive to interference.

---

[1] Monitors are a very important operating system concept invented by Per Brinch Hansen and Tony Hoare in the early 1970s.

EXAMPLE 13.4	Car parks for a viewpoint

Problem   There is a famous viewpoint in the vinelands of Savanna that has two car parks at its two access roads. We would like to keep track of how many cars enter each car park and also how many cars in total visit the viewpoint.

Solution   Create an applet that shows a picture of the view as well as counters of the number of cars in the three places. At a later date, Savanna Conservation may decide to limit the number of cars at the viewpoint, in which case the car parks will serve as buffers. We should bear this in mind when designing the system. The choice of an applet rather than application is made to show how threads interface with applets; we shall not be using the features of a browser, and the program can run in an applet viewer.

Design   There are three different counters to consider. The main one, that of the viewpoint, 'belongs' to the applet itself. The other two are to operate independently and therefore reside in two separate additional threads. However the threads are identical in every respect except name (West and East car parks), so we define one thread class and instantiate it twice.

Algorithm   The main algorithm is the running of the car parks. Entering the viewpoint is done by calling a method that updates the total number of cars and displays (shows) it. Because the `enter` method can be called by two threads, potentially simultaneously, and because it updates a variable, we declare it as synchronized, thereby ensuring that the variable does not get corrupted.

Program   The program follows.

```
import java.io.*;
import java.applet.*;
import java.awt.*;
import java.util.*;


public class CarPark extends Applet {

   /* The Car-Park applet by J M Bishop January 1998
    * ==================== Java 1.2 August 2000
    *
    * Simulates a viewpoint with two car parks.
    * Reads and shows an image of the view.
    * Illustrates threads and a synchronized method.
    * Can be run simply in appletviewer.
    */


   Image im;
   ViewPoint view;
```

```
Random delay = new Random();

public void init () {

  // Get the image
    im = getImage(getCodeBase(),"reserve.jpg");
  // Ensure that the image has been received before
  // the constructor returns.
    MediaTracker tracker = new MediaTracker(this);
    tracker.addImage(im, 0);
    try { tracker.waitForID(0);}
    catch (InterruptedException e) {}
    Font f = new Font ("SanSerif",Font.PLAIN,24);
    setFont(f);

    view = new ViewPoint("View",150);
    new CarThread("West",0).start();
    new CarThread("East",300).start();
}

class CarThread extends Thread {
//---------------------------

  int cars;
  int x;
  String pos;

  CarThread (String s,int n) {
    pos = s;
    x = n;
  }

  public void run () {
    while (true) {
      cars++;
      show(x,cars,pos);
      view.enter();
      try {sleep (factor(x));}
      catch (InterruptedException e) {}
    }
  }
}

class ViewPoint {
//-------------
```

```
    int x;
    int cars;
    String pos;

    ViewPoint (String s,int n) {
      x = n;
      pos = s;
    }

    synchronized void enter () {
      cars++;
      show (x,cars,pos);
    }
  }

// Utilities
// ---------
  public void paint (Graphics g) {
    g.drawImage(im,0,0,this);
  }

  void show(int x, int cars, String s) {
    Graphics g = getGraphics();
    g.setColor(Color.orange);
    g.fillRect(x,300,120,50);
    g.setColor(Color.black);
    g.drawString(s+" "+cars,x+5,330);
  }

  int factor (int x) {
    return Math.abs(delay.nextInt()%5000+x);
  }

}
```

Should `show` also be synchronized? No, `show` is a passive method, merely taking parameters and displaying them. The rectangles are on different parts of the screen so no conflict is possible. Suppose `show` also had statements to `print` values. Would the output lines become entangled? Fortunately not, because print and all similar methods in the `PrintWriter` class are declared as `synchronized`. Therefore only one method can be using them to affect the `System.out` object at any time.

Testing   Figure 13.8 shows the output from the program, running under an applet viewer. The HTML contains only the applet tag, as the image is drawn by the applet, not by the HTML.

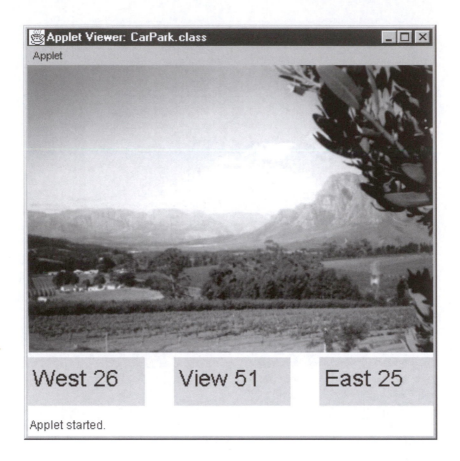

Figure 13.8 *The car parks for the view site showing the counters.*

Signalling between threads

Protecting shared resources is one aspect of synchronization. The other is indicating to a thread when a condition that it is waiting for has been met. The methods involved are shown in the form overleaf.

If a thread finds that it cannot continue because the object it is busy with is not quite in the right state, it calls `wait` from within a synchronized method belonging to that object. The thread will then be placed on a queue associated with the object.

A thread that has altered some relevant data or conditions in an object should call `notify` or `notifyAll`. This will give the waiting threads a chance to recheck their conditions for getting on the queue. Some of them may then be able to run at the next opportunity provided by the operating system.

Synchronization methods

`wait ();`
`notify ();`
`notifyAll();`

`wait` suspends the current thread, adding it to a queue of threads waiting to run on the object. `notify` wakes up the first thread on the queue which is waiting to run on this object. `notifyAll` wakes up all the threads on the queue.

In theory, threads that are waiting should eventually be notified that they can run. In practice, this depends on careful programming, considering all possible combinations. It is quite possible to construct a program where a certain condition does not get set and we find thread one waiting for thread two which is waiting for thread one. This situation is called **deadlock** and means of detecting and preventing it are covered in courses on operating systems and concurrency. Java can detect some logical errors, particularly if `wait` and `notify` are used with unsynchronized methods. In this case an `IllegalMonitorStateException` will be thrown.

The next, rather extensive, example shows how threads of different kinds can be started up at runtime and synchronized to achieve a common goal.

13.4 Inside the `Display` class

The `Display` class has been a mainstay of our programming development throughout this book. Now at last we are going to look inside it. Although it does not have any extra threads, it does use thread methods to set up a small monitor which watches over the Ready button. Let us first look at the structure of the class, then at this and other interesting techniques used inside `Display`.

The structure of the `Display` class

The `Display` class, at 220 lines, is really a very modest utility. It consists of the eight public methods (with some extras through overloading), only three private methods, and two supporting classes. The private methods and their functions are:

- `initializeDisplay` – handles all the GUI initialization of the window, setting up a scroll pane for input and a text area for output, as well as the Ready and Close buttons;

- `getEntry` – performs the work common to the three public get methods;

- `insertPrompt` – does the same for the three overloaded public prompt methods.

The table of input values

The values that are input via the display are maintained by it in a hash table, as shown in Figure 6.16. The table has an interesting structure. The key is a string, as we have seen, and could be something quite long, such as 'Pet tag name'. The values are objects of the following class:

```
private class Data {
  TextField field;
  String value;
}
```

As soon as a new input field is requested via a prompt, a field is created and added to the input section. The reference to this field forms part of the entry in the table. The other part is the value that is supplied to the `prompt` method. Notice that we retain the value as a string. This makes rewriting it in the text field more accurate from the user's point of view. If we had stored numbers, we would have been faced with the need to decide on a format for them, which may not be what the user had in mind, and could never have been general enough.

The `getEntry` method is interesting. It is used by `getInt`, `getDouble` and `getString` to check whether the label supplied is valid, and to get a copy of the current data from the table. The method with one of the `get`s is:

```
private Data getEntry (String s) {
  if (table.containsKey(s))
    return (Data) table.get(s);
  else {
    outDisplay.append("\nERROR: No such input label: "+s+"\n");
    return null;
  }
}

public int getInt (String s) {
  Data d = getEntry(s);
  return Integer.valueOf(d.value).intValue();
}
```

Notice that the error message is sent to the output section, which is a fairly user-friendly thing to do.

When does the table get updated? Firstly, we will have noticed that it is not necessary to press return after making changes in a data field. However, pressing the Ready bar acts as a general 'return' and it is in response to this event that the input section is scanned. The `ready` method includes the following loop:

```
// copy all the values from the boxes to the table
   for (Enumeration e = table.keys(); e.hasMoreElements();) {
     String name = (String) e.nextElement();
     Data d = (Data) table.get(name);
     d.value = d.field.getText();
     table.put(name, d);
   }
```

Having stored the reference to each text field in the table, we can very easily pick off the values from the GUI.

The ready watcher

One of the most interesting parts of the `Display` class is its `Watcher` class. The logic behind the watcher is this. When the program reaches a `ready` call, it transfers control to the `Display` class, which gets ready to read the values from the input section. However, the `Display` class must wait until such time as the user physically presses the bar. In other words, we have to synchronize with the `actionPerformed` method which responds to the bar being pressed.

The synchronization is performed in a monitor which has the form:

```
class Watcher {

  private boolean ok;

  Watcher () {
    ok = false;
  }

  synchronized void watch () { // called by ready
    while (!ok) {
      try {wait(500); }
      catch(InterruptedException e) {}
    }
    ok = false;
  }

  synchronized void ready () { // called by actionPerformed
    ok = true;
    notify();
  }
}
```

The watch method uses a thread wait to continuously go round and consider whether the boolean ok has been set or not. As soon as the bar is pressed and the event picked up by actionPerformed, the ready method is called which sets ok and notifies anyone waiting in this monitor. watch comes round, re-evaluates ok and is then able to continue.

The full listing of Display follows:

```
package javagently;

import java.awt.*;
import java.awt.event.*;
import java.util.*;
import java.io.*;

public class Display extends Frame implements ActionListener {

  /* Display by J M Bishop July 1999
     *******
   * is a simple class that provides facilities for
   * input and output on a window.
   * The data values are entered in boxes in the input section.
   * Different data choices can be entered if the
   * driving program asks for them.
   * There is an optional integration with the Graph class

   * Interface
   * =========
   * new Display (title)   - sets up a new Display object with a title
   * println (string)      - prints a string in the output section
   * prompt (label, value) - sets a box in the input section with the
                             given label
   * ready (message)       - prints a message then enables reading from
                             the boxes
   * getDouble (label)     - reads the double value that was set with
                             that label
   * getInt (label)        - gets the int value that was set with
                             that label
   * getString (label)     - reads the string value that was set with
                             that label
   * reposition (graph)    - takes a graph and places it on the bottom
                             of the input section
   */

  private String title;

  public Display (String t) {
    /* the alternative constructor -
```

```
       has a title */
    title = t;
    initializeDisplay();
}


  private Hashtable table = new Hashtable(10);
  private int xwidth, yheight;
  private Button okButton, closeButton;
  private TextArea outDisplay;
  private Panel inDisplay;
  private ScrollPane inPane, outPane;
  private Watcher okWatcher = new Watcher();
  private boolean graphInFront;
  private Graph graph;


  private void initializeDisplay () {
    xwidth = 640;
    yheight = 480;
    setSize(xwidth,yheight);
    setTitle(title);
    setLayout(new BorderLayout());
    Panel p = new Panel ();
      p.add(new Label("INPUT"));
      p.add(new Label("OUTPUT"));
    add(p,"North");
    p = new Panel (new FlowLayout(FlowLayout.CENTER,15,0));
      inPane = new ScrollPane(ScrollPane.SCROLLBARS_ALWAYS);
        inPane.setSize(xwidth/2 - 40, yheight - 100);
        inDisplay = new Panel(new GridLayout (0,2,10,10));
        inPane.add(inDisplay);
      p.add(inPane);
      outDisplay = new TextArea(24, 40);
      p.add(outDisplay);
    add(p,"Center");
    p = new Panel(new BorderLayout());
      okButton = new Button("Ready");
      okButton.addActionListener(this);
      okButton.setEnabled(false);
      p.add("Center",okButton);
    closeButton = new Button("Close");
      closeButton.addActionListener(this);
      closeButton.setEnabled(true);
      p.add("East",closeButton);
    add("South",p);
      addWindowListener (new WindowAdapter () {
      public void windowClosing(WindowEvent e) {
```

```
        System.exit (0);
      }
    });
    setVisible(true);
    graphInFront = false;
  }

public void reposition (Graph g) {
  // makes the graph smaller and puts it on the bottom
  // half of the input section
  g.setLocation (30, yheight/2-30);
  g.setSize(xwidth/2 - 40, yheight/2-15);
  graphInFront = true;
  graph = g;
}

public void actionPerformed (ActionEvent e) {
  if (e.getSource() == okButton) {
    okWatcher.ready();
  } else
  if (e.getSource() == closeButton) {
    System.exit(0);
  }
}

private class Data {
  TextField field;
  String value;
}

private Data getEntry (String s) {
  if (table.containsKey(s))
    return (Data) table.get(s);
  else {
    outDisplay.append("\nERROR: No such input label: "+s+"\n");
    return null;
  }
}
public int getInt (String s) {
  Data d = getEntry(s);
  return Integer.valueOf(d.value).intValue();
}

public double getDouble (String s) {
  Data d = getEntry(s);
  return Double.valueOf(d.value).doubleValue();
}
```

```
public String getString (String s) {
  Data d = getEntry(s);
  return d.value;
}

private void insertPrompt(Data d, String s, TextField t) {
  Panel p;
  p = new Panel(new FlowLayout(FlowLayout.RIGHT));
   p.add(new Label(s));
   inDisplay.add(p);
 t.addActionListener(this);
   t.setEditable(true);
   p = new Panel(new FlowLayout(FlowLayout.LEFT));
   p.add(t);
   inDisplay.add(p);
 d.field = t;
}

public void prompt (String s, int n) {
  Data d = new Data();
  TextField t = new TextField(10);
  insertPrompt(d, s, t);
  d.value = Text.writeInt(n,0);
  t.setText(d.value);
  table.put(s, d);
}

public void prompt (String s, double n) {
  Data d = new Data();
  TextField t = new TextField(10);
  insertPrompt(d, s, t);
  d.value = Double.toString(n);
  t.setText(d.value);
  table.put(s, d);
}

public void prompt (String s, String n) {
  Data d = new Data();
  TextField t = new TextField(n.length()+2);
  insertPrompt(d, s, t);
  d.value = n;
  t.setText(d.value);
  table.put(s, d);
}

public void ready (String s) {
  outDisplay.append(s+"\n");
  okButton.setEnabled(true);
```

```
      setVisible(true);
      if (graphInFront) graph.toFront();
      okWatcher.watch();
      // copy all the values from the boxes to the table
      for (Enumeration e = table.keys(); e.hasMoreElements();) {
        String name = (String) e.nextElement();
        Data d = (Data) table.get(name);
        d.value = d.field.getText();
        table.put(name, d);
      }
    }


   public void println (String s) {
       outDisplay.append(s+"\n");
   }


  class Watcher {

  private boolean ok;

  Watcher () {
    ok = false;
  }

  synchronized void watch () {
    while (!ok) {
      try {wait(500); }
      catch(InterruptedException e) {}
    }
    ok = false;
  }

  synchronized void ready () {
    ok = true;
    notify();
   }
  }


  }
```

13.5 Case Study 9: Walkman Hire

Savanna Museum is going to introduce a modern system of hiring out Walkman tape players that visitors can listen to instead of having guided tours of the exhibits on display. At the entrance to the museum, there is a counter where a variable number of volunteer helpers are on duty at any one time to hire out the Walkmen. The charge is one graz. Visitors arrive in groups of between 1 and 10 and wait until the correct number of Walkmen is available. We would like to simulate the system in advance, to see how many Walkmen will be needed for a given arrival rate of visitors.

Discussing the solution

How does one begin to tackle a simulation such as this? The stepping off point is to draw a diagram of the real-life set-up, and to use this to identify the objects and their interactions. Figure 13.9 gives a start.

The day begins with the museum opening with a given number of Walkmen, and then counter threads being created, one for each helper available. The museum is a monitor class with two synchronized methods: hire and replace. The counter helpers call hire, and when their request for a given number of Walkmen is satisfied, they create a new visitor thread, simulating the idea of a visitor group wandering around the museum on its own.

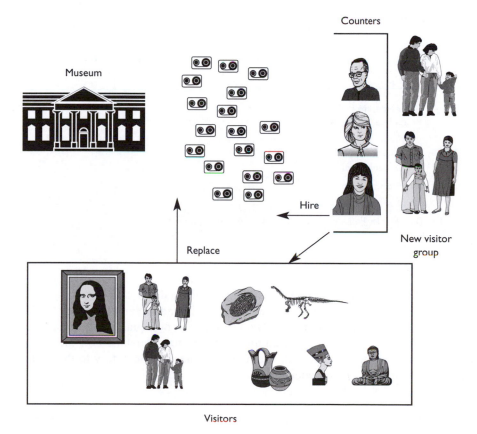

Figure 13.9 *Layout of the museum simulation.*

The visitors drop their Walkmen directly off at the museum exit, without joining counter queues again. This has the effect of replenishing the number of Walkmen for hire, and may enable a helper to satisfy a request.

For example, suppose there are only two Walkmen left. In the diagram, neither group at the counter can proceed, and must wait. Then suppose the group looking at the Mona Lisa decides to go home. They deposit their Walkmen and one or other of the groups will be satisfied, though not necessarily on a first come, first served basis. The pool will then be down to one or zero again.

Class design

This time we shall not draw a detailed model diagram, but rather indicate the interaction of the objects of the four classes at a high level. Figure 13.10 gives such a diagram. Synchronized methods may be marked with an S in the corner. `WalkmanHire` instantiates the `Museum` class. It also starts up the counters as threads. The counters start up `Visitor` threads as needed. Counters hire Walkmen from the museum object, and visitors replace them.

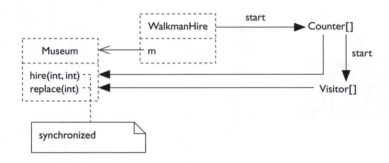

Figure 13.10 *High-level object diagram for the Walkman program.*

Synchronized objects

Now consider the synchronization parts of the program in detail. `hire` and `replace` are the two methods that control the number of Walkmen and the amount of cash taken as deposits. Obviously, the sum of these two must always be equal to the initial amount. Here is what the class looks like. Read the comments to understand how the `hire` and `replace` interact. `Museum` provides some rudimentary commentary to the user as to how the hiring process is proceeding.

```
import java.io.*;

class Museum {
```

```
Museum (int w) {
    walkmen = w;
    cash = 0;
  }

  synchronized void hire (int c,int n) {
    // If there are not enough Walkmen left,
    // wait until someone at another counter returns
    // some and notifies us accordingly.
    // If the returns are not enough, we'll carry on
    // waiting.
    System.out.println("Counter "+c+" wants "+n);
    while (walkmen < n) {
      try { wait(); }
      catch (InterruptedException e) {}
    }

    // Hire out the Walkmen and take the deposit.
    // Let the customers at this counter "walk away"
    // by relinquishing control of the monitor with
    // a notify call.
    walkmen -= n;
    cash += n;
    System.out.println("Counter "+c+" acquires "+n);
    System.out.println("Pool status:"+
      " Deposits "+cash+" Total "+(walkmen+cash)
      + " Walkmen "+walkmen);
    notify ();
  }

  synchronized void replace (int n) {

  // Always accept replacements immediately.
  // Once the pool and deposits have been updated,
  // notify any other helper waiting for Walkmen.
  System.out.println("Replacing "+n);
 walkmen +=n;
 cash -= n;
 notify ();
  }

 private static int walkmen;
 private static int cash;
}
```

Calling the `hire` part of `Museum`, we have the `Counter` threads. Once their needs have been satisfied, they create a new `Visitor` thread and then sleep for a while before serving another batch of customers. Both the number of visitors in a group and the time between groups are based on random numbers.

```
class Counter extends Thread {

  Counter (Museum m, int q) {
    museum = m;
    queue = q;
  }


  public void run () {

    // Decide how many Walkmen are needed for a
    // group of visitors and attempt to hire them
    // (waiting until successful). The visitors are
    // sent off on their own to walk around (by
    // starting a new Visitors thread which runs
    // independently.)
    while (true) {
      int w = a(7);
      museum.hire(queue, w);
      new Visitors (museum, w).start();

      // Wait a bit before the next people arrive
      try {sleep(a(100));} catch(InterruptedException e) {}
    }
  }


  Museum museum;
  int queue;
}
```

The `Visitors` threads simulate the groups walking around for a random time, viewing the exhibits and then returning the Walkmen directly to the `Museum` object. The `replace` method is synchronized so that there may be a small wait if a `Counter` thread is busy completing the hiring out of Walkmen at that precise moment, but otherwise the visitors can get on their way without queueing.

```
class Visitors extends Thread {

  Visitors (Museum m, int w) {
    museum = m;
    groupSize =·w;
  }
```

```
public void run () {

   // The group walks around on its own for 50 time units.
   // You may need to alter this figure to suit your computer.
   // They then replace all their Walkmen and leave.
   // The thread dies with them.
   try {sleep((int) (Math.random()*1000)+1);}
        catch(InterruptedException e) {}
   museum.replace(groupSize);
 }


 Museum museum;
 int groupSize;
 }
```

Finally, there is the main program itself. This is responsible for starting the `Museum` and `Counter` threads. In order to let the user change the size of the simulation, the numbers of Walkmen and counters can be set from the command line. By default they are 50 and 3 respectively.

```
class WalkmanHire {

 /* The Museum Walkman Hire program      J M Bishop Jan 1997
    simulates the hiring of Walkmen from a fixed pool for G1
    each. There are several helpers at different counters
    handling the hire and replacement of the Walkmen.

    The number of Walkmen in the original pool is 50
    and the number of helpers serving is 3,
    but these can be overridden by parameters at runtime
    e.g. java WalkmanHire 100 8.
    The cash float starts at zero.

    Illustrates monitors, with synchronize, wait and notify.
    Shows a main program and two different kinds of threads
    running simultaneously.
  */

 public static void main (String [] args) {

   // Get the number of Walkmen in the pool
   // and open the museum for business.
   if (args.length >= 1)
     pool = Integer.parseInt(args[0]);
```

```
    else pool = 50;
    Museum m = new Museum (pool);
    // Get the number of helpers
    // and open the counters.
    if (args.length >= 2)
      helpers = Integer.parseInt(args[1]);
    else helpers = 3;
    for (int i=0; i<helpers; i++)
      new Counter (m,i).start();
    }
    static int pool;
    static int helpers;
  }
```

Testing

The program produces text output. Let us consider just a small part of it, at a point where the number of Walkmen is getting low. We number the lines for reference.

```
1.   Pool status: Deposits 15 Total 20 Walkmen 5
2.   Counter 1 wants 5
3.   Counter 1 acquires 5
4.   Pool status: Deposits 20 Total 20 Walkmen 0
5.   Counter 2 wants 7
6.   Counter 0 wants 2
7.   Counter 1 wants 4
8.   Replacing 1
9.   Replacing 2
10.  Counter 0 acquires 2
11.  Pool status: Deposits 19 Total 20 Walkmen 1
12.  Replacing 6
13.  Counter 2 acquires 7
14.  Pool status: Deposits 20 Total 20 Walkmen 0
15.  Counter 0 wants 5
16.  Counter 2 wants 1
17.  Replacing 1
18.  Replacing 5
19.  Counter 0 acquires 5
20.  Pool status: Deposits 19 Total 20 Walkmen 1
21.  Counter 2 acquires 1
22.  Pool status: Deposits 20 Total 20 Walkmen 0
23.  Counter 2 wants 2
24.  Counter 0 wants 7
25.  Replacing 7
```

```
26. Counter 1 acquires 4
27. Pool status: Deposits 17 Total 20 Walkmen 3
28. Counter 2 acquires 2
29. Pool status: Deposits 19 Total 20 Walkmen 1
```

The program was set running with a pool of 20 Walkmen and with three counters (0, 1 and 2). At the beginning of this extract, there are five Walkmen left. Counter 1 wants 5 and gets them, leaving none. At that point each of the counters puts in a request, and all are blocked until some groups start returning sets. On line 8, one set was returned to the pool, but this was not enough for any of the waiting threads, so they continue to wait. On line 9 another two come back. By line 10, there are three sets in the pool so the thread from counter 0 can continue. Notice that this was not the first one queued: counter 2 requested 7 on line 5, but still has to wait. Fortunately, on line 12, six more Walkmen come back, making seven in all, so that group can now continue. The pool, however, is back to zero again.

Study the rest of the output, and run the program yourself with different parameters to get a feel for the dynamics.

SUMMARY

In order to handle networks and user interaction better, Java provides for multithreading. A class can extend from `Thread` and objects of that class will run independently and concurrently via their own `run` methods. A `run` method generally has a loop and should be able to end normally. Communication among threads is via method and variable access. If there is a chance that threads might interfere with each other, the methods they call are declared as synchronized. Java then guarantees that a thread in a synchronized method will finish before another is allowed into any synchronized method in the same object. To control threads so that one can wait for another, there are two thread methods, `wait` and `notify`.

In this chapter we introduced one new keyword:

```
synchronized
```

and the API for the `Thread` class as follows:

```
Thread        wait
  start       notify
  run         notifyAll
  sleep     Display
  yield
```

There were the following new forms:

Thread creation
Thread methods
The `run` method of a thread
Synchronized method
Synchronization methods

and two new exceptions:

```
InterruptedException
IllegalMonitorStateException
```

QUIZ

13.1 A thread could be inactive because it

    (a) is unlucky
    (b) could be waiting for a share of processing time
    (c) could be waiting for information
    (d) answer (b) or (c)

13.2 To implement threads, a programmer needs to

    (a) do nothing, because the threads are transparent
    (b) just initiate the thread objects and let them run
    (c) make sure that there is enough memory and other resources for the threads to work
    (d) instantiate the threads, keep them synchronized and detect when they should finish

13.3 The nucleus of a thread is the

    (a) `run` method
    (b) `start` method
    (c) `Thread` class
    (d) `Runnable` interface

13.4 In the `Spots` thread, in example 13.1, what is the effect of the following lines of code?

```
try {
  sleep (500);
}
catch (InterruptrdException e) {
}
```

    (a) the program slows down after 200 iterations of the loop
    (b) the computer is put into sleep mode for 500 seconds
    (c) the thread stops for 500 milliseconds, after which an `InterruptedException` is thrown by the `sleep` method, and execution continues
    (d) the thread yields execution to another waiting thread for half a second

13.5 Certain operations in a threaded program need to be synchronized

    (a) to prevent deadlock
    (b) to allow them to change the system's time

(c) to allow the synchronized method, which contains code that modifies global variables or the program state, to finish execution completely before another method is called

(d) so that they do not have to wait at a red traffic light at every intersection

13.6   The `Display` class has neither an inner class extending `Thread`, nor a `run` method. How, then, does it have the attributes of a thread?

(a) It has a `ready` method

(b) It has a `watcher` class which calls wait and notify

(c) all main methods are threads

(d) answers (a) and (b)

13.7   In which package is the `Thread` class declared?

(a) `java.util`

(b) `java.lang`

(c) `java.io`

(d) `java.applet`

13.8   A thread ends when

(a) the program that created it ends

(b) it calls `stop()`

(c) it reaches a natural conclusion, e.g. its loop finishes

(d) all other threads of that class end

13.9   To start a new car park in Example 13.4, we could say:

(a) `new CarThread ("North", 450);`

(b) `new CarThread ("North", 450).start ();`

(c) `new ViewPoint ("View2"), 450);`

(d) `new ViewPoint ("View2"), 450).start();`

13.10   The `Display` class uses the following data structure to keep track of data items that can be input:

(a) linked list

(b) array

(c) hash table

(d) vector

PROBLEMS

Note: The first four problems do not rely on synchronization.

13.1   **British traffic lights.** In Great Britain, there is a fourth phase on every set of traffic lights. Between red and green, both the red and yellow lights come on. Alter the program in Example 13.2 to take this into account.

13.2   **Duke catching for real.** The catching the Duke program (Example 12.4) used pseudo-animation in that the image only moved when the mouse moved, albeit in a seemingly random way. Change the program so that there is a thread moving the duke.

13.3   **Shape animator.** The Shape Selector system of Problem 11.1 enables shapes to be placed on a screen. Using ideas from the Spot program (Example 13.1) and the Catching the Duke program (Example 12.4) enhance the program so that at any stage the shapes can be made to move around the screen. Do this in Swing, and add a slide bar to control the speed of movement.

13.4   **Working watch.** In Problem 10.1, we designed the face of a digital watch. Now using a thread, make it work, with the digits clicking over and the buttons for resetting and displaying being active at the same time.

13.5   **Visible Walkmen.** The Walkman program (Case Study 9) could really do with a user interface that (a) shows how the Walkmen come and go, and (b) has a control panel so that the arrival of parties can be under the user's control, rather than generated automatically. Create such a user interface to run as an additional thread in the system.

13.6   **Broken Walkmen.** It could well happen that visitors find Walkmen that are no longer working when they finish. Instead of handing them back directly, we ask them to go back to the counter and hand them in specially. How would the model diagram have to change if we did this, and what methods would be needed? Implement this change and also add a `curator` class which comes round periodically and collects broken Walkmen, returning them later.

13.7   **VIP visitors.** Some visitors are VIPs and should not have to queue long for walkmen. Add another function to the `Curator` class to bring in such VIP groups occasionally and let them get Walkmen with a higher priority. Show on comparative sample outputs the effect that they would have.

13.8   **Viewpoint full!** Savanna Conservation is concerned about the number of cars going up to the viewpoint in Example 13.4. See if you can extend the program so that the viewpoint has a maximum number of places and cars can only enter from the car parks if there is space. If not, they use the wait synchronization method to queue. When a car leaves (after a random time spent looking at the view), the car parks are notified that another car can come in.

CHAPTER 14

Networking

14.1 Connecting via the Internet

Java was built to access the network. It has extensive features for network programming at various levels from connecting via URLs or sockets to accessing remote methods (RMI) and Java database connecting (JDBC). Because Java makes such connectivity so easy, we can justify including it in an introductory text such as this one, especially since we shall examine these new ideas by using examples in the usual *Java Gently* way.

All four methods for connecting are part of the Java core APIs and are available in the standard JDK and any browser that supports Java 1.2. Specifically, we shall be using the packages `java.net`, `java.rmi` and `java.sql`.

URL connections

Java has a class called URL which enables the data referred to by a URL on the Internet to be downloaded, and some interaction with the resource to be achieved. Given a string, Java will create an appropriate URL which can then be used to establish a

URLConnection. The connection enables interaction as defined by the resource's protocol, perhaps via input–output streams.

The form for creating a URL is:

URL creation

```
URL urlid = new URL (urlstring);
URL urlid = new URL (urlbase, urlstring);
```

The first form attempts to create a URL from the string given. If no such URL exists, a MalformedURLException is raised.

The second form allows relative URLs so that from an existing URL object, new expanded ones can be formed.

For example,

```
URL info = new info
  ("http://u/java/Book/chap13/Spots.java");
```

We can also use a URL connection to our local machine, in order to get around the restriction that applets cannot read local files. Because we are accessing the C drive, it is clear that we are actually using a local file, but via the Internet technology. So we could set up

```
URL data = new data
  ("file:///C|/books/jges/chap8/rates.data");
```

In order to maintain independence for the applets and their files, we can have relative URLs, which is the way we would normally do things. First, we would get the URL from where the applet came using an applet method, getCodeBase, and then get the file relative to it, e.g.

```
URL info = new URL (getCodeBase(),"rates.data");
```

URLs can also be relative to the page that loaded the applet, using another applet method, getDocumentBase(). The constructor makes sure that you have the correct syntax for forming a URL. If not, a MalformedURLException is thrown. It is therefore usual to put the declaration in a try-statement and catch the exception.

To access the resource at the URL, we shall have to set up a connection. If the resource is a text file, then we can create an input stream to it. The relevant form for achieving this is:

Creating a URL connection

```
URLConnection connection = URLid.openConnection();

BufferedReader readerid = new InputStreamReader
                (connection.getInputStream());
Stream streamid = new Stream
                (connection.getInputStream());
```

---

connection is an object established from the given URLid.
It is used to get an input stream, which is then passed either to
    InputStreamReader, producing a BufferedReader, or to
    Stream, to produce a Stream object.

The reader or stream now acts as any normal input source. Summarizing the above, we can postulate a method that will handle all the connecting, given a file name and returning a BufferedReader. It would be:

```
BufferedReader connectTo (String fileName) {

/* A method to connect a filename to a BufferedReader
 * via the Internet. Uses the display for error messages
 */
  BufferedReader fin = null;
  try {
    URL dataFileURL = new URL(getCodeBase()+fileName);
    display.println("Connecting to "+dataFileURL);
    URLConnection con = dataFileURL.openConnection();
    try {
      fin = new BufferedReader(new InputStreamReader
            (con.getInputStream()));
    }
    catch (IOException e) {
      display.println("File "+fileName+" could not be opened");
    }
  }
  catch (Exception e) {
    display.println("Unexpected error when connecting");
  }
  return fin;
}
```

ConnectTo sends messages to the display, but could easily be changed to send them to the console via System.out.

| EXAMPLE 14.1 | Converter applet |

Opportunity   The directors of Savanna Travel see the opportunity of offering the currency converter program on the Internet, so that prospective travellers can see what foreign exchange they will get for their trip.

Response   Convert the program developed in Example 11.3 into an applet as per the instructions in Section 12.1. Create an HTML file and access it via a browser from anywhere on the Internet. The applet will be loaded into the HTML page.

Program design   The initial changes to the program in Example 11.3 follow the steps outlined in Section 12.1 and Example 12.1. However, once the main program is removed, there is no need to keep the rest of program in a separate class, so we may as well consolidate into a single class.

There is only one further alteration. Since the applet may be running on a computer in one city and the travel agent is in another city, we have a problem with the `rates.dat` file. It will be on the travel agent's computer and cannot be opened in the usual way. The good news is that the file can be read in the ordinary way, provided we first connect to it via the Internet, as described above.

The `Rates` class does not change for the applet version, which looks like this (with the unchanged method bodies not given in full):

```java
import java.awt.*;
import java.awt.event.*;
import java.util.*;
import java.io.*;
import java.applet.*;
import java.net.*;
import javagently.*;

public class ConverterGUIApplet extends Applet
         implements ActionListener, ItemListener{

  /* The Converter Applet      by J M Bishop Dec 1998
   * --------------------          Display version July 1999
   *                               GUI version July 1999
   *                               Java 1.2 August 2000
   * Keeps the exchange rates from one currency into
   * many others and enables currency exchanges to be
   * estimated.
   *
   * Illustrates the use of a simple GUI with
   * choice boxes, text field, buttons, text area
```

```
 * and labels.
 */
 ... declarations as before

    public void init () {
      ... as before
    }

    public void actionPerformed (ActionEvent e) {
      ... as before
    }

    public void itemStateChanged(ItemEvent e) {
      ... as before
    }

    void transaction () {
      ... as before
    }

  void readIn() {
     try {
     // Setting up access to the rates file via the internet
     URL ratesFileURL = new URL(getCodeBase()+"rates.data");
     URLConnection con = ratesFileURL.openConnection();
     Stream fin = null;
     try {
       fin = new Stream(con.getInputStream());
     }
     catch (IOException e) {
       resultField.append("rates.data file not found\n");
     }
   }
   ... as before
 }
}
```

Testing   We have added a little bit of text around the applet, to illustrate how it is embedded in HTML. The creation of the HTML was done in the editor of Netscape in a wysiwyg fashion, and the resulting file stored as `Converter.html`. This file is the one we open when we want to access the applet. If it was stored on a web server, we could access it via a web address. The output, running in Microsoft Internet Explorer browser, is shown in Figure 14.1.

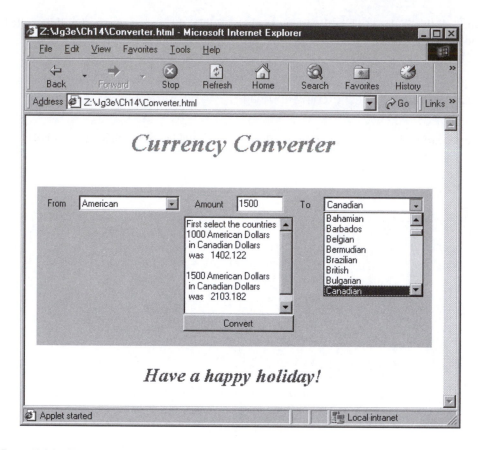

Figure 14.1 *The converter applet running under Microsoft Internet Explorer.*

Fetching images

How do we fetch images? In fact, there is a very easy way using the services of the awt, and in particular of the `awt.image` package. The form is:

Fetching an image

```
Image imageid = createImage((ImageProducer)
                imageURL.getContent());
```

`getContent` returns the entire contents of the file.
The contents of the file are type cast into a class that conforms to the
    requirements of the `ImageProducer` interface.
In a `Frame` object the `createImage` method is called to convert an
    `ImageProducer` interface object to an `Image` object.

Once all this is done, when the frame is made visible, the `paint` method will be called and the image shown.

Fetching an image

Illustration   The following program illustrates the fetching of an image from a URL.

```java
import java.awt.*;
import java.awt.event.*;
import java.awt.image.*;
import java.net.*;

public class FetchImage extends Frame {

  /* Fetch an image program  by J M Bishop Jan 1997
   * ======================  Java 1.1
   *                         updated B Worrall Aug 2000
   *
   * Fetches a jpg or gif image into a window.
   * Illustrates use of awt.image. */

  private Image image;

  public void paint(Graphics g) {
    g.drawImage(image, 50, 50, this);
  }

  public static void main(String[] args) throws Exception {
    new FetchImage(args[0]);
  }

  FetchImage (String name) throws Exception {
    URL imageURL = new URL(name);
    image = createImage((ImageProducer) imageURL.getContent());
    setSize(300, 300);
    setVisible(true);
    addWindowListener(new WindowAdapter () {
      public void windowClosing(WindowEvent e) {
        System.exit(0);
      }
    });
  }
}
```

Testing To test out the program, we run it with a known image file name, as in:

```
java FetchImage file:/u/java/Book/chap14/Fluffy.jpg
```

A window will open up (as is usual with awt programs) and the kitten's image will be displayed therein. The window can be closed by clicking the Close box, because we have included a `windowClosing` method for this purpose.

14.2 Ports and sockets

In the previous section, we concentrated on connections via high-level URLs. Java provides another level of connection, that of ports and sockets. A **port** is an abstraction of a physical place through which communication can proceed between a server and a client. The server is said to provide the port, and the client links into it.

Operating systems have processes assigned to specific ports, with server software that runs continuously, listening for anticipated messages of particular kinds. Ports are generally known by numbers. For example, under Unix, connecting to port 13 will return the date and time of the computer. Other ports provide for receiving and sending mail, checking the status of the computer, finding out who is logged on, and so on. Most of the time these ports will not be available to mere users, as security could be impaired. However, there are many vacant ports which we can use where we can create our own services.

Such a service will be a multithreaded Java program which provides sockets on the given port. A **socket** is an abstraction of the network software that enables communication in and out of this program. A Java socket can be created if we have a valid computer Internet address and a valid port number. Several sockets can be created on a single port, enabling many clients to make use of the service provided, as shown in Figure 14.2.

Once a socket has been created, the client and server communicate in whatever way has been arranged. In Java, the simplest method is to establish an ordinary stream from

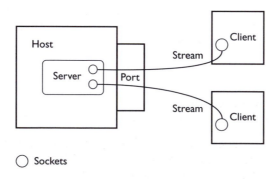

Figure 14.2 *Diagrammatic view of ports and sockets.*

the server to the client. Thereafter, the server can use read and print methods to get and send data.

If the client is a Java program then it will also have a socket and streams that match those of the server. Alternatively, the client could be an existing program such as telnet, or the server could be an existing service such as the time of day. The form associated with setting up a socket is:

Creating sockets

```
ServerSocket listener = new ServerSocket (port);
Socket socketid = listener.accept();
Socket socketid = new Socket (host, port);
```

---

and the forms for attaching input and output streams to it are:

Streams for sockets

```
BufferedReader instreamname =
     new InputStreamReader (name.getInputStream());
PrintWriter outstreamname = new
     PrintWriter(name.getOutputStream(),true);
```

As mentioned before, we can also attach sockets via the `Stream` class. If we are creating a socket on the server side, we first set up a permanent listening socket on that port, based on the `ServerSocket` class. Then for each client that accesses the port, a separate socket of the `Socket` class is set up via the `accept` method. From the client's side, to create such a socket we instantiate the `Socket` class directly and indicate the host to which it must connect.

The two stream connections follow the same pattern as any other stream connections. The one difference is that the output stream indicates to the `PrintWriter` class that it must flush each line (the `true` parameter).

EXAMPLE 14.3   Opening a port

Illustration A simple program to act as a client accessing an existing server on a host is the following. In this case, we use port 13 which returns the time of the computer. The program uses the second form for creating a socket.

```java
import java.io.*;
import java.net.*;
import javagently.*;

class Ports {
  /* The Ports program            J M Bishop 1997
   * -----------------            updated August 2000
   *
   * For checking the response from various ports
   * on a remote computer.
   * Illustrates sockets
   */

  public static void main(String[] args) {
    String computer;
    int port;

    if (args.length > 0) computer = args[0];
    else computer = "syd.cs.up.ac.za";
    if (args.length > 1) port = Integer.parseInt(args[1]);
    else port = 13; // the clock port

    new Ports (computer, port);
  }

  Ports (String computer, int port) {

    System.out.println("Accessing port "+port+" on "+ computer+"\n");
    try {

    // Create a socket to the given port.
    // Set up an input stream to read what the socket on that
    // side provides.

    Socket t = new Socket(computer, port);
    Stream in = new Stream(t.getInputStream());

    // Read from the server until readLine
    // returns no more data
    while (true) {
      String s = in.readLine();
      if (s == null) break;
      else System.out.println(s);
    }
  }
  catch(IOException e) { System.out.println("Error" + e); }
 }
}
```

Testing   If we ran this program without parameters, it would default to the computer called syd.cs.up.ac.za and to port 13. The result would be the date and time printed out, such as:

```
Accessing port 13 on syd.cs.up.ac.za

Sun Aug 26 15:57:14 2000
```

We now consider how to create our own server program on a spare port. Ports above 8000 are usually spare, so we can use one of those.

EXAMPLE 14.4   Creating an ATM server

Problem   We would like to simulate the operation of ATMs (automated teller machines) connected to a bank, and handling the initial PIN (personal identification number) validation.

Solution   We shall set up a server on a vacant port. The service should allow multiple connections from clients representing ATM machines. The protocol between the server and a client should go something like this:

Server	Client
Welcome to Savanna Bank	
Please type in your PIN number or type CANCEL	1234
Incorrect PIN. Try again.	5678
Please start your transactions	

We only have a simulation here, so there is no database of clients in this service, and the PIN will be 5678, for all clients!

Design   If there are to be multiple clients then it is certain that they will be running at different speeds and will need their own threads within the server. This is no problem, as we have fully investigated how to set up threads in Chapter 13. The question is rather how to test the service. We could set up a Java client program similar to the one in Example 14.3, but actually there is an easier way: we can use another existing client, telnet. Telnet is a software program with a simple protocol which, in the absence of any other instructions, will read and write to a host, line by line. Thus we can telnet into our chosen port and type in lines one at a time.

Program   The program makes use of a class called InetAddress which represents Internet addresses, as well as their string equivalents. The server follows (with comments to explain what is happening at each stage).

```java
import java.io.*;
import java.net.*;
import javagently.*;

class ATMServer {

  /* A simple server program  by J M Bishop December 1996
   * =======================
   *                              Java 1.1 revised January 1998
   *                              Java 1.2 B Worrall August 2000
   * Allows multiple simultaneous connections.
   * Illustrates sockets and networking.
   */

  static final String magicPIN = "5678";
  static int port = 8190;
  InetAddress serverAddress = null;
  private boolean done = false;

  public static void main(String[] args) {
  // Set up the port address from the command line,
  // or default to 8190
   if (args.length > 0)
      port =Integer.parseInt(args[0]);
      new ATMServer (port);
  }


  ATMServer (int port) {

     try {
       serverAddress = InetAddress.getLocalHost();
     } catch (UnknownHostException e) {}

   // Initial printing on Server side only
   // using System.out

     System.out.println("****** SAVANNA BANK ********");
     System.out.println("Simulate an ATM session by "
           + "telnetting in to ");
     System.out.println(serverAddress.getHostName() +
           " on port "+port);
```

```
      System.out.println("from any number of different computers or");
      System.out.println("from different active Windows.");

  // Set up the server socket
    try {
      ServerSocket listener = new ServerSocket(port);

      int c = 0;
      while (!done) {

        // This is where the program waits for new clients
        Socket client = listener.accept( );
        c ++;
        System.out.println("Card inserted on " +
                  client.getInetAddress().getHostName());
        System.out.println("Starting a new client, numbered "
            +c);
        new handler(client, c).start();
      }
      listener.close();
    }
    catch (IOException e) {
      System.out.println("Port "+port+
        " may be busy. Try another.");
    }
  }

  void closeDown () {
    done = true;
  }

class handler extends Thread {

  private Socket toClient;
  private int id;

  handler(Socket s, int i) {
  // Remember the client socket number and client id number
    toClient = s;
    id = i;
  }

  public void run() {
```

```
try {
  Stream conin = new Stream (toClient.getInputStream());
  PrintWriter conout = new
    PrintWriter(toClient.getOutputStream(),true);

  conout.println( "Welcome to Savanna Bank");
  for (int tries = 0; tries < 3; tries++) {
    conout.println("Please type in your PIN "+
        "number or type CANCEL");
    String s = conin.readLine();
    System.out.println("Client "+id+":"+s);

    if (s.equals("SHUTDOWN")) closeDown();
    else if (s.equals("CANCEL")) {
      conout.println("Transactions halted. Goodbye.");
      break;
    }

    else if (s.equals(magicPIN)) {
      conout.println("Please start your transactions");
      break;
    }
    else
      conout.println("Incorrect PIN. Try again.");
  }
  System.out.println("Simulation complete. Thanks.");
}
catch (IOException e) {System.out.println("IO Error");}
      }
    }
  }
```

Each thread records its socket reference when constructed. It then asks for the input and output streams associated with that socket, which will give it access to the client that is on the other side. The handler sends an introductory message to the ATM and enters its loop, asking for a PIN three times. The client can also type CANCEL or there is a chance to stop the server (not generally advertised). When the loop ends, the socket to the client is closed and then the thread dies.

Testing   To run the server, we simply execute it as a normal Java program. If we want to telnet into the server as a client from the same machine (which is certainly possible) then we should run the server in the background using `java ATMServer &` or a separate window on a windowing environment. A typical session is shown in Figure 14.3. The kind of server represented in this example is taken further in Case Study 10.

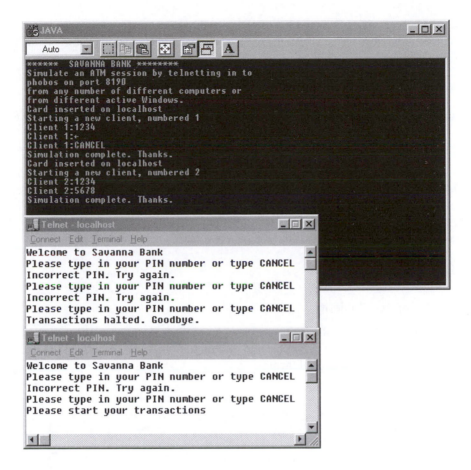

Figure 14.3 *The output from the ATM server and two simultaneous clients.*

14.3 Case Study 10: The Chatter system

In Example 14.4, each of the clients was completely independent. It would be nice to extend the system so that the messages typed in by one are relayed to each of the others by the server. Such a server is known as a 'chat program'.

Keeping track of clients

The first issue is how to keep track of clients within the server. Clients can sign on and leave at will, and the number of clients could be very hard to control or predict. It thus makes sense to envisage a linked list of clients rather than an array, since we know that we can add and remove from such a list without worrying about the number of elements.

If we declare

```
private static LinkedList clientList = new LinkedList();
```

where `LinkedList` is the class in the `java.util` package (discussed in Section 8.3) then adding a new client thread's reference to the list is done simply by:

```
clientList.add(client);
```

Now, how do we remove a client from the list? Clearly, the client must request such removal, once a BYE has been detected. The client knows what its socket reference is, and this is unique among the current clients. Therefore, the server can use the `LinkedList remove` method as follows, where s is the socket reference:

```
clientList.remove(s);
```

Broadcasting to all clients

Broadcasting a message to all clients requires a loop. Since the message has to be echoed to the originator as well, we do not have to differentiate between that client and the rest and we simply loop through all of them.

```
for (ListIterator list = clientList.listIterator();
                        list.hasNext();) {
  s = (Socket) list.next();
  p = new PrintWriter(s.getOutputStream(), true);
  p.println(name+": "+message);
}
```

For each client on the list, we get the corresponding output stream and send the message there.

Synchronizing activities

The removal and broadcast operations both access the list of clients kept by the server. Given that the removal operation will make fairly drastic changes to the list, it would not be wise for both operations to be active simultaneously. Therefore they are declared as `synchronized` and Java will ensure that once one has begun, it will be finished before the other is attempted.

A model diagram

This time, let us record a model diagram for the server and its handlers, as shown in Figure 14.4.

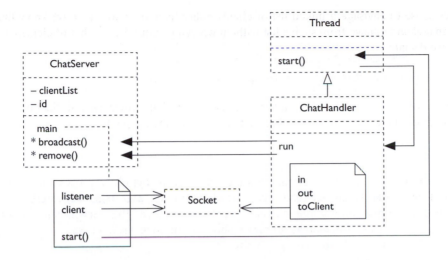

Figure 14.4 *Model diagram for the Chatter system (the asterisks indicate synchronized methods).*

The server

The code for the chat server therefore looks like this in full:

```
import java.io.*;
import java.net.*;
import java.util.*;
import javagently.*;

public class ChatServer {

  /* The Chatter program      by J M Bishop January 1997
   * ====================      Java 1.1 January 1998
   *                           updated August 2000
   *
   * Sets up a server for multiple conversations.
   *
   * Join in by typing
   * telnet x y
   * where x and y are the computer"s name and port as
   * given when the Chatter starts.
   *
   * Illustrates sockets, streams on sockets,
   * threads, synchronization and the use of lists (again).
   */

  private static LinkedList clientList = new LinkedList();
```

```
   private static int id = 0;

   public static void main(String[] args) throws IOException {
     // Get the port and created a socket there.
     int port = 8190;
     if (args.length > 0)
       port = Integer.parseInt(args[0]);
     new ChatServer (port);
   }

ChatServer (int port) throws IOException {
   ServerSocket listener = new ServerSocket(port);
   System.out.println("The Chat Server is running on port "+port);

   // Listen for clients. Start a new handler for each.
   // Add each client to the linked list.
   while (true) {
     Socket client = listener.accept();
     new ChatHandler(client).start();
     System.out.println("New client no."+id+
         " from "+ listener.getInetAddress()+
         " on client's port "+client.getPort());
     clientList.add(client);
     id++;
   }
}

synchronized static void broadcast(String message, String name)
     throws IOException {
   // Sends the message to every client including the sender.
   Socket s;
   PrintWriter p;
   for (ListIterator list = clientList.listIterator(); list.hasNext();) {
     s = (Socket) list.next();
     p = new PrintWriter(s.getOutputStream(), true);
     p.println(name+": "+message);
   }
}

synchronized static void remove(Socket s) {
/* Using the LinkedList remove method, removes the
 * first occurrence of the given socket object
 */
   clientList.remove(s);
   id--;
 }
}
```

There is one `ChatHandler` object for each client. It is a thread with a `run` method which first sets up the streams and then loops till a BYE is entered by a client.

```
class ChatHandler extends Thread {

  /* The Chat Handler class is called from the Chat Server:
   * one thread for each client coming in to chat.
   */

  private BufferedReader in;
  private PrintWriter out;
  private Socket toClient;
  private String name;

  ChatHandler(Socket s) {
    toClient = s;
  }

  public void run() {
    try {
      /* Create i-o streams through the socket we were
       * given when the thread was instantiated
       * and welcome the new client.
       */

      in = new BufferedReader(new InputStreamReader(
        toClient.getInputStream()));
      out = new PrintWriter(toClient.getOutputStream(), true);
      out.println("*** Welcome to the Chatter ***");
      out.println("Type BYE to end");
      out.print("What is your name? ");
      out.flush();
      String name = in.readLine();
      ChatServer.broadcast(name+" has joined the discussion.",
        "Chatter");

      // Read lines and send them off for broadcasting.
      while (true) {
        String s = in.readLine().trim();

        if (s.equals("BYE")) {
          ChatServer.broadcast(name+" has left the discussion.",
          "Chatter");
          break;
```

```
            }
            ChatServer.broadcast(s, name);
          }
          ChatServer.remove(toClient);
          toClient.close();
        }
      catch (Exception e) {
      System.out.println("Chatter error: "+e);
    }
    }


  }
```

A sample chat session

Once again we use telnet for the clients. The following could be a sample chat session, as recorded on the server's display.

```
Chat/Chatter>java ChatServer 8191 &
[2] 5802
Chat/Chatter>The Chat Server is running on port 8191

Chat/Chatter>telnet syd 8191
Trying 137.215.18.16 ...
Connected to syd.cs.up.ac.za.
New client no.0 on client's port 57889
Escape character is "^]".
*** Welcome to the Chatter ***
Type BYE to end
What is your name?
Nelson
Chatter: Nelson has joined the discussion.
Anyone out there?
Nelson: Anyone out there?
New client no.1 on client's port 1026
Chatter: Seagull has joined the discussion.
Hi Seagull
Nelson: Hi Seagull
Seagull: Hi Nelson, how's the coffee shop?
Great. Business is booming.
Nelson: Great. Business is booming.
Seagull: Oh well, bye for now
Seagull - you must type BYE to end
Nelson: Seagull - you must type BYE to end
Seagull: BYE
```

```
Try again
Nelson: Try again
Seagull: BYE
Chatter: Seagull has left the discussion.
BYE
Nelson: BYE
Chatter: Nelson has left the discussion.
Connection closed by foreign host.
```

Notice that we told telnet to look for the host called 'syd' and it translated this to a numeric Internet address, 137.215.18.16. The server, once it accepts the client, can get this Internet address and translate it back to its full string equivalent, in this case 'syd.cs.up.ac.za'. You can also use the special Internet address '127.0.0.1' to telnet into your own machine.

When running the chat server using telnet, some oddities may emerge when trying to say goodbye, or with the echoing or non-echoing of lines locally. It is worth experimenting to find out how your computers react.

14.4 Database connectivity

Databases are a cornerstone of computing in today's age. Java provides connectivity to databases via the JDBC (Java database connectivity). The JDBC allows a connection to be made to a database with no more fuss than connecting to a resource or image. However, Java also provides for SQL (standard query language) statements to be sent, and the results of queries to be interpreted on return.

In order to access a database we need a driver that can interpret both Java's JDBC protocol and that of the database itself. If the database vendor does not supply a JDBC driver, it is sure to have an ODBC (open database connectivity) driver, and Sun provides a bridge between the two. Therefore, to load a driver we use:

Loading a database driver

```
try {
  Class.forName ("driver name");
} catch (ClassNotFoundException c) {
    System.out.println("Could not load database driver.");
}
```

The driver name could be something like `sun.jdbc.odbc.-JdbcOdbcDriver`. The driver will be loaded as part of the `DriverManager` class, used in the next form.

Next, we open a connection to the database using the driver.

Connecting to a database

```
Connection con = DriverManager.getConnection (url, user, password);
Connection con = DriverManager.getConnection (database);
```

The first form is used to connect to a remote database. The second will access a local database (as described in the example below). Both use the driver previously loaded into the `DriverManager`.

Once the connection is successful, we can send SQL statements and get results back. The statements are formed as strings (which means they will not be checked for correct SQL syntax). Two of the options are:

Sending a statement to a database

```
Statement stat = con.createStatement ();
int result = stat.executeUpdate("SQL insert");
ResultSet rs = stat.executeQuery("SQL query");
```

Using the connection previously set up, a `Statement` object is instantiated.
The `executeUpdate` method will submit an INSERT type SQL statement, and return a result code as to whether it was successful or not.
The `executeQuery` method will submit a SELECT SQL statement, and return a `ResultSet` object. Then the result set can be processed in a loop, record by record.

EXAMPLE 14.5   The converter database

Problem   Savanna Travel has decided that the exchange rates for its currency conversion system should be kept on a database and updated there. Clients should be able to access the database to get the latest values.

Solution   We already have a converter program (developed in Examples 6.8, 11.3 and 14.1), so all we have to do is change it to access a database. In broad terms, Figure 14.5 shows how the one program would be split into: one to create the database from the existing text file, and the other to query it.

Pre-set-up   We are going to choose to use a very simple database available on all Windows systems. Before Java can load the relevant JDBC-ODBC driver, it must be acti-

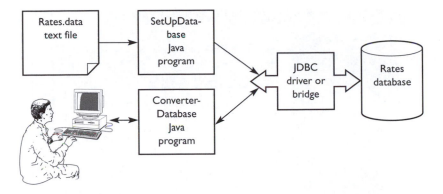

Figure 14.5 *Creating and accessing a database.*

vated on the computer. The next steps lead you through this process. Open the Windows Control Panel and double-click on ODBC Data Sources (32 bit). A window should open that contains the list of user data sources as in Figure 14.6. There will be entries such as MS Access Database and dBase Files. You will need to add your database to this list. To do this, click on Add... on the right-hand side of the dialogue box. Then, select the driver you use to access your database. In our example, we use an MS Access database, so we select Microsoft Access Driver (*.mdb) (Figure 14.7).

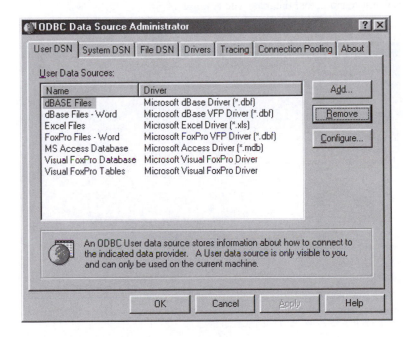

Figure 14.6 *ODBC data source administrator in Windows.*

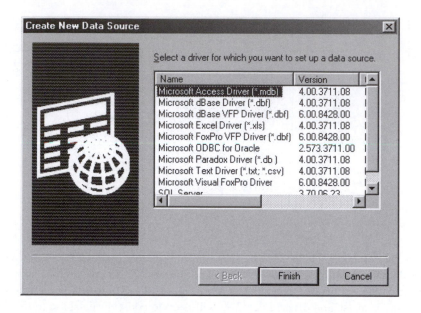

Figure 14.7 *Selecting a database driver.*

Another dialogue box will pop up, where you must supply your data source with a name, description and actual database file (Figure 14.8).

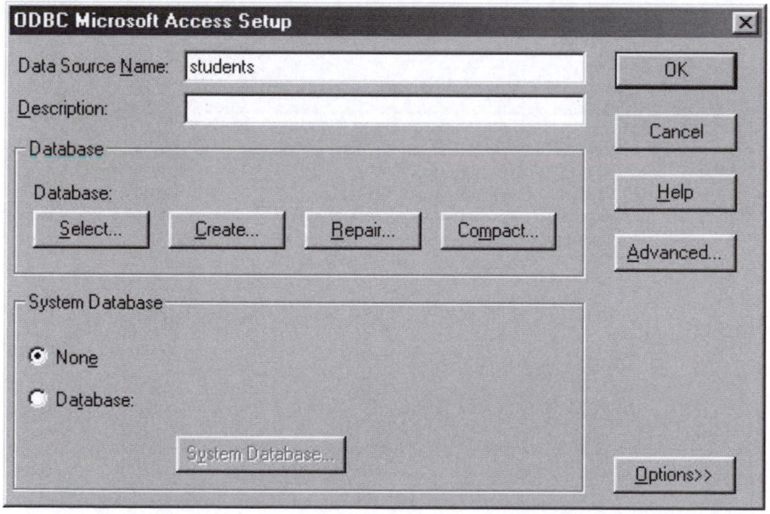

Figure 14.8 *Naming the new data source.*

Type in the name in Data Source Name (the screenshot shows 'students', but use 'Rates' for the `converterGUI` example), then click on Select... if you have already created a database, otherwise click on Create... .Both these options will pop up a file-select dialogue box, and you must choose a directory and name for the database. If the database has already been created, you need only to browse over to where it is stored, and then press OK. If it is a new database, browse to the directory where the database is to be stored, then type a name in the Database Name field.

If you want to add a user name and password to the database, click on Advanced... on the right-hand side of the dialogue box, and type in a user name and password for your database (Figure 14.9). These can be used in the text by changing the `DriverManager.-getConnection` as in the first form in this section. You can then save all the settings by clicking on OK in all the dialogue boxes.

Design of the set-up program The important SQL statements that the set-up program must send to the database are:

DROP TABLE rates   clear the data from the database
CREATE TABLE rates (metadata)   give the format, in terms of columns per field
INSERT INTO rates VALUES (values)   give values for one record

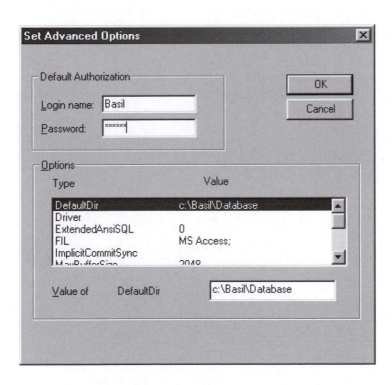

Figure 14.9 *Changing database authorization.*

The program otherwise follows the steps outlined in the forms above. It is:

```
import java.sql.*;
import javagently.*;
import java.io.*;

class SetUpDatabase {

  /* Database setup program by B Worrall August 2000
   * ====================== amended by J M Bishop
   *
   * Sets up a database of rates data
   * as read in. The database uses Sun's
   * jdbc:odbc driver to connect to a text based
   * Access Database.
   */

  private Connection conn;

  SetUpDatabase() {
    // Load JDBC-ODBC Bridge driver
    try {
      Class.forName("sun.jdbc.odbc.JdbcOdbcDriver");
    } catch (ClassNotFoundException c) {
      System.out.println("Could not load database driver.");
    }
    // Read the data from the text file and store it in the
    // database.
    try {
      OpenConnection();
      WriteData();
    } catch (SQLException s) {
      System.out.println(s);
    } catch (IOException i) {
      System.out.println(i);
    }
  }

  void OpenConnection() throws SQLException {
    conn = DriverManager.getConnection("jdbc:odbc:Rates");
    Statement s = conn.createStatement();
    String state = "DROP TABLE rates";
    try {
      // Delete old data if necessary (if no such data,
```

```
      // exception is flagged and we carry on)
      int temp = s.executeUpdate(state);
    } catch (SQLException q) {}

    // Create table with columns in database
    state = "CREATE TABLE rates (Code VARCHAR(3), Country VARCHAR(80), " +
      "Curr VARCHAR(30), Conv DOUBLE)";
    int temp = s.executeUpdate(state);
  }

  void WriteData() throws IOException, SQLException {
    Stream fin = new Stream("rates.data", Stream.READ);
    try {
      for (; ;) {
        Rates r = new Rates();
        r.setRate(fin);
        // add data into rates
        Statement s = conn.createStatement();
        String state = "INSERT INTO rates VALUES ("" +
                        r.code + "", "" +
                        r.country + "", "" +
                        r.currency + "", " +
                        r.conversion + ")";
        int rs = s.executeUpdate(state);
      }
    } catch (EOFException e) {}
  }
  public static void main (String [] args) {
    new SetUpDatabase();
  }
}
```

The program should read each line of the `rates.data` file and move the values, record by record, into the database in what is known as comma delimited format.

Updating the converter program   The main difference between the Converter Database program and those that went before, is that there is no hash table. However, there is still a reading-in section, because the the program must scan the database to extract all the country names to put in the two choice boxes in the graphical user interface. The code to do this is:

```
conn = DriverManager.getConnection("jdbc:odbc:rates");

// Do SQL query to get all data from the table
Statement s = conn.createStatement();
```

```
String command = "SELECT Country FROM rates";
ResultSet rs = s.executeQuery(command);

while (rs.next()) {
  String temp = rs.getString(1).trim();
  toChoice.addItem(temp);
  fromChoice.addItem(temp);
}
```

`ResultSet` objects do not need enumerators: they can be iterated over using just the `rs.next()` method call. The transaction method resembles its predecessors, with access to the hash table replaced by statements such as

```
Statement s1 = conn.createStatement();
String command = "SELECT Country,Curr,Conv FROM rates " +
                 "WHERE Country = "" + fromCountry +""";
```

obtaining the required values. The full program follows:

```
import java.awt.*;
import java.awt.event.*;
import java.util.*;
import java.io.*;
import java.sql.*;
import javagently.*;

class ConverterDatabase extends Frame
  implements ActionListener, ItemListener {

  /* The ConverterDatabase Program    by J M Bishop Dec 1998
   * ---------------------------       Display version July 1999
   *                                   GUI version July 1999
   *                      B Worrall Database version August 2000
   * Keeps the exchange rates from one currency into
   * many others and enables currency exchanges to be
   * estimated.
   *
   * Illustrates the use of jdbc connection to a database.
   */

  private Connection conn;

  Choice    fromChoice, toChoice;
  TextField amountField;
  TextArea  resultField;
  int       amount = 1000;
  String    toCountry, fromCountry;
  Button    goButton;
```

```
public ConverterDatabase () throws SQLException {
  // First set up GUI interface, but do not
  // setVisible.
  Panel p = new Panel (new BorderLayout());

    // left hand side panel
    Panel q = new Panel();
      q.add ("North",new Label ("From"));
      fromChoice = new Choice();
        fromChoice.addItemListener (this);
        q.add("Center",fromChoice);
      p.add ("West", q);
    // right hand side panel
    q = new Panel();
      q.add ("North",new Label ("To"));
      toChoice = new Choice();
        toChoice.addItemListener (this);
        q.add("Center",toChoice);
      p.add ("East",q);
    // Centre panel
    q = new Panel(new BorderLayout());
      Panel r = new Panel();
        r.add(new Label("Amount"));
        amountField = new TextField("1000 ");
          amountField.addActionListener(this);
          r.add(amountField);
          q.add("North",r);
        resultField = new TextArea(8,20);
          q.add ("Center",resultField);
        goButton = new Button ("Convert");
          goButton.addActionListener(this);
          q.add("South",goButton);
      p.add("Center",q);
  add(p);
  setTitle("Currency Converter");
  setSize(610,300);
  addWindowListener(new WindowAdapter() {
    public void windowClosing(WindowEvent e) {
      System.exit(0);
    }
  });
  // Call readIn function to open the connection
  // to the database, and to fill the Choice lists
  // with the country names.
```

```
      readIn();
  }


public void actionPerformed (ActionEvent e) {
  if (e.getSource() == amountField)
    amount = (int) Integer.parseInt(amountField.getText().trim());
  else
  if (e.getSource() == goButton)
    transaction();
}


public void itemStateChanged(ItemEvent e) {
  String s = (String) e.getItem();
  if (e.getItemSelectable() == fromChoice)
    fromCountry = s;
  else toCountry = s;
}


void transaction () {
  // Called when the go button is pressed
  try {
    // Create a statement to query the fromCountry
    // details for the conversion. Then execute the
    // query, saving the resuls in rs.
    Statement s1 = conn.createStatement();
    String command = "SELECT Country,Curr,Conv FROM rates " +
      "WHERE Country = "" + fromCountry +""";
    ResultSet rs = s1.executeQuery(command);
    rs.next();

    // As above, but for toCountry, and results stored
    // in rs2.
    Statement s2 = conn.createStatement();
    command = "SELECT Country, Curr, Conv FROM rates " +
      "WHERE Country = "" + toCountry + """;
    ResultSet rs2 = s2.executeQuery(command);
    rs2.next();

    // Add the conversion text to the resultField.
    // Notice how database methods are used to access
    // the data, as opposed to using a Hashtable's get
    // method.
    resultField.append(amount+" "+rs.getString(1)+" "+
      rs.getString(2)+
      "\n in "+rs2.getString(1)+" "+rs2.getString(2)+"\n was "+
```

```
        Text.format(amount/rs.getDouble(3)*
           rs2.getDouble(3),10,3)+"\n\n");
    } catch (SQLException q) {
      q.printStackTrace();
      System.exit(0);
    }
}

  void readIn() throws SQLException {
    // called at the end of the constructor
    // Open a connection with the database
    conn = DriverManager.getConnection("jdbc:odbc:rates");

    // Do SQL query to get all data from the table
    Statement s = conn.createStatement();
    String command = "SELECT Country FROM rates";
    ResultSet rs = s.executeQuery(command);

    // Iterate through rows in the table, adding the
    // necessary country names to the Choice lists
    while (rs.next()) {
    String temp = rs.getString(1).trim();
      toChoice.addItem(temp);
      fromChoice.addItem(temp);
    }

    // Now we can set the Frame visible
    setVisible(true);
  }

  public static void main(String[] args) {

    // Load the JDBC-ODBC Bridge driver
    try {
      Class.forName("sun.jdbc.odbc.JdbcOdbcDriver");
    } catch (ClassNotFoundException c) {
      System.out.println("Error loading JDBC-ODBC driver.");
      System.exit(0);
    }
    try {
      new ConverterDatabase();
    } catch (SQLException s) {
      s.printStackTrace();
    }
  }
}
```

Testing If we test the program, we find that as far as visible output on the GUI is concerned, there is no difference at all between the previous programs and the new database version. The difference now is that we have achieved separation of concerns: an administrator can update the `rates.data` file and run the `SetupDatabase` program while the `ConverterGUI` programs out there are running. As long as new countries are not added (which would affect the choice boxes) any new rates would be immediately available.

14.5 Accessing remote objects

Sockets give us the ability to transmit raw data across machines, and database connectivity enables the transmission of structured relational data. In between these two ends of the spectrum is the very common case of transmitting data that are typed, and checked, but that are formatted to suit the programmer, rather than a database. In the Java model, such data would obviously be in the form of objects.

In addition to being able to send objects around a network, Java also allows us not to send them! What this means is that we can have objects situated on one computer and merely access them there, calling their methods to perform operations on them as required.

This description fits in exactly with the client–server model. The server holds an object that the clients want to fetch or access. Java requires that the server registers or **binds** the object in a central **registry** on that computer. Then the client must know which computer to go to, and the name by which the object was registered, whereupon it can **look up** the object and get a reference to it. Thereafter the object can be used as if it were local, and the Java remote method invocation system (or RMI) takes care of all the protocol, transporting and checking of data back and forth. `java.rmi` is a core package in the JDK and is therefore available on all Java systems. The following forms show how a remote object is declared on a server, and how binding and look-up are achieved.

Remote object declaration

```
// common to the server and its clients
interface remoteInterfaceid {
  ... methods
}


// in the server
class remoteClassid extends UnicastRemoteObject
                    implements remoteInterfaceid {
  .. implementation of the methods
}
```

The `remoteClassid` defines the class of objects that satisfies the interface the clients will see, and is also part of the RMI system.

RMI binding

```
RemoteClassid remoteObjectid;
try {
    Naming.rebind ("Service name", remoteObjectid);
catch (Exception e) {
    System.out.println("Registry not found etc.\n"+e);
}
```

The *Service name* is entered in the registry alongside a reference to
the remote object given by *remoteObjectid*. The remote object
must be of a class that implements the Remote interface.

Any existing services of the same name are overwritten. To avoid this
happening, use bind instead of rebind.

The registry must be accessible, i.e. running somewhere in the current
program's path otherwise there will be an exception.

RMI look-up

```
RemoteInterfaceID localObjectId;
try {
 localObjectId = (RemoteInterfaceid)
 Naming.lookup (url + "Service Name");
}
catch (Exception e) {
 System.out.println("No such service or no registry\n"+e);
}
```

The client sees the type of the remote service only through a common
interface with the server, *RemoteInterfaceid*.

The client looks up the *Service name* in the registry to get a reference to the remote object into the *localObjectid* variable.

If either the registry or the particular service are unavailable, exceptions
are thrown.

Once the look-up has been successfully completed, localObjectid contains a direct
reference to the remoteObjectid across the Internet, but can be used just as any other
local object.

EXAMPLE 14.6　　Magic number server

Problem　Illustrate RMI with the simplest possible program.

Solution　Have a remote object that generates random numbers and is accessible through a server. Clients come in to get their 'magic' numbers.

Design　The system consists of a server on one computer and any number of clients on the same or other computers. Both use the `java.rmi` package. The server binds an object in the registry and the client looks it up. The development of the system proceeds in steps:

1. Define the `MagicNumber` class from which the remote objects will be the instantiated.

2. Define a corresponding `Transferable` interface which can be used by the client, because it cannot see the `MagicNumber` class directly.

3. Define the `MagicNumberServer` on one machine or in one directory on a machine.

4. Define a `MagicNumberClient` on another machine or in another directory.

5. Proceed with compiling everything, then put the remote object class, i.e. `Magic-Number`, through the **rmic** tool to create its stubs and skeletons. Through these, it can be accessed remotely.

6. Run the **rmiregistry** tool to create the object registry.

7. Run the server and then the clients.

Program　So first of all we have the object class:

```
import java.rmi.*;
import java.rmi.server.*;


/* A remote object    by J M Bishop Oct 1997
 * ================    Java 1.2 August 2000
 *
 * These objects can be registered on one machine and
 * accessed via the Internet and rmi protocol from other
 * machines. Compilation is a two-step process:
 *    javac MagicNumber.java
 *    rmic MagicNumber
 * The latter creates skeletons and stubs for the
 * remote object. To make it accessible on the network:
 * In Window 1 type:
 *    rmiregistry
```

```
 * The registry will stay running.
 * Then activate the server and client parts of the system.
 */

class MagicNumber extends UnicastRemoteObject implements Transferable {

  MagicNumber () throws RemoteException {
  }

  public String getNumber () throws RemoteException {
    return "Your magic number is "+ (int) (Math.random()*100);;
  }

}
```

To match this kind of object, we have the interface:

```
import java.rmi.*;

interface Transferable extends Remote {
  String getNumber () throws RemoteException;
}
```

Then the server:

```
import java.rmi.*;

public class MagicNumberServer {

  /* The Magic Number client-server system by J M Bishop Aug 2000
   * =====================================
   *                         adapted from the ThingServer Oct 1997
   *
   * Illustrates client-server using RMI
   * Run by typing:
   * In Window 2:
   *    java MagicNumberServer
   */

  public static void main (String args []) throws RemoteException {

    MagicNumber number = new MagicNumber ();

    try {
      Naming.rebind ("Magic Number Service", number);
```

```
    }
    catch (Exception x) {
      System.out.println("Could not bind or no such host etc"+x);
    }
    System.out.println("The Magic number service is running");
  }
}
```

And finally the client:

```
import java.rmi.*;
import java.rmi.server.*;

public class MagicNumberClient {

  /* The client part  by J M Bishop Oct 1997
   * ================  Java 1.2 update August 2000
   *
   * Activate the client by typing
   * In Window 3:
   *    java MagicNumberClient
   * which will default to the current machine, or
   *    java MagicNumberClient serverid
   * if the client is running on a different machine
   * from the server.
   */

  public static void main (String args []) {

  String computer;
  if (args.length == 0) computer = "127.0.0.1";
  else computer = args[0];
    try {
      Transferable t = (Transferable) Naming.lookup
                  ("rmi://"+computer + "/Magic Number Service");
      System.out.println(t.getNumber());
  }
  catch (Exception e) {
    System.out.println("Error "+e);
  }
  }
}
```

Because magic numbers are going to be dealt with across the network, they need special treatment, and Java wants to know about it. That is why `MagicNumber` imports `rmi` and `rmi.server` and indicates in its methods and constructor that a `Remote  Exception` could be thrown, for example if the server goes down.

Testing The system can be tested on one computer with several windows or background jobs or on different computers, without change. However, RMI programs need special treatment. First of all, we start up the registry by executing

```
rmiregistry
```

Then we execute the server:

```
java MagicNumberServer
```

Now clients can come in. If we type, in a new window,

```
java MagicNumberClient
```

back will come the output:

```
Your magic number is 69
```

A realistic example of RMI is given next in Case Study 11.

14.6   Case Study 11: The Airport Announcer system

The Savanna Airport Company has decided to computerize its announcements, rather than using an operator. Announcements come from two sources: airlines and the company itself. Airlines send out announcements as required regarding check-in, flight delays and so on. The airport is responsible for security messages which tend to be sent at regular intervals, automatically. We are therefore looking at a system with an initial model design as in Figure 14.10. The monitor handles the distribution of the messages, via loudspeakers as well as on the TV screens around the airport. To keep our example simple, we shall use a single monitor, operating as a scrolling line of text.

The airlines' applets

The system provides airlines with access to a set of applets. Each applet sets up a screen and asks for information which is then used to compose a message. For example, the Checkin applet asks for a flight number and destination. It then dispatches the message such as:

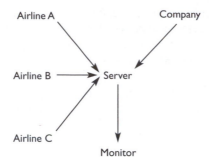

Figure 14.10 *Model for the Airport Announcer system.*

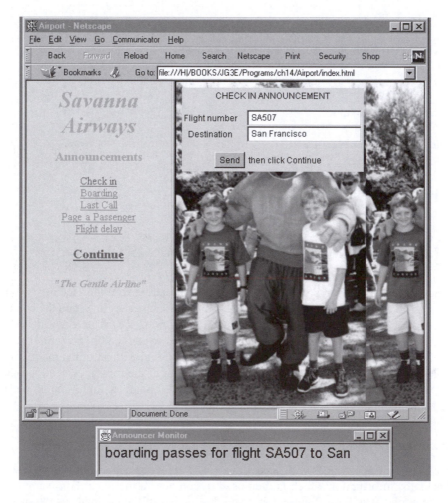

Figure 14.11 *The* Checkin *applet for the Airport Announcer system with the monitor below.*

'Will all passengers not yet in possession of boarding passes for flight SA567
to San Francisco please leave the queue and move directly to check-in 35 or 36.'

Other applets display messages for a boarding call, last call, flight delay and so. In each
case, only the necessary information is called for. The Checkin applet with the result of
its message is shown in Figure 14.11.

The applet is put on the right side of a double frame, where the left side always has the
menu of applets available. At start-up, the right side merely shows a background image,
as in Figure 14.12.

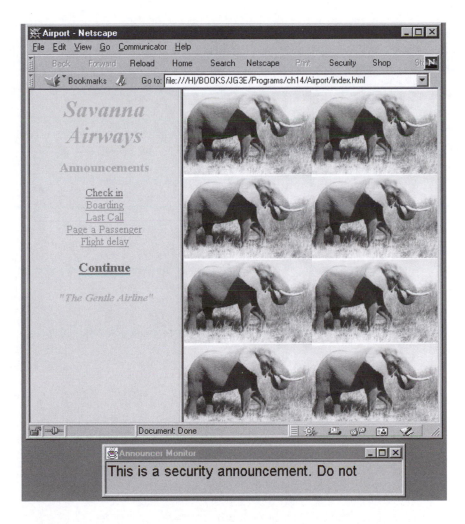

Figure 14.12 *The first screen for the Airport Announcer system, with a security announcement.*

Airline-side HTML

The applets for the airlines are run via browsers which handle the frames, menu and background pictures. The `index.html` file for the system is very short:

```
<HTML>
<HEAD>
  <TITLE>Airport</TITLE>
</HEAD>


<FRAMESET COLS="215,*">
<FRAME SRC="Contents.html" NORESIZE SCROLLING="NO">
<FRAME SRC="Applets.html" NAME="Applets">
</FRAMESET>


</HTML>
```

The Contents frame presents the menu, and is given by:

```
<HTML>
  <HEAD>
    <META NAME="Author" CONTENT="JM Bishop">
    <TITLE>Contents</TITLE>
  </HEAD>
  <BODY TEXT="#CE5831" BGCOLOR="#F1D7BE" LINK="#EF5310"
        VLINK="#974D0F" ALINK="#EF5310" SCROLLING="NO">

  <CENTER>
  <H1>
  <I><FONT COLOR="#00CC00"><FONT SIZE=+3>Savanna Airways
    </FONT></FONT></I></H1>

  <H2>
  <FONT FACE="Arial, Helvetica"><FONT COLOR="#00CC00"><FONT SIZE=+1>
  Announcements</FONT></FONT>
  </H2>

  <FONT COLOR="#E17100">
  <A HREF="checkin.html" target="Applets">Check in</A>
  <A HREF="Board.html" target="Applets">Boarding</A>
  <A HREF="Last.html" target="Applets">Last Call</A>
  <A HREF="Page.html" target="Applets">Page a Passenger</A>
  <A HREF="Delay.html" target="Applets">Flight delay</A>
  </FONT><BR>
  <BR>
```

```
    <H2>
    <FONT COLOR="#00CC00"><FONT SIZE=+1>
    <A HREF="Applets.html" target="Applets">Continue</A>
    </FONT>

     <I><FONT SIZE=+0>"The Gentle Airline"
   </FONT></FONT></FONT></I></H2>
   </CENTER>
     
</BODY>
   </HTML>
```

The target tag in an HTML link indicates which frame the page should be loaded into. We declared two frames, Contents and Applets. So the above code indicates that each of the applets gets loaded into the right hand, or Applets, frame.

Notice that the Continue link pulls up the original right frame background, in so doing overwriting the applet that has just been used. Each of the HTML links points to another HTML file which is very simple, just setting up a background and calling in the appropriate applet. Checkin's looks like this:

```
<HTML>
  <HEAD>
    <TITLE>Check in</TITLE>
  </HEAD>

  <BODY TEXT="#CE5831" BGCOLOR="#F1D7BE" LINK="#A76330"
        VLINK="#974D0F" ALINK="#EF5310" BACKGROUND="Genishot.jpg"
        SCROLLING="NO">

  <APPLET CODE="Checkin.class" WIDTH=260 HEIGHT=120></APPLET>
  </BODY>
  </HTML>
```

The system is now ready to have the applets and servers added.

The applets

The applets are straightforward in that they have text boxes to be filled in. To get a better layout than that provided by Grid layout (as shown in Figure 14.11) we use GridBag layout. Although we have avoided it up to now, there is really nothing terribly difficult about GridBag. The position of the components in the grid is arranged so that the left ones get the space they need and the right ones get the rest. This arrangement is ideal for label–text field pairs. The full text of the Checkin applet is:

```java
import java.awt.*;
import java.applet.*;
import java.awt.event.*;

public class Checkin extends Applet implements ActionListener {

  /* The Check in Message Applet    by L Botha and J Bishop
   * ===========================    Java 1.1 January 1998
   * receives the fields for the check in
   * message, constructs it and sends it
   * on to the rmi server which must be set
   * running first.
   */
  private Button sendButton;
  private TextField flight, to;

  public void init() {
    // the color is Java Gently's special orange, specified
    // as a hexadecimal number, taken from the HTML

    setBackground(new Color(0xF1D7BE));
    setLayout(new BorderLayout());

    add("North",new Label("CHECK IN ANNOUNCEMENT",Label.CENTER));

    Panel p = new Panel();
      // We use Grid Bag so that the labels and fields can be
      // different sizes

      GridBagLayout layout = new GridBagLayout();
      p.setLayout(layout);
      GridBagConstraints c = new GridBagConstraints();
      c.gridwidth = 1; c.gridheight = 1;
      Label flightLabel = new Label("Flight number");
        c.gridx = 0; c.gridy = 0;
        layout.setConstraints(flightLabel, c);
        p.add(flightLabel);
      Label toLabel = new Label("Destination");
        c.gridx = 0; c.gridy = 1;
        layout.setConstraints(toLabel, c);
        p.add(toLabel);
      flight = new TextField("", 20);
        flight.addActionListener(this);
        c.gridx = 1; c.gridy = 0;
        layout.setConstraints(flight, c);
```

```
        p.add(flight);
    to = new TextField("", 20);
      to.addActionListener(this);
      c.gridx = 1; c.gridy = 1;
      layout.setConstraints(to, c);
      p.add(to);

    add("Center",p);

  Panel q = new Panel();
    sendButton = new Button("Send");
      sendButton.addActionListener(this);
      q.add(sendButton);
      q.add(new Label("then click Continue"));
    add("South",q);
  }

  public void actionPerformed(ActionEvent e) {
    Object source = e.getSource();
    if (source == sendButton) {
      String message =
        "Will all passengers not yet in possession of "
      + "boarding passes for flight " + flight.getText() + " to "
      + to.getText() + " please leave the queue and move "
      + "directly to check-in 35 or 36.";
      AnnouncerClient.sendMessage(message);
      flight.setText("");
      to.setText("");
    }
  }
}
```

Connecting via RMI

Potentially, there could be many computers in this system. There are at least three – an airline, an announcer server plus monitor and the airport company – plus one more for each additional airline. The question is, how do the computers communicate? We could open sockets, but RMI is a more elegant solution, and surprisingly easy to set up and use.

Figure 14.13 gives a high-level diagram of the different classes that are required. The system is not symmetrical. The airline applets are coupled with a client that will dispatch a message to a local client on the same machine, but the airport company's client is based with the announcer because it is activated when the announcer wishes. It calls the company's server for an appropriate message.

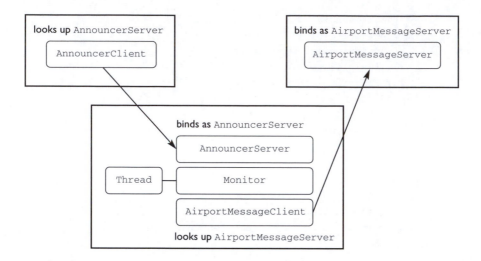

Figure 14.13 *Top-level model diagram of the Airport Announcer system, showing the different computers.*

The applet calls its client as follows:

```
AnnouncerClient.sendMessage (message);
```

The client reacts by looking up a remote interface to the announcer server and passing the message on, as in:

```
Announcer an = (Announcer)Naming.lookup
               ("rmi://localhost/AnnouncerServer");
an.sendMessage(message);
```

The server's version of `sendMessage` stores the message in an array of messages. It is necessary to do so, since messages could be coming in thick and fast, certainly faster than the monitor can announce them. The server, though, is passive: it receives messages and then waits for the monitor to ask for them when it is ready to display them.

The monitor is a thread, and can therefore run at the same time as the server is accepting more messages. It gets a message from either one of the servers as appropriate. If the announcer has messages, it gets one, otherwise it waits a few seconds and asks the airport client for a message. The client connects up to the server and gets a message. The `run` method of the monitor is active, and looks like this:

```
public void run() {
  boolean startdelay;
  while (true) {
    startdelay = true;
    if (server.hasMessage()) {
      String msg = server.getMessage();
```

```
      while (msg.length() > 0) {
      String displaymsg = formatString(msg);
      message.setText("");
      message.setText(displaymsg);
      if (startdelay == true) {
      try { Thread.sleep(1000); } catch (Exception e) {}
         startdelay = false;
      }
      try { Thread.sleep(200); } catch (Exception e) {}
        msg = msg.substring(1);
      }
      message.setText("");
      server.removeMessage();
    }
    try { Thread.sleep(5000); } catch (Exception e) {}
    String newmsg = AirportMessageClient.getMessage();
    if (newmsg != null)
      server.sendMessage(newmsg);
  }
}
```

`Server` refers to the `AnnouncerServer`. `Monitor` asks if it has a message. If not, it waits a while and gets a message from its other source, the airport company using a local client and the remote server. The airport company running the remote server can add different messages at different times and change the timing for them. At present the system is set up to present one of the following messages in rotation:

> 'This is a security announcement. Do not leave baggage unattended at any time. Baggage left unattended will be removed and destroyed.'
> 'Children are not allowed to play on the escalators or in the lifts.'
> 'The Airports Company welcomes you and trusts you will have a safe and pleasant journey.'

The full code for the system is given on the web site, but Figure 14.14 summarizes the system with a full model diagram.

Running the system

To run the system, we need the equivalent of three background processes (or windows) and a browser. In the first window we set up the RMI registry by typing:

```
rmiregistry
```

In the next two windows, we activate the two servers, which bind themselves to the registry, i.e.

```
java AnnouncerServer
```

```
java AirportMessageServer
```

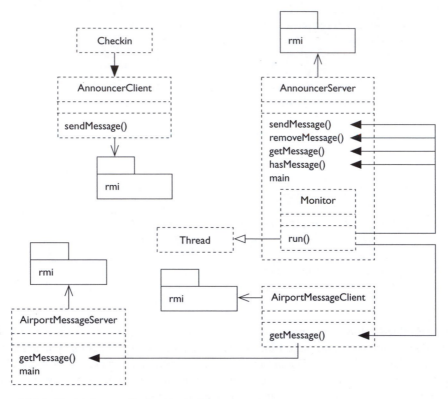

Figure 14.14 *Model diagram for the Airport Announcer server system.*

Then we enter the browser, opening `index.html`. The screen should give us Figure 14.12. If we click on <u>Check in</u> we will get Figure 14.11, and so on. The monitor window is started up by the `AnnouncerServer`, and is a small thin window through which the messages scroll. Try it out, and have fun!

SUMMARY

Java provides a variety of ways of connecting machines on the network, from URL connections to resources, to ports and sockets, database connectivity and remote objects. Each is supported by special classes and libraries and all are part of the standard Java language.

In this chapter, several new packages – `java.net, java.sql, java.rmi` and `java.rmi.server` – and their methods were introduced:

```
URL                              Class
  openConnection                   forName
  getContent                     DriverManager
URLConnection                      getConnection
  getInputStream                 Connection
Image                              createStatement
  createImage                    Statement
ImageProducer                      executeUpdate
ServerSocket                       executeQuery
  accept                         ResultSet
Socket                           Naming
InetAddress                        rebind
  getHostName                      lookup
  getLocalHost
```

New forms are:

URL creation
Creating a URL connection
Fetching an image
Creating sockets
Streams for sockets
Loading a database driver
Connecting to a database
Sending a statement to a database
Remote object declaration
RMI binding
RMI look-up

and there were some new exceptions:

```
MalformedURLException
ClassNotFoundException
SQLException
RemoteException
```

QUIZ

14.1 If `elephant.jpg` is an image file in the same directory as an applet which is currently running, a Java statement to access it would be:

    (a) `Image e = elephant.getImage();`
    (b) `Image e = getImage(this, elephant);`
    (c) `Image e = getImage(getCodeBase(), "elephant.jpg");`
    (d) `Image e = (MediaTracker) getImage("elephant.jpg");`

14.2 In the statement

```
a.b = a.createImage((ImageProducer)imagename.getContent());
```

what is the class of `imagename`?

(a) `URL`
(b) `ImageProducer`
(c) `Image`
(d) `Object`

14.3 In Example 14.4 (ATM server), a handler thread can call `server.closeDown()` if a special message is received. When will the server react to the message?

(a) immediately
(b) when it comes round its while-loop again
(c) after the next client has joined
(d) b and c

14.4 What is the difference between a socket and a server socket in Java's APIs?

(a) a socket resides on the client and a server socket on the server
(b) both reside on the server, but the server socket can listen for new clients
(c) `ServerSocket` is a class and `socket` is an object
(d) server sockets listen for new clients and sockets reside on both sides to make the connection

14.5 What is the URL tag for displaying an image?

(a) `<IMAGE = ...>`
(b) `<IMG SRC = ...>`
(c) `<IMG = ...>`
(d) `<DISPLAY .= ...>`

14.6 Suppose we have another class in Example 14.6 called `Secret`, which also implements the `Transferable` interface. Leaving out exception handling, a statement to bind `s`, an object of class `Secret`, in the RMI registry would be:

(a) `Naming.rebind (Secret, s);`
(b) `Naming.rebind ("Secret Service", s);`
(c) `s.rebind ("Secret Service");`
(d) `Naming.rebind (s);`

14.7 The `Socket` class is declared in the java package called

(a) `java.lang`
(b) `java.net`
(c) `java.util`
(d) `java.rmi`

14.8 If `con` is a database connection, then a Java statement to create an object to hold an SQL query would be:

(a) `String s = con.readln();`
(b) `Statement s = con.createStatement();`
(c) `Statement s = con ("SELECT");`
(d) `String s = con.create("SELECT");`

14.9　Before we can write database programs in Java, we need to

    (a)　set up a suitable JDBC driver
    (b)　set up a suitable JDBC or OBDC driver
    (c)　set up a suitable JDBC driver or JDBC:OBDC bridge
    (d)　call `Class.forName()`

14.10　The RMI compiler (rmic) must be run on

    (a)　all classes that are part of an RMI system
    (b)　only the client classes
    (c)　only the server classes
    (d)　only the remote object classes

PROBLEMS

Using connections and sockets

14.1　**Listing via HTML.** Create a Lister program as an applet, which accepts the name of a file coming in from a text field added to the applet's interface. Put the applet in an HTML page and have the HTML give a list of suggested files on a particular topic that can be fetched.

14.2　**Chatting clients.** The Chatter program (Case Study 10) provides a server only. Using the Ports program in Example 14.3 as a basis, create a Java program that can be started up on the client side and provide similar facilities to telnet.

14.3　**Chatting on the web.** Even after Problem 14.2, the user interface to the Chatter is rather basic. Try making the server into an applet and embody it in an HTML page that provides instructions, displays the output, and has a separate line for typing in input.

14.4　**Knock knock!** Using the ATM server as a basis (Example 14.4) write a server to play Knock! Knock! The game goes like this:

Client	Server
Knock knock	
	Who's there?
Amos	
	Amos who?
Amos Quito.	

Use telnet for the client again.

14.5　**Cellphone messages.** Create a system to handle cellphone messages. There is a central server which keeps track of registered cellphones. Each cellphone is a client which collects a message and a phone number sends the message to the server, which relays it to the correct phone. This system is very similar to the chat system (Case Study 10) except that the messages go out to a specific person rather than to everyone. You can represent the cellphones using the command line, or you can use a GUI interface such as that developed in Problems 10.3 and 12.10.

14.6　**Voicemail.** If a phone is switched off, then a message should be stored at the server. As soon as the phone is switched on, a system message is sent out saying that there are so many stored messages. The user can then retrieve them one by one. Implement such a system for the cellphone in Problem 14.5.

For database connectivity

14.7 **Pets database.** Using the methods described in Section 14.4, convert the Veterinary Tags system (Case Study 4 in Chapter 9 and Problem 12.9) to run on a database. The client applet should allow queries, and submission to a separate manager thread which handles updates. The manager can presumably then first check that the updates are valid before adding them to the database.

14.8 **House search.** An estate agent keeps a record of available houses for sale on a database. When a client comes along, a list of suitable properties by price range and/or by area can be printed out. Set up such a system. Start by defining a house object, and follow the steps in Section 4.4.

14.9 **Coffee shop database.** Nelson would like to investigate whether a database would be better than serialized linked lists (as in Problem 9.6) for having a truly permanent record of his inventory which can be queried by clients only, and updated by himself in his shop. Program a database for the coffee shop and write a report comparing the two approaches.

14.10 **Room bookings.** Going back to the Room Bookings system posed in the problems of Chapters 4 and 5, investigate putting the system on a database. All queries and updates should be available to everyone.

On RMI

14.11 **Room booking statistics.** Regard the program in Problem 14.10 as a server, and add to it a class called `RoomStats` which will access the database to find out statistics about room usage. Then set up a separate applet which communicates with the server via RMI calls to `RoomStats` methods. Such an applet could be used by management and should have ease of use in mind.

14.12 **Airport applets.** Write the remainder of the applets associated with the airport system.

CHAPTER 15

Data structures and algorithms

15.1 About data structures

We conclude our study of Java by looking ahead to a more advanced computer science course, and the study of data structures.

A **data structure** is a collection of **nodes** of the same class or type which is organized and accessed in a defined way.

A node would usually be an object, but could be as simple as an integer. The fact that the definition states that the nodes must be of the same class or type means that we can refer to a structure of that type, for example a list of coffees or a hash table of strings.

The linked list data structure that we built up in Section 8.2 was an *ad hoc* one, designed for the purpose. Another problem might require a very different data structure. In computer science, though, there are several recognized data structures that crop up again and again in solutions to problems. They have names and defined properties, and in a sense can be regarded as an extension of the basic data types of a language.

Java has recognized the importance of data structures and has supplied classes in its standard packages for a good number of them. Just to provide a checklist, Table 15.1 gives a canonical list of data structures, indicating those that are in Java and those that are covered in this edition of the book.

In this chapter we revisit linked lists in order to add some more features and give another example of their use. We also cover two more Java data structures classes – `Stack` and `BitSet` – and look at how queues can be implemented based on arrays.

Properties

Each data structure has properties relating to the following:

- relationship to other nodes;
- composition of a header node;
- point of addition of nodes – front, back or anywhere;
- point of deletion of nodes – front, back or anywhere;
- direction of scanning – none, forwards, backwards or other.

As we get to each data structure, we shall address these issues.

Table 15.1 *Table of data structures*

Data structure	Sample Java Class (if any)	*Java Gently* section
array	built-in	6.1, 6.2
extensible array	`java.util.Vector`	6.5
linked list	`java.util.LinkedList`	8.1, 8.3, 15.5
stack	`java.util.Stack`	15.4
queue		15.4
tree	`java.util.TreeMap`	
hash table	`java.util.Hashtable`	6.5
set	`java.util.Set, BitSet`	15.6
dictionary	`java.util.Dictionary`	
sequential file	`java.io.File...Stream`	4.5
random file	`java.io.RandomAccessFile`	

Representation

Data structures can be represented as either **arrays** of objects or as nodes **linked** by their references, as already shown in Section 8.2. The decision as to which method to employ depends on two factors. A linked representation has the advantage that the number of nodes in the structure can be completely flexible: with an array representation, the maximum number would have to be fixed. On the other hand, linked-based structures require space for the links, and these increase the overall size of the structure.

There is no inherent complexity related to the programming in either case, and we shall present both representations, endeavouring to show the underlying algorithms as independent of the representation. In so doing, we create **abstract data types** which have recognizable forms and properties, and can be used only as specified.

Algorithms

Two of the operations we will often need for a data structure as a whole are sorting and searching. Before we start on looking at the inner details of data structures, therefore, we complete our study of the basic algorithms that should be part of a computer scientist's toolkit. The list includes:

- a linear search and a faster one;

- a straight sort and a faster one.

A linear search was shown in Section 6.4 for arrays, and in Section 8.3 via iterators for linked lists. Straight sorting was also covered in Section 6.4. Both the faster algorithms we shall look at now make use of a basic computing technique – **recursion** – without which no textbook on programming would be complete.

What Java provides

As with data structures (see Table 15.1), Java provides for the fundamental algorithms we are about to discuss. There is a class called `Arrays` which has `binarySearch`, `sort`, `equals` and `fill` methods for arrays of every one of the eight primitive types as well as the superclass `Object`. Selecting only integers, these are defined in the following form:

Arrays class methods for int

`int binarySearch(int [] a, int key)`
`boolean equals (int [] a1, int [] a2)`
`void fill (int [] a, int val)`
`void sort (int [] a)`

Although one could use these methods exclusively, it is very useful to know how they work. The next two sections describe the insides of binary searching and quick sorting, and compare their performance with the linear versions.

15.2 Linear and binary searching

We can define a **sequence** as a data structure which has the property that each element is reachable after the previous one. In other words, the structure can be accessed in sequence. Examples of such structures would be an array, a list or a file stream. A hash table is not a sequence, however, although a Java hash table can be accessed sequentially via an enumerator.

If we have a sequence of values then we can search for a particular value by starting at the beginning of the sequence and comparing each element in turn. This is called **linear** searching, because we scan the sequence in a linear way.

The linear searching algorithm is an example of a double-exit loop: either the value is found in the sequence, or the end of the sequence is reached before the value is found. These kinds of loop were examined extensively in Section 5.2, where the sequence was the input data stream, and again in Section 8.3 for a linked list. Let us now translate that logic to searching an array.

The advantage of searching an array is that we know its length. We can therefore use a for-loop, together with the extra control it provides for stopping if not found. A first attempt at the linear search is:

```
int i;
for (i = 0; i< a.length; i++)
  if (a[i] == x) break;
```

Though simple and neat, this loop has an unfortunate defect: at the end we do not know if we exited the loop because we found the item or not. Now, if we are certain of finding the item, this is fine. But in the general case, we cannot be so sure. Notice also that we deliberately declared i outside the loop so that we could access a[i] afterwards.

That means that the algorithm returns two values: a yes/no indicator (or boolean, say) and an index. This makes it very difficult to parcel the search up into a method, since we can return only one value from a method (unless we return a multivalued object).

A possible technique is to return the index, but to set it to some out-of-range value if the item was not found. Possible values could be –1 or length. Instinctively this smacks of bad practice. An altogether better approach is to use a user-defined exception. Consider the following proposal:

```
class ItemNotFoundException extends Exception { }

item a [] = new a[n];

static int LinearSearch (item a [], item x)
                    throws ItemNotFoundException {
  for (int i = 0; i< a.length; i++)
    if (x.equals(a[i])) return i;
```

```
      // item not found: no normal return
      throw new ItemNotFoundException();
    }


    //Test the method
    try {
      int found = LinearSearch (a, x);
      // do what ever is necessary with a[found]
        ...
    }
    catch (ItemNotFoundException e ) {
      // react to x not being there
        ...
    }
```

The method is passed the array and the item being sought. It loops through the array, using the array's own length as a stopping condition (which makes the method nicely general), comparing each item with *x*. The comparison is done via a call to `equals`, since we are assuming here that the items are objects. If the item is found, we return immediately. If the loop eventually ends, we throw the exception.

The calling method has a try–catch pair. If the search is successful, the next statement is executed, whatever it is. If not, control transfers to the handler in the catch-part and alternative arrangements must be made. There is a test program on the web site which shows this method in action. We do not include it here, because we want to press on to the next search algorithm – the binary search.

Binary searching

If the data to be searched are ordered, that is, sorted, then there are more efficient searching methods than linear search. The archetypal one is called **binary search**. It involves splitting the sequence in half, and searching only that part where the value must lie. One can be certain about which half the value is in, because the sequence is assumed to be sorted.

For example, suppose we have the sorted sequence:

```
23 45 61 65 67 70 82 89 90 99
```

and are searching for the value 90. Informally, we could divide the sequence in two between 67 and 70 and see that 90 must be in the right-hand side:

```
23 45 61 65 67 70 82 89 90 99
```

We divide this subsequence in two between 89 and 90 and move to the right again:

```
70 82 89 90 99
```

The sequence we are interested in is now two long, but we still divide and move to the left, where we find 90:

$$90 \quad 99$$

This took four divides and compares, compared with nine with a linear search.

Clearly, binary search is faster *on average*, but not every time. If the value being sought was 23 (the first in the sequence), binary search would still start in the centre and move gradually to the left to find it. The best way to formulate such a binary search is by using a technique called **recursion**:

> **Recursion** allows us to describe an operation in terms of itself, based on modified data and with a stopping condition.

Using this idea, an algorithm for binary search is:

> **Binary search a sequence for x**
>   If the sequence has one element,
>   compare x with it and return found or not found.
>   Otherwise consider the element in the middle of the sequence.
>   If x < middle element, then **binary search** left subsequence for x
>   else **binary search** the right subsequence for x.

In many cases, the sequence or subsequence to be split will not have an even number of elements and so we adopt the convention that the extra element goes to the left subsequence. Looking at the algorithm, one can see that an improvement would be to add an additional condition in the second part, to consider whether the value being sought is in fact the middle element at the time.

Conditions for binary search

Binary searching relies on the values being ordered, but it also relies on being able to index the sequence. Thus, binary searching is not possible on files or lists. It works on arrays only.

EXAMPLE 15.1   Animated binary search

Problem In order to illustrate binary search, we shall develop a Java program to implement the algorithm above, and show the stages of the search as it develops.

Solution We start off with a sequence of numbers, and every time we split the sequence, we shall print out only those numbers left in the sequence. This begs the question of how we 'split a sequence'. The answer is that we do not! What we do is we keep only one sequence and indicate the left and right limits each time.

Algorithm   There is a slightly difficult part in splitting a sequence. If the sequence starts at 0, the midpoint is at $n/2$, where n is the last index. For example, for an array going from 0 to 9, $9/2 = 4$ is the midpoint. However, if a subsequence runs from j to k in a larger sequence, then the midpoint of the subsequence is at position $(j + k)/2$. You should verify that you understand why this is so.

Program   The program to animate the binary search follows. We have chosen to use character data stored as objects, but to preset it in the program. Remember to keep the data sorted, or the program will not function correctly. (Alternatively, slot in a sort procedure and sort the data first, just to make sure.)

The important part of the binary search method is its use of recursion, and we therefore list it separately first, with line numbers.

```
1.   static int binarySearch (item a [], item x, int left, int right)
2.             throws ItemNotFoundException {
3.     display(a,left,right);
4.     if (left==right)
5.       if (x.equals(a[left]))
6.         return left;
7.       else
8.         throw new ItemNotFoundException ();
9.     else {
10.      int mid = (int) ((left+right) / 2);
11.      if (x.equals(a[mid]))
12.        return mid;
13.      else
14.      if (x.less(a[mid]))
15.        return binarySearch (a, x, left, mid);
16.      else
17.        return binarySearch (a, x, mid+1, right);
18.    }
19. }
```

`binarySearch` will call itself with the left or right subsequence (lines 15 and 17) until the subsequence is of length one (detected on line 4). Then it either exits with an exception (line 6), or returns the index of this subsequence (line 5). The point of call was line 15 or 17, so the return comes back to one of these. Both result in the method reaching a natural end (line 19) and so a return to the previous point of call is made again. Once again, this could be line 15 or 17. Eventually, the very first call of `binarySearch`, which was made with the full sequence, will reach its natural end, and control will go back to the calling method. All along, the index value that was detected as holding the required item x is being passed back as the return value of the method.

binarySearch is declared as static because it is a method like mean or stdDev: it takes parameters and returns a value. However, it also makes use of an ancillary method, display, and a variable, counter. These therefore also have to be static. Why is counter not declared inside binarySearch? The reason is that it needs to retain a value that is independent of the recursion. If it were inside the recursive method, it would be reset to zero each time round the loop and not retain its count of how many times the search had iterated.

The main program and associated classes look like this:

```
import javagently.*;
import java.io.*;


class Animated {

  /* The animated binary search program by J M Bishop Jan 1997
   * =================================== Java 1.1
   *                                     improved August 2000
   * searches a sorted sequence for a given value
   * and shows the workings of binary sort.
   *
   * Illustrates recursion and user defined exceptions
   */

  static item a [] = new item [10];
  static int counter;

  static int binarySearch (item a [], item x, int left, int right)
  //---------------------
                          throws ItemNotFoundException {
    display(a,left,right);
    if (left==right)
      if (x.equals(a[left])) return left;
      else throw new ItemNotFoundException ();
    else {
      int mid = (int) ((left+right) / 2);
      if (x.equals(a[mid]))
        return mid;
      else
        if (x.less(a[mid]))
      return binarySearch (a, x, left, mid);
        else
      return binarySearch (a, x, mid+1, right);
    }
  }
```

```
public static void main (String args [])
                    throws IOException {

   BufferedReader in = new Stream(System.in);
   System.out.println("**** Testing the binary search ****");
   System.out.println("Type in 10 sorted characters "+
           "separated by spaces");
   for (int i=0; i<a.length;i++)
     a[i] = new item (Stream.readChar(in));

   // Loop to try several searches
   while (true)
     try {
       counter = 0;
       Text.prompt("Find what value?");
       item x = new item(Stream.readChar(in));
       System.out.println("The array is:");
       System.out.println("0 1 2 3 4 5 6 7 8 9");

       try {
         int found = BinarySearch (a, x, 0, a.length-1);
         // do what ever is necessary with a[found]
         System.out.println((char) x.data+
                " was found at position "+found
                +" in "+counter+" probes.");
       }
       catch (ItemNotFoundException e ) {
         // react to x not being there
         System.out.println((char) x.data+" was not found in "
           +counter+" probes.");
       }
     }
   catch (EOFException e) {break;}
 }

 static void display (item [] a, int left, int right) {
   for (int j = 0; j < left; j++)
     System.out.print(" ");
   for (int j = left; j <= right; j++)
     System.out.print((char) a[j].data+" ");
   System.out.println();
   counter++;
 }
}
```

```
class item {
// ---------
// the objects being sorted

  item (char i) {
    data = i;
  }

  boolean equals (item x) {
    return data==x.data;
  }

  boolean less (item x) {
    return data < x.data;
  }

  char data;
}
class ItemNotFoundException extends Exception { }
```

Testing   Several tests are shown, including one when the number was found, and one when it was not. Note that e and j were found in fewer probes than with a linear search, but that finding b took slightly more. A real advantage of the binary search is that it can always establish that an item is not there in far fewer probes than a linear search can. The exact number of probes is given by a formula which we shall discuss in the next section.

```
**** Testing the binary search ****
Find what value?e
The array is:
0  1  2  3  4  5  6  7  8  9
e g h j k m r t w y
e  0  9  4
e  0  4  2
e  0  2  1
e  0  1  0
e was found at position 0 in 4 probes.
Find what value?f
The array is:
0  1  2  3  4  5  6  7  8  9
e g h j k m r t w y
f  0  9  4
f  0  4  2
f  0  2  1
f  0  1  0
f was not found in 5 probes.
```

```
Find what value?k
The array is:
0  1  2  3  4  5  6  7  8  9
e  g  h  j  k  m  r  t  w  y
k  0  9  4
k was found at position 4 in 1 probes.
Find what value?t
The array is:
0  1  2  3  4  5  6  7  8  9
e  g  h  j  k  m  r  t  w  y
t  0  9  4
t  5  9  7
t was found at position 7 in 2 probes.
Find what value?
```

15.3 Quicksort and performance

There are many different algorithms for sorting, but one that is a classic because of its overall good performance is known as **Quicksort**. Sorting is based on the twin operations of comparing and exchanging; Quicksort is based on the principle that any exchange must take place over the greatest distance possible. Thus, instead of exchanging adjacent elements, we select elements that are at virtually opposite ends of the sequence. To do this, we adopt the split-in-half idea used in binary search. Basically, we split the sequence at a certain point and move all the bigger items to the right and the smaller items to the left, using 'long exchanges'. This done, we concentrate on each subsequence in turn, doing the same until only one item remains in each. Quicksort does not split each subsequence exactly in half, as binary search did, but divides on the position around which the last exchange was made.

Put in algorithmic terms, Quicksort is:

Quicksort
Provided the sequence has more than one item
   Choose an item as a pivot (e.g. the midpoint)
   Move all items less than it to the left
   Move all items more than it to the right
   Quicksort the left subsequence
   Quicksort the right subsequence

where the algorithm for the move is given in Figure 15.1.

Quicksort is quite complicated, and strangely enough, animating it, or performing an example in detail does not make it clearer. It is one of those algorithms that one has to understand in theory, and then accept as correct. It is, however, possible to program it quite concretely in Java.

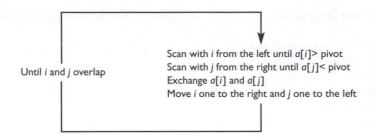

Figure 15.1 *Algorithm for a move in Quicksort.*

In Java, a recursive Quicksort is:

```
1. static item [] quicksort (Item [] a, int l, int r) {
2.    if (l < r) {
3.       display(a,l,r);
4.       int i = l;
5.       int j = r;
6.       int k = (int) ((l+r) / 2);
7.       Item pivot = a[k];
8.       do {
9.          while (a[i].less(pivot)) i++;
10.         while (pivot.less(a[j])) j--;
11.          if (i<=j) {
12.             item t = (item) a[i].clone();
13.             a[i] = a[j];
14.             a[j] = t;
15.             i++; j--;
16.          }
17.       } while (i<j);
18.       a = quicksort (a, l, j);
19.       a = quicksort (a, i, r);
20.    }
21.    return a;
22.}
```

Note some points about the programming. On line 7 we set up the pivot as a reference
to the middle element using assignment, but on line 12, we use `clone` to make a copy
of `a[i]`. Why the difference? The reason is that lines 12–14 are performing a swap of
the two elements, `a[i]` and `a[j]`. Before we wipe out `a[i]` on line 13, we need to
copy its contents.

   Like `binarySearch`, `quicksort` is a typed method, but this time we return an
array, rather than just one index. Therefore when it is called, it takes the array as a parameter and returns the new version as its result.

There is a test program for `quicksort` on the web. Here is some typical output:

```
**** Testing Quicksort ****
27 91 42 23 40 74 96 28 31 59
27 31 28 23
27 23 28
   27 28
      28 31
                    74 96 42 91 59
                    42 96
                       96 74 91 59
                          91 96
23 27 28 31 40 42 59 74 91 96
```

On each line, the method displays the subsequence it has been given to sort. The initial pivot, 40, is not considered after the first line, because we had shifted everything greater than it to the right and everything less than it to its left. That means that 91 and 42, which were originally on its left, would have swapped with 31 and 28 respectively. You can see the result on lines 2 and 6, which show the first two subsequences.

A look at performance

The need to look for different algorithms to solve the same problem stems from a desire for speed: newer algorithms may be faster and therefore, in everyone's eyes, better. What differences in speed are found? With searching and sorting algorithms, they can be quite considerable. Moreover, the speed of the algorithms is proportional to the number of items involved, and therefore can become quite significant once there are thousands or millions of items.

There are two ways of comparing performance: theoretical and experimental. Let us look first at the theoretical performance. We calculate the speed of an algorithm based on the number of 'basic operations' it has to perform. These basic operations are rationalized to include only comparisons and exchanges, and assessing the performance boils down to counting the occurrence of these inside loops.

Comparison of sorts

Consider selection sort which we dealt with in Section 6.4. The outer loop goes for $n - 1$, and includes $n - 1$ exchanges. The inner loop runs from *leftmost* to $n - 1$ and so reduces by one at each iteration. The number of comparisons is therefore:

$$(n - 1) + (n - 2) + (n - 3) + \ldots + 1 = n\,(n - 1)\,/\,2$$
$$= (n^2 - n)\,/\,2$$

To simplify matters, we ignore the coefficients in the number of exchanges and simply say that they are of the order n^2. If we add in the number of exchanges, the whole process is still dominated by the n^2 term.

Quicksort, on the other hand, uses a partitioning algorithm, which in rough terms involves $\log_2$ iterations. On each iteration, n comparisons are done, and roughly $n/6$ exchanges. Quicksort is therefore considered to operate at a speed proportional to $n \log_2 n$. In real terms, how does this compare with the order of performance of selection sort? Table 15.2 evaluates both formulae for various values of n. The difference is phenomenal. Suppose the unit of time for one iteration is 1 microsecond (10^{-6} s). Then for a million items, Quicksort will take 20 seconds, whereas selection sort will take around $11\frac{1}{2}$ days! It is interesting, though, that at this rate of 1 µs, the difference between the two sorts would not really be noticeable until n exceeds 1000. At this point, selection sort will take a full second, whereas Quicksort will take only 1/100 of a second. In an interactive environment, the difference may not even be noticed.

Table 15.2 *Comparison of the speed of selection sort and Quicksort*

n	Selection sort order n^2	Quicksort order $n \log_2 n$
10	100	30
50	2 500	300
100	10 000	700
1 000	1 000 000	10 000
10 000	100 000 000	130 000
100 000	10 000 000 000	1 600 000
1 000 000	1 000 000 000 000	20 000 000

So why don't we use Quicksort all the time? The answer is provided by the other performance indicator we have: space. Java methods occupy space in memory for their instructions, as well as for their data. Both the algorithms have roughly the same number of statements, so there is not much to choose on the instruction side. However, there is a big difference in data space used. Selection sort declares four local variables and uses them throughout. Quicksort declares eight local variables and parameters for each recursive call. Since recursive calls are stacked up, it may be in the worst case that for a million items, there are 160 items stacked up by Quicksort.

Yet even this is not a lot, and therefore we can probably conclude that the slight wariness with which ordinary programmers regard Quicksort is probably due to an unfamiliarity with recursion. Of course, Quicksort does not have to be programmed recursively, but the non-recursive version is even more awkward.

Comparison of searches

The two searches we looked at can easily be seen to have performances related to n (linear) and $\log_2 n$ (binary). Here, the difference in speed is even more dramatic than sorting (Table 15.3). Put in real terms, this means that to search a telephone directory of a million entries by means of binary search, we should be able find any entry in no more than 20 probes. Very much better than an entry-by-entry linear slog!

Table 15.3 *Comparison of the speed of linear and binary search*

n	Linear search order n	Binary search order $log2n$
10	10	3
50	50	6
100	100	7
1 000	1 000	10
10 000	10 000	13
100 000	100 000	16
1 000 000	1 000 000	20

Where is this leading?

The study of algorithms, and their analysis of performance, is a cornerstone of computer science, and a major part of a second computer science course. In addition to the two sorting algorithms mentioned here, you will learn other sorts such as bubble sort (very slow), merge sort and tree sort (very fast), and pigeonhole sort (extremely fast, but fussy). You will learn how to choose an algorithm for a given solution, and look at the limits of algorithms: how fast can they really get? It is a fascinating study, and we have merely touched on it here.

15.4 Stacks and queues

We now start on the first of our data structures – the humble **stack**. Informally, a stack is defined as its name suggests: it is a pile of items which gets added to and removed from its top. A stack is often drawn upright, as in Figure 15.2(a), although it can be drawn on its side as in Figure 15.2(b).

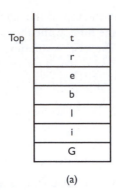

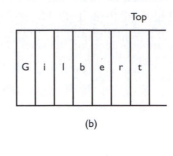

(a)

(b)

Figure 15.2 *Diagrams of stacks.*

Stack properties

Formally, we can detail the properties of a stack according to the criteria stated in Section 15.1 as:

- nodes are arranged in sequence;
- there is one end, the **top**;
- nodes are added to the **top**;
- nodes are removed from the **top**;
- the stack cannot be scanned: only the **top** node is visible. [1]

A stack can also be known as a LIFO or last-in, first-out list.

The Stack class

We are now in a position to define the stack as a class. Fortunately, Java provides such a class in its util package, with the following methods:

```
Stack

public class Stack extends Vector {
  public Object push (Object item);
  public Object pop () throws EmptyStackException;
  public Object peek () throws EmptyStackException;
  public boolean empty ();
```

---

[1] Actually Java cheats: it provides a method for searching through a stack (called search), but we shall ignore it here.

The `push` method takes the item and pushes it on to the top of the stack. The `pop` method returns the top item, 'popping' the stack at the same time, while the `peek` method returns just the top item, without popping the stack. The `empty` method determines whether there are any items on the stack. The `Stack` class is based on `Vector`, which means that a stack would be efficiently implemented as an array, and would not be restricted to a specific size.

The stack methods are defined for the superclass `Object`, so that we can put any class's objects on to a stack, and remove them, provided we provide the correct type cast. Although Java will not enforce it, we should restrict each stack to items of the same class.

The next example is a simple one, but serves to illustrate the effect of using a stack.

EXAMPLE 15.2   Reversing a sentence

Problem   Reverse a sentence of any length, word by word.

Solution   Stacks have the property that they can be used to reverse a sequence. Each word is put on the stack as it is read. Eventually when the sentence ends, the words will be stacked up, one on top of each other. We can then go through the stack again, popping the words off and printing them.

Program

```
import java.io.*;
import javagently.*;
import java.util.Stack;

public class Reverser {

  /* Testing the stack class   by J M Bishop Jan 1997
   * ----------------------    Java 1.1
   *                           updated August 2000
   * Reads a sentence and reverses it using a stack.
   * Illustrates push, pop and empty in Java's Stack class.
   */

  public static void main (String args [])
    throws IOException {
    new Reverser();
  }

  Reverser () throws IOException {

    Stream in = new Stream (System.in);
```

```
Stack S = new Stack();
System.out.println("**** Testing the Stack class ****");
System.out.println("Type in a sentence and end the input " +
    "(cntrl-D or cntrl-Z)");
System.out.println("The original sentence is: ");

while (true) {
  try {
    String word = in.readString();
    S.push(word);
  }
  catch (EOFException e) {break;}
}

System.out.println("The reversed sentence is:");
while (!S.empty())
  System.out.print (S.pop()+" ");
System.out.println();
  }
}
```

Testing Expected input and output would be:

```
**** Testing the Stack class ****
Type in a sentence and end the input (cntrl-D or cntrl-Z)
The original sentence is:
The curfew tolls the knell of parting day,
The reversed sentence is:
day, parting of knell the tolls curfew The
```

Uses of stacks

Stacks are useful for recording the state of a computation as it unfolds. A typical example is the evaluation of expressions which involve precedence and nesting. A stack is also the data structure that implements recursion. In a language such as Java, it is usually possible to use recursion with its implicit stack rather than an explicit stack. The next data structure is probably more useful in practice.

Queues

Although stacks are the simplest structures we have, their property of reversibility is not always useful. A more common data structure is one where the items can be removed in the same order in which they were inserted. Such a structure is known as a **queue** or FIFO (first-in, first-out) list.

In order to implement this property, a queue has to have two ends, indicating the front and back. New items are added on to the back, and items are removed from the front. Queues are usually drawn sideways, as in Figure 15.3(a). However, an innate property of queues is that they move forward: as an item is removed from the front, so all the other items behind it move up one. We can see immediately that such moving in an array implementation would be inefficient, and so we can already consider an alternative depiction of a queue as a circle. Here there is a fixed number of slots in the circle and the queue moves around it, as in Figure 15.3(b).

Queue properties

Formally, we can detail the properties of a queue as:

1. Nodes are arranged in sequence.

3. There are two ends, the **front** and **back**.

4. Nodes are added to the **front**.

5. Nodes are removed from the **back**.

6. The queue can be scanned from the front to the back.

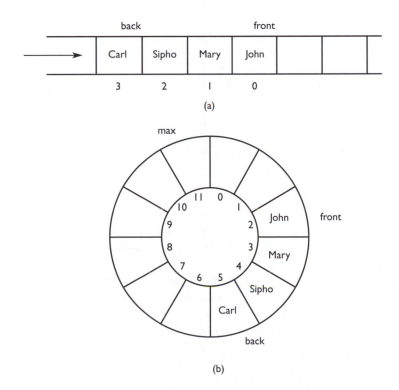

(a)

(b)

Figure 15.3 *Flat and circular queues.*

The queue abstract data type

We are now in a position to define the queue as a data type. As for stacks, we define it in terms of the superclass `Object`. However, Java does not have a predefined queue class, so we need to implement one. On what should it be based? The choices are an array, the `Vector` class or the `LinkedList` class. The last two will allow the queue to be of variable size. The `LinkedList` is probably more powerful than we need, since we do not need to remove elements anywhere in it, only at the front. `Vector` provides complete extensibility, but we actually want to control the queue by reusing elements that have been vacated, in a circular manner, as in Figure 15.3(b). In fact, a simple array is a good choice.

What should we do if the queue gets full or if an attempt is made to remove an element when it is empty? The correct response is to throw an exception. This we do, using one exception with a parameter for full or empty. As was done with the Java `Stack` class, we define `Queue` based on the `Object` superclass.

```
Bounded Queue

public class Queue {
    Queue(int n);
    void add (Object x);
    Object remove ();
    boolean empty ();
    boolean full ();

    void reset ();
    void succ ();
    boolean eol ();
    Object current ();
}
```

A property of a circular queue is that it is bounded, and we can specify the bound in the constructor. In an array implementation, any bound specified would have to be less than the maximum size of the array declared within the queue class itself. The `Add` method (sometimes known as enqueue) adds an item to the back. `Remove` takes the item off the front (providing such an item exists). This is sometimes known as dequeue. `Empty` checks for an empty queue, and `full` checks if all the spaces allocated to the queue have been used up.

Property 5 above indicated that we should be able to scan the queue, perhaps doing something to each item. For example, we may wish to print the queue out, or search for a particular item. Without more sophisticated language features, it is difficult to generalize the scanning operation. We therefore have to allow the user access to the queue itself. This can be done in a controlled way by insisting that all scanning operations use the four iterator methods, supplied with the class.

We now consider an example of the use of the above definition of a queue, *before* looking at how the queue itself is implemented. Java does not have a built-in queue class, so here we show how a data structure would be built from scratch.

EXAMPLE 15.3   Doctor's waiting room

Problem   A doctor has a small waiting room with a small number of chairs – say seven or so. Patients can come in and wait there, but once the seats are full, they tend to go away and come back later. Simulate this behaviour, so that the doctor can decide if it is essential to build a bigger waiting room.

Solution   We can set up a queue with a maximum size and randomly let patients arrive and be seen by the doctor. The state of the queue can be continuously displayed and when it is full, a signal can be made, and arrivals ignored until there is space again.

Algorithm   We can simulate what is happening with the algorithm of Figure 15.4. There is a 50% chance at each iteration that a patient will arrive (signified by checking whether the die throw is even) and there is a 30% chance that the doctor will be ready to see another patient (die is 1 or 2). There is also a 30% chance that nothing will happen (die is 3 or 5). We run the simulation for a set number of times and watch what happens.

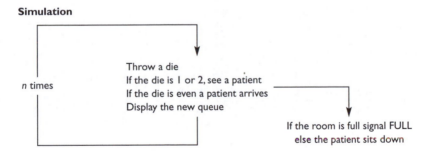

Figure 15.4 *The simulation of a doctor's waiting room.*

Program   The contents of the queue are the same simple integer. We know the queue is dealing with `Objects` and therefore apply the necessary casts.

```
import myutilities.*;

class WaitingRoom {
   /*  Simulation the Waiting Room   by J M Bishop    Jan 1997
    *  ---------------------------    Java 1.1
```

```
     *   Shows a queue growing and shrinking in response to
     *   random events.
     *
     *   Illustrates queues and home-made queue iterators.
     */

public static void main (String args []) throws QueueException {
    new WaitingRoom ();
}

WaitingRoom () throws QueueException {
  Queue chairs = new Queue (7);
  int patient;
  int choice;

  System.out.println("*** Doctor's Waiting Room Simulation ***");
  System.out.println("There are 7 chairs");
  System.out.println("Arrivals on 2,4,6; patients seen on 1,2");
  System.out.println();
  System.out.println("Time\tChoice\tPatient numbers");

  for (int i = 2; i<30; i++) {
    choice = (int) (Math.random()*6+1);
    System.out.print(i+"\t"+choice+"\t");
    display(chairs);
    try {
      if (choice == 1 || choice == 2)
        if (!chairs.empty())
          patient = ((Integer) chairs.remove()).intValue();
      if (choice == 2 || choice == 4 || choice == 6)
        chairs.add(new Integer(i));
    }
    catch (QueueException e) {
      System.out.println("\t\t\tWaiting room "+e.getMessage());
    }
  }
}

void display (Queue q) {
  if (q.empty()) System.out.print("Empty"); else
  for (q.reset(); !q.eol(); q.succ())
    System.out.print(((Integer) q.current()).intValue() +" ");
  System.out.println();
}
}
```

Testing A run could look like this:

```
*** Doctor's Waiting Room Simulation ***
There are 7 chairs
Arrivals on 2,4,6; patients seen on 1,2
```

Time	Choice	Patient	numbers				
2	1	Empty					
3	1	Empty					
4	6	Empty					
5	5	4					
6	4	4					
7	4	4	6				
8	5	4	6	7			
9	5	4	6	7			
10	1	4	6	7			
11	4	6	7				
12	4	6	7	11			
13	6	6	7	11	12		
14	4	6	7	11	12	13	
15	1	6	7	11	12	13	14
16	4	7	11	12	13	14	
17	6	7	11	12	13	14	16
18	6	7	11	12	13	14	16	17
		Waiting room Full					
19	1	7	11	12	13	14	16	17
20	1	11	12	13	14	16	17
21	5	12	13	14	16	17	
22	2	12	13	14	16	17	
23	1	13	14	16	17	22	
24	6	14	16	17	22		
25	3	14	16	17	22	24	
26	1	14	16	17	22	24	
27	1	16	17	22	24		
28	1	17	22	24			
29	4	22	24				

The room got full only once in this short run, but given the random nature of the 'die' throwing, completely different runs could be obtained. Notice that when we have a 2, the queue is both added to and removed from in one iteration. This circumstance occurs on lines 22–23.

Queues using arrays

The best array implementation for a queue is a circular one. The back of the queue starts at 0, and gradually moves up to the maximum size. Once there, the next position considered for adding is 0 again, provided a remove has taken place and there is no live data there. Because of this, the conditions for full and empty are not based on whether the indicators are 0 or max, but on a count of the number of live items. The full class definition for a queue, which can be added to the myutilities package, is:

```
package myutilities;

public class Queue {
  /* Queue abstract data type  by J M Bishop Jan 1997
   *                              updated August 2000
   * Implements a queue as a bounded circular array.
   * Has a set maximum of 100 elements. */

  public Queue (int m) {
    if (m <= maxQueue)
      size = m;
    else size = maxQueue;
    front = 0;
    back = -1;
    live = 0;
    reset();
  }

  public void add (Object x) throws QueueException {
    // throws an exception if the queue is full
    if (live < size) {
      back = (back + 1) % maxQueue;
      Q[back] = x;
      live++;
    }
    else
      throw new QueueException("Full");
  }

  public Object remove () throws QueueException {
    // throws an exception id the queue is empty
    if (live >=1) {
      Object x = Q[front];
      front = (front + 1) % maxQueue;
      live--;
      return x;
    }
  }
```

```java
    else
      throw new QueueException("Empty");
  }

  public boolean empty () {
    return live == 0;
  }

  public boolean full () {
    return live == size;
  }

  // Iterator methods
  public void reset () {
    now = front;
  }

  public void succ () {
    now = (now+1) % maxQueue;
  }

  public boolean eol () {
    if (back==maxQueue)
      return now == 0;
    else
      return now > back;
  }

  public Object current () {
    return Q[now];
  }

  private
  int size, // total vector capacity;
      front, back, // indicators
      live, // number of used spaces in the circular queue
      now; // position for displaying the queue
  private Object Q [] = new Object [maxQueue];
  static private int maxQueue = 100;


}

public class QueueException extends Exception {
  QueueException (String s) {super(s);}
}
```

Notice that all the data items are declared private in the queue, and are instance variables, to be replicated for each object.

Queues using lists

As with stacks, queues cannot be altered except at the ends, so the only advantage of using a list as a base for the queue is to obtain complete flexibility of the size. Notice that we would still provide a border facility, so that a queue can stop growing. The above class definition can be very simply translated into a version based on lists and is left as an exercise for the reader. The `WaitingRoom` program should run without change if the one class is replaced by the other.

15.5 Linked lists again

The simple list connector we developed in Example 8.2 had the odd property that by adding new items to the front, it stored data backwards. What we were really creating was a stack – a very neat data structure because it has only one indicator. If we would prefer to store the data in the correct order, then we need two indicators – one for the front and one for the back, as in a queue.

In fact, linked lists can be more general than either a stack or queue and can permit operations to occur not just at the ends, but anywhere in between. We saw this once we started using the `LinkedList` class in Section 8.3. To complete the discussion in the same vein as for stacks and queues, we continue with linked list properties and another example.

Linked list properties

Formally, we can define the properties of a list as follows:

- Nodes are linked together linearly in both directions, forwards and backwards.
- There are two ends to the list – the front and the back.
- Nodes can be added anywhere in the list.
- Nodes can be deleted anywhere in the list.
- The list can be scanned forwards or backwards.

These properties are embodied in the `LinkedList` class we have already mentioned in Chapter 8, except that we need more methods from that class to meet all the requirements. These extra methods are:

LinkedList (additional methods)

void addFirst(Object *objectid*)
void addLast(Object *objectid*)
void removeFirst()
void removeLast()
void add(**int** index, Object *objectid*)
void remove (**int** *index*)
int size()

The first four methods can be efficiently used to handle additions and deletions at the ends of a list.

To make changes elsewhere, we iterate through the the list, maintaining a count and then use the add with index method.

Size assists in this iteration process.

The following example makes excellent use of the advanced features of the Linked-List class.

EXAMPLE 15.4   Photograph line-up

Problem   A photographer is going to photograph a class of students, and wants them neatly arranged by height. The idea is to have the taller people in the back rows, and for each row to slope downwards from the centre. Given a class of students and their heights, we would like a plan of where each should stand.

Example   Each row should be lined up as shown in Figure 15.5.

Solution   We start by creating a single line of everyone in height order. Then, starting at the tallest, we peel off however many we want per row, and create a new list starting in the middle and adding alternately to the right and left. Suppose we label the people A, B, … where A is the tallest. Then a row of seven people would be arranged thus:

GECABDF

Algorithm   The algorithms make very good use of the list methods defined above. First, we consider how to create a list in height order. The result will be a list with the front pointing to the tallest person (Figure 15.6).

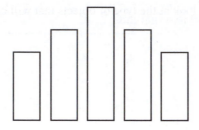

Figure 15.5 *Five people in a row in a photograph.*

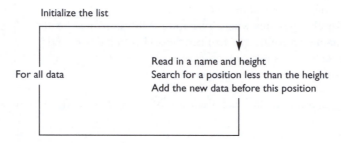

Figure 15.6 *Create an ordered list.*

Now we consider how to peel off a row and create the left–right effect. For ease of computation, we assume that the row will have an odd number of people. The algorithm is given in Figure 15.7.

Adding to the back equates to `addAfter(back)` and adding to the front becomes `addBefore(front)`. We can print out or display the line by calling the iterator methods. Then, we can erase the line and start with a new one. Erasing a list in Java is as simple as setting it to null, as then all the nodes that were associated with it will be garbage collected in a short while.

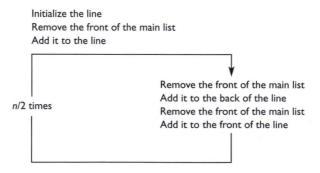

Figure 15.7 *Create a left–right sorted list.*

Program First of all, we look at the type of objects that will be stored in the list. It is:

```java
class Student {

  double height;
  String name;

  Student(double h, String s) {
    height = h;
    name = s;
  }

  public int compareTo (Object x) {
    if (name.equals(((Student) x).name))
      return 0;
    else if (height < ((Student) x).height)
      return -1;
    else
      return 1;
  }

  public String toString () {
    return ("\t"+height+"\t"+name);
  }
}
```

The `compareTo` method is defined so that students are equal if their names are equal, and otherwise their heights are compared. In other words, the class, as given here, does not allow two people with the same name.

As before, the program is surprisingly clean and short, since all the work is done in the well-defined list methods.

```java
import java.io.*;
import javagently.*;
import myutilities.*;
import java.util.*;

class Photo {

  /* The class photo program      by J M Bishop   January 1997
   * ========================      revised January 1998
   *                              revised for JFC August 2000
   *
   * Uses linked lists to set up the rows
   * for a class photo, based on height.
```

```
 *
 * Illustrates List handling.
 */

LinkedList studentList = new LinkedList();

public static void main (String args []) throws IOException{
  new Photo();
}

Photo () throws IOException {
  System.out.println("**** The Class Photo ****");
  lineUp();
  for (int row = 1; studentList.size() > 0; row++)
    pickOff (row);
}

void lineUp () throws IOException {

  Stream in = new Stream ("students.dat", Stream.READ);
  System.out.println("The students as read in are:");
  while (true) {
    try {
      double h = in.readDouble();
      String n = in.readString();
      Student s = new Student (h, n);
      System.out.println(s);

      // Find the place for the new entry
      int before = 0;
      for (ListIterator e = studentList.listIterator(); e.hasNext();) {
        if (s.compareTo(e.next()) > 0)
          break;
        before++;
        }

      // add the new entry
      studentList.add(before,s);
    }
    catch (EOFException e) {break;}
  }
  System.out.println("The students in height order are:");

  for (ListIterator e = studentList.listIterator(); e.hasNext();)
    System.out.println(e.next());
}
```

```
void pickOff (int row) {
  System.out.println("Row "+row+"\t");
  LinkedList line = new LinkedList ();
  Student s;
  s = (Student) studentList.removeFirst();
  line.addLast(s);
  for (int i = 0; i<rowSize/2; i++) {
    s = (Student) studentList.removeFirst();
    line.addLast(s);
    s = (Student) studentList.removeFirst();
    line.addFirst(s);
  }
  for (ListIterator e = line.listIterator(); e.hasNext();)
    System.out.println(e.next());
}

static final int rowSize = 7;
}
```

Testing   The program would process this and produce the following arrangement:

```
**** The Class Photo ****
The students as read in are:
        1.8   Danie
        1.58  Petra
        1.9   John
        1.55  Harry
        1.81  Mary
        1.75  Craig
        1.71  Sipho
        1.77  Diamond
        1.4   Tiny
        1.79  Michael
        1.76  Robert
        1.69  Elizabeth
        1.68  Lucy
        1.5   Sarah
The students in height order are:
        1.9   John
        1.81  Mary
        1.8   Danie
        1.79  Michael
        1.77  Diamond
        1.76  Robert
        1.75  Craig
```

```
        1.71  Sipho
        1.69  Elizabeth
        1.68  Lucy
        1.58  Petra
        1.55  Harry
        1.5   Sarah
        1.4   Tiny
Row 1
        1.75  Craig
        1.77  Diamond
        1.8   Danie
        1.9   John
        1.81  Mary
        1.79  Michael
        1.76  Robert
Row 2
        1.4   Tiny
        1.55  Harry
        1.68  Lucy
        1.71  Sipho
        1.69  Elizabeth
        1.58  Petra
        1.5   Sarah
```

The program has the restriction that the number of students must be a multiple of the row size, but this is a minor detail.

15.6 Bit sets

The last data structure that we shall consider is the bit set. As we know from mathematics, a set is an unordered collection of items of the same type on which operations such as union, intersection and membership are defined. Java has a `Set` class which encompasses these operations on Objects.

A bit set is different in that it is envisaged as a sequence of bits, each of which is known by number and can be turned on and off. Sets and bit sets are very similar in effect, but differ in the way they are used. In a set of integers, one could check whether it contained 8; in a bit set, one would check whether the 8th bit was on.

Some of the methods provided for Java's bit sets are given in the following form:

Bit sets

```
BitSet ();
BitSet (int n);

boolean get (int b);
void set (int b);
void clear (int b);
void and (BitSet s);
void or (BitSet s);
void xor (BitSet s);
```

After having created a bit set with a given size or by using the default, we can set, get and clear individual bits. Then we can also combine two sets using the three operations shown. For an explanation of the results of bit operations, go back to Section 3.6 on booleans.

Bit sets are fairly restrictive in that they can record only integer numbers. That is, we cannot have sets of characters, for example. We can now consider an example of the use of sets, in fact of arrays of bit sets in this case.

EXAMPLE 15.5   Training schedules

Problem Employees at Savanna Inc. attend training courses, and a record of each course attended or planned to attend is kept on a file. We wish to discover which employees are signed up for which courses, and which courses overall have been used. We would also like to know which employees need computer user codes, given a list of courses that will be using the computer.

Solution One could construct arrays with the name of each employee who has done a course. Alternatively, if both the employees and courses are identified by number, then sets can be used.

Algorithm Assume that the data have employee numbers followed by a list of course numbers. A typical file would look like this:

```
50   1 2 3
44   3 8 7
99   1
61   1 7
```

meaning that employee 50 is meant to attend courses 1, 2 and 3; employee 99 is meant to attend 1 only, and so on. We need to keep a set of employee numbers for each course, and a set of all courses taken. This is done with the data structures:

```
BitSet courses [];
BitSet schedules [];
```

The algorithm then consists of reading in a number followed by its courses. For each course, we add the employee number to the set in the `courses` array indexed by that course. Then we also add the course to the employee's record in the `schedules` array. The important statements are:

```
// Put employee n on course c
    courses[c].set(n);
// Put course c in employee n's schedule
    schedules [n].set(c);
```

Before we can set bits in a bit set, though, we must take care that the object has been created. For example, creating a new course set would be done like this:

```
// Create course c if not yet started
    if (courses[c] == null)
        courses[c] = new BitSet (employeeMax);
```

Program The program is arranged in three sections, each its own method, namely: `readIn`, `display` and `userCodes`. One aspect of this program, unrelated to bit sets, is how to read data that have a terminator such as the end of a line. The `Text` class will not work in this case because it is oblivious of ends of line. Never mind: by now we are able to write our own input routines, picking off numbers from a `StringTokenizer` as we want them.

Reading in starts by getting a whole line, then tokenizing it and counting the number of tokens (using a predefined method). After getting the employee number, a for-loop can be used to process each course as described above. This is done in the `readIn` method.

Getting in the list of courses that use the computer follows a similar pattern, and the students enrolled for that course are added into another bit set as follows:

```
codesNeeded.or(courses[c]);
```

The rest of the program is concerned with printing out the sets neatly.

```
import java.util.*;
import java.io.*;
import javagently.*;
```

```
public class Training {

 /* Training schedules program     by J M Bishop Jan 1997
  * =========================     Java 1.1
  *                               updated August 2000
  * Creates class lists and schedules for employees,
  * including a list of those who are taking special courses.
  *
  * Uses bit sets and its own StringTokenizers rather than
  * javagently's Text class.
  */

  BitSet courses [];
  BitSet schedules [];
  int employeeMax, courseMax;
  Stream in = new Stream (System.in);

  public static void main (String arg []) throws IOException {
    new Training ();
  }

  Training () throws IOException {

    // The main program declares two arrays of sets and then
    // calls the three static methods to read and print out
    // the data.
    System.out.println ("*** Training Schedules ****");
    System.out.print("What is the highest course number? ");
    courseMax = in.readInt();
    System.out.print("What is the highest employee number?");
    employeeMax = in.readInt();

    // Create an array of sets, one for each course
    // Each set will be EmployeeMax big
    // but is created later as the data is read in
    courses = new BitSet [courseMax];

    // Create an array of sets, one for each employee
    // Each set will be CourseMax big
    // but is created later as the data is read in
    schedules = new BitSet [employeeMax];

    System.out.println("Enter each employee's schedule as follows:");
    System.out.println("Employee number course numbers");
    System.out.println("Example 100 12 7 4 15");
```

```
      System.out.println("End with a blank line");

      readIn();
      display();
      userCodes();
   }

   void readIn () throws IOException {
     // Uses its own StringTokenizer since data is read a line
     // at a time. A blank line signifies zero tokens and
     // ends the reading of data.

     String s;
     StringTokenizer T;
     int n, c, ntokens;

     while(true) {
        s = in.readLine();
        T = new StringTokenizer (s);
        ntokens = T.countTokens ();
        if (ntokens == 0) break; // no more employees
        n = getInt(T);

        //Create a schedule for employee n
        schedules [n] = new BitSet (courseMax);
        for (int i=0; i<ntokens-1; i++) {
          c = getInt(T);

          // Create course c if not yet started
          if (courses[c] == null)
            courses[c] = new BitSet (employeeMax);

          // Put employee n on course c
          courses[c].set(n);

          // Put course c in employee n's schedule
          schedules [n].set(c);
        }
     }
     System.out.println("Data read in successfully.");
   }

   void display () {
   // prints each of the set arrays slightly differently.
   // calls printSet for printing a single set
```

```
System.out.println("The course lists");
System.out.println("=================");
for (int c =0; c<courseMax; c++) {
  System.out.print(c+': ');
  if (courses[c]==null) System.out.println("No students");
  else
    printSet(courses[c]);
}
System.out.println("The schedules");
System.out.println("=============");
for (int n = 0; n < employeeMax; n++) {
  if (schedules[n] != null) {
    System.out.print(n+": ");
    printSet(schedules[n]);
  }
 }
}


void userCodes () throws IOException {
  // A method to illustrate a bit set operation.
  // given a subset of the course numbers,
  // create the union (or) of all the employees
  // signed up for them and print that set.

  Text.prompt("Which are the computer-related courses?");
  BitSet codesNeeded = new BitSet(employeeMax);

  String s;
  StringTokenizer T;
  int c, ntokens;

  s = in.readLine();
  T = new StringTokenizer (s);
  ntokens = T.countTokens ();
  for (int i=0; i<ntokens; i++) {
    c = getInt(T);
    codesNeeded.or(courses[c]);
   }
  System.out.println("Employees needing usercodes");
  System.out.println("===========================");
  printSet(codesNeeded);
}


void printSet (BitSet b) {
  // Prints the members of a single bit set

  for (int i = 0; i < b.size(); i++)
```

```
      if (b.get(i)) System.out.print(i+" ");
    System.out.println();
  }

  int getInt (StringTokenizer T) {
    String item = T.nextToken();
    return Integer.valueOf (item.trim()).intValue();
  }
}
```

Testing A sample run would give:

```
*** Training Schedules ****
What is the highest course number? 10
What is the highest employee number? 100
Enter each employee's schedule as follows:
Employee number course numbers
Example 100 12 7 4 15
End with a blank line
50 1 2 3
44 3 8 7
99 1
61 1 7

Data read in successfully.
The course lists
================
0: No students
1: 50 61 99
2: 50
3: 44 50
4: No students
5: No students
6: No students
7: 44 61
8: 44
9: No students
The schedules
=============
44: 3 7 8
50: 1 2 3
61: 1 7
99: 1
Which are the computer-related courses? 2 3
Employees needing usercodes
===========================
44 50
```

This quick tour through algorithms and data structures emphasized that there is always more than one way of approaching the solution to a problem. In sorting and searching, we had linear or binary methods (with vastly differing performances). Recursion was also introduced as a means of expressing solutions in a simple and elegant way.

We can implement data structures via arrays or linked lists, with different effects. However, what we did manage to achieve is a defined set of properties for each data structure, which are adhered to no matter what the implementation chosen.

Four data structures were discussed — stacks, queues, linked lists and bit sets. The three Java-implemented ones — stacks, linked lists and bit sets — served as guides for the definition of the other one. In the examples associated with illustrating the data structures, some of the lesser-used Java features cropped up again: interfaces, tokenizers and user-defined exceptions.

QUIZ

15.1 If the linear search in Section 15.2 was to be used to search an array of integers, what line would you change?

    (a) `throw new ItemNotFoundException();`
    (b) `for (int i=0; i<a.length;i++)`
    (c) `if (x.equals(a[i])`
    (d) none

15.2 In the following list of numbers:

    8 17 25 35 41 52 60 75 86

how many comparisons would binary search take to find 35?

    (a) 4
    (b) 3
    (c) 5
    (d) 2

15.3 Binary search is always faster than linear search when the item being sought is

    (a) at the end of the list
    (b) at the start of the list
    (c) not in the list
    (d) in the second half of the list

15.4 If we pushed the numbers 1 to 10 onto two stacks, S1 and S2 alternately, and then took all of S1 followed by all of S2 off, what would be printed out? The code is:

```
Stack S1 = new Stack(5);
Stack S2 = new Stack(6);
for (int i = 1; i<=10; i+=2) {
  S1.push(i);
  S2.push(i+1);
```

```
    }
    while (!S1.empty())
     System.out.print(S1.pop()+" ");
    while (!S2.empty())
     System.out.print(S2.pop()+" ");
```

(a) 10 9 8 7 6 5 4 3 2 1
(b) 9 10 7 8 5 6 3 5 1 2
(c) 9 7 5 3 1 10 8 6 4 2
(d) 10 8 7 6 4 2 9 7 5 3 2 1

15.5 In the doctor's waiting room example (15.3), assume that each time period is 2 minutes. In the run shown here, how many minutes has the patient now first in the queue been waiting when the simulation ends?

(a) 2
(b) 12
(c) 10
(d) 20

15.6 To add a new item somewhere in the middle of a linked list, we

(a) have to iterate from the front to find the right place to use `add(index, object)`
(b) answer (a) or could maintain the current position and use it if relevant with `add(index, object)`
(c) use `contains` to find the right position as a reference and use that
(d) use `binarySearch` to find the right position and then use `add(index, object)`

15.7 In the waiting room example (15.3) how many time slots did patient number 12 wait before seeing the doctor?

(a) 10
(b) 9
(c) 11
(d) 1

15.8 The technique whereby a method can call itself is called

(a) iteration
(b) recursion
(c) introspection
(d) inverstion

15.9 Give a definition of a new bit set that will keep track of all courses taken by anyone in the training schedules example (15.5).

(a) `Bitset allCourses = new BitSet (courseMax);`
(b) `BitSet allCourses [] = new BitSet (courseMax);`
(c) `Bitset allCourses = new BitSet [courseMax];`
(d) `BitSet allcourses.setMax (courseMax);`

15.10 What would be a statement that can be added to the `readIn` method to update this set of all courses while a student's course particulars are being processed?

(a) `allCourses.bitOn(c)`
(b) `allCourses [c].set()`
(c) `allCourses.set(c)`
(d) none of these

PROBLEMS

15.1 **Speedier concordance.** How could the concordance of Problem 7.5 be speeded up with faster sorting and searching?

15.2 **Stack spy.** Suppose we wanted to print out the contents of a stack, without destroying them, and without using anything other than push and pop operations. Write a program to do this.

15.3 **Waiting statistics.** It is clear that some patients in Example 15.3 could wait a long time before being seen by the doctor. At each display, compute the total time waited by all the patients in the queue and print this out on the right-hand side.

15.4 **Queues with lists.** Implement a queue class based on linked lists. Test it out.

15.5 **Palindrome with a stack.** Solve the palindrome problem (7.2) using a stack rather than an array.

15.6 **Winning a raffle.** At a party, everyone is given a numbered raffle ticket. After supper, a number is drawn and the person with the number wins the prize, and so does that person's family. Write a program to read in people in families into lists, to organize a draw, and to print out the winning person and his/her family.

15.7 **Sorting lists.** Linked lists can be sorted as follows: Create a new list of the same kind. Add each element into it with a comparison as required. Then the new list is a sorted version of the old. Add such a sort method that uses lists from Chapter 8 and check that it works.

15.8 **Electronic diary.** Students at Savanna University have to undertake a group project in their third year. The number of groups and the number of students in a group vary from year to year. One of the difficult tasks at the beginning of the year is establishing when members of a particular group can meet and discuss their project, since they may be taking different courses and have different timetables. They would like to get computer assistance in arranging meetings. Making use of bit sets and linked lists, set up such an electronic diary program.

APPENDIX A

Modelling notation
for *Java Gently*

Part I Building blocks

Item	Long notation		Short notation

Class

Long notation:
```
Classid
----------
variables
----------
methods
```

Short notation:
```
Classid
```

object

Long notation:
```
objectid
----------
variables
----------
methods
```

Short notation:
```
objectid
```
```
:Classid
```

primitive variable

Long notation:
type x = value
type x

Short notation:
x = value
x

object variable

Long notation:
type x ——▶ | x |

Short notation:
x ——▶ | x |

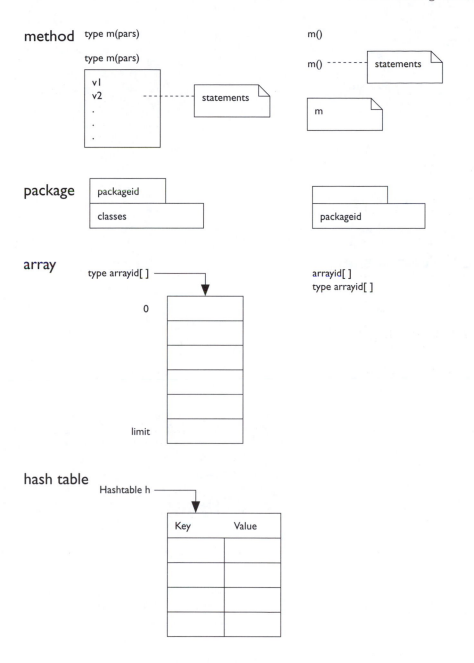

method   type m(pars)   m()

        type m(pars)   m() - - - - - - -   statements

        v1
        v2 - - - - - - - -   statements   m
        .
        .
        .

package   packageid   packageid

        classes

array   type arrayid[ ]   arrayid[ ]
                                     type arrayid[ ]

          0

      limit

hash table   Hashtable h

Key	Value

Interface

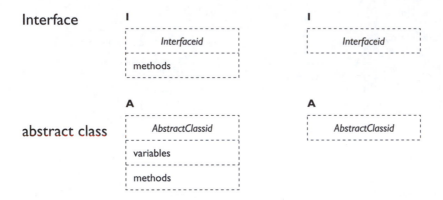

abstract class

Part II Associations

inheritance

instantiates

imports

method call

private

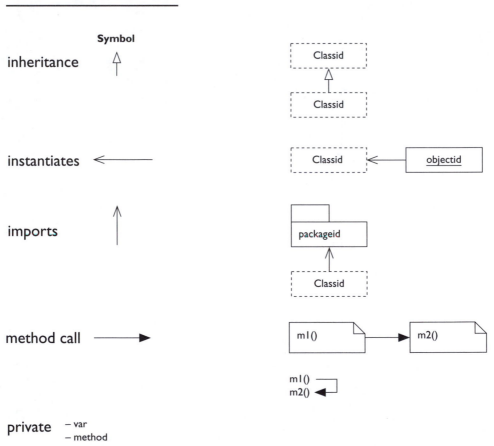

public   + var
           + method

reference ⟶

implements ----▷

x ⟶ | objectid |

| Classid | ----▷ | *Interfaceid* |

APPENDIX B

Collected syntax and semantic forms

The syntax and semantics of the Java language are provided in form diagrams on the pages indicated. The construction and use of the form diagrams is explained on pages 24–26.

APPENDIX C

List of programs, applets and classes

Animated	program	Example 15.1
ATMServer	threaded socket program	Example 14.4
Batch	class	Example 8.1, Case Study 3
ButtonTest	GUI program	Example 10.4
CarPark	applet	Example 13.4
CarThread	threaded class	Example 13.4
CatchM	applet	Example 12.4
ChatHandler	threaded class	Case Study 10
ChatServer	socket program	Case Study 10
Checkin	applet	Case Study 11
ChequeDetector	program	Example 7.2
Coffee	class	Example 8.1
Coffee2	class	Case Study 3
CoffeeShop	program	Example 8.1
CoffeeShop2	program	Case Study 3
Competition	applet	Example 12.3
Converter	program	Example 6.8
ConverterDatabase	database program	Example 14.5
ConverterGUI	GUI program	Example 11.3
ConverterGUIApplet	network applet	Example 14.1
ConverterSwing	GUI program	Case Study 7
Counter	threaded class	Case Study 9
Country	class	Example 9.2
Curio	class	Examples 2.3, 3.5, 5.2
CurioStore1	program	Examples 2.3, 2.5
CurioStore2	program	Example 3.5
CurioStore3	program	Examples 5.2, 5.3, 5.5

Currency	program	Example 7.4
CustomDates	program	Example 7.6
Display	javagently class	Sections 4.2, 13.4
DisplayWarning	program	Example 2.4
Dive	class	Example 6.2
DivingCompetition	program	Example 6.2
FetchImage	network program	Example 14.2
Filer	myutilities class	Example 4.9
Flag	graphics class	Example 2.2
FlagCanvas	graphics class	Example 10.3, Case Study 5
FlagCanvasMotif	graphics class	Case Study 5
FlagCanvasVerti	graphics class	Case Study 5
FlagMaker1	graphics program	Example 2.2
FlagMaker2	graphics program	Example 10.3
FlagMakerGUI	GUI program	Case Study 5
FleetCalculator	program	Example 2.6
Frequencies	program	Example 6.1
GoldExploration	program	Example 6.5
Graph	javagently class	Section 6.3
Greetings	program	Example 4.1
Greetings2	program	Example 4.4
HCFRepeat	program	Example 5.1
HighestValue	program	Example 4.5
LargeTemperatureTable	program	Examples 3.6, 4.3
LightBulbAnalysis	program	Example 6.4
LinkTest	program	Example 8.2
LotsaLabels	program	Example 3.2
MagicNumber	remote object class	Example 14.6
MagicNumberClient	remote program	Example 14.6
MagicNumberServer	remote program	Example 14.6
Museum	synchronized class	Case Study 9
Olympics	program	Example 4.10
OurInteger	class	Example 9.2
PartCodes	program	Examples 4.7, 4.8
Photo	program	Example 15.4
PizzaDelivery1	program	Case Study 1
PizzaDelivery2	program	Case Study 1
PlayGame	class	Case Study 2
Ports	socket program	Example 14.3
Queue	myutilities class	Section 15.4
RainfallHistogram	program	Example 3.4
RandomInvestigation	program	Example 3.1
Rates	class	Example 6.8, Case Study 7
ReadingsAverages	program	Example 4.6
Reverser	program	Example 15.2
RSPGame	program	Case Study 2

APPENDIX D

Answers to quizzes

2.1	(b)	2.2	(c)	2.3	(b)	2.4	(a)	2.5	(d)
2.6	(b)	2.7	(b)	2.8	(b)	2.9	(a)	2.10	(d)
3.1	(c)	3.2	(b)	3.3	(c)	3.4.	(a)	3.5	(b)
3.6	(a)	3.7	(c)	3.8	(d)	3.9	(c)	3.10	(d)
4.1	(b)	4.2	(c)	4.3	(c)	4.4	(d)	4.5	(c)
4.6	(b)	4.7	(d)	4.8	(b)	4.9	(b).	4.10	(a)
5.1	(b)	5.2	(d)	5.3	(d)	5.4	(d)	5.5.	(b)
5.6	(a)	5.7	(c)	5.8	(a)	5.9	(c)	5.10	(a)
6.1	(c)	6.2	(c)	6.3	(b)	6.4	(c)	6.5	(a)
6.6	(b)	6.7	(b)	6.8	(d)	6.9	(c)	6.10	(c)
7.1	(a)	7.2	(c)	7.3	(d)	7.4	(d)	7.5	(d)
7.6	(b)	7.7	(b)	7.8	(b)	7.9	(c)	7.10	(b)
8.1	(b)	8.2	(c)	8.3	(b)	8.4	(b)	8.5	(d)
8.6	(d)	8.7	(d)	8.8	(c)	8.9	(b)	8.10	(c)
9.1	(b)	9.2	(a)	9.3	(b)	9.4	(c)	9.5	(a)
9.6	(c)	9.7	(b)	9.8	(b)	9.9	(c)	9.10	(a)
10.1	(b)	10.2	(c)	10.3	(d)	10.4	(b)	10.5	(b)
10.6	(b)	10.7	(b)	10.8	(c)	10.9	(c)	10.10	(d)
11.1	(c)	11.2	(b)	11.3	(b)	11.4	(a)	11.5	(b)
11.6	(a)	11.7	(b)	11.8	(a)	11.9	(b)	11.10	(d)

12.1 (b)	12.2 (c)	12.3 (c)	12.4 (c)	12.5 (d)
12.6 (b)	12.7 (b)	12.8 (d)	12.9 (b)	12.10 (a)
13.1 (d)	13.2 (d)	13.3 (a)	13.4 (d)	13.5 (c)
13.6 (b)	13.7 (b)	13.8 (c)	13.9 (b)	13.10 (b)
14.1 (c)	14.2 (a)	14.3 (b)	14.4 (d)	14.5 (b)
14.6 (b)	14.7 (b)	14.8 (b)	14.9 (c)	14.10 (c)
15.1 (c)	15.2 (b)	15.3 (d)	15.4 (c)	15.5 (b)
15.6 (b)	15.7 (a)	15.8 (b)	15.9 (c)	15.10 (d)

Index

Programs, classes and forms are indexed separately in Appendices B and C. There is a list of examples in the Contents. Keywords, Java APIs, forms and exceptions are also indexed again in each chapter summary.